54th Yearbook of the National Reading Conference

Edited by

Beth Maloch
James V. Hoffman
Diane L. Schallert
Colleen M. Fairbanks
Jo Worthy
University of Texas at Austin

With the editorial assistance of

Samuel D. Miller
University of North Carolina, Greensboro

Sarah J. McCarthey
University of Illinois, Urbana-Champaign

Laura May
University of Texas at Austin

Angela Owens, Executive Director
National Reading Conference

Jenni Gaylord
JKG Studio Design

Published by
National Reading Conference, Inc.
Oak Creek, Wisconsin

2005

NRC YEARBOOK is published annually by the National Reading Conference, Inc., 7044 South 13th Street, Oak Creek, WI 53154, Tel: (414)908-4924

POSTMASTER:
Send address changes to NRC Yearbook, 7044 South 13th Street, Oak Creek, WI 53154.

SUBSCRIPTIONS:
Institutions: $80 domestic or $90 foreign (surface), per year, or, $140 or $155, respectively, as part of a combination subscription with *NRC's Journal of Literacy Research*. Foreign subscribers add $20 if airmail is preferred. Individuals who attended the 2004 annual conference receive the YEARBOOK as part of their registration. Quantity discounts available for use in university or college courses. Write for information.

PERMISSION TO QUOTE OR REPRINT:
Quotations of 500 words or longer or reproductions of any portion of a table, figure, or graph, require written permission from the National Reading Conference, and must include proper credit to the organization. A fee may be charged for use of the material, and permission of the first author will be secured.

PHOTOCOPIES:
Individuals may photocopy single articles without permission for nonprofit one-time classroom or library use. Other nonprofit educational copying, including repeated use of an individual article, must be registered with the Copyright Clearance Center, Academic Permission Service, 27 Congress Street, Salem, MA 01970, USA. *The fee is $1.25USD per article, or any portion, or any portion thereof, to be paid through the Center. The fee is waived for individual members of the National Reading Conference.* Consent to photocopy does not extend to items identified as reprinted by permission of other publishers, nor to copying for general distribution, for advertising or promotion, or for resale unless written permission is obtained from the National Reading Conference.

Microfiche copy is available from ERIC Reproduction Service, 3900 Wheeler Avenue, Alexandria, VA 22304. The YEARBOOK is indexed in *Psychological Abstracts, Index to Social Sciences & Humanities Proceedings* and *Educational Research Information Clearing House*. The NRC YEARBOOK is a refereed publication. Manuscripts must be original works that have been presented at the Annual Meeting of the National Reading Conference, and that have not been published elsewhere.

ISSN
ISBN 1-893591-07-7
Printed in the United States of America

National Reading Conference

Editorial Advisory Review Board
Fifty-fourth Yearbook of the National Reading Conference

Jane Hansen
University of Virginia

Janis M. Harmon
University of Texas, San Antonio

Colin Harrison
University of Nottingham, UK

Jerome Harste
Indiana University, Bloomington

Douglas Hartman
University of Connecticut

Kathleen Hinchman
Syracuse University

Rosalind Horowitz
University of Texas, San Antonio

Marcia Invernizzi
University of Virginia

Gay Ivey
James Madison University

Francine Johnston
University of North Carolina, Greensboro

George Kamberelis
University at Albany, State University of New York

Edward J. Kame'enui
University of Oregon

Rachel Karchmer
University of Delaware

Maureen Kendrick
University of British Columbia

Sharon B. Kletzien
West Chester University

Linda Kucan
Appalachian State University

Linda D. Labbo
University of Georgia

Diane Lapp
San Diego State University

Kevin Leander
Vanderbilt University

Lauren Leslie
Marquette University

Cynthia Lewis
University of Minnesota

Guofang Li
State University of New York, Buffalo

Marjorie Lipson
University of Vermont

Marla Mallette
Southern Illinois University

Joyce Many
Georgia State University

Prisca Martens
Towson University

Sarah McCarthey
University of Illinois, Urbana-Champaign

Lea McGee
University of Alabama

Sherri Merritt
University of North Carolina, Greensboro

Larry Mikulecky
Indiana University

Kathleen Mohr
University of North Texas

Karla Moller
University of Illinois, Urbana-Champaign

David W. Moore
Arizona State University

Ernest Morrell
University of California, Los Angeles

Darrell Morris
Appalachian State University

Barbara Moss
San Diego State University

David O'Brien
University of Minnesota

John O'Flahavan
University of Maryland, College Park

Donna Ogle
National-Louis University

Penny Oldfather
University of Georgia

Nancy D. Padak
Kent State University

Jeanne R. Paratore
Boston University

Leslie Patterson
University of North Texas

Eric Paulson
University of Cincinnati

Julie L. Pennington
University of Nevada, Reno

Deborah Price
Sam Houston State University

Taffy E. Raphael
University of Illinois, Chicago

JoyLynn H. Reed
University of Texas, Dallas

Ray Reutzel
Utah State University

Victoria Risko
Vanderbilt University

Laura R. Roehler
Michigan State University

Rebecca Rogers
Washington University in St. Louis

Kathleen Roskos
John Carroll University

Robert Rueda
University of Southern California

William H. Rupley
Texas A & M University

Rachel Salas
University of North Carolina, Greensboro

Mark Sadoski
Texas A & M University

Misty Sailors
University of Texas, San Antonio

David Schwarzer
University of Texas, Austin

Margaret Sheehy
University at Albany, State University of New York

Kathy G. Short
University of Arizona

Heidi Silver-Pacuilla
American Institute for Research

Lawrence R. Sipe
University of Pennsylvania

Laura Smolkin
University of Virginia

Dorothy S. Strickland
Rutgers University

William Teale
University of Illinois, Chicago

Sheila Valencia
University of Washington

Suzanne E. Wade
University of Utah

Gordon Wells
University of California, Santa Cruz

Haley Woodside-Jiron
University of Vermont

Shelley Hong Xu
California State University, Long Beach

54th Yearbook of the National Reading Conference

54TH NRC ANNUAL MEETING

Articles and Addresses Organized by Topic

DIRECTIONS FOR RESEARCH

DISCOURSE ANALYSIS

EARLY LITERACY LEARNERS

TECHNOLOGY AND NEW LITERACIES

Preface
54th Yearbook of the National Reading Conference

The 2004 NRC conference, set in San Antonio, took place against a political backdrop in which the nature and substance of literacy research has become suspect. Given the current state of politically-driven research agendas, the focus of the 54th annual NRC meeting—What is the past, present, and future of literacy research, and how is excellence in literacy research defined?—was a timely one, one also reflected in this volume. Papers included in the 54th NRC Yearbook suggest that literacy researchers continue to push for new and increasingly sensitive methodologies to address the ways in which policy is positioning teachers, schools, and researchers, as well as ways to examine the understandings of children, of teachers, and of pre-service teachers. Our methodologies are broadening and expanding, rather than folding under the pressure of increasingly narrow definitions of "scientific" research.

Of the 95 manuscripts we received, 25 are included here and reflect a range of theoretical perspectives, questions, and methodologies. Collectively, the 54th Yearbook includes papers on topics as diverse as the examination of children's literary responses to texts, critical analyses of policy initiatives, and an exploration of the reading processes of adult English Language Learners. The papers here include data-driven research reports, conceptual explorations of important issues, and papers delineating methodological approaches and techniques. They explore issues related to adolescent literacy, instructional techniques and approaches, uses of technology and new literacies, and reading and writing processes of children, adolescents, and adults.

In addition to these manuscripts, you will find the plenary addresses from the conference, the Oscar Causey and Albert Kingston award winners, a summary report of the conference from current president and the 2004 Conference Chair, Don Leu, and a complete list of presentations and their authors from the conference. The table of contents again lists the chapters first alphabetically and then by topic area. We have also included in this Yearbook an In Memoriam page. This year we lost five colleagues and friends of NRC far too soon. The recognition of these colleagues' contributions played a significant role at the conference this year; we wanted to represent and honor this recognition in the Yearbook, as a reflection of the 2004 conference.

As always, we have a long list of people to acknowledge. Our editorial advisory board went beyond the call of duty this year due to our high number of submissions. Almost all members of this year's board reviewed three manuscripts. We were again impressed with the level of detail and effort put into these reviews. Our organization and the field of literacy research benefits from such careful review and feedback. Sam Miller and Sarah McCarthey skillfully served as outside editors for manuscripts submitted by authors affiliated with the University of Texas at Austin. Laura May, our new editorial assistant, helped keep us on track and organized throughout this process. Assisting individual editors through the management and editing of manuscripts, Angela Hampton, Angela Bush, Kristy Leigh Hamm, Peggy Semingson, and Tara Bowman acted as graduate student assistant editors. Olivia Becerra provided administrative support, contributing at every stage of the process. Finally, Denise Rockhill and her colleagues at NRC Headquarters were tremendously helpful this year in facilitating and carrying out this process in a timely and organized manner.

Peter Mosenthal

Albert J. Kingston Award

The annual Albert J. Kingston Award for service to the National Reading Conference was established in 1985 to honor Albert Kingston for years of dedicated service to the NRC. Professor Kingston, an educational psychologist and reading specialist, was President of NRC from 1965-1966.

The Albert J. Kingston Award is about service: service to NRC and contributions of time, energy, and intelligence to our organization. Peter B. Mosenthal, the recipient of the 2004 Albert Kingston Award, certainly gave an abundance of all three. He was a member of the Publications Committee for 4 years, served on the editorial boards of JLR and the NRC Yearbook for 10 and 20 years respectively, reviewed program proposals for over 20 years, a prolific author and coeditor of prestigious research handbooks, and a recent President of NRC. In each of these roles Peter Mosenthal brought vitality and a very special sensibility and humor.

Two stories he told describe his wonderful sense of fun and his will to achieve:

He very nearly got fired his first year of teaching because he allowed his students to use crayons to color in the bubbles of the standardized achievement test—as it was, he had to pay the district $100 for his students to be re-tested.

When he was a little boy walking along the sidewalk near his local library, he saw an older boy carrying a huge stack of books under his arm. He thought to himself that he wanted to be like that older boy who was obviously very smart. He, of course, became that smart boy, and often said of this incident, "Sometimes passers-by make a difference in other people's lives."

This year's Kingston Award goes to Peter B. Mosenthal, who made a difference in many people's lives. He was, from the beginning, an intensely lively member of this organization. He made us laugh, most of the time on purpose. He infused every job he did with wit, and smartness, and charm. And he could give presentations—even his Presidential Address—that left us all exhausted from attempting to keep up with his fast-paced, energetic delivery.

I am immensely pleased to represent the selection committee and NRC in giving this award to Peter B. Mosenthal. We will miss him and know that he will never be replaced.

Accepting the award is Kathleen Hinchman.

Presented by Martha Rapp Ruddell
December 2004

Steven A. Stahl

Oscar S. Causey Award

The Oscar S. Causey Award recognizes outstanding contributions to reading research. Dr. Causey was the founder of the National Reading Conference and served as its president from 1952 to 1959. There were two recipients of this year's Causey Award.

Steven A. Stahl, recipient of the 2004 Oscar Causey award, pursued an extraordinarily diverse research agenda, resulting in seminal contributions to all five constituent areas of reading identified by the National Reading Panel. Researchers in the areas of phonological awareness, phonics, fluency, vocabulary, and comprehension will not travel far in the literature without encountering an important title of his, often one that has modified, sharpened, and occasionally redirected the course of inquiry. His insistence on strong theoretical grounding and methodological rigor became well known to the literacy research community and made him an exemplar of these qualities to students and colleagues alike. This insistence sometimes led him into principled debate with those whose work he felt did not reflect such attributes.

Stahl pioneered assessments of phonemic awareness and related stage theory to its development. He demystified phonics and helped its study regain cachet following the whole language era. John Readence, coeditor of *Reading Research Quarterly*, when Stahl's article, "Everything You Wanted to Know about Phonics" appeared, later called it the finest article on the subject ever written. Stahl referred to fluency as the "forgotten" component of reading and developed a highly successful approach to fostering it, called Fluency-Oriented Reading Instruction. To his first love, vocabulary, he made enduring contributions, such as examining the links between vocabulary and comprehension and distilling important lessons from an abundance of findings. Stahl's interest in comprehension extended well beyond its linkage to vocabulary, and his investigation of how multiple texts are processed advanced stage theory and has helped ground comprehension research in hypertext environments.

His distinguished career was guided by the belief that research must have the enhancement of student achievement as its primary goal. The work that sprang from this belief has been previously recognized by many institutions and organizations. In 2002, the American Educational Research Association presented him with the Interpretive Scholarship Award, for relating research to practice. In 2004, the International Reading Association awarded him the William S. Gray Citation of Merit, perhaps literacy's highest distinction.

His untimely passing underscores the significance of his accomplishments. He achieved so much in so short a time. We all wonder what other topics, issues, and dilemmas would have benefited from his insightful scholarship had he been with us longer. Even so, we are grateful for the time he spent with us and the insights he did bring us. All of us—not just his colleagues, but the thousands of teachers, children, and parents whose lives have been touched, and will continue to be touched, by his contributions to reading theory and pedagogy.

Victoria Purcell-Gates

Oscar S. Causey Award

The Oscar S. Causey Award recognizes outstanding contributions to reading research. Dr. Causey was the founder of the National Reading Conference and served as its president from 1952 to 1959.

A recipient of this year's Causey Award, Dr. Victoria Purcell-Gates, is an individual whose support and participation in NRC has for some time been substantial and substantive.

Victoria Purcell-Gates was marked by early career brilliance, including appointments at some of the most distinguished universities on the North American continent. The record of scholarship is extraordinary, encompassing studies of contrasting elementary classroom literacy environments, family literacy, and adult literacy. She has published significant monographs in each of these areas—real books! A couple of excerpts from the letter of recommendation:

- The work shows theoretical breadth, reflecting a grasp of constructivist and critical perspectives.

- A command of both qualitative and quantitative methodologies.

- Studies conducted in both the U. S. and abroad, significant both nationally and internationally.

Dr. Purcell-Gates can be characterized as an activist in several ways. First is her research focus on marginalized individuals and communities, reminding one of Freirean concepts and actions. Whatever the context of the problem, the story line highlights the needs of those who, for whatever reason, have been dealt a difficult hand. From the nominating letter – "I have been inspired by the nominee's commitment to those who struggle most as literacy learners, and I find that the work offers the hope that new avenues of research will bring us ever closer to knowing how to help these learners." Second is activism in the policy arena, including service dealing with substantive areas of literacy, but also attention to methodological matters – a report on behalf of NRC, for instance, on "The Role of Qualitative and Ethnographic Research in Educational Policy."

A brief professional sketch—graduate work at Berkeley, then a trip to Cambridge and the Harvard Graduate School of Education, which proudly announced in 1996 the receipt of the Grawemeyer Award for *Other People's Words: The Cycle of Low Literacy* (Purcell-Gates, 1995), a case study of an Appalachian family's struggles. In the summer of 2003, Dr. Purcell-Gates volunteered as a classroom aide with Migrant Head Start. Sounds like the beginning of another set of experiences, which gives special meaning to the idea of "participant observation." Other significant monographs include, *Now we read, we see, we speak: Portrait of Literacy Development in an Adult Freirean-based Class* (Purcell-Gates, 2000), and just released, *Print. Literacy Development: Uniting Cognitive and Social Practice Theories* (Purcell-Gates, Jacobson, & Degener, 2004).

Following a visit to Michigan, Dr. Purcell-Gates moved most recently to the University of British Columbia to occupy the Canada Research Chair in the Faculty of Education. Asked about a research program, she answered, "I have to get to know the Canadian context... The community needs to be part of the research.... Everyone who is collecting data needs to find a way to work in that community and give something back." A consistently high ethical standard....

Much more could be said, but to the point. It is my delight to announce the recipient of the 2004-05 Oscar Causey award, a person who blends so many admirable qualities, intelligence, commitment, and grace, Professor Victoria Purcell-Gates.

Presented by Robert Calfee
December 2005

Purcell-Gates, V. (1995). *Other people's words: The cycle of low literacy.* Cambridge, MA: Harvard University Press.

Purcell-Gates, V. (2000). *Now we read, we see, we speak: Portrait of literacy development in an adult Freirean-based class.* Mahwah, NJ: Lawrence Erlbaum Associates.

Purcell-Gates, V., Jacobson, E., & Degener, S. (2004). *Print literacy development: Uniting cognitive and social practice theories.* Cambridge, MA: Harvard University Press.

The Role of Wisdom in Evidence-Based Preschool Literacy Curricula

Lea M. Mcgee

University of Alabama

Early Reading First, a portion of the No Child Left Behind (U.S. Congress, 2001) legislation, authorized $245 million between 2002 and 2004 to develop "preschool centers of educational excellence" (2004 Application for New Grants for the Early Reading First Program, A-1). While the draft guidelines for Early Reading First for each of the three years of funding between 2002 and 2004 have remained the same, there have been two changes in the language of the requirements in Selection Criteria for the grants in 2002 versus 2004 which prompted the focus of this paper.

In both 2002 and in 2004, the Application for New Grants for the Early Reading First Program specified that Early Reading First grantees would use "language and literacy activities based on scientifically based reading research that supports the age-appropriate development of-

- Oral language (vocabulary development, expressive language, and listening comprehension);

- Phonological awareness (rhyming, blending, segmenting)

- Print awareness; and

- Alphabet knowledge (letter recognition) (for example, 2004, p. B-2)."

However, there were differences between 2002 and 2004 in the categories of Selection Criteria and in the language used within these categories. In 2002, grantees were evaluated on the Quality of Project Activities (or Services) where the level of early literacy achievement was not specified (see 2002, p. E-6). In contrast, in 2004 (in a Selection Criterion not included in the 2004 Quality of the Project Design) grantees were evaluated on their plan for insuring that children in the project would develop:

(A) Recognition, leading to automatic recognition, of letters of the alphabet;

(B) Knowledge of letter sounds, the blending of sounds, and the use of increasingly complex vocabulary;

(C) An understanding that written language is composed of phonemes and letters, each representing one or more speech sounds that in combination make up syllables, words, and sentences;

(D) Spoken language, including vocabulary and oral comprehension abilities;

(E) Knowledge of the purposes and conventions of print. (Application for New Grants for the Early Reading First Program, 2004, p. E-10)

While the broad categories of oral language, phonological awareness, print awareness, and alphabet knowledge were still referenced in other places in the 2004 document (for example, B-12), grantees were evaluated on their attention to these more specified achievement levels.

In addition to the shift from more general expectations to higher and more specified levels of child outcomes, there was also a shift away from a call for "activities and services" to a call for using "the curriculum" to deliver instruction in 2004. The Quality of Project Design Selection Criteria in 2004 required applicants to:

> Outline *the curriculum's* defined scope and sequence and describe how it is structured, systematic, and aligned to support the development of children's oral language, phonological awareness, print awareness, and alphabet knowledge. (italics added, p. E-10)

These two shifts prompted me to ask three questions which focus specifically on alphabet knowledge and phonemic awareness:

1. What level of alphabet knowledge and phonemic awareness is enough to prepare children for success in kindergarten?

2. What methods of teaching, materials, and activities have researchers found effective in teaching phonemic awareness and alphabet knowledge to three- and four-year-olds?

3. How well do early language and literacy curricula match conclusions about instructional goals and the methods, materials, and activities found to be effective in reaching those goals?

I focus on alphabet knowledge and phonological awareness for two reasons: (a) it narrowed my task to a (barely) manageable size; and (b) because it has been the topic of so much interest and controversy. I do not, however, want to imply that these two components of emergent literacy are more important, more crucial, or more central to the task of learning to read and write. In fact, oral language and comprehension are emerging as far more crucial than we previously have believed (Storch & Whitehurst, 2002; Dickinson, McCabe, Anastasopoulos, Peisner-Feinberg, & Poe, 2003).

GOVERNMENT-SPONSORED REVIEWS OF RESEARCH: WHAT DO THEY SUGGEST?

In order to answer the first question, I first examined recommendations of the Committee on the Prevention of Reading Difficulties in Young Children summarized in *Preventing Reading Difficulties in Young Children* (Snow, Burns, & Griffin, 1998) in order to determine the level of alphabet knowledge and phonemic awareness we can reasonably expect in preschool. In the chapter titled "Preventing Reading Difficulties Before Kindergarten," Snow and her colleagues reviewed three preschool phonological training studies. From this review they concluded, "It is clear that instruction in phonological awareness ought to be accompanied by training in letters and letter-sound associations also. Children who *enter school* with these competencies will be better prepared to benefit from formal reading instruction" (p. 154-55, italics added). One of the three phonological awareness training studies examined in their chapter included a 1989 study by Byrne and Fielding-Barnsley, although none of Byrne and Fielding-Barnsley's subsequent works (e.g., Byrne, 1992; Byrne & Fielding-Barnsley, 1990, 1991, 1993, & 1995) were discussed in this chapter. The second study quoted in their chapter was an unpublished manuscript (Dorval, Joyce, & Ramey, 1980), and the third study was actually conducted in inner-city kindergartens (Brady, Fowler, Stone, & Winbury, 1994). To further complicate matters, in the chapter summary, the authors significantly altered the way they discussed letter and phonological awareness outcomes for preschoolers, they stated: "Ideally, . . . children [will] have acquired some specific knowledge of letters, [and] . . some capacity to play with and analyze the sound system of their native language" (p. 170).

Next, I turned to *The Report of the National Reading Panel* (2000) for its recommendations on expected outcomes in preschool. In its section on "Alphabetics," the authors drew conclusions about levels of instruction in phonological awareness that are appropriate for different ages of children. They concluded that, "The reason to teach first-sound comparisons is to draw preschoolers' or kindergartners' attention to the fact that words have sounds as well as meanings. A reason to teach phoneme segmentation is to help kindergartners or first graders generate more complete spellings of words" (p. 2-31). First-sound comparisons involve selecting the names of pictures or spoken words that have the same initial sound--what Byrne and his colleagues (Byrne & Fielding-Barnsley, 1991) call phoneme identity and Bradley and Bryant (1985) call sound categorization.

Together these two large-scale, government-sponsored reviews of research suggested that children in preschool should begin the journey into learning the alphabet and acquiring phonological awareness. However, neither provided convincing evidence of how far that journey should take them, although the *Report of the Reading Panel* (2000) suggested a possible ending point for phonological awareness.

REVIEW OF THREE BODIES OF RESEARCH

Next, I examined three bodies of research in order to address my three questions:

1. Research which has described what preschoolers know and can do (descriptive studies);

2. Research which has examined what is critical for preschoolers to know (longitudinal studies); and

3. Research which has examined what preschoolers can learn to do (instructional or training studies).

The first body of research includes qualitative and quantitative studies describing young children as they engage in literacy activities in their homes or preschools. These included, among many: Barone's (1999) case studies of young children exposed to crack/cocaine; Fox and Routh's (1975) study of preschool children's ability to segment sentences into words and words into syllables and phonemes; Chaney's (1992) study of metalinguistic skills in three-year-old children; and Lonigan, Burgess, Anthony, and Barker's (1998) study of two- to five-year-old children's phonological sensitivity at different levels of linguistic complexity.

Several studies suggested that four-year-olds, especially from middle-income families, learn a great deal about alphabet letters (e.g., Mason, 1980; Worden & Boettcher, 1990; Treiman, Tincoff, Rodriguez, Mousaki, & Francis, 1998). Treiman and her colleagues examined the knowledge of individual alphabet letters and letter-sound correspondences among 660 preschool children in three locations in the United States. Children in California assessed in the late 1980s knew a mean of 54% of the upper case letter names compared to preschoolers in Detroit assessed in the mid 1990s who knew a mean of 74%. Children knew fewer letter-sounds (in California a mean of 6 letter sounds and in Detroit a mean of 9). Thus, middle-class four-year olds typically knew a range of 14-19 upper case alphabet letters, fewer lower case letters (a mean of 10), and fewer letter-sounds (a range from 6 to 9) (Treiman et al., 1998; Worden & Boettcher, 1990).

While Treiman and Kessler (2003) argued that preschoolers learn letter-names from informal experiences, such as singing the alphabet song or reading alphabet books at home or in preschool, Bloodgood's (1999) research suggests another important pathway for the beginning of alphabet letter learning. Bloodgood studied the development of children's ability to recognize and write their name as well as their development of a variety of early literacy concepts. Her study showed that children's alphabet learning emerged later than, and was related to, their awareness and skill in recognizing and writing their name.

Numerous studies have demonstrated that preschoolers are capable of demonstrating various levels of phonological and phonemic awareness. For example, Lonigan and his colleagues (Lonigan, Burgess, Anthony, & Barker, 1998) found that 26% of two-year-olds, 14% of three-year-olds, and 39% of four-year-olds knew rhyme. In contrast, no two-year-olds could identify a word that began with a different phoneme from a set of three words, 9% of three-year-olds could do this, and only 34% of four-year-olds--all these children were from middle-income families. Only 10% of four-year-olds from low-income families could perform this task.

While this body of research documented the kinds of early conventional concepts related to language and literacy, and provided some information about the percentage of children who could complete the assessment tasks ultimately, it was not very helpful in answering the question of what level of alphabet knowledge and phonemic awareness is sufficient at the end of preschool to reasonably predict success in kindergarten. These researchers did not address either theoretically or empirically the level of knowledge that matters at kindergarten entry.

So, I turned next to examine longitudinal research intended to predict later reading and writing performance from earlier performance. These researchers search for variables that account for unique variance after variables such as verbal skills, IQ, age, and SES have been controlled. In preschool these included alphabet recognition, phonological awareness, name writing, and concepts about print and vocabulary. A classic example of this kind of research is Maclean, Bryant, and Bradley's (1987) study of the relationship between preschool children's knowledge of nursery rhymes and their later phonological development. Other examples include the work of Bowey (1995), Lonigan, Burgess, and Anthony (2000), Storch and Whitehurst (2002), and Muter, Hulme, Snowling, and Stevenson (2004).

Surprisingly, I found that predictor studies were quite uninformative in answering my question of how much phonemic awareness and alphabet knowledge is enough. To illustrate, the following is a summary statement typical of the longitudinal studies I examined: "Our results are clear (a) in demonstrating the critical roles of phoneme sensitivity and letter knowledge for the development of early word recognition skills, and (b) in demonstrating that for reading comprehension, as might be expected, vocabulary knowledge and grammatical skills play additional significant roles" (Muter, Hulme, Snowling, & Stevenson, 2004, p. 679).

The only researchers, out of the many longitudinal studies that I read, who took a stance on how much alphabet knowledge and phonemic awareness ought to be expected in preschool were David Dickinson and his colleagues (Dickinson, McCabe, Anastasopoulos, Peisner-Feinberg, & Poe, 2003). These researchers were predicting the later reading and writing achievement of Head Start children and found these children had very low levels of preschool language and literacy development. They noted that the mean receptive vocabulary score for the children in their study was in the 19th percentile. Print and phonological skills for these children were similarly depressed. In contrast, they suggested that children who have experienced one or two years of preschool should have been able to recognize familiar environmental print words in context, discriminate words from non-words (letter, number, and symbol strings), write their name, and identify many alphabet letters. Similarly, they argued that children should have been able to produce rhyming words and delete ending sounds from words. While most of these recommendations seem reasonable, it is important to note that there is considerable controversy over whether the use of deletion of phonemes is an adequate measure of preschool phonological awareness. Blachman (2000), for example, concluded that "more complex manipulation of phonemes, such as is required in the deletion and rearrangement of phonemes in a spoken words, is actually the result of learning to read and spell" (p. 494) suggesting, as did *The National Reading Panel* (2000), that segmenting phonemes is more appropriate at the kindergarten and first-grade level where instruction in reading is provided.

Finally, I examined training studies, in which preschool children were taught alphabet letters, phonological awareness, or sound-letter correspondences, for further insights into how much alphabet knowledge and phonemic awareness can be expected in preschool. Two lines of research emerged as critical in addressing this question: the series of studies conducted by Treiman and her colleagues (e.g., Treiman, Weatherson, & Berch, 1994; Treiman, Tincoff, & Richmond-Welty, 1996, 1997; Treiman, Tincoff, Rodriguez, Mouzaki, & Francis, 1998; Treiman & Kessler, 2003); and those conducted by Byrne and his colleagues (Byrne & Fielding-Barnsley, 1989, 1990, 1991, 1993, 1995, 2000; Byrne, 1998; Byrne, Fielding-Barnsley, & Ashley, 2000). However, before reviewing these two critical lines of research, I review a few phonological awareness training studies in which preschoolers reached awareness of phonemes, for reasons that will become apparent later in this paper.

Lundberg and his colleagues (Lundberg, Frost, & Peterson, 1988) taught Danish preschool children who were actually six and seven years old to manipulate words, syllables, rhymes, and finally phonemes. The gains children made in phonological awareness produced higher levels of reading and spelling in Grade 1. This groundbreaking study was replicated with five-year-old kindergartners in Germany (Schneider, Kuspert, Roth, Vice, & Marx, 1997), but not with preschoolers. One innovative study conducted by Ukrainetz and her colleagues (Ukrainetz, Cooney, Dyer, Kysar, & Harris, 2000) showed how preschoolers and kindergartners were taught phonemic awareness embedded within shared reading. The teacher read aloud a book with several rhyming words and stopped every second page to help children identify two rhyming words, isolate each of their beginning phonemes, segment each of the words into phonemes, and count the number of phonemes. In a study using a more explicit approach, Justice and her colleagues (Justice, Chow, Capellini, Flanigan, & Colton, 2003) increased preschoolers' ability to segment phonemes during six weeks of game-like instruction. In both these studies, instruction was effective in improving children's phonemic awareness. It is not clear, however, whether this increase in awareness made a significant difference in children's reading and spelling because the children were not followed into kindergarten and first grade. Nonetheless, these studies demonstrate that it is possible for four-year-olds to become aware of phonemes and to manipulate them with teacher support.

Acquiring Alphabet Knowledge: The Legacy of Rebecca Treiman and Her Colleagues

Most of Treiman's long career has been devoted to uncovering the role that alphabet letter names play in literacy acquisition. In order to put her research into context, I return to 1975 when Richard Venezky published "The Curious Role of Letter Names in Reading Instruction." He reviewed several studies including those in which researchers taught children alphabet letters and then assessed their ability to decode words. For the most part, these researchers found no enhanced decoding resulted from merely teaching children to name the alphabet letters. Based on these and other studies conducted with adults who were taught to discriminate among shapes with or without learning names for the shapes, Venezky concluded, "a heavy emphasis on letter-name learning in either pre-reading or initial reading programs has neither logical nor experimental support" (1975, p. 19). Adams (1990) reached the same conclusion in her review of research. Thus, it is not surprising that we have had so few alphabet training studies in the last 30 years.

However, Treiman took a different route to investigating the role of letter names in literacy development. Rather than teaching children alphabet letters, she demonstrated, in a series of studies, how the alphabet name knowledge that children already had acquired influenced their performance on reading and spelling tasks. In one study (Treiman & Rodriguez, 1999) children were taught to read words with simplified spellings (like those used by Ehri and Wilce, 1985). Children learned to associate a word with each of the spellings. The word learned for the letter name spellings included the name of the letter in the word (BT for the word /bee/ /t/). The word learned for letter-sound spellings included letters associated with the sounds at the beginning and endings of the word (BT for the word /b/ ai /t/). The word learned for visually distinctive spellings included letters not associated with the word, but the letters were written in various sizes to make them more memorable (B T for ham).

Preschool and kindergarten children who could read no words at the onset of the study were able to learn to read the simplified spellings. They learned more words with letter-name spellings than either words with visually-distinctive spellings or words with sound-related spellings. Thus, Treiman and her colleagues concluded that children must be using their knowledge of letter names to boost their word reading. In other studies Treiman and her colleagues demonstrated that children's letter name knowledge influenced their spelling (e.g., Treiman, Sotak, & Bowman, 2001; Treiman, Tincoff, & Richmond-Welty, 1996; Treiman, Weatherston, & Berch, 1994).

Treiman and her colleagues also demonstrated that knowing alphabet letter names plays a role in learning sound-letter associations. In one study (Treiman, Tincoff, Rodriguez, Mouzaki, & Francis, 1998), preschoolers were taught the sounds of 10 alphabet letters using paired associate learning methods. Children included in the study knew the names of the letters used in the training, but they knew few or none of their sounds. Three kinds of letters were included in the study: letters in which the sound normally associated with the letter is found at the beginning of the letter name (CV letters such as d and v); letters in which the sound is found at the end of the letter name (VC letters such as l and m); and letters in which the sound is not found in the letter name (other letters such as w and y). Children performed better with CV letters than VC letters, and better with VC letters than other letters. Treiman believed that the only way to learn to associate the letter shape with either its name or sound was through rote memory, and paired associate learning is the most effective method for helping people learn to associate two seemingly unrelated and non-meaningful items. Therefore, she argued that if children's performance was based on memory alone, then children should have performed equally well on all three kinds of spellings. They did not, and Treiman concluded that without any direct instruction, children were able to deduce relationships between letter names and sounds.

Share (2004) replicated this study with Israeli children who spoke no English (Share, 2004). Both Treiman and Kessler (2003) and Share concluded that children must be able to segment the sound out of the letter name. However, it could be that children notice that similar vocal gestures are used to say a letter name and its sound--something that Murray (1998) has argued. Nonetheless, these studies demonstrated that children first acquire knowledge of some alphabet letter names, followed by the ability to use this knowledge of specific letters to learn to spell, read, and discover letter-sound relationships. Once children have acquired some alphabet letter recognition, they can use this knowledge strategically in principled learning, particularly of letter-sound relationships, rather than relying on mere rote memory.

However, in summarizing what children must learn in order to first recognize alphabet letters, Treiman and Kessler (2003) stated that "rote memorization of shape-name pairs is the only option with languages like English, where the shapes of almost all letters are, from the child's point of view, arbitrary" (p. 119). Thus, she and her colleague argued that rote learning was the only pathway to learning to recognize alphabet letters by name. The way to increase the effectiveness of letter-name learning, they suggested, was to increase children's familiarity with the stimulus (the letter shape) or the response (its name), thereby increasing the speed with which children will memorize the pairing. Paired associative learning is the most efficient way to learn non-meaningful pairs, thus alphabet recognition instruction should capitalize on these techniques.

But is the stimulus, the letter shape, something that must merely be memorized? Gibson and her colleagues (Gibson, Gibson, Pick, & Osser, 1962; Gibson & Levin, 1975) demonstrated that children learned to discriminate among alphabet letters using an ever-increasing awareness of letter features such as straight or curved lines, open or closed letters, and orientation. Murray (1998) suggested that learning alphabet letters might be learning alphabet identities, in which children learn the features that distinguish one category (e.g., C) from other categories (e.g., U) through example and non-example.

Thus, becoming familiar with letter stimulus (letter shapes) must involve learning about letter features so that the categories of different letters (for example, C and U) can be distinguished from one another. Researchers have shown that children learn confusable letters (letters which share features) later than less confusable letters (Treiman et al., 1998). Nonetheless, in order to learn the alphabet letter names, children must get past the obstacle of confusable letter features. I would expect that effective alphabet letter instruction would confront children with letter features. Children would examine or write examples and non-examples of particular letters, possibly talking about how the letter features are alike or different, in order to make letter shapes more familiar. I would argue that combining attention with letter features and discriminating confusable letters should be included as a part of paired associative learning techniques. Thus, I would expect that children would learn sets of 2-6 letters together because paired associate learning methods are more effective with a small number of pairings to be learned.

Now I turn to two recent studies in which researchers have taught children several early language and literacy concepts including alphabet letters. Roberts (2003) and her colleague (Roberts & Neal, 2004) taught preschool English Language Learners whose home language was Spanish or Hmong several early literacy concepts in two different treatment groups. Children in the letter-rhyme group learned to identify 16 alphabet letter names using a series of what I would call "table top" games during "letter of the week" instruction. These consisted of finding the target letter in a bag of letters and feeding it to a puppet, finding the letter in the children's names, matching letters, and writing the letter with teacher guidance. The children were also taught rhyming by listening to rhymes and jingles, judging whether words rhymed, matching rhyming words, and generating rhymes. Children in the comprehension group were introduced to a story a week, taught vocabulary from the story, and participated in activities which drew attention to story events, sequence, and vocabulary. The researchers argued that both of the instruction procedures were explicit. At the end of the sixteen-week instructional program, children in the letter-rhyme group learned more alphabet letters and children in the comprehension group learned more vocabulary. No other differences were found. In a similar study with more emphasis on rhyme and teacher-modeled fingerpoint reading, Roberts (2003) found that the letter-rhyme children learned more alphabet letter names whereas the comprehension group learned more vocabulary and concepts about print.

In both studies, the instruction in alphabet recognition proved effective. In the letter-rhyme treatment group, 58% of the children knew 13 or more of the 16 letters taught and the mean of the entire group was 11 out of 16 (Roberts & Neal, 2004). These researchers pointed out these children learned 50% of the alphabet names, a performance similar to what Worden and Boettcher (1990) found with middle class children. This seems remarkable given that all of the children in these two studies were identified as non-English speaking at the beginning of the instruction.

Other techniques for teaching alphabet letter recognition have also been successfully employed. Justice and her colleagues (Justice et al, 2003) taught low-income children, many with oral language difficulties, to recognize alphabet letters by teaching them to write and recognize letters in their names, sing the alphabet song while pointing to the alphabet letters, and play alphabet letter games. In a different study Justice and Ezell (2002) read aloud big books using prompts that focused on alphabet letters (e.g., "Where is the letter B on this page?" "Does anyone see any letters in their name?" "What two letters are the same on this page?"). In both studies children increased their ability to name alphabet letters.

Notice that the kind of instruction for learning alphabet letter names provided in these studies was not much like the paired associate techniques and focus on letter features that I laid out as optimal. Letters in these studies were not taught in groups. For example, in the Roberts studies (Roberts, 2003; Roberts & Neal, 2004), one letter a week was taught and no explicit mention of review across weeks was mentioned in the study--although surely this was done. In no study were letter features discussed, and confusable letters were not addressed. However, letters were written frequently during instruction, and children sang the alphabet song. Clearly, much research is to be done in order to discover the most effective ways to teach children alphabet letter names, especially for children who find this difficult.

However, I am confident from the studies that I have reviewed, and others I will now turn to, that we can expect preschoolers to learn from 50-75% of the alphabet letter names before the end of preschool. The benefit of knowing this many letters is that learning the remainder of the letters should be quicker and easier (suggesting another study that ought to be conducted). Further, as shown by Treiman and her colleagues (Treiman et al., 1998), this level of alphabet knowledge will allow children to acquire awareness of sound-letter relationships more strategically, and as I will argue next, facilitate acquiring phonological awareness.

Acquiring Phonemic Awareness: The Legacy of Brian Byrne and His Colleagues

In 1989, Brian Byrne and his colleague Ruth Fielding-Barnsley began a series of studies aimed at answering the question: What is the minimum amount of information, including phonemic awareness, that young children need in order to acquire a rudimentary understanding of the alphabetic principle? (Byrne & Fielding-Barnsley, 1989, 1990, 1991, 1993, 1995; Byrne, 1996, 1998; Byrne, Fielding-Barnsley, & Ashley, 2000) Byrne (1998) defined the alphabetic principle as awareness that the letters which comprise printed words stand for individual sounds which comprise spoken language (p. 1). In a series of small-scale experiments, he and his colleague(s) taught children a series of skills using paired associate learning. For example, the children learned to segment the words *sat* and *mat*, and then they learned to read *sat* and *mat*. Next, the children were tested to determine if they had acquired the alphabetic principle on a transfer task. In this task, children were shown a printed word (such as *sow*), and asked whether the word was *sow* or *mow*. Finally, children learned letter-sound associations (i.e., m says /m/ and s says /s/). Again children were given the transfer test. Finally, children were taught the names of the two critical letters. In some experiments children were taught phoneme identity instead of phoneme segmentation. For phoneme identity, children practiced matching and sorting words with the same beginning phoneme.

In every experiment, children performed above chance on the transfer test only after: (a) learning to read the words mat and sat; (b) learning the letter-sound associations of m and s; and (c) acquiring phoneme identity. Thus, these researchers concluded that phoneme identity and knowledge of letter-sound relationships were the minimal concepts required to induce the alphabetic principle. Murray's (1998) research with kindergartners provides some additional support for this hypothesis. Byrne and Fielding-Barnsley's research clearly demonstrates that the easiest level of phonemic awareness that matters in helping children reach the critical insight to reading (i.e., the alphabetic principle) is phoneme identity, although this needs to be accompanied by knowledge of letter-sound relationships.

These results led Byrne and Fielding-Barnsley to develop a program for teaching phoneme identity, which they called *Sound Foundations* (1991). They evaluated its effectiveness on children's development of phonemic awareness, acquisition of the alphabetic principle, and on later reading and writing performance in a larger-scale training study. The treatment consisted of teaching children to recognize six phonemes in initial and final positions in words. Children in the treatment group were taught in small groups of 4-6 by Ruth Fielding-Barnsley for 20 minutes once a week for 12 weeks using pictures presented on large posters and worksheets. Children in the control group used the same materials as the treatment group; however, they were taught to sort pictures by semantic categories rather than by first or last phoneme.

Children in the treatment group scored higher on a posttest of phoneme identity both for the phonemes that were included in the lessons and for phonemes that were never taught. Only 32% of the children in the control group reached the criterion level; whereas, 95% of the treatment children reached criterion on this assessment. Only 15% of the children in the control group reached criterion on the alphabetic principle transfer task; whereas, 47% of the treatment children reached criterion on this same task--which was not included in the instruction.

A follow-up study of children in kindergarten (Byrne & Fielding-Barnsley, 1993) showed that treatment children were better than the control children on final phoneme identity but not initial, and that they were also better at pseudoword identification. In grades 1 and 2 (Byrne & Fielding-Barnsley, 1995) treatment children were still better at identifying pseudowords in first grade and better at comprehension as well in grade 2. Differences favoring the treatment group children were still found in a follow-up study when the children were in fifth grade (Byrne, Fielding-Barnsley, & Ashley, 2000) on word attack and identifying irregular words.

In 1995 Byrne and Fielding-Barnsley reported the results of an additional instructional study of classroom teachers who implemented the *Sound Foundation* program using whole group instruction. Teachers did not implement the program with as much fidelity as in the original study, and the results were less promising. Only 52% of the treatment children reached criterion on the phoneme identity test compared to the 95% who achieved it with more intensive, small-group instruction delivered by the researcher.

There are other differences between the original study and the classroom study that merit close attention. The original study included middle-income children with a mean expressive vocabulary score of 110. These children knew a mean of 12.6 alphabet letters at the onset of the study. A sizeable proportion of the children had high levels of phoneme identity before the study began. In the 2000 report, these researchers revealed that they had assessed whether each child was secure in the concept of phoneme identity at the end of each of the preschool instructional lessons. In order to be secure, children had to identify correctly every picture in the poster and worksheet that began with the target sound. Twenty-six of the sixty-four treatment children were judged to be secure in the very first lesson and remained secure for the remainder of the instruction.

For the classroom study, information about children's initial levels of literacy knowledge is not described. However, it could be that children began instruction in the classroom study with lower levels of literacy knowledge. This hypothesis is supported by the results of a study by Whitehurst and his colleagues (Whitehurst, Epstein, Angell, Payne, Crone, & Fischel, 1994; Whitehurst, Zevenbergen, Crone, Schultz, Velting, & Fischel, 1999) in which they implemented Sound Foundations in Head Start classrooms in the United States.

Whitehurst and others (1994, 1999) attempted to intensify phoneme identity instruction by teaching children the Sound Foundations program three days a week over a longer period of time, although instruction was delivered in whole group settings. However, at the beginning of this study, children's alphabet knowledge and their ability to identify same-different sounds were below normal. The mean score of oral vocabulary ranged from 86 to 90 among the different treatment groups. Thus, it seems clear that the Head Start children began Sound Foundations with considerably lower expressive vocabulary levels, less alphabet knowledge, and lower than normal levels of phonological awareness compared to children in the Australian study (Byrne & Fielding-Barnsley, 1991).

Differences in both the starting levels of skills of the children and the intensity of the instruction could explain the difference in results between the Australian study and the Head Start study. Whitehurst and his colleagues (1994) did find differences between the treatment and control group in both preschool and kindergarten (although not second grade), but not the dramatic differences found in the Australian study. It could be that the children in the Head Start study were less responsible to the instruction within *Sound Foundations* because they did not have sufficient levels of literacy knowledge at the onset to take advantage of this instruction. Perhaps they lacked sufficient potential to learn what was taught.

Byrne and his colleagues argued that children's responsiveness to instruction is based on whether they have the potential to learn what is taught in instruction (Byrne, Fielding-Barnsley, & Ashley, 2000). Responsiveness to instruction, actually learning what is taught, is as Treiman and others (1998) have argued, is a function of the effectiveness of instruction and children's "ability to learn from and make sense of the instruction" (p. 1536). Children may need to have acquired a certain threshold of knowledge in order to learn from and make sense of certain kinds of instruction (Byrne, 1998).

There is research suggesting that alphabet letter knowledge may, indeed, act as a threshold enabling children to acquire phonological concepts (Stahl & Murray, 1994). For example,

Johnston, Anderson, and Holligan (1996) showed that there is a strong relationship between knowing some alphabet letters and being able to perform phonemic awareness tasks. These researchers identified children who could not name any letters versus those who could identify one or more letters. They also identified children who could not segment or delete even one phoneme versus those who could. They found 25 children who knew one or more letters and could also segment or delete one or more phonemes. These children knew a mean of eight letters. They also found a group of 17 children who knew one or more letters but could not segment or delete a single phoneme. They knew a mean of fewer than two letters. There was only one child who could segment or delete at least one phoneme who knew no alphabet letters. These results indicate that children's knowledge of alphabet letter names, even a few, is related to their being able to perform phonemic awareness tasks. Treiman's argument (Treiman & Kessler, 2003) that knowing some alphabet letter names facilitates children's awareness of letter-sound relations suggests a possible mechanism by which alphabet letters provide the potential to learn phonemic awareness. Knowing a threshold number of letters (more than two at least) may provide the potential to notice the phonological properties of a letter name including its phoneme, and thus to operate at the level of phoneme at least unconsciously. This in turn enables children to acquire the more conscious competency of letter-sound knowledge and phoneme identity. This may explain why phonological training studies that have also included instruction in letter-sounds have found superior effects compared to instruction without letter-sound instruction (*Report of the National Reading Panel,* 2000). Knowing a few letter names facilitates children's awareness of the phonological properties in a letter name and facilitates learning letter-sound associations. Learning letter-sounds and discovering, at the intuitive level, phonological properties of letter names provides the potential for and facilitates the acquisition of more explicit phonemic awareness. This may also explain why preschoolers in Read's (1975) study were able to discover how to spell words before being able to read. They may have used alphabet letter knowledge to identify sound segments in words.

The concept of "potential to learn," for example, the potential to learn alphabet letter names or letter-sounds or phoneme identity, is a concept that deserves more research. Of course, potential to learn is entirely dependent on what is to be taught. I am suggesting that knowing some alphabet letters, perhaps eight or more, provides the potential to acquire some phonological awareness. Using letters in phonemic awareness instruction, drawing explicit attention to the phoneme embedded in the letter name, and drawing explicit attention to vocal gestures when saying both the phoneme and letter name may enable children who already know some letter names to acquire initial phonemic insights. Thus, learning some alphabet letters may enable children to take advantage of more complex instruction, such as acquiring a concept of phoneme identity. Similarly, singing the alphabet song and learning to recognize, write, and spell their names may enable children to take advantage of the more complex letter-name instruction.

A recent review of longitudinal and training studies in phonemic awareness also supports this conclusion. Castles and Coltheart (2004) argued that no study has actually demonstrated that phonological awareness has been taught prior to any emergence of literacy knowledge including letter recognition. Further, they argued there was no evidence to suggest that syllable manipulation or segmenting words into sentences were related to later development in phonemic awareness. This conclusion is supported by another review of research on rhyme instruction and its role in learning to read and spell (Macmillan, 2002).

Therefore, I conclude that the levels of alphabet knowledge and phonemic awareness that can be expected to emerge at the end of preschool are:

1. recognition of 50-75% of upper and lower case alphabet letters (Bloodgood, 1999; Treiman & Kessler, 2003; Worden & Boettcher, 1990; Roberts 2003; Roberts & Neal, 2004)

2. phoneme identity of 6 or more phonemes (Byrne & Fielding-Barnsley, 1991, 1993, 1995; Justice et al., 2003; Lundberg et al., 1988; Ukrainetz et al., 2000)

3. knowledge of 6-9 letter-sound relationships (Treiman & Kessler, 2003; suggested by Byrne & Fielding-Barnsley, 1991, 1993, 1995)

4. rudimentary use of the alphabetic principle in reading new words in familiar rhyming word families (Byrne & Fielding-Barnsley, 1991; Byrne, Fielding-Barnsley, & Ashley, 2000) and spelling words using early invented spellings (Read, 1975).

EFFECTIVE PHONEME IDENTITY INSTRUCTION

The second question that framed this paper was: What does research reveal about effective instruction in alphabet knowledge and phonemic awareness? In order to answer this question, I reexamined any research study in which preschool children were taught alphabet recognition, phoneme identity, letter-sound relationships, rudimentary word reading, or invented spelling. However, because of length constraints, I will only describe one set of research-based assumptions that I deduced related to instruction in phoneme identity:

1. Begin instruction when children know some alphabet letters, perhaps 8 or more letters (Johnston, Anderson, & Holligan, 1996).

2. Begin instruction when children know the names of the alphabet letters associated with the phonemes to be taught (Treiman & Kessler, 2003).

3. Teach a small set of 5 to 6 phonemes including CV non-continuants and VC continuants (Byrne & Fielding-Barnsley, 1991; Treiman & Kessler, 2003).

4. Use continuants early in instruction (Byrne & Fielding-Barnsley, 1991).

5. Draw attention to the phoneme in the letter name (Treiman & Kessler, 2003).

6. Draw attention to vocal gesture in both the phoneme in isolation and in words (Murray, 1998).

7. Make explicit that certain words are alike because they have the same phoneme (Byrne & Fielding-Barnsley, 1991; Murray, 1998; Byrne, 1998).

8. Focus on the phoneme at the beginning and then the end of words (Byrne & Fielding-Barnsley, 1991).

9. When more than one phoneme is acquired, have children sort or match pictures by phoneme (Byrne & Fielding-Barnsley, 1991; Murray, 1998).

10. When a child does not acquire phoneme identity after several days of instruction, consider the child's potential to learn and provide enabling activities (Byrne, 1998).

11. Segue from phoneme identity instruction to letter-sound instruction in each lesson so both are coordinated in order that both letter-sound learning and phoneme identify are boosted at rates beyond rote learning (Treiman & Kessler, 2003; *The Report of the National Reading Panel,* 2000).

THE CASCADE OF INSIGHTS

Based on this list of critical preschool competences and on my lists of assumptions about effective instruction derived from research, I propose a model of preschool early literacy curriculum, which I call, based on Byrne's suggestion (1998, p. 140), The Cascade of Insights. Figure 1 presents this model curriculum, an unfolding of increasingly complex concepts which I argue should define the preschool curriculum in teaching alphabet knowledge and phonemic awareness (obviously not the entire early literacy curriculum). First, instruction should focus on activities that seem to enable both the acquisition of alphabet letter naming and phonemic awareness. Research suggests these Enabling Activities would include: singing the alphabet song (Treiman & Kessler, 2003), reading alphabet books (Murray, Stahl, & Ivy, 1996); listening to and reciting nursery rhymes and singing songs with rhyme (MacLean, Bryant, & Bradley, 1987); and

Figure 1 The Cascade of Insights

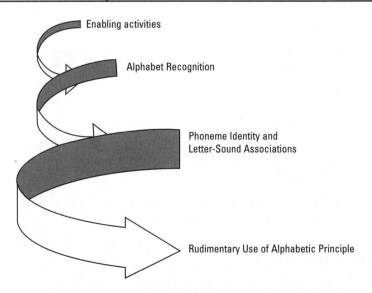

Enabling activities

Alphabet Recognition

Phoneme Identity and
Letter-Sound Associations

Rudimentary Use of Alphabetic Principle

learning to recognize, write, and spell names (Bloodgood, 1999). Reading and attending to the letters in environmental print may also be enabling (Cronin, Farrell, & Delaney, 1999; McGee, Lomax, & Head, 1988); however, some researchers have found that environmental print does not lead children to more sophisticated understandings (Masonheimer, Drum, & Ehri, 1984). Tapping syllables, segmenting sentences into words, and learning rhyming words may also be in this category (Lundberg et al, 1988; Schneider et al., 1997). It is clear that some, although few, young children can and do develop these concepts even without instruction (MacLean, Bryant, & Bradley, 1987; Lonigan et al, 1998); however, no research has shown that children *must* learn these skills before moving to the level of phoneme or even whether doing so makes it easier to learn about phonemes (Castles & Coltheart, 2004; Macmillan, 2002). Brady and her colleagues (Brady, Fowler, Stone, & Winsbury, 1994) commented that having kindergartners segment sentences into words seemed to confuse children; Schneider and his colleagues (Schneider, Kuspert, Roth, & Vise, 1997) who replicated the Lundberg et al (1988) study with German kindergartners, found that shortening the length of time spent in rhyming instruction and lengthening the amount of time spent on analyzing phonemes had more effect on later reading and writing development. Van Kleek and her colleagues (Van Kleek, Gillam, & McFadden, 1998) discovered that preschoolers who spent an entire semester learning rhyme yielded no better rhyming skills than children who merely participated in their regular instruction, although the same amount of time spent on phoneme instruction was powerful in increasing phonemic awareness. Further, Byrne and Fielding-Barnsley's extensive line of research demonstrated that children can go directly to the level of phoneme without practice with larger linguistic units.

Enabling activities should accelerate children's learning of alphabet letter names. Once children acquire some alphabet name knowledge, and research suggests that it might be the acquisition of eight or more alphabet letter names (Johnston, Anderson, & Holligan, 1996), phoneme identity instruction may begin. However, Byrne and Fielding-Barnsley's (1991) research implied that this instruction can wait until some children have higher levels of alphabet knowledge and some children have already developed some level of phonemic awareness from more informal activities before initiating instruction for all children. Letter-sound instruction should occur simultaneously, and be coordinated with, phoneme identity instruction. Instruction should capitalize on children's knowledge of letter names and demonstrate how to use vocal gestures to discover letter-sound relationships. Letter sound and phoneme identity instruction should focus on a small group of letters and phonemes so that children are quickly led to the alphabetic principle. When letter-sounds and phoneme identity are achieved, children should be introduced to rudimentary alphabetic principle activities. Children can identify whether a word like *mat* says *sat* or *mat* and be guided in how to turn the word *mat* into *fat*. This is precisely Byrne and Fielding-Barnsley's transfer of the alphabetic principle task with the instructional components of scaffolding and problem solving (which they never included). In addition, children could be guided to invent spellings as another appropriate rudimentary use of the alphabetic principle.

TO WHAT EXTENT DOES A RESEARCH-BASED
CURRICULUM REFLECT THE RESEARCH?

Because of length constraints I review only one curriculum, *SRA Open Court Reading* (Bereiter, Campione, Carruthers, Hirshberg, McKeough, Pressley, Roit, Scardamalia, Stein, & Treadway, 2003), because of its strong claim to being research-based (p. vi-vii). I will only address the contents of two portions of this curriculum—Phonological and Phonemic Awareness and Alphabetic Principle.

This curriculum is divided into 160 lessons divided into 8 units of 20 lessons each. Every lesson in the Phonological and Phonemic Awareness section of the curriculum, which I will refer to as PA lessons, includes two parts: a finger play or song (many of which include rhyming words), and a sound activity. During Lessons 1-51, PA sound activities introduce children to differentiating among sounds that are loud and soft, animal sounds, and environmental sounds. Children identify first and last picture, first and last environmental or animal sound, and segment sentences into words. Thus, for 51 lessons, children focus on sounds in their environment, sounds that animals make, loud and soft sounds, and segmenting words into sentences. We currently have no research suggesting that these activities are helpful in acquiring phonological awareness and at least two reviews that suggest they are not (Castles & Coltheart, 2004; Macmillan, 2002).

On the 52nd lesson in this curriculum, children are introduced explicitly to the concept of rhyme. Prior to this lesson, in 21 lessons, teachers are told: "Have children identify rhyming words" found in the finger plays or songs. Thus, in 21 lessons, children are asked to perform a phonological task that they have not been taught in this systematic curriculum.

Beginning in Lesson 61, a new component is added to instruction: lessons in Alphabetic Principle. The lessons in Alphabetic Principle follow directly the lessons in PA. In PA Lessons 61-86 children are taught to identify rhyming words and to orally blend compound words like cupcakes or two-syllable words like pencil. In Alphabetic Principle Lessons 61-86, children are taught letter-sound associations for letters. Notice that the level of linguistic unit called for in PA lessons is the syllable, while the linguistic unit called for in Alphabetic Principle lessons is the phoneme. It is not until Lesson 87 that children begin to blend single onsets and rimes and, therefore, operate at the level of phoneme during both PA and Alphabetic Principle lessons. Thus, for 26 lessons, the level of phonological functioning expected in PA is different from that expected in Alphabetic Principle lessons. Children are taught eight letter-sound associations (phonemes) before ever being taught to perceive phonemes in PA instruction. It could be that this is intentional. Children may use rote memory to learn letter-sound relationships and doing so may increase their awareness and ability to perceive phonemes. However, research suggests that children can be more strategic in learning letter-sound relationships than merely relying on rote memorizing (Treiman & Kessler, 2003).

In Units seven and eight, children are taught to blend and segment two- and three-phoneme words. These are activities which *The Report of the National Reading Panel* (2000) suggests are more appropriate for kindergarten or first grade.

This curriculum never directly teaches phoneme identity. The activities included in the

Alphabet Principle portion of each lesson came closest to allowing children to develop this concept. Children practice judging whether a phoneme is located in spoken words by holding up a letter card when they hear their teacher say a word with the target phoneme. However, in the entire curriculum, the teacher never is directed to make explicit that these words are all spelled with the same letter because they have the same phoneme. Nonetheless, it is certainly the case that children might infer this concept from the variety of instruction that is provided. Further, teachers are also never directed to make connections between what they are teaching or have already taught during either PA or Alphabetic Principle lessons or vice versa despite the fact that these two lessons are always taught one after the other. Children are never directed to listen for phonemes in letter names and vocal gestures are not described.

It is important to note that this curriculum is based on the research of Lundberg and others (1988) and replicated by Schneider and others (1997). Nevertheless, I have revealed that there are portions of this research-based curriculum that are not supported by research. Children are asked to perform tasks with linguistic units before they are explicitly taught to perceive those units. A large portion of the PA lessons focuses on linguistic units, such as environmental sounds and syllables, for which we have no research to indicate its usefulness (Macmillan, 2002). It could be that the Lundberg and others' (1988) and Schneider and others' (1997) success with this kind of curriculum is due to the very small amount of time the curriculum devotes to phoneme level processing. There is also a lack of coordination between PA instruction and Alphabetic Principle instruction so that the boost that children could acquire through coordinating these activities is lost (Treiman & Kessler, 2003). Finally, the curriculum teaches children segmenting and blending two- and three-phoneme words, skills which *The Report of the National Reading Panel* (2000) suggests are more appropriate in kindergarten and beyond.

Thus, I would argue that we would not be wise to use this evidence-based curriculum, and probably any evidence-based curriculum, with strict fidelity. Fidelity, for research purposes and for Reading First purposes, means that teachers are expected to use the curriculum materials without substitution or modification and to implement the instructional practices only as specified in the curriculum. Yet, as I haven shown, this curriculum, while clearly having direct ties to research in some places, has components without result support.

Before I draw my final conclusions, I want to describe a child for whom preschool really mattered. Quinlan entered a preschool in Alabama that primarily serves children from low-income families with a standard score of 65 on an expressive vocabulary test. He knew no alphabet letters, could only identify the front and back of a book, did not know rhyming words, and could not write his name. He ended preschool with a standard vocabulary score of 76, could write his name in conventional form, knew 26 upper case and 25 lower case letters, could rhyme, could identify and isolate phonemes in words, and could invent spellings with one or two letters. His kindergarten teacher called him "her best student." He is lucky to have attended a preschool in which his teacher was skillful in helping children learn what they must while also encouraging their playful and unconventional explorations of print. All children, like Quinlan, deserve a long line of successes rather than a string of failures. We cannot wait until the end of an intensive intervention program to discover that 35-45% of the children in the program are treatment resisters (Torgesen, 2000). Instead we must frequently consider children's potential to learn and modify our instruction to allow children to develop this potential rather than teaching the curriculum.

In conclusion, I ask, what is the role of wisdom in the face of public policies recommending, even requiring, use of a curriculum based on scientifically-based research? While wisdom has been defined in different ways by different researchers, in general, it is considered to be the use of extensive knowledge and experience to make ethical decisions that promote the good for everyone rather than for just a few (e.g., Baltes & Staudinger, 2000; Sternberg, 2003). In our case, as NRC members, this means we must have extensive knowledge of research and extensive experience with children and teachers in classrooms where learning occurs. If we are not wise about the use of research in instruction, who will be? If we are not wise about identifying which components of a curriculum are based on research and which components are not, who will? If we are not wise enough to communicate to the public that no curriculum can ever be entirely based on research--we simply don't have all the research we need, then who will do so? As members of NRC, we must be wise.

REFERENCES

Adams (1990). *Beginning to read: Thinking and learning about print.* Cambridge, MA: MIT Press.

Barone, D. (1999). *Resilient children: Stories of poverty, drug exposure, and literacy development.* Newark, DE: International Reading Association.

Baltes, P.B., & Staudinger, U.M. (2000). Wisdom: A metaheuristic (pragmatic) to orchestrate mind and virtue toward excellence. *American Psychologist, 55*(1), 122-136.

Blachman, B. (2000). Phonological awareness. In M.L. Kamil, P.B. Mosenthal, P.D. Pearson, & R. Barr (Eds.), *Handbook of reading research: Vol. 3.* (pp. 483-502). Mahwah, NJ: Lawrence Erlbaum Associates.

Bloodgood, J.W. (1999). What's in a name? Children's name writing and literacy acquisition. *Reading Research Quarterly, 34*(3), 342-367.

Bowey, J.A. (1995). Socioeconomic status differences in preschool phonological sensitivity and first-grade reading achievement. *Journal of Educational Psychology, 87*(3), 476-487.

Brady, S., Fowler, A., Stone, B., & Winbury, N. (1994). Training phonological awareness: A study with inner-city kindergarten children. *Annals of Dyslexia, 44,* 26-59.

Bradley, L., & Bryant, P. (1985). *Rhyme and reason in reading and spelling.* Ann Arbor: The University of Michigan Press.

Byrne, B. (1992). Studies in the acquisition procedure for reading: Rationale, hypotheses, and data. In P. Gough, L. Ehri, & R. Treiman (Eds.), *Reading Acquisition,* (pp. 1-34). Hillsdale, NJ: Lawrence Erlbaum.

Byrne, B. (1996). The learnability of the alphabetic principle: Children's initial hypotheses about how print represents spoken language. *Applied Psycholinguistics, 17,* 401-426.

Byrne, B. (1998). *The foundation of literacy: The child's acquisition of the alphabetic principle.* East Sussex, UK: Psychology Press.

Byrne, B., & Fielding-Barnsley, R. (1989). Phonemic awareness and letter knowledge in the child's acquisition of the alphabetic principle. *Journal of Educational Psychology, 81*(3), 313-321.

Byrne, B., & Fielding-Barnsley, R. (1990). Acquiring the alphabetic principle: A case for teaching recognition of phoneme identity. *Journal of Educational Psychology, 82*(4), 805-812.

Byrne, B., & Fielding-Barnsley, R. (1991). Evaluation of a program to teach phonemic awareness to young children. *Journal of Educational Psychology, 83*(4), 451-455.

Byrne, B., & Fielding-Barnsley, R. (1993). Evaluation of a program to teach phonemic awareness to young children: A 1-year follow-up. *Journal of Educational Psychology, 85*(1), 104-111.

Byrne, B., & Fielding-Barnsley, R. (1995). Evaluation of a program to teach phonemic awareness to young children: A 2- and 3-year follow-up and a new preschool trial. *Journal of Educational Psychology, 87*(3), 488-503.

Byrne, B., Fielding-Barnsley, R., & Ashley, L. (2000). Effects of preschool phoneme identity training after six years: Outcome level distinguished from rate of response. *Journal of Educational Psychology, 92*(4), 659-667.

Castles, A., & Coltheart, M. (2004). Is there a causal link from phonological awareness to success in learning to read? *Cognition, 91,* 77-111.

Chaney, C. (1992). Language development, metalinguistic skills, and print awareness in 3-year-old children. *Applied Psycholinguistics, 13,* 485-514.

Council for Exceptional Children (2004). *No child left behind act of 2001: Reauthorization of the elementary and secondary education act.* Retrieved February 2, 2005, from, http://www.cec.sped.org/pp/OverviewNCLB.pdf

Cronin, V., Farrell, D., & Delaney, M. (1999). Environmental print and word reading. *Journal of Research in Reading, 22*(3), 271-282.

Dickinson, D.K., McCabe, A., Anastasopoulos, L., Peisner-Feinberg, E.S., & Poe, M.D. (2003). The comprehensive language approach to early literacy: The interrelationships among vocabulary, phonological sensitivity, and print knowledge among preschool-aged children. *Journal of Educational Psychology, 95*(3), 465-481.

Dorval, B., Joyce, T.H., & Ramey, C.T. (1980). Teaching phoneme identification skills to young children at risk for school failure: Implications for reading instruction. Unpublished manuscript, University of North Carolina, Chapel Hill.

Ehri, L.C., & Wilce, L.S. (1985). Movement into reading: Is the first stage of printed word learning visual or phonetic? *Reading Research Quarterly, 20,* 16-179.

Fox, B., & Routh, D.K. (1975). Analyzing spoken language into words, syllables, and phonemes: A developmental study. *Journal of Psycholinguistic Research 4*(4), 331-342.

Gibson, J.J., Gibson, E.J., Pick, E.D., & Osser, H. (1962). A developmental study of the discrimination of letter-like forms. *Journal of Comparative and Physiological Psychology, 55,* 897-906.

Gibson, E.J., & Levin, H. (1975). The psychology of reading. Cambridge, MA: MIT Press.

Johnston, R.S., Anderson, & M., Holligan, C. (1996). Knowledge of the alphabet and explicit awareness of phonemes in pre-readers: The nature of the relationship. *Reading and Writing: An Interdisciplinary Journal, 8,* 217-234.

Justice, L.M., Chow, S., Capellini, C., Flanigan, K., & Colton, S. (2003). Emergent literacy intervention for vulnerable preschoolers: Relative effects of two approaches. *American Journal of Speech-Language Pathology, 12,* 320-332.

Justice, L.M., & Ezell, H.K. (2002). Use of storybook reading to increase print awareness in at-risk children. *American Journal of Speech-Language Pathology, 11,* 17-29.

Lonigan, C.J., Burgess, S.R., & Anthony, J.L. (2000). Development of emergent literacy and early reading skills in preschool children: Evidence from a latent-variable longitudinal study. *Developmental Psychology, 36*(5), 596-613.

Lonigan, C.J., Burgess, S.R., Anthony, J.L., & Barker, T.A. (1998). Development of phonological sensitivity in 2- to 5- year old children. *Journal of Educational Psychology, 90*(2), 294-311.

Lundberg, I., Frost, J., & Petersen, O.P. (1988). Effects of an extensive program for simulating phonological awareness in preschool children. *Reading Research Quarterly, 23*(3), 263-355.

Maclean, M., Bryant, P., & Bradley, L. (1987). Rhymes, nursery rhymes, and reading in early childhood. *Merill-Palmer Quarterly, 33*(3), 255-281.

Macmillan, B. (2002). Rhyme and reading: A critical review of the research methodology. *Journal of Research in Reading, 25,* 4-42.

Mason, J. (1980). When do children begin to read: An exploration of four year old children's letter and word reading competencies. *Reading Research Quarterly, 15,* 203-227.

Masonheimer, P.E., Drum, P.A., & Ehri, L.C. (1984). Does environmental print identification lead children into word reading? *Journal of Reading Behavior, 16,* 257-271.

McGee, L., Lomax, R., & Head, M. (1988). Young children's written language knowledge: What environmental and functional print reading reveals. *Journal of Reading Behavior, 20,* 99-118.

Murray, B.A. (1998). Gaining alphabetic insight: Is phoneme manipulation skill or identity knowledge causal? *Journal of Educational Psychology, 90*(3), 461-475.

Murray, B.A., Stahl, S.A., & Ivey, M.G. (1996). Developing phoneme awareness through alphabet books. *Reading and Writing: An Interdisciplinary Journal, 8,* 307-322.

Muter, V., Hulme, C., Snowling, M.J., & Stevenson, J. (2004). Phonemes, rimes, vocabulary, and grammatical skills as foundations of early reading development: Evidence from a longitudinal study. *Developmental Psychology, 40*(5), 665-681.

National Institute of Child Health and Human Development. (2000, April). *Report of the National Reading Panel: Teaching children to read* (NIH Publication No. 00-4769). Retrieved February 2, 2005 from http://www.nichd.nig.gov/publications/nrp/smallbook.htm

Read, C. (1975). *Children's categorization of speech sounds in English.* (Research Report No. 17). Urbana, IL: National Council of Teachers of English.

Roberts, T.A. (2003). Effects of alphabet-letter instruction on young children's word recognition. *Journal of Educational Psychology, 95*(1), 41-51.

Roberts, R., & Neal, H. (2004). Relationships among preschool English language learner's oral proficiency in English, instructional experience and literacy development. *Contemporary Educational Psychology, 29*(3), 283-311.

Schneider, W., Kuspert, P., Roth, E., Vise, M., & Marx, H. (1997). Short- and long-term effects of training phonological awareness in kindergarten: Evidence from two German studies. *Journal of Experimental Child Psychology, 66,* 311-340.

Share, D.L. (2004). Knowing letter names and learning letter sounds: A causal connection. *Journal of Experimental Child Psychology, 88,* 213-233.

Snow, C.E., Burns, M.S., & Griffin, P. (Eds.). (1998). *Preventing reading difficulties in young children.* Washington, DC: National Academy Press.

Stahl, S.A., & Murray, B.A. (1994). Defining phonological awareness and its relationship to early reading. *Journal of Educational Psychology, 86*(2), 21-234.

Sternberg, R.J. (2003). *Wisdom, intelligence, and creativity synthesized.* New York: Cambridge.

Storch, S.A. & Whitehurst, G.J. (2002). Oral language and code-related precursors to reading: Evidence from a longitudinal structural model. *Developmental Psychology, 38*(6), 934-947.

Torgesen, J.K. (2000). Individual differences in response to early interventions in reading: The lingering problem of treatment resisters. *Learning Disabilities Research & Practice, 15*(1), 55-64.

Treiman, R., & Kessler, B. (2003). The role of letter names in the acquisition of literacy. In R.V. Kail (Ed.), *Advances in child development and behavior* (Vol. 31, pp. 105-135). Oxford: Academic Press.

Treiman, R., & Rodriguez, K. (1999). Young children use letter names in learning to read words. *Psychological Science, 10*(4), 334-338.

Treiman, R., Sotak, L., & Bowman, M. (2001). The roles of letter names and letter sounds in connecting print and speech. *Memory & Cognition, 29,* 860-873.

Treiman, R., Tincoff, R., & Richmond-Welty, E.D. (1996). Letter names help children to connect print and speech. *Developmental Psychology, 32*(3), 505-514.

Treiman, R., Tincoff, R., & Richmond-Welty, E.D. (1997). Beyond zebra: Preschoolers' knowledge about letters. *Applied Psycholinguistics, 18,* 391-409.

Treiman, R., Tincoff, R., Rodriguez, K., Mouzaki, A., & Francis, D. (1998). The foundations of literacy: Learning the sounds of letters. *Child Development, 69,* 1524-1540.

Treiman, R., Weatherston, S., & Berch, D. (1994). The role of letter names in children's learning of phoneme-grapheme relations. *Applied Psycholinguistics, 15,* 97-122.

Ukrainetz, T.A., Cooney, M.H., Dyer, S.K., Kysar, A.J., & Harris, T.J. (2000). An investigation into teaching phonemic awareness through shared reading and writing. *Early Childhood Research Quarterly, 15*(3), 331-355.

U.S. Congress (2001). *No child left behind act of 2001.* Public Law 107-110. 107th Congress. Washington, DC: Government Printing Office.

Van Kleeck, A., Gillam, R.B., & McFadden, T.U. (1998). A study of classroom-based phonological awareness training for preschoolers with speech and/or language disorders. *American Journal of Speech-Language Pathology, 7*(3), 65-76.

Venezky, R.L. (1975). The curious role of letter names in reading instruction. *Visible Language, 9*(1), 7-23.

Whitehurst, G.J., Epstein, J.N., Angell, A.L., Payne, A.C., Crone, D.A., & Fischel, J.E. (1994). Outcomes of an emergent literacy intervention in Head Start. *Journal of Educational Psychology, 86*(4), 542-555.

Whitehurst, G.J., Zevenbergen, A.A., Crone, D.A., Schultz, M.D., Velting, O.N., & Fischel, J.E. (1999). Outcomes of an emergent literacy intervention from head start through second grade. *Journal of Educational Psychology, 91*(2), 261-272.

Worden, P.E., & Boettcher, W. (1990). Young children's acquisition of alphabet knowledge. *Journal of Reading Behavior, 22*(3), 277-295.

"New" Literacies: Research and Social Practice

Michele Knobel
Montclair State University, USA

Colin Lankshear
James Cook University, Australia

THE CONCEPT OF "NEW" LITERACIES

Talk of "new" literacies is usually associated with textual practices mediated by new computing and communications technologies (CCTs) (Asselin, 2004a; Smolin & Lawless, 2003). We think it is important, however, to resist defining new literacies *exclusively* in terms of CCTs. To do so marginalizes a diverse range of recently emerged and evolving textual practices that have integral places in the ways that many people negotiate their *contemporary* everyday lives but that are not (necessarily) mediated by new technologies. Defining new literacies exclusively in terms of new technologies may deflect researchers' attention from some highly contemporary text-mediated social practices and delegitimate their significance as objects of literacy research that looks to the future as well as to the present. Consequently, in this chapter we discuss examples of both types.

At the same time, however, the examples we have chosen of new literacies that do not necessarily presuppose CCTs are ones that, nevertheless, have been greatly augmented, facilitated, and proliferated by new technologies. While it is important not to marginalize new practices that do not necessarily involve CCTs, it is equally important to acknowledge and validate the massive and growing significance of CCTs within contemporary "literacyscapes" (Leander, 2003).

Following Street (1984), we conceive literacy as "social practices and conceptions of reading and writing" (p. 1). From this perspective there are *many* literacies, construed as identifiable *forms* that reading and writing take within varying social contexts and under varying social conditions. Such forms vary according to the people involved, their purposes, circumstances, cultural ways, available tools, and so on. Literacies come and go as changes occur regularly and from place to place within the constitutive conditions of doing textual work. The idea of new literacies is associated with such changes.

Consequently, ascriptions of *new* literacies are relative and contestable. There is always some place from which to question particular identifications or ascriptions of new literacies (cf., Leu, 2000). We take an uncomplicated and open approach to new literacies, and think of them as identifiable forms of textual practices that occur on a scale and with a degree of social significance that both invite recognition and are more or less chronologically recent. Within this broad frame we distinguish between (new) literacies that might be regarded as "ontologically" new and literacies that, while being chronologically recent, are *not* necessarily ontologically new.

Ontologically new literacies constitute or are constituted by a new kind of "stuff." They constitute a new *kind* of phenomenon (Lankshear & Knobel, 2003), such as when the laborious production of texts by hand, one by one changed to include the mass production of texts following the invention of the printing press. In our own times, this order of change is associated with the emergence of "post typographic" forms of text production, distribution, and reception using digital electronic media.

Different levels of change have accompanied the explosion of digital electronic media. At one level, reading and writing involve new *operations*, such as constructing and following hyperlinks between documents and/or images, sounds, movies; using semiotic languages (such as those used by the characters in the online episodic game Banja, or emoticons used in email, online chat space or in instant messaging); or manipulating a mouse to move around within a text; or interpreting file extensions and identifying what software will read each file. On this level, changes may occur quite rapidly. For example, in the early 1990s reading online involved operations, such as the ability to navigate a text-only interface, use keyboard-based commands to follow hyperlinks, master a set of programming language commands that would download document files to one's computer, and so on. Today, however, reading online using a graphical interface like Internet Explorer or Safari requires different operations. These include reading the different elements of a webpage—the various buttons, menus and go-to bars of an Internet browser; distinguishing between internal and external hyperlinks; understanding cursor-initiated behaviors on-screen; knowing how and when to launch or use different media within a given online space (e.g., play a video, download an audiofile, copy an image); and being able to troubleshoot "broken" hyperlinks, and so forth.

When we focus on the operational and/or technological aspects of new (post-typographic) literacies as in the preceding paragraph, we only get part of the picture. We find that reading involves new kinds of operations. The larger point, however, is that new kinds of social *practices* emerge as well. People begin to develop and to participate in text-mediated practices that simply *did not exist before* because they *could not*. These are practices such as rating news report texts in (close to) real time, disseminating "reputation" information globally about a buyer or seller, weblogging alternative versions of events to those published in official media reports, warchalking, and so on. For us, literacies such as warchalking and weblogging are quintessential examples of *ontologically* new literacies. That is, they are chronologically recent literacies that are *new in kind*.

Not all chronologically recent literacies are new in this ontological sense, however. There exist, for example, literacies that are chronologically recent but that have emerged independently of digital electronic media. Notable examples include fan fiction (fanfic), manga comics and zines. In Figure 1 we present a range of what we regard as significant new literacies and categorize them according to whether or not they are ontologically new in the sense described above.

In the remainder of this paper we will discuss fan fiction, manga, online chat, and weblogs; provide short "state of the art" research statements for each of them; and briefly describe and illustrate some leading edge ways in which online chat and weblogs can be integrated into processes for researching new literacies. Before turning to our four selected new literacies, however, we think it is useful to clarify our own orientation toward new literacies research. This orientation shapes what we do and do not say and how we do or do not say it in this paper.

Figure 1 Short classification of some new literacies

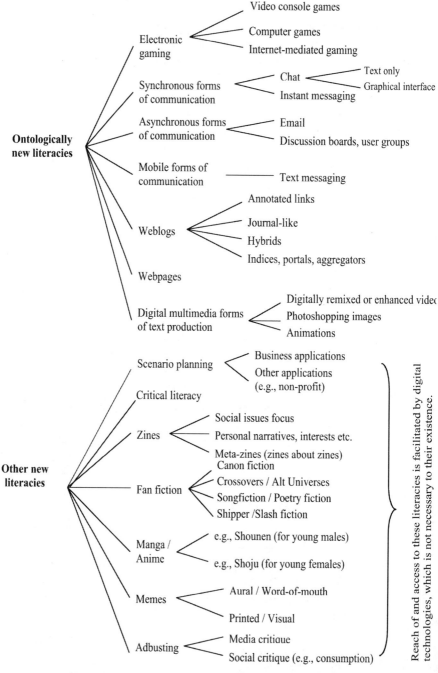

RESEARCHING NEW LITERACIES

While we think of ourselves first and foremost as educators, we are wary of the extent to which a great deal of literacy research is driven by "applied" concerns. That is, educational researchers are encouraged to investigate, say, (new) literacy practices with an eye toward arriving at findings intended to inform classroom curriculum and pedagogy more or less directly. Although there is certainly a valid and important place for such "applied" orientations to literacy research, we are often personally dismayed by the results of applied research. By the time it ends up as off-the-shelf teaching and learning packages, or as highly functional statements, the original practices have been leached of much of their richness and vitality in the attempt to "deliver" useful and relevant applications and strategies for teachers who, for whatever reasons, believe they need them.

In contrast to this functional, applied orientation, we believe it is important with respect to so-called new literacies to emphasize research that seeks to understand contemporary practices in their own right, on their own terms and, so far as possible, from the perspectives of insiders to those practices that, to a large extent, entails researchers becoming insiders/practitioners themselves. Based on reflections of our own and other colleagues' experiences as *users* of new literacies research, we think the most important contribution research in this area can make to enhancing teaching and learning is *indirect*. Research that provides rich accounts of new social practices mediated by new technologies and multimodal texts can help inform teachers and others involved in education about what the world, beyond the school gates that is mediated by these technologies and texts, *is like*. The more such knowledge and understanding educators have the better position they are in to judge how best to integrate (or not) new technologies into school work.

During the 1990s we read everything we could locate that offered insider accounts of cybercultures. These were mainly *not* texts written by academics or by people who would regard themselves as (highbrow) researchers of technoliteracies. They were accessible, "down home" descriptions of people's experiences in MUDs and MOOs, in Silicon Valley start up companies, of hackers and great hacks, of inventors and innovators, of programmers and sysops and bulletin board hosts, of geeks, and so on. We lost ourselves in the wonder, mystery, and sheer magic of how strings of 0s and 1s could produce sound, color and movement in conjunction with magnets and lasers. We read it simply because it was interesting, and in the process we learned things we regard as among the most important and valuable things we have ever learned. And we read almost *none* of it with a view to thinking about how we could directly apply it in our lives. We were moved by a sense of wonderment and wanted to know.

Every day, in diverse ways, this knowledge helps us in our work and in wider aspects of our lives. This is rarely, however, in direct, functional, or *applied* ways. Instead, it provides us with concepts and examples developed by insiders that help us make sense of things we see and read about or that provide clues about what to look out for in the way of trends and changes and where to go to find out what is going on. We still have to do the interpretive work and "nut out" specific applications. But, we have a worldview and a bit of a knowledge base from which to do so.

We think that this is how research can work best to contribute to classroom practice: to make available rich examples and useful concepts to educators that they can draw on in working out how to "do" good pedagogy. Speaking personally, we would like to see a moratorium on research that delivers activities and modules and professional development "tricks" designed for classroom application. In place of such material, we would prefer to see research that provides rich and theorized accounts of cultural practices that enable and encourage educators to experience them from the inside, as participants. Teachers are then in an optimal position to make productive connections between learners' prior knowledge and experiences, the potential of new technologies to expand student learning, their own knowledge and theory relevant to teaching and learning, and the learning goals and outcomes to which they are committed.

The brief accounts of some new literacies that follow have been written in this spirit. They are intended to provide introductions to fanfic, manga, chat and weblogs to colleagues, who may not be knowledgeable about them, from the standpoint of two researchers who believe educators should be informed about such social practices. We are not advocating that teachers try to import them (directly) into classroom practice. Rather, we think that having some knowledge of such practices may be useful for teachers in a way analogous to how being informed about learners' funds of knowledge can be useful in reflecting upon how to go about one's pedagogical work.

FAN FICTION WRITING

In fan fiction, or "fanfic" to aficionados, "devotees of a TV show, movie, or (less often) book write stories about its characters" (Plotz, 2000, p. 1). These stories chronicle alternative adventures, mishaps, or even alternate histories/futures for main characters, relocate main characters from a series or movie to a new universe altogether, create "prequels" for shows or movies, fill in plot holes, or realize relationships between characters that were only hinted at, if that, on screen.

Today's fanfic writers innovate on myriad screen and book texts. Besides the various Star Trek series, television shows currently attracting large numbers of fanfic writers include *Scarecrow and Mrs. King, Andromeda, Angel, JAG, Lizzie McGuire,* and *Xena: Warrior Princess.* Popular movies include *Star Wars, Moulin Rouge, X-Men* and *Pirates of the Caribbean,* and books include *Les Miserables, Phantom of the Opera, A Series of Unfortunate Events,* and the Bible.

The origins of fanfic are generally dated to the late 1960s. The Star Trek television series, which first aired in 1966 and rapidly gained a cult following, is credited with helping to establish fan fiction as a distinct genre. From the first episode fans wrote their own stories set within the Star Trek universe and using key Star Trek characters. They would then mimeograph and bind their stories into handmade books or magazines (precursors to today's zines) and distribute them at Star Trek fan conventions. Since then, fanfic has become an established genre and the subject of academic study (see, for example, Jenkins, 1992; Somogyi, 2002). Women make up the majority of fanfic writers, and their stories tend to pay relatively little attention to developing the plotline in comparison to developing dialogue and carefully crafting a range of relationships among characters. These relationships may be heterosexual or same-sex, particularly romantic relationships between males (Gillilan, 1999; Rehak, 2003; Trainor, 2003). This emphasis on relationships is a well-defined sub-category of fan fiction, known to aficionados as "Relationshipper" (or "Shipper") stories. The following is a reasonably typical sample of popular fanfic writing. (All texts are copied verbatim from websites.)

Author: quicksilver2402004

Xena: The Tale of a Murder

Disclaimer: The creators charcters in no way belongs to me except Kyra, Astella, Linden, Thainlen and other characters that I created. If anyone finds any errors in this story or your confused about something you can let me know by emailing me at [email address deleted] and I will be happy to fix or explain it.

Introduction:
Rain fell through the black sky and hit against the trees and bushes. Rain fell into puddles creating a splashing sound. A pale light shone through the forest as a wagon with one horse trotted through the path. Sitting on top, sat two people who both had a hooded cloak on. The horse that was pulling the wagon was a dark grey color with green eyes and a white mane. The horse who could see and hear better than the humans looked left and right making sure it wouldn't fall over any debris the storm had left a few hours before. The horse stopped suddenly making the two people grab the wagon's bar that was in front of them. The horse neighed turning its head looking at the cloaked figures. One of the cloaked figures climbed over the seat and walked towards the horse. The horse neighed again as if telling the stranger something was wrong.

"What is it Selena???" said the male voice.

The horse neighed motioning its head toward the left. The man removed the hood revealing a handsome face with dark blue eyes and short black hair. Rain droplets slid down his face. He turned looking at the other cloaked figure that was walking towards him. "Selena senses something over there," said the man to the cloaked figure. The cloaked figure removed their hood revealing a young woman with purple eyes and long brown hair.

"Astella should we look?" asked the man. "Yes".

The man pulled his sword out of his scabbard making a sound of metal being sharpened which revealed a 18 inch silver Wakizashi Sword which had a leather hilt. Lighting flashed and thunder rumbled as he and Astella walked into the direction the horse had pointed out to them. They walked through wet trees and stopped. A sound was heard.

"Did you hear that Linden? It sounded like crying." Asked Astella. "Yes. It came from over there." Whispered Linden motioning towards a group of giant pine trees. Lighting flashed revealing a hole below one of the trees. Astella and Linden crept towards the tree looking around to make sure it wasn't a trap. Thunder mixed in with the crying as they walked towards the tree. A loud bang of thunder sounded off making Astella and Linden jump. Linden and Astella walked to the hole and knelt in front of it. Lighting flashed showing what was inside. It was a baby. It was lying on its back wrapped up in blankets. The baby cried and moved its little arms back and forth. Linden and Astella exchanged surprise looks. Astella reached for the baby and held it in her arms. (www.fanfiction.net/ s/2013938/1/; accessed Feb 5, 2005)

In many ways, fanfic is a contrived communal practice of reading and writing (Plotz, 2000). Prior to the Internet becoming a mass medium, fanfic was circulated person to person among relatively small circles of aficionados and subjected to sustained critique. Authors received peer comments and suggestions for improving their stories. Today, however, fanfic narratives in the tens of thousands are posted in open public forums on the Internet to be read and reviewed online by anyone who cares to do so.

FANFIC RESEARCH

Most research on fan fiction to date has been undertaken within English literary studies, cultural studies (including women's studies) and media studies. Perhaps the best known study is Henry Jenkins' (1992) ethnography of media fan sub-cultures, *Textual Poachers: Television Fans and Participatory Culture* (see also, Jenkins, 1988). Drawing on de Certeau (1984), Jenkins explored how fans take resources from commercial culture and rework them to serve alternative purposes. Rather than seeing them as cultural dupes, thoughtless consumers, or social misfits, Jenkins portrayed fans as active producers and skillful manipulators of content from commercial programs, nomadic poachers, and *bricoleurs* constructing their own culture from borrowed materials. Subsequent studies have focused on fan fiction as a sub-culture or as an element of "alternative" culture, drawing on survey-based demographic profiles of fan fiction groups, participant observation of fan fiction gatherings, and interviews with fans and fan fiction writers (cf., Gillilan, 1999).

Fan fiction has also been studied from the standpoint of copyright issues, as a sidebar in larger text-based studies of feminist resistance and/or critique (e.g., Westcott 2003), and as text or genre. The latter involves analyzing fanfic productions and the original artifacts to which they respond in terms of content, narrative styles and strategies, rhetorical moves, cultural capital, cultural production, and so on (e.g., Jancovich, 2002; Vrooman, 2000). Recent research has extended to studies focusing on fans writing about computer or video game characters, like Lara Croft from *Tomb Raider* (e.g., Rehak, 2003).

Most fan fiction studies published in the past 5 years use Internet-based fanfic writing archives and fan fiction discussion boards as their database (e.g., Pearson, 2003; Pereira de Sá, 2002; Trainor, 2003). This research suggests that the emergence of Internet-based fanfic archive and review sites on a large scale is attracting a visible new stratum of pre-teen writers who did not exist in the era of fan fiction conventions, when adults dominated the ranks of fanfic authors (Rehak, 2003).

Few published studies of fan fiction as a *literacy practice* exist (cf., Black, 2004; Chandler - Olcott & Mahar, 2003a, 2003b; Trainor, 2003). Indeed, fan fiction writing has attracted negligible attention in the field of education research, notwithstanding the growing research interest in adolescent writing. And despite the fact that the incorporation of themes and motifs from popular culture within the texts of very young children is often encouraged and quite well-documented (e.g., Dyson, 1997; Marsh, 2005), investigation of fan fiction writing within classrooms beyond the early years is conspicuous by its absence. Indeed, within upper grades of elementary schooling, narrative writing grounded in reworking television series or movie plotlines tends to be cast as "poor writing," lacking in imagination and creativity. It is rarely considered in terms of intertextuality, "media mixing" and the like, despite the importance attached to such literary techniques within high school English classes in relation to "the canon" (cf., Lankshear & Knobel, 2002).

An example of student fan fiction encountered in the course of our own research and writing provides a supporting illustration for our orientation to new literacies research as described above. This example comes from work produced by a thirteen-year-old, non English-speaking migrant student (Tony) in his final year of elementary school. Tony had emigrated from Taiwan to Australia with his parents six years previously. He was the only ESL learner in the case. His teacher was conscientious by any standards. She expressed concern about the absence of support for ESL learners in the school and worried about having Tony in her class, perceiving his English as inadequate for school learning and believing she did not know how to help him. To illustrate her concerns she pulled a fat wad of A4-sized paper, covered in handwriting and stapled in one corner out of a drawer. She dropped it on the desk, sighed, and asked rhetorically, "What do you do with that? It doesn't even make sense!"

Tony had been working on this text, an adventure narrative, for more than a month by the time he handed it in. The learning context involved a genre-based language syllabus, and the class was working on narrative. His teacher said by the time she saw it as a draft it was far too long for her to conference properly (i.e., to give him feedback about his text, identify its strengths, and suggest how to improve it as a basis for subsequent work in class). She had filed it in his assessment portfolio and said she was not going to grade it because it was too long and it was now too close to the end of the year to find time for marking it and giving feedback. She felt she simply did not have time to correct his English and explain what was wrong with his turn of phrase.

The following excerpt, which typifies the character of the text as a whole, comprises the orientation to his narrative: orientation, conflict, resolution, and coda being the four structural features of narrative as defined in the syllabus.

Author: Tony (Taiwanese mandarin speaker)

Doom: Part 1

In the dark Ages, Europe was broke into many different countries.

In the Kingdom of Khimmur, King Little, the ruler of Khimmur, gave a mission to one of the brave warriors, Jake Simpson.

His missions was to defeat Shang-Tsung. Shang-Tsung was an evil person. He tried to rule the whole china, but he never did it, so he went to Europe. Now he is planning to take over the whole Europe. And he has three warriors.

Kung-Lao, before he was a dragon, then Shang-Tsung made him \into a/ human Raiden, God of Thunder.

Gora, a 2000 year old giant with four hands.

Shang-Tsung also took control of lots of things. He has a vas number of soldiers.

Snow Witch, Lizard King and Baron Sukumvit were also Shang-Tsung's helpers, because Shang-Tsung promised to Share the power with them.

And the Warlock of Firetop Mountain, was guard for Shang-Tsung's Rich.

"So I will send you to attack Shang-Tsung" said King Little.

"Isn't there anyone going with me?" asked Jim.

"Oh, I nearly forgot to tell you about this" said King Little "There will be two Martial Arts Master from the great Empire of Han, Chung-Hi-San-Wu and Lee-Quan-Lin will go with you. They were send by the Emperor of China".

This excerpt from Tony's narrative reveals a most unfortunate teaching and learning situation. Tony's teacher's refusal to engage with his text can be seen as uninformed and misguided both in terms of the official purposes of the curriculum and her own serious endeavor to develop a pedagogical approach equal to those purposes (Lankshear & Knobel, 2002). The excerpt above reveals much about Tony's literacy proficiency that actually directly contradicts his teacher's appraisal of it. At a surface level, it is evident that he has a competent grasp of a range of important writing conventions. These include compiling lists, paragraphing, direct speech conventions, punctuation, and controlling the genre structure of a narrative. His use of '\ /' marks show that he has mastered the convention for inserting text into a sentence already handwritten. Likewise, a word he was not sure how to spell is underlined, another "school" writing practice. His vocabulary negates our interpretation of his teacher's assessment of his command of English; namely, that Tony had minimal command of English in his writing. His text contains some systematic errors in tense, with plurals, and with some prepositions. By the same token, our investigation of the class as a whole suggested that, in terms of conventional print literacy indicators, Tony's literacy competence was considerably greater than several of his native English-speaking classmates (see ibid.).

Even a cursory glance at Tony's text reveals to anyone with relevant insider knowledge that he has produced a complex intertextual narrative: in effect, a fanfic text that builds on his insider status within video gaming and pen and paper based role-play simulations Discourses. For example, the characters, "Shang-Tsung," "Raiden," and "Kung Lao," are all characters in Mortal Kombat, an adventure game from the early 1990s originally produced by Nintendo (and now available as a computer game as well). Kung Lao is described on the Mortal Kombat official website as "a troubled young warrior from the Order of Light Temple. He is a skilled Mortal Kombat fighter with incomparable focus and strength. Kung Lao was raised alongside other children from the temple and trained from birth to fight in the Mortal Kombat wars…" (see www.mortalkombat.com). Similarly, the character "Gora-Gora" can be found in the Nintendo game, *The Ultimate Evil*. Subsequent references in Tony's narrative to a skeleton army (and not appearing in the excerpt above) echoes a range of skeleton armies found in different Nintendo games, including *Dungeon Keeper II*. Later, characters from the video and computer game DOOM appear in Tony's adventure, such as Demon Queen and the Barons of Hell. The Warlock of Firetop Mountain makes an early appearance in the narrative as a character, and the character's name is actually the title of the first Fighting Fantasy Gamebook produced in the 1980s by Steve Jackson and Ian Livingstone. The reference to Snow Witch in the excerpt above echoes another Fighting Fantasy Gamebook by Ian Livingstone (1984) entitled *Caverns of the Snow Witch*. Lizard King and

Baron Sukumvit, other characters making an early appearance in Tony's text, are also from the Fighting Fantasy Gamebook series. This series of books—60 in all—were enormously popular "quest" games that came with dice and maps and required role-playing and a large amount of reading to plot and navigate the adventures written into them.

This case provides an example of how awareness of cultural forms, such as fanfic and the cultural artifacts that beget them, could potentially provide teachers alternative perceptions of who learners are and what they can do. The world of school is awash with perceptual frames born of stereotypes, ascribed deficits, convenient "throwaway" lines, and pop-explanations (e.g., "there is no language in the home," "s/he is not ready for learning") that can readily distort how teachers see learners. Similarly, a relatively confined range of classroom literacies can easily limit understandings of the concrete forms that abstract constructs such as "narrative" assume in the world and of their relative power and significance in the various dimensions of everyday life. Research designed to provide rich, theorized, concrete accounts of new literacies in their own right and on their own terms are potentially useful antidotes to perceptual biases as well as potentially fruitful sources of understandings, pointing toward spaces where classroom literacy activity can meet learners on productive pedagogical ground.

MANGA

Manga is a graphic narrative genre that is most easily described as "Japanese comics." Manga, in its current form, has its origins in the stylized and often humorous outline drawings by sixth century Shintoist monks to illustrate calendar scrolls (Sanchez, 2003). The term "manga" itself (which translates roughly into "whimsical pictures" in English) was first used to describe a particular style of illustration in the late seventeenth century developed by a Japanese artist, Hokusai, who rebelled against traditional woodblock style Japanese printmaking, working with French and Dutch art and art theory to develop a style of drawing that comprised finely detailed, free-flowing characters and landscapes (i.e., "man," meaning undisciplined and free form, and "ga," meaning drawing or image; Wiedeman, 2004, p. i). Hokusai's chief goal for his new drawing style was to create meaningful *and* entertaining art pieces (ibid.). Manga really came into its own, however, in the late 1940s and early 1950s. Comic strips were popular in Japan soon after they first began appearing in U.S. newspapers early in the 20th century; however, the growing worldwide popularity of Disney animations, cinema techniques, and the ready availability of Marvel and DC comics in Japan after World War II helped to shape manga into a distinct and highly popular graphic-and-text genre.

Most manga are published in serial form and are produced in black and white. Early manga tended to focus on action-packed adventure or sci-fi stories for boys (i.e., shounen manga) or romance stories for girls (i.e., shoujo manga) (Allen & Ingelsrud, 2003). In the 1970s, manga aimed at adult Japanese readers began to be produced and included violent or taboo themes and a wide range of anti-heroes, along with sometimes sharp social critique (Allen & Ingulsrud, 2003). New categories of manga began to appear during this period, including pornographic manga and homoerotic manga, as well as much more prosaic instruction manual manga and textbook manga.

Manga began to be translated into English during the late 1980s and quickly gained popularity among young people (e.g., especially the *Yu-Gi-Oh!* and *Dragon Ball Z* graphic novels, and the *Shonen Jump* serial collections). In English speaking countries, manga fans (known as *otaku*) tend to be adolescents and young adults, with females comprising a sizeable proportion of readers (Lent, 2004). The largest market for manga outside Japan is the U.S., where young people spent approximately $100 million on manga in 2002 (Lent, 2004).

Many parents and educators in English-speaking countries have denounced manga as being too violent for young people to read, and as responsible for "dulling readers' minds" (Lent 2004, p. 39). On the contrary, manga are highly complex texts. They require English-language readers to learn to read comic frames from right-to-left (see Figure 2) and to operate a range of challenging meaning *conventions* like recognizing the "signification" of different sized-frames. For example, a narrow, page length frame can denote time passing or direction in a journey, while a two-page single frame can signal something momentous is about to happen. The illustrator can also shift the reader's point of view from that of "outsider, looking in" to "viewing the scene from the perspective of the different characters in the story," and the reader needs to be able to recognize, make sense of, and keep up with rapid changes in point of view (see Figures 2 and 3) (Allen & Ingulsrud, 2003, p. 679).

The widespread popularity of commercial manga has generated a sub-culture of "amateur manga"—manga drawn by fans that adds to or produces new versions of existing manga—and which, in Japan and the U.S. at least, are distributed at manga markets or comics conventions. These markets and conventions have also become an important source of peer feedback on manga aficionados' narrative plot development and their drawing techniques (e.g., tips on fine-tuning perspective, on capturing a range of facial expressions, on adding realistic shine to hair). Amateur manga writers are particularly serious about their artwork and regularly form social networks or "circles" devoted to constructively critiquing each other's manga drawings. Most highly prized within these circles are original drawings, rather than copies of existing manga artwork (which is often what manga fans— *otaku*—usually begin with).

Figure 2 A diagram showing the typical 'reading path' for manga texts (courtesy of SHONEN JUMP Magazine, © VIZ Media, LLC)

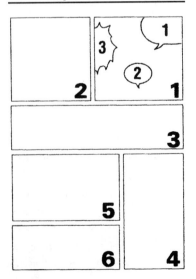

The development of graphic interfaces for online browser software has seen a significant change in the original face-to-face nature of otaku circles as they have moved online and have become more widely distributed. Otaku use the Internet to exchange their artwork and feedback

Figure 3 Two pages from Dragon Ball Z (Vol. 18, pp. 14-15).

Dragon Ball Z
DRAGON BALL © 1984 by BIRD STUDIO/SHUEISHA Inc.

via discussion boards or email discussion lists. Chandler-Olcott and Mahar (2003a) provide excellent examples of the kind of art-focused critique that takes place between manga fans in their case study of Eileen, a 13-year-old aspiring manga artist. Eileen scans and posts an original drawing to an email discussion list and received the following feedback:

> The background is kinda simple, which is actually a pretty good idea. You might want to add something towards the bottom of the picture to balance all the items you have floating around at the top…. Also, his chest is either really small, or really smushed. Either way, it's not a good look with large biceps (those are the ones on the top of the arms, right? I get confused sometimes). Not to be crude, but he needs more shading in the crotch area. It seems there's nothing there from knee to knee. Otherwise I love the expression, specially the grin. It totally sets the mood to scare some people. Or freak them out, whatever. And like usual, nice shiney hair, Very pretty. (Mailing list posting, December 7, 2001) (p. 360).

Research on Manga

To date, research on manga has focused mainly on content analyses of manga texts, stylistic analyses of artistic techniques employed in manga drawing, and the examination of manga texts as leisure reading choices. This research corpus can be organized around several categories of interest. Key manga research categories include: (a) studies of artwork and art style, including the cinematic qualities of manga drawings (e.g., Adams, 1999; Darling, 2001; Toku, 2001); (b) work that investigates manga as an historical barometer (e.g., Gilson, 1998; Morris-Suzuki & Rimmer, 2002; Nakar, 2003); (c) studies that address manga in relation to gender, identity and/or sexuality (e.g., Fujimoto, 1991; Ito, 1994, 2002; Perper & Cornog, 2002); (d) investigations of manga in terms of or in relation to ideology and propaganda (e.g., Kinsella, 1999); (e) studies of manga as popular culture artifacts (e.g., Grigsby, 1998); (f) studies of manga as reading material and learning resources (e.g., Allen & Ingulsrud, 2003; Frey & Fisher, 2004; Nagata, 1999); and (g) amateur manga production as a social practice (e.g., Black, 2004; Chandler-Olcott and Mahar, 2003a).

Much of the existing research corpus on manga focuses on *adult* manga readers and writers (e.g., Allen & Ingulssrud, 2003; Ito, 1994, 2002). This is slowly changing. Researchers are increasingly studying online amateur manga writing/drawing sites, as well as young people's engagement with animated manga or *animé* (cf., Black, 2004; Chandler-Olcott & Mahar, 2003b). Few studies, however, address amateur manga production from the standpoint of manga involving processes that pay careful attention to art and entertainment. Moreover, there is a notable lack of research that focuses on young people's engagement with manga as readers and writers/artists, and their manga-related practices in relation to their other media engagement and social relations. Increasingly, these networks and practices tend to blur boundaries between physical space and cyberspace boundaries. They offer rich potential for understanding how young people present themselves as readers, writers, and reviewers in their everyday lives (cf., Chandler-Olcott and Mahar, 2003a, 2003b; Livingstone & Bober, 2001). A further noteworthy silence in the research literature is around studies that explore both the complexity of manga texts and their enduring popularity as leisure reading texts, even among young people who struggle with reading at school.

The research corpus that *does* exist indicates that reading, writing and drawing manga are closely bound up with identity and popular culture. One key contribution of current manga studies is a greater understanding of the role women are playing in shaping the content and direction of what has traditionally been a male-oriented genre. On the other hand, most studies to date tend to treat manga as relatively static popular culture artifacts, rather than as integral dynamic aspects of social practice and identity. This, too, seems to be changing. Some of the most recent ethnographic-type studies of young people's engagement with manga underscore the importance of paying attention to the *fluidity* of their manga (and animé) production and discussion that spans paper-based, television, video game and Internet media (Ito, 2001; Chandler-Olcott & Mahar, 2003b; Thompson, 2004).

POST – TYPOGRAPHIC EXTENSIONS OF MANGA AND FANFIC

Studying new literacies is a complex undertaking, made the more so by the transition of fan-based practices like manga and fanfic into virtual domains through the uptake of electronic media that greatly extend the reach of these practices across time and space.

As a distributed and collaborative social practice, fanfic has expanded exponentially with the development of graphic interfaces for Internet browser software, the increased availability of low-cost, large-bandwidth, and high-speed Internet access services, availability of free or close-to-free discussion board hosting, and the development of a range of multimedia capable communication applications online (e.g., Instant Messenger software that enables users to exchange large files) (cf., Brooker, 1999; Hamming, 2001; Jones, 2000).

Ethnographies of young people engaging in fan-based activities such as manga drawing and fanfic writing show participants employing a wide range of electronic and analog technologies in a multimodal network of communication and interaction (cf., Ito, 2001, in press; Chandler-Olcott and Mahar, 2003a, 2003b). Thomas' (2005) ongoing study of adolescents' new literacy practices shows how collaborative fan fiction writing may be accompanied by role-playing that is "enacted" via Instant Messaging or on discussion forums during the development of new chapters in an ongoing narrative. Similarly, blog posts are written from the perspective of key characters in a narrative, and story-related conversations take place between authors using voice chat applications. Youthful fanfic authors create multimedia story "trailers," soundbites and "teasers'" to "advertise" new narrative episodes as they test and develop new story lines, characters, and experiences for their characters (Thomas personal communication, February 8, 2005; cf., anyaka.blogspot.com and personal.edfac.usyd.edu.au/staff/thomasa).

Similarly, amateur manga artists/writers and otaku have used the Internet to complement interactions and exchanges in the physical space of conventions and circles. Manga Internet sites like the *Online Manga Webring* (j.webring.com/hub?ring=onlinemanga) index the websites of individual manga author/artists-fans. These sites showcase their owners' comics, galleries, reviews, etc., and provide quick links to online discussion and feedback forums, as well as online tutorials for learners. The identity implications generated by the complex dynamics surrounding the mediation by the Internet of social practices like manga and fanfic are diverse and interesting. One notable trend is toward young people, regardless of their cultural heritage, taking on Japanese aliases and manga-style avatars for their online identities and interactions.

Such examples, which are growing rapidly in virtual spaces of adolescent popular culture, inform ever-expanding understandings of new electronic technologies as *relationship and communication technologies* more than *information* technologies (cf., Rheingold, 2003). This insight is important because schools (over)emphasize the "information" dimension of new technologies at the expense of their communication and relationship potentials. Moreover, as will become apparent in the following section, the ontological and chronological newness of contemporary literacy practices are writ large in online communication and, particularly, in *synchronous* online communication.

SYNCHRONOUS ONLINE COMMUNICATION

Synchronous online communication is a catch-all term used to describe a range of Internet-based software interfaces and services that enable people to communicate directly and more or less immediately with each other in real time, even if geographically separated. Internet Relay Chat

(Chat) is the longest running and probably the best-known synchronous communication application. It involves dedicated web spaces and purpose-built interfaces that enable "chatters" to register with a chat service and converse with each other by keying texts into the chat software system (see Figure 4).

Examples of Synchronous Online Communication: From Chat to Palace to ActiveWorlds

Continually evolving online interaction services and interfaces are rapidly displacing text-based chat as a preferred communication medium. Foremost among these is instant messaging (IM). IM combines the direct communication and file sharing elements of email with the immediacy of chat. IM interfaces enable users to see when friends or colleagues are online and to converse with them via text in real time. Popular IM interfaces include AOL's Instant Messenger, Yahoo!'s Messenger, and MSN Messenger. A user subscribes to one or more IM services and creates an alias that can be added to other people's "buddy lists" as part of a private communication network. IM service settings allow users to make their IM alias available *publicly*, so that anyone can locate them and send them a message or *privately*, where only those to whom a user has given their alias can contact them. The speed of IM means that messages tend to be short and peppered with abbreviations and acronyms and to contain homophonic text (mixes of letters and numerals to make words) and emoticons (small icons for signaling emotions).

Instant messaging lends itself to diverse purposes. In our own academic work we find it useful for developing arguments and ideas through instantaneous exchange of fragments that build a plan for writing or produce draft passages that can be copied and pasted into a final document, and so on. This process is typically accompanied by instantaneous file transfers of relevant materials that we are reading as part of the process of "working up" the idea in question. At the other

Figure 4 A screen shot of the 30s chat group on Yahoo!. Retrieved November 28, 2004, from chat.yahoo.com.

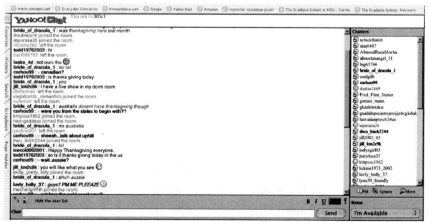

extreme, instant messaging is simply keeping in touch, a routine social exchange with an intimate (e.g., describing what's going on, what I am doing now, how I felt about X, etc.). Very often, instant messaging is just one ingredient in a multitasking mix. The program runs in the background and is updated when an alert from the task bar signals a new incoming message. The following interview excerpts illustrate how youth engage in such multitasking.

> (L)et me tell you what my friends and I seem to be doing a lot lately when we're on [the computer] after school. Especially my friend Sarah, she was the first rl [real life] friend that came to my talker, so she and I have been doing this together for a few years now. Well, Sarah and I go home, and she calls me on the phone when she's ready to log on later. We keep the phone conversations going while we log on and decide where to go. We're always on my talker, but sometimes we go idle there to visit other places [online]. I keep telling dad I need a bigger monitor, because I end up with so many windows open that I can't always follow what's going on in each one. Then we do about six different things at the same time.

> We'll have my talker open, our icq on [IM], we have the role-playing MOO we've just joined open, we have our homework open (which I am pleased to report, we both get done at the end of the night, and its sooooo much more fun doing it this way!), we have the palace open [a virtual world chat space], we have our own private conversation windows open for different friends, and we have our phone conversation going on at the same time. And that is not to mention having conversations with mom or dad, popping out for drinks and nibbles, and having my music on in the background. Then, depending what's going on, we have hysterics over the phone together as we manage the activities going on in each window. (Thomas, 2004)

Figure 5 A sample screen shot from The Palace
(source: unknown)

Graphic interfaces for chat exchanges are genetically related to text-based MUDs (multi-user domains) and MOOs (multi-object oriented domains), which are virtual environments comprising "rooms," objects, character descriptions and real-time character interactions carried out by typing conversations into a chat-like pane on the screen. Graphic interface chat exchanges linear text entries in the chat pane for two-dimensional images (although text-based chat can be enabled as well). These images are used in two ways: for signifying specific rooms or areas within a space or virtual environment (e.g., a backyard pool scene, a haunted mansion), and as "stand ins" or "avatars" that represent each chatter within a given space. These avatars are often customizable. Participating in graphic interface chat spaces usually requires downloading client software that will run the interface on the user's computer while remaining connected to a server that hosts interactions among participants. Popular graphical interface chat services include Palace (thepalace.com) and Microsoft Chat (chat.msn.com/ns.msnw).

Three-dimensional virtual worlds are another take on real time chat and graphical interface chat environments. Using a 3D programming language (e.g., VRML), 3D virtual worlds enable users to create and manipulate their avatars within a given landscape (that has depth and often obeys the laws of physical spaces; e.g., users have to "climb" ladders, slide down slopes, etc.) and to interact with other users' avatars in real time. Perhaps the most well-known virtual world is ActiveWorlds.com, which also lets users create their own 3D world where others can meet and interact. Other popular virtual chat worlds include TheSimsOnline.com, Worlds.com, Moove.com, and Cybertown.com.

Synchronous Online Communication Research Foci

Research tends to focus on the following areas: (a) online synchronous communication and gender (e.g., Bowker & Lieu, 2001; Calvert et al., 2003; Constantin et al., 2002; Herring, 1993; Lee, 2003; Witmer & Katzman, 1997); (b) the language of synchronous communications, especially abbreviations, emoticons and phonetic dialects or linguistic features of interactions (e.g., Greenfield & Subrahmanyam, 2003; Grinter & Palen, 2002; Walther & D'Addario, 2001; Witmer & Katzman, 1997); (c) roles and relationships and the social conventions of language use in online synchronous spaces/discourse analysis (e.g., Herring, 1993, 2004a, 2004b; Herring and Martinson, 2004; Jones, 2001, 2004; Panyametheekul & Herring, 2003; Vallis, 1999, 2001, 2002); (d) foreign or second language learning (e.g., Belz & Kinginger, 2003; von der Emde, Schneider, & Kötter, 2001; Weininger & Shield, 2003); (e) collaborative learning, including self-reflection (especially in relation to MOOs and MUDs) (e.g., Anderson, DeMeulle, & Johnston, 1997; Murfin, 2001); (f) user statistics (e.g., Shiu & Lenhart, 2004); (g) identity and/or subjectivity (e.g., Bechar-Israeli, 1995; Thomas, 2004; Unsworth et al 2005); and (h) interpersonal interactions and relationships or community (e.g., Grinter & Palen, 2002; Hu et al., 2003; Jacobson, 1999; Tidwell & Walther, 2002).

WEBLOGS AND WEBLOGGING

A weblog, or "blog" for short, can be defined as "a website that is updated frequently, with new material posted at the top of the page" (Blood, 2002a, p. 12). Blogs began back in the early 1990s as websites that listed annotated hyperlinks to other websites containing interesting, curious, hilarious and/or generally newsworthy content located by the publisher of the weblog. Early blog publishers, "bloggers," tended to be computing "insiders," partly because some knowledge of webpage and hyperlink coding was needed for posting material to the Internet.

In 1999, however, weblog publishing tools and web hosting became available on a large scale through Pitas.com and Blogger.com. This made it relatively easy for Internet users who were less familiar, or not comfortable, with using hypertext markup language and the principles of web design for coding and designing their own weblogs, and spawned a new mass generation of bloggers. This new generation was much more diverse than the original blogging generation. Many began using weblogs as a medium more like regularly updated journals than indices of hyperlinks, and postings could document anything and everything from what the blogger had for lunch that day, movie and music reviews, descriptions of shopping trips, the latest illustrations completed by the blogger for offline texts, and the like. Posts can combine photographs and other graphics along with text and hypertext.

Today, many weblogs are hybrids of both journal entries and annotations or indices of links or some mix of musings or anecdotes with embedded hyperlinks to related websites (see Figure 6). Blood describes this new use of weblogs as being concerned with creating "social alliances" (Blood, 2002b, p. 7). In other words, weblogs are largely interest-driven and intended to attract readers who have (or would like to have) similar, if not the same, interests and affinities. Individual weblog entries ("posts") are accompanied by the date (and sometimes the time) they were posted in order to alert readers to the "currency" or "timeliness" of the log. Some bloggers choose to update several times a day, while others may update every few days or once a week or so.

Figure 6   Screen shot of Manolo's Shoe Blog. Retrieved February 11, 2005, from shoeblogs.com.

Most weblog front pages contain at least two columns. One houses weblog postings ordered chronologically from the most recent entry to the least recent entry. Entries are archived after a given period (e.g., a few days, a week, a month). Blog posts are usually quite short, often no more than a few lines to each post. The second column acts as an index of hyperlinks to other weblogs or to websites that the blogger likes, recommends, or otherwise sees as related in some pertinent way to their own blog. This index is usually divided into subcategories and generally runs along lines of interest. Some bloggers include advertising on their sites, as graphic ads or as hyperlinks to commercial sites. (See Figure 6.)

There are two basic types of posts: those that include hyperlinks to other blogs or websites, and those that don't. Posts that include hyperlinks may begin with a link followed by a brief commentary beneath it in a form very similar to an annotated bibliographic entry. Hyperlinked posts may also include quotes from the information or text to which they are linking in the manner of a "sound bite" in order to give readers a sense of what they will find when they follow the link.

Blogs are created and maintained for very diverse purposes. These include, but are far from exhausted by, (combinations of) the following: to publish personal diaries/journals; to provide alternative accounts of events and other phenomena to those of mainstream media; to teach and learn media, to sell products, to provide information on current news events, to critique mainstream broadcasting of news events, to distribute corporate news and updates, to parody other blogs and other media, to express personal opinion, to archive memories (e.g., photo blogs, audio blogs, video blogs), to augment fanfiction writing or drawing, to archive or index profession-related materials (e.g., hyperlinks to relevant policy documents and news reports etc.), to augment hobbies and pastimes (e.g., collecting items, techno-gadgetry, genealogy studies, sport), to notify fans of popular culture events and information (like band tour dates, author readings and book events, art and design world developments), to create fictional characters or lives (e.g., found photo albums are used to invent a fictitious life, hoax blogs that deliberately mislead readers), and so on.

A good sense of the nature and range of weblogging at its most sophisticated can be gleaned from a quick tour of blogs like Stevenberlinjohnson.com (a blog of annotated links and commentary), BoingBoing.net (a collective blog offering "a directory of wonderful things") and Littleyellowdifferent.com (a journalesque blog).

Stevenberlinjohnson.com

Steven Johnson is a leading Internet commentator and author who co-founded and edited the legendary online magazine Feed.com in the late 1990s. He might best be described as an Internet public intellectual. A semiotics major from Brown University and author of books on interface culture and brain theory, Johnson's weblog (stevenberlinjohnson.com) began on November 11, 2002 and has become a popular source of opinion on matters relating to Internet culture, politics, brain theory, urban development in New York, hi tech news, landscape architecture, and design in general.

Carefully archived back to its inception, Johnson's blog emphasizes economy and clarity in its design, is rich in hyperlinks on topics covered in his regular posts (currently 2-3 per week), and keeps Johnson's work and personal profile strongly in the foreground. At the time of writing, the right hand column featured a small color photo of Johnson, a brief descriptive promotional statement for his latest book, a short list of links to some of his recent published essays, a list of topics covered in his recent postings, small cover photos of his first two books with hyperlinks to their listings on Amazon.com, a calendar of his appearances in U.S. towns to promote his latest book, a list of sites and publications (with hyperlinks) he has written for, a relatively short (18 items) list of links to other people's blogs, a search tool for trawling Johnson's blog, and hyperlinks to his blog archives.

After even a short time exploring Johnson's blog a savvy reader will have a good sense of:

1. How Johnson wants to be seen publicly; the blog does important identity construction and presentation work.

2. Why Johnson operates a blog; reasons range from self promotion and advertising to enhancing his presence in the money and attention economies (in his inaugural blog posting in November 2002 Johnson referred to blogs as vanity sites), to taking a position on current issues he sees as important.

3. Some potentially powerful "affinity maps;" e.g., constellations of influential people in the blogosphere who take center/center right/right wing positions on global political issues (and by default one can generate maps of blogerati— famous bloggers—who advocate left of centre views on global political issues).

4. A particular perspective on a range of technological innovations.

BoingBoing.net

BoingBoing.net is jointly authored by four previously well-established writers. It was overall winner of the 2004 Bloggies contest, an annual, peer-reviewed awards event that recognizes outstanding weblogs or elements of weblogs. At the time of researching this blog (February, 2005), BoingBoing.net was ranked as the most popular weblog on Technorati.com's ranking system, registering 17,810 direct links to its content from other websites. BoingBoing prides itself on showcasing the weird and wonderful. Content is eclectic, and includes annotated links to: (a) images of portraits made entirely from used bubblegum; (b) a website where you can print out full-colour patterns and instructions for assembling paper-based, miniature vintage video game machines; (c) news of recent developments in the digital art world (e.g., hypertext artworks etc.); (d) company plans to print advertising text on individual Pringle's potato chips; (e) a new low-carbohydrate potato developed for dieters; and (f) a webpage featuring news items about and pictures and video clips of people falling down.

BoingBoing also alerts readers to new technogadgets, particularly artifacts associated with wireless computing and entertainment. Its focus on gadgetry, the weird, and the wonderful is complemented by serious and astute commentary on and predictions about popular technologies and social networking. All four authors are likewise committed to social critique and community development projects. At the time of writing, recent posts include: (a) a summary account from

Cory Doctorow of proceedings and developments at the International Broadcast Treaty negotiations meetings at the United Nations building in Geneva; (b) commentary on e-voting; (c) endorsement of critiques of the Federal Communications Commission rulings in the U.S.; (d) developments in creative commons laws concerning free noncommercial use of archived media materials; (e) comments on the importance of free wireless access for mobile computer users; and (f) summaries of wi-fi projects in developing countries.

BoingBoing's authors clearly are committed to keeping readers abreast of actual and anticipated developments within technology, art, and communication access fields. They provide links to diverse types of posts on other blogs about such developments and also provide their own firsthand accounts whenever possible. Consequently, BoingBoing becomes the first port of call for many readers who want to stay in touch with techno-trends, technology-mediated projects in developing countries, digital art developments, and related themes. As well-reputed commentators on technology and communications-related news and with their extensive social network of colleagues in journalism and areas of technology development, BoingBoing's authors can also provide readers with authoritative accounts of topics that might otherwise go unnoticed in mainstream media venues, such as national and international policy negotiations and agreements and heavy-handed copyright actions on the part of giant corporations.

Littleyellowdifferent.com

The weblog *Little.Yellow.Different* (littleyellowdifferent.com) won the overall Bloggies award for excellence in 2003. It began in June 2000 and is authored by Ernie Hsiung, a 28-year-old, self-described overweight, short, gay, Chinese American web designer and developer who works for Yahoo!. *Little.Yellow.Different* is a regularly updated, journal-like space that Hsiung uses to inform his readers about such things as renovations he is making to a recently purchased apartment, events going on in his life (e.g., buying his apartment, appearing on a television game show, making a trip to Disney World, subscribing to cable television, starting his new job with Yahoo!), aspects of his relationships and interactions with his parents and relatives, and his ideas and views on elements of popular culture. Although many journal-type weblogs, which tend to be heavy on accounts drawn from the author's life and light on annotated hyperlinks, have been criticized on the grounds of being somewhat banal celebrations of mediocrity and the microinformation of everyday life, *Little.Yellow.Different* has attracted a strong following of readers who are keen to read Hsiung's semi-regular, often hilarious—but often *serious* and "pointful" fun, accounts of what has been happening to him lately.

Reading this blog over even a short period of days is enough to reveal important recurring themes in the posts. These include: (a) different challenges and benefits to be had from growing up Chinese American; (b) contrasts between Hsiung's own experiences growing up Chinese American and media representations of Chinese Americans (including Chinese American representations of Chinese American culture); (c) gay cultural practices (including spoofing his own gay identity by confessing certain musical tastes, romantic attractions, interior decorating motifs and, so on); (d) comments on popular culture trends and events; (e) finding the humour in almost everything that happens to him; and (f) keen-eyed observations on a range of social relationships, including those he has with work colleagues, friends, family and relatives, and so on. Hsiung's accounts of navigating American and Chinese cultures are often deeply ironic (and infinitely patient) and regularly offer insights into what it means to be on the receiving end of the American mainstream's tendency to homogenize "Asians." His practice of recounting word-for-word dialogue in his blog posts becomes the perfect medium for both unveiling cultural ignorance on the part of others and for making pointed social commentary without resorting to blunt-edged, heavy-handed criticism. For example, he recounts an exchange at work as follows:

Engineering lead: We don't have a lot of time to finish this project. It's a good thing another country has implemented an avatar system already.

Ernie: (looks through code) Uhm, this is a lot of code. And these javascript comments are in Korean.

Engineer: But aren't–

Ernie: ...I'm Chinese.

Engineer: Oh. This project is still due next Tuesday.

Little.Yellow.Different is less overtly political and global than blogs such as Steven Johnson's and less openly concerned with intellectual freedom and rights as blogs such as BoingBoing.net. Nonetheless, it is common for Hsiung's posts to attract 30 or more comments from readers. Comparisons across weblogs show that this is a high level of traffic per post.

Weblog-related Research

To date there has been relatively little formal academic research undertaken on weblogs, although a torrent of studies seems imminent, many of which seem likely to focus on the use of weblogs in schools. Some of the more readily identifiable areas of current weblog research include: (a) success within the blogosphere and blog networks (Kumar et al., 2003; Shirky, 2003); (b) genre analysis of blogs (Herring, et al., 2004); (c) blogging and gender (Huffaker, 2004; Huffaker & Calvert, in press); (d) blogging as a research tool (Mortenson & Walker, 2002); (e) blogs and communities (Asyikin, 2003; Carl, 2003); and (f) institutional uses of blogs (Asselin, 2004b; Lamshed, Berry, & Armstrong, 2002; Schroeder, 2003).

Detailed case studies of bloggers themselves and their decisions about what to blog and why, how their blogs should look, and what role their blogs play in their everyday lives comprise a notable absence within the corpus of blog-related research to date. Some initial forays in this direction have been made using survey research designs (Carl, 2003). Nevertheless, detailed, ethnographic case studies would provide useful windows on the social role blogs play in people's online and offline lives. The need for this kind of research will increase as more people move to mobile blogging (or moblogging), using wireless multimedia communication devices such as mobile phones, personal digital assistants (PDAs), and mobile computing devices. In this context blogging is becoming a widespread mobile information/communication/social practice. As with so much new literacies research in other areas, notoriously absent in the current corpus is a focus on young people from low socioeconomic status families and/or marginal cultural groups and their weblog uses and productions.

USING WEBLOBS AND CHAT TO RESEARCH NEW LITERACIES

Many Internet applications, weblogs and chat in particular, have an interesting reflexivity for researchers of new literacies, because they can be used as instruments and other kinds of resources within the very process of researching new literacies (and anything else for that matter). Work currently being done by Thomas (2004) in Australia, who is investigating ways in which children construct their identities in multimodal digital worlds, is an excellent example of how weblogs and chat spaces, among other online media, can be used as research tools. For the past four years, she has been studying young people aged 10 to 16 from the U.S., Canada, Australia, the UK, Holland, Finland, and Germany. The range of multimodal worlds in which the young people participate includes websites and weblogs, MUDs and chat services (e.g., IM, chat, and what are referred to generically by participants as "talkers" or "palaces"), video games and graphic virtual worlds or "palaces" made possible by interactive software such as *The Palace*. Themes under investigation include the ways online literacy practices shape identity, children's reports about embodiment as it occurs in digital worlds, the ways children exercise power and control in such environments, the development of relationships with others within digital space, the type of capital associated with existing in digital worlds, and the gender differences in online discursive and social practices. The study aims to illuminate ways in which children's online lives are intimately connected to their sense of self and their developing identities as subjects of the new media age.

Thomas employs a variety of online data collection techniques in which uses of chat and weblogs figure prominently. For example, she does a lot of synchronous electronic interviewing using chat (text-based as well as palace), and says, "I like doing synchronous interviews on the palace because I can take a line of questioning and pursue it a little to get depth, and also see their behavior with avatars, movement, body placement, off screen influences and so on" (Angela Thomas, personal communication, November 12, 2004). This method, however, has limitations, some of which are overcome by using her weblog as a space for participants to record their responses: "Sometimes the blog posts [being asynchronous] give them more time to reflect and consider a question and the response can be astonishingly brilliant and open up a whole new line of thought for me." In an interesting adaptation, Thomas uses blog posts to "check out" "her theorizing" against her participants' thoughts and experiences:

> Sometimes when I am reading theory, I try and write up a kid-friendly question that relates directly to that theory on the blog to try and stimulate the kids to engage with it a bit. Sometimes it works, other times it doesn't. Other times I deliberately disclose something personal in an attempt to inspire a deeper level of response from them about their 'self.' (Thomas, personal communication, November 12, 2004)

Besides collecting synchronous and asynchronous responses to questions and prompts she has devised herself, Thomas also engages in virtual participation by logging group conversations online, which provides her with transcripts. She makes screenshots and movie screen captures of her participants' activity on the Palace (see Figure 5 earlier), records asynchronous discussions in which participants are involved in their role playing game forums and copies role playing posts they make in these forums, and collects artifacts in the form of avatars, quotes, and signature files.

Thomas's weblog, *E-selves: Cyberkids, literacy and identity ... and other commentary about literature, pop culture, education and amusing Internet myths* (anyaka.blogspot.com), is a dynamic working site that has been carefully customized to meet her research purposes, as well as to enact and communicate other dimensions of her identity. The posts column is used to record and report data collected in the ongoing e-selves project, as well as to provide information and point of view on a range of personal interest topics. In addition to housing the links to archives, the right hand column provides information about Thomas's published work, work in progress, her research keywords, links to other sites of personal interest, links to courses she teaches, and a tag board that is used by her research participants (and anyone else who wishes to) for communicating in real time (or to be picked up later if no one else is "there" at the time).

Among the many features of the use of chat and weblog by Thomas and other online researchers that merit comment, one stands out in particular. This is the quality of data that can be obtained when these online applications are used well. We will conclude by citing at length an example of a synchronous interview response that provides rich insights into how young "insiders" understand what they are doing as they enact identities in multimodal worlds.

> The funny thing was that the way I talk-write in cyber started flowing over into my social life. I've found myself writing notes to people in real life with stuff like "brb" and "irl" in them! *smile*. I tried all sorts of talk-write styles until I found what I was comfortable with. The way it looked on the screen was very important to me. I am sure it has changed over the years, depending on new invented ways of playing with ASCII, being able to use icons and images and so on. It also changes of course from one cyberworld to the other, but I really worked hard to present the real 'me' in text/icon/ascii for the first talkers I lived in.

> Maybe I should explain to you why I just said 'of course' when I was talking about how I talk-write changes from one cyberworld to the other. My teachers tell me that those words are <puts on a teacher voice> 'no substitute for a well constructed argument young lady!' Typical. I suppose they're right, so here goes. What I mean is this. In my own talker for example, I want to present myself as the 'me' that I imagine myself to be. My words have to look *just so*, I use certain non-conversation words and icons to portray the way I might behave, like *giggles* or <rolls eyes> and those sorts of expressions. Its an aesthetic thing, my words and actions, the images, music, web design – they all have to look a particular way to reflect how the inner me is. My friends at school who also log into my talker tell me that I am much more open and expressive in cyber. I think that's because you just have to type a lot to let people know you.

> ...

> I need to make a confession right now, I am talking to you but at the same time I am talking to this cool guy Matt who I know from school, and trying to do some homework – an essay, for which I am hunting some info on the web – you

know, throw in some jazzy pics from the web and teachers go wild about your 'technological literacy' skills. Big deal. If they ever saw me at my desk right now, ME, the queen of multi-tasking, they'd have no clue what was happening (from interview with 'Violetta'. "I am Violetta today, I am feeling bright yellow and somewhat creative").

LIMITATIONS AND AGENDA: FINAL WORDS

This paper barely scratches the surface of the terrain of actual and potential new literacies research. At the very least, so far as an educationally useful mapping is concerned, we would ideally look at research that covers information, communication, and leisure/recreation/entertainment dimensions of new social practices and conceptions of reading and writing. Such scope is well beyond us here. The most we can do is gesture toward the need for a comprehensive mapping that can provide an overview of the current state of the art, and to note that at least one such project is in process (Leu, et al., forthcoming).

We conclude by making a call for further research into new literacies, and suggest that so far as possible this should be research undertaken in the first instance simply for the purposes of knowing more about trends of genuine interest and significance. In the not-so-short run this will be the research that has most to offer teachers and learners who believe that their vocation is to educate in the present with an eye to tomorrow *and* to the decades ahead.

REFERENCES

Adams, J. (1999). Of mice and manga: Comics and graphic novels in art education. *Journal of Art & Design Education, 18*(1), 69-75.

Allen, K. & Ingulsrud, J. (2003). Manga literacy: Popular culture and the reading habits of Japanese college students. *Journal of Adolescent & Adult Literacy, 46*, 674-683.

Anderson, R. DeMeulle, L., & Johnston, J. (1997). Plugging in: Using on-line collegial dialogue for self-study. *Teaching Education, 8*, 129-37.

Asselin, M. (2004a). New literacies: Towards a renewed role of school libraries. *Teacher Librarian, 31*,1481-1782.

Asselin, M. (2004b). *Weblogs at the Institut St. Joseph.* Paper presented at the International Conference of Educational Multimedia, Quebec City, Quebec, Canada.

Asyikin, N. (2003). *Blogging life: An Inquiry into the role of weblogs in community building.* National University of Singapore. Retrieved November 29, 2004, from permanenthiatus.net/ thesisblog/prop.html.

Bechar-Israeli, H. (1995). From <Bonehead> to <cLoNehEAd>: Nicknames, play, and identity on Internet relay chat. *Journal of Computer-Mediated Communication, 1*(2). Article 2. Retrieved from http://jcmc.indiana.edu/vol1/issue2/bechar.html May 13, 2005.

Belz, J. and Kinginger, C. (2003). Discourse options and the development of pragmatic competence by classroom learners of German: The case of address forms. *Language Learning, 53*, 591-647.

Black, R. (2004). Access and affiliation: The new literacy practices and of English language learners in an online anime-based fan fiction community. Paper presented to the National Council of Teachers of English Mid-Winter Conference, Berkeley, CA.

Blood, R. (2002a). Weblogs: A history and perspective. In Editors of Perseus Publishing (Eds.). *We've got blog: How weblogs are changing culture* (pp. 7-16). Cambridge, MA: Perseus Publishing.

Blood, R. (2002b). Introduction. In Editors of Perseus Publishing (Eds.). *We've got blog: How weblogs are changing culture* (pp. i-x). Cambridge, MA: Perseus Publishing.

Bowker, N., & Lieu, J. (2001). Are women occupying positions of power online?: Demographics of chat room operators. *CyberPsychology & Behavior, 4*, 631-644.

Brooker, W. (1999). Internet fandom and the continuing narratives of *Star Wars, Blade Runner* and *Alien*. In A. Kuhn (Ed.), *Alien Zone II: The spaces of science fiction cinema* (pp. 50-72). London: Verso.

Calvert, S. (2002). Identity construction on the Internet. In S. Calvert, A. Jordan, & R. Cocking (Eds), *Children in the digital age: Influences of electronic media on development* (pp. 57-70). Wesport, CT: Praeger.

Carl, C. (2003). *Bloggers and Their Blogs: A Depiction of the Users and Usage of Weblogs on the World Wide Web*. Unpublished Masters dissertation. Georgetown University, Washington D.C. Retrieved November 29, 2004, from cct.georgetown.edu/thesis/ChristineCarl.pdf

Chandler-Olcott, K. & Mahar, D. (2003a). Tech-savviness' meets multiliteracies: Exploring adolescent girls' technology-mediated literacy. *Reading Research Quarterly, 38*, 356-385.

Chandler-Olcott, K. & Mahar, D. (2003b). Adolescents' anime-inspired "fanfictions": An exploration of multiliteracies. *Journal of Adolescent & Adult Literacy, 46*, 556-566.

Constantin, C., Kalyanaraman, S., Stavrositu, C., & Wagoner, N. (2002). Impression formation effects in moderated chatrooms: An experimental study of gender differences. Paper presented at the 88th annual meeting of the National Communication Association, New Orleans, LA.

Darling, M. (2001). Plumbing the depths of superflatness. *Art Journal, 60*(3), 76-89.

de Certeau, M. (1984). *The practice of everyday life*. Berkeley and Los Angeles, CA: University of California Press.

Dyson, A. (1997) *Writing superheroes: Contemporary childhood, popular culture, and classroom literacy*. New York: Teachers College Press.

Frey, N. & Fisher, D. (2004). Using graphic novels, anime, and the Internet in an urban high school. *English Journal, 93*(3), 19-44.

Fujimoto, Y. (1991). A life-size mirror: Women's self-representation in girls' comics. *Review of Japanese Culture and Society, 4*, 53-57.

Gillilan, C. (1999). *Zine fans, zine fiction, zine fandom: Exchanging the mundane for a women-centered world*. Unpublished doctoral thesis, University of Colorado at Boulder.

Gilson, M. (1998). A brief history of Japanese robophilia. *Leonardo, 31*, 367-369.

Greenfield, P. & Subrahmanyam, K. (2003). Online discourse in a teen chatroom: New codes and new modes of coherence in a visual medium. *Journal of Applied Developmental Psychology, 24*, 713-738.

Grigsby, M. (1998). *Sailormoon: Manga* (comics) and *anime* (cartoon) superheroine meets Barbie: Global entertainment commodity comes to the United States. *Journal of Popular Culture, 32*(1), 59-80.

Grinter, R. & Palen, L. (2002). Instant Messaging in teen life. *In Proceedings from Conference on Computer Supported Cooperative Work 2002*. New York: ACM Publishers. Retrieved February 4, 2005, from http://cs.colorado.edu/~palen/Papers/grinter-palen-IM.pdf.

Hamming, J. (2001). Whatever turns you on: Becoming-lesbian and the production of desire in the Xenaverse. *Genders, 34*. Retrieved February 8, 2005, from http://www.genders.org/g34/g34_hamming.html.

Herring, S. C. (1993). Gender and democracy in computer-mediated communication. *Electronic Journal of Communication, 3*(2), np. At http://www.cios.org/getfile/Herring_v3n293

Herring, S. (2004a). Computer-mediated discourse analysis: An approach to researching online behavior. In S. Barab, R. Kling, & J. H. Gray (Eds.), *Designing for virtual communities in the service of learning* (pp. 442-446). New York: Cambridge University Press.

Herring, S. (2004b). Online communication: Through the lens of discourse. In M. Consalvo, N. Baym, J. Hunsinger, K. Jensen, J. Logie, M. Murero, & L. Shade (Eds.), *Internet Research Annual, Volume 1*. New York: Peter Lang.

Herring, S. & Martinson, A. (2004). Assessing gender authenticity in computer-mediated language use: Evidence from an identity game. *Journal of Language and Social Psychology, 23*(4), 424-446.

Herring, S., Scheidt, L., Bonus, S., & Wright, E. (2004). Bridging the gap: A genre analysis of weblogs. Paper presented at the 37th Hawai'i International Conference on System Sciences, Los Alamitos. Retrieved November 29, from http://www.blogninja.com/DDGDD04.doc

Hu, Y., Smith, V., Westbrook, N., & Wood, J. F. (2003). Friendships through IM: Examining the relationship between Instant Messaging and intimacy. Paper presented to the Communication Technology and Policy Division of the Association for Education in Journalism and Mass Communication (AEJMC), Kansas City, MO.

Huffaker, D. (2004). *Gender similarities and differences in online identity and language use among teenage bloggers.* Unpublished Masters thesis. Graduate School of Arts and Sciences, Georgetown University, Washington, DC.

Huffaker, D. & Calvert S. (2005). Gender, identity and language use in teenage blogs. *Journal of Computer-Mediated Communication.* Retrieved November 25, 2004, from http://www.eyec.com.

Ito, K. (1994). Images of Women in Weekly Male Comic Magazines in Japan. *Journal of Popular Culture, 27*(4), 81-95.

Ito, K. (2002). The world of Japanese ladies' comics: From romantic fantasy to lustful perversion. *Journal of Popular Culture, 36*(1): 68-85.

Ito, M. (2001). Technologies of the childhood imagination: Media mixes, hypersociality, and recombinant cultural form. Paper presented to the Society for the Social Studies of Science meeting, Boston. Retrieved November 25, 2004, from http://www.itofisher.com/PEOPLE/mito/Ito.4S2001.yugi.pdf.

Jacobson, D. (1999). Impression formation in cyberspace: Online expectations and offline experiences in text-based virtual communities. *Journal of Computer-Mediated Communication, 5*(1) Article 3. Retrieved May 13, 2005, from http://jcmc.indiana.edu/vol5/issue1/jacobson.html

Jancovich, M. (2002) Cult fictions: Cult movies, subcultural capital and the production of cultural distinctions. *Cultural Studies, 16*, 306-322.

Jenkins, H. (1988). Star Trek rerun, reread, rewritten: Fan-writing as textual poaching. *Critical Studies in Mass Communication, 5*(2), 85-107.

Jenkins, H. (1992). *Textual poachers: Television fans and participatory culture.* New York: Routledge.

Jones, R. (2001). Beyond the screen: A participatory study of computer-mediated communication among Hong Kong youth. Paper presented to the Annual Meeting of the American Anthropological Association, Washington D.C., November 28-Dec. 2.

Jones, R. (2004). The problem of context in computer mediated communication. In P. Levine & R. Scollon (Eds), *Discourse and technology: Multimodal discourse analysis* (pp. 20-33). Georgetown University Press, Washington, DC.

Jones, S. (2000). Histories, fictions and Xena: Warrior princess. *Television & New Media, 1*, 403-418.

Kinsella, S. (1999). Pro-establishment manga: Pop-culture and the balance of power in Japan. *Media Culture & Society, 21*, 567-572.

Kumar, R., Novak, J., Raghavan, P., & Tomkins, A. (2003). On the bursty evolution of blogspace. Paper presented at the 12th Annual World Wide Web Conference, Budapest, Hungary. Retrieved November 24, 2004, from http://www2003.org/cdrom/papers/refereed/p477/p477-kumar/p477-kumar.htm.

Lamshed, R., Berry, M., & Armstrong, L. (2002). *Blogs: Personal e-learning spaces.* Australia: Binary Blue. Retrieved November 29, 2004, from http://binaryblue.com.au/docs/blogs.pdf

Lankshear, C. & Knobel, M. (2002). DOOM or Mortal Kombat? Bilingual literacy in the "mainstream" classroom. In L. Diaz Soto (Ed.), *Making a difference in the lives of bilingual/bicultural children* (pp. 31-52). New York: Peter Lang.

Lankshear, C. & Knobel, M. (2003). *New literacies: Changing knowledge and classroom learning.* Buckingham and Philadelphia: Open University Press.

Leander, K. (2003). Writing travellers' tales on new literacyscapes. *Reading Research Quarterly, 38*, 392-97.

Lee, C. (2003). *How does Instant Messaging affect interaction between the genders?* The Mercury Project for Instant Messaging Studies at Stanford University. Retrieved May 13, 2005, from www.stanford.edu/class/ pwr3-25/group2/pdfs/IM_Genders.pdf

Lent, A. (2003). Far out and mundane: The mammoth world of manga. *Phi Delta Kappa Forum, 84*(3), 28-41.

Leu, D. (2000). Literacy and technology: Deictic consequences for literacy education in an information age. In M. L. Kamil, P. Mosenthal, P. D. Pearson, & R. Barr (Eds), *Handbook of reading research, Volume III* (pp. 743-770). Mahwah, NJ: Erlbaum.

Leu, D., Coiro, J., Knobel, M., & Lankshear, C. (forthcoming). *Handbook of research on new literacies*. New York: Erlbaum.

Livingstone, I. (1984). *Caverns of the snow witch*. New York: Puffin.

Livingstone, S., & Bober, M. (Eds) (2001). *Children and their changing media environment: A European study*. Mahwah, NJ: Lawrence Erlbaum.

Marsh, J. (Ed.) (2005). *Popular culture, new media, and digital literacy in early childhood*. London: RoutledgeFalmer.

Morris-Suzuki, T., & Rimmer, P. (2002). Virtual memories: Japanese history debates in manga and cyberspace. *Asian Studies Review, 26*(2), 147-164.

Mortenson, T., & Walker, J. (2002). Blogging thoughts: Personal publication as an online research tool. In A. Morrison (Ed.), *Researching ICTs in Context* (pp. 249-279). Oslo: Intermedia Report.

Nagata, R. (1999). Learning biochemistry through manga: Helping students learn and remember, and making lectures more exciting. *Biochemical Education, 27*(4), 200-203.

Nakar, E. (2003). Memories of pilots and planes: World War II in Japanesse manga, 1957-1967. *Social Science Japan Journal, 6*(1), 57-76.

Panyametheekul, S. & Herring, S. (2003). Gender and turn allocation in a Thai chat room. *Journal of Computer-Mediated Communication, 9*(1) Article 8. Retrieved May 13, 2005, from http://jcmc.indiana.edu/vol9/issue1/panya_herring.html

Pearson, R. (2003). Kings of infinite space: Cult television characters and narrative possibilities. *Scope: An Online Journal of Film Studies*. November. Retrieved November 23, 2004, from http://www.nottingham.ac.uk/film/journal/articles/kings-of-infinite-space.htm

Pereira de Sá, S. (2002). Fanfictions, comunidades virtuais e cultura das interfaces. Paper presented to the Sociedade Brasileira de Estudos Interdisciplinares da Comunicação, XXV Congresso Brasileiro de Ciências da Comunicação, Salvador/BA, 1-5 September. Retrieved November 24, 2004, from http://intercom.org.br/papers/xxv-ci/np08/NP8SA.pdf

Perper, T. & Cornog, M. (2002). Eroticism for the masses: Japanese manga comics and their assimilation into the U.S. *Sexuality & Culture, 6*(1), 3-126.

Plotz, D. (2000). Luke Skywalker is gay? Fan fiction is America's literature of obsession. *Slate*. Retrieved November 19, 2004 from http://slate.msn.com/id/80225.

Rehak, B. (2003). Mapping the bitgirl: Lara Croft and new media fandom. *Information, Communication & Society, 6*, 477-496.

Rheingold, H. (2003). *Smart mobs: The next social revolution*. New York: Basic Books.

Sanchez, F. (2003). HIST 101: History of manga. AnimeInfo.org—Anime University. Retrieved November 24, 2003, from http://www.animeinfo.org/animeu/hist102-11.html

Schroeder, R. (2003). Blogging online learning news and research. *Journal of Asynchronous Learning Networks, 7*(2), 56-60.

Shirky, C. (2003). Power laws, weblogs and inequality. Retrieved June 7, 2003, from http://www.shirky.com/writings/powerlaw_weblog.html

Shiu, E. & Lenhart, A. (2004). *How Americans use instant messaging*. Pew Internet and American Life Project Report. Retrieved November 24, 2004, from http://www.pewinternet.org/PPF/r/133/report_display.asp

Somogyi, V. (2002). Complexity of desire: Janeway/Chakotay fan fiction. *Journal of American & Comparative Cultures*. Fall-Winter. 399-405.

Smolin, L. and Lawless, K. (2003). Becoming literate in the technological age: New responsibilities and tools for teachers. *Reading Teacher, 56*, 570-577.

Street, B. (1984) *Literacy in theory and practice*. Cambridge: Cambridge University Press.

Thomas, A. (2004). *e-selves@palace.kids: Literacy and Identity in a Virtual Community*. Unpublished dissertation, Charles Darwin University, Darwin, Northern Territory, Australia.

Thompson, M. (2004). Intersecting literacies: Adolescent girls' identity around anime and fan fiction. Paper presented to the National Council of Teachers of English Midwinter Conference, Berkeley, CA.

Tidwell, L. & Walther, J. (2002). Computer-mediated communication effects on disclosure, impressions, and interpersonal evaluations: Getting to know one another a bit at a time. *Human Communication Research, 28*, 317-348.

Toku, M. (2001).What is manga? The influence of pop culture in adolescent art. *Art Education, 54*(2), 11-17.

Trainor, J. (2003). Critical cyberliteracy: Reading and writing *The X-Files*. In J. Mahiri (Ed.) *What they don't learn in school: Literacy in the lives of urban youth* (pp. 123-138). New York: Peter Lang.

Unsworth, L., Thomas, A., Simpson, A., & Asha, J. (2005). *Children's literature and computer based teaching*. London: Open University Press.

Vallis, R. (2001). Applying membership categorization analysis to chat-room talk. In A. McHoul and M. Rapley (Eds.), *How to analyse talk in institutional settings: A casebook of methods* (pp. 86-99). London: Continuum.

Vallis, R. (1999). Members' methods for entering and leaving #IRCbar: A conversation analytic study of Internet relay chat. In K. Chalmers, S. Bogitini, & P. Renshaw (Eds.), *Educational research in new times* (pp. 117-127). Flaxton: PostPressed.

Vallis, R. (2002). *Sense and sensibility in chat rooms*. Unpublished doctoral thesis, University of Queensland, Brisbane, Australia.

von der Emde, S., Schneider, J., & Kötter, M. (2001). Technically speaking: Transforming language learning through virtual learning environments (MOOs). *The Modern Language Journal, 85*, 210-225.

Vrooman, S. (2000). *Generic negotiation: An investigation of audience response in romantic 'X-Files' fan fiction*. Unpublished doctoral thesis, Arizona State University, Tempe

Walther, J., & D'Addario, K. (2001). The impacts of emoticons on message interpretation in computer-mediated communication. *Social Science Computer Review, 19*, 323-345.

Weininger, M., & Shield, L. (2003). Promoting oral production in a written channel: An investigation of learner language in a MOO. *Computer Assisted Language Learning, 16*, 329–349.

Westcott, J. (2003). *Reassessing women in mainstream science fiction film and television, from 'When Worlds Collide' to 'Alien'*. Unpublished master's thesis, Queen's University at Kingston, Ontario, Canada.

Wiedemann, J. (2004). Introduction. In A. Masano (Ed.), *Manga design* (pp. i-iii). Cologne: Taschen.

Witmer, D., & Katzman, S. (1997). On-line smiles: Does gender make a difference in the use of graphic accents? *Journal of Computer-Mediated Communication. 2*(4). Retrieved November 25, 2004, from ascusc.org/jcmc/vol2/issue4/witmer1.html

Pattern Recognition:
Learning from the Technoliteracy Research

Ilana Snyder

Monash University

A few months ago, I read William Gibson's (2003) most recent book, *Pattern Recognition*. It is a novel about a world mediated by the use of new technologies: surveillance, information, games, chatrooms, and much more. If you have not read anything by Gibson, try him: you are in for a treat.

Why not Google him and see what you come up with? His official website has a blog and information about his projects, old and new. One that has always intrigued me is *AGRIPPA, A Book of the Dead*. This is a longish poem written in 1992 which included a floppy-disk that displayed the text only once, then became unreadable. Perhaps the tale of the self-destructive disk was just one of the many apocryphal stories that have grown up around Gibson, but it certainly was a provocative concept in a world notable for its capacity to produce an infinite number of copies.

In the blog Gibson refutes another apocryphal story--that he writes with a manual typewriter. As the tale goes, Gibson shuns the use of the technologies that are central to his fiction, including the Internet. However, Gibson states unequivocally in his blog that since the coming of the Web in the mid 1990s, he has and continues to enjoy long sessions on the Internet.

It is Gibson's capacity to create new words and to invest old ones with new meaning to which I draw your attention. He has named some of the cultural touchstones of the techno-society in which we now live. In *Neuromancer*, published in 1986, he coined the words *cyberspace* and *the matrix*, both introduced on the second page:

> A year [in Japan] and he still dreamed of cyberspace, hope fading nightly. All the speed he took, all the turns he'd taken, and the corners he'd cut in Night City, and still he'd see the matrix in his sleep, bright lattices of logic unfolding across the colorless void. (pp. 10-11)

Neuromancer is about the human-machine interface created by the growing use of computers and computer networks. It is set in the near future in decayed city landscapes like those portrayed in the film *Blade Runner*. At the heart of *Neuromancer* is the urban rage of cyberpunk subculture.

Some critics dismissed *Neuromancer* as deriving from William S. Burroughs' novels, such as *Nova Express*, and Raymond Chandler's *The Big Sleep*. But I would argue that *Neuromancer* is historically significant. Gibson's allusions to contemporary technology set a new standard and his vision of a nightmare world marked by urban decay, rampant crime, and corruption everywhere helped create a new genre of fiction: cyberpunk.

His terminology continues to pop up everywhere; there was a computer virus called *Screaming Fist*, and the Internet is sometimes referred to as *The Matrix*. More commonly, however, it is called *Cyberspace*:

> Case was twenty-four. At twenty-two, he'd been a cowboy, a rustler, one of the
> best in the Sprawl. He'd been trained by the best, by McCoy Pauley and Bobby
> Quine, legends in the biz. He'd operated on an almost permanent adrenaline high, a
> byproduct of youth and proficiency, jacked into a customer cyberspace deck that
> projected his disembodied consciousness into the consensual hallucination known as
> the matrix. (Gibson, 1986, pp. 11-12)

'Bright lattices of logic unfolding across the colorless void'; 'a consensual hallucination'. Great stuff!

In 1993, Gibson published the first book in his trilogy, *Virtual Light*, then in 1996, *Idoru*, set in Japan, and finally in 1999, *All Tomorrow's Parties*. By the late 1990s, it had become an in-joke in some academic circles that an article on the cultural significance of new technologies had to include a reference--perhaps a genuflection is a more accurate term--to William Gibson.

And I have a confession to make: I am one of those academics who did just that (and am doing it again here!). I called the chapter I wrote for a book titled *ICT, Pedagogy and the Curriculum*, edited by Avril Loveless and Viv Ellis, 'Hybrid Vigour': Reconciling the Verbal and the Visual in Electronic Communication* (Snyder, 2001). My focus was on the new texts associated with the use of digital technologies. I wanted to make the following point, now familiar to us all. In the age of print the word was dominant; by contrast, in the age of the Internet, verbal and visual elements combine in all sorts of new formations. The result is that the ways in which we represent the world and communicate with each other--in other words, the ways in which we make meaning--are dramatically altered. This is how I managed to sneak Gibson in: At the beginning of *All Tomorrow's Parties*, William Gibson's 1999 final book in his cyber-noir trilogy, Rydell is still a security guard at the Lucky Dragon convenience store in LA. As he does his routine curb check outside the store, Rydell notices:

> a Japanese girl standing out there with a seriously amazing amount of legs,
> running down from an even more amazingly small amount of shorts. Well, sort
> of Japanese. Rydell found it hard to make distinctions like that in LA. Durius
> said hybrid vigour was the order of the day, and Rydell guessed he was right. (p.
> 10)

With his inimitable inventiveness, Gibson submits the idea of 'hybrid vigour' to explain the constitution of the stunning female product he beholds in the street. It seems that the Japanese girl is breathtaking because of her mixed racial and ethnic origins. 'Hybrid vigour' also encapsulates an intrinsic component of the new forms of representation and communication discussed in this chapter. It is the very hybridity of the textual formations that gives them their force. Coming to understand the nature of this 'hybrid vigour,' while at the same time allowing it to flourish in the context of curriculum and pedagogical practices, provides a major challenge for English teachers.

It is Gibson's inventiveness with language to which I am particularly partial which brings us back to his most recent book with which I began today: *Pattern Recognition*. The protagonist is Cayce Pollard--an expensive market research consultant: *a cool hunter*. Her clients want to know what will work commercially and they pay her big money to find out.

Cayce--a boyfriend had insisted on comparing her to Helmut Newton's nude portrait of Jane Birkin--is in London on a job. But she is also offered another assignment: to investigate some absorbing video fragments, known as *the footage*, that have been appearing on the Internet. A subculture has grown around these bits of footage. People, including Cayce, discuss them endlessly on the Internet, arguing passionately about the narrative that might be assembled once all the fragments are made available. Cayce's new employer wants to understand how that kind of 'brand loyalty' can be created--a potential gold mine if it could be reproduced.

But then her friend's apartment (the ultimate in cool design) is burglarized and her computer hacked and the story gets going. Cayce's father, Win Pollard, ex-security expert and probably CIA, disappeared on 9/11; he took a taxi in the direction of the World Trade Centre and is presumed dead. She is still numb at his loss and, as much as for him as for any other reason, she refuses to give up this new job which takes her to Tokyo and to Moscow. Cayce follows the trail of the mysterious film to its source and in the process learns about her father's death.

I do not want to give too much more away in case you decide to read it--just enough to provide a sense of the compelling plot and the striking global cities in which the book is set. My purpose in presenting these details, however, is more complex than simply suggesting a good book to read. There are several concepts central to the book which I have chosen to use as lynch pins for my analysis of the technoliteracy research literature. I have already mentioned several of them:

1. Cool hunter--"There is cool to be hunted, here [Camden Town], and Cayce has clients in New York willing to pay for a Cayce Pollard report on what the early adaptors in this crush are doing, wearing, or listening to" (p.38). As Cayce explains later to her allies, Magda and Voytek: "I consult on design ... And I hunt 'cool' ... Manufacturers use me to keep track of street fashion" (p.86).

2. The footage--Fragments of film that gain meaning only at the end of the novel when details of the context in which they were created and the intention of the film maker are revealed. There are several other terms that Gibson uses to great effect.

3. The mirror world--When Cayce arrives in Camden Town, London, jet-lagged after her flight across the Atlantic, she depicts the UK as the 'mirror world:'

   The plugs on appliances are huge, triple-pronged, for a species of current that only powers electric chairs, in America. Cars are reversed, left to right, inside; telephone handsets have a different weight, a different balance; the covers of paperbacks look like Australian money. (pp. 2-3)

4. Semiotic neutrality--Cayce admires Damien's flat in Camden Town as an achievement in 'semiotic neutrality': "He'[d] kept his decorators from decorating." Like Cayce's apartment in New York, it is "carefully cleansed of extraneous objects ... she has fewer things in her apartment than anyone" (p.89).

5. Pattern recognition--This is the title of the book and focus of this presentation. As Cayce explains to Magda and Voytek, "It's about a group behavior pattern around a particular class of object. What I do is pattern

recognition. I try to recognise a pattern before anyone else does" (p.86).

I hope by now you are trying to puzzle out what I am planning to do with these ideas from Gibson's latest invention. But before I explain, let's cut to the chase. If we want to learn from the technoliteracy research, we need to think carefully and critically about the ideologically volatile contexts within which our work in literacy and technology studies is located. We need to devise smart strategies to guide our reading of the research. This involves being able to identify the rhetorics that permeate discussions of the new technologies, both within and outside the institution of education: to recognize the patterns.

Once we can recognize these patterns--that is, understand the powerful and potentially persuasive ways in which language is being used to shape our thinking about the use of new technologies--our attention can turn to the important work of extracting from the research, the implications for teaching and learning. Released from limited and limiting ways of viewing the use of technology in literacy education, we can decide what changes to curriculum and pedagogy are warranted and what changes are possible.

As you have probably guessed by now, I am not going to present a formal overview of the technoliteracy research literature. If you are interested, there are many excellent reviews available in books and journals. Rather, I ask an apparently simple question: What are the rhetorical patterns discernible in the research and policy literature about the use of information and communication technologies (ICT) for educational purposes?

By *research*, I mean the systematic studies that practitioners, researchers, and theorists have conducted to investigate the application of ICT in literacy education. By *policy*, I mean more than just the officially mandated policy documents but also the policy *environment* that influences the shape and timing of policies as well as their evolution and outcomes. By *technoliteracy*, I mean the use of new technologies for literacy purposes. Embedded in this term is the understanding that literacy has always been technologized and that literacy and technology are so interconnected that to speak of them separately is increasingly meaningless. I could have used other perhaps more popular terms, such as *digital* literacy or *electronic* literacy, but I have chosen *technoliteracy* because it symbolizes the interdependencies of the two concepts by combining "technology" and "literacy" to form a single word.

Implicit in the question, what are the rhetorical patterns discernible in the research and policy literature about the use of ICT for educational purposes, is the belief that if you can recognize the patterns you can avoid being seduced by them.

As an international guest to this conference, I have decided to concentrate on Gibson's "mirror worlds"--Australia, the UK, and South Africa in particular--where plugs are different, people drive on the left-hand side of the road, and where research approaches to investigate the educational applications of ICT are similar but not exactly the same as here in the US. Then I have something to say about cool hunters, but you will have to wait until the end of this presentation to find out just what.

PATTERN RECOGNITION:
WHAT ARE SOME OF THE DOMINANT PATTERNS?

The Technology 'Revolution'

A statement about the scale and speed at which online forms of communication have entered all aspects of our lives has become almost mandatory in articles and books about the use of ICT in literacy education:

> We live in a constantly changing world that continues to be shaped and mediated by the new information and communication technologies. Speed, instantaneity, flexibility, mobility, on-the-spot readjustment, perpetual experimentation, change devoid of consistent direction and incessant reincarnation are some of the hallmarks, not only of Web literacy practices, but also of real-life social and cultural practices. (Snyder, 2002, p. 173)

Of course, the danger with the repetition of such statements is that even though many facets of them ring true, their predictability in the literature can render them glib and empty. The hyperbolic language, that shapes the big claims about "revolutions," "radical" changes, "unprecedented speed," and "transformations" needs to be scrutinized.

The Techno-Enthusiasts / Techno-Demonizers Continuum

Dividing the world into those who love technology and those who fear or abhor it is another common pattern. When computers first arrived in schools in the late 1970s, there was a little skepticism and a lot of euphoria. The cries of the pessimists who warned of the technology's inevitable dehumanizing effects were drowned out by the enthusiastic rhetoric of *techno-evangelists* who believed that simply giving students computers to use as writing machines would improve the quality of their writing.

However, we now know that early predictions that the use of computers and then later, the Internet, would *transform* education systems were simply incorrect. Such claims and others like them, that characterized the early days of uncritical *boosterism*, ignore the deeply complex and contextualized ways in which information technologies are embedded in local and global structures of commerce, industry, and education.

Yet at the same time, we know that the "technological revolution" has lead to changing cultural practices by reshaping the way we work, play, form relationships, and communicate. We need to consider carefully and with dispassion the claims of those who wax lyrical about the technologies' powers on the one hand, and the claims of those who demonize them on the other. That is why I find the metaphor of a continuum useful. Where would you place yourself on the continuum before you have read the research and policy literature? Where would you place yourself after you have read the research and policy literature?

Technological Determinism

"Technological determinism" represents a particular way of talking about the power and influence of technology. It assumes that qualities in the computer medium itself are responsible for changes in social and cultural practices. The perception of technology as an autonomous agent of change is not new.

"The compass made Europe's colonization of the world possible." "The printing press caused the Reformation." Such popular narratives convey a strong sense of technology as a driving force of history. In the popular discourse of technological determinism, the "technology" is made the subject of an active predicate: "The automobile created suburbia;" "The Pill produced a sexual revolution." And in the case of ICT: "The Internet has democratized access to information;" "ICT have transformed education." In each example, a complex event is made to seem the outcome of a technological innovation.

I recently saw a wonderful American film called *My Architect: A Son's Journey*, about the life and work of Louis Kahn. The film introduced me to the notion of "architectural determinism"-- which was apparently discredited a long time ago as a simplistic approach to exploring the complex connections between buildings and the people who inhabit them.

It should be apparent what I think about this pattern: grandiose claims about the influence and power of any technology need to be interrogated since they build on the spurious premise that technology is directly responsible for changes that affect social relations. They overlook the human agency integral to all technological innovation and rely on an interpretative frame in which any notion of control over technology disappears.

When we recognize this pattern of looking at technologies in deterministic ways, we can query the technocratic belief that computers and networks will make a better society and that access to information, better communications, and electronic programs can cure social problems. ICT are articulated in many ways in our educational system, ranging from liberatory to oppressive. We need to be on the lookout for the many forms that technological determinism can assume and then interrogate the assertions.

Policy Agendas

Policy documents emerge from particular contexts and therefore have particular agendas. It is up to us as teachers to recognize the patterns. In the mirror world, national and state technology policy documents no longer simply rely on the rhetoric of "improving" and "enhancing" teaching and learning with the use of ICT. They present the use of ICT for educational purposes in both reductive and expansive ways. In Australia, policy documents range from those that are prescriptive, instrumental and talk about competencies to those that refer to the social and cultural importance of introducing young people to technology.

A principal aim is often the promotion of "technological literacy," but from a purely instrumental perspective. The emphasis is on the economic and social "transformations" that have made technology skills central to the future employment of students and to the importance of technological innovation in Australia's economic wealth. In the context of the overwhelming emphasis in such documents on the connection between the labour market and technology, we need to keep in mind issues related to equitable access to technology. We know of course that in the US and in the mirror world, access to and capacity to use ICT remain unequal.

Many reports contain strong assertions that technology can "catalyze" much needed changes in the content, methods, and overall quality of teaching and learning processes, encouraging the replacement of lectures with inquiry-oriented practices. But some of these claims are doubtful, given that technologies can just as easily stifle innovation, or be associated with the return to some superseded practices in classrooms. In other words, technological determinism too often flavors policy documents. Being aware of the pattern is what is important.

Commercial Imperatives

When we consider the influence of commercial imperatives, it is almost inevitable that we focus on the profound impact of the US on the mirror world, particularly when we take into account the global reach of organizations such as Microsoft.

In *The Road Ahead*, published in 1995, but still of interest as exemplifying this pattern, Bill Gates presents himself as 'an ordinary man who made good', a possibility, he suggests, open to anyone with a little bit of luck and a lot of hard work. However, although he claims not to be an expert on matters educational, as he never completed his college degree at Harvard, Gates proceeds with some assurance in this book to make remarkable claims about the educational benefits of ICT. And he expresses his views within the frame of the familiar rhetorics of the language of "democratization," "empowerment," "enhanced learning," "economic productivity" and "improved futures"--patterns I have already mentioned.

The result is something quite chilling as it is difficult to distinguish between Gates, the hugely successful businessman, and Gates, the self-acclaimed authority on education. In the chapter on education, the language of commercialism and the business world is inseparable from the disinterested social and cultural objectives of democratic education.

There is big money in education for hawkers of hardware, software, and strategies. The corporations have made their move on the education sector, and we have to recognize the patterns of their incursions. The aim is to open education up as a new frontier for business activity and entrepreneurship. Teachers should be in no doubt that their profession and occupations are under attack by unfriendly forces.

We also need to be aware of the extent to which the push to technologies in education is intimately tied up with interests most eager to undermine the tradition of public education. In the mirror world of Australia, John Howard was recently returned for a fourth term. His education policy is designed to weaken the public sector and to encourage the move to private education. And in Australia, where more than 30% of students K-12 attend schools in the private sector, and where the schools in that private sector often market themselves on the basis of technological resources and training, this is a pattern that needs to be identified and questioned.

Different Accounts of Technoliteracy Education

There are patterns evident in the different ways of explaining literacy and technology education in the research and policy literature. There are psycholinguistic accounts and social accounts of technoliteracy. The psycholinguistic accounts, that have characterized literacy studies in the past, mistakenly assume that technoliteracy is simply a basic skill, easily transmitted by teachers and inherently powerful.

By contrast, social accounts acknowledge that the communication landscape has changed and continues to do so. They recognize that multiple languages and multiple cultures within nation states are accompanied by increasing diversity in the modes and media of communication. While the impact of cinema and television is apparent even in the poorest households, the impact of computers and the Internet is progressively shifting literacy practices around the world, changing the mix of signs, symbols, pictures, words, sounds, and gestures.

Another pattern we need to recognize is the over-use of the adjective "new." Technoliteracy practices do not simply represent a break with the past; old and new practices interact in far more complex ways producing hybrid rather than wholly new practices. More and more, the literacy landscape is dominated by multimodal textual formations and practices. As educators we need to be aware of the continuities with earlier forms but also of the ways in which both the context and the medium for literacy education change where they are caught up in the use of ICT.

In books and articles that focus on the use of new technologies for literacy education, again, we can observe different patterns. There are those who advocate learning at-a-distance and those who argue that face-to-face learning is the only approach to education for the future. There are also those who suggest that striking an effective balance between the two is essential. These are the patterns of the discussion in the literature.

But it is probably better to avoid seeing these debates as either/or, as allowing them to be constructed in such a way stifles useful discussion. The bottom line is that ICT are being used both within formal education systems and in society more broadly, to a greater and lesser extent, depending on the global location. When they are available in schools, finding ways to use them well seems a worthwhile goal. And, in situations where resources are scarce, the imperative is to find creative ways to do more with less.

The Shape of the Questions Researchers Ask

There are discernible patterns in the kinds of questions that researchers asked back in the early 1980s and, it seems, continue to ask: "Does the use of computers for writing improve the quality of students' texts?" "What is the impact of ICT on literacy education?"

The title of Richard Andrews' book, *The Impact of ICT on Literacy Education*, published earlier this year in the mirror world, represents a problematic way of looking at the complex relationship between the use of technology for literary purposes and the associated influences. However, his systematic analysis of the relation between ICT and literacy does offer useful reflection on the coming together of the domains of ICT and education.

The review concentrates on these five areas: (a) the relation between ICT, literacy learning, and learners whose first language is not English; (b) the impact of ICT on reading and literature in general; (c) the relation between ICT and the moving image; (d) outcomes evidence on the effectiveness of the use of ICT in literacy learning programs, predominantly drawn from experimental studies; and (e) the specific impact of 'networked ICT' on literacy learning.

Andrews' survey of the research literature provides an important corrective to excessive optimism about the use of technology in literacy education. He found that for some learners the use of ICT brings no improvement in educational outcomes.

Moreover, Andrews concludes that in some instances educational practices and learning are made worse. His findings might have a sobering effect on the enthusiasts who claim that teaching can more closely target the needs of individual learners, that curriculum can be diversified and enriched, and that different teaching styles can be catered to.

Andrews proposes that randomized trials should precede further investments in ICT for literacy education. As I've already suggested, the basic question informing this research overview is problematic. Classrooms are not laboratories and to think that experimental research is the answer, despite the attitudes of the major funding bodies in the UK where Andrews works and here in the US where many of you live, disregards all that we have learned about the importance of taking account of the social and cultural context in which our work is located.

Experimental research designs do not capture the complex, interactive and dialogical character of literacy learning and teaching. A carefully designed qualitative approach is more likely to provide an appropriately nuanced picture of what happens when ICT are used in literacy education. More useful questions are: (a) How best can educators utilize ICT to achieve teaching/learning objectives that are socially and culturally empowering?, and (b) If ICT are changing the nature of literacy, how can control, mastery, and pedagogy attached to the new literacies be incorporated into classroom teaching?

Interrogating the Narratives About the Use of ICT in Literacy Education

These rhetorical patterns are not exclusive to the research literature. Similar patterns are evident in the narratives that abound about the use of ICT in classrooms. Again, we need to recognize the patterns of these narratives if we are to use them for our own purposes rather than be used by them.

There is a problem with narratives created to explain the history of the use of computer technology for educational purposes as a neat series of chronological and causally linked events. Histories of educational technology presented in this way may be comforting in the familiarity of their patterns, but they don't help us to understand the complexities and nuances.

Equally problematic are the creation myths--take those about the Internet or the birth of hypertext, for example--dominated by the rhetoric of founding fathers and institutions. Although they are appealing in their simplicity, romanticism, and elegance, this approach to history also has its limitations.

Even when the stories are told by eminent sociologists such as Manuel Castells (1996, 2001), they need to be interrogated. According to Castells, in the last two decades of the twentieth century, a related set of social transformations took place around the world. Together these transformations constituted the formation of a new type of social structure that Castells calls the network society. Integral to the network society is a new technological paradigm centered around the use of ICT.

In Castells' view, the new technologies represent a greater change in the history of technology than those associated with the Industrial Revolution or with the previous Information or Print Revolution. He argues that we are only at the beginning of this technological revolution; as the Internet becomes a universal tool of interactive communication, and as nanotechnology and the biology revolution make possible what was only recently impossible, the world will change dramatically and irreversibly. We need to think about Castells' assertions about the massive changes of the current era that he links directly with the use of ICT. We cannot afford to ignore them, but we might not necessarily accept them uncritically.

There are also other stories--stories about real people in real situations-- "situated," as the proponents of the New Literacy Studies approach say, in contexts of use and practice. They are about the changes to educational practices associated with the use of ICT; they are often about successes and failures. They demonstrate that the changes are happening very unevenly, within and between nation states, in both the developed and the developing world. Even in the developed world, the enthusiasm of corporations and governments for the promise of enhanced communication networks does not always pay off as expected.

Again, a diversion from the mirror world, and again, I have a story about Bill Gates. When Gates tried to halt the exodus of people from rural areas to the cities, by wiring rural America, the outcome was much less than he desired. In a classic instance of well-meaning but narrow understandings of access and the complex relationships between ICT and society, Bill Gates predicted in 1996 that the Internet would help rural people stay put, in part because they would have the same advantages as city people in the virtual world.

He made that prophecy in *The Road Ahead*, a book already mentioned, the cover of which shows Gates standing in the middle of an empty highway in remote eastern Washington. But when Gates, the richest man in the world, returned recently to the land of no stoplights as part of the last phase of a five-year philanthropic effort to put computers in every poor library district in the United States, he acknowledged that the road ahead was full of blind curves. There is scant evidence that the wiring of rural America has done anything to make Gates' prediction about population flight come true. The new computers may even be aiding the exodus from rural America, as people go online to find jobs far away (Egan, 2002).

In the developing world, there are parallel stories of both success and failure when ICT are used. Heeks (1999) describes an example of each in South Africa where there have been efforts to use ICT to help alleviate poverty.

In 1995, a project was begun by the Office of the Premier in North-West Province to provide information to six rural communities through touch-screen computer kiosks. The kiosks provided general demographic and economic information about the province, details of main government programs, and speeches by the Premier and by Nelson Mandela. This did not meet community needs and it became apparent that this had been more a public relations exercise than a development initiative. The project was scrapped in 1997.

In 1995 a project was begun by the local government in Alexandria township (near Johannesburg) to create a database of local resources. All township organizations were asked to provide details, a process often organized by school children as homework. The database was made accessible over the Internet. Not only did it provide information about local capabilities to community members, it also enabled community enterprises to win contracts from larger firms in Johannesburg.

While material provision is clearly important, these two instances suggest something of what else might be required to make a difference: consideration of issues related to ownership and commitment, consultation, appropriateness, negotiation, relevance, and purpose, as well as technical know-how and availability (Snyder & Beavis, 2004).

CONCLUSION

We need to tell stories about the use of ICT. The stories, however, are probably neither of simply successes or failures; we need accounts and interpretations that are more nuanced. We need researchers to explore the complexity of technology-mediated literacy practices in the contexts of their own locations and experience. They need to describe their developing understandings as teachers using ICT, as well as the responses of their students, and the learning that went on between them, as together they investigate what it means to do literacy in the age of the Internet. There are many other narratives about ICT and literacy education from the mirror world.

I have concentrated to a large extent, on what William Gibson calls the "mirror world." In reality, however, we live in a globalized world, and what I have done is somewhat artificial as there are meanings and understandings emerging from the research that are trans-global. We need to recognize the patterns in the research and policy literature if we are to use them for our own purposes rather than be used by them. As the people in Gibson's book, *Pattern Recognition*, eventually discover about "the footage," there is no single, coherent, completely satisfying narrative about the effective use of ICT in literacy education, but some are better informed and thus more useful than others.

As well as determining which stories are more useful, I invite you all to become "cool hunters." Seek out those who use these technologies creatively for multiple literacy purposes and who know what can be done with them. The young people in your classes are perfect targets; consider what they are already doing with the new technologies and allow this knowledge to provide a foundation for curriculum reform. In *Pattern Recognition* (Gibson, 2003), Cayce discovers important information about the intruders into her flat by looking at the browser history on her computer that they hacked into. Perhaps we should look at the browser histories of our students, but with their permission: Where do they go when they cruise the Internet? Where have they been?

So let's be cool hunters--not necessarily to bring what the young people enjoy outside of school into the classroom but at the very least to recognize the patterns. Let's see what they are doing. Let's see what kinds of literacy practices they are engaging in. We need to understand students' use of technology and new media. We need to learn from the young--to let them be our informants. Our challenge is to find ways to utilize what ICT have to offer in productive ways but, at the same time to become, together with our students, critical and capable users: to engage in pattern recognition.

I never did manage to weave "semiotic neutrality" into my text, so I have left it to the end. Achieving a state of semiotic neutrality in a world dominated by the calculated and often insidious use of logos and symbols, all carefully designed to encourage us to conform to certain patterns of behavior, is a challenge. As an employee of Monash University, I am advised to use the Monash "brand" slide template for presentations. As you have seen, I did not conform. But, of course, the slide you are now looking at is shaped by another template, Microsoft's PowerPoint. Semiotic neutrality *really* is a challenge. William Gibson was onto something when he used it to critique a world gone mad with consumerism and branding.

REFERENCES

Andrews, R. (2004). (Ed.). *The impact of ICT on literacy education*. London & New York: Routledge.

Castells, M. (1996). *The rise of the network society, volume 1, The information age: economy, society and culture*. London: Blackwell Publishers.

Castells, M. (2001). *The Internet galaxy: reflections on the Internet, business and society*. Oxford: Oxford University Press.

Egan, T. (2002). NYTimes.com Article: 'Bill Gates views what he's sown in libraries', November 6, 2002. Retrieved on November 10, 2002 from http://www.nytimes.com/2002/11/06/national/06GATE.html?ex=1037574814&ei=1&en=8621c72f4b3c387f

Gates, B. (1995). *The road ahead*. Hammondsworth: Penguin.

Gibson, W. (1986). *Neuromancer*. London: Grafton Books.

Gibson, W. (1993). *Virtual light*. Hammondsworth: Viking (Penguin).

Gibson, W. (1996). *Idoru*. Hammondsworth: Viking (Penguin).

Gibson, W. (1999). *All tomorrow's parties*. Hammondsworth: Viking (Penguin).

Gibson, W. (2003). *Pattern recognition*. New York: Berkeley Books (Penguin).

Heeks, R. (1999). Information and Communication Technologies, Poverty and Development. Institute for Development Policy and Management, University of Manchester. Retrieved on November 10, 2002 from http://idpm.man.ac.uk/wp/di/di_wp05.htm

Snyder, I. (2001). 'Hybrid vigour': Reconciling the verbal and the visual in electronic communication. In A. Lovelace & V. Ellis (Eds.), *ICT, pedagogy and curriculum: Subject to change* (pp. 41-59). London: RoutledgeFalmer.

Snyder, I. (2002). Communication, imagination, critique: Literacy education for the electronic age. In I. Snyder (Ed.), *Silicon literacies: Communication, innovation and education in the electronic age* (pp. 173-83). London: Routledge.

Snyder, I. & Beavis, C. (Eds.). (2004). *Doing literacy online: Teaching, learning and playing in an electronic world*. New Jersey: Hampton Press.

The Mind (and Heart) of the Reading Teacher[1]

Robert Calfee

University of California Riverside

In his tribute to Oscar Causey, Al Kingston (1961) wrote, "by deed and example, Professor Causey served to inspire others, particularly young men and women, to the pursuit of knowledge in the field of reading. Many of these young people have grown to professional maturity as a result of his example and aid. Similarly, the National Reading Conference [NRC], which he nurtured during the shaky years . . . has developed as an organization of national repute" (p. 75-76). Professional maturity, and the respect that it engenders, is the theme of the present work, which will attempt to connect the research activities that have become the NRC hallmark to the labors of the tens of thousands of reading teachers who are the centerpiece of many of these research activities.

What does the teacher of early reading need to know, do, and feel in order to fulfill his or her responsibilities? Answers to this question might take many forms, depending on how one views the task and context. In this paper I focus on primary grade teachers in regular classroom settings. From one perspective, the reading teacher is a semi-professional whose job is to follow the manual, attending to the tasks of classroom management along the way. Another image emphasizes the teacher's care and concern for children, along with his or her skill in establishing environments that foster the natural development of language and literacy. A third view, the emphasis in this paper, imagines a professional with significant technical knowledge about the language-literacy domain and informed sensitivity to the developmental progression of young children as they move through the elementary grades. This last image is by no means a simple joining of the first two perspectives, although both are important parts of the picture. Complicating the "professional" picture, one is hard put, since the demise of the normal school, to find an academic locus for the development of reading professionals. Where and how are teachers to learn what they need to know? And while it is possible to identify and study exceptional reading teachers (e.g., Pressley, Allington, Wharton-McDonald, Block, & Morrow, 2001), rarely does the image of a professional community emerge from these investigations. Think about what it would mean to investigate the work of medical doctors in the Eighteenth Century, before the sciences of medicine had evolved, before knowledge and skill had reached today's sophistication--and levels of public trust.

This paper looks partly to the past, partly toward the future. It is partly personal--an opportunity to recount my own development as a reading researcher--but largely professional--a description of how concepts and experiences have led to a particular conception of the reading teacher, in which knowledge, skill, and passion commingle. Following a brief resume of my career, I propose a "basic principle," a vision of literacy for our society, and then sketch a framework of literacy education designed to promote the principle. Empirical studies of programs built around this framework have been the focus of my research for the past few decades, and I will mention

[1] Portions of this work were supported by grants from the Spencer Foundation (1999-00046) and the Interagency Educational Research Initiative (9979834)

63

some of this work. Like most such efforts, which run contrary to most current practice and policy, they have failed the "scalability" test. Despite promising episodes here and there, the programs have tended to disappear over time, and have seldom spread to other locations. The ideas rest on teachers rather than packages, and one explanation for the lack of scalability is that teachers are simply not capable, in the aggregate, of acting as professionals. For evidence to the contrary, I look back to artifacts from the early Twentieth Century revealing expectations far greater than today's characterization of "teacher quality." After a brief exploration of the implications of this review for current policies and practices, I conclude with some puzzlements, predicaments, and possibilities.

A ROAD WITH MANY FORKS

Receipt of the Causey Award, an enormous honor, led me to ruminate about my past. This paper accordingly has an historical flavor, reflecting my years as a researcher, but also mindful of the loss of several colleagues during the past few years. Career awards focus attention on the individual, but every awardee can name dozens if not hundreds of others whose contributions have been of seminal importance; for me, the list includes mentors, colleagues, former students, and most especially, those classroom teachers who exemplify the concepts from the paper.

My career as a reading researcher began in the 1960s when, as an experimental cognitive psychologist, I became intrigued by the psychology of reading. The field has a long history, of course, but several events ongoing at that time sparked my interest. Dick Atkinson, who advised my doctoral work at UCLA, was establishing a computer-assisted instruction (CAI) program at Stanford. The federal government was allocating significant funding for educational research in several areas, but especially reading, for individual researchers, but also through university centers and regional laboratories. I moved to Wisconsin-Madison as an assistant professor in Psychology, where Dick Venezky (whom I had met at Stanford the preceding year) showed up at my office door. He had just joined the departments of Computer Sciences, English, and Linguistics. Following several delightful discussions, we decided that the field of pre-reading could use our help, and so we walked down the street to the Wisconsin Research and Development Center, where we garnered funding to study kindergarten literacy, the beginning of a long and productive collaboration, professional and personal. The massive, multi-year First Grade Reading Studies were going on at that time (Bond & Dykstra, 1967), but the field of pre-reading was relatively dormant. Reading readiness was the accepted wisdom; some children were ready to read as six-year olds (perhaps even younger), but others needed more time. Assessment of basic perceptual capacities-- visual, auditory, and linguistic--provided a means to determine readiness, to decide who was ready and who was not. Our studies provided evidence contradicting these beliefs and practices, and introduced the concept of phonemic awareness, which several years later was to become quite popular (Calfee & Norman, 1999).

Following my move to the Stanford School of Education in 1969, I continued the pre-reading investigations, which emphasized assessment, but began to examine classroom instruction, the basis of literacy acquisition for most children. The "Reading Diary" was an effort, through detailed and extensive observation of numerous classrooms, to trace growth in decoding skills during first grade, and to relate student growth to curriculum and instruction (Calfee & Piontkowski, 1980). The study proved extremely frustrating, mostly because of what appeared to be a blooming-buzzing chaos in the classroom. Two constants emerged. One was the centrality of the teacher's manual as the source of discourse activities during the reading lessons with teacher's questions and students' answers largely determined by the basal scripts. The other was the primary dependence of achievement trends on the student's entry point. In a foreshadowing of the Matthew effect (Stanovich, 1986), detailed monthly assessments revealed that the students who did well when they entered the class progressed more rapidly than the students who were low to begin with, some of whom seemed to make little or no progress during the entire year. Aside from assignment to a reading group, decisions about curriculum and instruction seemed unrelated to student learning rate. These patterns puzzled me, but I assumed that I was simply not looking at the data properly. After all, my preparation was in psychology; along with several other colleagues who made a similar shift at about the same time, we soon discovered that we had a lot to learn about classrooms and schools.

About ten years after arriving at Stanford, during a spring visit to Graystone Elementary School in San Jose, an event occurred that was to profoundly affect my career (for the full story, cf. Calfee & Patrick, 1995). The principal, Jean Funderburg, spent the morning with me as I traveled through classrooms to observe reading lessons. Along the way, I asked students and teachers to comment on the activities. "What are you learning?" "What are you teaching?" For both students and teachers, the question took them aback, students with a shrug, teachers with unease ("Did I do something wrong?"). In her office after the visit, Funderburg asked, "Is there a basal series that emphasizes understanding? Kids ought to be able to tell why they are doing what they are doing." My response was that textbook series were generally similar to one another, and that understanding came not from textbooks but from teachers. By the 1980s, studies by Shulman and his colleagues at the Michigan State University *Institute for Research on Teaching* had shown that teacher decision-making was largely procedural, guided by routines like the Initiate-Respond-Evaluate or IRE pattern (Cazden, 1988) that allowed teachers to maintain control while moving through the content.

Funderburg raised several other concerns: the literacy curriculum was simplistic and boring; the emphasis on reading meant that writing received little attention (and was disconnected from reading); struggling readers never seemed to "get it"; motivation and interest declined throughout the grades. Also on her mind was the arrival of the Whole Language movement. What to do? My research experience was not especially helpful at this juncture, but I turned to what I knew for a response. Teachers might benefit from cognitive learning principles (increasingly referred to as "constructivism"; Richardson, 2005), from a moderate dollop of linguistics (including a brief look at the history of the English language), and most especially from acquaintance with rhetoric (ideas and techniques for the use of language as a tool for thinking and communication). I had begun to suspect, correctly as it turned out, that these three domains were largely missing from teacher preparation programs, nor were they central considerations in the design of basal readers.

Our discussion led to a weeklong workshop with Graystone faculty in early summer. My research team (doctoral students who had been accomplished teachers) and I developed ideas and overheads from the three domains, relying on the faculty (and Funderburg) for strategies and tactics that translated the ideas into classroom actions. As the summer progressed, the team created *The BOOK for the Reading Teacher*, a loose-leaf "work in progress" notebook, which was presented to the faculty as a guide for constructivist literacy instruction. The team and I were regular visitors during the school year, partly as observers, partly as resources, partly as researchers. The changes seemed revolutionary to all of us, and the spring test scores increased. We were elated--reforming literacy instruction seemed easy!

During the quarter century since Graystone, the platform that emerged during that experience--we eventually labeled it READ-Plus--has served to support and direct my research. By no means a program, READ-Plus is instead better understood as a set of ideas and techniques designed to provide teachers with a view of literacy instruction that is "professional" by several criteria. First, it builds on established research findings, not the "fully tested" variety to be found in the *What Works* clearinghouse, but the kind of studies that build on theory-guided experimentation and concept-based scholarship. Second, the program emphasizes adaptability rather than prescription; in essence, the classroom teacher conducts action research throughout the day and week, guided by the framework, with the aim of ensuring that every student becomes a competent and motivated reader and writer. Third, the teacher operates as a member of a school-wide professional community; much as medical doctors compare notes, puzzle over unexpected problems, and critique one another's work, so teachers make the time to review lesson designs, observe instruction, and evaluate patterns of student learning. READ-Plus was grounded in classroom realities, but as I realized the importance of professional skill and knowledge, my focus shifted to the roles of adults--teachers, principals, and district administrators--and the ways in which formal language might support their thinking and communication.

A VISION THING

Literacy means different things to different people; reading, in particular, has many construals. One definition emphasizes basic print skills, such as portrayed in the stage theory proposed by Chall (1983). As popularly interpreted, the idea is that the young child first acquires the ABCs (the alphabetic symbols), then the sounds associated with the various symbols (phonemic awareness), next the idea of letter-sound strings as words (often by means of onset-rime patterns), and finally to sentences and stories (increasingly through restricted or "decodable" texts). The instructional emphasis shifts from phonics to comprehension as the child moves through the stages. Of course, children who have trouble in the early stages may take quite a while to get to the "good stuff." In the stage model, the goal of early reading instruction is fluency and automaticity in translating print to some form of spoken language that the reader can eventually use for other purposes. The content used for skill development is of secondary importance; interesting material is desirable, a criterion that has challenged publishers since the days of Dick and Jane. Writing is a related but secondary curriculum goal, to be taught separately and later in the child's development.

In the *No Child Left Behind* policy, reading achievement is defined by externally mandated tests, principally standardized multiple-choice instruments or speed-based systems such as DIBELS (www.dibels.org). The national goal is to ensure that all children perform at or above national norms on these instruments within the next decade or so.

Whether any schools will be able to meet NCLB requirements is presently a matter of considerable debate, but my aim here is to explore an altogether different vision of literacy, one that emphasizes different outcomes, different goals, and different means to achieve those goals. While it reflects a personal perspective, I think that that the vision warrants consideration as an alternative perspective during these troubled times for public schools:

> THE VISION--To ensure that all children *** have the opportunity *** to acquire the level of literacy *** that allows them full participation in our democratic society *** depends on a corps of teachers who possess extraordinary minds *** and hearts.

The parsing is an effort to highlight several key points in the statement. For present purposes, I will focus on four elements. First is "level of literacy," by which I mean to emphasize the interrelatedness and functionality of several language and literacy components. Literacy is not a grab bag of skills that allow the individual to "do something;" instead, literacy within this vision entails a distinctive way of thinking and communicating, to be incorporated in all aspects of curriculum and instruction from the earliest days of schooling. "Full participation in our democratic society" implies (for me) the notion that the learner, from the beginning, gains a sense of the freedoms and responsibilities that are the American ideal. Today's classrooms are typically the antithesis of democracy; public schooling is the longest sentence that can be assigned short of a felony. Something seems fundamentally wrong with the notion that young students should be taught to do what they are told for years on end, with the expectation that they will somehow become "free and responsible." The challenge in this proposition is especially great given the diversity found in virtually all of today's classrooms. I am not proposing anarchy in the classroom. Rather, the goal is to transform the chaos found on the first day of kindergarten into classroom cooperatives—students and teachers--who have learned to work together.

The next part of the statement centers around teachers' minds and hearts. "The mind of the reading teacher" (Calfee, 1984) proposed a mental model based on concepts of cognitive organization and function current at the time. Briefly, the idea was that the competent reading teacher called upon several domains of skill and knowledge in handling classroom practice: curriculum objectives, instructional strategies, assessment techniques, management tactics, and so on. My thinking was that teachers acquired a schema containing these elements during preparation and practice, and that they relied on this shared knowledge base to guide practice and as a basis for professional dialogue. I was clearly mistaken. Exchanges with experienced teachers during READ-Plus workshops (also cf. Calfee & Drum, 1979; Fraatz, 1987) revealed a quite different mental organization, one shaped by a hodgepodge of ideas, activities, and folk wisdom. Which is not to downplay the value of the "wisdom of practice," to the contrary. But the expository foundations for professional exchanges were missing; in their place were marvelous stories of students, colleagues, and experiences.

Upon reflection, I have come to realize that these stories, while they may not fit a cognitive model, provide the foundation for a mostly missing ingredient in research on teachers and teaching--the heart. A consistent feature of my talks with teachers is the passion with which they approach their work, and the ways in which daily they tend to the needs of "other people's children" (Delpit, 1996). Teacher motivation is not on any syllabus that I have encountered, nor is the topic featured in workshops and conferences. The *Third Handbook of Research on Teaching* includes a chapter on "The Cultures of Teaching" (Feiman-Nemser & Floden, 1986) touching on the issue. In the *Fourth Handbook of Research on Teaching*, Noddings (2001) provides a brief (but compelling) historical analysis of "The Caring Teacher," and Hansen's (2001) chapter on "Teaching as a Moral Activity" contrasts the intellectual and moral facets of teaching, raising several pertinent issues. Recruitment and selection frequently give romanticized attention to the intrinsic rewards of working with children and young people, and my sense is that one of the primary reasons for leaving the field is a candidate's realization that spending every day with crowds of kids is not especially satisfying. While teachers are generally held in high respect, external incentives--salary and working conditions--are not exceptional. Accordingly, although I can call upon little systematic research to inform the topic, it seems important to include it in the picture.

A CONCEPTION CONSISTENT WITH THE PROPOSAL

What might be the shape of a "level of literacy allowing full participation in a democratic society?" What does the teacher of early reading need to know and do to ensure that all children acquire the skill, knowledge, and inclination associated with such a conception of literacy? An adequate answer to this question clearly goes beyond the scope of the present paper, but several features of the READ-Plus platform incorporate elements from my thinking (Calfee & Patrick, 1995; Calfee & Drum, 1986). First, the proposal is not to introduce a new "reading program." Plenty of these are available, and a half century of research confirms unequivocally that the teacher more than the program is the key element determining student achievement. Rather, the platform is a comprehensive framework for professional development centered around literacy as the acquisition of a *formal language register* (Calfee, 1982). One consequence of this focus is the notion that reading, writing, and language development are integrated, bound together by principles found in the rhetoric. The framework is *developmental*, which means movement through a common set of curriculum elements from the earliest years onward. In contrast to the stage model, the idea is that all curriculum elements progress in parallel across the grades, in ways and with materials appropriate to particular students. While certain general progressions make sense, the framework does not rest on the lock-step objectives found in typical scope-and-sequence charts. Rather, *curriculum, instruction*, and *assessment* (CIA) are interwoven domains for promoting student learning. The intention is that instructional strategies are consistent with curriculum goals, and that assessment practices provide valid information about learning outcomes. Finally, the foundations for the framework rest on principles from research in the *social-cognitive* tradition, a particular version of what is referred to as constructivism. These ideas, generally associated with

Vygotsky (1962), emphasize the impact of learning in social settings that foster reflection and metacognitive awareness.

These four fundamental domains--formal language and the rhetoric, developmental progressions, the CIA triad, and social-cognitive learning--each constitute substantial fields of study in their own right. Each can be located in university catalogues, sometimes within departments, sometimes spanning multiple disciplines. Seldom are they connected with one another. In particular, the CIA domain, typically found in Education, tends to be distributed over different courses; rarely are the three topics found elsewhere in the university.

To illustrate the challenge confronting the college student considering a career in elementary teaching, consider the topic of *formal language*, a fancy label for the special ways in which language is used in schools, businesses, or courts. Several contrasts distinguish this register or style (also referred to as "academic language") from the casual style used in everyday conversations: (a) the speaker provides more explicit detail about his or her thoughts, so that the dialogue can stand on its own; (b) the various elements tend to be organized and "marked," in order to support memory; and (c) exposition serves as the primary structure, with narrative excerpts illustrating and enlivening. Where can teacher candidates learn about this domain in their course work? You were first introduced to the techniques when you entered kindergarten and participated in show-and-tell. Later, freshman English contributed more ideas and techniques. The field of study for college students stretches from English departments (courses in the rhetoric) through Linguistics and on to Anthropology. For the aspiring reading teacher, this stretch can be daunting. Each group of scholars employs a different vocabulary and explores distinctive issues, most with little interest in the practical implications for the teacher confronting a group of 25 diverse first-graders. At my campus, for instance, here is the catalogue entry for the introductory course in Linguistics: "The nature of language; language structure; grammars; the languages of the world; historical and comparative linguistics; interdisciplinary approaches, including anthropology and psycholinguistics." Ten weeks and four units.

So what might the university do to prepare the reading teacher? Candidates for the elementary credential are likely to be reasonably literate, but are probably unacquainted with most of the domains mentioned above. They can surely "read and write," but have probably given little thought to the ways in which they use language differently in causal conversation versus more serious discussions. Little in their preparation program is likely to cover this contrast, and if they take the initiative to put together a program on their own, the result is likely to be considerable frustration. All of the pieces exist somewhere in the mix, but the candidate--a novice--has to pick and choose, organize in a coherent framework, and connect to the practical realities that are still on the horizon. Consider the area of phonology, which provides information about the articulation of speech sounds. The candidate would need to know about the area, locate one or more relevant courses, and take on the challenge of seeing how a professor's particular interests (e.g., variations in Slavic fricatives) might apply to the first grade setting. The bottom line--most graduates of elementary teacher programs enter the classroom with thin and scattershot preparation in the fundamentals of language and literacy.

Professional Development: Curriculum

READ-Plus was an effort to pull together key concepts from these domains into an efficient and compelling package, establishing a professional foundation that would allow experienced teachers to connect their current practices with a developmental and social-cognitive model. Implementation began (typically) with a late summer workshop for a school staff (including the principal), followed by a series of follow-up sessions throughout the year, supported by district staff with advice from the research team.

Workshops began with a conceptual overview covering principles of learning and thought, language and literacy. While most ideas were generally new to many participants, a consistent reaction from evaluations was "Interesting stuff, but when are you going to tell us what to do?"

The next agenda item presented the language-literacy curriculum framework for the model: four separable language-literacy components (Calfee & Spector, 1981)--two at the word level and two at the passage level.

1. Phonology and phonics--the representation of English phonemes by printed symbols. In READ-Plus, the distinctive features included (a) the historical origins of English, based on Venezky's analysis of spelling-sound patterns (Calfee, 2005), (b) and consonant articulation as the basis for understanding "speech sounds." In WordWork, the consonant-vowel-consonant (CVC) pattern provides the foundation for constructing syllabic patterns by "gluing" the consonant bricks together with vowels.

2. Semantics and vocabulary--psycholinguistic research portrays the organization of "words" in conceptual networks, a variation on "six degrees of separation." In place of the vocabulary lists that begin most textbook lessons, the READ-Plus curriculum relies on graphic organizers for visual portrayal of various network structures, including webs and weaves. Again, students construct the networks around a topic, beginning with associations by group members, and then adding "textbook" items to the mix.

3. Narratives and stories--all kindergartners come to school with storehouses of stories, and can both comprehend and compose in this genre. They are less likely to know how to explain their understanding, and they lack a technical language for discussing what they know (e.g., character, plot, setting, theme).

4. Expositions and reports--as students move through the grades, they encounter more complex and unfamiliar genres, including informational texts, persuasive pieces, and explanatory passages. Comprehending and composing in these forms is essential for entry to academic disciplines--and acquaintance with the styles is also helpful to the adolescent presenting his or her case in traffic court, where it can be hazardous to address the judge as if she were a buddy.

These four elements constitute the READ-Plus curriculum. Each element is separable from the others, in the sense that the key concepts and relations comprising the domain are distinctive. Each domain consists of a large "chunk" that can be taught independently from the others. Most of the day, however, is spent blending the various elements in authentic project-oriented activities. The four components span the developmental spectrum from preschool through graduate work, assuming appropriate adaptation to development and individual differences. All four are important parts of the kindergarten day, and all four serve significant roles in high school classes. At the risk of redundancy, the model does not proceed from basic skills in kindergarten to thematic projects in high school, but moves all four domains in parallel from the earliest school experiences onward.

Two domains, phonology-phonics and exposition-reports, will illustrate the notion of developmental adaptability. In the primary grades, the primary task is to help young children grasp the notion that speech can be represented by printed symbols in a systematic manner, for decoding and for spelling. It helps to learn the letter names, providing a language for talking about the symbols. Acquiring the letter names depends on rote memory; lots of experiences in a variety of engaging settings (e.g., magnetic letters, ABC books, letter card games). Learning the "sounds" of English speech is another matter. They come in great variety (almost 50 distinctive phonemes), they are subject to dialectal variations, they can disappear in normal speech, and they are difficult to sort out as "parts" of a spoken word. They can be learned by rote, of course, but the WordWork technique is strategic. Children learn how English consonants are produced or articulated, arranging them as a matrix based on how and where a sound is produced, with the addition of voicing as a later refinement. For example, /p/ is a "popping" sound at the front of your mouth, while /n/ is a "nose" sound in the middle of your mouth. Students do not master the entire system before moving on; rather, they begin with a handful of consonants to introduce the concept, and then start building CVCs, at which point the concept of a vowel or glue-letter is introduced. For instance, you can build PAN by gluing /p/ and /n/ together with /aaaa/, stretching and exaggerating the series of articulatory components while thinking about what your mouth is doing along the way. Decoding and spelling become flip sides of the same coin; the preceding exercise is as much about one as the other. In this process, phonics depends not on rote memorization, but on reconstructing the alphabetic system.

Study of English orthography continues into the later grades in this model; phonics is never finished! The focus in the primary grades is on commonplace English words, which spring from Anglo-Saxon origins, CVCs that can be joined into compound words and augmented by syntactic affixes (-ed, -ing, -er/est, and so on). In the later elementary grades, students encounter increasing numbers of words from Latin and Greek origins in the content areas, social studies, science, and mathematics. These words are longer and more complex, but they also build on different morphological principles (e.g., root-plus-affix rather than compounds), as in *polymorphism*. These words are infrequent, they appear in specific contexts, and students need to learn different strategies for approaching them. The least efficient and effective approach is rote memory; unfortunately, textbooks typically begin with the "vocabulary" list, leading to learning that seldom lasts beyond the Friday spelling test. In addition to increased demands on spelling, decoding, and meaning, older students--for "full participation"--need to acquire competence with oral presentations. Today's high school graduates are notable for their lack of competence in this arena. Their arguments may be scattershot, but it does not matter because you often cannot understand what they are saying. They have not learned to articulate clearly, and so they bow their heads and mutter. The good news is that the techniques used in the primary grades for learning the concept of speech sounds also support effective enunciation--for speech, but also for song, for drama, and even for traffic court appearances.

The second example draws on the expository domain. Show-and-tell in the primary grades is ideally suited to development of competence in report making and giving. For many children, it can be a difficult experience, but they manage to get through it in an endearing if somewhat rambling fashion. When scaffolded by the skillful teacher, kindergartners can learn the basic strategy--identify a topic, pick a few things to say about it, and then sandwich these ingredients between an introduction and conclusion. The result may not seem particularly spectacular, but it provides the young child with a simple template for both comprehending and composing more complex assignments in the later grades, where familiarity with a handful of expository structures can help them cope with the enormous outpouring of content engendered by the standards movement (e.g., from California Grade Five History Content Standards: "Students trace the routes of early explorers and describe the early explorations of the Americas; Explain the aims, obstacles, and accomplishments of the explorers, sponsors, and leaders of key European expeditions and the reasons Europeans chose to explore and colonize the world [e.g., the Spanish Reconquista, the Protestant Reformation, the Counter Reformation]"). Most human beings are incapable of absorbing the deluge of material, and so skill in selection and organization is essential. At this point, the interplay between comprehending and composing becomes critical (Nelson & Calfee, 1998). When confronted by a technical report, the fully competent "reader" needs to digest the material, transform it in some fashion, and construct a new text displaying a genuine depth of understanding.

In the ideal context for the READ-Plus curriculum, reading and writing would seldom appear on the board as separate topics, but as embedded within more substantive domains such as literature, social studies and science, and so on. To be sure, selected topics, such as elements from phonics strategies, along with generic structures for vocabulary and texts, warrant a modest amount of dedicated instruction, but most of the time spent today on "reading" (and the sparse moments spent on writing) could be more effectively spent in studying topics that really matter over the long run--putting literacy into practice.

Instruction and Assessment

A few words about the other two components of the CIA trio. The instructional model is summarized by the CORE acronym: Connect, Organize, Reflect, and Extend (Miller & Calfee, 2004). The model is only partly sequential, and the teacher needs to move back and forth among the elements. CORE provides a basis for planning a 30-minute lesson, developing a multi-week project, or handling students' puzzled expressions during a one-minute fix-up activity. CORE is, in short, meta-instructional, a set of essential ingredients that can be flexibly employed to promote the acquisition and mastery of the academic register. Each component invites the teacher to draw upon students' experience and knowledge as the basis for acquiring new ideas and skills by drawing upon what students bring to the situation.

Each component incorporates well-established research findings from the past several decades. *Connect*, for instance, refers to instructional techniques for engaging students in discussion about their knowledge of a particular topic. Extracting thoughts and opinions can be difficult; Heath (1983) presents disheartening classroom dialogues among students who have not learned the "school game." Open-ended questions and respect for wait time are proven techniques for delving into prior experience, but are seldom in the basal scripts. Equally important is a classroom style that encourages and respects what students have to say, including their preconceptions, a style fostered by discussions around familiar topics like fast food favorites, local events, holidays, and so on. Standards-based curricula have no room for such fluff. A steady diet of IRE-based teacher talk leaves most students cautious about what they say, lest they offer the wrong answer to a pre-scripted question. More authentic discourse, in contrast, can reveal a great deal about what students already know and believe, and can enliven discussions. From my storehouse of anecdotes, a retained seventh grader offered his thoughts about the "weather," describing a TV news report about a volcanic explosion in the Pacific Ocean affecting weather around the world, including sunsets in New York City where he lived. My reaction to his story: This "connection" demonstrated that he watched the news, he recalled significant events, and he linked this information to his own experience. Not exactly what one would expect from a struggling reader.

Organize mirrors the structure of human memory, and the interplay between long-term and short-term memory. Human beings have unlimited capacity to retain attended events, but both storage and retention are managed through the limited capacity of short-term or working memory. Hence the K.I.S.S. principle—"Keep it simple, sweetheart." The READ-Plus design focuses attention on a few critical learning goals worth attention across all grades and subject matters, facilitating the teacher's work and fostering professional communication. The same principle holds for students as well; organizing lessons and projects around a small number of regularly appearing and essential goals makes it more likely that learning will occur. For instance, in the narrative genre, four elements—character, plot, setting, and theme--suffice to start the analytic process for most stories. Today's alternative is to slice-and-dice stories with detailed questions.

Reflection—thinking about what you are learning and how you are learning it—was the missing ingredient in my Graystone visit. Reflection, in Vygotsky's analysis, is inherently social. The metacognitive process evolves from experiences in which individuals "bounce ideas off one another." Reflection is hard work, as you struggle to bring to consciousness the thinking behind your thinking. The value of reflective learning comes when the student encounters new situations, where transfer often depends on studying the similarities or common elements in two situations. The reflective stance is engendered in social situations, where others wrestle with similar tasks. Opportunities for developing a reflective habit of mind require a noisy classroom, in which discourse patterns reveal mental processes.

Finally, the *Extend* component includes activities where students demonstrate that they can apply learning to significant problems in new settings. Extensions are inherently performance-oriented, for both process and product. Whether developing a dramatic script for Act IV of "Puss in Boots" or developing an entry for a science fair, extension calls upon students to construct something original, something that goes beyond the information given.

As is probably apparent, Extension is an important element in the READ-Plus assessment process. Assessment is teacher-driven in the model, a matter of ongoing action research (Hiebert & Calfee, 1989), in which the teacher identifies significant questions about student learning, captures background information on the fly, plans and conducts mini-experiments to determine the influence of variations, and confirms hunches through a mix of formative and summative indicators. Externally mandated tests may be part of the design, but in proper perspective and for clearly defined purposes.

Evaluation

The READ-Plus platform has been implemented in a variety of settings over the past few decades, in part or whole. These explorations have typically investigated particular research questions rather than program evaluation. Indeed, it is not clear what "program evaluation" would mean, given the adaptability inherent in the model. Several studies have been conducted around the Phonology-Phonics and Expository-Report components, with generally positive outcomes (Calfee, Norman, Trainin, & Wilson, 2001). These investigations have employed design-experiment methodologies, still in their infancy, offering the opportunity to explore technical as well as substantive issues (Calfee, Norman, Miller, Wilson, & Trainin, in press). In general, these studies demonstrate the efficacy of constructivist curriculum-instructional techniques in promoting students' acquisition of high-level concepts and skills, in sustaining these learnings across grades and content areas, and for promoting constructivist approaches that persist when program support is removed.

However, the studies also reveal the institutional vulnerability of the concepts. Beginning with the Graystone experience, and virtually without exception in later projects, changes that persisted for individual teachers have not held for schools. Indeed, initiating school-wide involvement in the READ-Plus concept has occurred relatively infrequently, and appears to depend on the principal. District-level support for innovative programs is a different matter, and, from my experience, is most easily achieved through the "installation" of packaged programs such as a textbook series. Mounting a program of genuine professional development is a daunting task, and requires a type of administrative planning and support that is rare in districts, especially those dealing with large numbers of students from at-risk environments, generally with inadequate resources.

The challenge for public schooling (for which literacy instruction is clearly a critical outcome) is to promote lasting reform in a conservative environment under conditions that are extremely stressful for all participants. The READ-Plus platform, like several other programs built around similar principles, requires substantial knowledge and skill from the classroom teacher and others involved in direct services to clients, to students and teachers. Today's elementary teachers have been prepared for the most part in a "methods" model: 3-5 ways to teach reading, most relying on prepackaged textbook materials, and advice on how to follow the instructions. University courses may present conceptual ideas from time to time, but these tend to be scattershot and seldom survive the turmoil of induction. Novice teachers are quickly introduced by colleagues to survival strategies, focused mainly on classroom management. Under these conditions, the idea of "literacy for participation in a democracy" must seem to verge on the ridiculous.

THE WAY THINGS USED TO BE

The notion of professional communities appears in contemporary discussions of school reform (e.g., Cochran-Smith, 2005; Darling-Hammond, 2005). READ-Plus is clearly designed around the notion of professional collaboration. Can we really expect the rank and file of elementary teachers to exert the additional time and energy required for participation outside of their classroom activities--especially with limited administrative support for such feisty endeavors, which may even run counter to official policies? I clearly believe that we can, and will offer a brief historical digression to support this proposition. Memories of my elementary teachers during the late 1930s bring forth images of remarkable individuals, who instilled in their students respect for the English language and its power to inform and persuade. They taught me about the historical origins of the language, an understanding of the difference between narratives and expositions, a hard-won realization that reading, writing, and speech were cut from the same cloth, and a fascination with words. Was I the product of an exceptional private school? Scarcely--I grew up in rural North Carolina, and attended a comprehensive school (first grade through high school) serving farmers' children. Most students did not finish the diploma, nor was that expected or necessary. There were no gifted classes. My teachers were graduates of normal schools, where they acquired knowledge and skill that they used to educate a diversity of students (no African-Americans, to be sure). I can't remember teacher's manuals, nor do I think we were assigned to groups, although I might be mistaken.

In any event, to buttress these personal memories in preparing for the presentation, I surveyed materials from several California normal schools (special thanks to Andrea Whittaker of San Jose State University and Jerry Treadway of San Diego State University for helping with this task), to get an idea of what was expected of candidates for the elementary teaching credential during the late 1800s through the 1930s. As a sample of my discoveries, here are sample questions from the Elementary Methods Exam from 1882 at San Jose Normal School (now San Jose State University): (a) State four distinct objects [sic] to be accomplished by the education of children; (b) State five distinct qualifications that should be possessed by every teacher; (c) What is meant respectively by teaching, educating, and training children?; and (d) From what primitives are the following words derived: *discord, corpuscle, confine, influx, abnormal.* From Grace Storm and Nila Banton Smith (1930), their coverage of important topics in first-grade reading included the following entries: (a) General purpose and specific objectives; (b) Reading in connection with the bulletin board, the blackboard, pictures, and the newspaper; (c) Oral and silent reading from charts and books; (d) Informal reading tests; (e) Phonetic analysis and word recognition; and (f) Independent and directed reading for pleasure (p. 148). Monroe's (1887) textbook on elementary reading provides teachers with details of articulation patterns for English consonants. Taylor

(1912) offers the following rhapsody in the preface: "An artistic reading teacher is one of the most valuable assets of a school. She [sic] is as rare as wisdom, which 'the gold and the crystal cannot equal.' Among a thousand instructors of youth how few there be who are cunning in the art of teaching beginners to read."

These examples are typical of material that I uncovered--substantial conceptual and technical information about the process of reading acquisition, and a high level of appreciation for the magnitude of the task and the contribution of the individual teacher. The candidates lacked access to the enormous body of research-based knowledge that has accumulated from the 1950s onward, but Huey's magnificent 1908 volume, *The Psychology and Pedagogy of Reading*, was available and frequently cited.

The times have changed since the 1930s. The emancipation of women has led to greatly enhanced career opportunities. The institution of a factory model of schooling has increased political and administrative centralization. Teacher associations have shifted their emphasis from professional issues to workplace concerns. The point is that, not that long ago, it appears that elementary teachers were expected to possess substantially more professional knowledge and skill than seems presently the case, along with greater autonomy and responsibility.

However valid these impressions, it seems worthwhile to pursue the goal of an enhanced professional corps of elementary teachers, including the proposition that their principal specialization should center around the promotion of high levels of literacy, with secondary attention to the other subject matters. How to pursue such a policy? One strategy would build around changes in the preparation programs for elementary teachers. The dimensions of such changes have been discussed by Wong-Fillmore and Snow (2000; also cf. Calfee & Scott-Hendrick, 2000), but they seem unlikely to come about in the next decade, given other pressures on universities and education schools. Another part of the equation is captured by the concept of school-wide change. The difficulty with the school-wide strategy is that genuine professional development requires substantial time, both within and across the years, while accountability pressures call for increased test scores "this spring," a time measured in months, with little chance of continuity from one year to the next.

Equally problematic, the indicators are out of joint. Standardized test scores do not assess "literacy for participation in a democratic society." For that matter, they gauge few if any outcomes approximating the higher levels of literacy presented in this paper. Nor do they attend to the sustaining effects of particular literacy practices. Future prospects would seem rather grim.

PUZZLEMENTS, PREDICTIONS, AND POSSIBILITIES

Given these reservations, why pursue the notion of a professional corps of elementary teachers? The focus of this pursuit is on individuals who possess an extraordinary capacity to promote the acquisition of literacy, although they may not necessarily claim exceptional expertise in other subject matter areas, not even mathematics. The first reason is that I think that the research supports this policy, and also provides practical advice about ways to implement the idea. Our field has learned a great deal during the past several decades about the business of helping all children to become fully literate. The second reason is that current policies and practices are bringing the nation to a critical juncture; within another few years, most public schools will have been designated as "under-performing," placing the entire system at risk.

And so, with some sense of urgency, I conclude by scattering a few loose ends to serve as points of departure for the future. A major *puzzlement*--the "heart thing." This topic has received little attention in my own research agenda, but as noted earlier, the emotional commitment of teachers to their work seems to provide the energy that sustains schools in hard times--the incredible devotion of individuals working under difficult circumstances with limited resources and erratic support (cf. Darling-Hammond, 2005). My colleagues and I are presently transcribing a series of videotaped seminars in which READ-Plus teachers discuss their efforts to ensure genuine success for all students; we know how to assess the displays of technical competence, but are finding it more difficult to capture the commitment. One impression from this activity is that, as a teacher gains knowledge and skill that supports success for all students, and when conditions provide opportunities to connect with other teachers around this core task, motivational outcomes emerge from the shared sense of competence and accomplishment.

Moving now to consider *predicaments*. For me, the most troubling news is that time keeps passing. The progress that we expected in the 1960s has been slow in coming. A related predicament, verging on frustration, is that research offering great promise has yet to be implemented--and is not even remembered. For instance, work in the 1970s and 1980s by the Center for the Study of Reading, the Center for the Study of Writing, The Institute for Research on Teaching, the Learning Research and Development Center, along with other individuals and programs of that time, is largely overlooked and often superseded by current policies. A final predicament is the persistent gap between ivory towers and brick buildings, between ideas and practice, between theory and engineering.

Finally, I put forward some *possibilities*. For my part, the good news is that there are plenty of significant questions to keep me--indeed, all of us in the Conference--busy in the years ahead. The question is, what questions to pursue for greatest impact, not as responses to current conundrums, but to position ourselves for the next round of opportunities. I remain intrigued by the potential from instilling the vision of literacy proposed above into the fabric of a network of elementary schools that can serve as models for the concept of an "inquiring school" (Calfee, 1992). My initial forays in this direction have not been especially promising. One principal responded, "We don't have time to think here." On the other side of the aisle, an academic colleague cautioned me that practitioners could not be trusted to make sound judgments, that only research-based, tightly prescriptive programs offered any promise. The "problem" inherent in this situation might be viewed as an inconvenience for both parties, but my inclination is to try to formulate it as a research question.

In any event, for the NRC band of brothers (and sisters), the continuing challenge is to apply our collective heads and hearts to the task of understanding the mysteries of literacy, to inform the challenges of practice, and to press for equitable policies. It's the least that we can do....

REFERENCES

Bond, G. L., & Dykstra, R. (1967). The cooperative research program in first-grade reading instruction. *Reading Research Quarterly, 2*(4), 348-427.

California Grade Five: History-Social Science Content Standards. *United States History and Geography, Standard 5.2.* Retrieved November 15, 2004, from www.cde.ca.gov/be/st/ss/histgrade5.asp,.

Calfee, R. C, Norman, K. A., Trainin, G., & Wilson, K. (2001). Conducting a design experiment for improving early literacy, or, what we learned in school last year. In C. Roller (Ed.), *Learning to teach reading: Setting the research agenda* (pp. 166-179). Newark DE: International Reading Association.

Calfee, R. C. (1982) Literacy and illiteracy: Teaching the nonreader to survive in the modern world. *Annals of Dyslexia, 32,* 71-91.

Calfee, R. C. (1984). Applying cognitive psychology to educational practice: The mind of the reading teacher. *Annals of Dyslexia, 34,* 219-240.

Calfee, R. C. (1992). The Inquiring School: Literacy for the year 2000. In C. Collins & J. N. Mangieri (Eds.), *Teaching thinking: An agenda for the twenty-first century.* (pp. 147-166) Hillsdale, NJ: Lawrence Erlbaum Associates.

Calfee, R. C. (2005). The exploration of English orthography. In T. Trabasso, D. Massaro, & R. C. Calfee (Eds.), *From orthography to school reform: A Festschrift for Richard Venezky* (pp. 1-20). Mahwah, NJ: Erlbaum.

Calfee, R. C., & Drum, P. A. (Eds.) (1979). *Teaching reading in compensatory classes.* Newark, DE: International Reading Association.

Calfee, R. C., & Drum, P.A. (1986). Research on teaching reading. In M. C. Wittrock (Ed.), *Third handbook on research on teaching* (pp. 804-849). New York: Macmillan.

Calfee, R. C., & Norman, K. A. (1999). Psychological perspectives on the early reading wars: The case of phonological awareness. *Teachers College Record, 100,* 242-274.

Calfee, R. C., & Patrick, C. (1995) *Teach our children well.* Stanford, CA: The Portable Stanford Series, Stanford Alumni Association.

Calfee, R. C., & Piontkowski, D. C. (1980). Reading diary part I: Acquisition of decoding. *Reading Research Quarterly, 16,* 346-373.

Calfee, R. C., & Scott-Hendrick, L. (2004). The teacher of beginning reading. *Contemporary Perspectives on Early Childhood Education, 5,* 87-117.

Calfee, R. C., & Spector, J. E. (1981). Separable processes in reading. In F. J. Pirozzolo & M. C. Wittrock (Eds.), *Neuropsychological and cognitive processes in reading.* New York: Academic Press.

Calfee, R. C., Norman, K., Miller, R. G., Wilson, K., & Trainin, G. (in press). Learning to do educational research. In R. J. Sternberg & M. Constas (Eds.), *Translating theory and research into practice.* Mahwah NJ: Lawrence Erlbaum Associates.

Calfee, R. C., Norman, K., Miller, R. G., Wilson, K., & Trainin, G. (in press). Learning to do educational research. In R. J. Sternberg & M. Constas (Eds.), *Translating theory and research into practice.* Mahwah NJ: Lawrence Erlbaum Associates.

Cazden, C. B. (1988). *Classroom discourse: The language of teaching and learning.* Portsmouth NH: Heinemann.

Chall, J.S. (1983). *Stages of reading development.* New York: McGraw-Hill.

Chambliss, M. J., & Calfee, R. C. (1998). *Textbooks for learning: Nurturing children's minds.* Oxford, UK: Blackwell.

Cochran-Smith, M. (2005). Constructing outcomes in teacher education: Policy practice, and pitfalls. *Education Policy Analysis Archives, 9*(11), 1-55.

Darling-Hammond, L. (2005). *A good teacher in every classroom.* New York: Guilford

Delpit, L. D. (1996). *Other people's children: Cultural conflict in the classroom.* New York: New Press.

Feiman-Nemser, S., & Floden, R. E. (1986). The cultures of teaching. In M. C. Wittrock (Ed.), *Third handbook on research on teaching* (pp. 505-526). New York: Macmillan.

Fraatz, J.M.B. (1987). *The politics of reading.* New York: Teachers College Press.

Hansen, D. T. (2001) Teaching as a moral activity. In V. Richardson (Ed.), *Handbook of research on teaching, 4th Ed.* (pp. 826-857). Washington DC: American Educational Association.

Heath, S.B. (1983). *Ways with words*. New York: Cambridge University Press.

Hiebert, E. H., & Calfee, R. C. (1989). Advancing the goals of elementary literacy through teacher assessment. *Educational Leadership, 46,* 50-52.

Huey, E. B. (1908/1968). *The psychology and pedagogy of reading*. Cambridge, MA: The MIT Press.

Kingston, A. J. (1961). Oscar S. Causey. *Journal of Developmental Reading, 4,* 75-76,

Miller, R.G., & Calfee, R.C. (2004). Making thinking visible: A method to encourage science writing in upper elementary grades. *Science and Children, 11*(6), 20-25.

Monroe, L. B. (1887). *How to teach reading: A manual for the use of teachers*. Philadelpha, PA: Cowperthwait & Co.

Nelson, N. N., & Calfee, R. C. (Eds.) (1998). *The reading-writing connection: The yearbook of the National Society for the Study of Education*. Chicago, IL: University of Chicago Press.

Noddings, N. (2001). The caring teacher. In V. Richardson (Ed.), *Handbook of research on teaching, 4th Ed.* (pp. 99-105). Washington DC: American Educational Association.

Pressley, M., Allington, R. L., Wharton-McDonald, R., Block, C. C., & Morrow, L. M. (2001). *Learning to read: Lessons from exemplary first-grade classrooms*. New York: Guilford.

Richardson, V. (2005). Constructivist pedagogy. *Teachers College Record, 105*(9), 1623-1640.

San Jose Normal School. (1882). *Elementary Methods Examination*. San Jose CA: (Author). The extracts are from the first two pages of the notebook.

Stanovich, K. E. (1986). Matthew effects in reading: Some consequences of individual differences in the acquisition of reading. *Reading Research Quarterly, 21,* 360-406.

Storm, G. E., & Smith, N. B. (1930). *Reading activities in the primary grades*. Boston MA: Ginn and Company.

Taylor, J. S. (1912). *Principles and methods of teaching reading*. New York: Macmillan.

Vygotsky, L. Y. (1962). *Thought and language*. Cambridge, MA: The MIT Press.

What Works Clearinghouse. Retrieved November 15, 2004, from www.whatworks.edu.

Wong-Fillmore, L. & Snow, C. E. (2000). *What teachers need to know about language*. Washington DC: Center for Applied Linguistics.

Investigating Methods of Kindergarten Vocabulary Instruction: Which Methods Work Best?

Rebecca Deffes Silverman

Harvard Graduate School of Education

NATIONAL READING CONFERENCE 2004
ABSTRACT FOR OUTSTANDING STUDENT RESEARCH AWARD WINNER

Early vocabulary knowledge provides an important foundation for children's reading development (National Institute of Child Health and Human Development [NICHD], 2000; Snow, Burns, & Griffin, 1998). Thus, the many children who enter school with limited vocabulary knowledge may be at risk for experiencing later difficulty in reading. In order to provide support for the language and literacy development of young children, researchers and educators must focus on identifying the most effective ways to build children's word knowledge.

Currently, in standard practice, teachers usually comment only cursorily on potentially unknown vocabulary words during storybook reading. When teachers do stop to discuss words with students, they typically just relate words to children's background knowledge or personal experiences. Researchers McKeown and Beck (2004) suggest that this kind of vocabulary instruction is not the most effective way to build children's vocabulary. These researchers advocate a method of instruction that is more direct and analytic, and they suggest that this method has much greater potential for teaching children words.

Beck, McKeown, and Kucan (2002) recommend that teachers engage children in such activities as comparing and contrasting words and evaluating word appropriateness in contexts other than the storybook. Other researchers (Juel & Deffes, 2004; Juel C., Biancarosa, G., Coker, D., & Deffes, R., 2002) have suggested that augmenting direct and analytic vocabulary instruction with attention to the letters and sounds of words may be even more effective than this kind of instruction alone. The objective of the study described here was to provide evidence about which methods of kindergarten vocabulary instruction are most effective. The study compared three methods of instruction during storybook reading: one based on standard practice typically seen in elementary classrooms ("Standard Practice Instruction"), one that attempted to replicate the more direct and analytic methods supported by Beck, McKeown, and Kucan (2002) ("Analytic Instruction"), and one that augmented this more direct and analytic method by anchoring instruction of vocabulary with attention to the letters and sounds in words ("Anchored Instruction").

The study consisted of a six-week read-aloud intervention in six kindergarten classrooms. The main research question guiding this study was the following: Are "Analytic" and "Anchored" vocabulary instruction methods more effective than "Standard Practice" instruction at promoting children's word learning? The study was conducted in a northeastern public school district located in a major metropolitan area. A total of 96 kindergarteners participated in the study. The sample of kindergarteners was demographically diverse: about a third of the sample received free or reduced lunch and nearly half of the sample was English language learners (ELL). Classrooms were assigned to one of the three instructional conditions. In each classroom, the intervention took place for 30 minutes a day, three days a week, for six weeks. The same six books were used and the same five words per book were targeted in all conditions.

In the Standard Practice condition, teachers discussed target words in a way that mirrors the kind of vocabulary instruction typically seen in kindergarten read-alouds. Teachers asked children about whether the story reminded them of something in their own lives and guided children to talk about the target words in the context of the story. As in the Standard Practice condition, teachers in the Analytic Instruction condition asked questions to help children think about the words in the context of the story and connect their experiences to the words in the story. Also, teachers guided students through activities which required them to think analytically about the meaning of the words in different contexts and in relation to other words. Teachers in the Anchored Instruction condition had children talk about words in relation to the story they were reading (as in the Standard Practice condition). Teachers engaged children in activities that had them actively analyze word meanings in various contexts (as in Analytic Instruction condition). Additionally, in the Anchored condition, teachers had children focus on the letters and sounds in the target words. To keep the intervention to 30 minutes per day in each of the conditions, less time was spent on discussion of the storybook in the Analytic and Anchored conditions than in the Standard Practice condition, and less time was spent on Analytic activities in the Anchored condition than in the Analytic condition.

Two classrooms were randomly assigned to each condition. Classroom teachers carried out instruction according to scripted curriculum for their condition. Instruction was observed and videotaped to document fidelity to the curriculum. Teachers demonstrated high fidelity to the curriculum. To control for children's general vocabulary knowledge and literacy, the Test of Oral Language (TOLD P:3) (Newcomer & Hammill, 1997) and the Dynamic Indicators of Basic Literacy Skills [DIBELS] letter fluency subtest (Good & Kaminski, 2002) were administered to the participants prior to the intervention. A researcher-designed vocabulary assessment, modeled on the TOLD P:3, was administered pre- and post-intervention to evaluate children's knowledge of the words taught in the intervention.

Analysis of Covariance (ANCOVA) revealed that, on average, the Analytic and the Anchored conditions enabled children to learn the words in the curriculum more effectively than the Standard Practice condition, regardless of the general vocabulary knowledge, letter-naming fluency, and background characteristics of the children. The effect sizes of the Analytic and Anchored conditions over the Standard Practice condition were greater than 1.0. The effect of the Analytic and Anchored conditions did not differ significantly.

The findings of this study lend support to the call of researchers such as McKeown and Beck (2004) for more direct and analytic vocabulary instruction in the early elementary grades. In this study, Analytic and Anchored instruction were equally effective. These findings suggest that incorporating a focus on the letters and sounds of words into analytic vocabulary instruction may not interfere with children's word learning. In fact, children may be able to simultaneously learn word meanings and the letters and sounds in the words. Further research investigating this possibility is needed.

Most teachers use storybook reading primarily to provide children with time to talk about stories and how their experiences relate to those stories. Given that research has shown that such conversations between adults and children can foster children's language skills, it is likely that standard practice does encourage children's language development (Bruner, 1978; Snow, 1983). The findings from this study suggest, though, that having children actively analyze words and their meanings is a more effective way to teach children words than discussion-based instruction alone during storybook reading time. Also, the findings of this study suggest the possibility that instruction targeting decoding skill and instruction focusing on word meanings can be delivered simultaneously. Thus, teachers may be able to use instructional time to meet multiple instructional objectives for children's early language and literacy learning.

REFERENCES

Beck, I., McKeown, M., & Kucan, L. (2002). *Bringing words to life: Robust vocabulary instruction.* New York, NY: Guilford.

Bruner, J. S. (1978). Learning how to do things with words. In J. S. Bruner & G. R. A. (Eds.), *Human growth and development.* Oxford, U.K.: Oxford University Press.

Good, R. H., & Kaminski, R. A. (Eds.). (2002). *Dynamic Indicators of Basic Early Literacy Skills* (6th ed.). Eugene, OR: Institute for the Development of Educational Achievement.

Juel, C., Biancarosa, G., Coker, D., & Deffes, R. (2003). Walking with Rosie: A cautionary tale of early reading instruction. *Educational Leadership, 60*(7), 12.

Juel, C., & Deffes, R. (2004). Making words stick. *Educational Leadership, 61*(6), 30.

McKeown, M., & Beck, I. (2004). Direct and rich vocabulary instruction. In J. F. Baumann & E. J. Kame'enui (Eds.), *Vocabulary Instruction: Research to Practice* (pp. 13-27). New York, NY: Guilford

Newcomer, P., & Hammill, D. (1997). *Test of Language Development, Primary 3, 3rd Edition.* Austin, TX: Pro-Ed.

National Institute of Child Health and Human Development. (2000). Report of the National Reading Panel. *Teaching children to read: An evidence-based assessment of the scientific research literature on reading and its implications for reading instruction.* (NIH Publication No. 00-4769). Washington, DC: U.S. Government Printing Office.

Snow, C. (1983). Literacy and language: Relationships during the preschool years. *Harvard Educational Review, 53*(2), 165-189.

Snow, C., Burns, S., & Griffin, P. (1998). *Preventing reading difficulties in young children.* Washington, D.C.: National Research Council.

Speaking Literacy and Learning to Technology, Speaking Technology to Literacy and Learning[1]

Annemarie Sullivan Palincsar

University of Michigan

Bridget Dalton

Center for Applied Special Technology, Wakefield, MA

As we prepare this review of research for publication in the *National Reading Conference Yearbook*, two billion Instant Messages are being sent daily, 92% of public school classrooms in the U.S. have access to the Internet, the U.S. College Board is introducing a test of technological literacy, Wikipedia, a free-content encyclopedia, is available in 57 languages, and the University of Michigan has negotiated with Google to digitize its seven million volume collection to be accessed via the Internet by anyone the world over. In short, one needn't look far to find examples of the continual reshaping of literacy by virtue of technologies. In fact, the evolution of literacy is a series of sociotechnical changes; from papyrus, to paper, to printing press, to electronic spaces, technologies have influenced how we use and make meaning with text.

To set the stage for this review, consider for a moment the multiple forms of literacy that are required to interpret and learn from a typical website. Upon first entering the site, the user must immediately interpret navigational cues and chart a path that will support knowledge building with the site. Frequently, the user can select from among several media links, simultaneously listening to and reading information, and activating simulations that also must be interpreted. The user must decode meaning-bearing icons. Mouse-overs may cause an image to pop up; that image may, in turn, expand to provide additional information. Graphs and diagrams may be called up and manipulated to address specific questions. All of this information must be coordinated, integrated, and evaluated for its credibility and relevance to the questions guiding the user. Color cues signaling glossary terms and links must be decoded. In addition, the user may have the option of participating in a forum discussion or forwarding the site to a fellow learner. The user is at once both reader and author, both consumer and generator of knowledge, engaging in both an individual and collective enterprise.

We chose to explore the intersection of literacy, learning, and technology, crafting our review as a travelogue. Our purpose was to transport the audience through various landscapes, resting at particular sites, and offering what John Urry (2002) has called the *tourist gaze*, that is, a socially organized and systematized way of looking on a set of different scenes or landscapes. Furthermore,

[1] The authors gratefully acknowledge Don Leu, the program chair who extended the invitation to us to prepare this review. We also extend sincere thanks to the following extraordinary colleagues who responded so generously to our requests for video clips and comments regarding their programs of scholarship: Donna Alvermann, Chip Bruce, Jim Gee, Margaret Hagood, Chuck Kinzer, Linda Labbo, Jay Lemke, Kevin Leander, Rich Mayer, Michele Knoebel, David Rose, David Reinking, Marlene Scardamalia, and Don Leu and the members of his research group: Jill Castek, Julie Coiro, Laurie Henry, and Melissa McMullen. Although we have not been able to do justice to their numerous contributions in this written document, the presentation of this review would not have been possible without the very capable and creative assistance of Kate Brigham, Linda Butler, Dan Densch, Alan Leney, and Nicole Strangman. Finally, we are grateful to Barbara Ladewski who painstakingly conducted the literature search reported in this paper replicating the Kamil and Lane's (1998) review.

we invited a number of scholars who have helped shape this terrain to join us in this travelogue. Although their ideas were presented via audio and video recordings in the conference presentation of this review, they will appear as edited quotations in this written document.

We delimited our search of *technology* to digital texts, that is, to "texts in digital forms displayed electronically on dynamically alterable surfaces such as computer screens" (Reinking, 1998, p. xx-xxi). We appropriated Jim Gee's definition of *learning*:

> For me there are two different ways to learn anything. One is a verbal way, to learn it in terms of words, where you know about the word, or just other words, something like a definition. But a second form of learning—a much deeper form of learning—is to learn concepts of words ...where you can see the world in terms of how that word would apply to the world either to engage in action or engage in dialogue with other people. That form of understanding is far deeper than just knowing the meaning of words. If you know the meanings of words verbally, just in terms of other words...you can pass a test on them, but you can't necessarily engage in action or dialogue with them. What we are after in schooling is surely situated understanding. So now the question becomes: How do you learn situated understanding of words? What is learning if what you are after is situated understanding? Well, the way that you learn situated understanding is by engaging in body and mind in the activities in which social groups engage. You affiliate with people in terms of their values, in terms of identity, how they look at the work they do; you learn to see the world the way they see it and that teaches you how to use the words that the group uses in their distinct ways (James Gee, personal communication, November 2004).

Delimiting our definition of *literacy* was somewhat more problematic. As Jay Lemke (1998) noted, "Literacies are legion. Each one consists of a set of interdependent social practices that link people, media objects, and strategies for meaning making" (p. 283). As we sought to define the terrain so that it would be manageable, we encountered the admonitions of literacy colleagues who kept pushing open the boundaries of literacy. For example, Margaret Hagood (2003) has argued that "notions of reading and text defined broadly must become an underlying premise rather than one for which we must continually argue" (p. 390). In addition, we were mindful of a burgeoning perspective called *new literacies*: "The new literacies of the Internet and other ICTs [information and communication technologies] include the skills, strategies, and dispositions necessary to successfully use and adapt to the rapidly changing information and communication technologies and contexts that continuously emerge in our world and influence all areas of our personal and professional lives. These new literacies allow us to use the Internet and other ICTs to identify important questions, locate information, critically evaluate the usefulness of that information, synthesize information to answer these questions, and then communicate the answers to others" (Leu, Kinzer, Coiro, & Cammack, 2004, p. 1572). Finally, we were mindful of Chuck Kinzer's reflections:

> In a sense, I'm not sure the term *becoming literate* is useful to us in our new, electronic and ever changing environment. Becoming literate is something that has been around actually for quite awhile, when we take a look at things such as emergent literacy and the understanding that vocabulary develops and continues to develop over time and that literacy in general changes and adapts as we go

through our lives and experience more types of literate behaviors. What I've been trying to wrestle with is the notion of *adaptive literacy*, modeled somewhat on the notion of adaptive expertise. If we think about becoming literate, that almost implies or presupposes that one can *become* literate - that there *is* a literacy standard or goal and eventually we will do things that will allow us to reach it or become it. I think the notion of *adaptivity* is actually very valuable. As new technologies evolve, we adapt the abilities and skills and literate knowledge that are needed for particular tasks and activity. But adaptive literacy also implies that we will need to adapt our literacy practices in terms of learning new ones. So, as technologies evolve, we need to adapt our behaviors in terms of learning new literacy skills, and those kinds of learnings continue to evolve. So this notion that literacy is a fixed point in time, and we become literate over time, is, in my mind, a little less productive than this notion of an adaptive set of skills and strategies, adaptive both in terms of what we do with them and also adaptive in terms of their changing nature (Charles Kinzer, personal communication, November 2004).

We delimited our review to research on technology in the teaching and use of literacy to advance the acquisition and development of knowledge about oneself and the world. We did not include in our review studies that focused solely on the acquisition of reading, writing, and oral language; nor did we review studies that focused on the acquisition of computer, Internet, or media skills. Our focus was on the application of these kinds of skills to the advancement of learning.

Method of Conducting Review

To conduct this review, we began with a close survey of the four primary literacy journals, *Journal of Literacy Research, Reading Research Quarterly, Written Communication,* and *Research on the Teaching of English,* essentially replicating the review that Kamil and Lane (1998) reported when they surveyed these journals from 1990-1995 and found that only 2.7% percent of the research articles published in these journals during that time addressed technology. As Figure 1 suggests, there has been only a slight increase, to 5.2%, in technology-related research articles published in these journals during the last eight years.

In addition to our search of these literacy journals, we conducted hand searches of *Cognition and Instruction* and the *Journal of the Learning Sciences* for the past five years. When we searched by topic, we surveyed the following: intelligent tutoring systems, hypermedia, assistive technology, and adaptive hypermedia systems. These topics took us to journals in computer science and information and computer technology. In addition, we consulted a number of recent handbooks. Finally, recognizing, as others have, that some of the most exciting work at the intersection of literacy, learning, and technology is being championed and conducted by teachers rather than researchers, we also attended to those venues that feature the work of teachers, such as *Reading Online's* "Teacher Voices" series, www.readingonline.org.

The scheme we chose to report our findings was to organize the research according to the purposes of the inquiry. Specifically, *ethnographic studies* have been conducted, in and out of school, for the primary purpose of capturing how technology shapes contexts, activity, and users and how users shape technology, context, and activity. *Psychological studies* have principally informed our understanding of how we learn with these new technologies. Finally, *intervention studies* have focused on changing the nature of the learner or the learning context and employing technology to achieve particular outcomes. Rather than attempt a global review of the studies that fell into these categories, we concentrated on a select number to identify general issues at the intersection of learning, literacy, and technology.

Ethnographic Studies: Capturing the Interactions Among Technology, Contexts, Activity, and Users

Ethnographic studies have played a key role in illuminating what is occurring at the intersection of literacy, learning, and technology. Their value is particularly salient when they are viewed synergistically. For example, Michele Knoebel reporting on her inquiry of students' out-of-school literacy activities observed:

> My commitment to sociocultural theories means that I'm not so much interested in looking at the effects of technology on young peoples' literacy proficiency at school, but rather, I'm much more interested in looking at what young people do when they're using new technologies, how their ways of being are tied to particular kinds of social purposes and are embedded within and woven into networks of social relationships. Some of the research I was doing in the 1990s took me into classrooms. What I noticed about most of the classrooms that we went into was that the computers they were using were usually equipped with scaled down child-friendly sorts of software. But when I went into the homes of the students I was studying, I noticed that they were all using full-scale adult

Figure 1   Percentages of technology-related articles, essays, and book reviews published in the last 10 years, percentage of U.S. classrooms with Internet access, and number of Instant Messages sent daily in 2004.

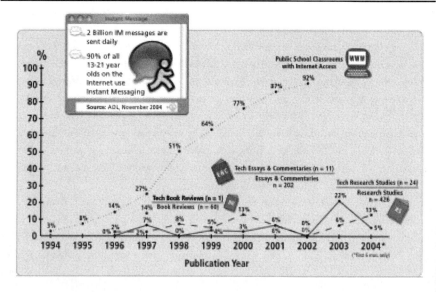

versions of software without any trouble at all. I remember one young man named Jacques who had had a long painful history of failure at school. He wasn't all that interested in using the computers at school, but he'd had access to some very powerful computer programs associated with business. And at home, he used the computer to produce a very proficient file with his mother and brother and very quickly established a thriving ongoing business. And it's cases like Jacques' that really underscore the importance of paying attention to how young people are using new technology in their lives in order to better understand some of the implications of these uses, and purposes, and practices for literacy education (Michelle Knoebel, personal communication, November 2004).

Kevin Leander has similarly documented the sophisticated skills, motivation, and persistence of adolescents as they engage in new literacies, crossing borders between out-of-school and in-school contexts. Literacy educators wrestle to identify the appropriate integration of popular culture into school literacy learning.

Donna Alverman (personal communication, November 2004) challenges her students to think about this integration by asking them: "If your principal interprets the new state standards in Georgia to mean that you must include media literacy in the curriculum, how would you attempt to bridge between your students' media readings of the latest TV reality shows and your own goals that you have for literacy learning in your own classroom?" In response, one of her students connects the TV reality show, *I'd Do Anything*, in which contestants take on unusual challenges in order to win a prize for someone they love, with Chris Crutcher's sports novels that explore self-sacrifice in caring relationships.

Ethnographic studies in school settings yield a mixed picture. Research reported by Wallace, Kupperman, Krajcik, and Soloway (2000) explored sixth grade students' activity on the web as they engaged in information-seeking within a unit of science study. Their results, which were consistent with those reported by Maya Eagleton and her colleagues in their study of Internet inquiry (Eagleton, Guinee, & Langlais, 2003), painted a rather bleak picture of students' use of technology to advance learning. Using audio and video records of online activity, Wallace and her colleagues found that their participants demonstrated low engagement with the subject matter, poor search and navigation strategies, and a tendency to reduce the task to that of searching for the keywords that yielded the smallest number of hits regarding their topic.

This is a striking contrast with the portrait painted in the inquiry conducted by Kinzer and Leu (1997) whose second grade participants revealed sophisticated understanding and use of the Internet and an array of technological tools (such as PowerPoint) in the conduct of research on topics in the social studies.

Finally, Labbo (2005), in collaboration with pre-school and kindergarten teachers, explored children's reading, viewing, designing, production, and publication of multimedia in the familiar context of engaging in language experience approaches to literacy instruction that are enhanced with the addition of digital technologies. She documented the ways in which the affordances of the technologies were changing the teaching and learning experience, for example, enabling multiple representations of one's ideas and facilitating revision of these presentations (see Figure 2), with improved language outcomes for children.

In summary, ethnographic research at the intersection of literacy, learning, and technology has revealed a complex and nuanced picture. Clearly, there is exciting potential at this intersection for both revealing and supporting learners' competence with literacy learning and use via information and communication technologies. On the other hand, there is work to be done to ascertain how the knowledge and dispositions that students reveal in out-of-school settings can be more purposely incorporated to advance literacy learning more generally and in school settings, in particular.

Psychological Studies: Informing Our Understanding of How People Learn with New Technologies

The preponderance of research informing our understanding of text comprehension has been conducted with traditional print text. There have been numerous and vivid attempts to capture the differences between traditional (print) text, multimedia, and electronic media and the implications of these differences for defining and studying literacy, broadly writ. Typically, while print literacy is described as linear, ordered, sequential, hierarchical, and logical, hypertext is characterized as fluid, spatial, decentered, bottom up, and playful (Burbulus, 2001; Ryan, 1999).

As Hegarty, Narayanan, and Freitas (2002) have noted, there is a tantalizing spectrum of choices that authors might make relative to the design of hypermedia presentations but few empirically validated guidelines for choosing among these capabilities. One might, for example, ask: Are diagrammatic presentations better than sentential representations? Are three-dimensional

Figure 2   Example of a child's multimedia representation in response to a language experience lesson.

representations better than two-dimensional? Are animated representations better than static? Are interactive better than non-interactive? In this section, we present a summary of the research conducted by Hegarty and her colleagues for the purpose of highlighting the model of inquiry in which they engage as well as reporting the findings of their work. We then proceed to summarize design principles derived from a complementary program of research conducted by Mayer.

Hegarty and her colleagues (Hansen, Schrimpsher, Narayanan, & Hegarty, 1998; Hegarty et al., 2002; Kozhenikov, Hegarty, & Mayer, 2002) have argued that because new media are studied in contexts using novel methods of instruction (e.g., discovery, collaborative learning, inquiry) and then are compared to traditional media in traditional contexts, there is a confounding. The overarching question guiding their program of research is whether multimedia presentations, including animations, commentaries, and hyperlinks, lead to different learning outcomes, when compared to traditional printed media, when both contain the same information and are designed according to empirically validated guidelines.

In a typical study conducted by this research group, the content would be a complex system, such as a mechanical system (e.g., a flushing cistern). They begin their research by studying the potential sources of comprehension problems learners might encounter specific to the content under study. This research informs the design of content hypothesized to ameliorate these difficulties. This content is then presented using different formats. Their participants are typically undergraduate students. Learning is assessed with an array of measures including: *mental animation questions* (i.e., asking students to predict how the motion of one component of a system will influence another), *function questions* (e.g., "what is the function of the float and float arm?"), *"fault-behavior" questions* asking how the system would behave were there to be a breakdown in one part of the system, and *"trouble-shooting" questions* that asks the learner to diagnose all possible problems with the system, given a set of symptoms. In one experiment (Hegarty, Quilici, Narayanan, Holmquist, & Moreno, 1999), the researchers compared the learning of students assigned to one of three conditions: a hypermedia manual (complete with hyperlinks and animations), and two text conditions.

They found no learning differences among the three groups, even though participants in the hypermedia group spent more time interacting with the content than did the groups in the text conditions. The researchers proposed that the additional information presented via the hypertext was possibly superfluous given the fact that a toilet tank is a common household item with which the participants were already sufficiently familiar. In a second experiment, they compared the effects of constraining the learner's use of the hypermedia manual with a condition in which the learner could navigate freely. While participants who viewed the navigation-restricted version spent more time in the system than did those in the free-navigation condition, the type of presentation did not affect performance on any of the four types of comprehension assessments. The authors cautioned that this was a limited test of navigational freedom due to the fact that the total number of sections to be navigated was relatively small (seven). In a third set of experiments, the authors queried the effects of (a) viewing a static diagram, (b) engaging in a mental animation (in which the learners studied the static diagram but then attempted to explain to the experimenter how it worked), (c) following the viewing of a static version with an animation of the system, accompanied by a verbal commentary, or (d) a condition that combined (b) and (c). The results indicated that viewing the animation and hearing the commentary significantly enhanced performance on the outcome measures. Furthermore, attempting to animate the machine mentally before viewing the animation enhanced the ability to describe how a machine works. What is the import of this research? Although some of their work does show that computer animation can facilitate learning, on the whole these studies suggest that merely translating information from a traditional print medium to a hypermedia system does not affect comprehension and learning when the content is held constant.

A second program of research addressing multimedia learning has been conducted by Richard Mayer and his colleagues and is summarized in Mayer (2001). This program of research has yielded seven principles regarding the effective integration of words and pictures: (a) Multimedia Principle—Students learn better from words and pictures than from words alone, (b) Spatial Contiguity Principle—Students learn better when corresponding words and pictures are presented near rather than far from each other on the page or screen, (c) Temporal Contiguity Principle—Students learn better when corresponding words and pictures are presented simultaneously rather than successively, (d) Coherence Principle—Students learn better when extraneous material is excluded rather than included, (e) Modality Principle—Students learn better when an animation is accompanied by spoken rather than printed text, (f) Redundancy Principle—Students learn better from an animation accompanied with spoken text rather than an

Figure 3 Screenshot illustrating embedded comprehension strategy supports (Palincsar et al., 2004).

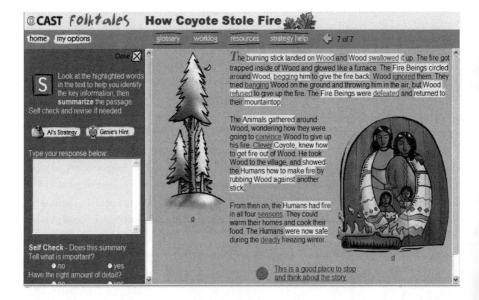

animation accompanied with spoken text and printed text, and (g) Individual Differences Principle—Differences in students' domain knowledge and spatial ability interact with the effectiveness of design elements.

Although research conducted in the psychological tradition has been very useful to raising questions about the processes in which learners engage when using new literacies and learning from multimedia, there is an important caveat regarding this research. Nearly all of the research done from a psychological perspective examining learning from hypermedia and multimedia has been conducted with university learners. We and our colleagues have been engaged in experimental studies in which we are investigating the learning processes and outcomes as fifth-grade students learn about light and vision from identical prose and diagrams in one of three digital environments. The design of these environments has been informed by descriptive research in which we investigated the interactions of struggling and typical readers as they learned from digitized narrative and informational text (Palincsar, Dalton, Magnusson, DeFrance, Proctor, Hapgood, Khasnabis, 2004). In one condition, students have access to text-to-speech and an online glossary. In a second condition, students are able to animate the diagram and are instructed in how to conduct an investigation using the diagram. In addition, they are supported in examining the relationship between the information presented in the prose and the diagram. In the third condition, students have the support of a coach as they engage in their inquiry with the prose and interactive diagram (see Figure 3).

In this study, we are interested in identifying the skills and strategies that students employ in this type of environment, the paths they create, the role that the interactive graphics and text play in their learning, the patterns of use as a function of such learner characteristics as literacy and language abilities and modality preferences. This research is bridge building from psychological to intervention research, to which we turn next.

Intervention Studies: Changing the Nature of the Learner, Text, Learning Context, and Learning Outcomes

Innovation often occurs in the margins, where dramatic gaps exist between desired outcomes and prevailing practices (Rose & Meyer, 2002). Accordingly, there is a strong line of research investigating the role of hypertext and digital reading environments for struggling readers. Within the special education community in particular, there is a commitment to using the power of technology to ensure that all children have access to the general education curriculum and, more importantly, that they go beyond access to meaningful participation and progress. A conceptual framework that has been helpful in guiding this work is Universal Design for Learning developed by David Rose and Anne Meyer (2002) among others.

Universal Design for Learning was originally stimulated by the universal design movement in architecture and environmental design. Ron Mace (1998), an architect with physical disabilities, introduced what was then a revolutionary idea but is now accepted in schools of architecture and design around the world. He argued that we should design from a universal perspective, that is, considering the needs of the broadest range of users from the beginning of the design process, rather than building and then retrofitting for those individuals for whom the usual ways of accessing and navigating spaces did not work, a practice all too prevalent in education where we retrofit curricula to meet the needs of individual students. So, now we all enjoy the fruits of universal design in our daily lives as we use curb cuts, view television captions, and listen to audio-taped books.

Just as a staircase represents a barrier for an individual with a physical disability, print, a one-size-fits-all technology, represents a barrier, rather than a gateway, to learning for many struggling learners. In the following quotation, Rose expands on the transformative capacities of digital text and media and speaks to an important change in national policy and the educational publishing landscape:

> The new technologies for literacies have a number of advantages. First, we are able to represent the text itself in very flexible ways that were not possible in print. Taking advantage of that flexibility means that we can have words talk themselves aloud for students who are blind or seriously struggling, in very individualized ways. We can make the text be whatever size a child needs. We can have the semantics of vocabulary link easily to its meaning. Even more importantly, the text now can be deeply structured with components shown to one child and not to another. We can individually support kids in becoming strategic readers, building in coaches and ways of providing students individualized feedback. The advantages of these wonderful, flexible, embedded texts have become apparent to a broad set of policy makers and educators, ushering in changes that are on the horizon. For example, the National Instructional Material Accessibility Standards stipulate to publishers that digital versions of traditional texts must be provided to states and school districts. We look to researchers in reading and literacy to help identify the features that need to be built into text to enable every student to comprehend and learn from text (David Rose, personal communication, November 2004).

How do we design optimal learning environments and tools that are responsive to the tremendous variation in learners, teachers and instructional contexts, goals and purposes, and texts? One way to approach the design of supported reading environments is to consider the various factors that contribute to any particular comprehension event. Consider the heuristic of reading comprehension, developed by the RAND Reading Study Group (2002) (see Figure 4).

In a digital environment, the relationship of these components and their contributions to a particular instance of comprehension can change dynamically. For example, students with decoding or fluency difficulties can use

Figure 4 A heuristic for thinking about reading comprehension (RAND Reading Study Group, 2002)

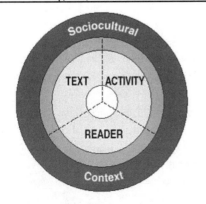

text-to-speech to gain access to the text, potentially freeing up cognitive capacity for meaning construction. An English language learner might use hyperlinked glossary terms and background knowledge links to help her read with understanding. The teacher can offload some coaching and guided practice through the use of computer avatar coaches who provide models and feedback. The notion of readability and what makes a text difficult or easy is essentially stood on its head in digital environments (McKenna, Reinking, Labbo, & Kieffer, 1999; Reinking, 1988).

From a universal design perspective, there are multiple ways to scaffold the learner such as, for example, providing access to the content, supporting strategic learning, enhancing engagement, and building self-awareness and efficacy. Most of the researcher-designed digital environments designed to improve comprehension provide multiple supports, combining representational supports (e.g., images and animated graphics to support prose vocabulary definitions, background knowledge links, graphic organizer overviews, or main idea statements), with supports for strategic learning (self-monitoring questions, note-taking tools, strategy coach-avatars) (Anderson-Inman & Horney, 1999; Boone & Higgins, 1992, 1993; Dalton et al, 2002; Reinking & Schreiner, 1985; Reinking, 1988). Figure 5 shows an example of a digital reading environment offering a range of supports.

Turning to the findings from research regarding these supportive environments, several researchers have investigated the potential of speech feedback, either through text-to-speech (TTS) or recorded digital speech, to support struggling readers' comprehension. The hypothesis is that

Figure 5 Screenshot illustrating embedded comprehension strategy supports (Dalton & Palincsar, 2005).

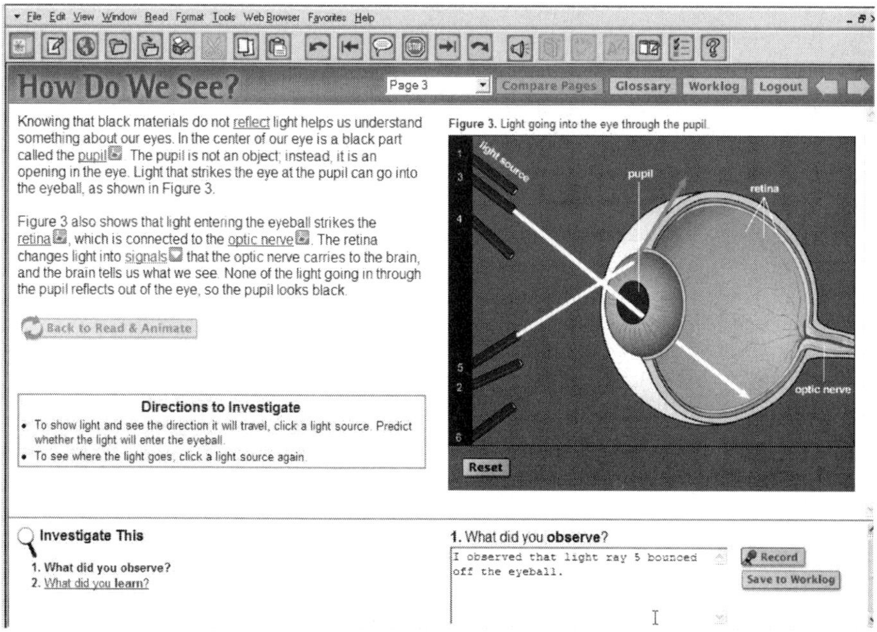

providing students more fluent access to the text will free up capacity for constructing meaning, thereby improving comprehension. Some have assessed students' comprehension within the supported text environment (Elkind, Cohen, & Murray, 1993; Lundberg & Oloffson, 1993), whereas others have also assessed transfer to comprehension of printed text (Aist & Mostow, 1997; Elbro, Rasmussen, & Spelling, 1996). If one looks across studies, TTS does not appear to influence comprehension. However, because it is possible to design digital environments that are responsive to individual differences, we can ask for whom do these environments work, and under what conditions? For example, positive results have been found in studies involving older students who were struggling readers (Lundberg & Olofsson, 1993) and who were using TTS to read digital texts over a sustained period of time, such as a class semester (Elkind et al, 1993).

Examining the outcomes of embedded learning supports designed to improve comprehension (for a review, see Dalton & Strangman, in press), we generally find that although there are positive effects on comprehension within the supported environment, some of which, in fact, transfer to improvement with print, the findings are mediated by a number of contextual variables such as the teacher's views on literacy and experience with technology integration, and the level of technology access for learners. Outcomes also vary in relation to student characteristics, highlighting the need for a more comprehensive model of reading and of the learner to guide the design of customized learning environments. Furthermore, given that ICTs (information and communication technologies) and new literacies represent a moving horizon, one that may always be somewhat in advance of our current school literacy practices, two key issues arise: (a) that of learner control, that is, how much support is pushed at the learner versus controlled by the learner; and, (b) how actively do we work to ensure near and far transfer to other digital environments and to print, a technology that will remain an important literacy in our society.

Before leaving the interventions portion of our review, we consider briefly a long-standing instructional project that has been under development for many years, with each generation of the research contributing important innovations: Computer Supported Intentional Learning Environment (CSILE), now referred to as Knowledge Forum (KF), designed and investigated by Marlene Scardamalia, Carl Bereiter, and their colleagues (Scardamalia, Bereiter, & Lamon, 1994). Underlying the design of this environment is the tenet captured in the following quote from Scardamalia (2004):

> Historically, learning has been an adequate objective for education because knowledge has not been thought of as growing, but rather in danger of being lost...the information revolution spells unprecedented growth in information ... and requires staying up to date as a prerequisite to contributing in your own right to the cultural wealth of society. Preparing students for knowledge generation represents a radically different challenge for education (p. 191).

Consistent with this perspective on learning, KF is designed as a multi-media community knowledge space in which students are supported by an array of tools designed to promote knowledge building. These tools include (a) annotation, citation, and reference links; (b) interconnected views through interlinking; (c) author assigned indices (e.g., keywords, titles, problem fields); (d) automatically assigned indices (e.g., author, date, semantic field); (e) knowledge scaffolding processes supporting theory refinement and constructive criticism; and (f) "rise above" notes presenting new ideas that represent an advance over previous ideas. Scardamalia and Bereiter are careful to note that the KF is not a collection of tools, but rather is an environment specifically designed to support inquiry, information searches, and creative work. The reader is referred to Scardamalia (2004) for an illustration of how KF represents an open environment, without predetermined boundaries or structures around ideas or activities, that, with the participation of contributors with diverse expertise, supports the emergence and refinement of big ideas.

Research on CSILE/KF has revealed significant, positive, differences on standardized tests of achievement, measures of depth-of-explanation for particular phenomena (such as extinction), graphical knowledge representation, beliefs about learning, depth of inquiry, and collaboration. While Knowledge Forum has been shown to be very successful at supporting many dimensions of literacy learning and knowledge building, it is also worth noting that not all implementations of CSILE/KF are equally effective; without careful monitoring and mediation by teachers, time spent in this environment can yield shallow learning (Lipponen, Rahikainen, Hakkarainen, & Palonen, 2002).

Teacher Research

While serving as co-editors of *Reading Online*, Dalton and Grisham recruited Michael Milone and Nicole Strangman to write an interview series featuring teachers who have developed outstanding projects integrating technology and literacy. These articles provide a window into the kind of innovative and impressive projects taking place in classrooms, using a variety of ICTs and situated in diverse learning contexts. In this section of the review, we share two of these projects in order to highlight a few emergent themes in new literacies in the classroom. The first project, entitled "A Digital Journey to Altoona's Past" (Strangman, 2002) is a collaborative project between Irene Huschak, a high school multimedia teacher in Altoona, PA, and high school English and computer science students. Together, they developed a collection of historically-based, interactive stories about their home town, with the reader actually being incorporated into each story as a character. The English students researched and wrote the stories and the computer science students developed the illustrations and web pages to bring them to life.

The second, and quite unique, project is called "The Many Faces of Alice" (Strangman, 2003). This project is the work of New York teacher Monica Edinger and her 4th graders. Every year, Ms. Edinger and her students study the book *Alice in Wonderland*, which is then showcased on a website. Ms. Edinger turns conventional literature study on its head: whereas most classrooms focus on printed text, with students reading the printed text and responding largely through writing, in Ms. Edinger's classroom, learning takes place in several modalities, with much less emphasis on the printed word. Ms. Edinger reads the book aloud, providing students with her own annotations, and a major focus is studying and responding to the book's illustrations. The unit culminates in a student-produced, Toy Theater production of the book that is digitally recorded and put on the Web.

As we conclude our review, we turn to identifying potential agendas that literacy researchers might productively pursue at the intersection of literacy, learning, and technology, as well as some of the design/methodological and theoretical issues germane to these agendas.

Possible Agendas to Guide the Scholarship of Literacy Researchers

We hope that this brief review has communicated the enormous richness of the terrain that is at the intersection of literacy, learning, and technology. Indeed, we hope the reader has come to share our amazement that so little attention is being paid to this area of inquiry, at least as reflected by the attention it is receiving in our professional journals. As we thought about directions this research might take, we had a few nominations we wished to make. The time is ripe for "border crossing," in which researchers, for example, apply the findings from the kinds of ethnographic research we reported to the design of intervention research. As another illustration, psychological research might productively be conducted investigating the process and outcomes of engaging in interventions that employ technology to advance literacy acquisition/development and learning.

In addition to studies that examine the application of technology for the purpose of specifically advancing computer and media literacy, it would also be worthwhile to investigate how computer and media literacy follow from engagement in learning for deep understanding and knowledge generation. It would be helpful to complement the decontextualized study of learning from hypertext/hypermedia with the study of real-world learning. Finally, there is significant research to be done identifying how technology can support diverse learners, such as students acquiring English as a second language, students with sensory impairments, and students with cognitive challenges, so that advanced knowledge building is the work of all students.

Methodological and Theoretical Issues

In terms of design and methodological issues, the time seems ripe for applying methods such as multi-dimensional scaling and small space analysis for the purpose of examining patterns of relationships among individuals, technologies, and learning environments. As Lemke (1999) has argued, we need to shift from a fixation upon technological tools to mapping the ecosocial systems of their use.

Drawing upon a methodological tradition that has received considerable attention in some areas of educational research such as science education, literacy researchers might explore the use of design experiments (Brown, 1992; Collins, 1992; Design-Based Research Collective, 2003) as a research methodology. The goal of design experiments is to engineer innovative learning environments and simultaneously come to understand salient aspects of human cognition and learning involved with those innovations. Design experiments would be fruitfully complemented by the conduct of intensive case studies of classrooms focused on the complex interaction among learners, teachers, information and communication technologies, and the context of individual classrooms in the service of learning.

There is an important role in this research arena for methods that provide more direct access to causal mechanisms. For example, logfiles that document each keystroke and every feature in a digital environment that is activated by the user can be used to examine the relationship between the activity in which the user engages and the outcomes of that activity. Eye-fixation studies, using web-cams, would be helpful to providing information about how the user approaches and navigates through complex digital environments, such as websites that offer many choices of where to begin and how to move through the environment. Think-aloud protocols would be a helpful complement, providing evidence about the reasoning and decision-making of the user.

The complexity of the research questions one is likely to ask and the instructional contexts in which one is likely to be working at this intersection suggest that there is an important role for collaborating across projects regarding, for example, the design and use of measures of engagement and learning, the coding and analyses of data sources, and the design of learning environments. Some of this complexity is revealed by examining the scholarship of the members of the New Literacies Research Lab, led by Don Leu, which is focused on the information and communication potential of the Internet for learning, as well as the new skills and strategies in reading, writing, and communication that are required by these new technologies. While Don's primary focus is on the development of a theoretical framework to guide the conduct of research on new literacies, the members of his research group have a range of foci: Laurie Henry investigates the skills that students use when searching for information; Julie Coiro studies the nature of reading comprehension and how it looks the same and different when reading on the Internet, within websites or while using search engines; Melissa McMullen investigates online collaborative learning, while Jill Castek investigates communication on the Internet, particularly in classroom contexts and how classroom teachers can facilitate reading and writing using communication vehicles developed for technologies.

There has been active discussion in the literacy community about the need for expanded definitions of literacy and new theories that place information and communication technologies (ICTs) at their center. Leu, Kinzer, Coiro, and Cammack (2004) have argued that for the past 500 years, literacy has emerged from a variety of social contexts but has primarily been shaped by the book and printing press. But today, both the social context and technologies are rapidly changing with ICTs and the Internet becoming the central technologies of literacy. Leu and his colleagues (2004, p. 15) have identified a set of ten principles to guide a theory of new literacies:

1. New literactices and ICTs are central technologies for literacy within a global community in an information age.

2. The Internet and other ICTs require new literacies to fully access their potential.

3. New literacies are deictic.

4. The relationship between literacy and technology is transactional.

5. New literacies are multiple in nature.

6. Critical literacies are central to the new literacies.

7. New forms of strategic knowledge are central to the new literacies.

8. Speed counts in important ways within the new literacies.

9. Learning often is socially constructed within new literacies.

10. Teachers become more important, although their role changes, within new literacy classrooms.

Leander (2003), similarly recognizing the need for grounding a theory of media in the cognitive and social processes by which knowledge is constructed, has proposed that cultural historical activity theory (CHAT), with its focus on "the analysis of mediation, material technologies, language, culture, and the relations between individual and systemic change" (p. 395) render it ideal for the study of ICTs.

Given the proportion of web-based text that is presented graphically, there is the need for theory that considers the syntactically- and semantically-dense properties of graphical representations. Finally, given the constantly changing nature of technology, there is a significant role for visionary theory.

CONCLUSION

As we bring this review to a close, we thank the scholars who served as generous "co-presenters" by responding to our queries and sharing their scholarship with us. In addition, following on Gunther Kress (2003) who noted that readers and writers become designers in these digital, multimodal, interactive environments, we acknowledge that we have been designers as we prepared this travelogue making decisions about the contours of the landscape, the studies upon which we would linger, and how we would represent the features of this scholarship.

We close with an observation from a member of the literacy community who has indeed been a visionary working at the intersection of literacy, learning, and technology: Chip Bruce. In a 1997 volume of the *Journal of Literacy Research*, Bruce wrote: "Technology is not just over there, but out there, at most in a distant suburb of literacy, if not on another planet" (p.). We wondered what Chip's sense of the state of literacy and technology was now, in the year 2004-2005.

> In 1996-97, I was fortunate to spend a year living in Beijing, and later, Brisbane, Australia. I was struck then by the way that the web, email, electronic bulletin boards, databases, digital photography, etc., were changing the *literacy* practices of young people. If we mean by literacy an assemblage of social practices through which people construct, represent, and share meaning, then young people there were engaged in a dramatic re-shaping of their literacies. They were:
>
> • learning English through the web;
>
> • using email, fax, and digital photography for political action;
>
> • developing new forms of jokes and story-telling;
>
> • playing games across the Internet;
>
> • finding new ways to construct and express their identities;
>
> • sharing their experiences of living in a changing China with those outside.

These activities were not unique to China, of course, but they were especially dramatic in the context of China then. I felt that we couldn't ignore those experiences. If we wanted to understand the meaning of literacy in the lives of young people, then we needed to focus more on what they were actually doing, on how their literacy was changing, and how their practices were in fact creating the new technologies of literacy.

In short, we needed to see technology as more than technique. The practices of young people around mobile phones, weblogs, e-zines, instant messaging, digital photography, network gaming, wireless networking, GPS, and more, are not simply means to accomplish pre-defined tasks, but new ways of being in the social and physical world.

Back in the US, the mainstream of literacy educators and literacy researchers were oblivious to what these events might mean. Many people conceived new information and communication technologies as irrelevant, or even antithetical, to the values they ascribed to literacy. They might, for example, acknowledge a role for computer-based instruction on an isolated literacy skill, but that very acknowledgement contained within it their view of the new technologies as reductionist.

The field of literacy has since made major strides in understanding the meaning and potentials of the new technologies. There are projects, programs, curricula, and analyses that accept the reality of the changes in social practices associated with multimedia, computers, the web, and such. But for many, technology still means specific techniques, which can be attended to or not.

Doing that compartmentalizes technology, and fails to comprehend its deeper connections to literacy. It also allows us to avoid such questions as:

• Who has access to these resources? controls the use? owns the content? judges the value?

• How are people transforming the tools?

• How are senses of community, play, and identity being reshaped?

• How do concepts such as story, meaning, communication, and knowledge need to be reexamined?

• How are the very means by which we enact literacy changing?

I'm speaking to you today from Tampere, Finland, not far from what must be cell phone heaven in Nokia. It reminds me of an eight-year-old who can send instant text messages, invent new linguistic forms, program the cell phone for international calls, download music and ring tones, surf the web on the phone, and more. She, along with millions of other young people around the world, are creating new literacies through technologies such as this. Meanwhile, the principal response of schools to cell phones has been to ban their use.

No! I'm not saying to put cell phones or iPods in every classroom! But, if we want to understand literacy, we cannot afford to ignore the lived experience of people who are remaking it right in front of us (Bertram "Chip" Bruce, personal communication, November 2004).

REFERENCES

Aist, G. S., & Mostow, J. (1997). *Adapting human tutorial interventions for a reading tutor that listens: Using continuous speech recognition in interactive educational multimedia.* Paper presented at the CALL '97 Conference on Multimedia, Exeter, England.

Anderson-Inman, L., & Horney, M. A. (1999). Electronic books: Reading and studying with supportive resources. *Reading Online* [Electronic journal]. Retrieved June 30, 2005, from http://www.readingonline.org/electronic/elec_index.asp?HREF=ebook/index.html

Boone, R., & Higgins, K. (1992). Hypermedia applications for content-area study guides. *Reading and Writing Quarterly, 8*, 379-393.

Boone, R., & Higgins, K. (1993). Hypermedia basal readers: Three years of school-based research. *Journal of Special Education Technology, 12*, 86-106.

Brown, A. L. (1992). Design experiments: Theoretical and methodological challenges in creating complex interventions in classroom settings. *Journal of the Learning Sciences, 2*, 141-178.

Bruce, B. C. (1997). Literacy technologies: What stance should we take? *Journal of Literacy Research, 29*, 289-309.

Burbulus, N. (2001). Paradoxes of the Web: The ethical dimensions of credibility. *Library Trends, 49*, 441-453.

Collins, A. (1992). Toward a design science of education. In E. Scanlon & T. O'Shea (Eds.), *New directions in educational technology* (pp. 15-20). New York: Springer-Verlag.

Dalton, B., & Palincsar, A. S. (2005). *Reading to Learn: Investigating general and domain specific supports in a technology rich environment.* Progress Report to IES

Dalton, B., & Pisha, B., Coyne, P., Eagleton, M., & Deysher, S. (2001). *Engaging the text: Computer supported strategy instruction for students with learning disabilities.* Final report to the U.S. Office of Special Education Programs.

Dalton, B., & Strangman, N. (in press). Using technology to support struggling readers' comprehension: A review of the research. In D. Reinking, M. C. McKenna, L. D. Labbo, & R. D. Keiffer (Eds.), *Handbook of literacy and technology* (2nd ed.). Mahwah, NJ: Erlbaum.

Design-Based Research Collective, The. (2003). Design-based research: An emerging paradigm for educational inquiry. *Educational Researcher, 32*(1), 5-8.

Eagleton, M. B., Guinee, K. & Langlais, K. (2003). Teaching Internet literacy strategies: The hero inquiry project. *Voices from the Middle, 10*(3), 28-35.

Elbro, C., Rasmussen, I., & Spelling, B. (1996). Teaching reading to disabled readers with language disorders: A controlled evaluation of synthetic speech feedback. Scandinavian *Journal of Psychology, 37*, 140-155.

Elkind, J., Cohen, K., & Murray, C. (1993). Using computer based readers to improve reading comprehension of students with dyslexia. *Annals of Dyslexia, 43*, 238-259.

Hagood, M. C. (2003). New media and online literacies: No age left behind. *Reading Research Quarterly, 38*, 387-391.

Hansen, S. R., Schrimpsher, D., Narayanan, N. H., & Hegarty, M. (1998). *Empirical studies of animation-embedded hypermedia visualizations* (Tech. Rep. No. CSE98-07). Auburn, AL: Auburn University, Department of Computer Science & Software Engineering.

Hegarty, M., Narayanan, N. H., & Freitas, P. (2002). Understanding machines from hypermedia and hypermedia presentations. In J. Otero, J. A. Leon, & A. C. Graesser (Eds.), *The psychology of science text comprehension* (pp. 357-384). Mahwah, NJ: Erlbaum.

Hegarty, M., Quilici, J., Narayanan, N. H., Holmquist, S., & Moreno, R. (1999). Multimedia instruction: Lessons from evaluation of a theory-based design. *Journal of Educational Multimeda and Hypermedia, 8*, 119-150.

Kamil, M. L., & Lane, D. (1998). Researching the relationship between technology and literacy: An agenda for the 21st century. In D. Reinking, M. C. McKenna, L. D. Labbo, & R. D. Kieffer (Eds.), *Handbook of literacy and technology: Transformations in a post-typographic world* (pp. 323-341). Mahwah, NJ: Erlbaum.

Kinzer, C., & Leu, D. (1997). The challenge of change: Exploring literacy and learning in electronic environments. *Language Arts, 74*, 126-136.

Kozhevnikof, M., Hegarty, M., & Mayer, R. E. (2002). Revising the visualizer-verbalizer dimension: Evidence for two types of visualizers. *Cognition and Instruction, 20*, 47-77.

Kress, G. (2003). *Literacy in the new media age.* New York: Routledge.

Labbo, L. D. (2005). From morning message to digital morning message: Moving from the tried and true to the new. *The Reading Teacher, 58*, 782-785.

Leander, K. M. (2003). Writing travelers' tales on new literacy scapes. *Reading Research Quarterly, 38*, 392-397.

Lemke, J. L. (1998). Metamedia literacy: Transforming meanings and media. In D. Reinking, M. C. McKenna, L. D. Labbo, & R. D. Kieffer (Eds.), *Handbook of literacy and technology: Transformations in a post-typographic world* (pp. 283-301). Mahwah, NJ: Erlbaum.

Lemke, J. L. (1999). Typological and topological meaning in diagnostic discourse. *Discourse Processes, 27*, 173-185.

Leu, D. J., Jr., Kinzer, C. K., Coiro, J. L., & Cammack, D. W. (2004). Toward a theory of new literacies emerging from the Internet and other information and communication technologies. In R. B. Ruddell & N. Unrau (Eds.), *Theoretical models and processes of reading* (5th ed., pp. 1570-1613). Newark, DE: International Reading Association.

Lipponen, L., Rahikainen, M., Hakkarainen, K., & Palonen, T. (2002). Effective participation and discourse through a computer network: Investigating elementary students' computer-supported interaction. *Journal of Educational Computing Research, 27*, 355-384.

Lundberg, I., & Oloffson, A. (1993). Can computer speech support reading comprehension? *Computers in Human Behavior, 9*, 283-293.

Mace, R. L. (1998). Universal design in housing. *Assistive Technology, 10*, 21-28.

Mayer, R. E. (2001). *Multimedia learning.* New York: Cambridge University Press.

MacArthur, C. A., & Haynes, J. B. (1995). Student assistant for learning from text (SALT): A hypermedia reading aid. *Journal of Learning Disabilities, 28*, 150-159.

McKenna, M., Reinking, D., Labbo, L., & Kieffer, R. (1999). The electronic transformation of literacy and its implications for the struggling reader. *Reading and Writing Quarterly, 15*, 111-126.

Palincsar, A. S., Dalton, B., Magnusson, S., DeFrance, N., Hapgood, S., Proctor, P., & Khasnabis, D. (2004, December). *Investigating verbal protocols for what they reveal about upper elementary students' text processing across narrative and informational texts.* Paper presented at the meeting of the National Reading Conference, San Antonio, TX.

RAND Reading Study Group. (2002). Reading for understanding: Toward an R & D program in reading comprehension. Santa Monica, CA, and Washington, DC: RAND Corporation.

Reinking, D. (1988). Computer-mediated text and comprehension differences: The role of reading time, reader preferences, and estimation of learning. *Reading Research Quarterly, 23*, 484-498.

Reinking, D. (1998). Introduction: Synthesizing technological transformations of literacy in a post-typographic world. In D. Reinking, M. C. McKenna, L. Labbo, & R. Kiefer (Eds.), *Handbook of literacy and technology* (pp.xi-xxx). Mahwah, NJ: Erlbaum.

Reinking, D., & Schreiner, R. (1985). The effects of computer-mediated text on measures of reading comprehension and reading behavior. *Reading Research Quarterly, 20*, 536-552.

Rose, D. H., & Meyer, A. (2002). *Teaching every student in the digital age: Universal design for learning.* Alexandria, VA: Association for Supervision and Curriculum Development.

Ryan, M. (1999). Cyberspace, virtuality, and the text. In M. Ryan (Ed.), *Cyberspace textuality: Computer technology and literary theory* (pp. 78–107). Bloomington, IN: Indiana University Press.

Scardamalia, M. (2004). CSILE/Knowledge Forum®. In A. Kovalchick & K. Dawson (Eds.), *Education and technology: An encyclopedia* (pp. 183-192). Santa Barbara: ABC-CLIO.

Scardamalia, M., Bereiter, C., & Lamon, M. (1994). The CSILE project: Trying to bring the classroom into World 3. In K. McGilley (Eds.), *Classroom Lessons: Integrating Cognitive Theory and Classroom Practice* (pp. 201-228). Cambridge: MA: MIT Press.

Strangman, N. (2002). Using technology to take young readers on a digital journey to the past. *Reading Online, 6*(3) [Electronic journal]. Retrieved June 30, 2005, from http://www.readingonline.org/articles/art_index.asp?HREF=/articles/voices/huschak/index.html

Strangman, N. (2003). Literary and visual literacy for all: A fourth-grade study of alice in wonderland. *Reading Online, 6*(7) [Electronic journal]. Retrieved June 30, 2005, from http://www.readingonline.org/articles/art_index.asp?HREF=/articles/voices/edinger

Urry, J. (2002). *The Tourist Gaze* (2nd ed.). Thousand Oaks, CA: Sage Publications, Inc.

Wallace, R. M., Kupperman, J., Krajcik, J., & Soloway, E. (2000). Science on the Web: Students online in sixth-grade classroom. *The Journal of the Learning Sciences, 9*, 75-104.

"That was Then, This is Now": Place, Time, and Shifting Experiences of Rural Literacy

Marta Albert
Mark Jury
University at Albany-SUNY

We spent a school year and summer (2001-02) conducting ethnographic research in a Northeast rural area as part of a multistate, middle-school improvement effort in English Language Arts (ELA). Early in the process of observing an eighth grade English class whose teacher was a participant in the reform project, we grew interested in situating curricular and pedagogical change within a broader conversation centered on regional socioeconomic and cultural change, and the growing instability and uncertainty about the meaning of work in a transforming rural landscape. Such issues are intimately linked to people's perceptions of the goals and processes of schooling (DeYoung, 1995; Elder and Conger, 2000; Howley, 1997), and they led youth, teachers, administrators, parents, and other community members to express a mix of positive anticipation and deep dread over the future of the region as a kind of rural place. To begin to understand how participants understood and responded to the shifting social landscape, how they located themselves within it, we determined a need to assume a place-conscious research stance.

In what follows, we examine how *place* emerged as a focus of analysis in the study, and explore how the metaphor of *topography* helped us trace the effects of place on literacy practice. The first half of our discussion is directed towards theory and method. In the second half, we pay attention to three distinct ways in which place fundamentally structured our understanding. The first, and lengthiest, centers on Katie, a focal student; the second looks at issues of time in relation to place; and the third comments on Wal-Mart, a recurring reference and strong physical and symbolic presence in our inquiry.

SITUATING THE PLACE, PARTICIPANTS, AND OURSELVES

School and Communities

Lancaster-Hull Middle School, the seventh and eighth grade segment of a K-8 building, is located on the fringe of a small, industrial city and a vast wilderness area (all references are pseudonyms) (cf., Nespor (2000) on ethical quandaries within place-sensitive social research). The school's hyphenated name reflects its contemporary history as a consolidated school district, borne from the merging of schools in adjacent towns that each served as the educational hub for a smattering of villages and hamlets. An understanding of school as the heart of small town community permeated the narratives of many adults in the study, who recalled with mixed emotions the effect, after consolidation, of only one town retaining a functioning primary (K-3) school. The new school, Lancaster-Hull, did not reside physically inside, or even very close to, the main thoroughfares of either of the small towns for which it was named. A few miles to the north of the school were crossroads that marked a passage into the mountains; a few miles south led to "big box" stores (including Wal-Mart) located along a main state highway.

Several miles farther took one into the nearest small city, population 18,000, a city built along a sizeable waterway. We refer to the city simply as City, or the City, to reflect the dichotomous rural or city language that peppered many participants' responses; quite often, the actual language used was overtly derogatory. Vanderbeck and Dunkley (2003) discussed the pervasive geographic "othering" present in youth narratives. They viewed its use as a marker of a young person's relatively broad or circumscribed sense of possibility and opportunity, and the length to which youth might go to draw tighter or looser geographic boundaries to defend a sense of self. As physically close as the City was to our school study site, psychologically it seemed quite distant to many participants. For instance, Angie, one of our five focal students, stated outright, "I'm a (Rural) County person" during a discussion about prospects for work in the future. She positioned herself as decidedly not-City, yet paradoxically, she did this in the middle of a "truck tour" of the City, a tour structured by her fond childhood memories of visiting an aunt who had lived in the City and of her time playing in an urban park. She also narrated quite a bit of the City's labor and migration history based on her family-grounded knowledge of the City's industrial roots and its contemporary economic struggles. Her sense of the City contrasted with that of her peers, who spoke largely in negative terms about urban danger and violence. Placing herself in the landscape, guiding us, Angie challenged the racial and ethnic stereotypes that operated in the discourse of her peer group, even as she distanced herself from City residents through her firmly rural status.

In and around the City, industries focused on textile production and other goods have been in existence for more than a century. The school's population and surrounding area were predominantly White, yet the City had a significant African American and Latino community base with long ties to the area as well. Historically, the dominant economic activity and identity of the Lancaster-Hull population has been linked to farming, farming-related industries, and textiles. The ability to engage in home-based production piecework, as well as factory and service-sector jobs in the City, featured prominently in a number of labor and family histories.

Participants viewed the City as an accessible place for work and entertainment yet an undesirable place to live. Mulling over the City's meanings, they expressed regional work identities that were grounded in their own small-town places but that also embraced the opportunities for labor and leisure afforded by proximity to urban culture and commodities. The potential for tourist industries to boost the economy, and perhaps shape career futures for young people, also cropped up through interviews and in the demographic research we conducted. The area also abutted both a major state highway into a vast mountainous region and beautiful lakes that drew large numbers of summer residents and vacationers. In all, the region serving as home to Lancaster-Hull was linked concretely and symbolically to a diverse, dynamic set of historical, economic, and ethnoracial currents, all of which made their way into this study.

Participants, Data Sources, Place Resources

   Students in and around classrooms. Generally, we visited the focal classroom at least twice each week to observe, audiotape lessons and conversations, and write field notes about the reading, writing, and communication practices prevalent in the class. We interviewed 17 of 18 students individually and in small groups, and we collected written artifacts. Five students (two female, three male) emerged as key informants due to the interesting variety of literacy practices in which they chose to engage. Literacy was a force that positioned these focal participants as actors who drew others around them or as loners whose interests and practices shut others out. The ELA teacher involved in the reform project recommended a range of eighth grade students who seemed to be "struggling" with literacy, and these five, despite their literacy-related interests and talents, were part of this cohort because they had difficulty meeting the school's expectations of ELA competence. Like the ELA teacher, we were interested in this disconnect. In particular, we wanted to learn more about the resources that supported students' literate development, especially resources caught up in larger currents of change within the region.

   We observed key informants in all major subject area classes, in other formal and non-formal learning spaces in school (cafeteria, hallways, in-school suspension room, library, computer lab), and at home during the summer. We also met with and interviewed parents, adult friends of students, and area merchants, and we took "truck tours" with students to learn about the sites, spaces, and places that mattered to them in terms of their development. Finally, throughout the year we interviewed teachers and administrators. Memories of literacy events, transformations in learning identities, varied uses of reading and writing, and experiences of academic difficulty or failure served as narrative anchors around which we constructed stories from the student data. Based on these stories, we compared people's experiences and understandings, looking for themes and patterns that might enrich our understanding of change and development (Cortazzi, 1993). We searched transcripts of interviews with adults for resonant themes as well.

   Movement into and around the region. Our initial foray into data interpretation alerted us to the significance of place. This theme was echoed in our conversations across the year as we physically traveled the sites sprinkled throughout participants' texts. *Travel* actually became central to our understanding of the range of ways one might move (or not) through this rural space; it functioned as a symbol of place and displacement, of youth to adult transition, and of perceived educational risk. Travel "placed" students in the landscape that contained the school, the landscape altered by the changing socioeconomic composition of the school. The more we read within and across data sources and texts to build stories, the weightier places and ideas connected to place seemed to be in relation to students' uses of literacy (for a similar discussion in an urban context, see Moje, et al., 2004).

   Questions about the construction of literacy capacities or struggles crystallized as we drove along diverse paths to and from Lancaster-Hull. During our travels, we considered how specific movement in specific ways "mapped" experiences of place--for us, as researchers, and for the youth and adults of our study--beyond the institutionally created boundaries of the maps we had purchased initially to find our school site (Aitken, 2001). As educators who'd come into rural areas from suburban neighborhoods, we each had learned quickly the profound way in which distance and travel shaped youth aspirations and opportunity structures in rural communities. Getting through and to places via car, truck, bike, horse, four-wheeler; using high-speed internet access or dial-up modem, or having no online access or computer at all; traversing specific landscapes on state highways or backroads to get to malls, relatives, friends; taking trails to the lakes and mountains; getting online to download poems or be part of gaming communities; driving the interstate to work: sheer movement through and beyond the region mattered enormously in the lives of our focal participants. It grew clear that we needed to think harder about the material tensions of change and stability in relation to student learning and struggle.

PERSPECTIVES ON LITERACY PURPOSES AND PROSPECTS

Skill and Development: Student Views

How students understood literacy competence and struggle materialized for us as they narrated their learning and literacy biographies, discussed their ideas of meaningful and desirable work, and deliberated about what "being rural" meant to them. They told compelling stories that depicted how they were simultaneously drawn to the mountainous landscapes "out the back door," as one young woman put it, even as the City beckoned from "the front door." Students shared notebooks, writing and cartoon journals, and computer network folders containing written artifacts from many years. Consummate tour guides, students explained the contexts of production and ably compared and contrasted compositions as representations of their skill or lack of it. Importantly, they also responded to these texts as icons of their identity in other times and places--times when they more or less struggled or felt they excelled as learners. Over and over, we noted how students' renditions of their text use and their textualizing work drew from valued place resources, led to the production or imagination of new places, provided reflective space to consider less well-known meanings about place, and served as arenas to examine the meaning of disparate places (from towns from their past, or areas where they might live and work as adults).

Literacy Theory

To make sense of these experiences, we first turned to situated literacy theory, sociocultural psychology, and activity theory, because each emphasizes how behaviors arising through and in particular time-space locations actually "stretch" well beyond those locations (Dreier, n.d., p. 12, quoted in Jury, 1999; see also Engestrom, 2001; McDermott, 1993). We considered the nesting of identity and experience across the multiple social domains that supported, impeded, or produced learning and particular practices of literacy for these rural students (Leander, 2002; Levinson, Foley, & Holland, 1996; Weis & Fine, 2000). Interviews and observations allowed us to investigate changed or changing levels of participation by individuals (and thus changed and changing learning identities) depending upon the nature of activity in the focal classroom site, other school spaces, or the composition of social networks inside and outside of school (Lave, 1993; Reder, 1994). Rural education and critical geography theories enabled us to extend such perspectives, to flesh-out the contours of place influences on people and activity.

Place-Based Pedagogy

For more than a century, rural educators have wrestled to figure out how to define and adapt to global forces of change and how to resist rhetoric that discounts the value of rural schooling, as economic restructuring alters landscapes that have long provided form and content for rural identity (DeYoung & Lawrence, 1995; Howley, 1997; Kleibard, 1995). In this study, we saw that students' capacities were valued as useful capital in a variety of ways depending upon the meanings they, other youth, and adults assigned to them, and many times valued capacities were afforded or made visible through opportunities that were present because of place-based resources and shared, place-oriented understandings. Overall, students made it clear that investments in learning developed, in part, based upon their uses of place in the present and their sense of the possibilities learning might hold to enable them to sustain, or leave, specific places in the future.

Rural educators who advocate for place-based pedagogy see it as "a way to address the decline of many rural communities, including the out-migration of young people, by preparing students to live productive and fully engaged lives in their home communities" (Gibbs and Howley, 2000, ¶ 1). Place-based curriculum advocates (e.g., Foxfire [Wigginton, 1985] and the affiliates of the Rural School and Community Trust) stress that locations matter in making learning "authentic"--that is, linked to familiar or imagined roles in known worlds--and helping to focus education on local purposes, particularly in rural areas where the very existence of "places" increasingly come under threat (Colchado, et al., 2003; Emekauwa, 2004). From this perspective, place and its preservation plays, or should play, a guiding role in teaching and assessment of student learning.

Topography: A View from Critical Geography

Place-based and other rural commentators suggest it is crucial to consider the difficulties communities face in sustaining rural lifeways while responding to regional and global change. Much of what we learned in this study indicated that rural lifeways are complex and dynamic in themselves, not merely as a reaction to external forces, but due to internal variations that lead people to experience the rhythms of rural life differently. Topography is a geographical term that refers to the study and representation of land features, including both surface features, "the shape and elevations of terrain," and relationships among "natural and human-made features" (Topography, 2001-04). This is an apt term to capture the tension we identified between rural education's focus on place-persistence and critical geography's idea that rural places are dynamic, complicated, and multifaceted.

In critical geography, places are formed at the intersection of competing interests and histories, and the residual meanings of places often compete with, or make possible, what increasingly are being studied in literacy research as "spatialized" activities (Leander & Sheehy, 2004). Landscapes are material, physical entities; as the topographical image suggests, they also are multidimensional, "real" yet also imagined; historically resonant; embodied, lived, and constructed; and as emotional as they are rational-technical. Landscapes mark and are marked by change in use and value across time, and they defy easy binaries. For instance, increased mechanization and concentration within traditional economies in the Lancaster-Hull region, such as agriculture and forestry, have significantly altered physical landscapes and the experience of land. Indeed, such changes tend to bolster talk of the need to "think globally" in rural areas. Yet landscapes in this site, as elsewhere, also foster immaterial sensibilities that can be transmitted between generations; when that occurs, they become sources of identification and commitment. Such sensibilities shape attachments, subjectivities, and life purposes and practices (Berry, 1978, 1990; Cross, 2001; Jury, 1999; Tuan, 1974). Alternatively, place ideals also develop as responses *against* the rigidities of place, and lead to other sorts of identification (Sibley, 1995).

Place sensibilities give content to, specify, people's aspirations and sense of trajectory, and they are far from the two-dimensional representations that serve to locate places on maps. Critical geographers consider place as encompassing conventional "purified" representations of stability, as well as identities and boundaries that are only "provisionally stabilized," more fluid than permanent (Murdoch & Pratt, 1997, pp. 66-67). The meaning of place is never self-evident, continuous, or uncomplicated, but the fact that places have meanings and residual histories should not be discounted. As Cresswell (2004), Massey (1994), Sibley (1995), and other geographers have suggested, place is more than a mere outgrowth of planning patterns or economic uses, as traditional spatial science discusses it, and more than the concentration of particular sets of practices that critical spatial theory suggests it is. Places are kinds of "layered locations" structured by multiplicity, producing certain continuities, but also disjunctures, and volatile ideas of "belonging" (Lippard, 1998, cited in Cresswell, p. 40; also Taylor, 2004). Changing practices may lead to new spaces being created that boldy or gently refashion existing places; in contrast, new spaces may take shape without much altering a place, because they may or may not "stick" (Ruddick, 1996) in a place over time. In the next sections, three cases of place-literacy intersections help illustrate these ideas.

KATIE: CHANGING PLACES?

Literacy/Difference

For eighth grader Katie, Lancaster-Hull had always been a place of nonbelonging and displacement, reading and writing a refuge. In many conversations with us, study participants referred to a communal "lost identity," and they cast this loss in one or more ways. Katie's story was a launching point to consider the meaning of shifting centers and peripheries—psychic, educational, economic—that form a place already complex and not merely, as others' comments often suggested, newly complex. The activities that led to Katie's veritable disembedding and re-embedding in the body of the school developed only as she was able to fashion a place-based form of agency. Katie accomplished this self-fashioning by challenging the problematic aspects of a small school that she felt dealt poorly with difference. Her challenge took shape by middle school through her textual practices, which were localized in activities sponsored, or barred, by her school, and regionalized through a sustained effort to link out-of-school activity, integral to her development, to school.

In Katie's experience, school was a source of intolerance to difference from the earliest grades. More directly, school was a site that produced stigma and marginality. Katie had a noticeable physical difference that she adamantly refused to term a handicap. Texts served as a refuge from stigma; reading both grew from and forged Katie's social relations with adult family members and eventually with adults more generally. Katie repeatedly marked her literary interests and habits as both outside many normative practices of school and as practices that spurred her growth. She mobilized literacy in ways that reinforced, but also celebrated, her sense of being different. It took until sixth grade for Katie to connect to school via an English teacher. This woman, Katie told us, noticed her difference and used a joking manner to engage Katie, to build a relationship in which she was recognized more fully. She also used texts to help link Katie to a peer. Thus, texts mediated her first friendship and helped sustain it as well.

Textual Panic

Through literacy practices, many youth we met transgressed the norms of places, including the norm that certain interests could not be carried into spheres where they did not typically reside lest they upset behavioral rules tied to one's age, status, and position in a structure of authority (Cresswell, 2004). We heard of such transgression from Katie, a prolific reader who described being censured for reading inappropriately adult novels in school. In nearly every class we observed, Katie could, at some point, be seen sneaking a chance to read from a thick novel typically tucked in the pages of a textbook. She misplaced one of these novels and found it had been discovered at the highest level:

> [the principal] read it and explained to me that I'm not allowed to lose this book, I'm not allowed to show this book to the other kids because it's not appropriate and their parents would probably not approve. Yes, my parents would approve of it but other parents won't. *So I'm not allowed to lose my books anymore!*

The loss of the book signaled the possibility of moral disruption. Despite the social network this textual practice embodied—linking her to both her in-school friend who had similar reading taste and to adults at home who shared reading material with her—the disciplinary response re-located Katie as a child among children, positioned her as a source of contamination, and marked her interest as considerably outside the bounds of acceptability in a place with considerable power to define and regulate what was "literate." Importantly, this regulation also controlled what might be seen as developmentally correct for youth in general. Lesko (2001) warned such responses reflect a vision of development that holds time at its epistemological center, regardless of evidence that developmental norms vary as a function of sociohistorical and cultural conditions. Lesko suggested what is seen as typical or appropriate for a young person ought to be interpreted on this basis rather on the basis of more narrow, age-based norms.

'Horse Sense' and Literate Competence

Apart from moral boundaries, certain spheres for literate practice seemed to be restricted unless they could be proven worthy of the norms and needs of a place. Once again, Katie's experience was instructive. She undertook an eighth grade science class assignment focused on horse-worming medications, a project that spanned several months and culminated with inclusion in a school-wide science fair. Her work required extensive research into pharmaceuticals, chemistry, and physiology; it also involved close negotiation with the owners of two stables where Katie taught riding to younger children, especially since she needed access to horses and the *material* where one might find horse worms! Already her employers, the stables' owners also became a part of Katie's research culture; they shared expertise and provided her with catalogs, supplies, and other resources needed to carry out the research with integrity. Further, both stipulated that Katie could *only* proceed if she could convince them her research would have something useful to contribute to their knowledge and their ability to maintain or improve the health of the horses. Katie thus was compelled both to learn the scientific method to demonstrate understanding in a school-based sense, and to learn and use it authentically, since her school-assigned project was shaped around real world interests and immediate needs. Her "success" relied on competence in both in- and out-of-school spheres; more precisely, "success," or learning, depended on Katie's ability to bridge the material interests of a non-school place to school itself, making school serve those "outside" needs.

Place thus fostered, and did not merely add value to, a school-rooted, problem-based learning activity. The project was made possible because of the affordances of a place, by Katie's investments in a place-based business (one she's keen to operate as an adult) that was, itself, part of a common place experience (horses are part of everyday life to many rural youth and communities). All of this gave the experience depth, texture, and meaning—for multiple participants, and along multiple dimensions. Katie outlined some of these dimensions when she related the ways in which the project was personally consequential. It called forth her best effort in relation to school literacy demands because she already felt invested in the stable work and recognized that it inspired ideas for her future that were weighty to her, even at age fourteen. Plus, the project was interesting. She stated, "I give my best effort every single day there [working at the stables]...just like my science fair project...I worked on it from January through March and it took me every one of those three months to do the project!" The project report could not contain "fluffy stuff" like the personal voice, she said, because the scientific report register required her to convey with precision how she used the scientific method to reach her conclusions. Accustomed to poetry writing, literary reading, and "stuffing [essays] full of information" when answering Document-Based Questions in her Social Studies class, Katie was challenged by this project on many levels. It reinforced her sense of intellectual competence, allowed her to link an authentic interest to a school literacy activity, and drew praise from and was inherently valued by teachers and the other adults critical to her growth. In this instance of bringing the rural "outside" into school, Katie excelled. The research writing stimulated and challenged her in forward-looking ways.

How and why this project mattered to Katie reverberated in other work we examined with her. Katie's computer network folder was filled with poems and stories she'd written over three years, and yet she still was barely passing eighth grade English. Comparing just two poems about horses, one written in sixth and the other at the end of seventh grade, Katie narrated a trajectory of genre and vocabulary development, literary sophistication, and awareness of how changing social practice influenced her literary process, purpose, and prowess. The poem written earliest was, Katie declared, full of "simple beauty…it gives you these images, it gives you that feeling…It just blurts it all out and lets you imagine. The simplicity is beautiful." The poem used adjectives such as "neighing" to describe the horses, but in hindsight, with the added expertise she'd gained in the field, Katie explained she'd now use the word "nickering" instead, a more precise term for one in the know of horses. "Oh trust me," Katie said, "if you're in the horse business you hear it *all* the time."

Katie, quite dis-fluent in the social world and in relation to many valued literacy practices of school and her peer group, was remarkably articulate about herself as both writer and "horse person." She had a rich vocabulary and a developing disposition to draw upon as she put to paper what she knew about this world. A significant part of her work in this world was that she taught riding to younger children, and this engendered respect for her skill and knowledge that she did not feel existed with her peers. Reading and discussing the latter of the two poems she shared, which compared in detail two horses from her worksite, as well as other poems with a narrative bent, Katie articulated what made these "more complicated" texts to her. The density of the images and themes was matched by more complex syntax, use of figurative language, and sophisticated vocabulary. Katie commented, "Like once in awhile I tried sticking in rhyming words? But not all the time….compared to other students, like I don't think they would use 'astonished' and 'undesirable,' things like that, that's like, you know, from my *reading*, those words I can specifically point out."

Katie reflected on the way her writing practices linked to her self-concept as a student, an intellectual, and a reader. As she explored the meanings of the activities she pursued, it became possible to link them to valued school literacy practices (prolific outside reading and writing). Yet clearly, as the earlier book infraction showed, it was not always possible for them to be valued in these ways. Katie insistently held close the generative sources that conditioned these activities—work in the community, shared text discussions with adults, and scientific research grounded in locale and her own place-rootedness. As she did this, we realized place could not be interpreted as a simple, geographic entity in relation to literacy, learning, and rural youth development.

THE PROBLEM OF PLACE AND TIME

Interacting with Katie and others underlined the complex forces that constructed this rural school; conceptually, there was a way in which the idea of complexity stood in contrast to an understanding of changing expressed by many. Participants talked of the need to be increasingly forward-looking in order to cope with *pending* changes and complexity, especially those changes connected to regional demographic transformation and bureaucratic mandates that were exerting pressure to alter curriculum and assessment practices. One level of discourse we heard revolved around what *used to be* (this, in fact, led us to borrow the popular title of the book read in our focal classroom, S.E. Hinton's *That Was Then, This Is Now*). Back then, before consolidation and before outsiders encroached on abandoned parcels and family farms, there was local decision-making, a small-town feel and communal support for education, collaborative and interdisciplinary teaching, and a sense of familiarity and camaraderie. What, then, characterized the present?

On one level, we heard a great deal about the influx of strangers from two demographic strata: middle class professionals looking for inexpensive housing, land, and the very small-town school experience that locals feared losing and a decidedly less popular group of strangers from the City, who moved to escape bad schools and violent communities. Participants expressed ambivalence towards both groups, each of which pushed against the known and the symbolic sense of *us*. Some adults conflated the new, wealthier demographic presence with rising educational standards and general social progress. We heard about this group as one bringing "culture" to the region, a sign similar to the effect of consolidation for one teacher and longtime resident, who saw in such change "healthy development" that generated a hedge against local students' "apathy." Others were more circumspect in their views, and described the newcomers as bossy and intruding. Angie, a focal student, associated the social hierarchy (which she and her friends deemed "preps, normals, and scumbags") with the outlook of the wealthier students, who held more social sway and were much less likely than she was to find themselves in trouble for minor infractions, she felt.

Threads of complexity were woven into constructions of past and present, as well as the future, interrupting any single or singular version of rural identity or "that was then" schooling, around which some narratives were organized. Many participants in our study were aware that the terms of community were unstable in an era of high mobility into and out of community regions. Massey (1994) suggested this instability is an inevitable and, ultimately, desirable perspective if we want to avoid conflating "identification of place with 'community'" (p. 153). Indeed, "what gives a place its specificity," Massey argued, "is not some long internalized history but the fact that it is constructed out of a particular constellation of social relations, meeting and weaving together at a particular locus" (p. 154).

Still, Lancaster-Hull youth and adults struggled to hold onto historical sources of community meaning and identity in light of current patterns of living that blurred known (and what seemed like natural) boundaries. Residential patterns in the region shifted, and work in traditional economies disappeared, only to be replaced either by good jobs well outside the region (resulting in higher rates of commuting to nearby suburbs and cities) or by local service-sector and retail jobs that were less secure and had little to do with the long-established occupational identity of the area, and much to do with a recasting of that identity. A former mill worker (and friend of a key informant) recounted Lancaster-Hull's regional economic history and noted that a center for the developmentally disabled was the county's current largest employer:

> [The Center], that's the main industry we got around here. If you don't work at [The Center], you'll be lucky if you get anything. You know, five, six dollars at McDonald's, and you still got to have an education, you gotta have a diploma. It's a nice place to live, but you've got to be able to afford to live. This area's for the retired and the retarded.

A topographical view, enmeshed as it was in our movement through the region, helped us begin to account for the dilemmas of mobility these rural youth and adults faced in changing times. Inherent to the notion of development is the idea that transitions are risky, especially when undertaken in sites in transition, places where historical sources of identity are threatened or in flux. Critical geographers of place try to account for the dynamic forces that shape experience, to make it possible to explore how transition might be understood simultaneously as a generative site and a source of conflict or risk. This is especially true under the conditions of intensified individualization that now shape development, whereby young people increasingly are responsible for gathering the qualifications needed to enter a sharply stratified adult world or face long-term social exclusion (Beck & Willms, 2004; Bynner, Chisholm, & Furlong, 1997; Dwyer & Wyn, 2001; Hodkinson, Sparkes, & Hodkinson, 1996; Morch, 1997). What anchoring is possible when familiar sources of identification and growth become dramatically unmoored?

WAL-MART: LAYERED LOCATION, COMPLEX TERRITORY

Central to our study of ELA reform was the idea that students' literacy experiences and identities evolve in relation to sites of practice undergoing transition (Nespor, 1997; Packer, 2000). Wal-Mart took on particular significance the more we revisited our data from this perspective, and we want to close with a brief account that explains why. A range of interviewees referenced Wal-Mart, so often that it seemed to function as a rich barometer of the meaning and purpose of literacy and rising educational standards, capturing differences in the way that people defined "good jobs" and viewed the relationship between education, human capital, and the potential to preserve a rural way of life. Located in a strip mall between the City and towns, the Wal-Mart of this study was flanked by a silo and overgrown pasture, and it faced an empty industrial park across the state highway. It marked a point of change between the landscape of the City, our students' "front door" view, and the fields, trailer parks, and scattered neighborhoods—leading eventually to farms, the lake, and mountains—that typified their "back door" view. People from the City and towns mingled at Wal-Mart, too, as workers and consumers; it was an unsettled, hybridized symbol and place (Stallybrass & White, 1986, p. 27).

Some youth referred to Wal-Mart as a place of potential adult employment, a site of possibility, but this perspective clashed with allusions by teachers and administrators, who invoked the store to speak to the importance of advanced literacy. With a "good" education, some adults suggested, youth could avoid a "Wal-Mart life," as one teacher said. "Do they really want to end up working at Wal-Mart?" several educators asked in response to our questions about how educational demands had changed and what the consequences were for students. An administrator explained the rationale for incorporating higher standards to provide visions apart from Wal-Mart work options. Marie, a teacher, noted that although some old-timers, who "have been…successful people in, within the boundaries of the district…see the need for more literacy," others resist change, and she could understand why, despite wanting her students to aim higher. To these "old minds…the blue collar workers," Wal-Mart presented options: "…you know we're always gonna need people to work in some of these positions," she mused, "and…there will always be a need for the mechanics, and for, you know, the greeters at Wal Mart, and the people to do those, the service positions."

For some parents and youth, such work had little to do with aspirations or a sense of intellectual potential, and everything to do with imagining how and where to live, to remain rural. Wal-Mart in this scenario figured as the embodiment of a potentially rewarding future, since Wal-Mart, the retail outlet, was a stable fixture, and the nearby distribution center signaled the possibility of better paying, more secure jobs, a chance to put down roots—a possibility. Wal-Mart thus served a role both biographically and semiotically. It was a site of personal location for some, a pragmatic tool for envisioning a productive adult work life in the region, but a sign, for others, of insufficient personal ambition, or the small and large-scale dislocations affecting youth. So many hopes and fears seemed to be channeled through Wal-Mart. Its strong presence signaled its vital role to our analysis of the "technologies" and "materiality" producing literacy on a local scale (Brandt & Clinton, 2002). It seemed to signify as well the unpredictable value of literacy at this historical juncture, in this place and at this time (Brandt, 2001).

CONCLUSION

Agrarian writers who challenge the assault of globalization often assert there is something distinctly humane about communities rooted in work with the land and the "commonplace" experiences of local participation and democratic action these structures present (see, for instance, Berry, 1978, 1990; Theobald, 1997). Although the camaraderie this view imagines may not be as apparent, perhaps, among neighbors with fewer economic ties and more portable means of sustainability, it is important to question discourse that sees "rurality" in totalizing ways when the "rural" encompasses broad human and cultural experience (Phillips, 1998). Here, the idea of topography came to function as a rich concept to probe the complexities we perceived.

Multiliteracy and poststructural theories delineate how one might feel rooted *and* experience the world and identity as shifting and fluid. Critical geography, topography, helped us think about these notions via *place*. It challenged us to suspend conclusions based upon any particular physical distinctions bounding place: classroom, school, town, county, city. These can mark, shortsightedly, what and who would be seen as "rural" or "literate," impose maps that erroneously shortchange the range of practices vital to rural youth as they navigate what can be "a conflict resulting from the perceived need to 'move out' in order to 'move up'" (Hektner, 1995, p. 12). Not to notice and analyze complexity would effectively mirror the ideology that is the burden of a placeless, standardized literate good. In our view, topography seems an apt tool to explore the depth, density, and presence of multiple formations at the heart of any particular place and the people who live (in) it.

REFERENCES

Aitken, S. (2001). *Geographies of young people: The morally contested spaces of identity.* New York: Routledge.

Beck, U., & Willms, J. (2004). *Conversations with Ulrich Beck.* Malden, MA: Blackwell.

Berry, W. (1978). *The unsettling of America: Culture and agriculture.* New York: Avon.

Berry, W. (1990). *What are people for? Essays by Wendell Berry.* San Francisco: North Point Press.

Brandt, D. (2001). *Literacy in American lives.* New York: Cambridge University Press.

Brandt, D., & Clinton, K. (2002). Limits of the local: Expanding perspectives on literacy as a social practice. *Journal of Literacy Research, 34,* 337-356.

Bynner, J., Chisholm, L., & Furlong, A. (Eds.). (1997). *Youth, citizenship, and social change in European context.* Brookfield, VT: Ashgate.

Colchado, J., et. al. (2003). *Engaged institutions: Impacting vulnerable youth through place-based learning.* Retrieved November 2004, from http://www.ruraledu.org/docs/kellogg/kellogg.pdf

Cortazzi, M. (1993). *Narrative analysis.* London: Falmer.

Cresswell, T. (2004). *Place: A short introduction.* Malden, MA: Blackwell.

Cross, J. E. (2001). What is 'sense of place'? Paper presented at the 12th Headwaters Conference, Western State College, November 2-4, 2001. Retrieved September 10, 2004, from http://www.western.edu/headwaters/archives/headwaters12_papers/cross_paper.html

DeYoung, A. J. (1995). *The life and death of a rural American high school: Farewell Little Kanawha.* New York: Garland.

DeYoung, A., & Howley, C. (1990). The political economy of rural school consolidation. *Peabody Journal of Education, Summer,* 63-89.

DeYoung, A., & Lawrence, B. K. (1995). On hoosiers, yankees, and mountaineers. *Phi Delta Kappan, Summer,* 104-112.

Dwyer, P., & Wyn, J. (2001). *Youth, education and risk: Facing the future.* New York: RoutledgeFalmer.

Elder, G. H., & Conger, R. (2000). *Children of the land: Adversity and success in rural America.* Chicago: University of Chicago Press.

Emekauwa, E. (2004). *The star with my name: The Alaska rural systemic initiative and the impact of place-based education on Native student achievement.* Retrieved November 15, 2004, from http://www.ruraledu.org/docs/Alaska-Rural_Systemic_Initiative.pdf

Engestrom, Y. (2001). Expansive learning at work: Toward an activity theoretical reconceptualization. *Journal of Education and Work, 14*(1), 133-156.

Gibbs, T., & Howley, A. (December 2000, EDO-RC-00-8). *World-class standards and local pedagogies: Can we do both?* Charleston, WV: ERIC Clearinghouse on Rural Education and Small Schools. (Publication prepared with funding from the Office of Educational Research and Improvement, U.S. Department of Education, under contract no. ED-99-CO-0027). Retrieved March 15, 2003, from http://acclaim.coe.ohiou.edu/rc/rc_sub/vlibrary/2_e_digs/World-Class.htm

Hektner, J. M. (1995). When moving up implies moving out: Rural adolescent conflict in the transition to adulthood. *Journal of Research in Rural Education, 11*(1), 3-14.

Hodkinson, P., Sparkes, A., & Hodkinson, H. (1996). *Triumphs and tears: Young people, markets, and the transition from school to work.* London: David Fulton.

Howley, C. (1997, April 30). Studying the rural in education: Nation-building, 'globalization,' and school improvement. *Education Policy Analysis Archives, 5*(12). Retrieved November 1, 2004, from http://epaa.asu.edu/epaa/v5n12.html

Jury, M. (1999). *Inventing work in a rural community: Exploring the social, historical, and cultural dimensions of school-to-work and work-to-work transitions.* Unpublished Doctoral Dissertation, University of California, Berkeley.

Kleibard, H. (1995). *The struggle for the American curriculum.* New York: Routledge.

Lave, J. (1993). The practice of learning. In S. Chaiklin & J. Lave (Eds.), *Understanding practice: Perspectives on activity and context* (pp. 3-34). New York: Cambridge University Press.

Leander, K. (2002). *Polycontextual construction zones: Mapping the expansion of schooled space and identity.* Retrieved August 20, 2004, from http://www.vanderbilt.edu/litspace/polycontext.pdf

Leander, K. M., & Sheehy, M. (Eds.). (2004). *Spatializing literacy research and practice.* New York: Peter Lang.

Lesko, N. (2001). *Act your age: A cultural construction of adolescence.* New York: RoutledgeFalmer.

Levinson, B., Foley, D., & Holland, D. (Eds.). (1996). *The cultural production of the educated person: Critical ethnographies of schooling and local practice.* Albany, New York: SUNY Press.

Massey, D. (1994). *Space, place, and gender.* Minneapolis: University of Minnesota Press.

McDermott, R. P. (1993). The acquisition of a child by a learning disability. In S. Chaiklin and J. Lave (Eds.). *Understanding practice: Perspectives on activity and context* (pp. 269-305). New York: Cambridge University Press.

Moje, E. B., Ciechanowski, K. M., Kramer, K., Ellis, L., Carrillo, R., & Collazo, T. (2004). Working toward third space in content area literacy: An examination of everyday funds of knowledge and discourse. *Reading Research Quarterly, 39,* 38–70.

Morch, S. (1997). Youth and activity theory. In J. Bynner, L. Chisholm, & A. Furlong, (Eds.), *Youth, citizenship, and social change in a European context* (pp. 245-261).

Murdoch, J., & Pratt, A.C. (1997). From the power of topography to the topography of power: A discourse on strange ruralities. In P. Cloke & J. Little (Eds.), *Contested countryside cultures: Otherness, marginalization, and rurality* (pp. 51-69). New York: Routledge.

Nespor, J. (1997). *Tangled up in school: Politics, space, bodies, and signs in the educational process.* Mahwah, NJ: Lawrence Erlbaum Associates.

Nespor, J. (2000). Anonymity and place in qualitative inquiry. *Qualitative Inquiry, 6,* 546-569.

Packer, M. (2000). *Changing classes: School reform and the new economy.* New York: Cambridge University Press.

Phillips, M. (1998). Theoretical approaches to rural restructuring: Social perspectives. In B. Ilbery (Ed.), *The geography of rural change* (pp. 31-54). Essex, UK: Longman.

Ruddick, S. (1996). *Young and homeless in Hollywood: Mapping social identities.* New York: Routledge.

Sibley, D. (1995). *Geographies of exclusion: Society and difference in the West.* New York: Routledge.

Stallybrass, P., & White, A. (1986). *The politics & poetics of transgression.* Ithaca, NY: Cornell University Press.

Taylor, L. (2004, September). Sense, relationship, and power: Uncommon views of place. *Teaching History, 116,* 6-13. Retrieved October 15, 2004, from http://www.findarticles.com/p/articles/mi_qa3900/is_200409/ai_n9410467

Theobald, P. (1997). *Teaching the commons: Place, pride, and the renewal of community.* Boulder, CO: Westview Press.

Topography. (2001–04). *The Columbia Encyclopedia (6th Ed.).* New York: Columbia University Press. Retrieved May 7, 2005, from www.bartleby.com/65/

Tuan, Y-F. (1974). *Topophilia: A study of environmental perception.* New York: Columbia University Press.

Vanderbeck, R. M., & Dunkley, C. M. (2003). Young people's narratives of rural-urban difference. *Children's Geographies, 1*(2), 241-259.

Weis, L., & Fine, M. (Eds.). (2000). *Construction sites: Excavating race, class, and gender among urban youth.* New York: Teachers College Press.

Wigginton, E. (1985). *Sometimes a shining moment: The Foxfire experience.* Garden City, New York: Anchor Press/Doubleday.

Vocabulary-Comprehension Relationships

James F. Baumann
University of Georgia

The relationships between reading vocabulary and comprehension have been recognized for well over 80 years (Anderson & Freebody, 1981). However, the exact nature of and theoretical explanations for associational or causal connections between word knowledge and comprehension vary (cf. Anderson & Freebody, 1983; Kame'enui, Dixon, & Carnine, 1987; Nagy, 2005; Stahl, 1991), as do the theoretical, empirical, and instructional implications of vocabulary-comprehension connections (Beck, McKeown, & Omanson, 1987; Graves, 1986; Nagy, 1988; Ruddell, 1994). These issues remain somewhat unresolved today. For example, the National Reading Panel (NRP, 2000) stated that "precisely separating the two processes [vocabulary and comprehension] is difficult, if not impossible" (p. 4-15), and the RAND Reading Study Group (RAND, 2002) expressed that the "relationship between vocabulary knowledge and comprehension is extremely complex" (p. 35).

There are several noteworthy classic works that review vocabulary-comprehension associations (e.g., Anderson & Freebody, 1981; Graves, 1986; McKeown & Curtis, 1987; Mezynski, 1983; Nagy, 1988; Rosenshine, 1980; Stahl & Fairbanks, 1986) as well as more recent works that address this topic (e.g., Baumann, Kame'enui, & Ash, 2003; Beck & McKeown, 1991; Beck, McKeown, & Kucan, 2002; Blachowicz & Fisher, 2000; Hiebert & Kamil, 2005; Nagy & Scott, 2000; NRP, 2000; RAND, 2002; Ruddell, 1994; Stahl, 1999). It is the purpose of this paper to examine the historic and contemporary literature identified and described in these reviews in order to synthesize what is known about the relationships between vocabulary and comprehension. Drawing from and building upon the structure and content of the extant reviews noted—with particular emphasis on the types of literature examined and the framework used by Anderson and Freebody in their 1981 seminal review—this retrospective review is organized into four sections: (a) research linking vocabulary and comprehension, (b) models to explain vocabulary-comprehension relationships, (c) research on vocabulary instruction and comprehension, and (d) a conclusion.

RESEARCH LINKING VOCABULARY AND COMPREHENSION

IQ and Vocabulary

The relationship between IQ and vocabulary is long-standing and strong, with correlations typically in the .70-.90 range (Minor, 1957, as cited in Anderson & Freebody, 1981, pp. 77-79; R. L. Thorndike, 1973-1974). Indeed, intelligence tests historically and contemporarily (e.g., the Kaufman, Slosson, Stanford-Binet, and Wechsler tests) include a verbal component or scale, which typically is some direct or indirect measure of word or concept knowledge. Thus, "verbal intelligence" has been and remains a kind of psychoeducational redundancy, linking concept knowledge to general understanding or comprehension. In fact, it has been argued (see Cunningham & Stanovich, 2003) that there is a strong—possibly reciprocal if not causal— relationship among vocabulary, intelligence, comprehension, and exposure to text through independent reading.

Early Descriptive Research

In a series of papers, Edward L. Thorndike (1917a/1971, 1917b, 1917c) reported on children's and adolescents' responses to comprehension questions about short paragraphs (for more detail, see descriptions and critiques of Thorndike's work by Allington, 1983, Nicholson, 1983, Otto, 1971, and Stauffer, 1971). In Thorndike's (1917a/1971) classic work titled "Reading as Reasoning," he acknowledged the relationship between vocabulary and comprehension, noting that "in correct reading (1) each word produces a correct meaning, (2) each such element of meaning is given a correct weight in comparison with the others, and (3) the resulting ideas are examined and validated to make sure that they satisfy the mental set or adjustment or purpose for whose sake the reading was done" (1917a/1971, p. 428). In other words, Thorndike argued that comprehension is dependent upon knowledge of the meanings of the constituent words. He noted, however, that although vocabulary knowledge may be necessary for comprehension, it is not automatically sufficient: "It appears likely also that a pupil may read fluently and feel that the series of words are arousing appropriate thoughts without really understanding the paragraph" (1917a/1971, p. 433). Thus, Thorndike's work set the stage for subsequent, more sophisticated analyses of the impact vocabulary knowledge has on reading comprehension.

Correlational Works Linking Vocabulary and Reading Comprehension

Davis (1944). Frederick B. Davis (1944) published a classic work, based on his 1941 dissertation data, titled "Fundamental Factors of Comprehension in Reading." Davis analyzed correlational data from nine reading "tests," administered to college freshmen, which represented comprehension processes and abilities deemed important by authorities in the field at that time. Two of the tests addressed vocabulary: "knowledge of word meanings" and the "ability to select the appropriate meaning for a word or phrase in light of its particular contextual setting" (p. 186). Davis reported that not only did these two tests correlate highly (.72) but also correlated well with most of the remaining nine tests (.28 - .71) (p. 187). Further, a factor analysis resulted in a powerful component primarily attributed to skill 1 (knowledge of word meanings), which led Davis to conclude that "Component I is clearly word knowledge (skill 1). Its positive loadings in each of the nine basic reading skills reflect the fact that to read at all it is necessary to recognize words and to recall their meanings. It is clear that word knowledge plays a very important part in reading comprehension" (p. 191). A second component, which Davis referred to as "reasoning in reading" (p. 191), included several skills that involved making inferences and integrating information. Davis argued that these two primary components were "measured with sufficient reliability to warrant their use for practical purposes" (p. 194). Davis concluded that "reading comprehension, as measured by the nine basic reading skills, is not a unitary ability" (p. 189), leading at least some in the field to argue that there was empirical support for discrete reading comprehension skills or abilities.

Reanalyses of Davis (1944). Two years following the publication of Davis's (1944) "Fundamental Factors" study, Thurstone (1946) published a report describing a reanalysis of Davis's data. Thurstone argued that the data revealed "a single common factor (reading ability)" (p. 185) that accounted for the association among the tests, rather than discrete reading comprehension skills. (In a later reanalysis Johnson, Toms-Bronowski, and Buss, 1983, likewise reported a single factor for Davis's 1944 original data.) Thurstone did note, however, that three tests, one of which was the vocabulary test, demonstrated specific, unique variances, and the general consensus in the field seemed to persist for quite some time that there were separately identifiable reading comprehension skills or components (Johnson et al., 1983).

Davis (1968). Davis (1968) replicated and extended his 1944 inquiry. Using eight tests (rather than the original nine tests or skills; two of the original nine were merged; see Davis, 1968, p. 512), which were elaborately field-tested and revised, Davis conducted a "uniqueness analysis" on data from 988 high school seniors. Davis reported again that "comprehension among mature readers is not a unitary mental skill or operation" (p. 542), noting that there were several discrete reading skills, with the largest proportion of the non-error variance (32%) associated with the vocabulary component. As in his 1944 study, Davis concluded that "memory for word meanings and drawing inferences from content" (p. 499) represented the most significant components, leading him to recommend that educators "make pupils familiar with the meanings of as many words as possible" and "encourage pupils to draw inferences from what they read" (p. 543) as instructional emphases.

Reanalyses of Davis (1968). Davis (1972) reanalyzed his 1968 data, reporting results that were essentially parallel to his 1968 analysis. At about this same time, two other analyses of Davis's 1968 data affirmed the power of vocabulary as a factor in reading comprehension but questioned the nature or presence of comprehension subskills or components. Spearritt (1972) reported that "word knowledge and three other skills were shown to be separately distinguishable" (p. 92). He noted, however, that the three comprehension components "were very highly correlated and thus could be predominantly measuring a single basic ability" (p. 92). R. L. Thorndike (1973-1974) identified three factors, the strongest of which involved word meanings and two others he had difficulty describing: "Beyond the separation of word knowledge, I must confess that I have been unable to make much sense of the patterning of the loadings" (p. 140). In fact, R. L. Thorndike even questioned whether vocabulary was distinct from comprehension ("But wait a minute! Is the ability that is measured by a word knowledge test reasoning-free?", p. 141), instead hearkening back to his father's, E. L. Thorndike's (1917a/1971), notion of "reading as reasoning," that is, as a unitary trait or process.

In his review of descriptive and empirical works that addressed the issue of whether there exist skill hierarchies in reading comprehension, Rosenshine (1980, pp. 540-543) conducted a thorough and insightful analysis of Davis's (1968) work and several reanalyses of it (Davis, 1972;

Spearritt, 1972). Rosenshine concluded that "*different analyses yielded different unique skills,* and only one skill was consistent across the three analyses: remembering word meanings" (p. 543). Thus, although debate persisted about whether comprehension was a unitary or multi-faceted trait (see Johnson et al., 1983, and Blachowicz's, 1983, commentary on Johnson et al.), there was little disagreement that vocabulary was an integral part of text comprehension.

Achievement test correlations. Research on achievement test and subtest data provides further support for a vocabulary-comprehension association. Various measures of reading comprehension and vocabulary knowledge, as measured by standardized assessments, correlate highly (see Bloom, 1976). As Anderson and Freebody (1981) note, an ambitious cross-cultural, cross-linguistic study also supported this connection. In 1973 R. L. Thorndike reported a study titled *Reading Comprehension Education in Fifteen Countries: An Empirical Study* in which data were gathered for 10-year-olds, 14-year-olds, and students in the final year of secondary education in countries as diverse as Belgium, England, India, Chile, Iran, Israel, Italy, New Zealand, and the U.S. Correlations between a test of word knowledge and two reading comprehension measures revealed that median obtained uncorrected correlations across countries were .59, .62, and .49 (range .31-.74) for the three age groups tested, respectively, and when corrected for unreliability, the values were .71, .75, and .66 (range .48-.86), respectively. Further, correlations were highest for English speaking countries (for details see R. L. Thorndike, 1973, pp. 61-63, and Table 4-7, p. 62).

Readability literature. By definition, readability—"ease of comprehension" or "prediction of reading comprehension" (Harris & Hodges, 1995, p. 203)—has a relationship to reading comprehension. Empirical analyses of readability formulas (see Klare, 1974-1975, 1984) are clear in determining that two factors, "a word or semantic variable and…a sentence or syntactic variable" (Klare, 1974-1975, p. 96) are prominent in predicting text comprehension, and that "the word or semantic variable is consistently more highly predictive than the sentence or syntactic variable" (Klare, 1974-1975, p. 96). However, the relationship between vocabulary and readability (or comprehension), no matter how irrefutable, "is a complex one" (Stahl, 2003, p. 241). For example, as Graves (1986, pp. 58-60) described in detail, research on simplifying vocabulary in texts has produced mixed results, with some studies showing significantly enhanced comprehension when texts contained more high-frequency words (e.g., Marks, Doctorow, & Wittrock, 1974; Wittrock, Marks, & Doctorow, 1975), others showing more modest effects when vocabulary is manipulated (Freebody & Anderson, 1983a, 1983b), and others showing no improvement as a function of vocabulary alterations (Nolte, 1938; Ryder & Hughes, 1985). Stahl (2003) stated that "simplifying vocabulary does not always make texts easier" (p. 246), although as Graves (1986) noted, the evidence generally suggests "that vocabulary difficulty can affect comprehension, that the effect it has is seldom a large one, and that a number of words have to be changed to produce the effect" (p. 59).

Summary

The evidence linking vocabulary and comprehension is both broad and long-standing. Whether descriptive in nature or from IQ and achievement test data, the readability literature, or a variety of correlational investigations, it is clear that word knowledge has an irrefutable association with text comprehension. Or as Johnson et al. (1983) concluded, "the works reviewed here indicate that vocabulary knowledge *is* critical to comprehension. If you don't know the words, you're not going to understand the passage" (p. 254). However, association does not imply causation (Beck et al., 1987), so we move to a discussion of models offered to provide theoretical explanations for the robust vocabulary-comprehension connections.

MODELS TO EXPLAIN VOCABULARY-COMPREHENSION RELATIONSHIPS

Researchers and theorists have proposed several models or explanations for the relationship between vocabulary and comprehension to guide theory-building and to explore possible causal connections. The first formal and elaborate articulation of potential explanations for vocabulary-comprehension associations was proposed by Anderson and Freebody (1981), who offered three positions or hypotheses: the instrumentalist, knowledge, and aptitude. Elaborations of these positions have been offered by Nagy and Herman (1987) and Stahl (1999), with critiques and extensions provided by Mezynski (1983), Stahl (1991), and Nagy (2005).

Instrumentalist

This position posits that "individuals who score high on a vocabulary test are likely to know more of the words in most texts they encounter than low scoring individuals," or "knowing the words enables text comprehension" (Anderson & Freebody, 1981, pp. 80-81). This position proposes a direct, causal connection between vocabulary and comprehension, which Stahl (1999, p. 4) represented graphically as "Vocabulary Knowledge ⇨ Reading Comprehension," and as Nagy and Herman (1987) stated, "this hypothesis predicts that teaching words should increase reading comprehension automatically" (p. 28).

Knowledge

This position hypothesizes that "performance on vocabulary tests is seen as a reflection of the extent of exposure to the culture" and "the knowledge view emphasizes conceptual frameworks or 'schemata'; individual word meanings are merely the exposed tip of the conceptual iceberg" (Anderson & Freebody, 1981, p. 81-82). The knowledge position suggests that a third factor, general knowledge of the world, influences both vocabulary and text comprehension. That is, "knowledge of the subject matter of a text plays an important role in the comprehension of that text, above and beyond the effects of knowing specific words" (Nagy & Herman, 1987, p.28), or as Stahl (1999, p. 5) conveyed, "Vocabulary Knowledge ⇨ Topic Knowledge ⇨ Reading Comprehension."

Aptitude

This position suggests that "vocabulary tests measure verbal *aptitude*," or "persons with large vocabularies are better at discourse comprehension because they possess superior mental agility"

(Anderson & Freebody, 1981, p. 81). In other words, like the knowledge hypothesis, vocabulary does not directly influence comprehension; rather, both are related to a common third factor, intelligence or general verbal aptitude in this case. Stahl (1999) depicted this as "Vocabulary Knowledge ⇔ General Ability ⇒ Reading Comprehension" (p. 6). Recently Nagy (2005) offered an extension of the aptitude hypothesis, the *metalinguistic hypothesis*, which posits that "part of the correlation between tests of vocabulary knowledge and reading comprehension is due to the fact that both require metalinguistic awareness—that is, the ability to reflect on and manipulate language" (p. 32). Nagy argued that the meta-ability to deal with the decontextualized nature of written language (i.e., no situational context, prosody, etc.) is a key ingredient in explaining word meaning and comprehension associations.

A Fourth Position: Access

In her review of vocabulary instruction studies, Mezynski (1983) proposed a fourth perspective, the *access* hypothesis, which suggests that comprehension is related to "accessing word meanings and in using those meanings efficiently in text processing," or the notion of "'automaticity' of word knowledge" (p. 254). This position, which Stahl (1991) referred to as "the *speed-of-access* hypothesis" (p. 158), is associated with the notion of automaticity in reading (LaBerge & Samuels, 1974), such that comprehension is related to vocabulary to the degree that a reader can locate and assign the semantic representation of words in text efficiently.

Analyses of, Modifications to, and Extensions of These Positions

Within their explication of the instrumentalist, aptitude, and knowledge positions, Anderson and Freebody (1981) acknowledged that "it would be naïve, indeed, to assume that one of the positions will turn out to be entirely right and the other two entirely wrong" (p. 82). They also noted that "no serious scholar in reading or related fields rigidly adheres to any one of these positions" (p. 89). Several scholars have compared and contrasted Anderson and Freebody's three positions and Mezynski's (1983) fourth position, resulting in various interpretations. Nagy and Herman (1987) pointed out limitations of the instrumentalist position while highlighting the importance of a schema-theoretic (knowledge hypothesis) perspective in explaining vocabulary-comprehension relationships. Stahl (1999) stated that "all three [of the Anderson and Freebody positions] say something about vocabulary and comprehension" (p. 7), while noting that there is empirical support for the instrumentalist hypothesis.

In an important paper titled "Beyond the Instrumentalist Hypothesis: Some Relationships Between Word Meanings and Comprehension," Stahl (1991) argued that "all four vocabulary-comprehension hypotheses seem too general" (p. 160) and that a new view was needed, which involved "looking at the vocabulary-comprehension relationship from a different perspective, that of the individual word's effect on understanding the individual passage" (p. 160). Ruddell (1994) proposed a broader, comprehension-process analysis view that draws from schema, transactional, and sociocultural theories to explain vocabulary knowledge and comprehension associations. Further, Ruddell argued that with respect to the schema component, the knowledge hypothesis "is an overarching construct that subsumes at least part of the other positions [instrumentalist, aptitude, access]" (p. 416). Kame'enui, Dixon, and Carnine (1987) also adopted a different perspective, arguing that each of the four "positions are of limited value to a more complete understanding of this elusive [vocabulary-comprehension] relationship, because they rely on single-factor explanations of a complex phenomenon" (p. 131). They proposed an alternate, pragmatic view—the *instructional design* position—that accounts for vocabulary instruction within "a broader context of instructional goals, task requirements, and learning outcomes within reading comprehension" (p. 132).

A New Position: The Reciprocal Model (Nagy, 2005)

Recently, Nagy (2005) argued that extant models mask the complexity of vocabulary-comprehension relationships in that they represent causality in a unidirectional manner (e.g., vocabulary knowledge directly affects comprehension as predicted by the instrumentalist hypothesis). Instead, Nagy asserted, that the vocabulary-comprehension relationship is bidirectional: "Having a big vocabulary does contribute to being a better reader. But being a good reader also contributes to having a bigger vocabulary" (p. 34). Acknowledging the Matthew effect for amount of reading and vocabulary development (Cunningham & Stanovich, 2003; Stanovich, 1986), Nagy described the *reciprocal model*, which he represented as a recursive process: "↷ Vocabulary   ⇨   Reading   Comprehension   ⇨   Volume   of   Reading   ↶" (p. 34). According to this view, vocabulary influences comprehension and vice versa, with both being mediated by the amount of reading one does.

Summary

Over the last 25 years, researchers and theorists have proposed a variety of models or hypotheses to explain the strong vocabulary-comprehension associations. The classic models are the instrumentalist, knowledge, and aptitude hypotheses (Anderson & Freebody, 1981), with additions or extensions represented by the access (Mezynski, 1983), instructional design (Kame'enui et al., 1987), and schema-transactional-sociocultural (Ruddell, 1994) positions. Most recently Nagy (2005) described a model characterizing a reciprocal relationship between vocabulary and comprehension. But what does the research reveal about the suitability of these models? We now turn to that issue.

RESEARCH ON VOCABULARY INSTRUCTION AND COMPREHENSION

There are classic (e.g., Petty, Herold, & Stoll, 1967), more contemporary (e.g., Beck & McKeown, 1991), and recent (e.g., Blachowicz & Fisher, 2000; Nagy & Scott, 2000) syntheses of instructional research on vocabulary which reveal many studies that address the relationship between vocabulary instruction and reading comprehension. This literature is presented here by describing and critiquing several significant and influential reviews that explored vocabulary-comprehension instructional effects. Many of these reviews and the underlying literature were predicated explicitly or implicitly on the instrumental hypothesis, so much of the intervention research attempts to describe the conditions under which teaching word meanings may or may not influence reading comprehension.

Mezynski (1983)

Mezynski (1983) provided one of the first systematic, detailed reviews of research examining the effects of vocabulary instruction on word learning and reading comprehension. She identified 8 studies, 7 of which involved instruction for middle-grade students (Grades 4-6), with 1 involving high school students. Mezynski noted that the studies varied considerably in design and measurement factors, including the number of words taught (6-1,800), duration of training (part of a day to a full school year), the training methods employed (e.g., flash cards, semantic associations), and the detail of description of methods and training programs. Mezynski's analysis revealed that all studies demonstrated gains in vocabulary knowledge for words taught, but only 4 of 8 studies demonstrated effects of vocabulary instruction on comprehension (e.g., Tuinman & Brady's, 1974, study revealed no effects whereas Beck, Perfetti, & McKeown's, 1982, study did). She noted that lexical access—manifest by the amount of practice with key vocabulary as in the Beck et al. study—seemed to be a critical factor in enhancing comprehension. Mezynski also commented that "the lack of effects of vocabulary training on reading comprehension may have been due, in many cases, to methodological problems" (p. 272), while noting that the greater the volume or emphasis on three factors seemed to distinguish studies that promoted comprehension: "(1) amount of practice given to the words, (2) breadth of training in the use of the words, and (3) the degree to which active processing is encouraged" (p. 273). These themes of methodological limitations and importance of practice, breadth, and active processing presaged conclusions reached by subsequent reviewers who examined an expanding instructional literature.

Graves (1986)

Within Graves's (1986) broad review of the literature on vocabulary teaching and learning, he included a brief but important section titled "Effects of Vocabulary Instruction on Reading Comprehension." He identified 14 relevant studies, 6 of which "failed to increase comprehension by teaching vocabulary" (p. 60). He stated further that a critical review of the 8 studies that did show positive effects, 5 were "questionable" in his estimation (e.g., due to limited descriptions of interventions, "comprehension" measures that were more like vocabulary tests, and mixed results or competing hypotheses for results), leading him to focus on the trilogy of studies by Beck, McKeown, and colleagues (Beck et al., 1982; McKeown, Beck, Omanson, & Perfetti, 1983; McKeown, Beck, Omanson, & Pople, 1985). Graves contended that these studies provided "convincing evidence that teaching vocabulary can increase comprehension of texts containing the words taught" (p. 61). He concluded that these works and related evidence suggested that vocabulary instruction that promotes comprehension should (a) be of considerable duration, (b) be multifaceted, (c) involve multiple encounters with words, (d) include semantic associations among words, (e) require active processing of learners, and (f) promote automaticity in word identification and semantic access.

Stahl & Fairbanks (1986)

Stahl and Fairbanks (1986) conducted a meta-analysis of research on the effects of vocabulary preinstruction on reading comprehension, that is, an examination of the utility of the instrumentalist hypothesis. They categorized studies according to three methodological and two setting factors. Method factors were (a) the degree of definitional and contextual information provided in the interventions according to a 5-point scale; (b) the depth of processing involving associational, comprehension, and generation tasks; and (c) the volume of exposure to taught words. Setting factors were (a) instructional organization (individual vs. group), and (b) instructional time. Dependent measures examined were reading comprehension (global or standardized measures vs. word-specific measures) and word knowledge (global, definitional word-specific, and contextual word-specific). Effect sizes were calculated for no-exposure controls (students who did not experience target words prior to post-tests) and no-instruction controls (students who studied target word definitions independently). For no-exposure controls, there was a mean effect size of .97 (41 effect sizes) for word-specific comprehension measures, indicating a strong effect of vocabulary instruction for passages containing taught words. For no-exposure controls, there was a mean effect size of .30 (15 effect sizes) for global measures of comprehension, indicating a modest effect of vocabulary instruction on general reading comprehension.

Stahl and Fairbanks (1986) noted, however, that not all instructional methods promoted comprehension. For instance, simply providing definitions, exposing students to a word only once or twice, or using drill-and-practice exclusively did not enhance comprehension. Instead, comprehension was promoted when word teaching involved deeper processing, students had multiple exposures to words, and students were provided both definitional and contextual information about words: conclusions generally in support of those drawn by Mezynski (1983) and Graves (1986). Stahl (1999) commented subsequently that the meta-analysis suggested that "vocabulary instruction does directly improve comprehension, thus validating the instrumentalist hypothesis" (p. 7). Stahl (1991) was also quick to point out, however, that there is literature in support of and that which challenges each of the three positions promoted by Anderson and Freebody (1981), making the vocabulary-comprehension relationship a complex phenomenon.

More Recent Reviews

Several more contemporary, broadly based reviews of research (e.g., Baumann, Kame'enui, & Ash, 2003; Beck & McKeown, 1991) on vocabulary learning and instruction support the general premises and conclusions put forth by reviewers such as Mezynski (1983), Graves (1986), and Stahl and Fairbanks (1986). Specifically, the evidence suggests that, in order to influence comprehension, there must be multiple encounters with words and instruction must be rich, involve active processing, and perhaps even extend beyond the classroom (Beck, McKeown, & Kucan, 2002).

Two recent commissioned reports also address research on vocabulary and comprehension: the NRP and RAND reports. The NRP (2000) embedded their review of "Vocabulary Instruction" (Chap. 4, Part 1) within the broader category of "Comprehension." The Panel identified 47 studies that complied with the NRP scientific criteria (p. 4-1). Given the variety of methodologies and variables and the relatively small number of studies in the data base, the Panel did not conduct a formal meta-analysis. The Panel's descriptive analysis, however, led them to assert that "vocabulary instruction leads to gains in comprehension," with the accompanying instructional recommendation that "there is a need for direct instruction in vocabulary items required for a specific text" (p. 4-4). The Panel also noted the importance of addressing vocabulary prior to reading and the effectiveness of active engagement in vocabulary learning tasks.

The RAND (2002) report also addressed vocabulary. Under the topic of what is known about comprehension instruction, the authors included a section titled "The role of vocabulary instruction in enhancing comprehension is complex" (pp. 35-39), elaborating that vocabulary-comprehension associations are confounded by "relationships among vocabulary knowledge, conceptual and cultural knowledge, and instructional opportunities" (p. 35). The authors noted further that the volume of studies on this topic is relatively small and that "some of the strongest demonstrations on the effects of vocabulary instruction in reading comprehension...used rather artificial texts heavily loaded with unfamiliar words. Little, if any, research addresses the question of which conditions—the types of texts, words, readers, and outcomes—can actually improve comprehension" (p. 36).

Summary

Reviewers of instructional research from Mezynski (1983) to the RAND Reading Study Group (2002) offer the consistent conclusion that word meanings can be taught but that it takes special circumstances for vocabulary instruction to influence comprehension. However, in spite of a general convergence of the nature of those circumstances, Beck and McKeown inquired in 1991, "Under what conditions will better comprehension be demonstrated? or even more importantly, In what way can an individual's ability to comprehend be improved by vocabulary instruction?" (p. 808). These questions remain relevant and lead to the conclusion of this review.

CONCLUSION

The research linking vocabulary and comprehension is broad and deep, with the overpowering, if not obvious, conclusion being that there is an incontrovertible link between the two. As has been shown, this conclusion is supported by strong connections between intelligence and vocabulary; numerous correlational and factor analytic studies demonstrating that vocabulary knowledge predicts reading comprehension; and the powerful role vocabulary plays in readability formulae. One must be cautious, however, in interpreting this associational evidence (NRP, 2000; RAND, 2002), and regarding models or hypotheses to account for vocabulary-comprehension associations, the field may not have a much better response today to the following questions Beck et al. (1987) posed 18 years ago:

> Correlational evidence is not causal. The causal links between vocabulary knowledge and reading comprehension are not well understood. For instance, are people good comprehenders because they know a lot of words [i.e., instrumentalist position], or do people know a lot of words because they are good comprehenders [i.e., aptitude position] and in the course of comprehending text, learn a lot of words [i.e., knowledge position], or is there some combination of directionality [i.e., reciprocal position]? (pp. 147-148)

Instructional research confirms that in order to enhance comprehension through vocabulary instruction, instruction must involve not just vocabulary in general but conceptually challenging, text-comprehension-central words (see Nagy, 1988, p. 33). Further, to promote comprehension, vocabulary instruction must go beyond simple definitional information and possess specific pedagogical characteristics. For example, Beck et al. (2002, p. 73) refer to such characteristics as including frequent encounters, rich instruction, and extensions beyond the classroom; Stahl (1999, p. 30) describes effective comprehension-inducing vocabulary instruction as that which provides definitional and contextual information, active processing, and multiple exposures; and Nagy (1988, p. 10) describes such instruction as including the qualities of integrating word meanings with prior knowledge, providing repeated exposures to words, and promoting the meaningful use of instructed words. Although the labels may vary, there is converging evidence that to influence understanding, key vocabulary must be addressed ambitiously, meaningfully, and repeatedly.

It should be acknowledged, however, that the empirical basis for these findings is limited both in volume and ecological validity (NRP, 2000; RAND, 2002), so future research needs to explore this phenomenon in more authentic instructional environments. Further, as noted by the RAND Reading Study Group (2000), the intricacies of vocabulary instruction-comprehension associations demands future research

> that examines how the relationship between vocabulary knowledge and reading comprehension depends on specific conditions, including the type of reader, type of text, proportion of unfamiliar words, their role in the text, and the purpose for reading or the outcome being considered. (p. 88)

It might be argued from the instructional research that the instrumentalist hypothesis is alive and well today, but we know that it's a bit more complex than simply suggesting that teachers teach lots of words to students before they read a selection and then comprehension will improve automatically (Stahl, 1991). We need to attend to the words chosen to teach and design specific types of instruction to promote text understanding. Given our knowledge of the importance of schema activation and development and the use of integrative approaches for vocabulary instruction in promoting comprehension, greater understanding may lie somewhere between the instrumentalist and knowledge positions or perhaps a hybrid of them (Nagy & Herman, 1987). Recently, Nagy (2005) iterated the notion that the instrumentalist, knowledge, aptitude/metalinguistic, and access hypotheses "are not mutually exclusive" (p. 38) but reflect the complexity of vocabulary-comprehension associations. Instead, Nagy argued, that the reciprocal model he describes accounts for this complexity and suggests the need for "comprehensive literacy programs" (p. 40) that provide for long-term, multifaceted vocabulary instruction that includes "teaching individual words; extensive exposure to rich language, both oral and written; and building generative word knowledge" (p. 28) (see also Graves, 2000).

Just as it is argued that greater complexity is needed in intervention research, so, too, it is important to explore complexity further in subsequent model building (Kame'enui et al., 1987; Nagy, 2005; RAND, 2000; Ruddell, 1994; Stahl, 1991). As Stahl (1991, p. 183) noted, subsequent to Anderson and Freebody's (1981) ground-breaking work, "we have resolved some of what might be called 'first generation' questions about vocabulary knowledge and its effects on reading comprehension" (p. 183). However, he argued, that it is important to "move beyond these initial hypotheses" (p. 183) and explore the intricate ways in which word knowledge influences text comprehension.

In 1917, E. L. Thorndike lamented that "little attention has been paid to the dynamics whereby a series of words whose meanings are known singly produces knowledge of the meaning of a sentence or paragraph" (1917/1971, p. 425). Given contributions to our understanding about process and pedagogy by subsequent 20th century researchers and theorists such as Davis, Thurstone, Spearritt, and R. L. Thorndike and more contemporary visionaries such as Anderson and Freebody, Beck and McKeown, Nagy, and Stahl, our knowledge base has expanded considerably. Although we cannot argue today that "little attention has been paid" to vocabulary-comprehension associations, vexing issues remain, and more theoretical and empirical work is required to solve the word meaning-text comprehension conundrum.

REFERENCES

Allington, R. L. (1983). A commentary on Nicholson's critique of Thorndike's: Reading as reasoning—A study of mistakes in paragraph reading. In L. M. Gentile, M. L. Kamil, & J. S. Blanchard (Eds.), *Reading research revisited* (pp. 230-234). Columbus, OH: Merrill.

Anderson, R. C., & Freebody, P. (1981). Vocabulary knowledge. In J. T. Guthrie (Ed.), *Comprehension and teaching: Research reviews* (pp. 77-117). Newark, DE: International Reading Association.

Anderson, R. C., & Freebody, P. (1983). Reading comprehension and the assessment and acquisition of word knowledge. In B. Hutton (Ed.), *Advances in reading/language research: A research annual* (pp. 231-256). Greenwich, CT: JAI Press.

Baumann, J. F., Kame'enui, E. J., & Ash, G. (2003). Research on vocabulary instruction: Voltaire redux. In J. Flood, D. Lapp, J. R. Squire &, J. Jensen, (Eds.), *Handbook of research on teaching the English Language Arts* (2nd ed.) (pp. 752-785). Mahway, NJ: Lawrence Erlbaum.

Beck, I. L., & McKeown, M. G. (1991). Conditions of vocabulary acquisition. In R. Barr, M. Kamil, P. Mosenthal, & P. D. Pearson (Eds.), *Handbook of reading research: Volume III*, pp. 789-814). New York: Longman.

Beck, I. L., McKeown, M. G., & Kucan, L. (2002). *Bring words to life: Robust vocabulary instruction.* New York: Guilford.

Beck, I. L., McKeown, M. G., & Omanson, R. C. (1987). The effects and uses of diverse vocabulary instructional techniques. In M. G. McKeown & M. E. Curtis (Eds.), *The nature of vocabulary acquisition* (pp. 147-163). Hillsdale, NJ: Erlbaum.

Beck, I. L., Perfetti, C. A., & McKeown, M. G. (1982). Effects of long-term vocabulary instruction on lexical access and reading comprehension. *Journal of Educational Psychology, 74,* 506-521.

Blachowicz, C. L. Z. (1983). A commentary on Johnson, Toms-Bronowski, and Buss's critique of F. B. Davis's study: Fundamental factors of comprehension in reading. In L. M. Gentile, M. L. Kamil, & J. S. Blanchard (Eds.), *Reading research revisited* (pp. 259-261). Columbus, OH: Merrill.

Blachowicz, C. L. Z., & Fisher, P. (2000). Vocabulary instruction. In M. L. Kamil, P. B. Mosenthal, P. D. Pearson, & R. Barr (Eds.), *Handbook of reading research: Volume III* (pp. 503-523) Mahwah, NJ: Erlbaum.

Bloom, B. S. (1976). *Human characteristics and school learning.* New York: McGraw-Hill.

Cunningham & Stanovich (2003). Reading matters: How reading engagement influences cognition. In J. Flood, D. Lapp, J. R. Squire &, J. Jensen, (Eds.), *Handbook of research on teaching the English language arts* (2nd ed.) (pp. 666-674). Mahway, NJ: Lawrence Erlbaum.

Davis, F. B. (1944). Fundamental factors in reading comprehension. *Psychometrika, 9,* 185-197.

Davis, F. B. (1968). Research in comprehension in reading. *Reading Research Quarterly, 3,* 499-545.

Davis, F. B. (1972). Psychometric research on comprehension in reading. *Reading Research Quarterly, 7,* 628-678.

Freebody, P., & Anderson, R. C. (1983a). Effects of vocabulary difficulty, text cohesion, and schema availability on reading comprehension. *Reading Research Quarterly, 18,* 277-294.

Freebody, P., & Anderson, R. C. (1983b). Effects on text comprehension of differing proportions and locations of difficult vocabulary. *Journal of Reading Behavior, 15,* 19-39.

Graves, M. F. (1986). Vocabulary learning and instruction. In E. Z. Rothkopf (Ed.), *Review of research in education,* vol. 13 (pp. 49-89). Washington: American Educational Research Association.

Graves, M. F. (2000). A vocabulary program to complement and bolster a middle-grade comprehension program. In B. M. Taylor, M. F. Graves, & P. van den Broek (Eds.), *Reading for meaning: Fostering comprehension in the middle grades* (pp. 116-135). Newark, DE: International Reading Association.

Harris, T. L., & Hodges, R. H. (Eds.). (1995). *The literacy dictionary: The vocabulary of reading and writing.* Newark, DE: International Reading Association.

Hiebert, E. H., & Kamil, M. L. (Eds.) (2005). *Teaching and learning vocabulary: Bringing research to practice.* Mahwah, NJ: Lawrence Erlbaum.

Johnson, D. D., Toms-Bronowski, S., & Buss, R. R. (1983). A critique of F. B. Davis's study: Fundamental factors of comprehension in reading. In L. M. Gentile, M. L. Kamil, & J. S. Blanchard (Eds.), *Reading research revisited* (pp. 247-270). Columbus, OH: Merrill.

Kameenui, E. J., Dixon, R. C., & Carnine, D. W. (1987). Issues in the design of vocabulary instruction. In M. G. McKeown & M. E. Curtis (Eds.), *The nature of vocabulary acquisition* (pp. 129-145). Hillsdale, NJ: Erlbaum.

Klare, G. R. (1974-1975). Assessing readability. *Reading Research Quarterly, 10,* 62-102.

Klare, G. R. (1984). Readability. In P. D. Pearson (Ed.), *Handbook of reading research* (pp. 681-744). New York: Longman.

LaBerge, D., & Samuels, S. J. (1974). Toward a theory of automatic information processing in reading. *Cognitive Psychology, 6,* 293-323.

Marks, C. B., Doctorow, M. J., & Wittrock, M. C. (1974). Word frequency and reading comprehension. *Journal of Educational Research, 67,* 259-262.

McKeown, M. G., Beck, I. L., Omanson, R., & Perfetti, C. A. (1983). The effects of long-term vocabulary instruction on reading comprehension: A replication. *Journal of Reading Behavior, 15,* 3-18.

McKeown, M. G., Beck, I. L., Omanson, R., & Pople, M. T. (1985). Some effects of the nature and frequency of vocabulary instruction on the knowledge and use of words. *Reading Research Quarterly, 20,* 522-535.

McKeown, M. G., & Curtis, M. E. (Eds.). (1987). *The nature of vocabulary acquisition.* Hillsdale, NJ: Lawrence Erlbaum.

Mezynski, K. (1983). Issues concerning the acquisition of knowledge: Effects of vocabulary training on reading comprehension. *Review of Educational Research, 53,* 253-279.

Minor, J. B. (1957). *Intelligence in the U.S.* New York: Springer.

Nagy, W. E. (1988). *Teaching vocabulary to improve reading comprehension.* Newark, DE: International Reading Association.

Nagy, W. E. (2005). Why vocabulary instruction needs to be long-term and comprehensive. In E. H. Hiebert & M. L. Kamil (Eds.), *Teaching and learning vocabulary: Bringing research to practice* (pp. 27-44). Mahwah, NJ: Lawrence Erlbaum.

Nagy, W. E., & Herman, P. A. (1987). Breadth and depth of vocabulary knowledge: Implications for acquisition and instruction. In M. G. McKeown & M. E. Curtis (Eds.), *The nature of vocabulary acquisition* (pp. 19-51). Hillsdale, NJ: Erlbaum.

Nagy, W. E., & Scott, J. A. (2000). Vocabulary processes. In M. L. Kamil, P. B. Mosenthal, P. D. Pearson, & R. Barr (Eds.), *Handbook of reading research: Volume III* (pp. 269-284) Mahwah, NJ: Erlbaum.

National Reading Panel. (2000). *National Reading Panel: Teaching children to read: An evidence-based assessment of the scientific research literature on reading and its implications for reading instruction* (NIH Publication No. 00-4754). Washington, DC: National Institute of Health and National Institute of Child Health and Human Development.

Nicholson, T. (1983). A critique of Edward Thorndike's study: Reading as reasoning—A study of mistakes in paragraph reading. In L. M. Gentile, M. L. Kamil, & J. S. Blanchard (Eds.), *Reading research revisited* (pp. 218-227). Columbus, OH: Merrill.

Nolte, K. J. (1938). Simplification of vocabulary and comprehension in reading. *Elementary English Review, 14,* 119-124, 146.

Otto, W. (1971). Thorndike's *"Reading as reasoning"*: influence and impact. *Reading Research Quarterly, 6,* 435-442.

Petty, W., Herold, C., & Stohl, E. (1967). *The state of the knowledge about the teaching of vocabulary.* Cooperative Research Project No. 3128. Champaign, IL: National Council of Teachers of English. (ERIC Document Reproduction Service No. ED 012 395)

RAND Reading Study Group. (2002). *Toward an R & D program in reading comprehension.* Santa Monica, CA: RAND Corporation.

Rosenshine (1980). Skills hierarchies in reading comprehension. In R. J. Spiro, B. C. Bruce, & W. F. Brewer (Eds.), *Theoretical issues in reading comprehension.* (pp. 535-554). Hillsdale, NJ: Erlbaum.

Ruddell, M. R. (1994). Vocabulary knowledge and comprehension: A comprehension-process view of complex literacy relationships. In R. B. Ruddell, M. R. Ruddell, & H. Singer (Eds.), *Theoretical models and processes of reading* (4th ed.) (pp. 414-447). Newark, De: International Reading Association.

Ryder, R. J., & Hughes, M. (1985). The effect on text comprehension of word frequency. *Journal of Educational Research, 78,* 386-291.

Spearritt, D. (1972). Identification of subskills of reading comprehension by maximum likelihood factor analysis. *Reading Research Quarterly, 8,* 92-111.

Stahl, S. A. (1991). Beyond the instrumentalist hypothesis: Some relationships between word meanings and comprehension. In. P. J. Schwanenflugel (Ed.), *The psychology of word meanings* (pp. 157-186). Hillsdale, NJ: Erlbaum.

Stahl, S. A. (1999). *Vocabulary development.* Cambridge, MA: Brookline Books.

Stahl, S. A. (2003). Vocabulary and readability: How knowing word meanings affects comprehension. *Topics in Language Disorders, 23,* 241-247.

Stahl, S. A., & Fairbanks, M. M. (1986). The effects of vocabulary instruction: A model-based meta-analysis. *Review of Educational Research, 56,* 72-110.

Stanovich, K. E. (1986). Matthew effects in reading: Some consequences of individual differences in the acquisition of literacy. *Reading Research Quarterly, 21,* 360-407.

Stauffer, R. G. (1971). Thorndike's "Reading as reasoning": a perspective. *Reading Research Quarterly, 6,* 443-448.

Thorndike, E. L. (1917a/1971). Reading as reasoning: A study of mistakes in paragraph reading. *Journal of Educational Psychology, 8,* 323-332. (Reprinted in *Reading Research Quarterly,* 1971, 6, 425-434).

Thorndike, E. L. (1917b). The psychology of thinking in the case of reading. *Psychological Review, 24,* 220-234.

Thorndike, E. L. (1917c). The understanding of sentences: A study of errors in reading. *Elementary School Journal, 18,* 98-114.

Thorndike, R. L. (1973). *Reading comprehension education in fifteen countries: An empirical study.* New York: Wiley.

Thorndike, R. L. (1973-1974). "Reading as reasoning." *Reading Research Quarterly, 9,* 135-147.

Thurstone, L. L. (1946). A note on a reanalysis of Davis' reading tests. *Psychometrika, 11,* 185-188.

Tuinman, J. J., & Brady, M. E. (1974). How does vocabulary account for variance on reading comprehension tests: A preliminary instructional analysis. In P. Nack (Ed.), *Twenty-third National Reading Conference Yearbook* (pp. 176-184). Clemson, SC: National Reading Conference.

Wittrock, M. C., Marks, C., & Doctorow, M. (1975). Generative processes in reading comprehension. *Journal of Educational Psychology, 67,* 484-489.

Why Critical Discourse Analysis in Literacy Research

Leslie Burns

University of Kentucky

Ernest Morrell

University of California, Los Angeles

While students in America's schools are acquiring literacy at unprecedented rates and levels, we know that a divide grows between the literacy skills of marginalized students and the increasing literacy demands of a print- and technology-rich society (Alvermann, 2001). Those who are unable to acquire literacies of power are significantly hindered in their ability to enjoy engaged citizenship or professional membership. We also know from social theory (Morrow & Torres, 1995) and educational sociology (Bowles & Gintis, 1976; Oakes, 1985) that the gap between the "haves" and "have-nots" is largely determined by race and class and that schools often reproduce the very inequality they might intend to eradicate (Kozol, 1992; MacLeod, 1987).

Philosophers such as Bakhtin (1986) and Foucault (1972) have argued that meanings are constructed through social languages or discourse. These socially constructed meanings are not neutral and often privilege some while marginalizing or excluding others. Drawing upon the work of Foucault and Bakhtin in the context of the recent literacy crisis in schools, it becomes important for literacy researchers and educators to understand how classroom discourses shape meaning in ways that promote the social reproduction of inequality. Additionally, we need to understand how classroom discourses are situated within larger metainstitutional discourses that shape, limit, or preserve problematic representations of reality. However, it is not merely enough to understand the role of discourse in social reproduction. Literacy researchers are also called to intervene in, challenge, and deconstruct oppressive discursive structures to facilitate more empowering engagements with institutionalized discourses or the creation of alternative ones. We associate this language study and language praxis with the term critical discourse analysis (CDA).

This article considers new directions for CDA in literacy research as well as additional purposes for the methodological and analytic tool in literacy pedagogy, literacy policy, and literacy praxis. We begin by theorizing CDA. We then discuss new possibilities for CDA in literacy research. We consider two examples that range from the analysis of the development of critical language awareness among urban youth to the investigation of standards documents and the archive of texts that construct a discipline such as English education.

The next section examines CDA as a pedagogical tool, looking at its uses in a teacher education program interested in preparing teachers for diverse urban contexts. Section three looks at CDA as a policy tool. We draw upon the example of the construction of guidelines for the preparation of English teachers. The final section considers CDA as a tool for praxis. We examine a summer research program where urban teens employed the tools of CDA to advocate for social justice. We conclude the paper with comments for literacy researchers interested in considering

CDA as a tool to promote student and teacher efficacy and to engage in scholarship in the pursuit of equity and educational justice.

CDA: AN INTRODUCTION

CDA is one variant of a number of practices that fall under the rubric of "discourse analysis." These variations overlap in terms of method and methodology and are used across disciplinary boundaries. Given their appearance in a number of contexts, along with the multiplicity of ways in which the term *discourse* can be used, we begin by briefly reviewing what we mean by *critical* "discourse" analysis. We begin with the latter term.

Meanings for discourse are diverse and contested. In her exploration of discourse as a concept in academic research, Mills (1997) reviewed the ways in which it has been defined across competing theories. She points out its broadest definition as simply "verbal communication" (p. 2). Additionally, discourse has been defined as conversational talk, formal speech or writing on a particular subject, or a linguistic unit greater than one sentence, reflecting the origins of the word as a linguistic concept. Ultimately, our conception of the term is most closely aligned with Fairclough (1992a) who commented:

> Discourse constitutes the social. Three dimensions of the social are distinguished--knowledge, social relations, and social identity--and these correspond respectively to three major functions of language...Discourse is shaped by relations of power and invested with ideologies. (p. 8)

The other term involved with CDA, *critical*, is contingent on the view of discourse above as it relates to ideology. CDA construes discourses as ideological because they are used to represent the systems of thought, manifested in language that groups and individuals use to identify themselves, filter information, and interpret meaning. As ideological systems, discourses tend to reproduce themselves along with the conditions necessary to sustain them. Further, CDA does not treat ideology as either "good" or "bad"; rather, it recognizes that ideology is not intended to be opposed to some concept of "the truth" that would otherwise render the term biased. At the same time, CDA asserts that an ideology *is* positive or negative depending on whether it helps to achieve some desirable end in a desirable way. This is a matter of perspective that highlights a mostly "inescapable Us/Them dichotomy" in CDA and an underlying belief that, from a critical perspective, some ideologies are "better" than others when the social project involves an attempt to achieve equity (van Dijk, 2004). The key is to maintain a stance wherein the researcher recognizes that ideologies and discourses interact in unpredictable ways and that even "positive" ideologies may have negative or unanticipated effects.

In CDA, the term critical also distinguishes this method from others because of its interest in change and intervention. Although it is true that all forms of discourse analysis pay attention to the social implications of the texts they study (Jaworski & Coupland, 1999), not all forms of analysis are focused on affecting practice. As such, it is significant that CDA places the term critical at the forefront. Whereas other types of discourse analysis are primarily designed to *describe* discourse, CDA seeks to understand and change discourse processes in order achieve equitable social relations.

CDA as Method

As Fairclough described it (1992b, 1995, 2003; Chouliaraki & Fairclough, 1999), CDA attempts to bridge the divide between direct and indirect forms of discourse analysis. By direct forms of analysis, we mean those forms that deal directly with close linguistic analysis, while by indirect we mean those forms that deal with the contextual aspects of discourse. The method of CDA involves a triad structure to guide research. It assumes that discourse is both constrained and enabled by social structures and by culture and proceeds by examining relationships between (a) texts as speech acts (texts as ideological recordings of communication events), (b) discursive practices around a text (processes of producing, writing, speaking, reading, and interacting), and (c) the sociocultural context in which these practices occur and within which resulting texts circulate and regulate (contexts as coming with their sets of rights and obligations that affect what is likely to be said or not said (Fairclough, 1995).

CDA views texts as speech acts; that is, they affect how language gets used and how meaning gets made. Texts are further viewed as both products of discourse communities and as producers of discourse communities, operating dialectically to aid in the identification and representation of the group. Texts get used to talk desired realities into being, and in doing so, they develop and set forth the terms and norms for who gets to talk, what they may say, how they may say it, what they should value, how they may think, and how they may behave. Given the powerful effects that a text can have in shaping subjectivities, it becomes important to understand how texts reify ideological discursive positions and tools (Fairclough, 1989).

The work of CDA proceeds from the identification of a text as part of a social event or a chain of events that occur in a network of social practices. The text is then articulated with other texts that may come before or after it in a discursive chain in order to help establish the context of the analysis. After identifying the genre or mix of genres that constitute the text, the analyst might next characterize the text's orientation to difference and also attempt to determine the level of intertextuality in the text--that is, whether and how other relevant texts and references are included or excluded by the text being studied.

Having described the context, genres, orientations to difference, and levels of intertextuality, the analyst might identify the assumptions at play in a text that have implications for the representation of reality, truth, and value--a focus on the ideological orientations of a text. In addition to these moves, a critical discourse analyst might describe the semantic, grammatical, and lexical relations of a text--that is, how the actual construction of words, clauses, and sentences is accomplished. These activities may be accompanied by efforts to determine the grammatical mood, the kinds of statements a text makes, and the purposes of those statements in the context of the social event. Next, the analyst might identify the discourses a text draws on and discuss the features that characterize those discourses and represent social events in particular ways. Finally, a critical discourse analyst might identify and evaluate the styles involved with the construction of a text, truth claims and their modalities, and values that a text conveys.

The process described above is not intended to totalize the practices of CDA, and the sequential organization of our overview is artificial; this is not intended as a rigid procedure. Depending on the level of analysis and point of entry into a text, a critical discourse analysis may or may not involve detailed linguistic analysis. Many discourse analysts focus on the use of social theory to construct explanatory critiques of texts (Bhaskar, 1986, cited in Chouliaraki & Fairclough, 1999) rather than linguistic descriptions of them. Both types of analysis are useful (and any given analysis is likely to include a mixture of the two), but in these latter cases, the focus of analysis will be on the identification of ideological positions, discourses and styles, and the value systems and power relations set up within a text and the social event it accompanies.

NEW DIRECTIONS FOR CDA IN LITERACY RESEARCH

The Discourse of Standardization

Much CDA in literacy research has focused on the level of classroom interactions. The first example of new directions in CDA research is drawn from the recent work of Burns (2005) on the analysis of *Guidelines for the Preparation of Teachers of the English Language Arts*, created by the National Council of Teachers of English (NCTE, 1996). At a macrolevel of analysis, Burns' CDA of the NCTE *Guidelines* began with a historical analysis of the English teaching profession. This level of analysis proceeded via the examination of archival documents and institutional histories; for example, Burns began with a review of NCTE histories written by Hook (1979) and Applebee (1974) along with a comprehensive review of texts associated with language arts curriculum from the late 1800's to the present. The development of such an archive enabled Burns to establish an argument regarding the episteme of English education, that is, "the sets of discursive structures as a whole within which [the profession] thinks" (Foucault, 1972). These historically situated discursive structures provided the ideas, concepts, and language used by English teachers to frame talk about what they do and believe and effectively provided a "common sense" network of ideologies that insiders used to make sense of their practices. Because this archive helped to establish the professional episteme, it also helped establish the knowledge context or "regime of truth" in which the creation of NCTE's guidelines occurred (Foucault, 1979, p. 46).

The epistemic historical analysis that Burns conducted around NCTE *Guidelines* provided a number of insights. First, elements of the archive established the privileged position of literature instruction in language arts curriculum, a position it has held from the beginning of the subject in US schools. This finding turned out to be crucial for the rest of the study by providing strong evidence that NCTE's discussions of literacy were dominated by a conception of functional literacy (the decoding and encoding of printed texts) that is associated with a focus on printed literary texts such as novels and short stories. In addition, the finding of a literary focus connected the development of English curriculum policy to a number of historical ideological positions, such as the treatment of canonical literature as a proxy for religious practice in public schools and as an instrument of social indoctrination and the "Americanization" of minority populations at the turn of the 20th century in the United States (Bailey, 1991; Mathieson, 1975; Protherough & Atkinson, 1991).

At the level of sociocultural context, Burns' study revealed a different kind of insight. By examining the various genres used in the composition of the *Guidelines*, as well as by examining the institutional structures within which the *Guidelines* were drafted, the analysis showed some of the ways in which social practices shaped the eventual play of meanings in the published text. For example, the acknowledgements and introduction of the NCTE *Guidelines* indicate an emphasis on professional experience and also on consensus in their discussions of authorship and intention. A reliance on experience rather than expertise in the development of the *Guidelines* suggested a treatment of knowledge that relied more on practice and tradition than on research and theoretical bases, while an emphasis on consensus suggested the submersion of alternative conceptions, dissent, or marginal points of view. Finally, an investigation of the genres used to create the *Guidelines* showed that the form of the text itself, a formal policy document, militated against the rationalization and justification of its own contents, thereby weakening its own arguments regarding disciplinary stability and rigor.

At the level of textual analysis, Burns' analysis produced findings that demonstrated particular ways in which the genres of the text, the historical roots of its topics, and the institutional structuring of its production manifested in ways that were not predictable or intentional. For example, even though the *Guidelines* articulated progressive visions of new knowledge in the language arts around diversity and technology, NCTE's focus on literature as the center of language arts curricula tended to make new knowledge marginal and supplemental, when such knowledge might otherwise have been treated as "new." In addition, close textual analyses helped to demonstrate how, although NCTE attempted to account for new knowledge, its "outsider" approach to discourses of technology led to a reproduction of the status quo and a loss of relevance for current curricula in the literate lives of students (Lankshear & Knobel, 2003). Finally, the textual analysis demonstrated convincingly how discourses of accountability had colonized NCTE's *Guidelines* and led the authors to frame their policies as resistant to such accountability. While on one level this frame of resistance or accommodation could be seen as desirable, the analysis indicated that such an accommodation to accountability actually led to a conservative position that served the interests of accountability while impeding the ability of the profession to account for knowledge and change.

Becoming Critical Researchers

Although most research in CDA is intended to show how prevalent discursive formations alienate and marginalize members of peripheral populations, we are arguing for another consideration of critical discourse analysis as the analysis of *critical discourse*--a way of assessing how marginalized populations have appropriated a language of empowerment. Morrell (2004) took as his data source a six-year summer program where urban teens were apprenticed as critical researchers of urban and educational inequality. The seminar brought students, teachers, and parents from urban communities throughout Los Angeles to a local university to design and carry out critical research projects on issues of immediate concern to these communities. Students were chosen from the most underperforming schools in the city. They were selected only for interest in the program, providing students with a wide range of life and educational experiences.

The students worked in groups of four or five on research teams led by teachers from the local schools. Throughout the five week seminar the students read seminal works in the sociology of education and critical methods of educational research; they developed research questions, read relevant literature, collected and analyzed data, and created research reports; and they presented these reports to university faculty, policymakers, and on occasion, to regional and national conferences of educational researchers and practitioners. Students also wrote individual papers where they contemplated the practical applications of their research to the issues in their own communities.

Morrell (2004) was interested in how students were appropriating the language and tools of critical research and how this appropriation translated into the acquisition of academic literacies. Additionally, Morrell sought to understand the relationship between changing participation in the critical research-focused community of practice and the development of empowered identities of these teens. As part of the data collection enterprise, he recorded observational notes and videotaped seminar sessions and students' experiences in the field. He also collected individual journal assignments, individual essays, and group research projects. Finally, Morrell and his colleagues invited distinguished education and social science faculty members to sit on the panel and to evaluate the quality of the students' papers and presentations.

Morrell interviewed faculty to get a sense of whether the students successfully appropriated the dominant discourses of social science research. The faculty responded overwhelmingly in the affirmative. He next analyzed student generated texts and classroom conversations to determine the change over time in reference to issues of social justice, in use of the language of social science research, in reference to themselves and their peers as critical researchers, and in their implied or expressed sense of agency. Specifically, he coded organizationally across activity settings, chronologically across time periods, and analytically across literacy events to understand how students incorporated the language of social theory and sociology into their discussions of educational inequality and into their research design, data collection, and data analysis. Additionally, Morrell analyzed these conversations and texts for references to critical research and the process of becoming a critical researcher, in seeking to understand the relationship between the mastery of empowered academic discourses and the identity development of these students as researchers and intellectuals.

Morrell also coded student work for any and all discussions of language, text, discourse, and power. He analyzed student texts and conversations primarily for *critical language awareness* (Fairclough, 1995), that is, where students showed an understanding of the uses of language and power. He looked for student explanations of ideology or language hegemony, where students revealed an understanding of how discourse shapes meaning, how they are shaped by discourses, and how they see themselves as shapers of discourse. Morrell (2004) was able to demonstrate a positive relationship between apprenticeship as critical researchers, the mastery of dominant discourses, and the development of a counterdiscourse of urban youth as intellectuals and agents of social change.

CDA AS A PEDAGOGICAL TOOL

In addition to functioning as a useful research theory and method, CDA has a number of pedagogical implications. Noting changes in economic structures and the expansion and monopolization of communications media, in addition to changes in power relations, Fairclough (1995) pointed out that schools are "heavily involved in these general developments affecting language in its relation to power" (p. 220), and argued that this "problematic of language and power" is "fundamentally a question of democracy" (p. 221). He argued that if individuals are to deal productively as citizens with the challenges of the social world, they need to be educated toward the development of a critical language awareness that "develops their capacities for language critique, including their capacities for reflexive analysis of the educational process itself" as well as analysis of the larger social, cultural, and linguistic contexts in which education occurs (p. 221). Burns's (unpublished) recent work on multiculturalist discourses in an English education classroom illustrated some of the ways in which CDA might become a tool both for teachers to use in the assessment of their students' talk and also for students to use in reflecting on their own education experiences as they learn to teach within school contexts.

Critical language awareness as a pedagogical tool may perhaps be most powerful when it is used as a form of metadiscourse in classroom discussions. By metadiscourse, here, we mean taking a step back from the discussion of a given topic to talk about the ways in which group members are using language to make meaning that embodies assumptions and beliefs or ideological positions. In the nearly all White class of preservice teachers Burns taught and studied, for example, ideological and culturally situated perspectives on race and ethnicity had a marked impact on the ways the class made sense of multiculturalist research, diversity in classrooms, and the nature of literacy and linguistic diversity. For example, many White students professed a value for diversity but did not view themselves as part of that diversity and therefore spoke as "outsiders" to that topic. Alternatively, some students used pluralist conceptions of multiculturalism to argue that while "awareness" of diversity was important, the only necessary accommodation in classrooms was for teachers to be inclusive of their students during activities. Others who were less comfortable with discussions of race frequently shifted the conversation by using the term "American" as a proxy code for "White" or "English speaking," while others argued that assigning labels such as White or Black created difference where there should not be any. Each of these positions informed students' understandings and uptake of course material and led to significant levels of conflict and variation within the class both among students and between Burns (as the course instructor) and his students.

Via the use of CDA, Burns was able to use video-recordings of this classroom discussion to revisit what had happened and begin to unravel the complex array of discourses that were at play during this talk about race and multiculturalism in the teaching of English. By examining the students' backgrounds, the content of the course, the structure and physical arrangement for the discussion, and his own pedagogical moves during the class, Burns was able to begin making more sense of his students' talk than he could have in the process of more informal reflections. CDA offered the lenses and procedures Burns needed to begin recognizing patterns and variations across student responses and to recognize the needs of individual students for developing conceptual understandings of diversity and multiculturalism that could be useful to them in their later work as classroom teachers. Furthermore, the analysis led him to critique his own positions and practices as an English educator and helped him to understand the ways in which his own position reflected various power relations between himself, his students, and the institutional program that framed their interactions. CDA highlighted the ways in which Burns's own positions and roles shaped what he said in the context of the class discussion and underscored the discursive structures that affected what his students might have said in an institutionalized program that valued multiculturalism highly.

In addition to highlighting the ways in which personal identities and institutional positions affected the ways in which they talked about race and multiculturalism, Burns's analysis of this classroom interaction led his students to begin an ongoing discussion about the structure and content of their university program. Their attention to the sociocultural context of their discourse drew attention to the fact that their curriculum did not provide important opportunities to learn about linguistics, history, cultural theory, and English as an academic discipline that would otherwise have shaped their talk and understanding differently. They discovered a number of ways in which knowledge necessary for the teaching of English had been "occulted" due to the way their curriculum had been designed. This discovery led them to become much more aware of the ways in which school curricula were not neutral. As Fairclough (1995) asserted:

> Critical language study and critical language awareness can…be reflexively applied within educational organizations to the practices of such organizations. … Accordingly, such reflexive work could involve learners and teachers in analysis of and possible change in their own practices, as speakers and listeners (and viewers), writers and readers. (p. 227)

While Burns notes that his own study described above does not constitute a pedagogical exercise in critical language awareness per se, it does highlight some of the practices that such awareness work might entail, and it points to the value of such work in enriching learners' and teachers' understanding of education as critical work. The absence of critical language awareness in teacher education programs has allowed critiques of critical pedagogy in schools that show how such projects can simply replace one oppressive system with another, and the teaching of such awareness could help to mitigate this problem and stress what Fairclough notes as:

> The difficulty in contemporary society in being entirely confident about the target, in the sense of what needs changing, and what it needs changing to. People on the ground must make up their minds about these complex issues, as they will whether critical language work is in progress or not. (1995, p. 231)

CDA AS A POLICY TOOL

In addition to its functions as a tool for research and pedagogy, CDA holds promise as a policy tool. A major implication of Burns's (2004) work analyzing teacher preparation guidelines is that, complementary to its function as a research tool, CDA could be used *in the process* of text construction to address the complexities inherent in the production of policy texts, which are intended to shape, direct, sustain, and reproduce educational practice. In this context, CDA becomes a tool for aligning textual components, addressing problems of intertextual representation, and mitigating or resolving the problems and limitations of various policy genres. The reflexive role of CDA allows it to play a powerful role in the pragmatics of educational policy and curriculum design.

One of Fairclough's (1989, 1995) primary goals in the use of CDA was the creation of spaces that allow for talk across difference. Particularly in policy discussions, where consensus models frequently interrupt the articulation of differences, CDA can help to ensure that discourse proceeds along lines that lead to *more* if not *total* critical discourse. As described by Habermas (1973), a context of absolute critical discourse is one in which all parties and interests are represented equally and free of constraining relations of power. According to Habermas, this totally inclusive critical discourse is impossible to achieve; however, a context of critical discourse is still a worthy goal and one worth striving for. CDA provides a set of tools and dispositions that enable social groups involved in conversations across difference to *better* and more completely involve concerned parties and to place them on more equal footing toward the achievement of equitable outcomes.

In addition to the potential for CDA to function as an inclusionary device for policy conversations, it also has the capacity to allow for the pragmatic design and administration of curricula and policy. As Cherryholmes (1988, 1999) has noted, *all* curricula are temporal, contingent, flawed, and historical; as such, they are limited in their sustainability--what was effective and desirable fifty years ago (or twenty, or ten, or even five) is unlikely to be effective and desirable now. By using critical discourse analysis as a means of periodically revisiting curricula and policy, it becomes possible to reevaluate their effectiveness and make judgments about what needs changing, how it might be changed, and what the consequences of change might be. As Fairclough (2003) states, any change in policy that might result in social transformation has winners and losers. As educators making curricular decisions that affect millions of people's access to literacy and opportunity, CDA should be indispensable. Particularly when it is used in combination with resources from the various social sciences, CDA can be a powerful instrument for social equity from *within* the construction of education policies, not just a powerful instrument for reaction *to* them.

CDA AS PRAXIS

To consider CDA as a tool for praxis, we draw upon Gee's (1999) ideas for making students social theorists of social languages and Freire's (1970) problem-posing dialogic pedagogy based on a project of collaborative inquiry rooted in a praxis of social change. Toward these ends we examine

Morrell's (2004) summer seminar project, which set out to develop urban teens' ability to use CDA to make sense of the dominant institutions that circumscribe their existence. This sense of "critical" in CDA is resonant with the streams of critical theory that are concerned with power and the locus of revolutionary thought and action. Critical pedagogues have envisioned a practice where students play an active role in the construction (and reconstruction) of meaning. Kincheloe and McLaren (1998) and Morrell (2004) have theorized critical qualitative research as involving marginalized populations as collaborators in research, not merely as objects of research.

If CDA is to follow in this tradition, and if it is to become an authentic tool for social change, then it cannot exist merely as a tool for sanctioned researchers to make sense of the alienating potential of dominant language. Rather, CDA must be shared with marginalized populations and used with them and by them in the struggle for social justice and empowering identity development. In this final section we will return to the research seminar to understand the practice and outcomes associated with apprenticing urban teens as critical discourse analysts.

During the summer seminar of 2000, one student group investigated urban youth access to the media and the media's portrayal of urban youth. Toward these ends, the teen researchers interviewed media representatives, but they also performed a content analysis of all of the major daily newspapers published during the week of the Democratic National Convention, paying close attention to the context of the descriptions of urban youth as well as the adjectives and nouns that were associated with urban youth, other young people involved in the official convention, and protests of the convention. The results of the content analysis were powerful, if not surprising.

The research activity itself was an important and powerful one for these teens in that it provided them with language and tools to change their own relationship to the media that played such an important role in their lives. The activity became social praxis when the student researchers used their research as a pedagogical and advocacy tool. They presented their research to teachers, university faculty, and elected officials; they wrote editorials in their school newspapers; and they developed curricular materials for incoming freshmen to make them more critical and engaged consumers of media discourses. In this praxis, the teens developed a language to critique media discourses but they also employed print and electronic media to promote viable counternarratives.

CONCLUSION

Critical Discourse Analysis is an analytic tool that has much to offer for literacy research and education. While CDA is being applied with increasing frequency in literacy studies, we argue that we have only scratched the surface in that regard. We hope that we have made the argument for more studies of critical language awareness among marginalized school populations, as well as studies of literacy education and literacy research as discourses in and of themselves. Additionally, we would like to push the field by advocating for the use of CDA as a tool for literacy pedagogy, literacy policy, and literacy praxis. We argue that CDA as a tool offers tremendous potential for training teachers, for affecting policy conversations, and for transforming classroom instruction to facilitate the literacy empowerment of our most marginalized populations. These uses represent praxis in its truest sense: using a theoretical and conceptual tool to act more powerfully upon the world in ways that increase student and teacher efficacy and humanize our curricula and our scholarship.

REFERENCES

Alvermann, D. (2001). *Effective literacy instruction for adolescents.* Executive summary and paper commissioned by the National Reading Conference. Chicago: National Reading Conference.

Applebee, A. (1974). *Tradition and reform in the teaching of English: A history.* Urbana, IL: National Council of Teachers of English.

Bailey, R. (1991). *Images of English: A cultural history of the language.* Ann Arbor, MI: University of Michigan Press.

Bakhtin, M.M. (1986). *Speech genres and other late essays* (Trans. Vern McGee), C. Emerson & M. Holquist (Eds.), Austin, TX: University of Texas.

Bowles, S., & Gintis, H. (1976). *Schooling in capitalist America: Educational reform and the contradictions of economic life.* New York: Basic Books.

Bhaskar, R. (1986). *Scientific realism and human emancipation.* London: Verso.

Burns, L. *Pieces of where they come from: Multiculturalist discourses in learning to teach.* Unpublished manuscript.

Burns, L. (2005). *Moving targets: A critical discourse analysis of literacy, ideology, and standards in English language arts teacher preparation guidelines.* Unpublished doctoral dissertation. Michigan State University, East Lansing.

Cherryholmes, C. (1988). *Power and criticism: Poststructural investigations in education.* New York: Teachers College Press.

Cherryholmes, C. (1999). *Reading pragmatism.* New York: Teachers College Press.

Chouliaraki, L., & Fairclough, N. (1999). *Discourse in late modernity: Rethinking critical discourse analysis.* Edinburgh: Edinburgh University Press.

Fairclough, N. (1989). *Language and power.* London: Longman.

Fairclough, N. (1992a). *Critical language awareness.* London: Longman

Fairclough, N. (1992b). *Discourse and social change.* Cambridge: Polity Press.

Fairclough, N. (1995). *Critical discourse analysis: The critical study of language.* London: Longman.

Fairclough, N. (2003). *Analysing discourse: Text analysis for social research.* London: Routledge

Foucault, M. (1972). *The archaeology of knowledge.* New York: Pantheon.

Foucault, M. (1979). *Discipline and punish: The birth of the prison.* New York: Vintage Books.

Freire, P. (1970). *Pedagogy of the oppressed.* New York: Continuum.

Gee, J. (1999). Learning language as a matter of learning social languages within discourses. Paper presented to the annual meeting of the American Educational Research Association, Montreal, Canada.

Hook, J.N. (1979). *A long way together: A personal view of NCTE's first sixty-seven years.* Urbana, IL: National Council of Teachers of English.

Jaworski, A., & Coupland, N. (Eds.) (1999). *The discourse reader.* New York: Routledge.

Kincheloe, J., & McLaren, P. (1998). Rethinking critical qualitative research. In N. Denzin & Y. Lincoln (Eds.). *Handbook of qualitative research: Strategies of qualitative inquiry* (pp. 260 – 299). Thousand Oaks, CA: Sage.

Kozol, J. (1992). *Savage inequalities: Children in America's schools.* New York: Perennial.

MacLeod, J. (1987). *Ain't no makin' it: Aspirations and attainment in a low-income neighborhood.* Boulder, CO: Westview.

Lankshear, C., & Knobel, M. (2003). *New literacies: Changing knowledge and classroom learning.* Philadelphia: Open University Press.

Mathieson, M. (1975). *The preachers of culture: A study of English and its teachers.* Totowa, N.J.: Rowman and Littlefield.

Mills, S. (1997). *Discourse: The new critical idiom.* London: Routledge.

Morrell, E. (2004). *Becoming critical researchers: Literacy and empowerment for urban youth.* New York: Peter Lang.

Morrow, R., & Torres, C. (1995). *Social theory and education: A critique of theories of social and cultural reproduction.* Albany, NY: SUNY Press.

National Council of Teachers of English. (1996) *Guidelines for the preparation of teachers of English language arts.* Urbana, IL: NCTE.

Oakes, J. (1985). *Keeping track: How schools structure inequality.* New Haven: Yale.

Protherough, R., & Atkinson, J. (1991). *The making of English teachers.* Philadelphia: Open University Press.

van Dijk, T. (2003). *Ideology and discourse: A multidisciplinary introduction.* Internet Course for the Oberta de Catalunya (UOC). Retrieved June 15, 2005, from http://www.discourse-in-society.org/ideo-dis2.htm.

Wixon, K., Dutro, E., & Athan, R. (2004). The challenge of developing content standards. *Review of Research in Education, 27,* 69-107.

Investigating Digital Curricular Literacies: Resolving Dilemmas of Researching Multimodal Technologically Mediated Literacy Practices

Geraldine Castleton
University College, Worcester UK

Claire Wyatt-Smith
Griffith University, Australia

Three propositions introduce this paper: first, that the literate capabilities of students as they graduate or simply leave school are increasingly important to the cultural, social, and economic development of contemporary information-economy nations; second, that the world today is a complex communication environment, reflecting the rapidly changing, cross-modal demands of activities in a wide range of sites, including those related to work, leisure, and the home; and third, despite the importance attributed to literacy, in general, and to integrating information communication technologies into curriculum, in particular, there is a paucity of research that brings together literacy, curriculum, and information communication technologies. These three foci have been central to our work with a longitudinal study (2003-2007), funded by the Australian Research Council (with Wyatt-Smith as Chief Investigator and Castleton as Partner Investigator), that has concentrated on what we call students' *digital curricular literacies* (DCL). This term draws together the concept of curricular literacies that highlights the discipline-specific literacy demands of different curriculum areas (Wyatt-Smith & Cumming, 2003) with new ways of being literate, that is comprehending, interacting with, and constructing meaningful hypermedia and multimedia texts in dynamic, non-linear, digital environments. The ongoing longitudinal study is an investigation of the products and processes associated with *how* and *how well* students engage with existing knowledge and create new knowledge in online environments. In this paper, following a brief overview of the goals of the longitudinal study, we explore some of the interesting conceptual and methodological issues we have encountered in capturing multimodal data, including the talk students engage in as they work online. Of special interest to the project and to this paper is how the acts of investigating "the new literacies" (Leu, Kinzer, Coiro, & Cammack, 2004) of the classroom call for new research literacies where information communication technologies afford research insights not otherwise available.

BACKGROUND: OVERVIEW OF LONGITUDINAL STUDY

The large-scale study against which this discussion is set involves 16 schools, with two classes and approximately 50 students from each school. The student population in Australia is characterized by diversity and, accordingly, the school sites were selected to ensure inclusion of a range of demographic variables, including cultural and linguistic backgrounds and ethnicity. The study aims to explore the nature of students' digital curricular literacies and to identify the features of classrooms and schools that are associated with enhancing students' literacy and learning capabilities as they work in online curricular environments.

In its initial stage, the study investigated how and how well students in the first and third year of high school (aged approximately 13 and 15 respectively) used the Internet to research information, including locating, reading, comprehending, and evaluating information about a given environmental problem. Also central was how and how well the students composed an online text to convey relevant information about the problem and to present a feasible solution to a nominated audience. Accordingly, in the first year of the study, the research team of university researchers and teachers developed a cross-curricular web-based research activity. Its curricular or content focus was the impact of plastic bags on the environment and strategies/solutions to reduce that impact, chosen because of its links to contemporary topics of study in a range of curricular domains in high schools. The activity involved students in (a) locating and evaluating "suitability for purpose" of specific information from web-based resources identified in the task, (b) independently researching for additional online information, and (c) creating a multimodal digital text for a specific audience to convey knowledge about the problem and the proposed solution(s).

Taking a situated perspective to the study of online curricular environments, the study is generating a broad-gauged database on an increasingly important aspect of high school students' literacy and learning capabilities against which practice, theory, and policy can be assessed. To establish the parameters for the database, three main types of data are being collected:

1. Process data: screen tracking of students' online activity as they work on a research task searching for information, synthesizing that information, and finally creating a multimodal digital text to demonstrate their learning on the topic;

2. Product data: the students' completed multimodal digital texts; and

3. Survey data: questionnaires filled out by the students, their parents, and their teachers to provide background information on school policies and practices about information communication technologies (ICT) and students' out-of-school ICT use.

All students participating in the study have been providing and continue to provide product and survey data with a sample of students (approximately eight per class) also providing process data. In addition, interaction data in the form of audio-recordings from a small sub-sample of students working in pairs are being gathered to investigate how these students work collaboratively in undertaking the online research task.

The focus of this paper is on some of the conceptual and methodological issues that we have encountered to date in our efforts to record, code, and analyze students' process data, that is, the real-time video record of their screen activity as they work online, as well as the new research opportunities afforded by the technology applied in the project.

EXAMINING STUDENTS' LITERACIES:
EXPLORING AVAILABLE CONCEPTUAL FRAMEWORKS

The project began with frameworks relating to literacy, multimodal environments, and curriculum, reflecting our focus on students' demonstrated literacies in engaging with curricular knowledges online. In keeping with the main concerns of this paper, we will not extend our discussion to curriculum frameworks here. The published research shows that there is considerable interest in identifying and mapping different aspects of literate practice (Chandler-Olcott & Mahar, 2003; Cope & Kalantzis, 2000; Green, 1988, 1999; Hasan, 1996; Luke, Freebody, & Land, 2000 (following Freebody & Luke, 1990); Smolin & Lawless, 2003; Unsworth, 2002). Although there are points of difference in these writings, of more immediate interest is the shared recognition of how learners need to develop a range of literate capabilities that allow them to engage effectively within educational, community, and networked settings.

Beyond this, several writers including Lankshear and Knobel (2003) and Leu (2000) have pointed to the limited research about new literacies of the Internet and other information communication technologies (ICTs). Leu and colleagues (2004) made the strong statement that "what we know about new literacies from the traditional research literature must recognize that we actually know very little" (p. 1571), and Lankshear and Knobel argued that literacy theorists have, to date, failed to address effectively the implications of new literacies that are emerging from technological, economic, and other changes including globalization.

Although the call for research on new literacies is pressing, what is also clear is how, at present, "we lack a precise definition of what new literacies are" (Leu et al., p. 1571). In the main, literacy frameworks, including those influential in current Australian curriculum documents and standardized testing programs, have tended to extrapolate from a conventional print base. Insofar as existing theoretical frameworks have been originally conceptualized in relation to reading and print, they do not automatically have relevance to the new and emerging literacies of the Internet and other information communication technologies. Clearly, the longitudinal study, with its systematic investigation of actual practice, has a role to play in addressing this recognized need for theory development in relation to multimodal technologically-mediated literacy practices.

Existing Frameworks of Literacy Practices

To illustrate the point, it is useful to consider the shifts that have occurred in the framing of the study. Initially, the project worked with the conceptual framework devised by Freebody and Luke (1990; Luke & Freebody, 1999) that identified how the desired repertoire of practice and capabilities can be thought of as four interrelated "roles": (a) *Code Breaker*: the practices required to "crack" the codes and systems of written and spoken language and visual images; (b) *Meaning Maker*: the practices required to build and construct cultural meanings from texts; (c) *Text User*: the practices required to use texts effectively in everyday situations; and (d) *Text Analyst*: the practices required to analyze, critique, and evaluate texts in order to understand the values promoted by the text. In its initial formulation, the four roles were designed to apply to reading, and more specifically, reading of print, with the expanded application to literate capabilities being a more recent iteration. By design, the roles serve to identify the repertoire of capabilities or resources that a reader needs to access and use to make meaning of print material, extending to critical engagement. Although the framework has been taken up in some Australian states to inform literacy pedagogy, currently there are no large-scale, longitudinal studies showing the usefulness of this framework for analyzing the processes on which students rely as they engage with multimodal online literacies in schooling. For this reason, the framework was taken to provide a useful starting point for examining the product data, that is, in investigating student-generated multimodal texts, once stabilized as final text.

Specifically, the four roles model allowed us to take account of the overall text effectiveness for purpose as well as the range of textual-linguistic and visual features serving that purpose (Jewitt, 2003; Kress, Jewitt, Ogborn, & Tsatsarelis, 2001). What it did not permit was close scrutiny of the processes in which students engaged as they interacted with online resources, including those of the Internet, and with one another in the classroom environment.

Green's 3D model (1988, 1999) shared with the four roles model the notion of literacy as an ensemble of social practices and included three dimensions: operational, cultural, and critical, taken to overlap, intersect, and be interdependent. For the longitudinal study, this framework was also informative insofar as it had been influenced in its development by Green's (1988) research into the relationships between literacy and subject or content area learning and was subsequently developed in response to the increasing "technologization" of literacy (see Bigum & Green, 1993).

Conceptualizations of Literacies in Online Environments

Although the four resources model and the 3D model provided working concepts for researching the capabilities that young people need to bring to bear on reading, comprehending, and writing online, we identified that they were not, of themselves, sufficient for analyzing the literate capabilities students relied on to progress through an online curricular task, negotiating and creating multimodal forms. Of more direct relevance were three multiliteracies concepts of the New London Group (NLG) (1996) and the developing conception of new literacies that Leu and colleagues (2004) have begun to frame. In relation to the work of the New London Group, our study drew on the concepts of (a) design and its related concern with multimodality, (b) hybridity, and (c) intertextuality, with the first of these giving emphasis to how any semiotic activity uses "Available Designs," including linguistic, visual, audio, gestural, spatial, and multimodal resources for meaning making, to create "The Redesigned," or a new set of meanings. The NLG (1996) members suggested that this Designing process

> transforms knowledge by producing new constructions and representations of reality. Through their coengagement in Designing, people transform their relations with each other, and so transform themselves.... Transformation is always a new use of old materials, a rearticulation and recombination of the given resources of Available Designs. (p. 76)

From this perspective, text construction or composing of any kind can be seen to be what Chandler-Olcott and Mahar (2003) refer to as a "blend" of an individual creative process and a social process.

The two other concepts, hybridity and intertextuality, are related to these processes, with hybridity defined as the articulation in new ways of "established practices and conventions" and intertextuality being "the potentially complex ways in which meanings ... are constructed through relationships to other texts, discourses, genres, and modes of meaning" (NLG, 1996, p. 82). With regard to the Internet, Zembykas and Vsasidas (2005) argued that its hypertext/hypermedia nature "allows users to move with unprecedented ease from document to document, accessing images, text, and sound, and to form new paths as they explore connections and co-construct knowledge" (p. 70). Although we acknowledge that these three concepts were originally developed within the multiliteracies pedagogical framework, collectively they can be directly applied to our investigation of student transactions with digital resources.

Our developing conception of digital curricular literacies was also informed by the work of Leu and colleagues (2004) who made the following proposal:

> The new literacies of the Internet and other ICTs [information communication technologies] include the skills, strategies, and dispositions necessary to successfully use and adapt to the rapidly changing information communication technologies and contexts that continuously emerge in our world and influence all areas of our personal and professional lives. These new literacies allow us to use the Internet and other ICTs to identify important questions, locate information, critically evaluate the usefulness of that information, synthesize information to answer those questions, and then communicate the answers to others. (p. 1572)

In keeping with this definition, Martin (2004) argued that the Internet and other forms of information communication technologies have changed conceptions of knowledge as well as the ways in which we acquire knowledge, exemplifying his point by noting how the use of search engines mediates the process of finding knowledge.

The scope of Leu and colleagues' conception of new literacies is aligned with our expectation that new theoretical perspectives could emerge from the literacies that we observe in situ, especially how students engage with the visual, linguistic, spatial, and audio resources afforded in online environments. This expectation is already emerging from our study of student learning using our tripartite lens of literacies, curricular knowledges, and information communication technologies. There is the need for a multiperspectival, multitheoretical approach that takes account of changing perspectives on the nature of knowledge itself and curricular knowledge in particular, and incorporates insights from learning and the role of cognitive and metacognitive processes, and from understandings of the inherently social nature of learning in classrooms. These new perspectives will allow for the changing nature of learning in networked classrooms where the distinctions between local and global, as well as actual and virtual, blur.

Limitations of Existing Literacies Frameworks

One of the challenges of the current research project is the limited empirical base available for understanding what new literacies look like. Preliminary analysis of data collected during the pilot of the project highlighted the need to conceptualize online literate capabilities in new ways.

The project therefore offers support to the call put forward by Leu and colleagues (2004) for developing new theorizations of these literacies that make information communication technologies focal, rather than importing perspectives evolved in other contexts to the ICT environment. By bringing together a concern for online literacies and their role in mediating the acquisition, evaluation, organization, and utilization of knowledge, the Australian study takes up the argument put by Leu and colleagues for multiple perspectives that capture sociolinguistic concerns as well as cognitive and ontological aspects of new literacies. In this way, it seeks to theorize new literacies by drawing on innovative research applications of the technologies in classroom practice.

The study has a related interest in developing ways of assessing students' demonstrations of new literacies, another area that has received little emphasis to date. Early work in the area by Johnson (2003) and Jewitt (2003) emphasized the potentially interrelated aspects of visual, audio, gestural, and spatial modes of meaning that challenge the privileging of any single mode, and in particular, the longheld dominance of the written linguistic mode as the determinant of literate accomplishment. Our work points to how assessment of new literate practices calls for a rethinking of literacy as multimodal design, with what is valued becoming students' demonstrated capabilities to combine different meaning systems and channels of communication. From this vantage point, there is a need to rethink the complex of (re)presentation and the implications of this for both learning and assessment.

Framework for Understanding Multimodal Environments

In the case of multimodal environments, the project started with the work of Corbel (1999) who extrapolated from conventional print-based literacies to identify four categories that reflect the distinctive environment in which online curricula activities occur. *Orientation* refers to the indicators that a text gives about its size, the actions available, and the user's current location within the current text and in relation to other potentially relevant texts. *Interaction* includes navigation and searching, involving the student's capacity to locate, view, manipulate, and follow "modules" of text linked with others in different ways. *Modification* involves the student's ability to add or modify an existing text using the available features of the application. *Integration* involves managing multiple online documents, such as opening and closing documents, moving from one to another effectively, etc. Corbel's key components have been incorporated, though considerably extended, into our conceptualizations and framework for capturing, describing, and analyzing students' online activity, to which we now turn.

METHODOLOGICAL CONSIDERATIONS
IN RESEARCHING NEW LITERACIES

How we conceptualize literacy and learning in online curricular environments is linked in fundamental ways to what counts as appropriate methods for investigating literate capabilities. In our work to date, this linking has raised a number of important issues. Already it has become clear that a longitudinal large-scale study that is designed to generate empirical data of students' literate capabilities in online curricular contexts necessarily involves new research literacies capable of engaging two key questions:

1. How do we systematically observe, record, collect, and collate quality screen activity data, as well as talk and other interactions, when students are working online?

2. How do we address researcher uncertainties about what we are seeing and how can we best code, describe, and analyze it, using a mix of qualitative and quantitative approaches?

Beyond a need for rethinking what counts as data, our longitudinal study has called for a dynamic approach that can take account of and engage with the mix of technological and methodological challenges of working in school sites.

In addressing the above questions, we have had to rethink our own research literacies, including the selection of tools for collecting and collating digital data, as well as the ways of working inductively and theoretically with these data. A key innovation of the research to date is the use of screen tracking software, in this case, *Camtasia Recorder* (available from www.techsmith.com), to produce real-time digital video recordings of students' screen moves as they undertake research and create texts in online environments. Camtasia Recorder also has an

Figure 1 A student's work in progress

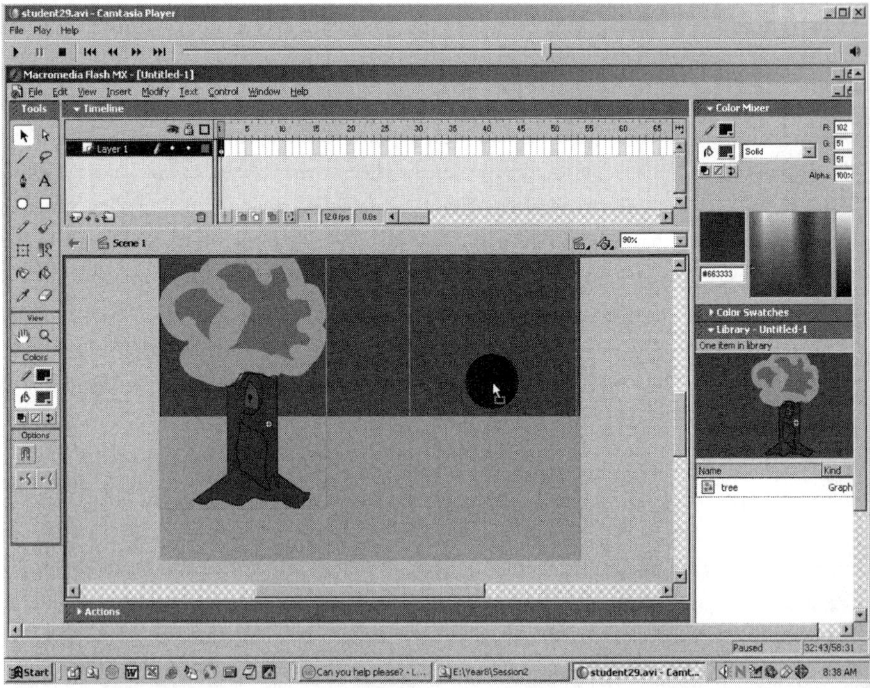

audio taping capacity that we used to capture talk at the computer of a sample of students who worked in pairs on their online task. The screen tracking capacity provides a move-by-move, real-time trail of individuals' decisions as they read, search, locate, and evaluate information, while sometimes concurrently organizing and representing ideas, moving to acts of transforming and designing. It is the software, installed on the school network and then on each student's computer, that generates and makes available for analysis the authentic records of individual students' digital curricular literacies. Figures 1 and 2 capture a student using Flash animation in the construction of his webpage. In the first image (see Figure 1), the video captures the screen on which he is currently working and the tools he is using. The slide bar at the top marks the progression of time whereas the dot in the image shows the moment-in-time position of the cursor. The second image (see Figure 2) records the completed animation undertaken in the next session a day later.

After a significant period of data collection, we are able to report that as a research tool, the software has proven effective, though time intensive, at collection and analysis stages, with its strength lying in ensuring the integrity of the process data. Its main potency lies in how it can capture the interactive nature of working online as students move backwards and forwards, to and fro, between search engines, multiple sites, task requirements, and software programs chosen for constructing meaning.

Figure 2 Same student work now completed

An Approach to New Literacies Integrating Process and Product

Although the mix of data types discussed above has made it possible to apply a range of methodologies, both quantitative and qualitative, the most significant challenge we have encountered to date is how to develop a principled and manageable methodology for coding students' actions captured in the process data. In terms of precedents, there have been a few studies that have involved the coding of data related to digital technologies. For example, working from a situated cognitive perspective, Barab, Hay, and Yamagata-Lynch (2001) proposed a coding methodology for studying the uses to which new technologies can apply to support learners in developing transferable knowledge in teaching and learning contexts. Chandler-Olcott and Mahar (2003) also developed a coding framework, this time using a multiliteracies perspective to capture an adolescent girl's use of modes in technology-mediated literacy practices. Although these studies are useful in illustrating approaches to sectioning data and parsing them down to codes, a distinctive feature of the current study is how it relies on computer technology as a data collection tool. Given this, one of the main challenges is how to develop the coding to engage with the multimodality of student work, and how students move between and orient to different media such as graphic/video images, text, music, and other sound effects. The main challenge is to capture and generate rich accounts of the patterns of interconnection inherent in the data. This involves, in part at least, what Zembylas and Vrasidas (2005) described as coming up with ways to analyze the transformations caused by information communication technologies in education.

Essentially, we are aiming to freeze, though temporarily, actions that are inherently dynamic, tracing for example, how students engage with digital resources, from searching the Internet for information through to designing their webpages. According to Zembylas and Vrasidas (2005), "the hypertext/hypermedia nature of the Internet allows users to move with unprecedented ease from document to document, accessing images, text, and sound, and to form new paths as they explore connections and co-construct knowledge" (p. 70). The coding methodology developed for the project is necessarily a construct on our part, beginning with inductive analysis, and then shifting to theoretically driven passes through the process data. Our unit of analysis therefore is the students' observable actions as they work with curricular knowledges online. As an interpretive framework, the coding acts as a shared lens on which researchers on the team rely to keep a running record of the sequence of actions, capturing them for the purposes of analysis, as mentioned above. A key characteristic of the project, then, is the capacity provided by the software to capture students' products, enabling thick descriptions of student outcomes as well as the ability to review, again and again, the process students have undertaken to arrive at the product.

Emerging Framework of New Literacies

In locating new literacies and multimodality at the center of the longitudinal study, we are developing codes around the notions of (a) *reading as inquiry*, (b) *designing and representing* in networked environments, and (c) *managing* operational aspects of networked environments. In relation to *reading as inquiry*, of interest are the strategies students use to locate online information related to the problem set in the task, evaluate it for both credibility (Haas & Wearden, 2003) and usefulness, and then synthesize, drawing from various resources. Four features of students' online reading processes have been the focus of our attention: (a) retrieval of relevant information from online resources provided as part of the task; (b) initiation and use of search strategies to locate additional relevant web-based information; (c) ways of recording findings of searches; and (d) ways of recording how students evaluate information, its "believability" and fitness for purpose. The concept map and evaluation matrix included in the task to assist students to make their thinking and decision-making visible has given us some insight into students' higher-level information processing strategies.

Broadly speaking, the *designing and representing* codes focus on the processes students use as they make decisions about how to represent and communicate their new knowledge. Theoretically, the codes draw on the multiliteracies notions of the NLG (1996) outlined above, namely design (including multimodality), hybridity, and intertextuality. Working from this position, the codes address the following: (a) the typography used in designing multimodal digital texts, including the articulation in new ways of "established practices and conventions" (NLG, 1996, p. 82); (b) evidence of working with several modes, including the actions students take in operating in a single mode and in bringing together written and visual language, and other audio and visual effects; and (c) evidence of intertextuality operating both as linking within the site and to external sources, and as "the ways in which meanings ... are constructed through relationships to other texts, discourses, genres, and modes of meaning" (NLG, 1996, p. 82).

The third element of the framework for coding process data, *managing* networked environments, seeks to address how students manage the procedural aspects of working online. To some extent, students' ways of managing files, including how and where they save, are determined by school network configurations, with most students directed to save to their individual folder on the school network. Similarly, the speed of the school network and its stability are factors beyond the students' control. These aspects are of interest in our study insofar as such institutional factors have impact on the time it takes a computer to perform a task, as well as how students are required to operate in the networked environment.

The three elements of the framework are taken to be interdependent, all being of equal importance in exploring and coming to understand the transactional and transformational relationships between literacy education, technology, and curricular learning in schooling. The point is that currently research has little to say about how and how well students access and use knowledge on the Internet, reading to determine not only relevance but also credibility. Further, little is known about how students carry forward what they have learned, working multimodally and by combining different semiotic systems to construct new texts.

Insights into New Literacies Emerging from Preliminary Analysis

The current study provides a picture of how students have widely divergent repertoires of practice when working online, lending support to Chen and McGrath's (2003) observation that "students were found to have diverse knowledge construction processes and considerable variation in their ability to use hypermedia for knowledge representation" (p. 33). Specifically, the data have brought to light a wide range of capabilities in designing, representing, and managing information. Emerging from the 2004 data is a picture of how some students choose to invest considerable time and effort in what are essentially the aesthetic aspects of designing, paying considerably less attention to the curricular knowledge they convey. Also of note is how the technical aspects of importing and transforming visual materials are not uniformly well controlled, with few student texts showing a capacity to bring a holistic, critical perspective to how various modes converge for effect.

Further, the knowledge and skills of students cover a considerable range, both in terms of how they access and use knowledge online and also how they take on the role of designer to convey their new knowledge. There are, for example, those students who have considerably well developed technical skills that enable them to import and modify images with ease, and yet the content of their texts, that is, the information that they convey, is limited. Conversely, there are students who have demonstrated little, if any, capacity to work with visual materials but have demonstrated abilities to locate and retrieve relevant content information. For these students, the format of choice is not a multimodal document but a unimodal text privileging written language.

IMPLICATIONS FOR ESSENTIAL
LITERACIES FOR THE KNOWLEDGE AGE

What is becoming clear from our own and others' work is that the most crucial skills required for the knowledge age are those of location, interpretation, synthesis, and transformation of information, gained from often complex sources, into meaningful knowledge. Essential literacies for this knowledge age include multimodal authoring skills involving a range of semiotic systems and incorporating multi-mediated critical analysis. Crucial literacy capabilities include navigation skills and exploration strategies as well as the ability to (de)construct verbal and visual images, and the capacity to evaluate how they weave together for maximum effect. Our observation and analysis of students at work in online environments highlights the urgency of expanding our conceptions of literacy and literacy learning to accommodate recognition of literacy as multimodal design. Failure to do so means that pedagogical and assessment practices may continue to ignore, or fail to give due acknowledgement to, the varied and ever-expanding knowledge and skills base of students in contemporary classrooms.

At this stage of the study, clear messages for effective pedagogical practices around the use of information communication technologies in classrooms have already emerged. These include the importance of ensuring that the integration of new technologies involves the purposeful inclusion of a range of applications for critical and creative purposes. It is evident that the nature of the problem-solving task has succeeded in engaging the students as designers, both critically and creatively, in the process of knowledge construction. The inclusion of attention structures, such as a concept map and decision matrix, can assist in shaping students' selective and reflective thinking as they undertake multimodal transformations. We look to further opportunities that the data analysis will provide to inform how teachers can ensure students undertake challenging tasks involving experimentation that will result in reflection on and transformation of their learning.

It is also evident that the affordance of computers as part of the research design provides researchers with new ways of documenting and understanding new literacies. Through the use of screen-capture software, we are given a window onto the integration of action with output, as students move backwards and forwards through the process of reading as inquiry, designing, representing, and managing information, all contributing to knowledge creation.

CONCLUSION

The longitudinal study that we are conducting starts from the assumptions that literacies are multiple in nature and that new forms of strategic knowledge and ways of working online are central to the quality of student outcomes. A related assumption is that learning is socially constructed, and in schools, this social construction occurs in pedagogical and curricular contexts. Much remains to be learned about what such assumptions look like in practice and how they are (or are not) realized in the work that goes on in online learning environments, as students explore the (hyper)textual and social worlds that such spaces make available.

Furthermore, we are only just beginning to consider how we might effectively research these new multimodal, technologically mediated practices. The contribution of this study at one level will be the development of new research literacies and methodologies for contemporary research and more specifically, for researching how students work with knowledge in online environments. At another level will be an empirical map of what students at various year levels can be expected to achieve in new literacies, based on a large corpus of data, bringing with it implications for policy, teacher education, and professional development. Central to this work is the recognition that the multimodal character and transformational nature of learning online reshapes traditional concepts of curriculum, pedagogy, and assessment in both fundamental and profound ways.

REFERENCES

Barab, S., Hay, K., & Yamagata-Lynch, L. (2001). Constructing networks of action-relevant episodes: An in situ research methodology. *The Journal of the Learning Sciences, 10*, 63-112.

Bigum, C., & Green, B. (1993). Technologizing literacy: Or interrupting the dream of reason. In A. Luke & P. Gilbert (Eds.), *Literacy in contexts: Australian perspectives and issues* (p. 4-28). Sydney, Australia: Allen & Unwin.

Chandler-Olcott, K., & Mahar, D. (2003). "Tech-savviness" meets multiliteracies: Exploring adolescent girls' technology-mediated literacy practices. *Reading Research Quarterly, 38*, 356-385.

Chen, P., & McGrath, D. (2003). Knowledge construction and knowledge representation in high school students' design of hypermedia documents. *Journal of Educational Multimedia and Hypermedia, 12*, 36-61.

Cope, B., & Kalantzis, M. (Eds.). (2000). *Multiliteracies: Literacy learning and the design of social futures.* London: Routledge.

Corbel, C. (1999). *Computer literacies: Working effectively with electronic texts* [Office 97 version]. Sydney: National Centre for English Language Teaching and Research, Macquarie University.

Freebody. P., & Luke, A. (1990). "Literacies" programs: Debates and demands in cultural context. *Prospect, 5*(3), 7-16.

Green, B. (1988). Subject-specific literacy and school learning: A focus on writing. *Australian Journal of Education, 32*, 156-179.

Green, B. (1999). The new literacy challenge? *Literacy Learning: Secondary Thoughts, 7*, 36-46.

Haas, C., & Wearden, S. (2003). E-credibility: Building common ground in web environments. *L1 - Educational Studies in Language and Literature, 3*, 169-184.

Hasan, R. (1996). Literacy, everyday talk and society. In R. Hasan & G. Williams. (Eds.), *Literacy in society* (pp. 377-424). London: Longman.

Jewitt, C. (2003). Re-thinking assessment: Multimodality, literacy, and computer-mediated learning. *Assessment in Education: Principles, Policy & Practice, 10*, 83-102.

Johnson, D. (2003). Activity theory, mediated action, and literacy: Assessing how children make meaning in multiple modes. *Assessment in Education: Principles, Policy & Practice, 10*, 103-131.

Kress, G., Jewitt, C., Ogborn, J. & Tsatsarelis, C. (2001). *Multimodal teaching and learning: Rhetorics of the science classroom.* London: Continuum.

Lankshear, C., & Knobel, M. (2003). *New literacies: Changing knowledge in the classroom.* Buckingham, UK: Open University Press.

Leu, D., Jr. (2000). Literacy and technology: Deictic consequences for literacy education in an information age. In M. L. Kamil, P. Mosenthal, P. D. Pearson, & R. Barr (Eds.), *Handbook of reading research* (Vol. III, pp. 743-770). Mahwah, NJ: Erlbaum.

Leu, D., Jr., Kinzer, C., Coiro, J., & Cammack, C. (2004). Towards a theory of new literacies emerging from the Internet and other information and communication technologies. In R. B. Ruddell & N. Unrau (Eds.), *Theoretical models and processes of reading* (5th ed., pp. 1570-1613). Newark, DE: International Reading Association.

Luke, A., & Freebody, P. (1999). A map of possible practices: Further notes on the four resources model. *Practically Primary, 4*(2), 5-8.

Luke, A., Freebody, P., & Land, R. (2000). *Literate futures: Review of literacy education.* Brisbane, Australia: Education Queensland.

Martin, A. (2004). [Review of the book New literacies: Changing knowledge and classroom learning]. *Journal of eLiteracy, 1*, 61-65.

New London Group. (1996). A pedagogy of multiliteracies: Designing social futures. *Harvard Educational Review, 66*, 60-92.

Smolkin, L., & Lawless, K. (2003). Becoming literate in the technological age: New responsibilities and tools for teachers. *The Reading Teacher, 56*, 570-577.

Unsworth, L. (2002). Changing dimensions of school literacies. *Australian Journal of Language and Literacy, 25*, 62–77.

Wyatt-Smith, C., & Cumming, J. (2003). Curriculum literacies: Expanding domains of assessment. *Assessment in Education: Principles, Policy & Practice, 10*, 47-60.

Zembylas, M., & Vrasidas, C. (2005). Globalization, information and communication technologies, and the prospect of a "global village": Promises of inclusion or electronic colonization. *Journal of Curriculum Studies, 37*, 68-83.

Reading First: Hidden Messages, Omissions, and Contradictions

Karen S. Evans
Marquette University

Nancy T. Walker
University of La Verne

When Public Law 107-110, now known as the No Child Left Behind (NCLB) Act, was passed in 2002, we were naturally interested in how it would affect education in the United States. As reading professors, we were particularly interested in how the Reading First (RF) portion of the NCLB Act would affect teachers, students, and ourselves. While we were hopeful that RF would provide the necessary funding and professional development to enact positive changes in students' reading abilities, we also were skeptical that RF alone would be sufficient to result in the level of improvements required in the types of schools that were being targeted by the law. Consequently, we decided to research RF to better understand its potential for changing reading instruction and students' reading abilities. Therefore, the purpose of this paper was to conduct a critical policy analysis of the Reading First (RF) grant proposals submitted by nine states. A previous analysis of 13 grant proposals (Bell, 2003) assumed a more functionalist perspective which we believe may have influenced the type of results that were found. We assert that applying critical policy analysis (Giroux, 1989) procedures to the RF grants revealed additional insights regarding the impact this policy is likely to have on reading education.

THEORETICAL FRAMEWORK

Functional Policy Study

Functionalism reflects our inclination to see schools, and society, as systems (Edmonson, 2001, p. 620). Functional Policy Study reflects a positivist view that facts are separate from human values. It explores the measurable effects of a policy within a particular context and is characterized by the research questions, what is, and what works (Edmonson, 2002). This area of research is applicable in early stages of educational research but is limiting without other layers of analyses which address gender, race, class struggles, and power. In the context of this study, we used a functionalist analysis when examining the contents of each state's reading application to first answer the question, what is reading instruction as defined by the nine states' RF grant applications?

Critical Policy Study

In contrast, critical policy study considers the social, historical, and political aspects of policy; who benefits from a policy; and who is left out. Examinations of policy focus on inequalities and injustices that result from domination and oppression. Consequently, power is a central tenet of critical policy analysis.   Such analysis explores how power is used to produce different meanings and practices that often reproduce existing power structures (Giroux, 1989). Rather than focus on what is, the critical policy analyst asks the research questions: what has been, why, and what might be (Edmondson, 2002, 2004).   "Critical analyses allow us to consider the consequences of particular research for the children, teachers, schools and communities that are implicated as we consider broader contexts and ideological visions for the future of schools" (Edmondson, 2002, p. 17).

METHOD

This research was conducted qualitatively to describe a social phenomenon (reading policy) as it occurs in the United States (Marshall & Rossman, 1995).   We utilized purposeful sampling (Merriam, 1998) as to which states would participate in grant analyses in order to obtain geographical, cultural, and population diversity.   The nine states selected were: California, Colorado, Florida, Iowa, Michigan, Nebraska, New York, Texas, and Wisconsin. This sample, although small in number, does allow for diversity in several different areas.   For example, the sample includes states from different geographical regions of the United States (i.e., East and West Coasts, Midwest, South, and Southeast), different state populations (i.e., heavily populated states with numerous metropolitan cities and states that are primarily rural with far less population), and different cultural representations (states with high concentrations of minority ethnic populations, and states with primarily Caucasian populations).

ANALYSIS

In a preliminary analysis, each grant was downloaded from the Internet and thoroughly read. We catalogued the year each state was in the grant process and utilizing a functional analysis, examined three areas of focus: curriculum materials, assessments, and professional development. We chose to focus on these three areas because they were the ones most likely to have direct impact on reading instruction, teachers, and students. Charting the information in these three areas allowed us to gain an initial answer to the functionalist question "What is" the vision of reading instruction in each of the nine states.   Content analyses (Spradley, 1980) were conducted on these three areas to look for similarities and differences across states, and to gain an in-depth understanding of each state's grant proposal.   After this level of analysis was completed, we compared notes (triangulation) to confirm similarities and differences across the nine states. Preliminary constructs emerged in the three areas of focus.

Following this initial functionalist analysis, we used a critical policy lens to analyze the proposals. Looking carefully at the theoretical constructs that underscore critical policy, we selected three main critical policy issues as the basis for our next level of analysis. These three theoretical constructs (i.e., Prescription/Control, Reaction, and Contradictions) became our coding categories for a second content analysis. During this second content analysis, it became apparent that we needed to add another critical policy construct to our coding categories—that of What's Missing. As Stevens (2003) suggests, what is missing is often as important as what is there. In our analysis, what was missing provided hidden (and not-so-hidden) messages as to what is valued and considered important in reading instruction and assessment.

FINDINGS

We will explain our findings and address each area of focus (curricular materials, assessment, and professional development) within each of our theoretical constructs (control, reaction, and contradiction). States are identified by a randomly assigned letter to retain their anonymity. Since RF is a national policy, our goal was to explore collectively the vision of reading instruction represented across all the states not to analyze any one individual state. Another reason for maintaining anonymity is because this research project had Human Subjects approval.

Prescription/Control

A primary goal of critical policy study is to expose sources of domination and oppression (Edmundson, 2004). Consequently, our analysis explored ways in which the proposed RF policies would control or prescribe the teaching of reading and possibly oppress those involved in reading instruction, including teachers, students, parents, and administrators. To make the data from this category more manageable, we further divided it into four main areas: Curriculum and Instruction, Assessment, Professional Development, and Higher Education. The potential for RF policies to "control" in each of these three areas is discussed below.

Curriculum and Instruction. Consistent with the federal guidelines for RF, all states required the adoption of a core reading program based on SBRR (Scientificaly Based Reading Resesarch). This requirement in itself could be viewed as a form of control since the way reading and research were defined by the National Reading Panel, which formed the basis for the RF legislation, has been called in to question (Allington, 2002; Garan, 2004; Stevens, 2003). Furthermore, the adoption of a common core reading program represents a potential form of prescription evidenced by the rationale for such a program given by one state: "[A core program is needed] so that all teachers teach the same to all students across all classrooms" (State A, p. 48). There was variation in the amount of control exerted by states over the selection of core reading programs. Some states required Local Education Agencies (LEAs) to select from a list of 2-5 reading programs that had been approved at the state level as meeting the SBRR requirement. Other states had a list of "recommended" programs, and other states allowed LEAs to select their own program, as long as it fulfilled the SBRR requirement. All states, however, required the use of the *Consumer's Guide to Evaluating a Core Reading Program: A Critical Elements Analysis* (Kameenui & Simmons, 2000) for evaluating core reading programs to determine whether they were based on SBRR. Given that the Consumer's Guide is consistent with the view of reading and research found in the NRP's report, this requirement, while not as stringent as requiring specific core programs, does represent another form of potential control.

Another form of prescription found in many proposals was the belief that reading skills are best taught hierarchically, as recommended by the Consumer's Guide (2000, p. 35). This criteria was found in most states' proposals, and can be illustrated by the following example:

> Skills like phonemic awareness and letter knowledge are particularly important predictors of the ease with which children acquire word reading accuracy and fluency, while broad oral language facility (vocabulary in particular) becomes critically important to the growth of reading comprehension skills once children learn to read words efficiently (emphasis added) (State A, p. 22).

In other words, higher order skills, such as comprehension, synthesis, analysis, and evaluation, cannot be addressed until students have first mastered the basic skills of phonics.

Assessment. The majority of states required the use of specific assessment measures for assessing outcomes, progress monitoring, and diagnostic purposes, and there was tremendous consistency among the states regarding which assessment measures were required (i.e., DIBELS, ITBS, Peabody).   Ease of administration and use of required assessments appeared more important than developmentally appropriate assessment practices. At least one state (State B) required the use of the ITBS in kindergarten, and another state explained that:

> To avoid the need for individual administration by teachers, [mandated norm-referenced instrument for assessment of outcomes] will be a group-based test in Grades 1-3, with a different approach for Kindergarten necessitated by the difficulties of reliably administering group-based assessments to young children (State C, p. 49).

In other words, it was not the fact that it is developmentally inappropriate to give such assessments to kindergarten-aged children that was problematic; rather, it was the fact that such assessments cannot be reliably administered in a group setting.

The hierarchical view of reading instruction also was reflected in the way state documents described assessment. For example, State A explained:

> Unfortunately, we can't assess children's ability to derive meaning from text for the purpose of early identification. Most kindergarten and first-grade children, whether or not they will eventually develop reading problems, can't read "authentic" stories to answer questions about meaning. Fortunately, we can assess performance on precursor skills in the early grades to identify children who will experience difficulty deriving meaning from text in later grades (p. 45).

While students may not be able to read authentic texts themselves, they certainly can have stories read to them and have their listening comprehension assessed through techniques such as questioning and retellings.   Once again, however, the overarching concern with the ability to administer group-based assessments would preclude such types of assessment practices. Moreover, a hierarchical notion of reading, with its emphasis on teaching phonemic awareness and phonics at these grade levels, eliminates the need for assessing comprehension since that is viewed as a higher-order reading skill that should only be taught once the basic decoding skills have been mastered.

Professional Development. The way control was evidenced in states' professional development plans was similar to that found in Curriculum/Instruction and centered around the requirement of a common, commercial reading program based on SBRR. Most states required professional development conducted by agencies that had been selected at the state level and met the SBRR requirement. For instance, State B required 50 hours of professional development by basal publishers, and State E used the professional development component of one of the state's recommended basal programs to provide all of the state-required professional development. Thus, a large portion of professional development time focused on learning how to implement the selected core reading program, the required assessments, and research-proven instructional strategies. While such objectives could be considered worthwhile, a critical policy lens reminds us that the types of instructional strategies and assessments possible are specific to those that meet the stringent requirement of the RF's definition of reading instruction and scientifically based research.

Higher Education. Aspects of prescription were found in how the proposals addressed higher education institutions and teacher preparation programs. The proposals consistently required teacher education programs to align their course curricula with SBRR and include only effective research-based reading practices. Moreover, some states (States C and E) required teacher education programs to submit all reading course curricula which would then be reviewed to determine if the content was consistent with SBRR and the essential components of reading instruction. If not, the state would make recommendations for course adjustments and revisions and provide faculty with training. Another state (State F) required all reading courses to address the elements of SBRR and have a significant targeted field experience component where candidates spent time actually applying these elements. Faculty was expected to be on-site with the candidates, supervising and aiding them in their development. What is different from a critical policy perspective, however, is the level to which issues of curricula and faculty expectations are now being mandated by the state. Moreover, it is likely that issues of academic freedom are likely to arise with such stringent curricula expectations and state-level oversight of course content.

Reaction

The second analysis category was that of reaction. An important component of critical policy analysis is to examine the social, historical and political aspects that inform a policy's creation. One such dominant value is that policy is typically a reaction to a trend or phenomenon in society (Shannon, 2000). In the case of RF, a common trend in society was the assumption that previous programs and policies were failures (i.e., the Reading Excellence Act), that public schools were failing, and that teachers were not doing their jobs. As a result, policies like RF call for an increased surveillance of their work as a reaction to the perception that they are not following the rules. Underlying this reactionary thinking appears to be an overall mistrust of teachers—that they cannot be trusted to follow the rules and do their work without a large degree of control and surveillance. As a policy rooted in a Conservative ideology, it is not surprising that numerous examples of reaction to these current societal trends were found in the proposals. The reaction category was subdivided into the smaller categories of Curriculum/Instruction and Higher Education.

Curriculum/instruction. The reaction to the assumption that teachers are not doing their jobs was represented in all proposals. The most common example of this reaction was the requirement that schools could not simply "layer" a new core program on top of an existing "non-research based" program. This requirement was overtly stated in almost every proposal and appears to suggest that teachers currently are using programs that are completely lacking in any research base and furthermore, cannot be trusted to use the new research-based program if the old programs are still accessible. This notion that teachers are not following the rules of using scientifically based reading practices, and even worse, using nonscientific instructional practices, was further illustrated in State D's proposal by the statement:

> [There is a] need to implement systematic change in their schools and classrooms that is based on the findings of SBRR, not on philosophy, ideology, or unproven theories of reading and reading instruction. ... The continued use of instructional practices that do not yield the desired result of improved or accelerated reading achievement is indefensible" (p. 17).

State E stated that LEAs must include a description of their plan for helping teachers change to a more appropriate model of instruction, which appears to suggest that teachers currently are teaching inappropriately with inappropriate materials.

Another example of reaction in the proposals seemed to suggest that not only can teachers not be trusted, they also are not very intelligent. For example, State G stated that, "The detailed analysis of a comprehensive reading program is a highly technical and complex task that requires expert evaluation in order to be considered valid" (p.57). State G required LEAs to arrange for "intense and comprehensive professional development on the use of instructional materials, including the core reading program. The initial training must be sufficient to fully prepare teachers to use these materials in a highly proficient manner from the first day of the school year" (p. 71). The requirement for professional development to extensively train teachers how to use the core reading program was a common one among states. Given that the types of core programs recommended by many states are fairly prescriptive, this requirement seems to suggest that teachers must be lacking expertise in how to teach reading to require this level of training in order to effectively use a scripted, highly detailed instructional manual.

The notion that teachers needed to be monitored to ensure that they were following the rules was also present in the proposals. For example, State H stated that "critical to what happens in the RF classroom will be whether or not teachers hold to the fidelity of the instructional program in reading" (p. 14). To ensure such fidelity, State B required RF classrooms to be observed once a month to record the materials, time allotment, and the instructional methods and formats utilized. The purpose for these observations was to observe for "proper implementation of the comprehensive reading program and materials" (p. 47). Observations can be an effective way to provide constructive feedback to teachers; however, these observations seem to serve more of a surveillance purpose to make sure teachers are following the rules and teaching the right way.

Higher Education. The notion that teachers cannot be trusted and are not doing their job was not reserved merely for K-3 teachers; higher education and faculty in teacher preparation programs were equally suspect. Two states in particular, however, most clearly stated the reactionary belief that higher education could not be trusted to make such changes on their own, and that teacher preparation programs were in large part to blame for why teachers were unable to successfully teach reading, and consequently, not doing their job: "Even with regulatory revisions, preservice models are not adequately preparing future teachers for the instruction of evidence-based reading instruction. Higher education institutions need technical assistance in revamping preservice curriculum and instructional experiences" (State G, p. 22). "Far too many beginning teachers leave colleges of education unprepared to deliver reading instruction as defined by [SBRR]. These teachers must be retrained and retooled when they enter public schools" (State C, p. 21).

What's Missing/What's Important

Two important goals of critical policy analysis are to examine what the policy offers and what it denies, and who the policy benefits and who is left out. In relation to reading instruction, this translates to what type of reading instruction is possible, based on what is mandated by states' RF grant requirements, and who is most likely to benefit from such instruction. This category then, illustrates what and who was left out of the RF grants. Such omissions are important in critical policy analysis since what is missing helps reveal what the grant authors valued and conversely, what they did not.

Limited English proficiency students. A major area of omission in most grants was how states would address their limited English proficiency (LEP) students. States were likely to discuss the need for reading instruction that specifically addressed the needs of LEP students; however, when examining their actual plan for instruction and professional development, there was an overwhelming lack of specifics as to how states would actually implement instruction and professional development that targeted LEP students. The few states that did provide an outline of their professional development curricula revealed that LEP students were not a priority. For example, State I required a three-day training institute for all teachers. LEP students were 1 out of 14 items to be addressed during those three days, which raises concerns regarding how such an important and complex topic could be adequately covered in such a timeframe.

As superficial as such coverage might be, at least State I made LEP students a clear area of focus for professional development. Other states omitted it from their RF plan completely. For example, in its section, "How is [State B] Faring," it was stated that of the state's 47,252 LEP students, 68% of 4th graders, and 81% of 7th graders scored moderate or low on the state's reading assessment as compared to 40% and 47% of non-LEP students respectively. There was also great overlap between the location of bilingual programs and the geographic regions of RF eligible LEAs. Therefore, it would appear that LEP students represent an area of need in this state, but yet the state's RF grant did not address this issue anywhere in its discussion of Current Gaps, nor in its plan for instruction, assessment, or professional development. We found it even more surprising that a consideration of issues surrounding LEP students was completely absent in the documentation from a state that has a large and growing population of LEP students. This state did discuss its Current Gaps, reasons for why one-third of its schools were still failing, planned RF activities, and planned new professional development. In none of these areas, however, were LEP students mentioned.

Reading Instruction. When analyzing what states planned for reading instruction and professional development, it became immediately clear that states focused on the NRP's five areas of reading instruction (i.e., phonemic awareness, phonics, fluency, vocabulary, and comprehension) to the exclusion of any other area of reading development or instruction. For example, silent independent reading, discussion, using writing to facilitate comprehension, the use of quality literature and multicultural literature, and children's attitudes towards literacy were missing from every state's RF proposal.

Moreover, when one such practice was discussed (i.e., silent independent reading), it was to expressly advocate that it not be included in the curriculum:

> Silent independent reading should not be used in place of direct instruction in reading. Even though studies have found a strong relationship between reading ability and how much children read, scientific research has not demonstrated that silent independent reading (such as SSR – Silent Sustained Reading and DEAR – Drop Everything and Read) with minimal feedback or guidance improves fluency or reading achievement (State D, p. 24).

This ignoring of "hundreds of correlational studies that suggest independent reading does promote fluency, vocabulary, and comprehension" (Yatvin, Weaver, & Garan, 2003, p. 31) reveals the degree of influence of the NRP's report on RF proposals. Since the NRP confined its investigation of reading research to only experimental and quasi-experimental studies, all correlational and observational research was omitted. Consequently, any instructional practice supported by such research also was omitted from states' RF proposals.

Texts. Reading, or at least reading comprehension, cannot be taught without texts; however, not a single RF proposal addressed the importance of text in its discussion of reading instruction or planned professional development activities. RF claims to have as a goal to meet the reading needs of all students—regular education, special needs and LEP students alike. It seems rather naïve to assume that the same text from the same core reading program will be equally appealing to such a diverse group of students, or equally appropriate to meet such a wide range of instructional needs.

Contradictions

Critical policy analysis seeks to reveal contradictions that exist within policies. Consequently, our analysis explored the contradictions that were present both within individual RF grants, and across grants. Numerous contradictions were found; however, we chose to emphasize the following two contradictions that were most commonly found across various state grants: Independent Research Requirements and Local Control.

Independent Research Requirements. RF guidelines and the Consumer's Guide both require states to use a scientifically based reading program. All state RF proposals required LEAs to select a core reading program that had independent, empirical research to support that it was based on SBRR. Currently, however, there is no independent research to support the use of a commercial reading program (Yatvin, Weaver & Garan, 2003) as "alternative approaches to instruction have not been compared with the approaches of commercial programs as to their overall effectiveness" (Wisconsin State Reading Association, 2003, p. 1). Furthermore, many publishers lack the resources to carry out large-scale studies in the effectiveness of their materials. Nevertheless, some major publishers of basal programs have compiled pages of data that purportedly demonstrate the effectiveness of their programs. However, getting these results published in peer-reviewed journals has proven nearly impossible (Cassidy & Cassidy, 2004, p. 1)

Local Control. Several states specifically talked about their decision to not require a specific core reading program so that districts could continue to exercise their local control with respect to instructional materials. These states did specify, however, that districts should provide clear evidence that the selected program was consistent with SBRR, and use the Consumer's Guide to evaluate their selected program. Given the narrow definition of both reading and research represented in the RF guidelines, it remains suspect as to how much local control districts would actually have in selecting a core reading program.

DISCUSSION

The main purpose of this study was to conduct a critical policy analysis of the RF grants in nine states to interpret their impact at the national, state, and local levels of education. As educators and researchers, it is important to ask different questions regarding the impact policy has on education. Questions concerning what the policy offers and what it denies, who the policy benefits and who is left out, capture the impact of policy. Furthermore, we need to consider "how power is used to define the parameters of particular questions, to set the rules of particular practices, and to shape particular agendas."(Edmondson, 2002, p. 188). In the previous sections, we outlined what is missing in the proposals, who is left out, and who is in control. In this final section, we outline the potential concerns that resulted from our analyses of RF.

Our analyses suggest that although the essential five components emphasized in RF are certainly important, they are not the only components necessary to a quality reading instructional program. We found six areas of concern that should be addressed. First, SBRR controls curriculum in the areas of textbook selection and the hierarchical progression of reading skill instruction, yet fails to address silent independent reading, writing to facilitate comprehension, and the use of quality literature. Second, addressing LEP students appears to be another missing component in many of the grant proposals. Gaps exist in professional development, curriculum, instruction, and assessment. Third, there is shared concern regarding assessment among educators. RF has the potential to take us on the "low road" (McGee, personal communication, December 21, 2004) of using a limited range of assessments (such as only using DIBELS without considerations of vocabulary or comprehension) to narrow curriculum and focus instructional time. Echoing McGee's concern regarding assessment, the International Reading Association has expressed support for NCLB and RF but has recommended multiple forms of assessment for measuring the success of our children and their schools (Farstrup, 2004). Fourth, basal publishers dominated the professional development section of the grant proposals and targeted SBRR instructional strategies and assessments. As discussed in our analysis of the RF grants, critical policy analysis reminds us there are other components of reading instruction not addressed in SBRR. Fifth, higher education is impacted with professors being pressured or required to align their reading courses with SBRR and the essential components of reading instruction. Such pressure has the potential to threaten academic freedom. Finally, according to McGee (personal communication, December 21, 2004), RF may take us on the "low road" where teachers are told to teach with fidelity to the curriculum only, not allowed to make alterations in instruction or materials, and not included in decisions regarding the instruction of individual children. These teachers are treated as if they are lacking intelligence in both the sense they are not able to judge whether an activity in a curriculum is based on actual research or ill-fitted to the needs of their children, and in the sense that they have no right to speak up about curriculum or instruction for the children they teach. We see this as a concern since "Any reform plan that strips teachers of their professional autonomy in instructional decision making lessens the likelihood that teachers will accept professional responsibility for the failure of their instruction to produce positive results" (Allington, 2002, p. 36). This becomes a very real possibility since RF essentially takes the decision-making process for selecting instructional programs and assessments out of teachers' hands.

Our analyses addressed questions such as what is missing from the RF grant proposals, who is left out, who maintains control, and who is left voiceless? Through answering such questions, our research has provided a glimpse of the future of reading instruction for teachers, students, and educators in the United States.

REFERENCES

Allington, R. (2002). *Big brother and the national reading curriculum.* NH: Heinemann.

Bell, M. (2003). The International Reading Associations' review of RF Grant recipients. *The Reading Teacher, 56*(7), 670-674.

Cassidy, J., & Cassidy, D. (2004, December). What's hot, what's not for 2005. *Reading Today, 22,* 1.

Edmondson, J. (2004). Reading policies: Ideologies and strategies for Political engagement. *The Reading Teacher, 57*(5), p. 418-428.

Edmondson, J. (2002). Asking different questions: Critical analyses and reading research. *Reading Research Quarterly, 37*(1), 113-119.

Edmonson, J. (2001). Taking a broader look: Reading literacy education. *The Reading Teacher, 54*(6), 620-629.

Farstrup, A. E. (2004, December). IRA and No Child Left Behind: Support and shared concerns. *Reading Today, 22,* 7.

Garan, E. (2004). *In Defense of Our Children.* Portsmouth, NH: Heinemann.

Giroux, H. (1989). *Schooling and the struggle for public life: Critical pedagogy in the modern age.* Minneapolis, MN: University of Minnesota Press.

Kameenui, E.J. & Simmons, D. (2000). *Consumer's guide to evaluating a core reading program: A critical elements analysis.* Eugene, OR: Institute for the Development of Educational Achievement.

Marshall, C. & Rossman, G.B. (1995). *Designing qualitative research.* Thousand Oaks. SAGE. Wisconsin State Reading Association, (July, 2003). National Council of Teachersof English: 2002 Resolution on the Reading First Initiative, WSRA Update, 16(8), 1-3.

Merriam, S.B. (1998). *Qualitative Research and Case Study Applications in Education.* San Francisco: Jossey-Bass.

Shannon, P. (2000). "What's my name?" A politics of literacy in the latter half of the 20th century in America. *Reading Research Quarterly, 35,* 90-107.

Spradley, J.P. (1980). *Participant observation.* New York: Harcourt Brace.

Stevens, L. (2003). RF: A critical policy analysis. *The Reading Teacher, 56*(7), 662-668.

Wisconsin State Reading Asociation, (July, 2003). National Council of Teachers of English: 2002 Resolution on the Reading First Initiative, Wisconsin State Reading Association Update, 16(8), 1-3.

Yatvin, J., Weaver, C., & Garan, E. (2003). Reading First: Cautions and Recommendations. *Language Arts, 81*(1), 28-33.

Thematic Analysis as a New Tool for
Genre Assessment in Early Literacy Research

Zhihui Fang
The University of Florida

The past decade has witnessed a growing interest among the National Reading Conference (NRC) membership in studying young children's understanding of and control over common school-based genres. Unlike the mainstream literacy research that has traditionally focused on such topics as phonological awareness, spelling, decoding, fluency, vocabulary, and comprehension, this strand of scholarship explores children's understanding and use of the forms and functions of two predominant elementary school genres--narrative (story) and informational (report). These studies have generated new insights and implications beyond those offered by the mainstream research.

Despite this surge in genre-based early literacy research, methods of conceptualizing and analyzing genres remain limited. The purpose of this paper is to introduce a new tool for analyzing genre that has the potential to expand our conception of genre and enrich our understanding of children's genre competence. Before proceeding further, I present a brief review of genre and genre-oriented early literacy (PreK-3) studies.

BRIEF REVIEW OF GENRE AND
GENRE-BASED EARLY LITERACY RESEARCH

According to Gunther Kress (1999), the term "genre" originated with Aristotle, who used it to distinguish major literary forms. The term was later used as a classificatory device with an emphasis on stereotyped conventions. In more recent accounts, genres refer to "abstract, socially organized ways of using language" (Hyland, 2002, p. 114). Genres are abstract in the sense that they are textual enactment of social contexts. They are social and purposeful in that they are created by people in their social interaction in order to achieve certain goals (Christie & Martin, 1997). Moreover, genres are predictable and recognizable because the relative regularity with which social life is conducted results in "recurrent use and typification of conventionalized forms" (Hyland, 2002, p. 114). Finally, genres are also flexible and subject to manipulation in that they respond to immediate contexts of situation and participants' intentions. Given the social origin of genres, different genres "'have', convey, and give access to different degrees and kinds of social power" (Kress, 1989, p. 11).

Scholars (e.g., Cope & Kalantzis, 1993; Martin, 1989) have suggested that knowledge of school-based genres is critical to success in school. In addition, recent studies (e.g., Cox, Shanahan, & Tinzmann, 1991; Cox, Fang, & Otto, 1997) have documented a significant relationship between genre knowledge and other aspects of literacy development. This line of research underscores the need for and importance of examining children's knowledge of school-based genres. Over the past 15 years, a considerable number of such genre-oriented early literacy studies have been conducted by NRC members. These studies explore children's genre competence by examining the texts they compose (orally or in writing) in response to requests for instantiating particular genres. A recent review of this research literature (Fang & Ruan, 2003) identifies two major approaches to the conceptualization and assessment of genre: (a) genre as content organization, and (b) genre as linguistic conventions.

Genre as Content Organization

In this approach, genre is conceptualized and operationalized as content organization using a two-dimensional "tree" diagramming system. This approach focuses on the relationship of ideas among individual clauses and on the hierarchical structure of the entire discourse. It draws upon the earlier work on discourse organization of prose by cognitive psychologist Bonnie Meyer (1975), which was later adapted by Judith Langer (1985) and others (e.g., Cox, Shanahan, & Tinzmann, 1991). Early literacy studies that use this approach to conceptualize and analyze genre include, among others, Newkirk (1987), Chapman (1994), Zecker (1996), and Donovan (2001). From the perspective of genre as content organization, developing competence in basic elementary school genres means, for example, composing progressively more complexly organized stories (e.g., from basic records and statements to recount and narrative) and reports (e.g., from label and list to hierarchical attribute series and paragraphs).

Genre as Linguistic Conventions

In this approach, different genres are viewed as comprising distinct sets of schematic and/or lexicogrammatical conventions. Schematically, for example, stories and reports both consist of obligatory stages (e.g., initiating event, sequent events, and final event for story vs. topic presentation, description of attributes, characteristic events, and final summary for report) and optional stages (e.g., placement, finale and moral for story vs. category comparison and afterword for report). Lexicogrammatically, stories and reports employ different participants (specific participants for story vs. generalized participants for report), verb types (action verb for story vs. relational verb for report), verb tense (past tense for story vs. present tense for report), and conjunctions (temporal conjunctions for story vs. logical conjunctions for report). They also differ in their use of other lexical and syntactical features (e.g., literary-sounding language and co-referential cohesive ties for story vs. technical language and co-classificatory cohesive ties for report). Early literacy studies that adopted this approach include Hicks (1990), Pappas (1993), Fang (1998), Duke and Kay (1998), Kamberelis (1999), and Donovan (2001), among others. They drew upon the work of Australian scholars (e.g., Derewianka, 1990; Halliday & Hasan, 1976, 1989; Hasan, 1989; Martin, 1989) and American researchers (e.g., Biber, 1991; Chafe, 1985; McCabe & Peterson, 1991; Stein & Glenn, 1979). They focused on how prototypic children's compositions (oral or written) were in relation to the text types requested. Thus, from the perspective of genre as linguistic conventions, development in genre competence means increase in the number of genre-specific schematic stages (especially the obligatory ones) and/or lexicogrammatical features included in children's production.

Studies using these two approaches have yielded important, though sometimes inconsistent and even contradictory, information about children's competence in school-based genres (Fang & Ruan, 2003). They have contributed much to the development of genre-based pedagogies that take into consideration the social and developmental needs of young children. Inconsistent findings between studies are often seen as a function of variability in task conditions, scoring procedures, and sampling characteristics (Mosenthal & Kamil, 1991). However, as Fang and Ruan (2003) have pointed out, such disparities may also be indicative of more deep-rooted problems in genre analysis. One such problem concerns the identification of text organization or its schematic structure. In the above two approaches, the criteria for identifying the structural boundaries of texts are not particularly well defined. Paltridge (1994) suggests that many factors, both linguistic and cognitive, may be *simultaneously* at work when analysts attempt to relate perceptual categories (i.e., perception of structural boundaries of text) to textual components (i.e., actual language of text). Thus, Crookes argues that it is difficult to validate such genre analyses "to ensure that they are not simply products of the analysts' intuitions" (Crookes, 1986, cited in Hyland, 2002, p. 116). A related criticism of these two approaches is their tendency for oversimplification by overlooking authorial intents and multi-functionality of text segments (Hyland, 2002). Third, the two approaches in question are, while effective in distinguishing between different genres, not as sensitive to variations within the same text type. In other words, they may not be particularly effective in differentiating the quality of texts within the same genre. For example, it is theoretically possible for a text to have a hierarchically well-organized structure and yet still be judged as unsuccessful because of weakness in its use of lexicogrammar. By the same token, it is also conceivable that a text can sometimes be less than effective (due to absence of certain rhetorical features), despite inclusion of all the genre-specific structural and lexicogrammatical features noted earlier.

These limitations do not render the two approaches to genre analysis invalid; rather, they suggest that genre is a much richer and more complex discursive construct. In order to gain new insights into children's genre competence, new tools for analyzing and assessing genres are needed. One such tool is thematic analysis. Thematic analysis has been applied in studies of advanced literacy (e.g., Berry, 1995; McKenna, 1997; Whittaker, 1995), but is rarely used in early literacy research. The rest of this paper introduces and exemplifies this method of genre assessment.

THEMATIC ANALYSIS FOR GENRE ASSESSMENT

What is Theme?

The term "theme" is used here not in the literary sense of plot, but as a construct in systemic functional linguistics that reveals how a clause in English is organized as a message. According to Halliday and Matthiessen (2004), theme is "the element which serves as the point of departure for the message; it is that which locates and orients the clause within its context" (p. 64). The remainder of the message, the part of the clause in which theme is developed, is called "rheme." In English, theme typically contains familiar information, that is, information that has already been given somewhere else in the text or is familiar from the context. On the other hand, rheme contains unfamiliar/new information, i.e., information that has not been mentioned previously in the text. Although scholars differ on just how much of what comes first in a clause counts as theme (c.f., Ghadessy, 1995a; Vande Kopple, 1991), those working within the framework of systemic functional linguistics generally agree that theme can be identified as "the elements up to and including the first experiential element at the beginning of a clause" (Schleppegrell, 2004, p. 68). Thus, as is shown in Table 1 below, different grammatical elements can serve as clause themes.

There are three types of themes: topical, interpersonal, and textual (Halliday & Matthiessen, 2004). The topical theme realizes the ideational meaning, or content, of a clause. Each clause must have, and can only have, one topical theme. Topical themes are either "unmarked" or "marked." An "unmarked" topical theme is one that is conflated with the grammatical subject of the clause, such as *He, The burning of trash...themselves all,* and *you* in clauses (1), (2), and (4), respectively. A marked topical theme, such as *By thinking carefully and choosing wisely* in clause (3), is one that does not simultaneously serve as the grammatical subject for the clause.

The topical theme can be preceded by other elements in the clause. These are elements that realize either interpersonal or textual meanings of a clause. Clause elements that typically serve as interpersonal themes are modal or comment adjuncts (e.g., *probably, fortunately, of course, in my opinion*), vocative (e.g., *John*), and finite verbal operators (e.g., *do, is, can, shall*). Textual themes are realized through continuatives (e.g., *yes, oh, well, now*) and conjunctions (e.g., *and, or, but, while, since, in case, even if*). In clause #4, for example, the topical theme "you" is preceded by two textual themes (conjunction: *and*; continuative: *well*) and two interpersonal themes (vocative: *John*, finite verbal operator: *do*).

Theme plays a major role in the development of text, distribution of information, and representation of experience. Analysis of themes can thus yield valuable information in the assessment of genre. Like other tools, thematic analysis enables researchers to distinguish one genre from the other. However, it is also a potentially more powerful tool in that it provides important insights into the ideational, interpersonal and organizational patterns of a text at once. As Martin (1995) notes, "Theme in English means more than what the message is about and ... significant patterns of information flow through Theme in ways that are critical to an interpretation of the

Table 1 Theme and Rheme in Sample Clauses

THEME	RHEME
He	bounced out of bed.
The burning of trash, the trucks that haul trash to landfills, and even the landfills themselves all	cause air pollution.
By thinking carefully and choosing wisely,	industry and individuals can protect the air living things need.
And well, John, do you	know why?

meaning of a text" (p. 254). Moreover, as this paper shall demonstrate later, thematic analysis is especially effective for differentiating effective texts from less effective texts within the same genre. Its power as a tool for genre assessment derives from its conception as a clause-level construct. Halliday (1982) points out that clause is both a constituent and an instantiation of text. As such, clause, like other semiotic units, inherits properties from the text and embodies "all the semantic components from which the text is built …" (Halliday, 1982, p. 230). The choice of what should serve as the starting-point for the constituent clauses of a text (i.e., theme) thus "reflects the range of meanings conveyed by the text as a whole, including interpersonal, textual and representational meaning" (Webster, 1995, p. 270).

Using Thematic Analysis to Differentiate Genres

Scholars (e.g., Fries, 1981; Ghadessy, 1995b) have suggested that there is a direct relationship between the structure of clause messages and genre. Theme offers speaker/writer options about what meanings to prioritize in a text and what to package as familiar and what as new. Patterns of thematic choices in a text "provide good clues about the genre of that text" (Vande Kopple, 1991, p. 339). They realize not only meanings about the organization of the communicative event, but the experiential content and interpersonal distance involved (Eggins, 2004). Analysis of themes can, thus, help us see organizational differences in texts and understand the choices a speaker/writer has made in presenting information and developing argument (Schleppegrell, 2004). Different genres have different ways of presenting information, enact different role relationships between speaker/writer and listener/reader, and structure text differently. They tend to highlight or prioritize different kinds of information and form distinct thematic patterns. As Fries (1995) has claimed, "patterns of thematic progression do not occur randomly but are sensitive to genre" (p. 7). In other words, different thematic patterns correlate with different genre types.

For example, topical themes in the narrative genre (e.g., stories) tend to involve specific participants. They are typically short and pronominalized, and often preceded by interpersonal and textual themes. The informational genre (e.g., reports), on the contrary, tends to thematize generalized participants. Its topical themes are typically lexicalized and often lengthy and abstract.

Table 2 Thematic Patterns in Narrative and Informational Genres

THEME	NARRATIVE	INFORMATIONAL
Topical*	Specific/concrete participants	Generalized/abstract participants
	Pronominalized/short nouns	Lexicalized/lengthy nouns
	Shifting and reiterating	Zig-zagging or reiterating
Textual	Many continuatives and conjunctions with generalized meanings	A varied set of conjunctions with precise/restricted meanings
Interpersonal	Many finite verbal operators and modal/comment adjuncts	Rare use of finite verbal operator and limited use of modal/comment adjuncts

* For the sake of simplicity, only unmarked topical themes are analyzed in this paper.

They are rarely preceded by textual or interpersonal themes. In terms of methods of thematic development, topical themes in the narrative genre tend to shift frequently from one participant to another, although each can also be repeated. Topical themes in the informational genre are sometimes reiterated as well, but more often feature what Eggins (2004) has called a "zig-zagging" pattern of development (see Figure 1), meaning that the rheme of one clause gets to become the theme for the next clause. The differences in thematic patterning between these two basic elementary genres are summarized in Table 2.

Figure 1 The zig-zagging pattern of thematic development*

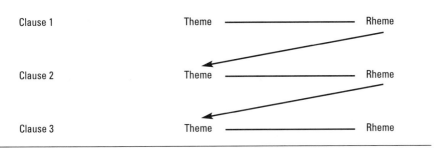

*adapted from Eggins (2004, p. 324)

Table 3 Sample Texts in Narrative and Informational Genres

TEXT 1 (NARRATIVE)	TEXT 2 (INFORMATIONAL)
It was a typical morning for Tigger. He bounced out of bed, bounced through his bath, bounced out his front door, and hurled himself across the Hundred-Acre Wood in a series of leaps and bounds that carried him easily over even the tallest trees until he arrived at the home of Winnie the Pooh. As soon as Pooh opened his front door, before he could say so much as "Good morning, Tigger!" or "My, aren't you looking particularly well today!" Tigger threw his arms around the portly bear, and they rolled head over heels across the floor into Pooh's parlor. (from Talkington, 1994, p. 11)	Recycling, along with reducing and reusing, also reduces the amount of trash that must be burned or hauled to landfills. The burning of trash, the trucks that haul trash to landfills, and even the landfills themselves all cause air pollution. To reduce air pollution, many people keep their cars well tuned. Well-tuned cars use gas more efficiently and produce fewer pollutants. As older cars wear out, many people replace them with more modern, fuel efficient ones that pollute less. Modern cars produce 95% less pollution than cars built 30 years ago. Many industries are working to reduce air pollution. Some find ways to reduce the amount of energy they use. Others reduce air pollution by changing how they make things. (from Scott Foresman, 2000, p. C67)

A comparison of the two sample texts in Table 3 illustrates these differences. Text 1 is an excerpt from a fantasy story for elementary-aged children, *Winnie the Pooh's Bedtime Stories* (Talkington, 1994). Text 2 is an excerpt from an elementary science textbook, *Science* (Scott

Table 4 Themes in Text 1 and Text 2

CLAUSE	TEXT 1	TEXT 2
1	It	Recycling, along with reducing and reusing,
2	He	The burning of trash, the trucks that haul trash to landfills, and even the landfills themselves all
3	(he)	To reduce air pollution
4	(he)	Well-tuned cars
5	and (he)	and (they)
6	until he	As older cars
7	As soon as Pooh	Many people
8	before he	Modern cars
9	or "My, aren't you	Many industries
10	Tigger	Some
11	and they	Others

* Only main clauses (e.g., …*Tigger threw his arms around the portly bear; Many industries are working to reduce air pollution*), hypotactic clauses (e.g., *until he arrived at the home of Winnie the Pooh; As older cars wear out*), and paratactic clauses (e.g., … *[he] bounced through his bath; …and [they] produce fewer pollutants*) are analyzed here. Embedded clauses (e.g., … *that carried him easily over even the tallest trees; … that pollute less*), which function as constituents of other clauses, are not parsed out for further analysis.

Table 5 Thematic Patterns in Text 1 and Text 2

THEMATIC FEATURES		TEXT 1	TEXT 2*
	Topical Theme	11	11
Features	generalized/abstract participant vs. specific/concrete participant	0:11	10:0
	lexicalized/lengthy noun vs. pronominalized/short noun	2:9	7:3
	method of development	shifting and reiterating	zig-zagging
	Textual Theme	6	2
Features	continuative	0	0
	conjunction	6	2
	Interpersonal Theme	2	0
Features	finite verbal operator	1	0
	modal/comment adjuncts	0	0
	vocative	1	0

* Text 2 has one marked topical theme in clause #3.

Foresman, 2000). Each text contains 11 clauses and thus 11 topical themes (see Table 4). Their thematic patterns are presented in Table 5. As Table 5 reveals, there are two interpersonal themes in the fantasy text, but no such themes in the report text. Moreover, the fantasy text uses three times as many textual themes as the report text. The topical themes used in the two texts are also very different, with the fantasy text thematizing mostly specific participants (e.g., *Tigger, Pooh*) and pronouns (*he, they*) whereas the report text thematizing mostly generalized participants (e.g., *well-tuned cars, many people*) and lexicalized/lengthy abstract nouns (e.g., *recycling, the burning of trash… landfills themselves all*).

Furthermore, as Table 4 shows, the topical themes in the fantasy text shift frequently, from "it" (used as the grammatical subject of an impersonal verb) and "he" (referring to Tigger) to

Table 6 Sample Report Texts

TEXT 3 (MODEL REPORT)	TEXT 4 (GOOD REPORT)	TEXT 5 (POOR REPORT)
Fish are ectotherms that live in water and use gills to get oxygen. Gills are fleshy filaments that are filled with tiny blood vessels. The heart of the fish pumps blood to the gills. As blood passes through the gills, it picks up oxygen from water that is passing over the gills. Carbon dioxide is released from blood into the water. Most fish have fins. Fins are fanlike structures used for steering, balancing, and moving. Usually, they are paired. Those on the top and bottom stabilize the fish. Those on the side steer and move the fish. Scales are another common characteristic of fish, although not all fish have scales. Scales are hard, thin, overlapping plates that cover the skin. These protective plates are made of a bony material. (from Glenco/ McGraw-Hill, 2000, p. 579)	Alligators are big reptiles with big mouths and sharp teeth and come from an egg and are thought that they lived in the prehistoric days. They eat meat, birds, fish, and some other water animals. The alligators fight for their water hole and are hunted for their skin and for fun. They can get to be very long. They stay a long time in the water and bath very near to the water. They can not live in the land for very long or they will dry out and turn white. Some alligators are all black and some are red and white. They are very very rare. They care their babies till they grow up. They sometimes carry their babies in their mouths. (written by a fourth grader)	Did you know that alligators live in the water? I would like to live in the water, would you? Hey and guess what, alligators like to eat all sorts of things, but their best things to eat are raw foods like humans, birds, any animal that lives under the water. They eat all kinds of stuff. If you saw an alligator, what would you do? Would you run? If I saw an alligator, I would scream and run as fast as I can. Alligators are a kind of dinosaur. Did you know that? I did not know until I read a book about them. Then I was amazed. All alligators don't live in the water. Some can live on land, but they mostly live in the water. Well, now that you know about alligators you can go home and tell your parents about alligators and maybe your mom and dad will be happy. (written by a fourth grader)

"Pooh," and back to "Tigger," and then onto "they" (referring to both Tigger and Pooh). The report text, on the other hand, shows a zig-zagging pattern of thematic development. The rhemes of clauses 1 (*the amount of trash that must be burned or hauled to landfills*), 2 (*cause air pollution*), 3 (*keep their cars well tuned*), 7 (*more modern, fuel efficient ones that pollute less*), and 8 (*cars built 30 years ago*) are promoted to become the themes of clauses 2 (*the burning of trash, the trucks that haul trash to landfills, and even the landfills themselves all*), 3 (*to reduce air pollution*), 4/5 (*well-tuned cars*) and 6 (*old cars*), 8 (*modern cars*), and 9/10/11 (*many industries/some/others*), respectively. Taken

Table 7 Themes in Model Report and Student Reports

CLAUSE	TEXT 3 (MODEL REPORT)	TEXT 4 (GOOD REPORT)	TEXT 5 (POOR REPORT)
1	Fish	Alligators	Did you
2	Gills	and (they)	alligators
3	The heart of the fish	and (they)	I
4	As blood	they	would you
5	it	they	Hey and guess
6	Carbon dioxide	The alligators	alligators
7	Most fish	and (they)	But their best things to eat
8	Fins	They	They
9	Usually, they	They	If you
10	Those on the top and bottom	and (they)	what
11	Those on the side	They	Would you
12	and (they)	or they	If I
13	Scales	and (they)	I
14	although not all fish	Some alligators	and (I)
15	Scales	and some	Alligators
16	These protective plates	They	Did you
17		They	I
18		till they	until I
19		They sometimes	Then I
20			All alligators
21			Some
22			but they
23			Well, now that you
24			you
25			and (you)
26			and maybe your mom and dad

*Only main clauses (e.g., *Fish are ectotherms*), hypotactic clauses (e.g., *As blood passes through the gills*), and paratactic clauses (e.g., ... *and [they] use gills to get oxygen*) are analyzed here. Embedded clauses (e.g., ... *that live in water*), which are constituents of other clauses, are not parsed out for further analysis.

together, the thematic differences between the two sample texts suggest, as do results from analyses of other linguistic corpora from more advanced texts (Ghadessy, 1995a; Taylor, 1983), that different genres utilize different choices and patternings of themes.

Using Thematic Analysis to Assess Children's Genre Competence

Not only is thematic analysis effective in differentiating between genres, it can also be used to assess how close children's text production approximates a target genre. It is a particularly useful tool for distinguishing successful texts from less successful ones within the same text type. To demonstrate this, three reports are presented in Table 6 and analyzed thematically. Text 3 is a "model" report about fish excerpted from a sixth-grade science textbook (Glencoe/McGraw-Hill, 2000). Texts 4 and 5 were composed by two fourth graders who were requested to assume the role of a scientist and write an informational report on the alligator, a favorite and familiar animal to them, for an audience who is unfamiliar with the creature. (Misspellings in these two texts have been corrected for ease of reading.) Text 4 was judged as "good" and text 5 "poor" by the students' language arts teacher.

The themes for the three reports are listed in Table 7. A comparison of the thematic patterns among the three texts is presented in Table 8. As is evident from these tables, the three reports are very different in their thematic choices. First, the "good" student report and the "model" report

Table 8 Comparison of Thematic Patterns in Model Report and Two Student Reports

THEMATIC FEATURES		TEXT 3 (MODEL)	TEXT 4 (GOOD)	TEXT 5* (POOR)
	Topical Theme	16	19	26
Features	generalized/abstract participant vs. specific/concrete participant	16:0	19:0	9:16*
	lexicalized/lengthy noun vs. pronominalized/short noun	13:3	3:16	6:19
	method of development	zig-zagging	reiterating	shifting
	Textual Theme	3	8	13
Features	continuative	0	0	3
	conjunction	3	8	10
	Interpersonal Theme	1	0	5
Features	finite verbal operator	0	0	4
	modal/comment adjuncts	1	0	1
	vocative	0	0	0

* Text 5 has one marked topical theme in clause #5.

* The term "you" can refer to the reader audience or have a general, indefinite meaning (Berry, 1995). The ratio in the table is derived from interpreting "you" as having genuine second person reference. If, however, the alternative interpretation is adopted, the ratio of generalized/abstract participants vs. specific/concrete participants would be 18:7.

both thematize generalized participants (e.g., *fish* and *gills* for text 3 and *alligators* and *they* for text 4), whereas the "poor" student report thematizes mostly specific participants (e.g., *I, you, your mom and dad* for text 5). According to Berry (1995), themes in texts 3 and 4 can be characterized as "informational themes" because they foreground the organization of the content by including a word/phrase that refers to something which can be regarded as an aspect of the topic. On the other hand, themes in text 5 are appropriately characterized by Berry (1995) as "interactional themes" in that they foreground the interactiveness of the discourse by including a word/phrase that refers to the writer or reader(s), or to a group of people which include the writer or reader(s). Second, whereas the "model" report thematizes mostly lexicalized nouns (e.g., *gills, blood, fins*), both student reports thematize mostly pronouns (e.g., *they* for the "good" report and *you* and *I* for the "poor" report). Third, while only 19% (3 out of 16) of the clauses in the "model" report contain a textual theme, the percentage is much higher for the two student reports (42% for the "good" report and 50% for the "poor" report). Fourth, whereas both "model" and "good" reports tend to minimize the use of interpersonal themes (especially those realized by finite verbal operators and vocatives), the "poor" report uses it in nearly 20% of its clauses.

In terms of thematic progression, unlike the "model" report that features a zig-zagging pattern of thematic development, the "good" student report features a reiteration pattern and the "poor" student report uses a shifting pattern. Specifically, in the "model" report, the rhemes in clauses 1 (*gills*), 2 (*tiny blood vessels*), 3 (*blood*), 5 (*oxygen*), 7 (*fins*), 9 (*paired*), 14 (*scales*), and 15 (*hard, thin, overlapping plates that cover the skin*) are picked up to become themes in clauses 2 (*gills*), 3 (*the heart*), 4 (*blood*, which is repeated in clause 5), 6 (*carbon dioxide*), 8 (*fins*, which is repeated in clause 9), 10 (*those on the top and bottom*) and 11 (*those on the side*, which is repeated in clause 12), 15 (*scales*), and 16 (*these protective plates*), respectively. Such thematic progression allows the topic to be effectively developed and makes the text more interesting to read. In sharp contrast, the topical themes in the "good" student report, *alligators/they,* are repeated throughout the text, making the report a bit monotonous and dry to read. In the "poor" student report (text 5), the topical theme shifts among *you, alligators,* and *I*. Other topical themes in text 5 include *guess* (marked), *their best things to eat,* and *your mom and dad.* Such rapid shifting of topical themes suggests that the text is unplanned and resembles spontaneous oral storytelling.

In summary, the above analysis demonstrates that differences in thematic choices and patternings result in qualitative differences among the three sample reports. This supports Berry's (1995) argument that thematic analysis has the potential to distinguish successful from unsuccessful writing in the target genre. Text 5, which uses thematic options and patterns resembling those in the story, is less mature as a report genre than text 4, which is less expert and sophisticated than text 3.

CONCLUSION

This paper introduces a new method of analyzing and assessing genre for early literacy research. It demonstrates that thematic analysis is a potentially powerful tool for differentiating between the two basic elementary school genres (story vs. report) and for assessing children's competence in these genres. Dovetailing with the theoretical perspective that grammatical and lexico-semantic properties of themes are different for different genres (Fries, 1995; Ghadessy, 1995b), thematic analysis provides valuable insights as to the meaning and texture of story/report and allows us to better understand how texts are characteristically constructed and contexts accordingly construed in these two basic elementary school genres.

Future research can apply this tool to other elementary school genres (e.g., procedures, explanation, argumentation), under other conditions (e.g., developmental/longitudinal research, intervention studies), and with more diverse student populations (e.g., special needs students, students with limited English proficiency). This research will contribute to not only the description of general tendencies of thematic patterning in different school-based genres, but our understanding of the challenges that particular genres pose to students. In addition, studies employing multiple methods of genre assessment (e.g., content organization, linguistic conventions, thematic patterning) should be encouraged. This will allow for triangulation of findings and ultimately give us a more accurate description of genre features and a more complete picture of children's genre competence. Finally, because genre is simultaneously social, conventional, and flexible (Kress, 1989/1999), future studies should also address this inherent tension of genre by investigating how children creatively adapt and appropriate characteristic thematic patterns and linguistic conventions of particular genres to accommodate the immediate needs of author, context, and audience. By viewing genre as discourse recontextualization (see, for example, Wollman-Bonilla, 2000), researchers will be able to explore more fully how, when, where, and why genre is used as well as the outcomes or significance of such use. Taken together, these future explorations should, according to Elster (2004), help us continue to refine and revise models of genre competencies, and expand our understanding of genre development, genre assessment, and genre practices.

REFERENCES

Berry, M. (1995). Thematic options and success in writing. In M. Ghadessy (Ed.), *Thematic development in English texts* (pp. 55-84). London: Pinter.

Biber, D. (1991). Oral and literate characteristics of selected primary school reading materials. *Text, 11*(1), 73-96.

Chafe, W. (1985). Linguistic differences produced by differences between speaking and writing. In D. R. Olson, N. T. Torrance, & A. Hildyard (Eds.), *Literacy, language, and learning: The nature and consequences of reading and writing* (pp. 105-123). Cambridge, England: Cambridge University Press.

Chapman, M. (1994). The emergence of genres: Some findings from an examination of first grade writing. *Written Communication, 11*(3), 348-380.

Christie, F., & Martin, J. (1997). *Genre and institutions: Social processes in the workplace and school.* London: Cassell.

Cope, B., & Kalantzis, M. (1993). *The powers of literacy: A genre approach to teaching writing.* Pittsburgh, PA: University of Pittsburgh Press.

Cox, B., Fang, Z., & Otto, B. (1997). Preschoolers' developing ownership over the literate register. *Reading Research Quarterly, 32*(1), 34-53. [Reprinted in R. Ruddell & N. Unrau (Eds.), *Theoretical models and processes of reading* (5th ed., pp. 281-312). Newark, DE: International Reading Association]

Cox, B., Shanahan, T., & Tinzmann, M. (1991). Children's knowledge of organization, cohesion, and voice in written exposition. *Research in the Teaching of English, 25*(2), 179-216.

Crookes, G. (1986). Towards a validated analysis of scientific text structure. *Applied Linguistics, 7*, 57-70.

Derewianka, B. (1990). *Exploring how texts work*. Maryborough, Victoria (Australia): Primary English Teacher Association.

Donovan, C. (2001). Children's development and control of written story and informational genres: Insights from one elementary school. *Research in the Teaching of English, 35*, 394-447.

Duke, N., & Kays, J. (1998). "Can I say 'once upon a time'?": Kindergarten children developing knowledge of information book language. *Early Childhood Research Quarterly, 13*(2), 295-318.

Eggins, S. (2004). *An introduction to systemic functional linguistics* (2nd ed.). London: Pinter.

Elster, C. (chair) (December, 2004). Methods and issues in current genre research. Symposium presented at the annual meeting of the National Reading Conference. San Antonio, Texas.

Fang, Z. (1998). A study of changes and development in children's written discourse potential. *Linguistics and Education, 9*(4), 341-367.

Fang, Z., & Ruan, J. (2003). Young children's narrative and expository skills in oral and written composition: A partial review of genre-based early literacy research. Paper presented at the annual meeting of the National Reading Conference, Scottsdale, Arizona.

Fries, P. (1981). On the status of Theme in English: Arguments from discourse. *Forum Linguisticum, 6*, 1-38.

Fries, P. (1995). A personal view of Theme. In M. Ghadessy (Ed.), *Thematic development in English texts* (pp. 1-19). London: Pinter.

Ghadessy, M. (Ed.) (1995a). *Thematic development in English texts*. London: Pinter.

Ghadessy, M. (1995b). Thematic development and its relationship to registers and genres. In M. Ghadessy (Ed.). *Thematic development in English texts* (pp. 129-146). London: Pinter.

Glencoe/McGraw-Hill (2000). *Science Voyages: Exploring the Life, Earth, and Physical Sciences* (level red, Florida edition). New York: Glencoe/McGraw-Hill.

Halliday, M. (1982). How is a text like a clause? In S. Allen (Ed.), *Text processing: Text analysis and generation, text typology and attribution* (pp. 209-248). Stockholm: Almqvist & Wiksell International.

Halliday, M. (revised by Matthiessen, C. M. I.) (2004). *An introduction to functional grammar* (3rd ed.). London: Arnold.

Halliday, M., & Hasan, R. (1976). *Cohesion in English*. London: Longman.

Halliday, M., & Hasan, R. (1989). *Language, context, and text: Aspects of language in a social-semiotic perspective* (2nd ed.). Oxford: Oxford University Press.

Hasan, R. (1989). *Linguistics, language, and verbal art*. Oxford: Oxford University Press.

Hicks, D. (1990). Narrative skills and genre knowledge: Ways of telling in the primary school grades. *Applied Psycholinguistics, 11*, 83-104.

Hyland, K. (2002). Genre: Language, context, and literacy. *Annual Review of Applied Linguistics, 22*, 113-135.

Kamberelis, G. (1999). Genre development and learning: Children writing stories, science reports, and poems. *Research in the Teaching of English, 33*(4), 403-460.

Kress, G. (1989). *Linguistic processes in sociocultural practice*. Oxford: Oxford University Press.

Kress, G. (1999). Genre and the changing contexts for English Language Arts. *Language Arts, 76*(6), 461-469.

Langer, J. (1985). Children's sense of genre. *Written Communication, 2*(2), 157-187.

Martin, J. (1989). *Factual writing: Exploring and challenging social reality*. Oxford: Oxford University Press.

Martin, J. (1995). More than what the message is about: English Theme. In M. Ghadessy (Ed.). *Thematic development in English texts* (pp. 223-258). London: Pinter.

McCabe, A., & Peterson, C. (1991). *Developing narrative structure*. Hillsdale, NJ: Erlbaum.

McKenna, B. (1997). How engineers write: An empirical study of engineering report writing. *Applied Linguistics, 18*, 189-211.

Meyer, B. (1975). *The organization of prose and its effect on memory*. Amsterdam: Elsevier-North Holland.

Mosenthal, P., & Kamil, M. (1991). Epilogue: Understanding progress in reading research. In R. Barr, M. Kamil, P. Mosenthal, & P. D. Pearson (Eds.), *Handbook of reading research* (pp. 1013-1046). NY: Longman.

Newkirk, T. (1987). The non-narrative writing of young children. *Research in the Teaching of English, 21*(2), 121-144.

Paltridge, B. (1994). Genre analysis and the identification of textual boundaries. *Applied Linguistics, 15*(3),

288-299.

Pappas, C. (1993). Is narrative "primary"?: Some insights from kindergarteners' pretend readings of stories and informational books. *Journal of Reading Behavior, 25*(1), 97-129.

Schleppegrell, M. (2004). *The language of schooling: A functional linguistics perspective.* Mahwah, NJ: Lawrence Erlbaum.

Scott Foresman (2000). *Science.* New York: Scott Foresman.

Stein, N. L., & Glenn, C. G. (1979). An analysis of story comprehension in elementary school children. In R. O. Freedle (Ed.), *New directions in discourse processing* (Vol. 2, pp. 53-120). Norwood, NJ: Ablex.

Talkington, B. (1994). "Once upon a bounce" in *Winnie the Pooh's Bedtime Stories* (illustrated by John Kurtz). New York: Disney Press.

Taylor, C. V. (1983). Structure and theme in printed school text. *Text, 3,* 197-228.

Vande Kopple, W. J. (1991). Themes, thematic progressions, and some implications for understanding discourse. *Written Communication, 8*(3), 311-347.

Webster, J. (1995). Studying thematic development in on-line help documentation using the Functional Semantic Processor. In M. Ghadessy (Ed.), *Thematic development in English texts* (pp. 259-271). London: Pinter.

Whittaker, R. (1995). Theme, processes and the realization of meanings in academic articles. In M. Ghadessy (Ed.), *Thematic development in English texts* (pp. 105-128). London: Pinter.

Wollman-Bonilla, J. (2000). Teaching science writing to first graders: Genre learning and recontextualization. *Research in the Teaching of English, 35,* 35-65.

Zecker, L. (1996). Early development in written language: Children's emergent knowledge of genre-specific characteristics. *Reading and Writing: An Interdisciplinary Journal, 8,* 5-25.

Becoming More Effective in the Age of Accountability: A High-Poverty School Narrows the Literacy Achievement Gap

Kristin M. Gehsmann
National Institute on Leadership, Disability and Students Placed At Risk

Haley Woodside-Jiron
University of Vermont

Schools across the nation are facing one of the most ambitious educational agendas in our nation's history: the implementation of the No Child Left Behind Act of 2001 (PL107-110). No Child Left Behind (NCLB) exerts unprecedented pressures on schools to close the achievement gap among subgroups of students in key content areas, including reading and writing (Elmore, 2002). Few schools feel the impact of this legislation more than those with diverse student populations and high concentrations of poverty (M. Cohen & Ginsburg, 2001; Elmore, 2002; Snow, Burns, & Griffin, 1998). As policy researchers and literacy specialists, we are interested in the *process* of successful school improvement in high-poverty settings because there are so few detailed examples in the literature (M. Cohen & Ginsburg, 2001; Rosenshine, 2002). As the number of schools labeled "in need of improvement" increases throughout our nation, educational leaders and practitioners need a vision of how to grow more effective schools. Our research focuses on just that—high-poverty elementary schools that re-invented themselves in the face of accountability.

In this particular case study, we examine the improvement process in one high-poverty elementary school that was identified by its state department of education as under-performing in early literacy. Over the course of four years, early reading achievement in this school significantly improved and even exceeded the state's average performance in 2003 (see Figure 1). The story of

Figure 1 South Street's second-grade reading achievement compared with state averages 1999-2003

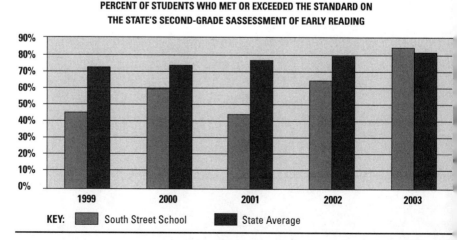

PERCENT OF STUDENTS WHO MET OR EXCEEDED THE STANDARD ON THE STATE'S SECOND-GRADE SASSESSMENT OF EARLY READING

KEY: South Street School   State Average

this school's improvement process gives researchers, practitioners and policy makers an insider's view of the complexity of school improvement, a set of lessons learned, and directions for further research.

BACKGROUND

Proficient reading is becoming an increasingly critical issue facing our schools and communities. While reading proficiency levels in the U.S. are stable, the gap among subgroups of students is wide, and the demand for a highly-literate public is mounting (Allington, 2002; Berliner & Biddle, 1996; Snow & Biancarosa, 2003). This demand calls for an increase in the reading achievement of all students and "more grievous consequences for those who fall short" (Snow et al., 1998, p. 1).

As reading proficiency becomes more critical to our nation's jobs and economy, we have seen early reading become a politically potent topic with "phonics bills" increasing exponentially across the nation (Patterson, 2000) and federal reading improvement grants mandating "scientifically based core reading programs" (U.S. Department of Education, 2003). NCLB calls for tougher standards, annual testing and strict accountability formulas that hold schools accountable for the adequate yearly progress (AYP) of all subgroups of students (U.S. Department of Education, 2002). The widespread efficacy of these policies has yet to be proven, and many researchers warn of their shortcomings (Amrein & Berliner, 2002; Elmore, 2002, 2003; Goetz, 2001; Linn, Baker, & Betebenner, 2002; Mintrop, 2003).

Even so, reading instruction in early grades merits our attention given the strong correlation between early reading difficulties and later reading failure (Blachman, Ball, Black, & Tangel, 1994; Francis, Shaywitz, Stuebing, Shawitz, & Fletcher, 1996; Snow et al., 1998). Poor children and minorities are especially vulnerable to early reading difficulties, particularly if they attend schools where 75% or more of the students are poor (Cohen & Ginsburg, 2001; Snow et al., 1998). Moreover, poor youth are six times more likely to drop out of school than their more economically advantaged peers (Children's Defense Fund, 2004). Dropouts commonly report a lack of the basic literacy skills needed to keep up with the demands of high school as a primary reason for dropping out of school (Kamil, 2003; Snow & Biancarosa, 2003).

High school dropouts face a constrained labor force with many blue collar jobs disappearing, or being filled by employees with some college experience or college degrees (Carnevale, 2001). America's high school dropouts are 72% more likely to be unemployed than high school graduates, and those who do work earn considerably less (Carnevale, 2001; U.S. Department of Labor, 2002). With more than 3,000 American students dropping out of high school each day (Alliance for Excellent Education, 2003), addressing the achievement gap in reading is a matter of equity and economic sustainability. It is an urgent concern for educators and policy makers alike.

This study examines the school improvement process in one high-poverty elementary school identified as "needing improvement" in early reading by its state department of education. The school, South Street Elementary School (a pseudonym), was purposely selected for study because of its demographic profile, its status as a school identified as "needing improvement" in early literacy, and its potential to show insight into one of the most pressing educational questions of our time: "How does an under-performing school become more effective?"

CONTEXT

South Street School is located in one of northern New England's few urban settings. South Street serves approximately 250 students in grades kindergarten through fifth and is arguably one the state's neediest schools. One hundred percent of the students at South Street receive free lunch (a typical indicator of poverty in American schools) and about 1 in 5 are English Language Learners (ELL)—mostly refugees newly relocated to the country by a missionary organization. Racial diversity at South Street is 14 times the state average and approximately 20% of South Street's students are eligible for special education services—nearly two times the state average (State Department of Education, 2003).

In 1999, less than one half of South Street's second-graders met or exceeded the state's standard in early reading—an assessment that requires students to read grade-appropriate text with accuracy, fluency and comprehension (State Department of Education, 2003). School principal Pat Jacobs (a pseudonym) described the school's climate at that time, "We were in crisis. We had thousands of visits to our planning [detention] room. Children were not succeeding in astronomically high numbers. It was violent. The place was a mess." Consequently, the school was identified as under-performing in early literacy by its state department of education in late 1999, and was later removed from its state's under-performing schools list in 2003 after posting an 89% increase in early reading achievement between 1999 and 2003.

METHODOLOGY

In this study, we used a grounded theory methodology (Glaser, 1992) to understand and describe the school improvement process at South Street School. Grounded theory is "a systematic, qualitative procedure used to generate a theory that explains, at a broad conceptual level, a process, an action, or interaction about a substantive topic" (Creswell, 2005, p. 396). By using constant comparative data analysis method (Creswell, 2005; Merriman, 1998), we generated an explanation of the improvement process at South Street School. While the South Street case might be considered instrumental (Stake, 1995), the findings of this study are intended to describe the improvement process at South Street School and identify directions for further research, rather than provide a "grand theory" (Cresswell, 2005).

Data Analysis and Collection

The central question of our inquiry was, "How did South Street School transform itself from being one of the lowest-performing high-poverty elementary schools in the state to a school that *exceeded* the state's average performance in early reading? We began our study with a semi-structured focus group interview (Patton, 2002) of the school's action planning committee in March of 2004. This committee contained a representative sample of the school's staff. After analyzing the transcript of this first interview, we refined our interview questions to include the following two questions: (a) What structures and practices improved student achievement in this context?, and (b) What motivated teachers and administrators to change their practice? We held two subsequent focus group interviews. In total, twenty teachers and one administrator participated, representing more than 90% of the certified staff. The three focus group sessions were an effective means for identifying the converging ideas and beliefs among the staff members.

Over the course of the next several months, we interviewed all kindergarten through third-grade teachers (n=6) about their individual perspectives on their school improvement process and literacy teaching. Additionally, we interviewed influential leaders and change agents including department of education officials, the building principal, the literacy specialist, and the school improvement coordinator. These interviews ranged in duration from 25 to 120 minutes. All interviews were audio taped and transcribed.

We independently coded the focus group and individual interview transcripts using inductive analysis, or open coding (Creswell, 2005; Patton, 2002). Subsequently, we compared and analyzed our individual codes through multiple iterations—each time analyzing the codes for consistency and the emergence of categories or themes (Creswell, 2005). Redundant and extraneous codes were eliminated through these comparisons and a member of the school's action planning committee verified our preliminary findings through member-checking (Patton, 2002).

Throughout our study, we acquired dozens of documents, including official correspondence between the state department of education and school officials, school action plans, a school climate report, newspaper clippings, internal correspondence, and assessment reports. We also conducted formal classroom observations in each kindergarten through third-grade teacher's classroom (n=6) for a minimum of two hours during a single literacy block. In addition to member-checking and investigator triangulation (Patton, 2002), these data sources were used interactively with our other sources of data to verify and expand our findings.

The results of our analysis are reported in four broad themes: context-based solutions, coherence, coaching, and compassion (see Figure 2). The following section describes these findings in rich detail, including the authentic voices of the participants.

FINDINGS

South Street School

At the time of identification, classroom instruction at South Street was described as "*very* different in each classroom" with teachers "doing their own thing." Struggling readers received the most fragmented instruction, according to special educators, because they worked with so many different people, many of them untrained para-educators, outside of the regular classroom. Teacher turnover was another challenge for the staff. In 1998 alone, nearly half of the teaching force (40%) resigned or transferred to other schools. It was not uncommon for new teachers at South Street to resign mid-year, leaving students with a succession of substitute teachers. Staff mobility made it difficult for sustainable change to occur. One teacher remarked, "We would start something and then someone would leave and we would never finish it… We were addicted to starting things."

When South Street was finally identified as needing improvement, the staff were not surprised, yet it was a difficult time. One teacher commented, "There was a major sense of panic. People were crying. It was very emotional. It was huge." Another teacher saw identification differently, "I felt like [the state] was saying this is a really hard job. This is a really hard place to work. This isn't like teaching in any other school." Differing perspectives and beliefs among staff members made moving forward a challenge.

Nine months after being identified, the school still had not developed a written plan of action as required by the state. Principal Jacobs explained the challenges she faced:

> Year one was a serious struggle. I think it was clear that the staff figured if they never wrote a vision, they'd never have to do the work. Given that, we could have been trying to write a vision for four years. It was that stuck. The staff were in such a deficit mode that we had to take care of their needs before they could come to the table and work with us. We had to learn how to listen to their concerns and remove all of the roadblocks put in our path.

Figure 2 Factors in South Street's improvement process

Context	Coherence
Context refers to an individual school's: • Demographics • History • Culture • Practices and Norms • Staffing and Leadership • Achievement Patterns • Resources, and • Expectations In short, context matters. South Street's school improvement plan was developed to match their unique context.	An alignment exists at South Street between standards, assessments, teaching practices, materials and professional development. There is a consistency in staffing, shared ownership of students, and an environment rich in dialogue and data. Participants frequently referred to coherence by saying, "We're on the same page now," or "We're speaking a common language." Coherence takes time, energy, resources, expert knowledge and leadership.
Coaching	**Compassion**
Coaching for shifts in behavior and beliefs includes: • Job-embedded professional development (including demonstration lessons and feedback) • Supervision and evaluation that is connected to the implementation of professional development and student achievement • Expert support for teachers and leaders • The monitoring of student achievement results and the use of assessment data to drive instruction. Coaching requires a balance of pressure and support.	Compassion is related to the human side of school improvement and how policy gets: • Developed • Communicated • Negotiated, and • Implemented. It also refers to an individual's or a group's capacity for empathy rather than blame. Compassion often leads to advocacy and action.

Student behavior was a prominent issue or "roadblock" at South Street. Over time, it became an excuse for low performance. One teacher admitted, "We would look at our [test] scores and be shocked and dismayed and everything else, but it was like, well, what do you expect?" Principal Jacobs elaborated, "Teachers were frustrated with student behavior… There was a culture here that [believed] if you just gave me the children that would behave then I could teach them." Principal Jacobs, just two years on the job, believed just the opposite, "I thought, if we could teach them, then they *would* behave." This visionary leader eventually made this belief a reality.

Today, two years after being removed from the state's under-performing schools list, the staff concede that being identified was a good thing because it meant that someone knew about them and their struggle wasn't a secret anymore. One teacher remarked, "Technical assistance was like a dark cloud with a silver lining."

Creating Coherence Out Of Chaos

Early in the initiative, Principal Jacobs collaborated with a school improvement coordinator from the state department of education. She also received a multi-year reading improvement grant from the state. This grant provided the much-needed funding and the expert support of a literacy specialist who visited the school one to two days per week. The principal, the school improvement coordinator, and the literacy specialist assembled a committee of teachers who would steer the school-based improvement initiative. The committee met regularly during the first year and studied student achievement data and the research on best practices in literacy. They shared their findings with the staff and provided suggestions for improving instruction. They also developed a multi-year plan for improving student achievement (see Figure 3).

One of the steering committee's first challenges was to persuade the district's leaders to stabilize the teaching force at South Street. In time, and after considerable pressure from the outside consultants, the superintendent was able to work with the teachers' union to eliminate limited teacher contracts in the school. Importantly, she also offered the South Street teachers the opportunity to transfer to other schools, or commit to four years of service at South Street—the term of their early literacy improvement plan. The staff who remained at South Street had to agree to implement the new literacy curriculum and assessments. They were also required to attend all of the professional development opportunities including an annual weeklong summer institute. While the improvement initiative targeted grades K-3, all teachers in the building were offered the same stipulations, known locally as, "the non-negotiables." Stipends and graduate credit were offered as incentives to stay at South Street. After much turmoil, the entire South Street staff committed to the new working conditions in early 2001.

In January of the same year, the district supported a benchmarking trip for action planning committee members to visit several successful high-poverty schools in New York City's acclaimed District #2. A staff member recalled her response to that experience:

> I walked into that school and I expected it to be about rules and consequences
> and that it was going to look like a prison… they didn't talk about kids like that
> at all. They really talked about instruction. It was about children and meeting

Figure 3   South Street's multi-year plan for improving student performance in literacy

Year One 2000-2001	Year Two 2001-2002
Big Idea: Good First Teaching—Reading Focus	**Big Idea:** Accountable Good First Teaching—Reading
Essential Questions:	**Essential Questions:**
1. What does good first teaching look and sound like?	1. How will teachers and learners be held accountable to the grade-level expectations?
2. What classroom materials are needed?	2. What "safety-nets" will be in place?
3. What routines and structures are necessary?	3. How will we meet the needs of all learners?
4. What are the expectations or goals?	4. How can we better use assessment to guide instruction?
5. How do teachers use assessment to guide instruction?	**Action Items:**
6. How do teachers and other stakeholders work collaboratively?	• Professional development plan to include book study, summer institute in Writing Workshop, ongoing training, classroom demonstration lessons and coaching
Action Items:	• Create timeline for implementing grade-level expectations
• Professional development plan to include book study, summer institute in Reading Workshop, ongoing training, classroom demonstration lessons and coaching	• Implement literacy assessment plan, reporting procedures, and literacy support team
• Establish grade-level expectations	• Pilot push-in model of services
• Establish assessment protocol and report out procedures	• Implement common planning, literacy blocks, and single grades
• Define balanced and comprehensive literacy instruction	• Develop a literacy materials closet
• Increase classroom literacy materials	• Improve lending library system
• Revise schedule for long literacy blocks and common planning	• Add literacy to after school programming
Create a plan for special education and Title 1 literacy instruction	• Create a teacher observation rubric for literacy block
	• Create a professional development/supervision and evaluation system connected to school's goals
	• District issues: budget, recruiting/retention, staffing

Year Three 2002-2003	Year Four 2003-2004
Big Idea: A Community of Learners— Parent & Community Partnerships	**Big Idea:** A Model for Excellence
Essential Questions:	Standards—Assessment—Instructional Strategies – Learning Opportunities—Professional Development —Professional Goals—Accountability— A Community of Learners
1. How do we engage parents in the school community?	**Essential Questions:**
2. How can parents share accountability for student learning?	1. What are we doing well with—what needs improvement?
3. What can we do better to serve the needs of transfer students, ELL students, minority students, etc.?	2. How will we sustain the systems, staffing levels, funding and high-quality professional development already in place?
4. Are me maximizing the expertise of all specialists?	3. How can staff members become teacher-leaders for the school and district?
5. Do we have meaningful ways for parents, volunteers and community members to contribute to improving the school and its climate?	4. How can school-based advocates organize and be persuasive in ensuring equity in the district's distribution of resources?
6. How do we better anticipate the needs and numbers of incoming kindergarteners?	5. Are all students achieving at high levels? What else can we do to meet the needs of all students?
Action Items:	6. Are there ways we can run the school more efficiently to leverage additional monies to support literacy initiatives?
• Professional development to include book study, summer institute in Word Study, ongoing training, demonstration lessons and coaching	**Action Items:**
• Pre-school story hour, parent access to the learning center, begin a parents' bookshelf	• Professional development to include book study, summer institute, ongoing training, classroom demonstration lessons, and coaching
• Parent involvement meetings and bulletin board	• Outside evaluation of the literacy program
• Extend literacy into the after school and summer programs	• Continuing contact/professional development in literacy
• School-wide homework policy	• Look to develop teacher leaders in key components of reading
• Report card revision—district committee	• Implement transfer student orientation plan
• Develop a system for improved coordination and communication between support services and classroom teachers	• Implement back-to-school orientation for new staff, students and families
• Make plans for sustainability and staff renewal	
• Develop a system for colleague visits	
• Delve deeper into curricular topics during grade-level meetings	
• Focus on transition planning for new students and fall orientation/assessment procedure for 2003	
• Develop an automated system for disaggregating data	

children's needs and knowing who they are as learners.... That trip gave me vision and a hope. Their kids looked just like ours and they can do it.... Everything seemed achievable.

The benchmarking trip was a motivating event for the team that attended, and Principal Jacobs' vision of "instruction first" and "literacy for all" started to gain momentum with the action planning committee members. However, widespread enthusiasm for the improvement initiative didn't occur until after the first summer institute. One teacher remembered, "It was hard to buy into the initiative until the trainers came and the quality of the training was so high that people were instantly engaged." Another teacher explained, "That was the most powerful professional development I'd ever done. The fact that every single teacher and administrator in the building was being trained in the same model of instruction at the same time was amazing." The common professional development provided teachers with a coherent plan for delivering literacy instruction throughout the grades.

The first summer institute at South Street focused on balanced literacy and the Readers Workshop approach developed by Lucy Calkins at Columbia University (Calkins, 2001). In subsequent summers, the staff studied Calkin's Writers Workshop (Calkins, 1994) and word study through Words Their Way (Bear, Invernizzi, Templeton, & Johnston, 2004). After several years of intensive training with staff developers and university professors from prominent East Coast universities, the teachers at South Street now speak about teaching and learning in precise terms. They recognize this accomplishment when they frequently say, "We're on the same page now," or "We all have a common language."

By the fall of the second year, being on the same page also meant sharing students and classroom space. The principal eliminated most of the special education and Title 1 pullouts—a change that affected more than a third of the school's students and every teacher. Regular education and special education teachers shared caseloads and all students were grouped flexibly within classrooms according to their individual needs. One special educator described the change this way, "There is a huge difference in the connection between special education and the regular classroom. We've worked to eliminate fragmentation as much as possible." Another teacher explained, "No kids are falling through the cracks now. We meet every month as a team and talk about *every* child that's not where we want them to be and we make a plan." Principal Jacobs believes that the full-inclusion model could not have happened without the common professional development, clear learning expectations, and the monthly monitoring of student achievement in literacy.

Eliminating fragmentation at South Street also meant replacing out-of-date books and literacy materials. Classroom libraries and an extensive lending library were purchased to support the implementation of South Street's three-block literacy framework that called for daily read alouds and guided reading, individual student book choice, extended amounts of time reading and writing, word study, and student response to reading. While most teachers viewed receiving the training, books and materials as "the most amazing piece," another teacher reminded them, "It was also a nightmare. We were in classrooms starting [in September] and we had all of this new information and materials. It was like being the pilot and trying to fix the plane at the same time."

This feeling of disequilibrium was commonly reported by participants throughout the course of our study—reminding us that coherence-making is always happening at the edge of chaos (Fullan, 2003).

Coaching

After the first summer institute on balanced literacy, teachers were expected to implement the new literacy curriculum and significantly improve student achievement in early reading. Incidentally, student achievement had slipped even more during the first tumultuous year of the improvement initiative (2000-2001). The "plane" could have crashed given the demands on the pilots, but it didn't. We wondered what made the difference. Several teachers pointed to the formal and informal coaching opportunities that existed after the training:

> That was a nerve-wracking fall implementing the summer training. Then we heard that the trainers were coming back. We wanted to look good and we wanted the literacy block to look the way it is supposed to. When the trainers came back to model lessons, we had teachers from various parts of the building in our classrooms observing - that was very motivating. People were looking at us. We received *very* positive feedback after many years of *very* negative feedback. It was just a real change.

Job-embedded professional development that included demonstration lessons and coaching became a regular part of the school's culture. A classroom teacher explained the importance of coaching, "We all need to be watched and given feedback, and set goals and deepen our understandings. We don't just learn by getting it the first time, we need to practice it, and then you change it and fix it."

Coaching for shifts in teaching behaviors took many forms at South Street. One teacher described how her students actually coached her: "I would see kids who would come in excited to learn and they would say, 'This is how my teacher did it last year,' and they would show it to me and I could see that it worked and because of that I was more apt to pick it up." Other teachers frequently identified students' increasing success and enthusiasm as important catalysts for changes in their instructional practices.

Teachers were not the only ones setting professional learning goals; Principal Jacobs aspired to become a better instructional leader. She met with the literacy specialist weekly to discuss the school's action plan, professional development priorities, and student achievement results. She conducted monthly observations of all certified staff and made daily rounds throughout the building, often stopping to talk to children about their reading work. It was not uncommon for Principal Jacobs to read aloud to the South Street students and staff. In fact, she shared favorite picture books in classrooms throughout the school each month. She also gave teachers regular and constructive feedback about their literacy instruction. Becoming a skilled instructional leader didn't happen instantly; it required coaching and support as well. Principal Jacobs explained:

> I conducted a huge number of observations—I observed every teacher, every month on some aspect of the literacy block. Sometimes I would say to the

literacy specialist, "There's nothing right. Where do I begin?" and she would say, "Okay, walk me through your observation. What did you notice? What's the one next thing this teacher needs to work on?" It was crucial to know the next piece people needed to work on. I mean there were a lot of things we all needed to improve upon, but we had to choose the *one* next piece so we didn't overwhelm people.

With help from the literacy consultant, Principal Jacobs and her staff learned how to support one another to improve student learning. A Title I teacher explained, "We talk about everything. …You can't get enough good minds wrapped around trying to help these children because they are so tricky [complicated] to teach." Another teacher remarked, "I knew I could get help right next door from a colleague because we all had the same training… I felt very supported in my own building." Coaching and collaboration are now the norm at South Street School. Working together helps the staff better meet students' needs and cultivate a culture of continuous learning and high expectations.

Compassion

The staff at South Street overcame many challenges throughout their initiative, including the difficulty of being identified as an under-performing school. One teacher recalled:

There were things about identification that didn't have to happen they way they did.…The [letters] were incredibly insulting, degrading, [and] demeaning… These judgments were made on high by someone who hadn't even been in the school … [At] first there was anger and [then] it was like, dammit, you can't tell us we're no good.

The early months of their initiative were so difficult that another teacher remarked, "It was like a major miracle that we got beyond that point." In some ways, it was a miracle. The research community offers little evidence that schools actually improve student learning in the face of high-stakes testing and identified failure (Amrein & Berliner, 2002; Amrein-Beardsley & Berliner, 2003; Mintrop, 2003).

In Mintrop's (2003) extensive study of 11 Kentucky and Maryland schools on probation, he found, "Rather than accepting criteria and judgments of the system, [the teachers] felt singled out as the ones who had to carry the "blame" for student learning and in turn externalized the causes for underperformance" (p. 22). Mintrop contended that teachers' disengagement was a serious inhibitor to progress. He also found that probation may prompt schools to "'harvest the low-hanging fruit,' … but [the schools] make few further inroads into the territory of instruction" (2003, p. 22).

Amrein and Berliner's study of 18 states with high-stakes testing policies arrived at similar conclusions. They wrote, "In all but one analysis, student learning is indeterminate, remains at the same level it was before the policy was implemented, or actually goes down when high stakes testing policies are instituted" (p. 2). Additionally, they pointed to a number of unintended consequences of high-stakes testing policies, including increased drop-out rates, teachers' and schools' cheating, and an increase in teachers leaving the profession (Amrein & Berliner, 2002). Although their findings were vigorously challenged (Rosenshine, 2003), Amrein and Berliner, who reanalyzed and expanded their data in 2003, defended their findings (Amrein-Beardsley & Berliner, 2003). While the debate about the utility and efficacy of high-stakes testing is unresolved, NCLB calls for strong accountability systems, annual testing, and prescriptive instructional solutions.

The teachers at South Street react strongly to some of these mandates: "It's always blame the teacher and praise the program. When are they going to get it right? Maybe you have to start praising good teaching. Maybe the policy makers need to look at good teachers." This is a recommendation that many researchers have emphasized in their work (Allington & Johnston, 2001; Darling-Hammond, 1999; Elmore, 2003; Pressley, Wharton-MacDonald, Collins-Block, & Morrow, 2001; Taylor, Pearson, Clark, & Walpole, 1999). Another teacher said, "It's going to take a lot of creativity and cleverness on our part to take what they say we have to work with and tweak it to the needs of our children and find the best in it and ignore the rest." A Title 1 teacher elaborated on the complexity of policy implementation:

> You can't treat South Street like you treat every other school. You can't say our kids' needs are the same as other children's needs. You need to look at the SES backgrounds of our children and their cultural diversity. It's impossible to teach a refugee child who does not have any English the same as a child who has been born and raised here and has had all of his needs met.

The staff at South Street believe that the search for "one size fits all" solutions to close the achievement gap is in vain.

Even with their success, the teachers at South Street School recognize that some students are still not achieving the standard. They explain, "It's fragile. We've only touched the surface. Even with all of the great things that have happened, it's still a hard place to work." These comments are not intended to convey blame or offer excuses as they once might have. Instead, these teachers are compassionate and they recognize there are factors that influence student achievement, many of which are out of their control. A South Street teacher explains:

> It's a bigger social issue. The children for whom this is not working [often] have such wretched home lives outside of this building, that they're just unavailable [for learning]. Until people start taking care of drugs, crime, and abuse, there will always be children who fail... I think if the government expects all children [to be] at standard, then they need to address the whole child. The whole child does not just exist within the school doors.

While it would be convenient to blame their students' parents for their children's school struggles, these teachers don't. They now realize that their students' parents would probably take a more active role in their children's education if they could. An ELL teacher describes the challenges these families face:

> There's a perception that people in poverty are not working hard enough... We live in a culture that blames victims... It's blaming poor people and it's blaming parents and then [they] go ahead and blame a profession, a predominantly female profession ... but let's look at the bigger picture. We need to look at what families are up against trying to get affordable housing, and jobs with their

limited education, and healthcare and transportation... You can't take a half-day to come to a conference at school when you work in the service industry. You'll lose a day of pay and you'll have to ride the bus back and forth... It's stressful enough [to raise children] when you *have* the resources!

This kind of compassion for children and families represents a shift in values and beliefs. The South Street staff have come to view school improvement as an expression of care and moral responsibility—a responsibility that they own, despite their frustrations with the system.

DISCUSSION

Lessons Learned

The South Street case study makes it clear that improving student achievement in reading is a challenging process at best. In the first phase of South Street's improvement initiative, Principal Jacobs worked with outside experts and her steering committee members to understand the needs of South Street's students and staff. They used data to drive their decision-making and they removed what they called "roadblocks" by providing people the training, materials, support, and resources they required to become successful. The committee selected their literacy framework carefully, noting that behavioral issues in the school were probably the result of students experiencing frustration with instruction that was either too difficult or ineffectively delivered. South Street's developmental approach to reading, writing and word study emphasizes differentiated instruction. In the words of one teacher, "This is a structure that really works for our kids... It's a really safe and wonderful way for our children to have choice and for teachers to get to know their students. It's very well thought out." South Street's improvement plan was designed to meet the needs of their unique context.

The staff at South Street consistently identify "being on the same page," or having what we call coherence and consistency, as a critical aspect of their success. They worked diligently to articulate and implement a common framework for literacy instruction. In addition to the state's assessments, they identified and implemented a local assessment plan to evaluate student progress and program effectiveness regularly. They also meet monthly to discuss all students who are below standard, including those who receive special education services. Achievement targets and intervention plans are developed at these meetings and the team reconvenes monthly to monitor the effectiveness of their recommendations.

Special educators and classroom teachers team-teach core subjects like reading, writing and word study to eliminate fragmentation and improve opportunities for flexible grouping and needs-based instruction. The teachers share common understandings about best practices, literacy development, and curricular goals. The staff are committed to working at South Street, and teacher turnover has temporarily been halted. Coherence and consistency were vital to this school's successful improvement initiative. We learned that coherence-making is an arduous process. It takes time—possibly years—energy, resources, commitment, expert knowledge, and instructional leadership.

At South Street School, coaching provided the support necessary for teachers to implement their new literacy framework. Monthly observations by the building principal and job-embedded professional development opportunities gave teachers positive feedback and constructive suggestions for improving their practice. A process that was not initially embraced is now revered as one of their most important practices. The staff recognize that some of the best coaches were their teaching colleagues and even students who motivated them by responding positively to the changes in instruction. The common professional development, clearly defined learning expectations, and coordinated local assessment plan allowed them to better collaborate and deepen their knowledge. Coaching helped teachers move research and standards into practice and build a community of continuous learning.

While the teachers of South Street know a lot about the improvement process, they understandably worry about sustaining their work. They say, "We look better and people are thinking we're okay. We may look better, but it's not easy. It's never going to be easy." Another teacher confessed, "I am exhausted at the end of the day." The teachers of South Street have devoted themselves to improving their skills and their students' achievement in reading for several years now. They have worked hard to replace frustration and low expectations with compassion and action. They've taken responsibility for factors within their sphere of influence, yet they acknowledge, "We're not done. Now we have to take on math ... I'm worried. How are we going to do it all?" Sustainability presents new challenges for the staff at South Street and the field (Fullan, 2003).

IMPLICATIONS

The South Street case illuminates the possibility of whole school improvement in high-poverty communities. Throughout the United States, thousands of high-poverty schools are identified by their state departments of education as needing improvement (Cohen & Ginsburg, 2001). It is time for the research community to respond with an unwavering commitment to conduct further research in these settings. We need a deep understanding of the challenges and opportunities these contexts have to offer. We must be timely in the dissemination of our findings, ensuring that they get to the people who need them most urgently—America's teachers.

We have a responsibility to learn more about what works, how to replicate powerful findings, and how to sustain improvements. The studies of effective schools and successful schools (Mosenthal, Lipson, Mekkelsen, Russ, & Sortino, 2001; Taylor et al., 1999) have given us a vision of what's possible in high-poverty settings, yet even these studies don't give us a plan for how to grow and keep more effective schools (Cohen & Ginsburg, 2001; Cuban, 1984; Rosenshine, 2002). We must learn more about the *process* of improving schools so all children in America (and beyond) have the chance to lead richly literate and productive lives.

As highlighted in current educational policy, improving teachers' skills is part of this equation. However, improved skills may not be enough. As we have seen from this case study and other studies of educational policy implementation and standards-based reform, teachers must have the *skill* and *will* to improve student achievement (Cimbricz, 2002; Cohen & Ball, 1999; Darling-Hammond, 1990, 1997; DeBray, Parson, & Woodworth, 2001; Spillane & Jennings, 1997). A South Street teacher emphasized this very point:

> You can take all of the scientifically based research in the world and you can have teachers who know every little move to make, but if they don't have the heart to work in a place like this, it won't make any difference. Every child will be left behind if that *heart* isn't there. And that's something that's really, really hard to mandate.

This teacher knows firsthand what distinguished policy researcher Milbrey McLaughlin noted nearly 20 years ago, "It is incredibly hard to make something happen, most especially across layers of government and institutions. It's incredibly hard not just because social problems tend to be thorny. It's hard to make something happen primarily because policy makers can't mandate what matters" (1987, p. 172). Skill and will are inseparable in successful policy implementation. This may explain, in part, why replication and sustainability are so persistently challenging. It is difficult to engender engagement and commitment from educators in a policy environment where they are at once the *targets* and *agents* of change (McLaughlin, 1987).

There is little dispute that education matters. So does a living wage, healthcare, affordable housing, high-quality childcare, proper nutrition, and personal safety. If we are serious about narrowing the achievement gap, we may need to consider a broader social policy that addresses the root causes of poverty and school failure. To accomplish this ambitious goal, it will be necessary to examine our power structures and competing discourses (Hoffman, 2000; Toll, 2002). We must engage disenfranchised participants, including educators and people of poverty, in the development and implementation of social and educational policy (Tyack & Cuban, 1995).

Policy is important. In a democratic society, our policy is an expression of our values and beliefs (Stone, 2002). Policy drives our actions, though not always in the most productive directions. In the case of South Street School, the state's accountability policy was implemented successfully through a process of negotiation. Inspired leaders listened, removed "roadblocks," provided resources and support, and held high expectations. Participants' actions, values and beliefs were often positively influenced by the policy and student achievement in reading increased. While it is infinitely complex, policy *can* work. The question that remains is: How can we make it work better for our schools and America's children?

REFERENCES

Alliance for Excellent Education. (2003). *Left out and left behind: NCLB and the American high school.* Washington, DC

Allington, R. (2002). *Big brother and the national reading curriculum: How ideology trumped evidence.* Portsmouth, NH: Heinemann.

Allington, R., & Johnston, P. (2001). Characteristics of exemplary fourth grade instruction. In C. Roller (Ed.), *Research on effective teaching.* Newark, DE: International Reading Association.

Amrein, A. L., & Berliner, D. (2002). High-stakes testing, uncertainty, and student learning. *Educational Policy Analysis Archives, 10*(18).

Amrein-Beardsley, A., & Berliner, D. (2003). Re-analysis of NAEP math and reading scores in states with and without high-stakes tests: Response to Rosenshine. *Educational Policy Analysis Archives, 11*(25).

Bear, D., Invernizzi, M., Templeton, S., & Johnston, F. (2004). *Words their way: Word study for phonics, vocabulary, and spelling instruction* (3rd ed.). Upper Saddle River, NJ: Pearson Merrill Hall.

Berliner, D. C., & Biddle, B. J. (1996). *The manufactured crisis: Myths, fraud, and the attack on America's public schools*. White Plains, New York: Longman.

Blachman, B. A., Ball, E. W., Black, R. S., & Tangel, D. M. (1994). Kindergarten teachers develop phoneme awareness in low-income, inner-city classrooms: Does it make a difference? *Reading and Writing: An Interdisciplinary Journal, 6*, 1-18.

Calkins, L. (1994). *The art of teaching writing* (2nd ed.). Portsmouth, NH: Heinemann.

Calkins, L. (2001). *The art of teaching reading*. New York: Addison-Wesley Longman.

Carnevale, A. P. (2001). *Help wanted... college required*. Washington, DC: Educational Testing Service, Office for Public Leadership.

Children's Defense Fund. (2004). *The state of America's children 2004*. Retrieved May 12, 2005, from www.childrensdefense.org/pressreleases/040713.aspx

Cimbricz, S. (2002). State-mandated testing and teachers' beliefs and practice. *Educational Policy Analysis Archives, 10*(2).

Cohen, D. K., & Ball, D. L. (1999). *Instruction, capacity, and improvement* (No. RR-43). Philadelphia: Consortium on Policy Research in Education at the University of Pennsylvania.

Cohen, M., & Ginsburg, A. (2001). *School improvement report: Executive order on actions for turning around low-performing schools*. Retrieved May 9, 2004, from www.ed.gov/offices/ous/pes/ibschools.pdf

Creswell, J. (2005). *Educational research: Planning, conducting, evaluating quantitative and qualitative research* (2 ed.). Upper Saddle River, NJ: Pearson.

Cuban, L. (1984). Transforming a frog into a prince: Effective schools research, policy and practice at the district level. *Harvard Educational Review, 54*, 129-151.

Darling-Hammond, L. (1990). Instructional policy into practice: "The power of the bottom over the top." *Educational Evaluation and Policy Analysis, 12*, 233-241.

Darling-Hammond, L. (1997). *Doing what matters most: Investing in quality teaching*. New York: National Commission on Teaching and America's Future, Teachers College, Columbia University.

Darling-Hammond, L. (1999). *Teacher quality and student achievement: A review of state policy evidence*. Seattle, WA: Center for Teaching Policy, University of Washington.

DeBray, E., Parson, G., & Woodworth, K. (2001). Patterns of response in four high schools under state accountability policies in Vermont and New York. In S. Fuhrman (Ed.), *From the capitol to the classroom: Standards-based reform in the states* (pp. 170-192). Chicago: The University of Chicago Press.

Elmore, R. (2002). *Unwarranted intrusion*. Retrieved March 31, 2003, from http://www.educationext.org/20021/30.html

Elmore, R. (2003). A plea for strong practice. *Educational Leadership, 61*(3), 6-10.

Francis, D. J., Shaywitz, S. E., Stuebing, K. K., Shawitz, B. A., & Fletcher, J. M. (1996). Development lag versus deficit models of reading disability: A longitudinal, individual growth curves study. *Journal of Educational Psychology, 88*, 3-17.

Fullan, M. (2003). *Change forces with a vengeance*. New York: Routledge Falmer.

Glaser, B. G. (1992). *Basics of grounded theory analysis*. Mill Valley, CA: Sociology Press.

Goetz, M. (2001). Standards-based accountability: Horse trade or horse whip? In S. Fuhrman (Ed.), *From the capitol to the classroom: Standards-based reform in the states* (pp. 39-59). Chicago: The University of Chicago Press.

Hoffman, J. (2000). The de-democratization of schools and literacy in America. *The Reading Teacher, 53*, 616-623.

Kamil, M. L. (2003). *Adolescents and literacy: Reading for the 21st century*. Washington, DC: Alliance for Excellent Education.

Linn, R. L., Baker, E. L., & Betebenner, D. W. (2002). Accountability systems: Implications of requirements of the No Child Left Behind Act of 2001. *Educational Researcher, 31*(6), 3-16.

McLaughlin, M. W. (1987). Learning from experience: Lessons from policy implementation. *Educational Evaluation and Policy Analysis, 9*, 171-178.

Merriman, S. B. (1998). *Qualitative research and case study applications in education.* Thousand Oaks, CA: Sage Publications.

Mintrop, H. (2003). The limits of sanctions in low-performing schools: A study of Maryland and Kentucky schools on probation. *Educational Policy Analysis Archives, 11*(3), 1-30.

Mosenthal, J., Lipson, M., Mekkelsen, J., Russ, B., & Sortino, S. (2001). *Elementary schools where students succeed in reading.* Providence, RI: The Lab at Brown University.

Patterson, F. R. A. (2000). The politics of phonics. *Journal of Curriculum and Supervision, 15*, 179-211.

Patton, M. (2002). *Qualitative research and evaluation methods* (3rd ed.). Thousand Oaks, CA: Sage Publications.

Pressley, M., Wharton-MacDonald, R., Collins-Block, C., & Morrow, L. (2001). *Learning to read: Lessons from exemplary first-grade classrooms.* New York: Guilford.

Rosenshine, B. (2002). Helping students from low-income homes read at grade level. *Journal of Education for Students Placed At Risk, 7*, 273-283.

Rosenshine, B. (2003). High-stakes testing: Another analysis. *Educational Policy Analysis Archives, 11*(24).

Snow, C., & Biancarosa, G. (2003). *Adolescent literacy and the achievement gap: What do we know and where do we go from here?* New York: Carnegie Corporation of New York.

Snow, C., Burns, M., & Griffin, P. (1998). *Preventing reading difficulties in young children.* Washington, DC: National Academy Press.

Spillane, J., & Jennings, N. (1997). Aligned instructional policy and ambitious pedagogy: Exploring educational reform from the classroom perspective. *Teachers College Record, 98*, 449-481.

Stake, R. (1995). *The art of case study research.* Thousand Oaks, CA: Sage Publications.

State Department of Education. (2003). *State school report.* Retrieved January 11, 2003, from http://www.state.vt.us/educ/new/html/maindata.html

Stone, D. (2002). *Policy paradox: The art of decision making.* New York: W.W. Norton & Company, Inc.

Taylor, B., Pearson, P. D., Clark, K., & Walpole, S. (1999). *Beating the odds in teaching all children to read* (No. 2-006). Ann Arbor: CIERA.

Toll, C. (2002). Can teachers and policy makers learn to talk to one another? In R. Allington (Ed.), *Big brother and the national reading curriculum: How ideology trumped evidence* (pp. 137-153). Portsmouth, NH: Heinemann.

Tyack, D., & Cuban, L. (1995). *Tinkering toward utopia.* Cambridge, MA: Harvard University Press.

U.S. Department of Education. (2002). *Stronger accountability.* Retrieved February 7, 2005, from http://www.ed.gov/policy/elsec/guid/secletter/020724.html

U.S. Department of Education. (2003, 2002). *Subpart 1 - Reading First.* Retrieved April 17, 2004, from www.ed.gov/policy/elsec/leg/esea02/pg4.html

U.S. Department of Labor. (2002). *So you are thinking about dropping out of school...* Retrieved October 6, 2002, from http://www.dol.gov/asp/fibre/dropout.htm

Adolescents' Punk Rock Fandom:
Construction and Production of Lyrical Texts

Barbara Guzzetti
Yunjung Yang
Arizona State University

Despite a recent increase in studies of students' interactions with popular culture as literate activity, few investigators have explored adolescents' construction or production of musical texts (e.g., Alvermann & Hagood, 2000; Alvermann, Hagood & Williams, 2001). Researchers who undertook this line of inquiry provided new insights into adolescent literacy by focusing on how young people interact with music and offered implications for classroom instruction. For example, Duncan-Andrade and Morell (2000) focused on hip-hop culture by relating its texts to poetry in an urban secondary English class, arguing that hip hop is an effective vehicle for developing students' critical and analytical thinking skills, particularly for those urban youth who have been marginalized. They posited that students are more inclined to develop literacy skills and strategies if they have culturally-relevant subject matter, calling for school-based literacy to include cultural values, self-awareness, and critical consciousness.

Other researchers have identified students' appreciation of musical texts and their music fandom as literate practice. Alvermann, Hagood, and Williams (2001) noted strategies used by a 14 year-old boy to obtain information about his favorite rappers, including positioning himself as competent, valuing social interactions with others around rap, taking up a stance of independence and self determination to locate, read, and share information about rap, and questioning. Moje (2004) argued that popular music was one of the most important funds of knowledge that Latino teens drew on in their lives. The New London group (1996) identified audio resources along with linguistic structures in their conceptions of literacy.

Alvermann and Hagood (2000) argued that studying fandom with young people can provide insights into how students construct their identities and illustrate how students create meanings from their personal interests. These researchers discovered that fan culture involves not only the consumption of lyrical texts, but also the production of these texts through parody and imitation in response to the professional media texts of fandom. Fans continually reread these texts, and, as a result, change their focus to the production of social knowledge and discourses.

Buckingham and Sefton-Green (1994) addressed the use of hardcore rap to foster students' critical discourse by investigating three pop music magazines produced by secondary students. These writers defined themselves in relation to wider social, cultural, and ideological forces by taking critical positions in discourse, claiming their tastes and identities, and intervening directly in popular culture forms. The study demonstrated that writing media texts can open a window to critical reflection and analysis.

PURPOSE

Despite these insights, little is actually known about how and why adolescents go about their enactment of music fandom. Not much is known about how young people critique, extend, or imitate lyrical texts, and how the production of these texts may help them in identity formation or play a role in developing and demonstrating critical literacy abilities. Hence, researchers have called for additional studies of adolescents' interactions with musical groups and their songs to explore how different tastes in music give young people different identities and place them in particular social groups (Alvermann & Hagood, 2000; Desmond, 1987).

The purpose of this study was, therefore, to address these under-investigated issues by exploring how adolescents engage with one genre of music, punk rock. Our research questions were: How do fans enact punk rock fandom? How do students construct their own pleasures through the critical consumption and production of musical texts? How do lyrical texts assist young people in forming and representing their identities?

Punk Rock

Punk rock fandom is particularly useful to study for these purposes because punk has been characterized not only as a genre of music with various subgenres, but also as a philosophy, a life style, and a way of representing one's self in the world (Azerrad, 2001). The relationship that young people have with punk has been referred to as impetus for self-discovery and self-definition (Greenwald, 2003). Punk is known as more than a music genre; it is also considered to be an entire cultural movement (Greenwald, 2003) with its own identity, values, and cohesion (Levine & Stumpf, 1983). Punk rock is characterized by freedom of expression, encouraging young people to create their own musical texts as empowerment of the individual and expression of identity. Accordingly, many punk songs are harsh political or emotional outcries of rebellion (Desmond, 1987). Punks have acted against the conventional by using dark imagery and symbols to impart fear and intimidation and to be thought provoking (Levine & Stumpf, 1983). These symbols, such as repulsive band names, iron crosses, swastikas and bikers' clothes are used to repel those in the mainstream culture or to challenge them.

Since its inception, much has been written about the history, philosophy, and genres of punk rock, such as emo or emotional punk, feminist punk, and political punk (e.g., Azerrad, 2001; Greenwald, 2003; Levine & Stumpf, 1983). Sirc (1997) noted that punk performers and songs are only as interesting as the emotions that they generate or the situations that they catalyze. Punk is valued more for its creative and empowering processes and its effects or outcomes that spur action than for its technically sophisticated products. Punk, as a genre of music and an act of transformation, is considered a form of free speech, representing how individuals want to live and take action toward the world.

THEORETICAL FRAMEWORK

This study of punk rock fans and their interactions about musical texts was informed by two theoretical frameworks. The first of these was literacy as a social practice, with a focus on literacy work as identity work (e.g., Gee, 1996; Street, 1995). Literacy practices are socially and culturally embedded, and are meaning-making processes, rather than simply acts of reading, writing, listening, and speaking (Gee, 1996; Street, 1995). Learning and practicing literacy are shaped by the social and cultural beliefs that students hold about the value and purposes of literacy, as well as by the activity (Scribner & Cole, 1981).

We considered it particularly important to study adolescents in their out-of-school literacy pursuits, for as Street (1995) suggests, to study youth only in school implies that they have no life outside of school. We also recognize that young people use literacy to form and represent their identities. Often, such identity work is done in communities of practice (Wenger, 1998) or affinity groups, recognizable by shared practices and language (Gee, 1996). Language is more than a mere set of rules for communication – it is an "identity kit" that signifies membership in a particular group. According to Gee (1996), "Discourses are ways of being in the world, or forms of life which integrate words, acts, values, beliefs, attitudes, and social identities, as well as gestures, glances, body positions, and clothes" (p. 127) and include all the ways of displaying membership in or allegiance to a particular social group or community.

A second framework that was complimentary to our view of literacy as a social practice resulted from our readings in cultural studies (e.g., Buckingham & Sefton-Green, 1994; Frith, 1996a; 1996b). We recognize that students' immersion in music allows them to interact with alternative texts other than the traditional texts that are typically found in school, thereby creating new sites of possibility for expression of identity. Buckingham and Sefton-Green (1994) focused on the relationship between music and identity, stating that "to claim particular tastes in popular music is thus to claim a particular social identity or, in some cases, multiple identities… people use music as a means of locating themselves socially, historically, and politically" (p. 64).

METHODS

Sample

This study was conducted as a case study, defined as the complete study of an integrated and bounded system (Stake, 1995). A purposive sample of two late adolescent (18 year old) females was selected as informants. These girls were chosen to participate based on their involvement in and proclivity to talk about punk rock. Both girls were avid punk rock fans with a long history of participation in punk-rock fandom and were exceptionally knowledgeable of and passionate about punk rock and its various genres.

One of the girls, Saundra (a pseudonym, as are all names herein) served as the primary informant for the study. We considered Saundra, a European-American teenager, who was thrust into a low socioeconomic area when her parents divorced, to be our main participant because of our long-standing relationship with her. Saundra had participated with us in prior research over the course of two past years. One of these investigations (Guzzetti & Gamboa, 2004a) focused on her co-production of a zine (a self publication created as an alternative to commercial magazines), *Burnt Beauty (BB)*, which was initiated by one of her friends. Although *BB* contained writings mainly focused on issues of social justice, Saundra's contributions to *BB* related to entertainment and punk rock. Saundra also was an informant for us in a related study (Guzzetti & Gamboa, 2004b) of her production of another zine, one that she initiated that focused exclusively on entertainment and punk rock. Over the course of four years, Saundra created four issues of this zine that she titled after a punk rock song, *Brutally Morbid Axe of Satan (BMAOS)* in which she reviewed punk rock bands, songs, and venues. In addition to her zining, Saundra played drums, guitar, and bass guitar in two punk rock bands, co-authored a punk rock song, co-produced a CD of her current band's songs, all using her stage name, a pseudonym with a sexual connotation. She also created brochures and informational material regarding punk rock.

During Saundra's senior year of high school, she asked a friend, Mrs. Eff (a self-selected pseudonym chosen after a comic book character) to collaborate with her in producing the third issue of her zine. Mrs. Eff was of Iranian and European - American descent, and went to the same high school as Saundra in the central area of a city in the Southwest. Mrs. Eff worked part time in a comic book store, an experience which influenced the format and content of her contributions to the zine. Mrs. Eff was knowledgeable about many different kinds of music because of her own efforts, as well as her family's and friends' expertise. Her grandparents were classically trained opera singers who taught at the university level and educated her and her parents about music. Her brother was a disc jockey, particularly knowledgeable about techno and hip hop, and her friends were "deeply submerged" into various genres of music.

During the course of the study, both girls graduated from high school and began their first year of college. Mrs. Eff attended a nearby community college in the city, while Saundra commuted to a local state university in a suburb. Although the girls were close friends with similar views, they had different dispositions. Mrs. Eff described herself as bipolar; Saundra considered herself to be on an even keel emotionally, with ups and downs that were not as dramatic as those Mrs. Eff experienced.

The Researchers

We had little knowledge of punk rock prior to meeting these informants. Barbara became somewhat familiar with punk rock through her prior studies of zinesters (Guzzetti & Gamboa, 2004a; 2004b) in which Saundra participated, but Yunjung, a native of Korea, had lived in the United States for only 4 years and had no prior knowledge about punk rock. Therefore, we were able to position ourselves as learners, allowing our informants to be our teachers or guides to the myriad facets of punk. Neither of us had any particular allegiance to or fandom of other genres of music; therefore, we were receptive to acquiring an interest in and appreciation of punk.

Data Collection

Data consisted primarily of interviews conducted in Saundra's home or in coffee houses and restaurants. We conducted four semi-structured interviews with both of the girls together, ranging from one and a half to three hours in duration. Four other semi-structured interviews were conducted with Saundra alone and were the same length as other interviews. These interviews were audio-recorded and transcribed to written record. Numerous informal interviews also were conducted by electronic communications, printed, and archived.

Our few observations focused on the girls' listening to and critiquing punk rock. These young women shared excerpts of songs with us and typed the lyrics to those songs for us. They shared their writings about punk rock, and consulted magazines and trade publications to illustrate their explanations. Following Buckingham's (1991) advice to get inside the experience of popular culture, we visited a popular punk rock venue to listen to and see punk rock performers and fans. We also frequented two stores devoted to punk rock memorabilia, records, tapes, CDs, publications, and clothing.

In addition to these data, we collected numerous documents as triangulation for the study. These included four issues of Saundra's zine, *BMAOS*; and the three issues of the zine that Saundra contributed to, *BB*. We also collected other commercial and self-made publications related to punk rock. Commercial publications included two issues of *Punk Planet*, a magazine for punk rock fans; and one issue of *Maximumrocknroll*, a commercial publication about rock music; and one issue of *Thrasher*, a magazine for skateboarders, in which Saundra's zine was reviewed. Self-publications consisted of four issues of Saundra's zine; Saundra's band's CD, titled *Genital Accident* and its pictures and liner notes; lyrics to the punk song she co-authored, *Dark and Buttery*; an informational brochure Saundra authored on punk rock, *Punk Rock for Beginners*; flyers advertising various punk bands and their appearances; and excerpts from Saundra's reviews of punk rock bands, recordings, and venues for her high school newspaper.

Data Analysis

These data were analyzed by inductive and thematic analysis. We began our analysis by reading and rereading the data which directed us to further data collection. Data were analyzed continually as they were collected through constant comparison (Glaser & Strauss, 1967). We also conducted a secondary analysis by searching our data for codes we developed from our theoretical frames, using a matrix procedure (Miles & Huberman, 1994).

In addition, we involved our participants in our data analysis. We asked the girls to define any terms with which we were unfamiliar to avoid translation into a language other than their own (Spradley, 1980). Finally, we conducted member checks with our informants, asking for their remarks on our transcriptions of data and our analyses of those data. These were conducted by e-mail, using track changes in Word. The girls filled in gaps in the transcriptions due to inaudible sections of the audiotapes; they corrected our misunderstandings (e.g., changing the name of a depressing indie movie they referred to from *Dancing in the Dark*, as we had it, to *Dancer in the*

Dark); and they elaborated on their interviews (e.g., adding, "cricket is like baseball in England; it uses a bat and a ball" in the section of the transcription where they had explained that a funny Lawnmower Deth song was about hitting people with cricket bats).

FINDINGS

Our first question asked how fans enact music fandom. We found that fandom was accomplished through personal displays, self education, and advocacy through teaching others. Our second question asked how young people construct their own pleasures through critical consumption and production of lyrical texts. We found that these girls had specific criteria for good and bad music and produced lyrical texts as a response through parody and imitation. Our third question addressed how musical texts assisted these students in identity formation and assertion. We found that political punk provided guidelines for their lives and served as a cushion against and a comfort in a commercial society and served as a refuge from other popular culture representations. These themes are elaborated on below.

Enacting Fandom

Personal displays. To explain how they indicated and enacted punk rock fandom, the girls took much time to educate us about the differences between dressing punk and dressing goth or hip hop, consulting magazines and trade publications to show us examples of the distinctions. They pointed out to us that their dress is a text to be read by others, referred to by researchers as symbols of inclusion or exclusion (Desmond, 1987) or markers of membership in an affinity group (Gee, 1996). To identify herself as a punk rock fan, Saundra wore jeans with multiple zippers, safety pins, and patches advertising punk rock bands, and punk rock t-shirts. During the course of the study, she shaved her hair into a Mohawk, a hair style that indicates punk rock fandom, as she described in her brochure, *Punk Rock for Beginners.* Mrs. Eff often dressed in kilts, plaids, leather, and black, styles also indicative of punk-rock fandom. Saundra confided their rationale for dressing this way:

> wearing the clothes sends signals to other people who are fans of the music so you can talk to those people…. If there was no punk rock style, no sort of common dress or anything, people would have to walk around and talk to everyone in order to find out if they were a cool person to talk to…I don't wear the buttons and have the patches so I can show people, "look at my musical taste; I'm so great 'cause I like these bands". It's just by looking at those things, it reminds me of the band, and I just feel warm and fuzzy inside again. Looking at the buttons will remind me of the music. (7/18/02)

Hence, for Saundra, some of these cultural symbols are more than just public indicators of membership in an affinity group (Gee, 1996). They are also personal reminders of the enjoyment of particular punk genres and bands. As such, they have covert as well as overt functions (Buckingham & Sefton-Green, 1994).

Saundra extended her identification with punk through stylistic choices in her performing life, as well. For example, Saundra's punk band often held theme nights, such as coming onstage as their favorite villains. Her band members decided to dress for their show as their favorite dead person on Halloween. Saundra chose to go as G.G. Allin, a deceased punk rock/shock rocker. Even when not in costume, on stage Saundra dresses even more extremely and distinctively as punk, wearing black leather, metal, and spiked dog-collar chokers.

Self-education. Mrs. Eff elaborated on how they engage in punk rock fandom beyond displays of identification and admiration. She described self-education as a primary way in which young people enact fandom. She explained that people like them who are passionate about punk rock generally will go out of their way to find out more about it.

Saundra became knowledgeable about many punk bands by looking them up on the Internet, reading about them, and finding their lyrics online, often copying them. She often acquired their recordings and downloaded their music, and typed the lyrics to selected songs that were important to her, transcribing by repeatedly listening to the songs. She usually discovered previously unknown bands by getting referrals and references from friends and her brother (who also had played in a punk rock band), and by discussing these bands with them.

Mrs. Eff was also able to extend her knowledge of punk in much the same way as Saundra did. Mrs. Eff relied on her social network of family and friends, including those she worked with at the comic book store for referrals to bands and songs. Mrs. Eff's boyfriend was a primary source of referral, and she often discussed the meanings and implications of lyrics with him, as well as with Saundra. These types of exchanges are typical between members of communities of practice as varying degrees of knowledge are represented within the group and its members learn from one another (Wenger, 1998).

Advocacy by educating. The girls also showed their enactment of punk fandom by their proclivity to teach others their knowledge of punk, and their desire to share their pleasures in punk music. One example of this was the informational brochure that Saundra created, *Punk Rock for Beginners.* This six-page booklet defines major genres of punk, such as Old School (political with messages of rebellion against the norm), New School (bands started in or after the 1990s, extremely trendy political punk), and Hardcore (loud, fast, and angry). Her booklet also explicated the style of dress of punk rock fans (e.g., Converse shoes, spikes, dyed hair, leather jackets, and zippers) and contained illustrations of representative hair styles, including a Devil's Lock, Mohawk, Bihawk, and Trihawk. Saundra also wrote advice on what to expect when attending a punk rock show (concert), included a quiz testing the reader's knowledge of famous punk performers, compiled a list of bands who have members that are also in other punk bands, and gave advice on ways to avoid being considered a poser, or someone who assumes to be knowledgeable about and appreciate punk, but lacks the substantive knowledge to be truly punk.

The zine, *Brutally Morbid Ax of Satan,* was another educational vehicle, the third issue of which was co-created by Saundra and Mrs. Eff. This issue contained regular features present in all issues, including an Obituaries section (punk venues, bands and performers who for various reasons no longer exist), and reviews, critiques of or stories about punk bands and CDs. Some of these reviews included the girls' emotional reactions, stimulated by particular songs or groups, as evidenced by Mrs. Eff's comments about the band Stereolab: "Some music makes me fall in love a little bit with no one particular each time I hear it" (p. 19).

Other reviews by Saundra in Issue Three extended the reviews she wrote for her high school newspaper and for *BB*, by analyzing the technical nuances of songs with comments like, "Something as small as the pitch of the vocals or just a tiny bit of the tone of an instrument will give certain songs away as a joke" (p. 17). Another feature in this issue of *BMAOS* was a tribute to the political and historical knowledge Saundra gained by listening to punk rock, called "Font of Knowledge." In this article, she contrasted the knowledge that she learned or was stimulated to learn by punk rock lyrics to the knowledge that she gained in school:

> The Love Canal. I remember reading something about this in dumb-kid history class my junior year, but no details. There was this canal in New York that was polluted and it caused some problems. Fortunately, there's a Flipper song called Love Canal that mentions exactly the kind of monster-like deformed flipper babies that have the Love Canal to thank for their birth defects! And so many people probably think that song is about vaginas (p. 5).

At times, Saundra related one lyrical text to another to piece together knowledge about a political or historical topic:

> Ronald Reagan: The Dayglo Abortions taught me to hate Ronald Reagan, but Mucky Pup taught me why. *Reagan Knew* by Mucky Pup is about the Iran arms-selling scandal that Ronald Reagan was mixed up in: "Oliver North was set up, and all of Congress knew it, yea Ollie North was set up and guess who made him do it! Reagan knew, Reagan knew, Ron told North just what to do, the government lied to hide the truth, Ron told Ollie: 'Boys, shred the proof!'" (p. 5).

These remarks lend insight into the power of lyrical texts by demonstrating the intertextual and metatextual nature of these adolescents' interactions with punk rock, reminders that musical texts are interpreted within the context of other texts and in a thematic relationship to other songs (McDonald, 1988). The girls' remarks illustrate that there is perhaps no better popular medium to create political awareness within young people than music. A song can create a sense of consciousness about a topic, giving the song a useful purpose (McDonald, 1988).

Critically Consuming and Producing Punk Rock

Critical consumption. Other researchers noted that young people not only read and reread lyrical texts, they also critically consume them; avid fans, as well as interpretative appreciators, judge the merits of the songs of those whom they admire (Lening, 1987). Adolescents have their own criteria for and conceptions of good music (Alvermann & Hagood, 2000). These young women identified the specific criteria that they use to evaluate punk rock texts. Those deemed worthy contained elements of creativity, passion, absurdity, humor, genuineness or sincerity, energy, emotionality or sentimentality, and empowerment. Songs with one or more of these characteristics were valued for their ability to evoke an emotional reaction or a physical response. For example, Mrs. Eff confided, "Sometimes the lyrics are so great, they just touch you, and you swear to God that the musician wrote that song just for you." She admired the group Tool, a metal band with a dark sound, but profound lyrics that were so depressing to her that they made her cry. Conversely, Mrs. Eff enthusiastically described a new genre of music she discovered, Trip Hop, that made her want to sing and dance.

Saundra also had emotional reactions to particular songs. She typed for us the lyrics to Black Flag's *Rise Above*, which speaks to resisting "society's arms of control," and wrote her reaction: "It was like a light shone down from heaven and angels started to sing. It really spoke to me." In a later interview she told us:

> I wish I'd wrote all the [Black Flag] songs myself because it speaks directly from my soul....It's things that I believe and you get this feeling in your stomach ...It makes you feel powerful when you listen to it because it's exactly what you're thinking, but they say it in words. (10/23/03)

The girls also admired songs that were playful or lifted their spirits, songs that were of various genres of music besides punk. For example, Mrs. Eff liked "fun music," such as Ween, a band she admired because, as Saundra stated, "They make fun of everything and everyone." Saundra described her excitement "like a big cartoon heart floating above my head" (10/23/03) when she heard an Oingo Boingo song, *Insanity*, for the first time. They laughed at lyrics of songs by Lawnmower Deth, British musicians who sing absurd lyrics about giant robots and people spanking each other with cricket bats. Saundra admired Parkway Wretch's song, *Tire Swing Blues*, a reminder to jilted lovers that they have friends who can repair damage done by broken romantic relationships, for its "excellent lyrics and positive message." The girls' responses drew them into emotional alliances with the performers (Frith, 1996a).

Just as these young women had criteria for good music, they could also characterize bad music. Bad music was most music played on the radio, commercialized music that sounded like everyone else's music, songs that are played too much, or songs that are insincere. Mrs. Eff characterized over-played and over-commercialized music by using an analogy:

> It's like American cheese; it's been processed so many different times, it's not cheese anymore. It's like if their lyrics had something to say and they were deep and meaningful [once] it doesn't matter anymore. (7/18/03)

Particularly important were the girls' distinctions between commercial and manufactured lyrics versus ones that were genuine. Genuine songs were ones that they sensed that the singer had written as sincere and personal expression. Commercial or insincere songs were those in which they knew the singer wasn't really singing from the heart and didn't really believe the lyrics. They considered Britney Spears' songs to be an example of bad music, as Saundra considered her tunes to be "truly pop and catchy, songs about being in love although you know she's not" that some people might take as a happy message, but as Saundra put it, "What it says to me is, 'I'm trying to make money.'" Mrs. Eff elaborated on this by stating:

> People that are depressed [like I am] are a little deeper because they are forced to think about things that other people aren't so their perspective on the world is changed, and they're forced to grow up quicker as opposed to people who just are all, you know, smiles and roses, and have this great perfect life, and never grow up, and never form

passionate feelings like audacity, and there's all these different things like audacity, there's fear, and there's pleasure, and there's sorrow, and there's good and evil, and there's rage.....and if you're like just growing up in this life where everything is perfect and you never need to take care of yourself, and you never get to learn those passions which is kind of like the same thing with Britney Spears songs, you know, they're all like this big freaking bowl of sugar, there's nothing more to it. (10/23/03)

Mrs. Eff elaborated on her conception of bad music by using another analogy:

> It just doesn't reach me in any way, Oh God, it's so empty. It's like, when you're trying to eat something good for yourself and you pick up a Snicker's[candy bar], and you eat it and it does nothing for you. It just puts crap in your system. (7/18/03)

Both Saundra and Mrs. Eff characterized commercialized music as "totally empty" music that has nothing to say, consisting of "false and packaged teen angst" (7/18/03). Mrs. Eff explained that money and popularity corrupt the writing style when the band's mission becomes the record company's mission—to make money—and songs are produced on a production schedule. As a result, the music becomes boring, producing certain ennui, even if the musicians have (in her words) "insanely good" skill levels. These comments speak to the ability of fans to evaluate music in an ethical way by critiquing lyrical texts for their authenticity or sincerity (Frith, 1996a). Incompetent and self indulgent music—including the "empty" music Mrs. Eff referred to—are two categories of bad music that fans identify (Frith, 1996a).

Producing punk rock. Saundra responded to lyrical texts she heard and critiqued by creating her own punk lyrics and writings. Her band produced 1,000 CDs which are sold in several local alternative music stores. Each of the songs on her CD also has a story with it in the liner notes preceding the lyrics that sets the context for and elaborates on those lyrics. In composing her lyrics, Saundra stated that she was inspired to write the words to *Dark and Buttery* by Anal Cunt's (AC's) songs. Although she co-wrote the lyrics, the original concept for the song was hers alone. The rhyme was characterized by the use of irony and appropriation, elements found in other punk songs. She described it as a "goofy, sick song" that is narrated rather than sung, with an extended outro or long ending. (2/13/04)

Written in a vein that imitates AC's style, with songs like, "I Sent a Thank You Card to the Guy Who Raped You"; "Sweatshops Are Cool"; and "I Snuck a Retard Into a Sperm Bank," Saundra's own titles and lyrics are ridiculously outrageous and mockingly offensive. Like AC, her style is to write in an unabashed and irreverent vein. Lyrics like these, according to Saundra, are not to be taken literally, but laughed at for their sarcasm and mockery that illuminate social problems and injustices in a facetious way. Saundra's production of these lyrical texts illustrates that making music is not simply a way of expressing ideas, but is a way of living those ideas (Hall & du Gay, 1996).

Using Musical Texts for Identity Formation and Representation

These young women identified political punk as providing guidelines for their lives, maturing their beliefs, and giving impetus for further involvement by political action or by exploring related ideas in other texts, such as musical texts. For example, Saundra spoke of her admiration for a song by Millions of Dead Cops, the lyrics of which embodied her outlook on society:

> Every time I hear it, I wish I was playing it and singing it. The lyrics are like, "Your authority and your power have turned us sick and sour, and your justice is a lie, and we're gonna fight you until you die."…Whenever I hear that song, it just makes me feel how angry I am, and I'm just so sick of the way life is forced down your throat, and you have no say in what you do to some extent…like the rules of life….you go to school, and then you get a job, and you earn money so you can buy things to keep yourself alive, and if you don't like that, then it's pretty much too bad. (10/23/03)

The girls shared songs that represented these ideas, as well as others that provided principles for living their lives, illustrating that music constructs identity (Frith, 1996a). These included a Millions of Dead Cops song, *America Is So Straight*, with lyrics that speak to the difficulty in trying to live a lifestyle outside the norm. Saundra cited Flipper songs as very life affirming with lyrics that speak to, "trying to be happy despite all of that." When Mrs. Eff expressed her fear of becoming caught in the trap of mediocrity, despite her perception of herself as less complacent and not as easily fulfilled as others, Saundra reminded her of the Black Flag song with its first line, "I won't believe that this is all" which Mrs. Eff said, "really sums it up for me." In turn, this lyric reminded Mrs. Eff of a Bjork song called, *There's More to Life Than This*. These discourses are reminders that "music gives us a way of being in the world, a way of making sense of it" (Frith, 1996, p.114) and "gives us a real experience of what the ideal could be" (Frith, 1996a, p.123).

The girls found messages in punk songs like these a cushion against and a comfort in a commercial society that has disappointed them, particularly by other popular culture representations that emphasize materialism. For example, Mrs. Eff confided that television programs like Who Wants to Be a Millionaire, Joe Millionaire, and Survivor made her depressed and cry, "the whole entire world is crumbling into ruins and I can't do anything about it…..that people watch shows like this and think it matters, and it makes their lives seem real." (10/23/03)

In addition to helping them form and represent their views, lyrical texts also spurned the girls to action in several forms. Mrs. Eff remarked that she attended more political protests when she was listening to political punk. Saundra subscribed to the e-mail list for the local anarchist coalition, a group with alternative views to government, such as those represented in some punk texts. Saundra also wore political punk t-shirts, such as one that quoted the title to a song by Bad Religion, *The Voice of God is Government*, and had posters of political punk bands like the U.S. Bombs on her bedroom walls. She also wrote about the messages of Millions of Dead Cops in the zine, *BB*, and discussed groups like the Dead Kennedys.

These activities showed the girls' activist natures and were representative of the call to action in political punk. Their actions and reactions are illustrative of the production of self as an object in the world. These girls engaged in the practices identified by Hall & duGay (1996) of self constitution (forming new philosophies from lyrical texts), reflection (relating lyrical texts to their everyday lives) and recognition (allowing songs to "speak" to them). Hence, identity construction through lyrical discourse was, for these girls, an act of power.

DISCUSSION

These students provided insight into how young people enact music fandom through learning and teaching. They demonstrated how meaning is enacted and shared among music fans, and how students use lyrical texts to represent their positions and their changing identities. This study demonstrates the social and cultural aspects of identity construction through music and the production of lyrical texts as literate practice.

Findings from this investigation support the incorporation of musical texts in literacy instruction in two complimentary yet distinct ways. First, these adolescents demonstrated that the music young people enjoy is often complex, richly metaphoric, and symbolic. The students in this study were making their own connections between the lyrical texts they enjoyed outside of school and their in-school instruction, supporting the notion that music is a logical bridge between popular culture and the school (Duncan-Andrade & Morell, 2000).

Second, lyrical texts provided these girls with a way to explore and represent their changing identities. The young women were empowered by music to make sense of the conflicts in their lives and in society using music to reflect on the nature of their lives. They were enabled to express their own visions and sense of self through their critical consumption and creative production of song lyrics. We believe that musical texts can provide a vehicle for other young people to explore their own identities and represent their personal values and ideas, as well.

Finally, we note caveats in incorporating musical texts in classroom instruction. Like Alvermann, Hagood, and Williams (2001), we agree that pleasure in lyrical texts is often individually defined, and the meanings that individuals construct from these texts are not necessarily shared meanings. Punk, with its irony, sarcasm, and dark imagery has the deliberate potential to be offensive. Punk rock, like any other genre of music, appeals to a particular subgroup of students and may not appeal to the mainstream.

Hence, lyrical texts, such as those of punk rock, might best accompany other texts in the curriculum that use similar literary elements. Punk uses satire, parody, and irony to convey its messages. Analyzing this critical and controversial music for both its devices as well as its content may lead to appreciation for this genre of music and result in conscious-raising discussions of esteem and power. Deconstructing such texts may encourage students to further their own knowledge of society and politics (Duncan-Andrade & Morell, 2000). Like the students in this study, critiquing these musical texts may also provide young people with the analytical tools to examine and evaluate messages in other texts of popular culture that permeate their everyday lives.

REFERENCES

Alvermann, D. E., & Hagood, M.C. (2000). Fandom and critical medial literacy. *Journal of Adolescent and Adult Literacy, 43*, 436-446.

Alvermann, D. E., Hagood, M. C., & Williams, K. B. (2001, June). Image, language, and sound: Making meaning with popular culture texts. *Reading Online, 4*(11). Available: http://www.readingonline.org/newliteracies/lit_index.asp?HREF=/newliteracies/action/alvermann/index.html.

Azerrad, M. (2001). *Our band could be your life*. Boston, MA: Little Brown & Co.

Buckingham, D. (1991). Teaching about the media. In D. Lusted (Ed), *The media studies book* (pp.12-35). New York: Routledge.

Buckingham, D., & Sefton-Green, J. (1994). *Popular culture goes to school.* London: Taylor & Francis.

Desmond, R.J. (1987). Adolescents and music lyrics: Implications of a cognitive perspective. *Communication Quarterly, 35,* 376-284.

Duncan-Andrade, J., & Morrell, J.E. (2000, April). *Using hip-hop culture as a bridge to canonical poetry texts in an urban secondary English class.* Paper presented at the meeting of the American Educational Research Association, New Orleans, Louisiana.

Frith, S. (1996a). *Performing rites: On the value of popular music.* Oxford, England: Oxford University Press.

Frith, S. (1996b) Music and identity. In S. Hall & P. du Gay (Eds.). *Questions of cultural identity,* pp. 108-127. London: Sage.

Frith, S. (1981). *Sound effects: Youth, leisure and the politics of rock and roll.* New York: Pantheon.

Gee, J. P. (1996). *Social linguistics and literacies: Ideology in discourses,* (2nd ed.) New York: Routledge-Falmer.

Glaser, B. J., & Strauss, (1967). *The discovery of grounded theory: Strategies for qualitative research.* New York: Aldine.

Greenwald, A. (2003). *Nothing feels good: Punk rock, teenagers, and emo.* New York: St. Martins press.

Guzzetti, B.J., & Gamboa, M. (2004a). Zines for social justice: Adolescent girls writing on their own. *Reading Research Quarterly, 39,* 408-437.

Guzzetti, B.J., & Gamboa, M. (2004b). Zining: The unsanctioned literacy practice of adolescents. In C. Fairbanks, J. Worthy, B. Maloch, J. Hoffman, & D. Schallert (Eds.), *53rd Yearbook of the National Reading Conference* (pp. 206-217). Oak Creek, WI: The National Reading Conference.

Hall, S., & du Gay, P. (Eds.), (1996). *Questions of cultural identity.* London: Sage.

Lening, J.S. (1987). Rock music and socialization of moral values in early adolescence. *Youth and Society, 8,* 363-383.

Levine, H.G., & Stumpf, S.H. (1983). Statements of fear through cultural symbols: Punk rock as reflective subculture. *Youth and Society, 14,* 425 -435.

McDonald, J.R. (1988). Politics revisited: Metatextual implications of rock and roll criticism. *Youth and Society, 19,* 485-503.

Miles, M. B., & Huberman, A. M. (1994). *Qualitative data analysis* (2nd ed.).Thousand Oaks, CA: Sage.

Moje, E. (2004). Working toward third space in content area literacy: An examinationof everyday funds of knowledge and discourse. *Reading Research Quarterly, 39,* 38-70.

New London Group. (1996). A pedagogy of mulitliteracies: Designing social futures. *Harvard Educational Review, 66,* 1, 60-92.

Savage, J. (1992). *England's dreaming: Anarchy, Sex Pistols, punk rock, and beyond.* New York: St. Martin's.

Scribner, S., & Cole, M. (1981). *The psychology of literacy.* Cambridge, MA: Harvard University Press.

Sirc, G. (1997). Never mind the Tagmemics, where's the Sex Pistols? *College Composition and Communication, 48,* 9-29.

Spradley, J. (1980). *Participant Observation.* New York: Holt.

Stake, R. (1995). Case Studies. In N.K. Denizen & Y.S. Lincoln (Eds.) *Handbook of qualitative research* (pp. 236-247). Thousand Oaks, CA: Sage.

Street, B. V. (1995). *Social literacies: critical approaches to literacy in development, ethnography and education.* London: Longman.

Wenger, E. (1998). *Communities of practice: Learning, meaning and identity.* Cambridge, UK: Cambridge University Press.

Spanish Speakers Learning to Read in English: What a Large-Scale Assessment Suggests About Their Progress

Lori A. Helman

University of Minnesota

The period of early literacy development is crucial for helping students become proficient readers and writers. When students do not develop literacy skills at a similar pace to their peers, they are at risk of falling further and further behind, and never "catching up" (Juel, 1988; Stanovich, 1986). Students who enter school with an oral language other than standard English are more likely to experience reading difficulties and to present a challenge for teachers to provide effective reading instruction that builds on their strengths and needs (Snow, Burns & Griffin, 1998; Tabors, 1997).

Hispanic-American students are the fastest-growing group entering public schools in cities, smaller towns, and rural areas of the United States (Population Reference Bureau, 2002). Unfortunately, accountability measures such as the National Assessment of Educational Progress (NAEP) show an achievement gap of 29 points between European-American and Hispanic-American students (U. S. Department of Education, NCES, 2004). To close the achievement gap, it is crucial for researchers and educators to understand the issues surrounding the beginning literacy development of this significant and growing population of students learning to read and write in English in U.S. schools.

In this paper, I report the findings from a statewide assessment of early literacy achievement administered in Nevada as part of its Reading Excellence Act (REA) partnership. Specifically, I focused my analysis on the reading and writing responses of Spanish-speaking English learners (ELs). I compared the nature and developmental timing of their literacy to monolingual English students in the same grade levels at the same schools. From these data, I draw implications for the assessment of and instruction for Spanish-speaking learners.

BACKGROUND

Of the school-aged population of English learners, 73% come from Spanish-language backgrounds (United States Census Bureau, 2002). Although the population of students learning English as a new language is growing rapidly in U.S. schools, much of the research on early literacy development documents the literacy growth of students with native English-language skills (see for example, Neuman & Dickinson, 2001; Snow, et al., 1998).

Students learn to read and write, and hone their advancing skills by continually applying their understanding of the structure of written language to reading and writing tasks (Bear & Helman, 2004). Students, who come to reading instruction in English without having it as a home language, may be affected by a variety of linguistic and other challenges. (August & Hakuta, 1997; Bialystock, 2001; Center for Research on Education, Diversity & Excellence, 2002; Cummins,

1998; Durgunoglu, Nagy, & Hancin-Bhatt, 1993; Durgunoglu & Verhoeven, 1998; Fitzgerald, 1995; Garcia, 2000; Moll & Gonzalez, 1994; Ovando & Collier, 1998; Valdés, 1996; Wong-Fillmore, 1991). The current study is guided by a model of literacy development that spotlights students' understandings at various stages of learning about written language in English. While this model does not encompass all of the psychosocial components of a broader view of literacy in society, it does elucidate a key aspect of literacy learning for students (i.e., the development of orthographic knowledge).

The Developmental Progression of Orthographic Knowledge

Literacy learning has been characterized as the internalization of ever more complex understandings about written language (Ellis, 1997; Henderson & Beers, 1980; Templeton & Morris, 2000). This development proceeds through a series of phases, or stages, that characterize students' understandings about print at a given time (Chall, 1983). These models delineate students' progress along a continuum beginning with a point of limited print awareness and moving to an initial understanding of the alphabetic principle (Morris, Bloodgood, Lomax, & Perney, 2003). Development then expands to full phonemic awareness and the representation in writing of all salient sounds. Development continues to grow as students understand spelling patterns that move beyond one-letter, one-sound approaches. Eventually, understanding blossoms into more advanced levels where an understanding of the spelling-meaning connection is necessary to be successful at literacy tasks.

The current study focuses on students in the beginning stage of reading development. The orthographic knowledge that students have at this stage can be characterized as "spelling by sound." Students challenge themselves to hear as many sounds as possible in a word, and to encode these sounds with letters they believe represent them. This is often a time of labored writing and reading, as skills have generally not been practiced enough to become automatic, and sight word knowledge is limited. The analyses throughout this study feature students' engagement with the sound layer of word knowledge, and how this knowledge interplays with beginning literacy behaviors.

Literacy Development for English Language Learners

Learning a written language while learning an oral language, and simultaneously becoming familiar with a new culture, is truly a formidable task. Comprehensive support for EL students must match the level of challenge they face (Center for Research on Education, Diversity and Excellence, 2002; Geva & Verhoeven, 2000). The current research into literacy learning for non-native speakers shows that the relationship is multi-dimensional, and varies depending on the tasks and background languages of the students involved (Bialystock & Herman, 1999). In other words, much depends upon characteristics of the student's home language, the characteristics of the language being learned, the instructional setting, and the specific demands of the literacy activities. Wu, et al. (1994) found that EL students need to have concrete experience and practice in the target language with a given discourse activity in order to be successful. Geva and Siegel (2000) suggest that a more accurate picture of second language reading development occurs when both underlying cognitive skills and the analysis of specific scripts are taken into account.

The oral and written characteristics of a student's home language and their relationship to English influence the ease or difficulty of second-language literacy development for young students. Because second-language learners in English bring phonological, syntactic, pragmatic, and vocabulary knowledge from their primary language (Bernhardt, 2000; Corson, 2001; Cummins, 1991; Fitzgerald, 1995; Garcia, 2000; Jimenez, 2004), similarities between how a student's first language is mapped to print and the written code of English can lead to support or confusion in the reading or writing process. Where there is similarity between a student's home language and English, there is greater support for the transfer of oral and written language skills. When the differences between languages are greater, a higher possibility for confusion exists (Goldstein, 2001). Durgunoglu and Verhoeven (1998) describe the complexity of supporting EL students to map sounds onto the letters in English, because it is difficult to hear individual sounds in the speech stream.

This background information about second-language literacy development has implications for early literacy screening for Spanish speakers. Two key areas stand out as potential areas of concern:

1. Students' oral language proficiency may limit their oral reading accuracy and comprehension. It may be difficult for students to understand the meaning of passages in texts if they do not understand specific words in English. It may be challenging for them to use context to identify unknown words when English syntactical structures may not be well established (Gregory, 1996).

2. Attempts to spell words may be affected by phonological distinctions between Spanish and English. Distinctive sounds between Spanish and English may lead to graphemic substitutions. Students who have some background knowledge of the Spanish alphabet may use letter name strategies that are different from monolingual English students.

METHOD

The context of the current study is the Nevada Reading Excellence Act (NREA) that operated for a three-year period from July 2001 through June 2004. In this partnership, 52 schools throughout the state were granted funding to participate in a variety of activities to support the early literacy achievement of their pre-K through third-grade students. As part of this project, the Phonological Awareness Literacy Screening (PALS) assessment (Invernizzi & Meier, 2001) was administered in the fall and spring at participating schools. This assessment included measures of developmental spelling, word recognition, and oral reading in context. After assessing each classroom of students, teachers or literacy specialists entered results into an on-line database, where scores were consolidated and could later be viewed on a class or school-wide basis.

The present study utilized a two-pronged approach to the data analysis: (a) an examination of the statewide quantitative PALS data that was submitted by individual schools, and (b) a qualitative analysis of individual responses of beginning readers from two focus schools.

Participants and Setting

Of the more than 18,000 NREA students who took the PALS 1-3 assessment in the spring of 2003, 4,692 were first graders, 4,711 second graders, and 8,621 third graders. Hispanic-American students accounted for 47.1% of this group, while European-American students made up 33.2%. The NREA population was predominantly low income (72.9%) and almost all were identified as Title 1 (96.6%). Approximately one in every four students (24.3%) was identified as limited-English proficient.

Instruments/Tasks

Two specific instruments provided data for the current study. The Phonological Awareness Literacy Screening (PALS) 1-3 is used nationwide to help identify students in need of extra support in their early literacy skill development (Invernizzi & Meier, 2001). The PALS assessment data used in this study measured three aspects of students' literacy knowledge: (a) a developmental spelling inventory evaluated students' orthographic knowledge in English; (b) a word recognition in isolation measure assessed students' ability to quickly recognize a series of grade-level words; and (c) an oral reading in context measure assessed students' fluency, accuracy, and comprehension on a graded passage of text. The word list consisted of 20 words. The score on the spelling assessment ranged from a possible 48 for first grade, 56 for second grade, and 64 for third grade. The PALS 1-3 assessments were developed based on a broad representation of student participation, and have been shown to be reliable and valid in regular field tests (Invernizzi & Meier, 2003).

The Language Assessment Scales-Oral (LAS-O), or its counterpart for grade 1 students, the Pre-LAS, assesses and categorizes students' oral English language proficiency. The LAS-O measures four primary language subsystems (i.e., phonemic, lexical, syntactic and pragmatic) to come up with a single summary score. Scores on the LAS-O range from 1 ("non-English proficient") to 5 ("fluent-English proficient") (De Avila & Duncan, 1994).

Procedure

The PALS 1-3 assessment was administered at all NREA grant schools to students in first through third grades between six weeks and two weeks before the end of the 2002-2003 school year. Literacy specialists, classroom teachers, and/or other support teachers administered the PALS and received written guidelines and in-service instruction in test administration.

The LAS-O assessments had been previously administered (per state mandate) to all students from non-English speaking households in Nevada. Test administrators varied by site, and may have included ESL and reading specialists, classroom teachers, and/or assistants. The LAS-O data were gathered from student records at the school, and entered into the PALS electronic database by school-based literacy coordinators.

My research involved two parallel avenues of data collection and analysis: analysis of statewide electronic data and visual analysis of 105 samples. In the statewide analysis, electronic data that represented numerical scores from the PALS 1-3 and LAS-O assessments were compiled following the assessment window. Demographic analyses were done on overall progress and trends for each ethnic group and for Spanish-speaking English learners. The statewide analyses also compared the overall scores of beginning readers from monolingual English-speaking and Spanish-speaking backgrounds on each component of the PALS early literacy assessment. Beginning readers were identified by their entry-level summed scores on the PALS 1-3 assessment.

The second set of analyses was conducted on 105 sample PALS 1-3 assessments from two NREA schools in the Reno metropolitan area. The populations of both of these schools represented typical NREA demographics (i.e., high percentage of Spanish-speaking students; socio-economic status representative of NREA as a whole; and the fact that students were learning to read and write in an English-speaking classroom). The qualitative samples represented approximately 20 first- and second-grade beginning readers selected from each of five categories of oral language proficiency based on their LAS test: Spanish speakers at LAS level 1; Spanish speakers at LAS level 2; Spanish speakers at LAS level 3; and, Spanish speakers at LAS level 4. English-only students were assigned to category 5. Having a representative sample from each of the language proficiency subgroups provided concrete examples of students' answers from the early literacy assessment.

Data analysis methods included descriptive statistics showing means, standard deviations, and correlations of the monolingual English and Spanish-speaking groups on various literacy tasks and in relation to demographic and language proficiency information. The response protocols of PALS 1-3 assessments were visually analyzed by the researcher, noting correct answers and miscues. Student responses were tallied and categorized to see if patterns existed based on language proficiency, EL status, and PALS' subtest scores. In order to compare the sample developmental spellings of Spanish speakers and monolingual English speakers, 19 matched-pair sets of assessments were identified from the 105 paper assessments in the focus sample to analyze in greater depth. Each Spanish-speaking student was matched to a monolingual English speaker based on his or her developmental spelling score and grade level.

RESULTS

In the following section, key overall findings are shared from the statewide electronic data. Next, results from the individual literacy tasks are presented through both the statewide quantitative data as well as the sample individual responses of beginning readers from two focus schools.

Statewide Overview

The statewide overview of results begins with a comparison of ethnic group performance, and then focuses on how EL students from Spanish-speaking backgrounds compared to monolingual English students. Next, relationships between assessment scores and language proficiency are shared. Finally, data are used to shed light on typical results for Spanish-speaking beginning readers.

Results indicated that ethnic groups in the NREA schools were not performing equally on the PALS assessment. On average, in grades one through three, the percentage of each ethnic group that did not meet benchmark levels was 23.3% for Asian-American students, 24% for European-American students, 27% for Native Peoples, 43% for African-Americans and 46.7% for Hispanic-Americans. Of critical concern is the fact that, even by third grade, 49% of Hispanic students were performing below grade-level benchmarks.

An examination of the data with a lens on the performance of students with limited proficiency in English yielded similarly discrepant figures. In Table 1, we present mean scores on PALS assessments across the three grade levels for Monolingual English European-American students ("EO") and Spanish-Speaking English Language Learners ("SS"). The SS students scored lower than their EO peers on every subtest of the PALS 1-3. On average, Spanish speakers: (a) read one level below their monolingual English schoolmates through the end of third grade; (b) recognized 3-4 fewer sight words from a graded list of 20; (c) represented fewer spelling features of English, as noted in their developmental spelling inventories; and (d) were identified as not meeting benchmarks at more than double the rate of monolingual English students.

The data from the second-grade NREA population, comparing the performance of EL students, organized by language proficiency level, with EO students, are presented in Table 2. The second-grade data are representative of the scores from grades 1-3. Higher student scores on English performance measures are associated positively with success on the component tasks of the PALS assessment. To illustrate, in the area of word recognition, the students in the LAS 1 category averaged 13.1 words correct on the second grade list while the LAS 4 students had a mean score of 16.5 words. The LAS 5 students who are classified as fluent English proficient, had the same average as monolingual English students.

The PALS data were also investigated, from a developmental perspective, in relation to the language-based groups. Students were classified as *emergent, beginning,* or *beyond beginning* based on their summed score for the PALS 1-3. Students at the beginning level of reading and the alphabetic stage of writing have a limited storehouse of sight-words, and use this reading vocabulary in combination with phonic decoding skills to read simple texts. Their spelling concentrates on the sound layer of word knowledge. Beginners read in a word-by-word manner, and have not yet developed fluent reading behaviors. Overall, in the NREA data, 36.8% of

Table 1 Mean Scores on PALS Assessments for EO and SS Students

	GRADE 1		GRADE 2		GRADE 3	
	EO	SS	EO	SS	EO	SS
Word recognition (out of 20 possible)	14.9	9.4	17.9	14.0	18.4	15.5
Spelling inventory	30.6	19.7	45.7	35.3	48.4	36.8
Oral reading in context	First grade	Primer	2nd - 3rd grade	1st - 2nd grade	2nd - 3rd grade	Second grade
Percent below benchmark	20	56	18	51	22	57

students at Grade 1 fit into the beginning reader category, 17.2% of second-graders were classified as beginning readers, and 15.6% of third-graders were so identified. A deeper analysis, however, demonstrates that the range of literacy levels did not distribute equally among the language groups. Table 3 outlines the distribution of students across the three literacy levels over first through third grade based on their language background.

Grade-level standards require students to be above the emergent literacy stage by the end of first grade, yet Table 3 indicates that 25.3% of Spanish speakers (compared to 4.8% of EO students) were still operating at the emergent level. And, while 93% of EO students were beyond the beginning reading level by the end of third grade, the percentage for Spanish-speaking students was 67.3%--a discrepancy of almost 26 percentage points.

Additional analyses indicate that, within the SS group, language proficiency is related to a student's literacy growth and classification (i.e., as an emergent reader, beginning reader or beyond). The data presented in Table 4 reflect second-grade students' literacy levels in relation to

Table 2 Grade 2 Means on PALS Tasks by Language Level

TASK	N	WORD RECOGNITION (OUT OF 20 POSSIBLE)	SPELLING INVENTORY	ORAL READING IN CONTEXT	ENTRY SUM SCORE
LAS 1	635	13.1	33.1	First to second grade	46.3
LAS 2	160	14.4	37.1	First to second grade	51.5
LAS 3	171	15.5	38.6	Second grade	54.1
LAS 4	98	16.5	40.7	Second grade	57.2
LAS 5	56	17.9	45.5	Second to third grade	63.4
English Only	1455	17.9	45.7	Second to third grade	63.6

Table 3 Distribution of NREA Students at Various Literacy Levels

GROUP[1]	N	% EMERGENT	% BEGINNING	% ABOVE
Grade 1	4519	13.7	36.8	49.5
Gr 1 EO	1519	4.8	28.7	65.8
Gr 1 SS	1065	25.3	46.4	27.7
Grade 2	4663	1.7	17.2	81.0
Gr 2 EO	1467	0.2	8.5	90.4
Gr 2 SS	1071	3.5	28.9	66.9
Grade 3	8601	1.8	15.6	82.5
Gr 3 EO	2560	0.4	6.6	93.0
Gr 3 SS	1806	4.8	27.9	67.3

[1] Students receiving services for Learning Disabilities, Developmental Delay, Emotional Disturbance and Mental Retardation were not included in these data.

language proficiency score. Readers beyond the beginning level account for 60% of LAS 1 second-graders, 71.9% of those who scored LAS 2, 76.6% of LAS 3 students, and, 83.7% of LAS 4 students. The data show that the lower the LAS score, the greater proportion of emergent readers in each group. The second-grade pattern is echoed in the first- and third-grade data as well. In the NREA data, 1,308 Spanish-speaking students were classified as beginning readers. Based on mean scores for this group, an example SS beginning reader might be expected to score 19 out of 48 possible points on the developmental spelling inventory, and correctly read 11 out of 20 words on the Grade 1 word recognition task. He or she would likely read instructionally at the Primer level. In the following section, data from the component tasks of the PALS assessments are shared to illuminate specific reading and spelling behaviors of Spanish-speaking beginning readers.

Patterns in the Component Assessments

Statewide numerical data from EO and SS beginning readers (N=2,038) were examined to compare commonalities and distinctions in students' responses. Response protocols of individual students' PALS 1-3 assessments from five language proficiency subgroups (N=105) were examined to provide a closer look at the reading and writing behaviors of beginning readers from Spanish-speaking backgrounds in comparison to the performance of monolingual English beginning readers. Highlights of these findings are presented in the following section.

Developmental spelling responses. An analysis of the spelling samples of EO and SS students showed that these beginning readers represented most beginning and ending sounds on the spelling inventory with the correct letters, correctly represented a majority of short vowel sounds in the spelling task, and were partially successful in spelling consonant blends and digraphs. Beginning readers did not use vowel combinations to represent long vowels.

The nature of the errors for different language groups did vary within the beginning reader samples. Spelling research over several decades has documented common errors in the developmental spelling of English speakers at the letter name/alphabetic stage of writing (Ganske, 1999). When these common English letter-name spellings were removed from the writing responses of the matched-sample group of monolingual-English and Spanish-speaking students, results showed that the Spanish-speaking group had a far greater percentage of spellings that varied from those documented in previous research. Specific words from the PALS spelling inventory that had the highest discrepancy of variant spellings between EO and SS students included *shade, slide, paint, chin, drive, wish,* and *brave.* These words were likely more difficult for Spanish speakers

Table 4 Grade 2 Students' Literacy Levels by LAS Score

LAS LEVEL	% EMERGENT	% BEGINNING	% ABOVE
LAS 1	5.0	34.2	60.0
LAS 2	2.5	25.6	71.9
LAS 3	1.8	21.0	76.6
LAS 4	0	16.3	83.7

because they contain sounds that are not present in Spanish, such as those associated with *sh, v,* and short *i* (Helman, 2004). In the individual PALS samples, Spanish speakers used a variety of strategies to represent difficult sounds in their alphabetic writing. On 22 occasions in the sample papers examined, Spanish speakers used E to represent the long *a*, such as PET for *paint*. Other variant spellings included: (a) using A or O to represent the long *I* (such as DRAF for *drive*); and (b) spelling out the diphthongized vowel sounds heard in the long vowels, such as SLAID for *slide*. In terms of consonants and digraphs, SS students sometimes confused *sh* and *ch*, and represented the sh sound with CH, HE, T, and TH, such as WICH for *wish*.

Word recognition responses. In the sample group of individual assessments that were reviewed, students from EO and SS backgrounds had similar patterns of responses in the word recognition task. A visual review and tallying by language group indicated that the words on the PALS list that were easiest or most difficult for beginning readers did not change by language background. For instance, the words *shadow* and *dance* were among the most difficult for students of both language backgrounds. What made a word difficult or easy to read for a monolingual-English beginning reader also appeared to make the word easy or difficult for Spanish speakers.

Oral reading performance. The average beginning reader in the current study read a Primer passage at an instructional level on the PALS assessment. Reading level placement did not correlate significantly with language background among beginning level readers. When subcomponents of fluency, accuracy, and comprehension were examined, however, differences and commonalities became more apparent between SS and EO students.

In Table 5, we present the correlations among language background and the oral reading measures of accuracy, fluency, and comprehension. In the first column we report the grade level of the beginning reader, and the passage level he or she is reading. For instance, Row 1 examines beginning readers from EO and SS backgrounds in first grade who are reading the Primer level passage. In this instance, there is a significant correlation between students' language background

Table 5 Correlations for Language Background and Oral Reading Measures

STUDENT GRADE/ PASSAGE LEVEL	ACCURACY	FLUENCY	COMPREHENSION
Gr 1/Primer	.116**	.032	.159**
Gr 1/1st	.162**	.174**	.242**
Gr 2/Primer	.198**	.04	.243**
Gr 2/1st	.120*	.076	.162**
Gr 2/2nd	.297**	.226**	.290**
Gr 3/Primer	.161	.201*	.172*
Gr 3/1st	.075	.143*	.145*
Gr 3/2nd	.297**	.219**	.225**
Gr 3/3rd	.273**	.241**	.270**

* Correlation is significant at the .05 level (2-tailed)   ** Correlation is significant at the .001 level (2-tailed)

and their accuracy, as well as between their language background and comprehension. Fluency measures, however, do not distinguish the performance of Spanish-speaking beginning readers from English-only beginners in this context.

At all grade and text levels, beginning readers' success at answering comprehension questions was highly correlated with language background. In the qualitative review of individual PALS assessments, this pattern was corroborated. For example, on the first grade passage, LAS 1 students answered between three and five comprehension questions correctly. No SS student correctly answered all six questions. For monolingual English students, the range was five to six questions correct. No EO student missed more than one comprehension question.

For the large data set of beginning readers presented in Table 5, statistical analyses of accuracy and fluency scores on the oral passages showed a patchwork of significant correlations with English learner status. Fluency scores always showed a significant correlation to English learner status when the reading passage was at the student's grade level (e.g., second-grade students reading a second-grade passage). Accuracy scores showed a significant correlation in 7 out of 9 analyses, but were not significant for third-graders reading Primer or first-grade passages. Qualitative reviews of the paper assessments of beginning readers did not produce any additional patterns in relation to fluency and accuracy in the performance of EO and SS students.

DISCUSSION

The current study examined a large data set of the PALS early literacy data to gain greater insight into the early literacy progress of Spanish-speaking students. When the data were disaggregated, it was discovered that not all students were meeting literacy expectations at comparable levels. Spanish speakers as a group were taking more time to progress through the stage of beginning reading. Language proficiency level in many cases was highly related to a student's success on various literacy tasks. Some tasks were especially difficult for English learners at the beginning stage of development, and others seemed to be equally challenging for EO and SS students. In the following section, results from the early literacy assessment are discussed in greater detail.

What Did the PALS Tell Us About Spanish-Speaking Students' Performance?

In data disaggregated by language background, Spanish speakers were shown to read one level below their grade-level peers and were much more likely to be identified as not meeting benchmark levels on the PALS tests. At all three grade levels, Spanish-speaking students were classified as beginning readers at significantly greater percentages than monolingual English students in their classes. Unfortunately, at the third-grade level, approximately 28% of Spanish speakers continued to perform at a beginning reading level. The monolingual English students in the current study are not setting an inflated standard of comparison for the EL students. If compared to grade-level peers in other communities across the nation, these NREA monolingual English students would be lagging in performance. This information tells us that there is a crisis in meeting state and national literacy expectations. In a time of increasing federal standards and expectations, Spanish speakers have an incredible hurdle to jump to keep up with benchmarks set for a generic national population. If standards are being held high for all students, it will take much more support than is currently offered for English learners to become successful.

What Did the PALS Tell Us About Spanish Speakers' Early Literacy Progres?

The current study provided data to help us understand the performance of beginning readers from a Spanish-speaking background in the NREA partnership schools. The average SS beginning reader was in the second grade, scored as limited-English proficient on the LAS-O test, and was identified as not meeting benchmarks on the early literacy assessment. This student read about 8 out of 20 of the words on the grade-level list, and scored at the instructional level on the Primer passage. In all likelihood, this SS beginning reader struggled more with comprehension questions than other components of the oral reading assessment. This student may have also used background knowledge he or she brought from the sounds and letters in Spanish to the writing of words on the developmental spelling inventory.

Some of these same descriptors would apply equally well for an EO student at the beginning reading level. Why, then, is this list of characteristics important for our understanding of literacy learning for Spanish speakers in particular? The differences in mean results for EO students as compared to SS students included the following: (a) EO students were, on average, younger--most likely in first grade; (b) EO students had slightly higher scores on the word recognition and spelling assessments; (c) EO students were not as challenged with the comprehension questions from the oral reading passages; and (d) the spelling attempts of EO students were likely to be more readily understood by English-speaking teachers because they were based on English letter names.

These differences are crucial for several reasons. To begin, most EO beginning readers are first graders, and first-grade teachers are much more likely to be prepared to meet the needs of students at a beginning developmental level. At later grade levels, pressures to perform on standardized assessments may rule the instructional agenda. Students' developmental levels may be ignored. Differentiated instruction may not always be in place. Students, who are operating at earlier developmental literacy levels beyond first grade, may suffer the consequences of not having instruction that is geared to their level of understanding.

Another relevant issue for meeting the needs of Spanish-speaking beginning readers concerns the diagnosis of comprehension skills. A classroom teacher may make the assumption from hearing students reading out loud that comprehension is occurring. This assumption is less likely to be true for English learners, who may have adequate accuracy and fluency on lower-level passages, but may not understand the vocabulary and content.

Finally, as demonstrated in the student spelling samples, SS students' developmental spelling attempts are likely to be as logical as those of English speakers, but because of a lack of familiarity with the Spanish sound system, a teacher may dismiss these spellings as not making sense.

What Was the Role of Language Proficiency in Success on Various Literacy Assessment Tasks?

The current study demonstrated the strong relationship of oral language proficiency on numerous early literacy tasks. Clearly, language proficiency had an impact on the early reading development of EL students as measured by the PALS 1-3. Specifically, students' LAS level were positively correlated to their scores on the word recognition, spelling inventory, and oral reading in context tasks. Oral language proficiency was associated with higher literacy levels. These data confirm previous research that identified second-language reading as complex and multi-level, with various components relying more on oral language than others (Bialystock & Herman, 1999; Garcia, 2000). These results clarify that, while it would be inappropriate to wait on literacy instruction for EL students until full oral-language proficiency has developed, literacy instruction must simultaneously be imbued with rich language teaching. Oral language is the foundation of literacy, and limited language proficiency constricts student success on many early literacy tasks.

LIMITATIONS OF THE STUDY

While the current study provided important data about student performance on an early literacy measure, several limitations must be acknowledged. First, the scope of the study involved early literacy behaviors that were assessed on the PALS 1-3 screening. This is a highly efficient and informational assessment, yet it does not measure the full picture of literacy development for each student (Jimenez, 2004). Ongoing informal assessment, observation of student behaviors and interviews, parent conferences, etc. would be required to truly understand each individual student's literacy journey with its many successes and challenges. Similarly, while a single LAS or Pre-LAS score was available to categorize a student's level of English proficiency, this was the only information available to correlate language level to performance on the PALS tasks. Information about when the LAS tests were given, by whom and how effectively was not known.

This study provides a large-scale picture contextualizing the performance of students from various demographic groups in a statewide context. To build on this, it would be valuable to investigate a smaller sample of EL students for a close inspection. This inspection would focus on the ways that students use language at home and school, and on the nature of students' literacy background in Spanish. It would also be useful to conduct in-class interviews that allow students to share their thinking about how Spanish influences their English reading and writing decisions.

INSTRUCTIONAL IMPLICATIONS

This exploration of results from the PALS early literacy assessment in the NREA offers direct implications for schools and teachers working with Spanish speakers. At the heart of the recommendations that follow lies the principle that the most effective teaching strategies will simultaneously acknowledge and build upon students' literacy development and background experiences. Background experiences include the oral and written language understandings that students bring with them to the classroom.

Apply a Developmental Perspective

Early literacy assessments give teachers information about the progress of individual students and allow teachers to cluster students based on similar developmental levels. For example, the classroom experiences of all beginning readers should include many opportunities to read text at their instructional level to gain fluency and accuracy and develop a greater sight word vocabulary.

Use Data to Target Instructional Resources

Schools, districts, and governmental agencies have a wealth of data available to them for identifying which students are succeeding in meeting educational expectations, and which are not. For example, interventions that are warranted by the results of the current study include setting up tutoring programs that are specifically designed for Spanish speakers. These programs might combine efforts to develop comprehension skills within beginning reading activities. Another possible innovation would be to provide professional development activities for teachers beyond the first grade to help them recognize the developmental level of beginning readers from diverse language backgrounds.

Build on the Language Resources Students Bring

Students from specific home languages and dialects may require extra support to build on their primary language and make connections to English. Teachers who have a basic understanding of the commonalities and differences both linguistically and socio-culturally between a student's home language and English will be able to build on this knowledge in the classroom. Teachers will recognize miscues that make sense, and guide students to consciously compare and contrast the two languages.

Look at Individual Student Needs

Teachers not only need to know what common problems for Spanish speakers might surface, they also need to consider individual assessments to apply this knowledge on an as-needed basis. The beauty of assessment data from an early literacy screening is that it not only gives teachers information about the performance of groups of students, it can also be used to tailor instruction to an individual student's strengths and needs.

Provide Rich Literacy Instruction That Encourages Language and Conceptual Development

EL students, generally, have no more time in their day at school than other students. Yet the expectations are for English learners to catch up and learn more than their monolingual peers. The only way this can happen is with exceptional teaching that builds oral language and concepts, incorporates thinking and discussion into literacy activities, and provides frequent opportunities to practice reading and writing at an appropriate developmental level.

CONCLUSION

This paper examined the progress of early literacy behaviors in Spanish-speaking students learning to read in English. Through this examination, it was found that Spanish-speaking beginning readers are progressing along the same developmental paths as students from monolingual English backgrounds, but at a different pace. In addition, being an English learner with a Spanish-speaking background has an influence on literacy learning in specific ways such as influencing developmental spelling attempts and making comprehension of reading passages more challenging. Early literacy assessments provide general information about the performance of groups, as well as detailed instructional information about individuals. The assessment results, in the current study, highlight the quantitative gaps in supporting early literacy goals for all students. These data can be used to guide attempts to improve teaching in the classroom and to shape thoughtful policy decisions at the administrative level.

REFERENCES

August, D., & Hakuta, K. (Eds.). (1997). *Improving schooling for language minority students: A research agenda* (Committee on Developing a Research Agenda on the Education of Limited English Proficient and Bilingual Students-Board on Children, Youth and Families). Washington, D.C.: National Academy Press.

Bear, D. R., & Helman, L. (2004). Word study for vocabulary development in the early stages of literacy learning: Ecological perspectives and learning English. In J. F. Baumann & E. J. Kame'enui (Eds.), *Vocabulary instruction: Research to practice.* New York: The Guilford Press.

Bernhardt, E. B. (2000). Second-language reading as a case study of reading scholarship in the 20th century. In M. L. Kamil, P. B. Mosenthal, P. D. Pearson, & R. Barr (Eds.), *Handbook of reading research, Vol. III* (pp. 791-811). Mahwah, NJ: Lawrence Erlbaum.

Bialystock, E. (2001). *Bilingualism in development: Language, literacy, and cognition.* New York: Cambridge University Press.

Bialystock, E., & Herman, J. (1999). Does bilingualism matter for early literacy? *Bilingualism: Language and Cognition, 2*(1), 35-44.

Center for Research on Education, Diversity & Excellence (CREDE). (2002). *Research evidence: Five standards for effective pedagogy and student outcomes.* (Technical Report No. G1). Santa Cruz, CA: University of California.

Chall, J. (1983). *Stages of reading development.* New York: McGraw-Hill.

Corson, D. (2001). *Language diversity and education.* Mahwah, NJ: Lawrence Erlbaum Associates.

Cummins, J. (1991). Interdependence of first- and second-language proficiency in bilingual children. In E. Bialystok (Ed.) *Language processing in bilingual children* (pp. 70-89). Cambridge: Cambridge University Press.

Cummins, J. (1998) *Linguistic and cognitive issues in learning to read in a second language.* Paper presented at Reading and the English Language Learner Forum, California Reading and Literature Project, Sacramento, CA.

De Avila, E. A., & Duncan, S. E. (1994). *Language Assessment Scales.* Monterey, CA: CTB Macmillan/McGraw-Hill.

Durgunoglu, A. Y., Nagy, W. E., & Hancin-Bhatt, B. J. (1993). Cross-language transfer of phonological awareness. *Journal of Educational Psychology, 85*(3), 453-465.

Durgunoglu, A. Y. & Verhoeven, L. (1998). *Literacy development in a multilingual context.* Mahwah, NJ: Lawrence Erlbaum Associates.

Ellis, N. (1997). Interactions in the development of reading and spelling: Stages, strategies, and exchange of knowledge. In C.A. Perfetti & L. Rieben (Eds.), *Learning to spell: Research, theory, and practice across languages* (pp. 271 – 294). Mahwah, NJ: Lawrence Erlbaum Associates.

Fitzgerald, J. (1995). English-As-A-Second-Language Reading Instruction in the United States: A Research Review. *Journal of Reading Behavior, 27*(2), 115-152.

Ganske, K (1999). The developmental spelling analysis: A measure of orthographic knowledge. *Educational Assessment, 6*, 41-70.

Garcia, G. E. (2000). Bilingual children's reading. In M. L. Kamil, P. B. Mosenthal, P. D. Pearson & R. Barr (Eds.), *Handbook of reading research, Vol. III* (pp. 813-834). Mahwah, NJ: Lawrence Erlbaum.

Geva, E., & Siegel, L. S. (2000). Orthographic and cognitive factors in the concurrent development of basic reading skills in two languages. *Reading and Writing: An Interdisciplinary Journal, 12*, 1-30.

Geva. E., & Verhoeven, L. (Eds.). (2000). Basic processes in early second language reading [Special Issue]. *Scientific Studies of Reading, 4*(4), 261-266.

Goldstein, B. (2001). Transcription of Spanish and Spanish-influenced English. *Communication Disorders Quarterly, 23*(1), 54-60.

Gregory, E. (1996). *Making sense of a new world.* London: Paul Chapman Publishing, Ltd.

Helman, L. A. (2004). Building on the sound system of Spanish: Insights from the alphabetic spellings of English-language learners. *The Reading Teacher, 57*, 452-460.

Henderson, E. H., & Beers, J. (Eds.) (1980). *Developmental and cognitive aspects of learning to spell: A reflection of word knowledge.* Newark, DE: International Reading Association.

Invernizzi, M., & Meier, J. (2001). *Phonological Awareness Literacy Screening 2001-2002.* Charlottesville, VA: The Rector and the Board of Visitors of the University of Virginia.

Invernizzi, M., & Meier, J. (2003). *Phonological Awareness Literacy Screening 2002-2003: Technical reference.* Charlottesville, VA: The Rector and the Board of Visitors of the University of Virginia.

Jiménez, R. (2004). More equitable literacy assessments for Latino students. *The Reading Teacher, 57*(6), 576-578.

Juel, C. (1988). Learning to read and write: A longitudinal study of fifty-four children from first through fourth grade. *Journal of Educational Psychology, 80*, 437-447.

Moll, L. C., & Gonzalez, N. (1994). Lessons from research with language-minority children. *Journal of Reading Behavior, 26*(4), 439-456.

Morris, D., Bloodgood, J. W., Lomax, R. G., & Perney, J. (2003). Developmental steps in learning to read: A longitudinal study in kindergarten and first grade. *Reading Research Quarterly, 38*(3), 302-328.

Neuman, S. B., & Dickinson, D. K. (2001). *Handbook of early literacy research.* New York: The Guilford Press.

Ovando, C. J., & Collier, V. P. (1998). *Bilingual and ESL classrooms: Teaching in multicultural contexts* (2nd Ed.) Boston: McGraw-Hill.

Population Reference Bureau (2002). *Children: English-speaking ability and Race/ethnicity.* Retrieved April 22, 2003, from http://www.prb.org

Snow, C. E., Burns, M. S., & Griffin, P. (1998). *Preventing reading difficulties in young children.* Washington, D. C: National Academy Press.

Stanovich, K. E. (1986). Matthew effects in Reading: some consequences of individual differences in the acquisition of literacy. *Reading Research Quarterly, 21*, 360-407.

Tabors, P. O. (1997). *One child, two languages.* Baltimore: Paul H. Brookes Pub. Co.

Templeton, S. & Morris, D. (2000). Spelling. In M.L. Kamil, P.B. Mosenthal, P.D. Pearson & R. Barr (Eds.) *Handbook of Reading Research: Volume III* (pp. 525-544). Mahwah, NJ: Lawrence Erlbaum Associates.

United States Census Bureau (2002). *Census 2000 supplementary survey.* Retrieved April 22, 2003, from http://www.census.gov/c2ss/www/Products/Rank/RankOL040.htm

United States Department of Education, NCES. (2004). *The nation's report card (NAEP).* Retrieved March 30, 2004, from http://nces.ed.gov/nationsreportcard/reading/results2003/raceethnicity.asp

Valdés, G. (1996). *Con respeto: Bridging the distances between culturally diverse families and schools.* New York: Teacher's College Press.

Wong-Fillmore, L. (1991). Second-language learning in children: A model of language learning in social context. In E. Bialystock (Ed.), *Language processing in bilingual children* (pp. 49-69). New York: Cambridge University Press.

Wu, H., De Temple, J. M., Herman, J. A., & Snow, C. E. (1994). "L'animal qui fait oink! Oink!": Bilingual children's oral and written picture descriptions in English and French under varying instructions. *Discourse Processes, 18*, 141-164.

Dialogical Caring Encounters Between Teacher and Students: The Role of Computer-Mediated Communication in Preparing Preservice Reading Teachers

Minseong Kim

University of Texas at Austin

Although the process of learning in an instructional environment requires a high degree of interpersonal connection between teacher and learner working together (Goldstein, 1999), the history of research on teaching has not fully addressed the relational nature of teaching and learning (Noddings, 2001; Prillaman & Eaker, 1994). Noddings (2001) even claimed that what most of the research on teaching has achieved so far is likely to separate teaching and learning rather than provide a careful look at the highly complex interrelationships between teachers and students through which learning is accomplished. To offer a possibility for explicating teaching and learning from a relational point of view, Noddings (1984, 1992) investigated teaching from a caring perspective. In her 1984 book, she described *caring* as a relationship between a person giving care (the one-caring) and a person receiving that care (the cared-for). For her, the meaning of caring goes beyond the actions that the one-caring takes that represent caring for the cared-for to include how the one-caring tries to open herself to the cared-for with full attention "to feel with or receive the other" (engrossment) (p. 30), further "allowing herself to be moved by the other's needs and feelings" (motivational displacement) (Noddings, 2001, p. 100). She emphasized the need for the cared-for in the relationship to give some sign to the one-caring that the cared-for has received the care, what she called *reciprocity*, in order to mark the relationship as a caring one. Indeed, caring is controlled by the cared-for, and without some sign that the cared-for recognizes the caring, Noddings would say that caring is not actually completed.

Although studies using the concept of caring have reported on the contribution of caring teacher-student relationships to changes in students' attitudes and performance (Goldstein & Lake, 2000; Pajares & Graham, 1998), their focus was on the participants' conceptions or definitions of caring, not on how actual caring relationships are developed. In addition, most of the research with a caring perspective has been conducted at the level of elementary, middle, or high school. Even in studies examining prospective teachers' opinions and beliefs about caring, the focus was on how these conceptions were likely to be based on what the prospective teachers had brought from their previous experiences with elementary, middle, or high school levels (e.g., Goldstein & Lake, 2000; Weinstein, 1998). Given that for student teachers, relationships with their college instructors or professors might be critical in influencing their conception of caring for their future students, examining caring at the college level could contribute to an understanding of the nature of teaching-learning relationships more broadly. Although there are a few such studies (e.g., Goldstein & Freedman, 2003), the construct deserves more attention, especially as it would illuminate how student teachers learn to care.

Relationships between teachers and students arise from myriads of ways of communicating how they feel and what they envision for each other. Language is one of the primary ways in which this communication takes place. As college classrooms increasingly make use of computer-mediated communication (CMC) environments, an interesting issue becomes how such an environment that depends solely on words on a screen can allow a teacher to show caring for students and for them to reciprocate in the relationship. Researchers have reported on the need of students to feel connected with their instructor in online learning (Burford and Gross, 2000) and on the personal and informal tone being carried even in purely text-based exchanges (Hawisher & Selfe, 1998; Herring, 1996; Kolb, 1996; Murray, 1991). Drawing on a Bakhtinian perspective, Assaf (2003) and Na (2004) elaborated on the nature of interactions in CMC and showed them to be dialogic. They noted that participants in CMC drew on the utterances of others to compose their own words, and that engaging in CMC was a process of situating oneself in relation to others' words. With their heavy reliance on a Bakhtinian approach to language, these two studies implied that teaching-learning relationships enacted in CMC need to be examined as dialogical relations, meaning that the very process of posting comments occurs in a chain of communication in which relationships with others are potentiated.

Drawing on the theoretical perspectives of caring from Noddings (1984) and of dialogue from Bakhtin (1979/1986), I focused on the perceptions and interpretations of teaching-learning relationships enacted in a CMC environment by undergraduate students, specifically preservice reading teachers, and their teacher educator. The following research questions guided my approach: 1) What is the nature of the dialogic messages in CMC in contributing to the development of teaching-learning relationships? 2) What role does CMC play in terms of creating and sustaining caring relationships?

METHOD

Participants and Setting

Data analyzed and reported in this paper were collected in the first semester of a three-semester reading specialization program. Participants were 25 prospective teachers (1 male, 24 female; 23 White, 1 Hispanic, 1 Indian; ages ranging between 20 and 24 except for one student of 30) and their leading teacher, Dr. Paul Jones (all names are pseudonyms). The students were taught as a cohort, which meant that the students took all of their courses together for three semesters. Dr. Jones taught the two courses I observed, Community Literacy and Reading Assessment, at a local elementary school. Having used bulletin board postings on TeachNet for several years for these two courses, Paul, as he encouraged the students to call him, gave the students a standing weekly assignment to post two messages, one for each course, in response to the required readings. He then responded to nearly all messages and the teaching assistants often responded to several as well.

Data Sources and Procedures

I collected data from the following sources: 1) classroom observations supplemented by audiotapes of every class session and daily field notes of the two classes; 2) a short survey asking background information such as age, ethnicity, reasons for choosing the reading cohort, and their past experiences with CMC; 3) text-based interviews with the students and the teacher conducted after several textual exchanges had taken place, with the purpose of gaining insight into the participants' thoughts and reasons underlying the words on the text; 4) three text-based interviews with five students and the teacher every other week after the first text-based interview had been conducted with all students; 5) printouts of all CMC texts; and 6) my own reflective research journal. Data from each source complemented each other and helped contribute to a holistic picture of the evolving teaching-learning relationships in the cohort.

In each text-based interview with the students and the teacher, I asked about which message they remembered most from among the recent weeks of postings. Next, I asked students what was their interpretation of the teacher's comments on their messages, and I asked the teacher about what had led to his responses to students' messages. Then, I asked the interviewee about specific passages that I had noted prior to the interview. I gave attention to places in the text where contextual or relational cues seemed to be present.

Data Analysis

Because I was interested in context, process, and meaning, I adopted a naturalistic paradigm reflecting an interpretive perspective (Lincoln & Guba, 1985). As a specific data analysis technique, the constant-comparative method of Strauss and Corbin (1990) was used. I began by reading the transcripts of the text-based interviews, referring at the same time to the postings mentioned by the students and the teacher during the interview. As patterns of students' perceptions of their teacher and of the teacher's perceptions of students in terms of relationships began to emerge, I identified, defined, and refined my categories by revisiting the data two or three times. Next, I read all the TeachNet postings organized by each case, which led me to postulate how each student had constructed his or her own understanding of the course content and how they were authoring themselves as future literacy teachers. Through these cross-case and within-case analyses, I constructed the three themes I present in the next section.

RESULTS

Theme 1: The Dialogic Nature of Messages in CMC: A Pre-Condition for the Development of Caring Relationships

From the teacher's and students' perspectives, the primary use of the CMC postings was for the students to provide evidence of having read and related what was read to their teaching and everyday life. However, as my analysis revealed, the postings took on a much more important function as the semester progressed. The dialogical nature of postings meant that a student's response to a class reading seemed formed within interactions between her or his past or ongoing experiences or beliefs and the assigned reading. Thus, a student's posting became a way to respond to the author of the assigned reading, to re-interpret his or her previous, present, and future life, and to allow the teacher to know him or her.

By using others' words, chosen from their assigned authors, the teacher, or other class members, the prospective teachers constructed their own meaning of the issues discussed in their assigned readings. For example, Cecilia, while responding to *Literacy and Schooling* by Judith A. Langer (1991), struggled with building her own definition of *literacy*. Her posting revealed that she was "confused about the definition of literacy," and that she was "unable to form a concrete idea of its meaning." But, as she read *Literacy and Schooling*, she began to realize what she was looking for in her own definition, which was that "it [the definition of literacy] varies depending on the society involved." Appreciating this possible variation, she was "relieved to read that, 'within a given society, several literacies can be valued, supported, and taught, in response to the needs of the various subcultures to which individual members belong or wish to belong.'"

Students' reading and responding to the weekly assigned reading encouraged them to look back on their past or forward to their future life, giving significance to all that had been given to them. Responding to *Life as Narrative* written by Jerome Bruner (1987), Nancy pictured what she would do with her students in her own classroom with the new knowledge gained from the reading, saying, "Just through this short study, I realized that every day in my future classroom I will have children describing themselves and their lives. I will note the way in which they speak and the words they use, and it will be a great (or maybe not so great) indicator into the way they structure experience." The dialogue with assigned readings seemed to contribute to students' realization of the importance of what they were doing as classroom activities, and their identification of themselves as future teachers, not just student teachers.

In addition to responding to the published authors of class readings, students appropriated the words of classmates as they made their CMC postings. In a description of how she had come to believe that "stories play a part in everyone's lives, young and old. It is how we can relate to others, to convey differing backgrounds and events to one another, and to enrich our lives," Edith referred to the words of her classmate, writing,

> Nancy had a very good point when she mentioned "Jesus used stories to convey messages in a more prominent way - a way that people could relate. When teaching, I should utilize this info and sometimes tell a captivating story with a related agenda underneath." I especially like the fact that she relates Jesus' teaching to the crowd to whom he was talking to a wonderful way of reaching our students once we are teachers. It is very important to remember who our audience is and how we can best reach them. If we can find different methods of reaching our students, they will be better equipped to learn.

Finally, postings showed their dialogical nature when students anticipated how their teacher might respond to them. Having read an article that deeply affected her, Jody decided to change her usual manner of posting and even alerted her teacher by saying, "This is a completely different way of responding to any of the articles but I really wanted to talk about how a few things really got me thinking about Frank my tutee." Although she stated in her interview that she had been nervous about this change, Paul responded with "I love it!"

These frequent negotiations of meaning in building their own understanding and finding their identity as future teachers seemed to illustrate Bakhtin's overarching construct of *intertexuality*, how any concrete utterance is "a link in the chain of speech of communication of a particular sphere" (Bakhtin, 1986, p. 9). For Bakhtin, the concept of dialogue does not necessarily require actual interactions among individuals but characterizes every message. In his view, verbal performance, whether oral or written, is always a response in some way to previous performances and, in turn, calls forth a response from others (Volosinov, 1973). Bakhtin's (1981) dialogism suggests that we are not only interacting with others when using language, we are also using others' words to represent our own meaning. When borrowing words from their classmates or the authors of their assigned readings, Cecilia, Nancy, and Edith adapted others' words to their own intention, their own accent, making them their own words to construct their own meaning, even as they anticipated their teacher's response to their postings.

Thus, in their very postings, the preservice teachers in Paul's cohort were showing how their words reflected a dialogue they were creating, first with the authors of the assigned readings, then with their fellow classmates, and finally with their teacher. I came to see that the dialogical echoes represented in each posting were important in triggering the teacher's response, acting as foundation for the cumulative effect of student-teacher interactions that eventually might develop into a caring relationship. The essence of Theme 1 is that by how they wrote, the students revealed who they were, how they were thinking, what they were feeling, and whether they would allow their teacher into the dialogue they were engaging with course concepts.

Theme 2: CMC Can Be a Place for Dialogic Encounters Between Teacher and Students

As I alluded to in the discussion of Theme 1, the dialogic nature of a message can invite others to come into contact with the meaning of the composer. The life of an utterance does not end with a message as uttered. Rather, it becomes an object of interpretation, support, and further development for others. As the semester progressed, the participants in this study felt that they were meeting each other when they were reading CMC responses. Even though they were not physically in the presence of their teacher, students were able to feel that he was there through his comments on TeachNet. Ruth, looking at Paul's comment embedded between sentences in one of her reading responses, vividly pictured him as if he were talking to her in the classroom. [Paul had the habit of responding to students simply by copying their message and inserting comments directly between the lines of their original message. In the examples that follow, Paul's responses appear in bold italic font inserted within and after each student posting. Quotes from interviews appear indented further in and marked with the date of the interview.]

From: Paul Jones /Re: Literacy and Schooling/February 16, 2004

Ruth writes:

"Although notions and uses of literacy vary among cultural groups, they also change within groups across time," (12).This quote made me think about someone who was trying to learn English, or any other language. *aha...our topic for tomorrow...*

> "See that just makes me think of Paul in class getting started and saying something and just standing there ready to surprise us. He didn't really, you know, go into it very much because we were going to talk about it the next day but I knew that I would be able to understand this quote and the reading and the topic better." (First interview with Ruth, 03/05/04)

Because she believed Paul was going to talk about this topic at the next class meeting, Ruth could accept that his response was very short. Her interpretation of this comment was not limited to the words, "aha, our topic for tomorrow..." Rather, she was anticipating what would take place the next day, that her understanding of the topic would grow, thereby showing how her teacher's words embedded between her own were shaping part of her life.

Students also could sense from what Paul wrote in response to their messages how seriously he took his teaching. For example, Paul wrote the following in response to Allison:

From: Paul Jones / Subject: Re: Learning to Read is Natural /January 29, 2004

Allison writes:

...I believe that many people often make the mistake of grouping oral and written language together. It is obvious that these two skills develop together and support each other and we as teachers should remember this fact while guiding our students in their development. *careful about what we consider as obvious...the obvious (what we think makes good sense) is often worth digging into deeply to examine how the obvious might be more complex than we thought.*

The teacher's focus on the word *obvious* told Allison that "he reads each and every sentence and thinks about what we said," which in turn allowed her to draw a certain image of her teacher. Paul's picking up on such details seemed to reveal a significant aspect of himself to another student, Michelle:

From: Paul Jones / Re: Learning to Read is Natural /January 29, 2004

Michelle writes:

.........I nanny for a five year old, and on fridays, *oh my...a child for your emergent literacy project* he comes home with his take home folder ready to show me his work for the week. It usually includes small beginner reading packets. And he loves to show me that he can read them. But to me it just looks like he has memorized the words that the class learned that week *(why "just"?)*. So I wonder, is that reading. Just seeing a word, recognizing it from memory. This article led me to believe that it is.

> "You know, when I read that, I was kind of thinking like, oh, you know, when you say words you don't mean it, or you say 'only' or 'just.' You know, you don't mean it, it's so small, but yeah, definitely that made me rethink, like, 'oh.' I mean,

because I guess we were talking about emergent reading. How, like, even though, even though they're just recognizing the McDonald's sign, it's still a step of reading. And I [wrote] 'just' and that's, like, his whole focus of his life. I mean, he's, like, 'just?' You know, so that definitely made me look. Oh, I shouldn't [say 'just']. Yeah, he really, really pays attention to what we're writing and really, uh, digs into it." (First Interview with Michelle, 03/11/04)

His reaction to the word *just,* the one slipped in by Michelle without much thought, showed how he read students' postings and what was important to him. Even though Paul's comment consisted of only two words, "why just?," for Michelle, it told her that the issue being discussed was significant to him at the level of "his whole focus of his life," which, as she stated, led her to pay more attention to how she used words.

Just as students seemed to feel that they were meeting Paul from his responses to their postings in TeachNet, Paul also perceived CMC as a place where he came to know students. In the first interview, he stated that as students from the prior cohorts went on in the program, he had "become so familiar with their voice." Simply by reading each student's responses, he could learn about a student's background, whether academic or cultural, her or his perspective on teaching, and so on. While students were trying to connect their reading to their prior knowledge or experiences, they could not help reveal different courses they had taken before entering this cohort, experiences they had had with reading, and what they had learned from all the activities set up by Paul.

Paul's growing knowledge about each student made him eager to know more about particular students. For example, his strong connections to South Africa from professional work in which he was currently engaged made him immediately interested in Tina who had cultural roots to the country and he frequently sought her out to hear about the kinds of cultural experiences she had had. As he was reading and responding to the following response of Tina's, his wanting to learn about her motivated him to "try to understand her experiences growing up."

From: Paul Jones/Re: Literacy and Schooling /February 16, 2004

Tina writes:

……I connected with this article in many ways. I did not go to public school during the elementary years and I always had attention from my teachers. I was in my own little 'culture' where everyone knew everything about everyone else. I did not have to explain to people that my family was different since my parents are from South Africa or why I was always traveling to visit family. They knew that I had no family nearby or what my parents did for a living. It was my culture. I was literate in that sense—I could read and write and knew a sense of my culture. When I observed other classrooms and saw the teacher not interacting with all the students I did not understand why since I had had that growing up. If anything this article has helped me to see a sense of what to do in my own classroom and how to act with the children to make them all more literate. **how much does it connect with you to South African society?? I am really curious about any connections you will make.**

However, Tina rarely met his need to know more about her. In reading one of her messages, Paul expressed feeling somewhat disappointed with her account of her own early reading experiences because he had expected her to show more appreciation of diversity than her posting showed.

From the examples above, CMC seemed to be a place where the students and the teacher could enter into a dialogic encounter, even if the degree of connecting with each other seemed to vary case by case. The TeachNet environment seemed to allow for a sense of a one-on-one interaction with the teacher that the in-class meetings did not as easily foster. In line with Noddings (1984), a dialogic encounter, even in a textual exchange, can provide opportunities to feel what the other is feeling or thinking about a certain topic, what she called *receptivity* or *engrossment,* one of the main characteristics of a caring person. With the possibility of meeting each other by reading and responding to each other's comments, students could know their teacher, develop a connection to him, and let him know what they were thinking and feeling in their postings, and the teacher had the potential of entering into a caring relationship with each student.

Theme 3: The CMC Dialogue is an Occasion for Authoring the Self and Others Within the Bi-Directional Influence of Caring Relationships

Thus, words in CMC allowed the teacher and students to join each other. In a Bakhtinian view (Clark & Holquist, 1984), the dialogic nature of an utterance allows it to bridge the gap between a self and an Other, a place where speakers can be aware of themselves through the eyes of another person. As we shape our words in the context of an anticipated response, the notion of who we are in relation to that response simultaneously shapes knowledge of self and others, what Bakhtin (1994) called *outsidedness.* In my study, the students seemed to be looking at themselves through their teacher's response to their postings, and the teacher, for his part, could see the growth of his students as future teachers, as shown through their hard work in their postings and other activities, becoming more aware of himself as a teacher, wanting to be a better teacher.

However, when one looks at him or herself through the Other's words, one cannot help but base his or her interpretation of those words on what has been constructed from previous contacts with the Other including textual exchanges in CMC and classroom interactions. In this study, the students used what they knew about Paul from classroom interactions and previous CMC exchanges to interpret his comments. They were picturing him as they interpreted his words in CMC as if he were talking in the classroom: "You can tell exactly, like, I can like, picture him saying it just the way he types it, and stuff" (Allison, first interview, 3/10/04). Also, students' interpretation of Paul's responses to their posting had an impact on their classroom interactions with him.

For the teacher, CMC could not be separated from other classroom contexts when it came to thinking about each individual student.

> "I can't separate them from each other. I mean, I can't separate a response I read one week and then watch them for three weeks working with kids and then read another response. Those two things are tied together because I've seen them now and I know them, you know, I can't imagine doing one without [the other]." (The third interview, 04/27/04)

With all his own past experiences and the knowledge he was gaining from his current interactions with the students, Paul seemed to be in a never-ending process of becoming a more knowledgeable and experienced teacher himself. When he responded to students' messages, these aspects of himself could not help but come out in his words, from which students felt how knowledgeable and experienced their teacher was.

For these students, TeachNet responses allowed the students to see their teacher's caring. Simply because Paul read and responded to their comments, the students perceived that he cared about them and felt that their work in posting was validated.

> "He'll answer your question sometimes there but it's nice to know that he actually takes the time to, like, when we take the time to write it, he actually takes the time to read it and respond to it, and that just makes you, you know, it's not like you are posting and he's just checking to make sure you did it. Like he actually reads it and it's amazing that he reads all of those, every single week and responds to all of them." (First interview with Jody, 03/27/04)

Melinda went on to say in her interview, "I think that's good for him to do. I mean, everybody, what everybody writes is important and he's validating that." Even with brief comments from their teacher, students could feel his presence in TeachNet, by which they felt validated for their work in posting. Also, they read from it "his wanting for everyone to be successful and to have the same experience" (First interview with Allison, 3/10/04).

Furthermore, what Paul responded to their postings in TeachNet sometimes played a role in students discovering abilities that they had not previously recognized.

From: Paul Jones /Re: Challenging Venerable Assumptions / February 22, 2004

Grace writes:

…Assumption One: English is the only legitimate medium for learning and instruction. "School curricula in this country have been developed primarily for native English speakers, thereby according primacy to English as the language of instruction." This reminds me of a story my mother told me about some of her fellow teachers. They were frustrated with the TAXS (**TAKS** [The Texas Assessment of Knowledge and Skills]*... but I like your's better)* system of testing for their students whose L1 was not English. We all remember the tests, instructions are given in English and after that the teacher is not allowed to help the students.

…Assumption Four: Error correction in process instruction hampers learning.

To be honest, this is something I have never considered until reading this article. My question is how do you know the defining line between hindering and helping a student? My school was big on the writing without rules or spelling. Proper punctuation, grammar or spelling was not emphasized as much as creative, free writing. To this day I am a terrible speller and rely on spell check to catch my mistakes. How do we know what the balance is? . . . *keep asking this question. Of course, you know also how much more important it is to be a good writer than a good speller . .but the two don't have to be set in opposition to each other. . . more to come.*

Because she had never been a good speller, Grace was very embarrassed when Paul, himself making a spelling error, pointed out her wrong spelling of TAKS. When Paul responded to her question about what the balance was between being a good speller and a creative writer, she felt relieved by his response because the question had bothered her for a long the time.

"So the first [part of his comment] was reassuring for me as a person because I am not a good speller and the second was something that I really feel like I need to keep in mind when I'm a teacher. That the two don't need to be in opposition to each other. So I feel like he hit both points when he responded to me on that. Just like on a personal level and then like a future educator level. So it was neat that he hit on something that I really did want to know about." (First interview, 03/04/04)

She felt reassured at a personal level, gaining confidence about her writing. In addition, his comment at the level of a future educator led her to realize that she would need to deal with both writing and spelling in her teaching. Coming to see herself from what Paul had said seemed to validate her as both a student and a future teacher.

Another student, Ruth, learned from Paul's response to her comment that she was doing something worthwhile. With his words, she could view herself as someone who was good at connecting the theories they were reading about with reality. This feeling of discovering herself to be "doing anything worth responding to the reading" made her "want to be a harder worker and look deeper into the reading," anticipating praise for her work.

From: Paul Jones/Re: Life as Narrative /Monday, February 09

Ruth writes:

"...Any story one may tell about anything is better understood by considering other possible ways in which it can be told," (36-7). This quote was one that made the whole article a lot clearer to me. I have grown up hearing that there are two sides to every story, but have never even imagined that the very same idea could be put into words like this. You live your life, and you see things as you want to see them... and I can only speak for myself, but I rarely, if ever, think about things from another person's perspective. ***this is at the heart of what it means to be a "critical thinker" ...***

"That was one of the first ones and it was just   I was at the point where I didn't really know him that well and for him to say something like that about me I was very taken aback for a second and reread it and I was, like, wow, I didn't even realize this was something that was so great. And he just gets in there and says it. It just makes me realize.. When I don't even think that I'm doing anything worth responding to and he says something like that... It makes me want to put the same effort if not more.... Because I want to, you know, I'd love to get a comment like that every time." (Text-based interview, 03/05/04)

These examples indicate that what students received from the teacher influenced their subsequent work. Because they perceived how much their teacher cared about their postings, their tutoring, and other course activities, they strove harder to meet and surpass his expectation.

For his part, seeing growth in students revealed in their CMC messages and in their tutoring with young readers led Paul to express his enthusiasm for them, such as "You are the most incredible group. You are unbelievably detailed in your poems [used in tutoring]." He said that they deserved the praise:

"Yeah, Yeah, they're a very incredible group. I mean, and believe me when that happens, it makes life fun and easy and exciting, and so you jump all over it and just say, 'oh my god, if this is where they are right now, there's so much exciting, so many exciting things that are going to happen next year with these folks.' It's exciting to think about." (Third interview, 04/27/04)

Students' hard work meant to him that "they see the importance of what they're doing at the moment and how it will enable them to get closer to that goal." However, he said that he would worry if he saw students working only to "do what he wants." As a way to carry this message to students, he was "much more responsive to and looking for evidence of hard work that's directed toward their own learning or directed toward the success of the students they're working with." That's why he often would respond with, "Great connection," "This is so great that you can reach back and see this," or "I never thought about this connection before," whenever he spotted that their work was directed to their own learning or their students. To describe what he felt about students' hard work, he used a line from the movie *As Good As it Gets*:

> "It makes you want to work (laughter) there's a stupid line from a movie. I use this all the time. Have you ever seen the movie? *As Good As it Gets*. I love that movie. Well, do you remember the scene where they're in the, they're in a restaurant and Nicholson is being weird. And she says, 'I need a compliment now. I need a compliment.' And he says, 'I started taking those pills the doctor ordered.' And she says, 'This is supposed to be a compliment about me not about yourself.' (laughter) And then he says, 'Yes, but the reason I started taking the pills is you make me want to be a better person.' And I think that's always the response to hard work is that it makes you want to be a better teacher." (Third interview, 04/27/04)

Although considered by the students as someone who was very knowledgeable in his field and loved what he was doing, Paul was nevertheless becoming a better teacher at every moment. Especially when he saw that his passion and love for teaching were reflected in the students, he stated that what they did "made him want to be a better teacher." Just as Nodding proposed that caring is completed when the cared-for indicates that caring has been received, in this study, each student needed to acknowledge or recognize the caring to maintain the caring relation, what is called *reciprocity*. No matter how much Paul appreciated his students or their learning, unless the students indicated some sign of receiving his care, such as by providing a more thoughtful connection to a reading or acknowledging what he was doing for the cohort, caring in Noddings' sense of the term would not be fulfilled. In this study, there were many places where the students revealed while responding to class readings how they had changed or grown as prospective teachers, allowing the teacher to know, from their words, how he had affected them. Through the CMC channel, students and the teacher had more chances to observe how much they were connected to each other than they would have if they had had only the one channel of in-class interactions.

DISCUSSION

While much more could have been presented from these data, my analysis here suggests that Noddings' concept of caring and Bakhtin's perspective on dialogue are useful for understanding more fully the nature of teaching-learning relationships, highlighting their dialogical nature in CMC environments to offer potential sites for building caring relationships. Such perspectives also appear useful for understanding better the process of the teacher's becoming devoted to students and students' becoming responsible as they see themselves reflected in their teacher's perception of them. As Assaf (2003) and Na (2004) have emphasized, CMC can be a place where the struggle for "authoring the self" and "ideological becoming" as a student and a caring teacher can be enacted. Even when CMC is mainly focused on intellectual meaning-making about a given topic, it offers increased opportunities for knowing about what others are feeling and thinking about a certain issue and can encourage students and teachers to enter into developing caring relationships. For teachers, CMC can afford opportunities for them to author their identities as a caring teacher in relation to students through dialogical interactions, while, for students, being in a continual process of mirroring themselves through the teacher's written comments helps them discover themselves as a student and prospective teacher.

Before turning to implications of these findings for theory and practice, I must mention two important qualifications on the findings. First, the data presented in this paper have not emphasized to any great extent the amount of variation across cases that were actually evident. Indeed, not all students developed the same kind of relationship with the teacher; a few students had a much more problematic response to meeting their teacher through TeachNet. However, I have not dwelled on such variation here because the focus of this paper was on showing the potential of CMC for contributing to a caring encounter between teacher and students. Second, it is important to acknowledge that there may have been some reactive effects from my presence among the class members, from my obvious interest in the relationship the students had with their teacher, and from my frequent questions about what they thought and felt about each other as revealed in their words. Such a process may very well have influenced the students to be more reflective than they would have otherwise been.

The findings of this study may have significant implications for Noddings' perspective on caring and teacher education. Noddings' (1984) descriptions of caring are deeply rooted in a relational point of view. The construct of reciprocity shows how important the role of the cared-for is to maintaining a caring relation. However, how the one-caring and the cared-for influence and need each other to develop their caring relation has not been much explored in Noddings' work so far. Drawing on a Bakhtinian perspective, this study provided some evidence of how dialogue can join the teacher and student, allowing each to author him or herself as the one-caring or the cared-for, and how CMC can provide a place for a dialogical encounter between students and their teacher.

Finally, the findings of this study indicated that the teacher's caring was reflected in the students' work with the young readers they tutored, thereby acting as a potential resource for relational as well as content knowledge about how teachers should care for their students. The possibility that prospective teachers' relationships with their professors in college might be projected in future relationships with their own students highlights the significance of what happens in teacher education programs.

REFERENCES

Assaf, L. C. (2003). *The authoring of self: Looking at preservice teachers' professional identities as reflected in an online environment.* Unpublished doctoral dissertation, University of Texas at Austin.

Bakhtin, M. (1981). *The dialogic imagination* (M. Holquist, Ed.; C. Emerson & M. Holquist, Trans.). Austin: University of Texas Press.

Bakhtin, M. (1986). *Speech genres and other late essays* (C. Emerson & M. Holquist, Eds., V. W. McGee, Trans.). Austin, TX: University of Texas Press. (Original work published 1979).

Bruner, J. (1987). Life as narrative. *Social Research, 54,* 11-32.

Burford, V. N., & Gross, D. D. (2000, November). Caring on-line: On-line empathy, self-disclosure, emotional expression and nurturing. Paper presented at the 86th meeting of the National Communication Association, Seattle, WA.

Clark, K., & Holquist, M. (1984). *Mikhail Bakhtin.* Cambridge: Harvard University Press.

Goldstein, L. S. (1999). The relational zone: The role of caring relationships in the co-construction of mind. *American Educational Research Journal, 36,* 647-673.

Goldstein, L. S., & Freedman, D. (2003). Challenges enacting caring teacher education. *Journal of Teacher Education, 54*(5), 441-454.

Goldstein, L. S., & Lake, V. E. (2000). "Love, love and more love for children": Exploring preservice teachers' understandings of caring. *Teaching and Teacher Education, 16,* 861-872.

Hawisher, G. E., & Selfe, C. L. (1998). Reflections on computers and composition studies at the century's end. In L. Snyder (Ed.), *Page to screen: Taking literacy into the electronic era* (pp. 3-19). New York: Routledge.

Herring, S. C. (1996). Two variants of an electronic message schema. In S. C. Herring (Ed.), *Computer-mediated communication: Linguistic, social and cross-cultural perspectives* (pp. 81-106). Amsterdam: Benjamins.

Kolb, D. (1996). Discourse across links. In C. Ess (Ed.), *Philosophical perspectives on computer-mediated communication* (pp. 15-25). Albany, NY: State University of New York Press.

Langer, J. A. (1991). Literacy and schooling: A sociocognitive perspective. In E. Hiebert (Ed.), *Literacy for a diverse society* (pp. 9-27). New York: Teachers College Press.

Lincoln, Y., & Guba, E. (1985). *Naturalistic Inquiry.* Beverly Hills, CA: Sage.

Murray, D. E. (1991). The composing process for computer conversation. *Written communication, 8,* 35-55.

Na, Y. (2004). A Bakhtinian analysis of computer-mediated communication: How students create animated utterances in graduate seminar discussions. *Yearbook of the National Reading Conference, 53,* 67-89.

Noddings, N. (1984). *Caring: A feminine approach to ethics & moral education.* Berkeley: University of California Press.

Noddings, N. (1992). *The challenge to care in schools: An alternative approach to education.* New York: Teachers College Press.

Noddings, N. (2001). The caring teacher. In V. Richardson (Ed.), *Handbook of research on teaching* (4th ed., pp. 99-105). New York: Macmillan.

Pajares, F., & Graham, L. (1998). Formalist thinking and language arts instruction: Teachers' and students' beliefs about truth and caring in the teaching conversation. *Teaching and Teacher Education, 14,* 855-870.

Prillaman, A. R., & Eaker, D. J. (1994). The weave and the weaver: A tapestry begun. In A. R. Prillaman, D. J. Eaker, D. M. Kendrick (Eds.), *The tapestry of caring: Education as nurturance* (pp. 1-11). New Jersey: Ablex

Strauss, A., & Corbin, J. (1998). *Basics of qualitative research: Techniques and procedures for developing grounded theory.* Thousand Oaks, CA: Sage.

Volosinov, V. N. (1973). *Marxism and the philosophy of language* (L. Matejka & I. R. Titunik, Trans.). Cambridge: Harvard University Press.

Weinstein, C. S. (1998). "I want to be nice, but I have to be mean": Exploring prospective teachers' conceptions of caring and order. *Teaching and Teacher Education, 14,* 153-163.

A Study of Adult ESL Oral Reading Fluency and Silent Reading Comprehension

Kristin Lems

National-Louis University

Fluency, a concept of interest to reading theorists and practitioners, has been called a *multi-dimensional reading construct* (Rasinski, 1990). The term *fluent reading* is generally used to refer to reading in which a high degree of automaticity has been reached, decoding is no longer effortful, and attentional resources can be focused on construction of meaning (Samuels, 2002).

Oral reading fluency is important due to its demonstrated robust correlation with silent reading comprehension and many measures of reading performance. Again and again, across different variables and populations, fluency scores strongly correlate with scores on many reading tasks (Kuhn & Stahl, 2002). As a result, fluency measures are used in a growing number of school settings for placement, norming, referral for special services, and as a gauge of individual and class reading progress (Blachowicz, Sullivan, & Cieply, 2001). Rebecca Barr (personal communication, February 2000) described the value of the fluency assessment succinctly: "It can provide enough information to confirm hunches, prompt further assessment, and begin the process of intervention." Fluency is assuming its rightful seat in the pantheon of key reading concepts.

In a neighboring but often non-intersecting field, teachers of English as a Second Language (ESL) work on developing second language (L2) proficiency in their students. Here, *fluency* is considered to be a proficiency and comfort level in all functions of the target language equal to that of one's native language, a meaning that differs markedly from the one used by literacy researchers. This paper adopts the concept of fluency found in reading research. Nonetheless, what both of these widely-differing concepts of fluency share is the idea of effortlessness, ease, and smoothness, a notion as important in L2 listening, speaking, reading, and writing as it is in first language (L1) reading, and whether the mode is silent or oral. In fact, fluency can be seen as a universal core language construct.

Beyond a simple correlation between oral reading fluency and reading comprehension scores, it has been shown that reading comprehension and fluency seem to be in a reciprocal causation relationship (Fuchs, Fuchs, Hosp, & Jenkins, 2001; Rasinski, 2003; Samuels, 1979; Stanovich, 1986). Moreover, fluency practice has positive washback on silent reading comprehension. Fluency building activities such as paired reading, timed repeated reading, Reader's Theatre, and poetry performance are becoming widely accepted in the integrated language arts classroom (Rasinski, 2003). Fluency building techniques are beginning to appear in textbooks and articles about English language learners as well (Anderson, 1999; Baker & Good, 1995; Li & Nes, 2001; Taguchi & Gorsuch, 2002; Taguchi, Takayasu-Maass, & Gorsuch, 2004).

However, adding oral fluency practice to the adult ESL curriculum may be premature because research has not yet established that there is a relationship between fluency and silent reading comprehension in adult English language learners. The purpose of this study was to examine whether there is a relationship between oral reading fluency and silent reading comprehension in these learners. Until that can be established or ruled out, using oral reading in ESL assessment or for classroom practice lacks construct validity.

The research questions guiding this study read as follows: (a) Is there a correlation between L2 adult oral reading fluency and silent reading comprehension? (b) Which measure of oral reading fluency correlates better with reading comprehension for L2 adults, a system of words correct per minute (WCPM) or a fluency rubric such as the Multidimensional Fluency Scale (MFS) of Zutell and Rasinski (1991)? (c) What can a more in-depth look at the miscues of seven English language learners at an intermediate proficiency level add to a description of oral reading by English language learners?

DEFINITIONS OF FLUENCY

There is considerable blurring in the conception of fluency in the literacy literature. Some simply call fluency "decoding plus comprehension" (Lipson & Lang, 1991). Some define fluency as "words correct per minute" (Hasbrouck & Tindal, 1992). Kame'enui and Simmons (2001) lament the "one size fits all" quality the term *reading fluency* has acquired. Shinn, Knutson, Good, Tilly, and Collins (1992), in a study of reading textbooks, found no distinction made between the constructs of fluency and decoding. It appears that, phrased in the words of frustrated researchers, "the unsettling conclusion is that reading fluency involves every process and subskill involved in reading" (Wolf & Katzir-Cohen, 2001, p. 219).

Thus, fluency seems not to be an absolute but an ability to interact with a variety of texts, for a variety of purposes. Lipson and Lang (1991) suggested, "Teachers are likely to be on firm ground if they ask not whether a student is fluent but rather, 'What can this student read fluently?' and 'Does the range of situations require expanding?'" (p. 225).

The Role of Fluency in Reading Models

The influential automatic information processing model of reading comprehension (Laberge & Samuels, 1974) assigns a prime role to fluency. In effect, the model describes an allocation of cognitive processing resources to the reading task, an allocation that evolves as proficiency increases from a focus on word recognition to a level of automaticity. Reaching this rapid, automatic level of word recognition thereby frees up cognitive resources for comprehension of text.

Stanovich's interactive compensatory model (Stanovich, 1980; Stanovich & Beck, 2000) presents fluent reading as a byproduct of, rather than contributor to, comprehension. In this model, a smooth (fluent) path to comprehension, with words rapidly accessible to the reader, allows a focus on comprehension, whereas a "hitch" in word processing requires the use of other strategic systems, including those based on knowledge of syntax, morphology, discourse, punctuation, and other kinds of literacy knowledge. In the interactive compensatory model, then, reading fluency has a comprehension component, as reflected in a description such as the following: "[a fluent reader is] able to perform two difficult tasks simultaneously...the ability to identify words and comprehend a text at the same time" (Samuels, 2002, p. 168). This model would also necessarily include prosody in its definition of fluency, given that prosody is another demonstration of knowledge of the syntax and discourse systems that are part of literacy.

Reading fluency takes on another role in reading models that posit reading as a transfer from oracy (oral language) to literacy (written language), with oral knowledge as the knowledge base for later literacy (Sticht & James, 1984). According to this theory, learning to speak emerges from listening comprehension, and both of these are preconditions to fluent reading, enabling a reader to comprehend a text through reading as easily as a listener can understand an oral text. Thus, fluent reading should allow readers to achieve the top limit of their language comprehension, and comprehension is assumed.

Gough and Tunmer's simple view of reading (1986) offers a formula for reading comprehension as follows: RC = D x LC, that is, reading comprehension (RC) is the product of decoding (D) and listening comprehension (LC), or what is sometimes referred to as general linguistic competence. This model, like the Sticht and James (1984) model, accounts for the importance of language competence in reading comprehension. If some of the features commonly ascribed to fluency, such as speed and accuracy, reside within the decoding part of the model, while other features of fluency, such as prosody, reside within the language comprehension part, the model could suggest that fluency is a feature common to both decoding and linguistic competence, and could serve as a bridge between the two.

Components of Oral Reading

Oral reading is the means by which the abstract construct of fluency is usually measured. It generally includes two or more of the following five measures: speed, accuracy, parsing, prosody, and comprehension, features at the same time both discrete and synergistic.

Speed is critical, in that, when text is read below a certain level of speed, reading comprehension is unlikely to occur. Rasinski (2000) observed that students who were referred to his reading clinic often scored only slightly below grade level in comprehension and word recognition, but their oral reading rate was significantly below that of their peers, making it impossible to keep up with their schoolwork. Based on a large sample, Hasbrouck and Tindal (1992) established widely-accepted grade level norms for oral reading in the second through fifth grades. However, norms for percentage of comprehension questions answered correctly vary considerably among researchers. Samuels (personal communication, March, 2003) pointed out that it is risky to establish norms unless text type and reading purpose are established as well.

Fluency is assumed by all researchers to require an accuracy measure. Goodman and Burke (1972) set up a complex miscue scoring inventory that has formed the basis of most scoring of oral reading performance ever since. An oral reading study in which speed was removed as a factor and only accuracy was charted failed to have much diagnostic power (Parker, Hasbrouck, & Tindal, 1992). Something about the synergy of speed and accuracy together appears to create a strong assessment tool.

The third construct, parsing, or "chunking," is the ability to separate text into meaningful phrase and clause units. Parsing is an important measure of the development of syntax knowledge, or the grammar of a language. In addition to natural breaks that follow syntax, punctuation provides signals for phrase and clause breaks, and mastery of these signals can be demonstrated through oral reading.

In 1991, Dowhower noted that prosody, which can be defined as reading with appropriate expression, was fluency's "neglected bedfellow" (p. 165). In several studies, she discovered a strong relationship between "expressive reading" and comprehension. As a result of such research, fluency rubrics, such as that of the National Reading Panel (2000) and the National Assessment of Educational Progress (NAEP) (Pinnell, Pikulski, Wixson, Campbell, Gough, & Beatty, 1995), include consideration of expressive reading, as does the Multidimensional Fluency Scale (MFS) (Zutell & Rasinski, 1991), included in a portion of this study.

Finally, some definitions of oral reading fluency include comprehension as a constituent. Samuels' (1979) description of proficient reading fluency included that the reader should be able to "comprehend while reading aloud" (Samuels, 1979, p. 406). Rasinski (1990) also defined reading fluency as "those surface level or observable behaviors during oral reading that are associated with comprehension" (p. 38).

Criterion Validity of Oral Reading

Many studies have found high criterion validity for oral reading as a proxy for reading comprehension. For example, in three different experiments, Deno, Mirkin, and Chiang (1982) found high correlations between oral reading tasks and standardized reading comprehension tests, levels higher than those with cloze or other direct measures. Oral reading fluency also correlated highly with both literal and inferential reading scores on standardized tests. In one controlled study, fluency samples were able to distinguish students with learning disabilities from those from impoverished socioeconomic backgrounds or students in general education (Deno, Marston, Shinn, & Tindal, 1983). Fuchs, Fuchs, and Maxwell (1988) found stronger correlations between oral reading scores and standardized tests of reading comprehension than between standardized tests and question answering, oral recall, and written cloze. Jenkins and Jewell (1993) found oral reading to correlate strongly with reading comprehension activities. Fluency was found to correlate well with teacher judgment of student progress (Hintze, Shapiro, & Conte, 1997). The same study also found that oral reading was a better measure of reading comprehension than orally answering questions on a silently-read passage, whether the reading program was basal, literature-based, or whole language-based. Several researchers reported that oral reading fluency correlations held up regardless of the nature of the text (Cahalan-Laitusis & Harris, 2003; Fuchs & Deno, 1992; Hintze et al., 1997). Shinn, Knutson, Good, Tilly, and Collins (1992) found that fluency measures correlate highly with any and all measures of reading comprehension, leading the authors to conclude that "oral reading fluency fits current theoretical models of reading well and can be validated as a measure of general reading achievement, including comprehension" (p. 476).

Espin and Foegen (1996) found that, by secondary school, learner outcomes such as ability to engage in higher order thinking skills and vocabulary knowledge are more important indicators of comprehension than oral reading, and Espin and Deno (1993) found that oral reading correlated only moderately with information-locating skills in more mature readers. Fuchs et al. (2001) described a "developmental trajectory of oral reading fluency [which] involves greatest growth in the primary grades, with a negatively accelerating curve though the intermediate grades and perhaps into high school" (p. 240). It may be that there is something like a "window of opportunity" for using fluency as a measure of reading comprehension.

Although there does not appear to be research on oral reading fluency and adult English language learners, two studies have validated oral reading in studies with Hispanic children. Baker and Good (1995) established the reliability and validity of using curriculum-based fluency assessments as measures of silent reading comprehension with second grade bilingual Hispanic students. In another study, Ramirez (2001) found higher correlations between silent reading comprehension and fluency than between silent reading comprehension and several other measures, including simple decoding, for fifth grade Hispanic English language learners (Ramirez, 2001).

READING BY ADULT ENGLISH LANGUAGE LEARNERS

Reading in a Second Language

Linguistics and bilingualism researchers have struggled to construct L2 reading models, finding the task difficult due to the incredible complexities involved. A model must account for such factors as L1 literacy level and educational experiences, the age at which L2 study commenced, sociocultural conditions under which both L1 and L2 are acquired and learned, the structural and phonetic differences between L1 and L2, and other features. While it is impossible to devote the time needed to explain these in this article, a few brief comments are in order.

A number of studies have corroborated that L1 literacy level is a key determinant of second language reading comprehension although the exact nature of the transfer between languages is not fully known (Bernhardt, 2000). Bernhardt and Kamil (1995) sketched a partial L2 reading model as follows: "Second-language reading is a function of L1 reading ability and second-language grammatical ability" (Bernhardt, 2000, p. 803). Nonetheless, even accounting for these factors, a great deal, perhaps 50%, of L2 reading proficiency remains unaccounted for at the present time (Bernhardt, 2005).

There is overwhelming evidence of transfer between languages. In fact, the central argument of those in favor of dual language, two-way immersion, and bilingual education programs rests on this important and extensive body of research. Research on the efficacy of transfer of cognitive and academic skills can be summed up nicely by the phrase, "you only learn to read once" (Anderson, 2003).

Fitzgerald's (1995) review of the research on L2 reading led her to the conclusion that, at least in academic tasks, L2 readers resemble L1 readers in substance, but process more slowly. She found that the more proficient an L2 reader becomes, the more his or her processing strategies resemble those of an L1 reader. She concluded that the differences were of degree, not kind. She also found that "considerable evidence emerged to support the [Common Underlying Proficiency] CUP model" (p. 186) proposed by Cummins (1979, 1981). The CUP model asserts that language knowledge is universal at its core and rests upon a common underlying competence possessed by all humans; what differs from one language to another is the set of surface manifestations, including phonology, morphology, vocabulary, syntax, discourse, and cultural features.

Differences in L1 and L2 Oral Reading

The need to disaggregate decoding, recoding, and meaning construction with L2 adult learners creates a more complicated landscape for assessing reading comprehension through oral reading than is the case with L1 children. At least three major factors can come into play when an L2 adult reads a text aloud, and these contrast with L1 oral reading in important ways.

Decoding without comprehension. In L1 reading, when an emergent reader of normal abilities is able to pronounce a decoded word aloud, the meaning of the word then becomes available for a semantic match. The L1 reader draws upon his or her oral word bank (the words in auditory memory) that the word signals, and makes a match with a known meaning (or develops a new one, possibly from context). A fluent L1 reader can identify the words in the text as whole units and simultaneously construct meaning from them, making an effortless match between a word's written form, oral form, and meaning, as long as the word is already familiar to the learner or can be construed from context.

However, even if an English language learner, literate in his or her L1, is able to transfer skills from L1 in order to decode English words successfully (that is, match sight and sound), it may still not be possible to make a semantic match with the word's sound, because some linguistic knowledge of the target language is missing. Learners may not realize that the word they have decoded is one they have heard, or they may not know the meaning of the word. An example of the former would be the word "listen," which has a silent "t." The learner may have heard the sounds /lISn/ but never learned that the word was spelled that way. Another example would be a reader who correctly decodes and pronounces the word "opossum" but simply does not know what an opossum is. Consequently, ability to read the word aloud may not necessarily access the word's meaning.

Comprehension without recoding (ability to pronounce). On the other hand, some L2 learners may be able to access the meaning of a word when reading it silently but be unable to pronounce the word when reading aloud because they do not know the phoneme-grapheme correspondences of English or cannot make the sounds. Nevertheless, they may know the meaning of the word. For example, most Americans would recognize the phrase on the U.S. dollar, "E pluribus unum" to mean "From many, one," and although they cannot pronounce it using Latin phonemes, or possibly at all, they can nevertheless comprehend it.

Decoding and pronouncing with negative transfer. A third possibility is some combination of the above, in which an L2 reader decodes and pronounces a word or string of words using his or her L1 knowledge in a way that interferes with the sound or meaning of the word in the target language. This can result from phonemic interference from L1, a false cognate, or other negative transfer from L1. For example, a native French or Spanish speaker may read the word "actually" and be confident that it means "at this time," because in those languages a word with similar spelling and sound does mean that. Thus, a word or string of words could be apparently correctly rendered, but not understood, or incorrectly rendered, but understood, depending on the nature of the interference.

In effect, what is being asked of L2 adult oral readers is to decode the graphemes of the connected English text and map them to both the English phoneme system and the reader's semantic knowledge, while simultaneously recoding those English phonemes into an oral performance, and to do it rapidly. On the basis of these considerations, therefore, one would predict that oral reading for L2 adults could tell us something about their L2 reading process, but that differences in L1 literacy level, language structures of L1, and decoding and recoding ability could confound the assessment.

METHOD

Participants and Program

This descriptive study looked at several measures of English language proficiency for 232 post-secondary ESL students in a five level semi-intensive academic ESL program at a private urban university in the Midwest. Because entrance to the program required a high school diploma, it could be assumed that the students were fully literate in their native languages. Learners consisted of both working adults and younger adults who had immigrated to the U.S. during high school and still needed to achieve a higher level of academic proficiency in ESL.

The first languages of the 232 students are summarized in Table 1. Those using the Roman alphabet included the speakers of Polish and Spanish, those using another alphabet included the speakers of Ukrainian and Bulgarian, and the Chinese students used Mandarin, a syllable-based logographic system with a phonological component (Li, 2002). In addition, there were ten students who represented other languages not disaggregated for the study.

The program had five levels of study, from total beginner (Level 1) to high intermediate/advanced students (Level 5). Academic in focus, its purpose was to prepare students for transition into undergraduate study at the university. The 14 hour per week, 10-week term included considerable study of grammar, reading and writing, language and computer lab, and conversation practice.

Of the 232 students in the study, 14 were in Level 1, 154 were in Level 3, and 64

Table 1 Participant Characteristics by First Language

FIRST LANGUAGE	NUMBER	PERCENT
Polish	143	61.6
Ukrainian	33	14.2
Chinese	23	9.9
Spanish (Mexican)	14	6.0
Bulgarian	9	3.9
Other	10	4.3
TOTAL	**232**	**100.0**

were at the advanced level, Level 5. Data from all the students were included in the first question of the study, regarding the possible correlation between oral and silent reading. The second question, comparing the use of two fluency assessment systems, words correct per minute (WCPM) and the Multidimensional Fluency Scale (MFS), involved 80 mixed level students. The third question, about the role miscue analysis can play in a description of intermediate students' oral reading, involved seven Level 3 students from mixed language backgrounds.

Procedure

Near the end of each quarter, a taped oral interview was conducted in the ESL program to evaluate students' English oral proficiency. Along with the existing interviews, a one-minute oral reading of a passage taken from the Level 3 reader that had not been used in the Level 3 curriculum was added at the end of the interview. The assessing teacher, who was not the classroom teacher, taped and timed the oral reading along with the interview. Later, the oral readings were replayed and coded by the researcher, using a system of words correct per minute (WCPM). Each oral reading was timed a second time, and miscues were deducted from the total words read in a minute. To insure uniformity of miscue coding, a key was created (Leu, 1982) that included substitutions, omissions, and insertions. The miscues were then classified in three ways: significant (meaning-changing) miscues, other miscues, and foreign accent features (comprehensible but with substitution of an L1 phoneme, such as pronouncing "thrift" "trift" or pronouncing the word "stopped" as a two syllable word). The foreign accent features were not counted as miscues and were not deducted from the total words read.

After each reader's words correct per minute (WCPM) score was obtained, it was entered into a statistics software program. The final exam score, used as the measure of silent reading comprehension, and the language lab final exam score, used as a measure of listening comprehension, were also entered for all 232 students. Later, 80 of the taped oral readings were rescored by two raters, using the MFS rubric instead of the system of words correct per minute. Analysis of the data included measures of central tendency and other descriptive statistics, correlations, and regression analysis. Finally, a subgroup of seven Level 3 learners was chosen from the 80 who had been evaluated using both fluency systems, and their miscue coding sheets examined qualitatively and in detail.

Validity and Reliability of Instruments

Words correct per minute (WCPM) is a well-established measure by which reading fluency has been measured and shown to correlate with silent reading comprehension. The use of a one-minute sample has also been validated, as Deno et al. (1982) stated: "When a global index of relative reading proficiency is the purpose of measurement, such an index can be easily obtained within 1 minute without using a standardized test" (p. 44).

The course final exam was used as the proxy for silent reading comprehension. It contained many features of standardized reading achievement tests, such as that students could not consult their notes or their classmates, it was timed, students were required to follow directions for several task types, and vocabulary knowledge played a key role in performance. Moreover, because the final exam was administered in the last week of the course, all students could be assumed to have had a similar instructional experience, adding further stability to the variable. The exams consisted of 15-17 pages, further improving reliability, and had been refined for use in the ESL program over a number of years.

The readability level for the reading passage was calculated using the Fry readability scale (Fry, 1977). Also, an approximate instructional reading level for each class level was established by calculating the readability levels of the reading passages on each final exam. Because no scale exists for adult English language learners at this time, the passages were matched with L1 children's grade levels (Fuchs, Fuchs, Hamlett, Walz, & Germann, 1993; Hasbrouck & Tindal, 1992). According to a well-established system for leveling texts (see Johns, 1997, for a description), the oral reading passage was at the frustration level for Level 1 students, instructional level for Level 3 students, and independent level for Level 5 students.

The language lab final exam used as the listening score was a two-page exam, based on content and structures taught in the language lab portion of the course. It consisted of listening to a series of short, taped items and responding with true/false, multiple choice, or one-sentence answers.

The Multidimensional Fluency Scale (MFS) (Zutell & Rasinski, 1991) uses three criteria in its rubric: pace, smoothness, and phrasing. The MFS has been used extensively in other research on reading fluency (Moskal, 2002; Pinnell et al., 1995; Rasinski, Blachowicz, & Lems, in press). The MFS ratings were scored by the researcher and a doctoral student in reading with a background in ESL and bilingual programs.

RESULTS

Descriptive Statistics

Among the 232 oral reading samples, there was a range in WCPM of 131 words between the lowest and highest fluency scores, indicating that WCPM can measure a wide range of differences in performance among literate adult ESL students. The final exam scores had a range of 47 percentage points with a mean of 81% (SD = 9.9), and the spread of the listening score was 72 percentage points, with a mean of 83% (SD = 10.9).

It was found that as learner proficiency in the program increased, so did the mean raw score for fluency. The mean WCPM increased by 23 words between Levels 1 and 3 and another 19 words between Levels 3 and 5. It appears that, just as is the case for L1 children, fluency rate increases in L2 adults studying English as their general language proficiency level increases.

When evaluated by first language, there were significant differences in WCPM, with speakers of Polish performing at the highest level, Chinese at the lowest, and the other language groups distributed in between, corresponding to the similarity of their written language to the English alphabet. However, there were no significant differences in mean performance among the language groups on the final exam and language lab final exam.

Correlations

When correlations were performed (see Table 2), a weak to moderate but highly significant correlation of .256 ($p < .001$, $N = 232$) was found between WCPM and the silent reading score (the final exam), and a somewhat higher correlation of .392 ($p < .001$, $N = 232$) between WCPM and the listening score (the language lab final exam).

When analyzed by level in program (see Table 3), the correlation between fluency measures and the reading score was stronger at Level 3 than Level 1 and stronger at Level 5 than Level 3. Using different presentations of the fluency components, speed alone was less predictive of the reading score than accuracy alone, and both speed and accuracy were less predictive than miscue ratio (MR), calculated by dividing miscues by total words read. The highest correlation between the reading score and a fluency measure was at Level 5, between MR and the reading score ($r = -.46$ $p < .001$). By Level 5, unlike Levels 1 and 3, the fluency measures become more strongly correlated with the reading score than with the listening score. This suggests that a threshold of listening comprehension may need to be reached before fluency measures are meaningful (Cummins, 1984).

When analyzed by first language, the strongest correlations were found for Hispanic students, with correlations reaching -.68 ($p < .01$) between miscue ratio (MR) and the reading score. On the other hand, no significant correlations were found between any of the fluency measures and the final exams (reading measure) or language lab final exams (listening measure) for the Chinese students. That these students did as well as the other first language groups on average on the reading measure but had considerably lower scores on the oral reading suggests that these students use some other means of constructing meaning from print that may not sample the oral forms of the words being read to access meaning.

Finally, the listening comprehension scores not only were correlated more highly with the reading scores than with the fluency measure, but were also more strongly correlated with the reading measure than any of the fluency measures were. Such a finding suggests that listening proficiency may have subskills that are found in both oral reading fluency and silent reading comprehension.

Table 2 Correlations for Measures of Oral Reading Fluency and Other Measures

MEASURE	FINAL EXAM (READING SCORE)	LANGUAGE LAB FINAL (LISTENING SCORE)
Words correct per minute (WCPM)	.26	.39
Total words read	.21	.35
Total # of miscues	-.29	-.30
Total # of significant miscues	-.30	-.32
Miscue ratio	-.31	-.41
Multidimensional Fluency Scale (MFS)	-.29	.46

n = 232 for all measures except MFS (n = 80); all correlations significant at p ≤ .001

Table 3 Correlations Between Measures of Oral Reading Fluency and Other Measures by
Level and First Language

MEASURE: WORDS CORRECT PER MINUTE (WCPM)	FINAL EXAM (READING SCORE)	LANGUAGE LAB FINAL (LISTENING SCORE)
Level 1 (n=14)	.04	.63*
Level 3 (n=154)	.27**	.38**
Level 5 (n=64)	.41**	.39*
Polish (n=143)	.24**	.24**
Ukrainian (n=33)	.10	.53**
Chinese (n=23)	.15	.51
Spanish (n=14)	.55*	.66*
Bulgarian (n=9)	.52	.76*
Other (n=10)	.30	.34
MEASURE: TOTAL # OF MISCUES	**FINAL EXAM (READING SCORE)**	**LANGUAGE LAB FINAL (LISTENING SCORE)**
Level 1 (n=14)	.06	-.01
Level 3 (n=154)	-.26**	-.25**
Level 5 (n=64)	-.42**	-.34**
Polish (n=143)	-.29**	-.14
Ukrainian (n=33)	-.11	-.42*
Chinese (n=23)	-.37	-.29
Spanish (n=14)	-.73**	-.72**
Bulgarian (n=9)	-.56	-.54
Other (n=10)	-.50	-.53
MEASURE: TOTAL # OF SIGNIFICANT MISCUES	**FINAL EXAM (READING SCORE)**	**LANGUAGE LAB FINAL (LISTENING SCORE)**
Level 1 (n=14)	-.11	-.19
Level 3 (n=154)	-.27**	-.23**
Level 5 (n=64)	-.40**	-.37**
Polish (n=143)	-.31**	-.17*
Ukrainian (n=33)	.00	-.54**
Chinese (n=23)	-.40	-.26
Spanish (n=14)	-.52	-.66*
Bulgarian (n=9)	.75*	.65
Other (n=10)	-.62	-.59
MEASURE: MISCUE RATIO	**FINAL EXAM (READING SCORE)**	**LANGUAGE LAB FINAL (LISTENING SCORE)**
Level 1 (n=14)	-.06	-.40
Level 3 (n=154)	-.29**	-.32**
Level 5 (n=64)	-.46**	-.37**
Polish (n=143)	-.31**	-.18*
Ukrainian (n=33)	.05	-.52**
Chinese (n=23)	-.30	-.25
Spanish (n=14)	-.68**	-.86**
Bulgarian (n=9)	-.75*	-.85**
Other (n=10)	-.43	-.46

n = 232; * p < .05; ** p < .01*

The second research question of the study was focused on which measure of fluency would correlate more highly with reading comprehension scores of L2 adults. Results indicated that the Multidimensional Fluency Scale (MFS) behaved like the WCPM measure in showing an increase with level in program. MFS correlated with silent reading comprehension at a level of .29, only slightly better than WCPM, and at the same level of significance. None of the subskills of the MFS (pace, phrasing, and smoothness), when disaggregated, had significantly higher correlations with the reading score than the total MFS score; however, when the subskills were put in a stepwise regression analysis to predict the reading score, pace was as strong a predictor (9%) of the reading measure as the total MFS score, whereas the other two subskills did not contribute to the prediction. Thus, prosodic features did not serve as predictors for silent reading comprehension performance. Like the other fluency measures, MFS was more highly correlated with the listening score than with the reading score. The correlation of MFS to listening ($r = .46$, $p < .001$) was the strongest correlation between any of the oral reading fluency measures and either silent reading or listening comprehension scores.

However, the MFS had low interrater reliability, just above chance on some of the submeasures. This is probably because of the subjective nature of the judgments the scale requires be made about pace, phrasing, and smoothness. Because WCPM and MFS scores are highly correlated with each other ($r = .88$, $p < .001$), the more reliable nature of the WCPM rating, especially when accompanied by a coding sheet, makes it preferable to the fluency rubric.

Miscue Analysis

A miscue analysis of the oral reading performance of seven Level 3 students from different language backgrounds indicated that all of the fluency measures failed to account for some of the characteristics of adult English language learners due to two factors: the varying degrees of difference between English and the L1 writing systems from which the students came and the issue of foreign accents that may "fossilize" early even though reading comprehension skills continue to increase.

By their nature, fluency scoring systems do not inform the rater whether a miscue derives from a problem with understanding the word's meaning or in pronouncing it, and with English language learners, this ambiguity becomes significant. For example, numerous participants in the study pronounced the word *used* with two syllables. It was impossible to know how many of them, both when they pronounced the word correctly and when they did not, understood that the word in this context meant "second hand." Further, it was impossible to know whether a mispronounced rendering was developmental, that is, able to be ameliorated, or had already reached a plateau and would remain as part of a permanent foreign accent.

The Role of Oral Reading Fluency in an L2 Adult Reading Model

From these data, attempts were made, using regression analysis, to build a model of L2 adult oral reading performance (when English is the L2). A model that combined listening comprehension and oral reading fluency was able to predict 46% of the variance in the silent reading comprehension scores in the sample overall, rising to as high as 54% when Level 3 students were examined alone; in other words, the listening score and fluency score (in the form of miscue ratio) when put together predicted nearly half of the performance on a reading measure. However, fluency variables added little explanatory power, so long as a listening comprehension variable was available.

One possibility is that oral reading fluency as a measure of L2 adult silent reading becomes significant only after a certain number of requisite skills are in place, such skills as a threshold level of listening comprehension (enough receptive oral vocabulary to access the English phonemic-semantic system to know what words mean when heard), a threshold level of decoding (enough knowledge of the English graphophonemic system to figure out how words sound), and a threshold of recoding/pronunciation (enough oral proficiency to pronounce some words in the English phoneme system). In such a model, the "window of opportunity," during which reading fluency is a sensitive assessment, would open after students reach an (as yet unspecified) minimum listening threshold and would close when students have achieved a mature level of silent reading, as is the case for L1 readers (Fuchs et al., 2001; Kuhn & Stahl, 2002). The opening may take place at different times for students from different L1 backgrounds, depending on their degree of familiarity with decoding and pronouncing the Roman alphabet, and on different learning styles.

Interestingly, in the study, the correlation between the listening comprehension measure and the silent reading measure remained relatively constant across levels, and the listening score alone predicted 29% of the reading score for Level 1 students, 25% for Level 3 students, and 28% for Level 5 students. It is interesting that the listening measure was written to match the difficulty level of the curriculum, so that the listening tasks became increasingly more advanced. However, the score retained about an equal correlation with silent reading as the students' level of proficiency increased. This is in contrast to the fluency measure's correlation with the reading score, which increased as proficiency increased. One can draw the conclusion that listening comprehension, which could be taken as a measure of linguistic competence, continues to be a stable measure that accounts for about 25% of reading comprehension across proficiency levels for these adult English language learners.

Reflecting on that phenomenon, one can see that the simple model of reading (Gough & Tunmer, 1986) described may have some relevance to second language learners. The formula in which RC (reading comprehension) = D (decoding) x LC (language comprehension) suggests that, once decoding and all of its complexities are taken out of the picture, the critical factor in reading comprehension may be linguistic competence, a concept somewhat similar in nature to listening comprehension.

For adult English language learners, then, it may be that oral reading cannot gauge decoding skills until the graphophonemic system, listening comprehension skills, including basic listening vocabulary, and L2 recoding skills are in place. Once these are in place, the fluency measure no longer correlates highly with silent reading comprehension because the learner is a literate adult and has presumably already reached a mature level of reading comprehension in L1, so that once

L2 decoding skills have been achieved, other adult reading strategies take over. Furthermore, L2 adult oral reading will always have the additional complication of the learner's foreign accent, which may make coding the oral performance more difficult and less reliable. The foreign accent issue certainly confounds a fluency rubric that includes a prosody measure because foreign accents often include not only different phonemes but different intonational patterns as well.

CONCLUSIONS AND DIRECTIONS FOR FURTHER RESEARCH

To make use of oral reading assessment on a large scale in adult ESL teaching, two pieces must be put in place: an instrument that can reliably factor in the "foreign accent" feature and statistically valid fluency norms for adult ESL students. A confirmatory study that includes a fluency measure, a listening comprehension measure, and a silent reading comprehension passage at independent reading level, using students from a post-secondary ESL program, would be a useful follow up to this research.

Although timed oral readings cannot powerfully predict L2 adult silent reading comprehension, their modest correlations with silent reading were highly significant ($p < .001$). The fluency scores can tell us several important things. First, an oral reading score is sensitive to progress across levels: as student language proficiency goes up, oral reading fluency should go up as well. Also, the fact that the fluency score was more strongly correlated with listening comprehension than with silent reading comprehension suggests that fluency may be a skill that indicates how well students are building bridges between their listening and reading skills. Third, hearing an individual student read aloud can give a teacher valuable insight into the student's learning processes. Consistent L1 vowel interference, for example, helps ESL teachers identify the need for more explicit instruction on vowel sound differences. Finally, the practice of oral reading in non-stressful contexts such as paired reading, choral reading, and repeated oral reading, can build confidence for L2 learners. This activity can be especially helpful to Chinese students for whom decoding in English is often an overwhelming and unfamiliar enterprise. ESL teachers of Chinese students may want to provide extra opportunities for those students to practice decoding and reading aloud, in order to get them to a level of speed and, ultimately, automaticity comparable to that of students from alphabetic first languages.

The study takes the first tentative steps in bringing the reading fluency construct to the field of adult and post-secondary ESL teaching, and its tantalizing findings raise as many questions as they answer. It is hoped that others will be inspired to address some of the questions and to take their own next steps in the journey.

REFERENCES

Anderson, N. (1999). *Exploring second language reading: Issues and strategies.* Boston: Heinle & Heinle.

Anderson, N. (2003, March). *Metacognition and the L2 reader.* Paper presented at the meeting of the Teachers of English to Speakers of Other Languages conference, Baltimore, MD.

Baker, S. K., & Good, R. (1995). Curriculum-based measurement of English reading with bilingual Hispanic students: A validation study with second-grade students. *School Psychology Review, 24,* 561-578.

Bernhardt, E. B. (2000). Second-language reading as a case study of reading scholarship in the 20th century. In M. Kamil, P. B. Mosenthal, P. D. Pearson, & R. Barr (Eds.), *Handbook of reading research* (Vol. III, pp. 791-811). Mahwah, NJ: Erlbaum.

Bernhardt, E. B. (2005). Progress and procrastination in second-language reading. In M. McGroarty (Ed.), *Annual review of applied linguistics* (pp. 133-150). Cambridge, UK: Cambridge University Press.

Bernhardt, E. B., & Kamil, M. (1995). Interpreting relationships between L1 and L2 reading: Consolidating the linguistic threshold and the linguistic interdependence hypotheses. *Applied Linguistics, 16*, 15-34.

Blachowicz, C. Z., Sullivan, D. M., & Cieply, C. (2001). Fluency snapshots: A quick screening tool for your classroom. *Reading Psychology, 22*, 95-109.

Cahalan-Laitusis, C., & Harris, A. (2003, April). *Oral reading fluency and optimal difficulty level of a literature-based reading curriculum.* Paper presented at the meeting of the American Educational Research Association, Chicago, IL.

Cummins, J. (1979). Linguistic interdependence and the educational development of bilingual children. *Review of Educational Research, 49*, 222-251.

Cummins, J. (1981). The role of primary language development in promoting educational success for language minority students. In California State Department of Education (Ed.), *Schooling and language minority students: A theoretical framework* (pp. 3-49). Los Angeles, CA: Evaluation, Dissemination, and Assessment Center.

Cummins, J. (1984). *Bilingualism and special education: Issues in assessment and pedagogy.* Clevedon, UK: Multilingual Matters.

Deno, S. L., Mirkin, P. K., & Chiang, B. (1982). Identifying valid measures of reading. *Exceptional Children, 49*, 36-45.

Deno, S. L., Marston, D., Shinn, M., & Tindal, G. (1983). Oral reading fluency: A simple datum for scaling reading disability. *Topics in Learning and Learning Disabilities, 2*, 53-59.

Dowhower, S. (1991). Speaking of prosody: Fluency's unattended bedfellow. *Theory into Practice, 30*, 165-175.

Espin, C. A., & Deno, S. L. (1993). Performance in reading from content area text as an indicator of achievement. *Remedial and Special Education, 14*, 47-59.

Espin, C. A., & Foegen, A. (1996). Validity of general outcome measures for predicting secondary students' performance on content-area tasks. *Exceptional Children, 62*, 497-514.

Fitzgerald, J. (1995). English-as-a-second-language learners' cognitive reading processes: A review of research in the United States. *Review of Educational Research, 65*, 145-190.

Fry, E. B. (1977). Fry's readability graph: Clarification, validity, and extension to Level 17. *Journal of Reading, 21*, 278-288.

Fuchs, L. S., & Deno, S. L. (1992). Effects of curriculum within curriculum-based measurement. *Exceptional Children, 58*, 232-242.

Fuchs, L. S., Fuchs, D., Hamlett, C. L., Walz, L., & Germann, G. (1993). Formative evaluation of academic progress: How much growth can we expect? *School Psychology Review, 22*, 27-48.

Fuchs, L. S., Fuchs, D., Hosp, M., & Jenkins, J. R. (2001). Oral reading fluency as an indicator of reading competence: A theoretical, empirical, and historical analysis. *Scientific Studies of Reading, 5*, 239-256.

Fuchs, L. S., Fuchs, D., & Maxwell, L. (1988). The validity of informal reading comprehension measures. *Remedial and Special Education, 9*(2), 20-29.

Gough, P. B., & Tunmer, W. E. (1986). Decoding, reading, and reading disability. *Remedial and Special Education, 7*(1), 6-10.

Goodman, K., & Burke, C. L. (1972). *Reading miscue inventory.* New York: MacMillan.

Hasbrouck, J., & Tindal, G. (1992). Curriculum-based oral reading fluency norms for students in grades 2 through 5. *Teaching Exceptional Children, 24*, 41-44.

Hintze, J., Shapiro, E., & Conte, K. L. (1997). Oral reading fluency and authentic reading material: Criterion validity of the technical features of CBM survey-level assessment. *The School Psychology Review, 26*, 535-53.

Jenkins, J. R., & Jewell, M. (1993). Examining the validity of two measures for formative teaching: Reading aloud and maze. *Exceptional Children, 59*, 421-432.

Johns, J. L. (1997). *Basic reading inventory* (7th Ed.). Dubuque, IA: Kendall/Hunt.

Kame'enui, E., & Simmons, D. (2001). Introduction to this special issue: The DNA of reading fluency. *Scientific Studies of Reading, 5*, 203-210.

Kuhn, M. R., & Stahl, S. (2002). *Fluency: A review of developmental and remedial practices* (No. 2-008). Ann Arbor, MI: Center for the Improvement of Early Reading Achievement. Retrieved September 25, 2002, from http://www.ciera.org/library/reports/inquiry-2/2-008/2-008.html

LaBerge, D., & Samuels, S. J. (1974). Toward a theory of automatic information processing in reading. *Cognitive Psychology, 6*, 293-323.

Leu, D. (1982). Oral reading error analysis: A critical review of research and application. *Reading Research Quarterly, 17*, 420- 437.

Li, L. (2002). The role of phonology in reading Chinese single characters and two-character words with high, medium, and low phonological regularities by Chinese grade 2 and grade 5 students. *Reading Research Quarterly, 37*, 372-374.

Li, D., & Nes, S. (2001). Using paired reading to help ESL students become fluent and accurate readers. *Reading Improvement, 38*, 50-62.

Lipson, M., & Lang, L. (1991). Not as easy as it seems: Some unresolved questions about fluency. *Theory into Practice, 30*, 218-227.

Moskal, M. (2002). *The effect of repeated reading on oral reading fluency when implemented by novice peer partners through collaborative student self-managed learning.* Unpublished doctoral dissertation, National-Louis University, Evanston, IL.

Parker, R., Hasbrouck, J. E., & Tindal, G. (1992). Greater validity for oral reading fluency: Can miscues help? *Journal of Special Education, 25*, 492-503.

Pinnell, G. S., Pikulski, J. J., Wixson, K. K., Campbell, J. R., Gough, P. B., & Beatty, A.S. (1995). *National Assessment of Education Progress: Listening to Children Read Aloud, 15* (Report No. 23-FR-04). Washington, DC: U.S. Department of Education, National Center for Education Statistics.

Ramirez, C. M. (2001). *An investigation of English language and reading skills on reading comprehension for Spanish-speaking English language learners.* Unpublished doctoral dissertation, University of Oregon, Portland.

Rasinski, T. V. (1990). Investigating measures of reading fluency. *Educational Research Quarterly, 14*(3), 37-44.

Rasinski, T. V. (2000). Speed does matter in reading. *The Reading Teacher, 54*, 146-151.

Rasinski, T.V. (2003). *The fluent reader: Oral reading strategies for building word recognition, fluency, and comprehension.* New York: Scholastic Professional Books.

Rasinski, T.V., Blachowicz, C., & Lems, K. (Eds.). (in press). *Fluency instruction: Research based best practices.* New York: Guilford Press.

Samuels, S.J. (1979). The method of repeated readings. *The Reading Teacher, 32*, 403-408.

Samuels, S. J. (2002). Reading fluency: Its development and assessment. In A. E. Farstrup & S. J. Samuels (Eds.), *What research has to say about reading instruction* (pp. 166-183). Newark, DE: International Reading Association.

Shinn, M.R., Knutson, N., Good, R.H., Tilly, W. D. & Collins, V. (1992). Curriculum-based measurement of oral reading fluency: A confirmatory analysis of its relation to reading. *School Psychology Review, 21*, 459-479.

Stanovich, K. (1980). Toward an interactive-compensatory model of individual differences in the development of reading fluency. *Reading Research Quarterly, 1*, 33-71.

Stanovich, K. E. (1986). Matthew effects in reading: Some consequences of individual differences in the acquisition of literacy. *Reading Research Quarterly, 21*, 360-407.

Stanovich, K., & Beck, I. (2000). *Progress in understanding reading: Scientific foundations and new frontiers.* New York: Guilford.

Sticht, T. G., & James, J. H. (1984). Listening and reading. In P. D. Pearson, R. Barr, M. L. Kamil, & P. Mosenthal (Eds.), *Handbook of reading research* (pp. 293-317). Mahwah, NJ: Erlbaum.

Taguchi, E., & Gorsuch, G. J. (2002). Transfer effects of repeated EFL reading on reading new passages: A preliminary investigation. *Reading in a Foreign Language, 14*(1). Retrieved January 1, 2005, from http://nflrc.hawaii.edu/rfl/April2002/

Taguchi, E., Takayasu-Maass, M., & Gorsuch, G.J. (2004). Developing reading fluency in EFL: How assisted repeated reading and extensive reading affect fluency development. *Reading in a Foreign Language, 16*(2). Retrieved January 1, 2005 from: http://nflrc.hawaii.edu/rfl/October2004/taguchi/taguchi.html

Wolf, M., & Katzir-Cohen, T. (2001). Reading fluency and its intervention. *Scientific Studies of Reading, 5*, 211-238.

Zutell, J., & Rasinski, T. V. (1991). Training teachers to attend to their students' oral reading fluency. *Theory into Practice, 30*, 211-217.

Exploring Computerized Text Analysis
to Study Literacy Policy and Practice

Leslie Patterson
University of North Texas

Kevin Dooley
Arizona State University

Shelia Baldwin
Monmouth University

Glenda Eoyang
Royce Holladay
Human Systems Dynamics Institute

Ruth Silva
University of North Texas

Joan Parker Webster
University of Alaska-Fairbanks

"The analysis of thought is always allegorical in relation to the discourse it employs... we must grasp the statement in the exact specificity of its occurrence; determine its conditions of existence, fix at least its limits; establish its correlations with other statements that may be connected with it, and show what other forms of statement it excludes" (Foucault, 1972, p. 27-28).

Foucault lays a grand challenge to any researcher studying human systems. Human systems are complex webs of connectedness (Buchanan, 2002), and these connections must somehow become opaque to us. In literacy studies, like other social sciences, we see two distinct epistemological approaches to uncovering these complexities. Quantitative studies attempt to capture the complexity of the observed system through mathematical sophistication. For example, survey-based research is used to statistically correlate literacy program design parameters with program outcomes through operationalizing the constructs on a numerical scale (Duke & Mallette, 2004). Conversely, qualitative studies attempt to comprehend the same event by depending on a human interpretation of these observed complexities. For example, a critical approach to literacy studies attempts to understand how language is used to maintain existing power structures per the interpretive lens of an individual researcher (Fairclough, 1992, 2003).

In literacy studies these webs of complexity manifest themselves as connections between and among written and spoken texts, individual and collective actions, and socio-cultural structures (for example, see Carspecken, 1996; Fairclough, 2003; Gee, 1999). Texts and social systems are mutually constitutive (Giddens, 1984), and within the system of learners, teachers, content providers, and family, "social organization is an emergent property of a (complexly) structured system of communicating individuals" (Corman, Kuhn, McPhee, & Dooley, 2002, p.159). The dynamics of literacy development can also be considered an emergent property of a social system or network (individual or group), which results from the complex adaptive processes (Davis, Sumara, & Luce-Kapler, 2000; Eoyang, 1997; Olson & Eoyang, 2001; Patterson, Cotton, Kimbell-Lopez, Pavonetti, & VanHorn, 1998) linking language, thought, and action (Davis, et al., 2000). Individual learning, shared learning among friends or colleagues, and evolving public opinion about policy issues represent emergent meanings at each of three levels, or scales.

The challenge for literacy researchers is to capture the dynamism, the multiplicity, and the contingency of these emergent realities. No wonder literacy researchers have had difficulty designing causal comparative studies that yield compelling findings with results that can generalize beyond the context under study. Even the most finely grained ethnographic case studies have not fully satisfied the need to understand the whole or the relationships among the parts. Literacy researchers have traditionally been creative and experimental in their epistemology (Duke & Mallette, 2001), and the field needs to continue to explore alternative research approaches in order to make sense of these complex networks. The purpose of this study is to examine the use of computerized text analysis within the analysis of policy documents, particularly as a bridge between quantitative and qualitative methods. Like a quantitative method, computerized text analysis is highly reliable, provides a means to quantitatively test the strength of hypothesized relationships, and discover patterns numerically. Like a qualitative method, computerized text analysis maintains the explicit connection to the text itself and still enables post-hoc latent and/or interpretive analysis. In order to explore the usefulness of computerized text analysis within the context of a literacy study, we investigate the emergent networks of meaning around the concept of "highly qualified teacher" as revealed in public messages by various stakeholders in the U.S. No Child Left Behind (NCLB) legislation.

CHALLENGES FACING LITERACY RESEARCHERS

Considerable challenges face literacy researchers who study the discourse that mediates literacy policy and practice. Sampling the overwhelming amount of data in these networks is the first challenge. Consider researching the concept "highly qualified teacher" introduced in the 2001 No Child Left Behind (NCLB) legislation. In order to use a discursive approach to understand the policies, the opinions and positioning of their proponents and detractors, and the translation and implementation of the concept within teacher preparation programs, a huge volume of texts needs to be examined--government documents, white papers, media articles, web sites, curriculum documents, conversations, e-mails, syllabi, rubrics, student work, test scores, portfolios, faculty meeting minutes, interviews, observations, and so on. The traditional approach of using human coders to synthesize the content of these texts becomes prohibitive as the volume of potentially relevant data increases. When faced with this challenge, researchers make decisions about sampling--focusing on one dimension of the discourse, a few salient topics, or small numbers of participants--a necessary practicality, but clearly a limiting factor.

Another distinct challenge for researchers is the interdependence among the participants--their massively entangled perceptions, understandings, dispositions, and behaviors. Linear causal relationships are rare. Nonlinear, reciprocal, and layered relationships comprise human social systems, and our current methodologies lack the complexity to help researchers unbraid these interdependencies. Another challenge for researchers is the dynamism of these systems. Current research methodologies allow us to see snapshots of parts of the system, but capturing movement in the system over time is more difficult.

A final challenge is that much of the analysis of qualitative data is not only laborious but also prone to reliability and validity problems (Krippendorf, 2004). Within a constructivist paradigm, such issues are moot, while within a positivist paradigm these issues can be fatal flaws. We take a moderated post-positivist stance that acknowledges both the constructed nature of reality and the pragmatic value of using data to understand social systems. Within such a framework, we must strive to use methods that better capture the complexity of the social system while addressing the challenges that we have laid out.

In this article we use two approaches to text/discourse analysis to examine the emergent properties of meaning-making related to the concept of "highly qualified teacher" as used in public messages related to No Child Left Behind legislation. Our research team is a cross-disciplinary group of researchers whose common interest is in how discourse mediates public opinion, policy development, and practice. Three of us are literacy teacher educators; one is a teacher educator focusing on cultural studies; two are practitioner/researchers from the field of organizational management; and one works in the field of management. One of us (Dooley) collaborated on the development of Centering Resonance Analysis (CRA), the computerized text analysis method used in this study. Space constraints in this article limit a full discussion of the findings of our analyses, so we focus here primarily on methodological decisions and implications. A future article will explain and discuss the findings in more detail.

COMPUTERIZED TEXT ANALYSIS AND CRA

There are two basic forms of content analysis. Manifest analysis examines only the words that actually occur in a text (surface structure); whereas latent analysis uses a human judge to interpret the deeper meaning of the textual content. Traditional human coding of texts is an example of latent content analysis. Because manifest content analysis can be made operational through explicit rules, it is open to be computerized. Through enabling computations to be done with the computer, one obtains "perfect" reliability (the same computer program will return the same results on the same input, always) and the amount of time it takes to study a text corpus, compared to latent human coding, is significantly reduced. However, a manifest analysis may potentially have low validity because assumptions behind interpretive rules end up being invalid, or at least incomplete. We shall address possible mitigations to this risk later in the paper.

All approaches to computerized text analysis involve common steps: (a) putting the text into electronic form, (b) removing words that contain little content (e.g. "the", "and", "of"), and (c) measuring the importance of words found in the corpus. The most common approach to step (c) is to equate the importance of a word with its frequency. More sophisticated techniques like Latent Semantic Indexing (Landauer, Foltz, & Laham, 1998) also take into account the co-occurrence of words within textual boundaries. Simple approaches based on word frequency suffer from a shallow description of the text, as they equate the text with a "pile of words." Conversely, most methods that use more sophisticated inferencing have to be "trained"; basically, the domain expertise of the researcher needs to be extracted and incorporated into the manifest rules of interpretation in order to "make sense" of the textual content.

Centering Resonance Analysis, or CRA (Corman et al., 2002) is a computerized text analysis method that uses natural language processing and computational linguistics to represent a text as a network (Danowksi, 1993; Carley, 1997), where words are nodes in the network and connections between nodes represent purposeful discursive connections by the author. Based on centering theory (Walker, Joshi, & Prince, 1998), CRA has been demonstrated to accurately model the concept map that an average reader creates when interpreting a text (Corman et al., 2002) and has been used in a variety of different research contexts (Dooley & Corman, 2002; McPhee, Corman, & Dooley, 2002; Dooley, Corman, McPhee, & Kuhn, 2003).

The underlying assumption of any network text model is that the discourse emerging from human systems can be conceptualized as networks of

Table 1 Centering Resonance Analysis results—the most influential words and word pairs, in descending order. Influence values range from 0 to 1.00.

WORDS		PAIRS	
teacher	0.36243	teacher-state	0.576
state	0.12230	teacher-school	0.557
school	0.09603	teacher-certification	0.416
education	0.07786	teacher-new	0.361
certification	0.05220	teacher-percent	0.321
student	0.04196	teacher-qualified	0.256
program	0.04175	teacher-quality	0.243
new	0.03980	teacher-program	0.227
percent	0.03544	teacher-education	0.169
available	0.03083	school-education	0.150
quality	0.02918	teacher-good	0.148
system	0.02916	teacher-student	0.122
teaching	0.02835	state-certification	0.102
good	0.02725	teacher-classroom	0.098
test	0.02708	teacher-academic	0.088
classroom	0.02244	teacher-system	0.085
report	0.02192	teacher-high	0.069
great	0.02185	teacher-subject	0.068
candidate	0.01884	teacher-preparation	0.060
research	0.01781	state-school	0.059
academic	0.01737	teacher-standard	0.048
high	0.01728	certification-system	0.040
qualified	0.01685	teacher-profession	0.038
study	0.01596	teacher-report	0.032
year	0.01590	teacher-teaching	0.031
science	0.01516	teacher-year	0.029
standard	0.01466	teacher-content	0.028
district	0.01463	teacher-alternate	0.028
subject	0.01449	teacher-public	0.027
title	0.01430	teacher-knowledge	0.026
brewer	0.01427	teacher-waiver	0.022

linked concepts. This idea mirrors the more latent approach of concept mapping (Miles & Huberman, 1994). Influential words are identified as such via their structural position within the network; in CRA, word importance is termed *influence* and is measured as the centrality-betweeness of the word within the corresponding CRA Network. Influential words have a special type of connectedness in the discursive network, one which contributes to the coherence of the text; influential words are the text's "center of gravity," and they act as boundary-spanners between otherwise disconnected concepts. CRA is potentially useful for studying how policy discussions are discursively framed because it provides a systematic and reliable way to identify words that are "influential," even though they may not be frequent. If we conceptualize the literacy system as a set of embedded and intersecting networks of people involving practitioners, theorists, politicians, and the public, then a network text analysis approach like CRA enables us to study the corresponding discursive networks of that human system. In the case of the NCLB highly influential teacher issue, these discursive networks are studied to find how language influences conceptual frameworks in policy and in practice.

Table 1 and Figure 1 display the results of the analysis of Rod Paige's Second Annual Report on Teacher Quality (2002). The analysis of the digital text yields a list of the highly influential words and word-pairs and a visualization of the CRA Network showing the links among these influential words. Table 1 displays the words and word-pairs with the highest influence values. Influence values range from zero to one, although in a typical-sized text, influence values above 0.10 are very large, between 0.05 and 0.10 large, and above 0.01, significant. The data are not statistical in that they represent the whole text, not a sample, and thus differences between word influence values have to be viewed in terms of "practical" significance.

Figure 1 is the map displaying the links between and among these words. The most influential words are near the top of the map; the less influential terms are mapped below. For example, in the CRA Network depicted in Figure 1, "teacher" and "state" are the most influential words in Paige's report. "School," "education," and "certification" are the second most influential concepts. Other influential concepts include "system," "student," "great," "program," "quality," "new," "report," "percent," "study," "available," "teaching," "good," "test," "research," "academic," "classroom," "high," "candidate," "science," "qualified," and "year." Obviously, this is a small percentage of all the words in that 66-page report, but they are the words that most often directly linked to other words. Assuming that meaning emerges from coherence or connectedness within a text, these are the concepts that convey the "meaning" in this report.

Researchers must also examine not only what is present in the list of influential words, but also what is absent. For example, this analysis suggests that, in Paige's definition of teacher quality, bureaucratic structures frame the definition of "highly qualified teacher." We find no mention of terms that focus on responsive decision-making or student-teacher relationships, words such as: "cultural responsiveness," "reflection," "individual differences," "professionalism," "professional development," "university," "in-service," "teacher union," and "teacher development." This text seems to focus on government as the sole arbiter of teacher quality; we find no mention of practitioners' or students' perspectives on teacher quality.

One common criticism of manifest analysis is that it can lack validity. In order to overcome this weakness, we suggest that latent and interpretive lenses should be applied, but *in conjunction with* the textual content being described by a manifest method such as CRA. In other words, we wish to use a manifest, computerized approach to understand patterns and complexities that would be beyond the capability of any research team to uncover with reliability, in part because of the large volume of text, and then apply latent analysis to make sense of those patterns. We explain an experiment to examine this sense-making in the next section.

Figure 1 Centering Resonance Analysis map of the Second Annual Report on Teacher Quality (Paige, 2003).

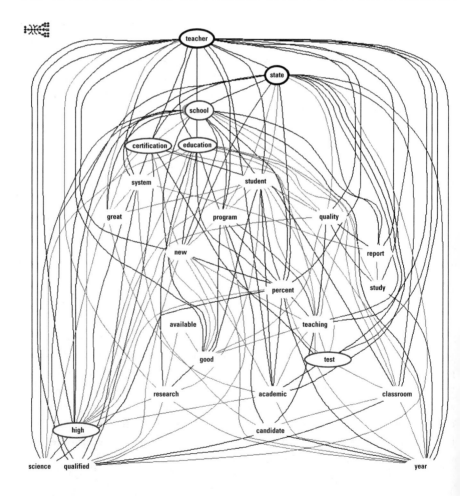

METHOD

In this investigation of the networks of meaning emerging around the term *highly qualified teacher*, Parker, Webster and Silva began by examining the actual definition as delineated in No Child Left Behind, using Fairclough's approach to critical discourse analysis (1992, 2003) as a frame. An important distinction in this analysis is the difference between the actual "construction" of the concept "highly qualified teacher" and its various "construals" by different stakeholders (Parker, Webster and Silva, 2004). How will the concept be represented, interpreted, and implemented at federal, state, and local contexts? Fairclough's (1992) analytical framework is both a method and a theory for studying *communicative* versus *strategic* use of language (Habermas, 1987) in discourse, as well as a means for gaining insight into the texts' relations to power and ideology (Foucault, 1977). By bringing together the linguistic (descriptive) features of the texts and making explicit the underlying social theoretical issues, Fairclough enables us to trace the "explanatory connections between ways … in which texts are put together and interpreted, how texts are produced, distributed and consumed" (1992, p.72).

For example, NCLB outlines a list of minimum requirements related to content knowledge and teaching skills that a *highly qualified teacher* should meet (all teachers, new and experienced): In general, under NCLB a highly qualified teacher must have: (a) A bachelor's degree, (b) Full certification and licensure as defined by the state, and (c) Demonstrated competency, as defined by the state, in each core academic subject he/she teaches. This is the official "construction"--the text that defines highly qualified teacher for state and local policy-makers and practitioners. Critical discourse analysis leads us to ask a number of questions about how that official definition will be construed by various stakeholders. For example, (a) When NCLB defines "highly qualified teacher," does this therefore imply a preempting of critique or the elimination of alternative definitions?; (b) How does one reconcile this absolute definition with the flexibility implied by the use of the phrase "defined by the state"?; (c) The requirements are prefaced with the phrase "In general." What are the exceptions; or what is the meaning of "in general" in this particular usage?; (d) What are the standards for "demonstrated competency"?; (e) Does "highly qualified" correlate with student achievement, learning or performance?; (f) Will there be some teachers who are more highly qualified than others because of diverse routes to certification?; (g) Will we get a tiered system of highly qualified teachers?; (h) How will state/district authorities explain this system to parents?; (i) What stakeholders will participate in the discussion about this concept, its official construction, and its public construal? Teachers? Parents? Students?; (j) Does this definition implicitly align with behavioristic orientations towards issues of mastery that view teachers primarily as executors of laws and principles of effective teaching as decided elsewhere, thus making teachers passive recipients of professional knowledge (Kleibard, 1973; Zeichner, 1983)?; and (k) Is a wide range of construals possible, and how will they affect implementation? Fairclough suggests that an initial step in critical discourse analysis is to analyze the language of the texts under investigation. Thus, to better understand the ways in which notions of "highly qualified teachers" were construed, we utilized CRA in combination with two different approaches--grounded theory and statistical modeling--to analyze 37 messages about "highly qualified teachers" from a range of stakeholders who were writing for various audiences. This initial analysis by Parker, Webster and Silva provided a critical frame for our subsequent inquiry (2004).

To identify the texts for analysis, the researchers searched the World Wide Web Internet in early March 2004. The terms used in the search were "nclb," "highly qualified," and "teachers." The MSN search engine, the ERIC and Electronic Collections Online (ECO) indexes were searched for online texts dated January 2001 through March 2004. The sources of the texts included private foundations, business-education coalitions, teacher unions, administrator associations, government agencies (including the Department of Education), and teacher educator associations, individual politicians, and professional journals. Two texts were eliminated because they did not focus primarily on the "highly qualified teacher" concept, leaving 37 texts for analysis.

Each of these texts were then analyzed using Crawdad Text Analysis System 1.1 software, which is based on CRA, and results were visualized and summarized, generating a variety of statistics and graphics. The data analysis process included the use of two distinct approaches performed in parallel, each of which took a different methodological approach: (a) Grounded theory, and (b) Exploratory statistical modeling.

The findings reported here resulted from the investigation of the use of CRA to document the network of meanings emerging from this discourse about the implementation of NCLB policies related to "highly qualified teachers." We adopted an experimental design for our research. First, three researchers with domain (literacy education) knowledge used CRA in a grounded-theory approach (Glaser & Strauss, 1967) where CRA results are used to focus a latent interpretation of the text. Second, a researcher not familiar with the research literature related to quality teaching or teacher development performed statistical modeling of the CRA results in order to determine what type of insight could be gained from an almost purely empirical perspective. Both analyses were done "blind" to one another in order to ensure a valid comparison. Finally, the entire research team responded to the findings and came to a consensus around the conclusions presented below.

Our focus in this chapter is on using the results to explore the methodological implications of our experiment. Therefore, a thorough presentation and discussion of the findings of this analysis is beyond the scope of this article. Findings are presented in summary form here to allow for more discussion of methodological issues but will be reported in greater detail elsewhere. We encourage readers to contact authors if more information on the findings is needed.

FINDINGS

Approach 1: Grounded Theory

First, each of the three researchers using this approach independently did what we called a "visual scan" of the maps of influential terms (like that in Figure 1) to identify patterns or themes. Periodic debriefings allowed the researchers to compare their observations, insights, and questions relevant to the guiding research questions. Because CRA was new to the researchers, these debriefing conversations were exploratory and generated more questions than answers and as many insights about the methodology and its implications as about the concept of "highly qualified teacher." New questions, inferences, and comments about the methodology were all recorded in a series of research memos written over the course of three months.

This visual scan of the maps yielded a list of similarities across these documents, a list of concepts or terms that were conspicuously absent, and a list of questions about each author's perspective, purpose, and audience. The initial analysis (displayed in the maps) identified the most highly connected, or influential, terms across all the texts: teacher, education, school, student, and state.

This list of terms is short, considering that these were identified as the most highly connected terms across 37 messages and hundreds of pages of text. That suggests that the discourse about "highly qualified teacher" does not represent a wide range of perspectives, although a survey of these authors' works (for example, Rod Paige, Linda Darling-Hammond, and Ted Kennedy) would suggest a range of stances and potential messages. Surprisingly, all these authors were using similar terms to talk about this concept. In other words, the networks of meaning emerging from this discourse were remarkably similar.

The analysis also yielded a longer list of terms that were identified as a second level of influence, according to the influence value within each text: certification, school, program, state, LEA (local education agency), education, university, study, policy, research, data, accountability, standard, department, state NCLB, teaching, student, child, and teacher.

Again, this yields a surprisingly short list (considering that the 37 texts comprise hundreds of pages), suggesting a great degree of similarity across these texts. These terms clearly prioritize bureaucratic frames for teacher quality--institutions, certification, accountability are referenced, rather than issues of teacher effectiveness or responsiveness to students. Four terms (teaching, student, child, and teacher) reference the teaching/learning act, but we see no reference to characteristics of effective or influential teaching--what teachers need to know or do. The focus is clearly on "qualification" of teachers, rather than on "quality" teaching.

This analysis generated five questions that could only be answered by returning to the original texts. Our next step was to read the entire original texts, focusing on those questions. Each text was read by two researchers, each of whom answered the following questions independently. We subsequently compared our answers, came to a consensus in response to each question, and developed a matrix to facilitate our comparison of these issues across the messages. Following are summaries of our conclusions in response to each question.

What concepts are NOT here that we might have expected to appear in discussions of "highly qualified teacher"? Terms having to do with "quality," "accountability," and "standards" are missing. Are they assumed? Inferred? Words that refer to students (individual differences, cultural diversity, responsiveness to student needs) are missing. Words that refer to teacher decision-making or the complexity of the teaching/learning act are also missing.

How does each author define "highly qualified teacher?" These maps of influential words, as well as the original texts themselves, indicate that these stakeholders begin with the official definition of "highly qualified teacher;" they do not address the complexity of high quality teaching. We suggest two possible interpretations of what we see as an over-simplification of the conceptual landscape.

First, perhaps these stakeholders are naïve about implementing policy in schools. Perhaps these writers set out expectations, and they trust states and districts to improve the status quo through mechanisms available to them. Maybe these writers are using these constructs to set broad boundaries or parameters within which local decision-makers can do what is "best" for teachers and learners; however, "best" is not defined.

A second interpretation is that these stakeholders have specific (and perhaps competing) agendas–their use of language seems to frame their messages in the broadest and least controversial terms appropriate to their target audiences. One example is that these texts seem to define "highly qualified" in bureaucratic terms (about certification requirements) rather than in more complex terms integral to the teaching/learning process.

Whom does the author hold responsible or accountable for decisions about highly qualified teachers? In focusing on government as the sole arbiter of teacher quality, the influential terms in these texts address three levels of government decision-making and implementation: federal, state, and school. Perhaps the assumption is that the federal policies in NCLB lay out the general blueprint, with individual states and local schools making the more specific policy decisions. For the most part, these documents seem to ignore school district-level decision-making structures. They talk about national/federal issues and "school" issues. Maybe these stakeholders collapse local layers of decision-making into "school" without distinguishing between district and campus levels.

Is the discussion referring to new or experienced teachers? These stakeholders focus primarily on the preparation and certification of new teachers. Only one of the texts focuses on experienced teachers' effectiveness and ongoing professional development.

Does the discourse include teachers' perspectives? In general, there is no acknowledgement that teachers might have an alternative perspective; neither is there any indication that teachers are or should be a part of the conversation about teacher quality. Two messages address campus-level decisions that should include teachers' input and participation in ongoing professional development. Those happen to be the most recent 2004 documents, so we can speculate about whether this suggests a shift in the discourse.

Does the use of these influential terms change over time? As mentioned before, this data set covers a fairly brief time span (2002-2004), but these data suggest that there may be more recent trends to define "highly qualified teaching" as related to student achievement and to include the need for teacher input into local decisions. This warrants further study.

Briefly, the findings of the analysis using the grounded theory approach suggested that:

(1) These stakeholders generally did not challenge the definition of "highly qualified teacher" set forth in NCLB.

(2) These texts focused on bureaucratic structures and policy issues, rather than research-based pedagogy or student-centered decisions.

(3) A few of the texts critiqued federal decisions, but the majority explained and recommended ways to comply with the federal mandates. All accepted the basic NCLB definition of "highly qualified teacher" as a starting point.

(4) Teachers' perspectives and any discussion of teacher autonomy or teacher professionalism were conspicuously absent.

Approach 2: Exploratory Statistical Modeling

This analysis focused on a methodological question: How much insight can be gained through application of statistical modeling techniques, independent of any background knowledge about these policy discussions? Approach 2 included these approaches: (a) Estimate tone (presence of positive versus negative words), intensity (presence of emotive words), and focus (high focus equates to few concepts being discussed in an integrative way of each text) (Dooley & Corman, 2004); (b) Develop an ontology (typology) of themes based on the most influential words and analyze theme influence values across the texts (Dooley & Corman, 2002), using ANOVA and correlation analysis, and (c) Use ANOVA to determine the relationship between thematic content and the political perspective of the source: neoconservative, neoliberal, managerial, progressive, or government (Apple, 2001). Here, we report on the analysis from the second approach listed.

This empirical analysis suggested a number of themes, or collections of influential words, that conveyed a common higher-level construct. The epistemological concept of a *theme* is similar to the concept of *latent constructs* that would be coded in latent content analysis, except they result from a manifest outcome of the statistical analysis, rather than a latent outcome of human interpretation. An example is the theme "assessment," which contains the words "standard," "data," "assessment," "test," testing, "exam," "score," and "evidence." Other themes identified with example words, include: (a) Cost: budget, money, fund, grant, cost; (b) Government: Paige, state, national; (c) Legal: law, policy, title, legislation; (d) Outcome: accountability, result, performance; (e) Partners: partnership, community; (f) Preparation: university, academic, preparation; (g) Program: NCLB, initiative, implementation; (h) Qualification: certification, qualified, experience; (i) Research: study, research, analysis; (j) School: school, principal, building, site; (k) Student: student, child, parent; (l) Subject: content, math, reading, English; (m) Teacher: teacher, classroom, union, faculty

Further analysis of the correlations between the themes themselves suggested there were two meta-themes: (a) The Policy: Cost, government, student, school, outcome, legal; and (b) The Teacher: Teacher, subject, research, qualification. These meta-themes were strongly negatively correlated--in texts where Policy themes were dominant, Teacher themes were not present, and visa versa, suggesting that policy and implementation were de-coupled within the public discourse. Interestingly, although this methodological approach was clearly different from the grounded theory approach, the findings were similar.

CONCLUSIONS

Public discussion of the official definition of *highly qualified teacher* has produced reactions from policy foundations, teacher education journals, professional organizations, parent bodies, and other interested groups. So, intended or not, the official construction has resulted in a variety of public construals which represent a range of perspectives on what it means to be a *highly qualified teacher* under NCLB, all represented in these texts. In our analysis, those construals, however, were surprisingly similar to the official construction. These texts revealed no significant critique of that definition and no clearly distinct alternative. These texts accepted the highly bureaucratic definition and did not invite alternative perspectives. Particularly significant was the absence of teacher agency or teacher perspectives in these construals. These construals focused on highly-qualified teachers (in terms of certification and accountability) rather than on high-quality teaching (in terms of professionalism or student learning). A continuation of Fairclough's critical discourse analysis (which is beyond the scope of this report) would take this investigation further to document the actual discursive practices in the implementation of policies, regulations, and procedures related to *highly qualified teacher* across the country, as well as the larger socio-economic and political structures that shape and are shaped by those discursive practices (1992, 2003).

The specific purpose of this article was to explore the use of computerized text analysis within a larger critique of how the concept *highly qualified teacher* is currently being defined and used in policy documents. The researchers used two approaches to text analysis: (a) grounded theory using a specific form of network text analysis, Centering Resonance Analysis (CRA), as an initial step to focus the interpretive analysis; and (b) exploratory statistical modeling of the CRA results. In this analysis of 37 texts that discussed the concept of *highly qualified teacher* within the context of the U.S. No Child Left Behind legislation, we compared a typical interpretive approach, grounded theory (using computerized text analysis as an initial step), to a pure manifest approach using computerized text analysis alone.

Several advantages stem from the use of computerized text analysis. First, software enables a large volume of text to be manifestly analyzed in a short period of time. It took only several minutes to analyze the several hundred pages of text in this experiment. Second, as a manifest approach, no training or a priori ontology was needed, so the method could be applied across the multiple genres found in our sample. Third, by quantifying word importance and linking it to a latent ontology (e.g. "tone" and "intensity" word lists), one can reliably combine qualitative and quantitative perspectives.

As with any tool, computerized text analysis provides one perspective. It is not a panacea for literacy researchers. Manifest content analysis (computerized or not) focuses on the surface structure of the text--not who said or wrote it, to whom, or for what purpose. To answer those questions, we need to use other approaches, such as grounded theory and critical discourse analysis. Grounded theory can include computerized text analysis as one tool for identifying recurring patterns worthy of further analysis and interpretation. Computerized text analysis such as CRA can be particularly useful in pointing to patterns across multiple texts which might not emerge in other text analysis approaches, and in this way can enrich the development of grounded theory.

Critical discourse analysis, as a theoretical frame, is essential if our purpose is to understand how particular texts influence and are influenced by discursive practices and larger social systems. A critical/interpretive perspective helps us consider the dialectics of discourse (Fairclough, 2003) and the complex interdependence of these texts and the lifeworlds of individual participants. If our purpose is to document and interpret the shades of meaning across official constructions of policy discourse and the construals by various stakeholders, we may begin with manifest analysis of multiple texts (computer assisted or not), but we must then move to other data sources and a focus on larger contexts.

In conjunction with other approaches and other tools, computerized text analysis promises to help literacy researchers map the meanings emerging from "the delicate and intricate organization of (human) networks" (Buchanan, 2002, p. 15). By studying those networks of meaning constructions and construals, literacy researchers may, in fact, come close to capturing the emergent dynamism, multiplicity and contingency inherent in the literacy policies and practices that shape our professional lives.

REFERENCES

Apple, M. (2001). *Educating the "right way": Markets, standards, God, and inequality.* NY: Falmer Press.

Barabasi, A-L. (2002). *Linked: The new science of networks.* New York: Perseus Publishing.

Berry, V., Hoke, M., & Hirsch, E. (2004). The search for highly qualified teachers. *Phi Delta Kappan, 85*(9), 684-689.

Buchanan, M. (2002). *Nexus: Small worlds and the groundbreaking theory of networks.* NY: W. W. Norton & Company.

Butler, J. (1990). *Gender trouble: Feminism and the subversion of identity.* New York: Routledge.

Carley, K. (1997). Extracting team mental models through textual analysis. *Journal of Organizational Behavior 18,* 533-558.

Carspecken, P.F. (1996). *Critical ethnography in educational research: A theoretical and practical guide.* New York: Routledge.

Corman, S., Kuhn, T., McPhee, R., & Dooley, K. (2002). Studying complex discursive systems: Centering resonance analysis of organizational communication. *Human Communication Research, 28*(2), 157-206.

Davis, B., Sumara, D., & Luce-Kapler, R. (2000). *Engaging minds: Learning and teaching in a complex world.* Mahwah, NJ: L. Erlbaum Associates.

Danowski, J. (1993). Network analysis of message content. In W. D. Richards & G. A. (Ed.), Barnett *Progress in Communications Science* (Vol.12, pp. 197-221). Norwood, NJ: Ablex.

Darling-Hammond, L. (2001). National Commission on Teaching and America's Future. *The research and rhetoric on teacher certification: A response to 'Teacher Certification Reconsidered.'* New York: Retrieved October 15, 2004 from, http://www.nctaf.org.

Dooley, K., & Corman, S. (2002). The dynamics of electronic media coverage. In B. Greenberg (Ed.), *Communication and terrorism: Public and media responses to 9-11.* Cresskill, NJ: Hamptom Press.

Dooley, K., Corman, S., McPhee, R., & Kuhn, T. (2003). Modeling high-resolution broadband discourse in complex adaptive systems. *Nonlinear Dynamics, Psychology, & Life Sciences, 7*(1), 61-86.

Dooley, K., & Corman, S., (2004). The dynamics of political messages. *Patterns 2*(8). Retrieved May 10, 2005, from http://www.hsdinstitute.org.

Duke, N., & Mallette, M. H. (2004). *Literacy research methodologies.* New York: The Guilford Press.

Duke, N. K., & Mallette, M. H. (2001). Critical issues: Preparation for new literacy researchers in multi-epistemological, multi-methodological times. *Journal of Literacy Research, 22,* 345-360.

Edmondson, J. (2004). Reading policies: Ideologies and strategies for political engagement. *The Reading Teacher, 57*(5), 418-428.

Eoyang, G. (1997). *Coping with chaos: Seven simple tools.* Circle Pines, MN: Lagumo Corporation.

Eoyang, G. (2001). *Conditions for self-organizing in human systems.* Unpublished doctoral dissertation, The Union Institute and University.

Fairclough, N. (1992). *Discourse and social change.* Cambridge: Polity Press.

Fairclough, N. (2003). *Analyzing discourse: Textual analysis for social research.* New York: Routledge.

Foucault, M. (1972). *The archaeology of knowledge.* NY: Pantheon.

Gee, J. P. (1999). *An introduction to discourse analysis: Theory and method.* New York: Routledge

Gergen, K. (1999). *An invitation to social construction.* London: Sage.

Giddens, A. (1984). *The constitution of society: Outline of the theory of structuration.* Berkeley, CA: University of California Press.

Glaser, B., & Strauss, A. (1967). *The discovery of grounded theory: Strategies for qualitative research.* Chicago: Aldine.

Goldstein, J. (1994). *The unshackled organization.* New York: Productivity Press.

Habermas, J. (1987). *The theory of communicative action: Lifeworld and the system: A critique of functionalist reason.* (Vol.2, T. McCarty, Trans.) Boston: Beacon.

Kaplan, L. S., & Owings. W. A. (2002). The politics of teacher quality: Implications for principals. *National Association of Secondary School Principals. NASSP Bulletin, 8* (6633), 22.

Kleibard, H. (1973). The question of teacher education. In D. McCarty (Ed.), *New perspectives on teacher education.* San Francisco: Jossey Bass.

Krippendorff, K. (2004). *Content analysis: An introduction to its methodology.* Thousand Oaks, CA: Sage.

Landauer, T. K., Foltz, P. W., & Laham, D. (1998). Introduction to latent semantic analysis. *Discourse Processes, 25,* 259-284.

McPhee, R., Corman, S., & Dooley, K. (2002). Organization knowledge expression and management: Centering resonance analysis of organizational discourse. *Management Communication Quarterly, 16,* 130-136.

Miles, M., & Huberman, A. (1994). *Qualitative data analysis.* Thousand Oaks, CA: Sage.

Olson, E.E., & Eoyang, G. H. (2001). *Facilitating organization change: Lessons from complexity science.* San Francisco, CA: Jossey-Bass/Pfeiffer.

Paige, R. (2002). *The secretary's second annual report on teacher quality.* Washington: Department of Education.

Patterson, L., Cotten, C., Kimbell-Lopez, K., Pavonetti, L, & VanHorn, L. (1998). The shared "ah-ha" experience": Literature conversations and self-organizing complex adaptive systems. *Yearbook of the National Reading Conference, 47,* 143-156.

Poole, M., Van de Ven, A., Dooley, K., & Holmes, M. (2000). Organizational change and innovation processes: Theory and methods for research. Oxford: Oxford Press.

Silva, R. (2001). *Teacher-as-researcher: contested issues of voice and agency in the creation of legitimized knowledge in teaching.* Unpublished doctoral dissertation. University of Houston, Houston.

Silva, R., & Webster, J. Parker. (2004, September). From rhetoric to reality: Do teachers have a role in translating national policy directives into action? Paper presented at The Oxford Ethnography and Education Conference, Oxford University, Oxford, UK.

Stacey, R. (2001). *Complex responsive processes in organizations: Learning and knowledge creation.* London: Routledge.

Stewart, I., & Cohen, J. (1999). *Figments of reality.* New York: Cambridge University Press.

Walker, M. A., Joshi, A. K., & Prince, E. F. (Eds.). (1998). Centering theory in discourse. New York: Oxford.

Webster, J. Parker. (2000). *Raising voices of practice through communicative action: Critical teacher inquiry as praxis.* University of Houston, Doctoral Dissertation.

Webster, J. Parker, & Silva, R. (2004, December). Interpreting networks of meaning from a critical perspective: Who benefits from the official definitions of highly qualified teachers? Paper presented at the National Reading Conference, San Antonio, TX.

Wise, A. (2003). Testimony to the Subcommittee on 21st Century Competitiveness, Committee on Education and the Workforce, U.S. House of Representatives, May 20, 2003. Retrieved February 21, 2004, from http://www.ncate.org/newsbrfs/wise_comments_may03.pdf

Willis, P. (1976). The main reality. University of Birmingham. Occasional Paper.

Willis, P. (1977). *Learning to labour: How working class kids get working class jobs.* London: Gower.

Zeichner, K. M. (1983). Alternative paradigms in teacher education. *Journal of Teacher Education, 34*(3), 9.

Resistance and Appropriation: Literacy Practices as Agency within Hegemonic Contexts

Kristen H. Perry
Michigan State University

Victoria Purcell-Gates
University of British Columbia

Poststructuralist scholarship emphasizes the importance of issues of power and control in education as it simultaneously rejects totalizing, universalizing, and essentializing narratives (Ninnes & Burnett, 2003). Poststructuralism offers an important theoretical framework for researchers who view literacy as social practice by recognizing that language plays a key role in power relationships; language is both constitutive and expressive of relations of power, and individuals are subject to multiple discourses within those relationships (Bell & Russell, 2000; Bourdieu, 1991; Canagarajah, 1999; Giroux, 1989). In recognizing the multiple ways in which issues of power relate to language and literacy practice (Barton & Hamilton, 1998, 2000; Cope & Kalantzis, 2000; Gee, 1996, 2001; Street, 2001a, 2001b), literacy scholars have increasingly taken up aspects of poststructuralist thinking. In rejecting universalizing narratives, these frameworks challenge cultural, social, and structural determinism and offer conceptualizations of power and hegemony that allow room for individual and collective agency and resistance (Canagarajah, 1999; Kincheloe & McLaren, 2000). The purpose of this paper, therefore, is to offer empirical data that support and expand current poststructural scholarship in literacy practices by examining issues of agency within hegemonic relationships across diverse cultural contexts.

Power itself is an ambiguous construct; yet critical scholars agree that it is neither monolithic nor universal (Kincheloe & McLaren, 2000). Power is a network of multiple but unequal points or nodes, and it does not exist without simultaneous resistance; that is, power and resistance are co-constitutive (Foucault, 1980; Ninnes & Burnett, 2003). The construct of hegemony describes the systems of power relationships where dominating groups wield power over others. These hegemonic power structures can involve political, economic, cultural, religious, educational, and other similar systems (Clayton, 1998; Giroux, 1992; Martin, 1998). Like the power relationships that make up these systems, hegemony is never total and complete, but rather is porous, leaving room for agency and resistance (Kincheloe & McLaren, 2000). In this paper, we argue that different types of hegemonic systems create room for different types of agency and resistance.

Agency is a key aspect of poststructural conceptualizations of subjectivity. That is, individuals have a range of available subject positions, and this subjectivity is fluid, dynamic, and negotiable (Canagarajah, 1999). McLaren (1994) also argued that subjects are active agents, capable of exercising deliberate actions in and on the world. While Gramscian notions of hegemony suggest that agency is partially involved in ensuring the conditions for class domination —that is, agents blindly accept hegemonic ideologies and therefore reproduce them (Martin, 1998)—others challenge the notion that the subjugated are somehow mystified and unaware of the power structures that lead to their condition (Canagarajah, 1999; Clayton, 1998; Giroux, 1989, 1992). These scholars have argued that dominated actors are often aware of power relationships and are able to consciously make decisions about their actions within those relationships. These conscious actions may take a variety of shapes, including appropriation of some dominant discourses and practices, as well as many forms of resistance against those practices or discourses. As a phenomenon, resistance is complex, multilayered, and socially constructed, and it is deeply connected to power relationships (Foucault, 1980). Poststructural resistance theories take seriously the various contexts of power, and in doing so, they become more open-ended than reproduction theories, which scholars critique as overly deterministic (Canagarajah, 1999; Clayton, 1998; Giroux, 1989, 1992; Kincheloe & McLaren, 2000). With this paper, we offer empirical data to support and extend these theories. Our analysis of agentive literacy practices illustrates the importance of context in shaping hegemonic relationships and multiple agentive responses to those power relationships.

THE CULTURAL PRACTICES OF LITERACY STUDY

The data for our analysis come from a collection of case studies that fall under the aegis of the Cultural Practices of Literacy Study (CPLS). Researchers working under CPLS conducted ethnographic case studies of literacy practices in diverse communities (Purcell-Gates, in press). These studies examined the multiple ways in which members of cultural communities practiced literacy, as well as the ways in which formal schooling appeared to influence literacy practices in these communities. This analysis, then, is based on data gleaned from seven of the case studies.

The CPLS Cases

Scholars from Botswana studying in the U.S. Molosiwa (in press) studied the literacy practices of four women from Botswana studying for advanced degrees in the United States. Some of the women in this study grew up in rural villages and were the children of uneducated parents; others were the children of teachers and civil servants. All were colleagues from the University of Botswana, thus representing the "educated elite." Molosiwa's study highlighted the hegemony of English language literacy practices in Botswana.

Farmers in Puerto Rico. Situating her study within a family of farmers, Mazak (in press) described the relationships among language, literacy, and power in Puerto Rico. In Puerto Rico, language issues are closely tied to political issues, and Puerto Ricans align with political parties that are pro-independence, pro-statehood, or pro-commonwealth. The focal participants in this study, brothers, came from an educated family of farmers who were highly involved in community organization. Although this family obtained high levels of education in English, they do not consider themselves English speakers.

Urban middle school students in an alternative school for "problem kids." Gallagher (in press) studied literacy practices of four ninth graders in an alternative middle school classroom, designed for students who had been identified as highly at risk for failure or dropping out of school. As one student explained to Gallagher, "You have to be bad or dumb to get in here." Gallagher's study focused on the unofficial and unsanctioned literacy practices that occurred in the classroom.

Chinese-American immigrants. Zhang (in press), examined the literacy practices of two Chinese-American bilingual immigrant families who chose to send their children to a Chinese enrichment school. These families, both affiliated with the state university, speak Chinese dialects at home and also speak English. The children of these immigrants either were born in the U.S. or came to this country at a young age, and they speak fluent English. Zhang's study examined the ways in which Chinese children appropriated literacy practices from home, community, and school environments.

The "Lost Boys of Sudan" in the U.S. Perry (in press) examined the ways in which three orphaned Sudanese refugee youth used literacy. These youth had been orphaned by the 20-year civil war in the Sudan—a war that was the result of the northern, Arab-dominated government imposing the Islamic religion, Islamic law, and the Arabic language on Black African, Christian southerners. The refugees lived for a decade or more in the Kakuma Refugee Camp in Kenya, where they received an education in English. Perry's study highlighted the community nature of literacy for the Lost Boys, as well as the ways in which language and power played out through literacy acts.

Cuban refugees in a Midwestern city. Rosolová (in press) compared the literacy practices of two Cuban refugees, a man who was an English language learner and a woman who was highly proficient in English. Both participants in the case study received five years of university education in Cuba and are literate in Spanish. Rosolová's study concluded that immigrant experiences with regard to English literacy practices vary and appear to be influenced heavily by family literacy practices in their native countries. Her study also demonstrated that many literacy choices centered around maintaining a sense of Cuban identity.

A young African-American girl in an urban context. Collins (in press) described the literacy landscape of Penny, a young African-American middle school girl. Penny lived in a government-subsidized housing project in the urban center of a university town. Penny, the youngest of nine children, repeated the fourth grade and attended an after-school literacy tutoring program that was run by the local university. Collins' study focused on the ways in which Penny imported and exported various literacy practices between her home, community, and school contexts.

Although each of these studies represented a different sociocultural context and community, all used a framework suggested by Luke (2003) to illustrate the complexity of literacy practices within each group. Each CPLS researcher investigated how participants had access to different discourses and used languages, texts, discourses, and literacies in homes, communities and schools. In cases that involved multilingual contexts, researchers also examined the ways in which participants had access to different languages and used languages within literacy events, as well as the ways in which language shaped or constrained literacy practices. For full details of the methodology employed for these case studies, and fuller definitions of important constructs such as "sociocultural community," see Purcell-Gates (in press).

One goal of the CPLS study is to aggregate data on literacy practices across context-sensitive case studies. We began this process by compiling data from each of these studies (and others) within a metamatrix. This matrix included demographic information about each participant, types of texts read and/or written, the language of the text, and the sociotextual domain of the text. Our definition of sociotextual domain integrates the concept of social domain—that is, domain as a social activity that reflects social relationships, roles, purposes/aims/goals, and social expectations—with linguistic and textual genre purposes. Thus, it captures genre factors such as purpose and text which, as we thought about our data, seem to codefine, or coconstruct, the social domains at the moment of mediation by the reading and writing of the different texts. These domains are fluid, floating, and overlapping rather than mutually distinct. The domain categories used in our analysis emerged from our data and included: interpersonal communication, entertainment, community organization, information, parenting, politics, school, work, and religion. This metamatrix then provided the basis for our analysis of literacy practices across the individual cases.

We observed that most of the cases in the larger CPLS project involved obviously disproportionate power relationships in some form. Some of these cases involved colonial or post-colonial contexts, such as graduate students from Botswana (a postcolonial African nation) who were studying in the U.S. and farmers in Puerto Rico (a formal territory of the U.S). Other cases involved ethnic minorities who had migrated to the U.S. for various reasons, such as orphaned Sudanese refugee youth, Cubans fleeing the oppressive regime of Castro, and Chinese-American immigrants. Still other cases involved (often) minority children who were non-voluntarily participating in the institution of formal schooling, such as at-risk urban youth in an alternative middle school, a low-income African-American teenager, and Chinese-American immigrant children attending both U.S. schools and an after-school Chinese enrichment program. Some of the relationships in these cases, such as the cases involving students from Botswana, farmers in Puerto Rico, families from China, and refugees from Cuba and the Sudan, represented power on a global scale. Relationships involving children from various communities in American schools represented power on a much smaller classroom scale, although these classroom-level power relationships certainly reflected the larger power relationships in society.

METHODS

We identified all of those practices which seemed "agentive" to us, within their individual contexts in the pool of data. This process of identification relied upon several data sources (a) the metamatrix of textual practices, described above, (b) transcripts of informant interviews from each of the case studies, and (c) narrative descriptions provided by the researchers within their final reports. This was an interactive process during which we clarified our intuitive sense of what it means for a language practice to be agentive, or to reflect agency. Based upon this analysis, we identified two types of responses to hegemony that we defined as agency within these cases: resistance and appropriation. Next, we listed the types of agentive acts in the data along with their sociocultural and sociopolitical contexts, looking for patterns. This process resulted in a patterning of agency within hegemonic contexts that, we believe, complicates the notion of hegemony and, at the same time, begins to clarify it.

FINDINGS

The results of our data analysis suggest particular patternings of agency through types of resistance and appropriation of literacy practices across each of the case studies.

Resistance

Our concept of resistance implies some form of rejection of the hegemonic discourse or ideology. Other scholars have included the notion of revolution in their concept of resistance; for example, Freire and Macedo's (1998) work implies this sense of resistance-as-revolution, particularly as applied to resistance through literacy practices. The data from our case studies did not provide instances of this particular construction of resistance. Rather, we identified two types of resistance: overt resistance and covert resistance. Overt resistance occurs when actors clearly and openly reject a hegemonic structure or discourse (Clayton, 1998). These are overt acts of refusal of some type--refusal to speak or to read/write within the linguistic hegemony. Covert resistance, on the other hand, is a much more subtle form of resistance, much like the "everyday" forms of resistance described by Clayton (1998) and others. Covert resistance largely passes "under the radar" of those in power. It involves language and literacy practices that are hidden from those in power.

Appropriation

Appropriation describes those acts by dominated groups where actors adopt a hegemonic practice for the agent's own purposes, rather than those purposes designated by those in power. We define appropriation as agentive for two reasons: dominated groups use the hegemonic practice for their own purposes, rather than for the purposes intended by the powerful, and the dominated group transforms the hegemonic practice itself, so that it no longer exactly matches the original practice. These actions result in a breaching of the hegemony and push against the hegemony. Below, we provide examples of each of these three types of agency as we present the ways in which hegemonic contexts appear to shape agentive acts, below.

The Patterned Nature of Agency in Response to Hegemony

We looked both within and across the seven CPLS cases in order to examine the ways in which groups used language and literacy practices as forms of agency. Our analysis revealed interesting patterns about the use of literacy practices in response to hegemonic power, particularly in terms of patterns of overt and covert resistance.

Overt Resistance and Appropriations within Diffuse Hegemonies

Overt acts of resistance occurred in cases that shared certain characteristics. Two cases in this study exhibited large proportions of agentive acts classified as overt resistance—Chinese-American immigrants, and Cuban refugees. Three other cases also involved acts of overt resistance, including Puerto Rican farmers, Sudanese refugees, and scholars from Botswana. Two cases, alternative middle school students and the case of a young African-American girl, did not exhibit any instances of overt resistance at all.

Appropriations showed similar patterns across cases. By far, the highest percentage of agentive acts from our data fell into this category. All seven of the cases included in this analysis showed acts of appropriation by participants. The cases involving refugees from the Sudan and farmers from Puerto Rico exhibited the highest proportions of appropriation. In both of these cases, we coded approximately 70% of the agentive acts as involving appropriation. Below, we discuss examples of agentive acts from each of these cases.

Chinese-American immigrants. Chinese-American immigrants exhibited overt resistance by choosing to shop at Chinese-owned stores, as opposed to mainstream American shops, and by sending their children to Chinese enrichment programs. Although most of the participants in the study could read English, they sought out Chinese-language newspapers and read the Bible in Chinese. In addition, parents in this community enrolled their children in a Chinese enrichment program, which not only taught Chinese language and Chinese arts, but also provided math classes in English. Each of these practices implies an overt rejection of certain American practices in favor of an attempt to maintain a Chinese identity.

Cuban refugees. The Cuban case showed similar patterns in terms of ethnic, national, or linguistic identity maintenance. Rosolová (in press) described how Lara made conscious choices about language and literacy, choices that reflected her desire to maintain a strong Cuban identity. Lara purposefully sought out books in Spanish to read for pleasure, despite the fact that she was fluent in English; she also preferred to read the Bible in Spanish, only reading an English Bible when one was not available to her in Spanish. An example of Lara's overt resistance came in this statement, "I refuse to read in English because I spend most of my day speaking and reading in English…When you spend all day speaking in a language that is not yours, you want to go back home and say, 'I am at home'" (Rosolová, in press). In addition, Lara forbade her children to speak "Spanglish," where Spanish and English are woven together. She insisted that her children choose either Spanish or English during a conversation, but not mix the two. Each of these choices indicated a desire to maintain an identity as a Spanish-speaking Cuban.

The cases from Puerto Rico, the Sudan, and Botswana also provided examples of overt resistance. Like the cases discussed above, acts of overt resistance in these cases implied a rejection of aspects of hegemonic power. Each of these cases also involved fairly high proportions of appropriations from the hegemonic system, and these appropriations revealed important characteristics of the hegemonic context.

Puerto Rican farmers. In this case, overt resistance took the form of purposively refusing to speak English, except within the domains of work and politics. Mazak (in press) described the strong hegemony of English and the context for resistance within Puerto Rico where English is the official language, imposed by the colonial power of the U.S. Puerto Rican schools use English in the Spanish-speaking country as the medium of instruction. One participant, Chucho, said, "They [teachers] wanted you to think in English, but I didn't think in English!" Refusing to speak English, therefore, is a very clear method of resisting the hegemony of the U.S. and English.

Language also provided the context for many appropriations in Mazak's case. Many of the appropriative acts of agency in this case involved agents acting as "brokers" in the community. For example, the brothers acted as English brokers for other farmers in the area by translating important information on pesticide containers. They also used information from the agricultural extension service to organize a community cooperative that essentially eliminated the "middle man." For this family, the business of farming provided an important impetus for appropriating hegemonic practices. The practice of acting as language brokers allowed the brothers to help their neighbors bypass "the system;" the neighboring farmers used U.S.-provided information that they otherwise would have been unable to understand, and this information helped to empower them. Another important domain of appropriative acts in this community involved politics. The family used their knowledge of English to read about Puerto Rican and world politics, often on the Internet; these farmers thus appropriated dominant political discourses in such a way as to challenge the hegemony of the United States.

Sudanese refugees. These participants also overtly resisted hegemony through rejection of language. Unlike each of the cases already described, however, they did not resist against the hegemony of a Western, English-speaking nation; rather, they directed their resistance toward the government of the Sudan. The refugees rejected the Arabic language and the Islamic religion of those in power in the Sudan. "It's [Arabic] a bad thing. It steals our language away in our minds," said one participant, Chol (Perry, in press). The Sudanese refugees saw English as a language of liberation and empowerment, rather than as a hegemonic language. Chol indicated that "English is important to communicate with many people around the world ... so that you can communicate with other African people." Arabic and English therefore stood in stark contrast for these orphaned youth; Arabic stole away their native languages, but English provided them with a voice through which to speak to the world.

This case exhibited a very high proportion of acts of appropriation, likely due to participants' beliefs that English and literacy were empowering. In this community, participants actively used literacy skills to research and write articles or letters to the editor (or, less often, speeches) about their experiences as refugees and about the oppressive regime in the Sudan. Participants eagerly read news media and participated in various Internet discussion boards about the situation in the Sudan. Sudanese refugees not only appropriated hegemonic discourses in the U.S. context, but they also had done so in their previous lives in refugee camps in Africa. Participants had few opportunities to learn to read and write in Dinka or other languages native to the Sudan, as a result of Kenyan language policies for education. One participant, Ezra, however, worked to translate school textbooks into Dinka in an effort to help refugees become literate in their own language, and he also wrote a grant proposal to obtain funds to build a small library in the refugee camp. In this case, Ezra appropriated the hegemonic discourses of Western schooling in order to promote local language literacies.

Scholars from Botswana. Participants in this study indicated that the hegemonic context of English literacy often conflicted with the cultural traditions of the Botswanan people. "The young generation is able to cope with such modern literacy practices but for people who were born in the

1960s, it is not easy. We are used to being told things verbally and keep them in our memories," said one participant (Molosiwa, in press). Acts of overt resistance in Botswana reflected this tension between the oral tradition and the hegemony of printed English. For example, the participants from Botswana issued invitations orally, consciously spurning the written practice introduced by the British. This preference, according to informants, appeared to be an act of overt resistance against the former colonial power, which introduced literacy to the country.

The tension between oral and written practices in Botswana also provided the context for appropriations. Molosiwa indicated that people in Botswana provided printed programs at funerals, a literacy practice taken from the British, but they used the local Setswana language instead of English. This case involved a *former* colonial power, demonstrating the fluidity of hegemony and acts of agency within it. This instance of appropriation suggested that contexts of indirect hegemonic systems may have provided more opportunities for subjects to appropriate and transform literacy practices than systems where the hegemonic power structure was direct and apparent. In this case, the hegemonic system was relatively nonthreatening, perhaps allowing participants to appropriate language and literacy practices for nonresistant purposes.

Resistance. The cases involving relatively high levels of overt resistance shared many characteristics. All but one case (farmers in Puerto Rico) involved immigrants to the U.S., and in several cases, acts of overt resistance appeared to focus on maintaining a national identity, such as Cuban or Chinese. In several of these cases, the United States and its geopolitical positioning and power provided the hegemonic context against which the participants resisted. This context is hegemonic in several aspects, such as language (English), economic system (capitalism), and educational system. English is the official national language in the U.S., although many languages are spoken in this country— some, like Spanish, spoken by fairly large percentages of the population. Many states and school districts have enacted policies to ensure that English remains the medium of instruction, even in schools where the majority of students speak a language other than English.

The educational system of this country likewise is a hegemonic system; although public education is free, it is also compulsory, and students therefore have very little say in whether or not they attend. In addition, the mainstream (largely White) middle class for the most part controls education by funding public schooling through tax dollars and by supplying the majority of teachers and administrators. However, unlike the hegemonic systems from which many participants came, part of the structure of the U.S. system is about freedom of speech and expression—U.S. hegemony is powerful, but it seems to allow room for overt resistance.

Appropriation. The cases that exhibit high proportions of appropriative acts of agency, particularly the Sudanese refugees and the farmers in Puerto Rico, share common characteristics. In each case, participants live in multilingual and multicultural contexts. The practices of the Sudanese refugees and the Puerto Rican farmers appeared to be responses to hegemonic contexts--the radical Islamic government of Sudan and the colonial power of the U.S. A sense of strife existed in both cases. In the Sudan, this strife was played out through warfare, genocide, and enslavement, while in Puerto Rico, the strife appeared in a highly charged political situation between groups who advocate independence, statehood, or the maintenance of commonwealth status. In both of these cases, participants held a clear and open political agenda, and our data suggest that political purposes such as these may frequently drive the choice of appropriation as a response to hegemony. Many of the literacy practices observed in these cases likely would not have existed without the particular hegemonic power situation in each context. Driven by political objectives, the participants in these cases appropriated literacy practices for their own purposes--purposes which were largely against a group in power (although not necessarily the group in power where the participants actually lived, as in the case of the Sudanese in the U.S.). In these two cases, at least, appropriation appeared to be an alternate method of resistance. Appropriation still differed from formal resistance, however, in that participants did not reject the practice or discourse, but they instead transformed the practice into a new form of resistance.

Diffuse hegemonies. Based upon the similarities in these hegemonic contexts, we suggest that these patterns represent *diffuse hegemonic relationships*. In diffuse hegemonies, the power of the dominant group is not as great or as apparent over the dominated as it is in more direct hegemonies. Dominated groups appear to have more "wiggle room" in diffuse hegemonic relationships. Diffuse hegemonies make overt resistance more possible, and participants appropriate more often from the discourses of power. This suggests that dominated groups may feel more comfortable accepting dominant ideologies and practices in diffuse hegemonies than in more direct ones. In this study, the contexts of Botswana, Puerto Rico, and the U.S. contexts of Chinese-American immigrants and Cuban and Sudanese refugees represented diffuse hegemonies.

Covert Resistance within Direct Hegemonies

In our data, cases that showed high proportions of covert resistance in contrast to other types of agency were typically cases where the hegemonic relationship was direct and apparent. For example, the two cases involving middle school students exhibited the most instances of covert resistance. In these cases, the hegemonic context typically did not allow room for overt resistance, and participants were also far less likely to appropriate practices from these contexts.

Alternative middle school students. The students in this case clearly did not enjoy school, and a large majority of the agentive literacy practices in this classroom involved covert resistance, practices that school authorities did not sanction (Gallagher, in press). The covertly resistant practices included writing and passing personal notes during lessons, reading nonschool and other unsanctioned literature during class time, and failing to turn in academic assignments. In addition, one participant wrote poetry in which she incorporated codes so that others would not be able to understand her meaning.

An African American pre-teen. Penny's agentive literacy practices exhibited the same patterns as those of the middle-schoolers described by Gallagher. Like the other middle-schoolers discussed above, none of her practices involved overt resistance. And, similar to the other middle-schoolers, Penny's practices of covert resistance involved passing personal notes in class. She also pretended to take notes and follow along in her textbook during lessons.

Resistance. Reflection on these settings led us to speculate that classroom contexts do not allow for acts of overt resistance. Therefore, participants resort to covert acts of resistance in order to subtly challenge the authority of their teachers and of the hegemonic system of formal schooling. Those in power did not permit students to openly defy them, and pretending to take notes in class or refusing to turn in assignments provided alternate ways for these students to reject the hegemonic discourse of schooling. Interestingly, both of the researchers involved in these two cases noted that student participants had negotiable relationships with those in power, their teachers and other authoritative adults. While it was clear that the adults in each case held the power in the classroom, students in both cases could negotiate some aspects of the student-adult power relationship. Indeed, the teacher in the alternative classroom sometimes appeared to "overlook" resistant behavior, such as passing personal notes. Despite the fact that students negotiated some aspects of the relationship with authority figures, it was also obvious that the students were subjugated in the sense that students are always subjugated. These students were nonvoluntary subjects (Ogbu, 1987, 1992), required to attend school regardless of whether or not they want to be there. The alternative middle school particularly emphasized this nonvoluntary status, the students described themselves as "bad or dumb," and attended this school as a "last chance" after being rejected by mainstream schools.

The single instance of covert resistance in the Chinese-American case study involved a student in her school context rather than in the larger community, supporting our conclusion regarding the hegemonic nature of classrooms. In this case, the student incorporated Chinese characters into an art assignment for her American school, characters that her American teacher likely could not read (Zhang, in press), but which may have held important meaning for the student in terms of her cultural and linguistic identity. In all of these cases, students were a clearly dominated, nonvoluntary population who were subjected to the hegemonic structure of schooling, thus rendering their resistance covert. In some instances, students had a negotiable relationship with those in power, complicating the hegemonic power structure relationship. However, such a negotiable relationship also may reflect the fact that no permanent structure existed against which to overtly resist, thus rendering all acts of resistance as covert.

Appropriation. Although covert resistance dominated acts of agency in these cases, the participants also engaged in limited acts of appropriation. Many of the students in both of the middle school cases used the Internet and school-style research skills to stay caught up on youth culture. Participants in Gallagher's (in press) study indicated that they read popular magazines and performed Internet searches to find song lyrics and to keep up-to-date on the latest information about popular musicians. One participant, Marshon, avidly played video games. He used a variety of resources, including the Internet, to help him achieve higher levels of play in the games. Collins (in press) wrote that Penny used the library to research hip-hop music lyrics via the Internet and to download and print the lyrics for herself. Although they might be surprised to recognize it, these middle school students actually appropriated practices that they learned in school, the very setting that they so covertly resisted. However, they transformed these skills by appropriating them in order to participate in youth culture, a purpose that remains largely unacknowledged or unsanctioned by formal schooling.

Direct hegemonies. Again, the commonalities in these contexts suggest that these hegemonic relationships are direct, rather than diffuse. In direct hegemonies, the powerful exert a great deal of power over the dominated. These hegemonies have a highly apparent power structure, making the powerful and the subjugated easily identifiable. Direct hegemonies may or may not be oppressive or repressive, but they typically do not allow for overt resistance. The dominated must resort to acts of covert resistance, and they appropriate relatively few hegemonic ideologies and practices. Both of the middle school cases represented direct hegemonies, as did participants' home situations in Cuba and the Sudan. The colonial situation in Botswana represented a direct hegemony before that country received independence.

THE RELATIONSHIP BETWEEN HEGEMON(IES) AND AGENCY

Based upon our analysis and the different patterns of actions we saw in response to hegemonic power systems, we suggest a more complex notion of hegemony in line with poststructuralist concepts of power relationships. Our data challenge Gramscian notions of hegemony as monolithic and deterministic (Clayton, 1998; Martin, 1998), and they illustrate that different types of hegemonies exist which are based upon the contexts of the systems involved. Hegemonies appear to be defined by the nature of the relationships between those in power and those who are dominated, rather than being defined solely by the political or economic structure of the context.

Our data also support poststructural theories suggesting that power and resistance occur together (Foucault, 1980; McLaren, 1989); resistance occurs in all hegemonic relationships, whether diffuse or direct. However, resistance and other forms of agency appear to take on different forms depending on the type of hegemonic relationship involved. Resistance in particular changes shape, given the context. Agents must consider both the possibility of resisting overtly, as well as what the potential cost might be for such resistance. Diffuse hegemonies seem to provide contexts where overt resistance is possible because the potential repercussions of such actions are relatively minor. For example, many of the U.S. hegemonic contexts in this study showed participants overtly resisting language practices; in this context, English is clearly hegemonic, but the U.S. system also guarantees freedom of speech. Diffuse hegemonies likewise appear to provide contexts where agents feel more comfortable appropriating hegemonic practices. Again, this may be due to the fact that the consequences of such appropriations are relatively minor. In contrast, direct hegemonies appear to provide little (if any) room for overt resistance. Because the consequences for overt resistance are great, agents must resist covertly. For example, in the alternative middle school, overt resistance might result in getting kicked out of the system entirely. In the native contexts of refugees from Cuba or the Sudan, overt resistance might result in political imprisonment or even death. Such high stakes appear to drive resistance underground, and they also may make participants less willing to appropriate practices or discourses from those in power.

As demonstrated in Figure 1, our analysis suggests that individuals may need to leave contexts where there are direct hegemonic relationships in order to be able to openly resist those hegemonic powers. The cases of refugees from Cuba and the Sudan strongly showed this pattern. In both of these cases, participants left direct hegemonic relationships for the U.S., which has a comparatively diffuse hegemonic structure. The new, diffuse hegemonic relationships appeared to allow more room for movement, choice, and resistance. Each of these cases showed high proportions of overt resistance in the U.S., resistance which likely would not have been allowed in their native contexts. The Sudanese emigration, in particular, appeared to allow refugees to overtly critique the Sudanese government. In this case, the diffuse hegemony of the U.S. also appeared to provide tools, practices, and discourses which participants could appropriate in order to resist the direct hegemony of their home country. This may also explain the higher degree of appropriations observed in these cases; that is, individuals may find great value in appropriating aspects of the diffuse hegemony because these appropriations allow them to better resist the direct hegemonic relationship of their home context.

In contrast to other cases, where participants moved from one context to another by changing physical location, the Botswana case represents a change of context over time. We speculate that Botswana's independence from Britain represents a shift from a direct, colonial hegemonic structure to a more diffuse hegemonic structure. Molosiwa (in press) indicates that there is a generational shift in attitudes towards English and literacy, an attitudinal shift which may reflect a similar shift in hegemonic context.

Clearly, what is considered hegemonic is shaped by context. Hegemony cannot be considered a single entity--it is not a political system, an economic structure, a language or literacy practice. Rather, hegemony is part of an overall system that is largely defined by the relationships

Figure 1 Direct and diffuse hegemonies, and the types of agency shown in each.

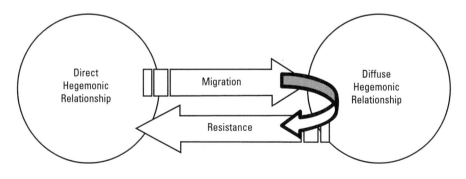

• Doesn't allow for overt resistance • Leads to covert resistance • Few, if any, appropriations	• Migration may enable overt resistance (from afar)	• Allows for overt resistance • Many appropriations

between those in power and those who are dominated or peripheral. In a similar vein, the hegemonic context also determines what can be considered agentive. Like hegemony, agency cannot be simply defined. What is an act of agency, and the manner in which it is shaped by dominated individuals and groups, may very well depend on the type of hegemonic relationship. Hegemony and agency, therefore, can be thought of as mutually constitutive.

Our reexamination and complication of the constructs of hegemony and agency may provide important insights for scholars and practitioners alike who recognize the role of power in language and literacy development and schooling. By recognizing that hegemony is not absolute, by recognizing that there are different types of hegemonic relationships, and that these different relationships enable and constrain agency in different ways, we may be able to move beyond the deterministic fatalism of many discussions of power and hegemony. We hope others will join us in continuing to theorize issues of hegemony and agency in ways that will allow both for more refined empirical investigations within these constructs that, in turn, may suggest pedagogical practices that will further the agency of students who find themselves stymied within hegemonic relationships.

REFERENCES

Barton, D., & Hamilton, M. (1998). *Local literacies: Reading and writing in one community.* London: Routledge.

Barton, D., & Hamilton, M. (2001). Literacy practices. In D. Barton, M. Hamilton & R. Ivanic (Eds.), *Situated literacies: Reading and writing in context* (pp. 7-15). London: Routledge.

Bell, A.C., & Russell, C.L. (2000). Beyond human, beyond words: Anthropocentrism, critical pedagogy, and the poststructuralist turn. *Canadian Journal of Education 25*(3), 188-203.

Bourdieu, P. (1991). *Language and symbolic power* (G. Raymond & M. Adamson, Trans.). Cambridge, MA: Harvard University Press.

Canagarajah, A.S. (1999). *Resisting linguistic imperialism in English teaching.* Oxford, UK: Oxford University Press.

Clayton, T. (1998). Beyond mystification: Reconnecting world-system theory for comparative education. *Comparative Education Review, 42,* 479-496.

Collins, S. (in press). Breadth and depth, imports and exports: Transactions between the in- and out-of-school literacy practices of an "at risk" youth. In V. Purcell-Gates (Ed.), *Cultural practices of literacy: Case studies of language, literacy, social practice, and power.* Mahwah, NJ: Lawrence Erlbaum.

Cope, B., & Kalantzis, M. (Eds.). (2000). *Multiliteracies: Literacy learning and the design of social futures.* London: Routledge.

Foucault, M. (1980). Power/knowledge: Selected interviews and other writings (C. Gordon, Ed. and Trans.). New York: Pantheon Books.

Freire, P. M., & Macedo, D (Eds.). (1998). *The Paulo Freire reader.* New York: Continuum.

Gallagher, D. (in press). "You have to be bad or dumb to get in here": Reconsidering the in-school and out-of-school literacy practices of at-risk adolescents. In V. Purcell-Gates (Ed.), *Cultural practices of literacy: Case studies of language, literacy, social practice, and power.* Mahwah, NJ: Lawrence Erlbaum.

Gee, J. (1996). *Social linguistics and literacies: Ideology in discourses.* London: RoutledgeFalmer.

Gee, J. (2001). Literacy, discourse, and linguistics: Introduction and what is literacy? In E. Cushman, E.R. Kintgen, B.M. Kroll, & M. Rose (Eds.), *Literacy: A critical sourcebook* (pp. 525-544). Boston: Bedford/St. Martin's.

Giroux, H. A. (1989). Schooling as a form of cultural politics: Toward a pedagogy of cultural difference. In H. A. Giroux & P. L. McLaren (Eds.), *Critical pedagogy, the state, and cultural struggle* (pp. 125-151). New York: University of New York Press.

Giroux, H. A. (1992). *Border crossings: Cultural workers and the politics of education.* New York: Routledge.

Kincheloe, J. L., & McLaren, P. (2000). Rethinking critical theory and qualitative research. In N.K. Denzin & Y.S. Lincoln (Eds.), *Handbook of qualitative research* (pp. 279-313). Thousand Oaks, CA: Sage Publications.

Luke, A. (2003). Literacy and the other: A sociological approach to literacy research and policy in multilingual societies. *Reading Research Quarterly, 38*, 132-141.

Mazak, C. (in press). Appropriation and resistance in the (English) literacy practices of Puerto Rican farmers. In V. Purcell-Gates (Ed.), *Cultural practices of literacy: Case studies of language, literacy, social practice, and power.* Mahwah, NJ: Lawrence Erlbaum.

Martin, J. (1998). *Gramsci's political analysis: A critical introduction.* London: Macmillan Press Ltd.

McLaren, P. (1989). On ideology and education: Critical pedagogy and the cultural politics of resistance. In H. A. Giroux & P. McLaren (Eds.), *Critical pedagogy, the state, and cultural struggle* (pp. 174-202). Albany, NY: State University of New York Press.

McLaren, P. (1994). Multiculturalism and the postmodern critique: Toward a pedagogy of resistance and transformation. In H. A. Giroux & P. McLaren (Eds.), *Between borders: Pedagogy and the politics of cultural studies* (pp. 192-222). London: Routledge.

Molosiwa, A. (in press). Language and literacy issues in Botswana. In V. Purcell-Gates (Ed.), *Cultural practices of literacy: Case studies of language, literacy, social practice, and power.* Mahwah, NJ: Lawrence Erlbaum.

Ninnes, P., & Burnett, G. (2003). Comparative education research: poststructuralist possibilities. *Comparative Education, 39*, 279-297.

Ogbu, J. (1987). Variability in minority school performance: A problem in search of an explanation. *Anthropology and Education Quarterly, 18*, 312-334.

Ogbu, J. (1992). Adaptation to minority status and impact on school success. *Theory into Practice, 31*, 287-295.

Perry, K. (in press). Sharing stories, linking lives: Literacy practices among Sudanese refugees. In V. Purcell-Gates (Ed.), *Cultural practices of literacy: Case studies of language, literacy, social practice, and power.* Mahwah, NJ: Lawrence Erlbaum.

Purcell-Gates, V. (Ed.) (in press). *Cultural practices of literacy: Case studies of language, literacy, social practice, and power.* Mahwah, NJ: Lawrence Erlbaum.

Rogers, A. (2001). Afterword: Problematising literacy and development. In B.V. Street (Ed.), *Literacy and development: Ethnographic perspectives* (pp. 205-222). London: Routledge.

Rosolová, K. (in press). Literacy practices in a foreign language: Two Cuban immigrants. In V. Purcell-Gates (Ed.), *Cultural practices of literacy: Case studies of language, literacy, social practice, and power.* Mahwah, NJ: Lawrence Erlbaum.

Street, B. (2001a). Introduction. In B. Street (Ed.), *Literacy and development: Ethnographic perspectives* (pp. 1-17). London: Routledge.

Street, B. (2001b). The new literacy studies. In E. Cushman, E. R. Kintgen, B.M. Kroll, and M. Rose (Eds.), *Literacy: A critical sourcebook.* Boston: Bedford/St. Martin's.

Zhang, G. (in press). Multiple border crossings: Literacy practices of Chinese-American bilingual families. In V. Purcell-Gates (Ed.), *Cultural practices of literacy: Case studies of language, literacy, social practice, and power.* Mahwah, NJ: Lawrence Erlbaum.

Commercial Reading Programs:
What's Replacing Narrative?

Linda M. Phillips
Martha L. Smith
Stephen P. Norris
University of Alberta

There has been a widespread appeal for the inclusion of more informational text in elementary reading programs and instruction. This appeal is motivated by claims that children's early reading material is dominated by narrative texts and by recognition of the importance of learning to read other types of text. Commercial reading programs provide a significant source of material used in reading instruction, yet there is little empirical research on the proportion of various text types within these programs. We conducted a systematic analysis of the types of text contained in three of the most widely used commercial reading programs in Grades 1 to 6 in Canada. A comparison of our results to those of previous studies confirmed that current programs contain less narrative than their predecessors. In order to determine whether informational text is replacing the gap created by the reduced amount of narrative, we paid particular attention to the presence of expository texts and other text types with informational qualities.

BACKGROUND

Commercial reading programs provided the dominant materials used for reading instruction in North American elementary classrooms throughout most of the 20th century (Dole & Osborn, 2003; Smith, Phillips, Leithead, & Norris, 2004). In spite of the literature-based movement of the 1980s and 1990s, recent survey and observational studies show that many teachers rely heavily on commercial programs for much of their reading instruction (Morrow & Gambrell, 2000; Moss & Newton, 2002). Thus, although not complete determinants of what happens in reading instruction, these programs are pervasive. Hence, it is imperative to study their content in order to make informed and appropriate instructional decisions.

Student texts for language arts/reading programs have changed dramatically over the last 25 years. A primary catalyst for change was the literature-based movement that had a significant effect on basal reading programs in the U.S. (Cullinan, 1987; McCarthy et al., 1995). The movement toward literature-based instruction called for the use of authentic texts in classrooms, a term that primarily referred to unedited and unabridged literature written by authors of children's books, although informational texts such as magazines and newspapers could also be included (McCarthy et al., 1995). Some state education departments called for literature-based reading programs and publishers of reading programs responded by producing anthologies that purportedly included large quantities of unabridged/original/authentic children's literature (Hoffman et al., 1994; McCarthy et al., 1995; Reutzel & Larsen, 1995).

There have been repeated calls for inclusion of more informational text in children's reading instruction (e.g. Christie, 1987; Duke, 2000; Pappas, 1991), following the height of the literature-based movement in literacy education. Although the definition of "literature" in literature-based reading instruction includes nonfiction informational books (Morrow & Gambrell, 2000), too often the range of literature that is provided consists mainly of narrative (fiction) texts (Moss, Leone, & Dipillo, 1997). The predominance of narrative in the early elementary grades has been challenged by calls for varied experiences with other text types, particularly expository or informational (Duthie, 1994; Littlefair, 1991; Yopp & Yopp, 2000). Arguments have been put forth regarding such a need (see Duke & Bennett-Armistead, 2003, for a summary). Foremost is the ubiquity of informational text in society, necessitating early exposure in order to build background knowledge, vocabulary, awareness of different text structures and features, and other types of knowledge essential for full access to literacy. Affective and motivational reasons have also been advanced (Doiron, 1994) as well as increased reading motivation and achievement (Guthrie et al., 1996). Gender concerns reinforce the need because evidence that boys are less enthusiastic about reading (particularly fiction) presents yet another serious challenge to the extensive use of fiction (Millard, 1997). Thus, there is a heightened awareness of the need for increased exposure to informational texts in the early grades.

Investigation into the types of writing included in commercial readers is limited, with the most extensive work done in the 1980s (e.g., Flood & Lapp, 1987; Flood, Lapp, & Flood, 1984) Schmidt, Caul, Byers, & Buchmann, 1984) and a few more recent studies (Moss & Newton, 2002; Murphy, 1991; Smith, 1991). Results of these studies point to a narrative or literary emphasis in the materials contained in reading programs. However, most existing research predates the contemporary push for inclusion of more nonfiction and informational texts in literacy instruction. Thus, it is not known how publishers have responded to recent calls in the literacy field and what sorts of text types students are exposed to through the use of student anthologies in commercial reading programs. Has the presence of narrative texts in anthologies waned as a result of the informational text movement? If so, has informational text waxed? What is replacing narrative?

METHOD

Data Sources

The current and most extensively used commercial reading programs in Grades 1 through 6 were identified by the ministries of education in all ten provinces and the three territories. Each identified at least one of the following programs: (a) *Cornerstones Canadian Language Arts* by Gage (1998-2001), (b) *Collections* by Prentice Hall Ginn Canada (1996-2000), and (c) *Nelson Language Arts* by Nelson Thomson Learning (1998-2001). Henceforth, we refer to these as Gage, Ginn, and Nelson. Complete program sets were obtained for this research.

Each set contained, in addition to Teachers' Guides and a variety of ancillary materials, a set of student books (anthologies). There were at least two student books per grade for each publisher with a total of 72 student books distributed as shown in Table 1. The text types of these student books were the focus of this investigation.

Unit of Analysis

All selections in each publisher's anthologies were inventoried by grade. Table 1 shows the distribution of the total 1,106 selections by publisher and grade. Each selection was nested in an instructional set that almost always contained ancillary pedagogical material such as introductory reading tips, author/illustrator information, responding activities, and associated student writings. Some instructional sets contained more than one selection. However, each selection was considered separately as a unit for analysis. All 1,106 selections were coded for this investigation.

Development of Classification Framework

To develop a classification framework, previous studies were examined (e.g., Flood & Lapp, 1987; Flood et al., 1984; Moss & Newton, 2002; Murphy, 1991; Schmidt et al. 1984; Smith, 1991). With the exception of Schmidt, et al. (1984), these studies had methodological commonalities with the work of Flood, et al. (1984, 1987). To optimize comparisons across time and to build on previous research, we utilized a methodology similar to that devised by the Flood, et al. (1984, 1987). Neuendorf's *Content Analysis Guidebook* (2002) was used as a general guide for procedures.

We endeavored to be comprehensive in our coding of text types. Each selection was coded for major genre/text type and subgenre in accord with standard usage. For example, we used narrative to mean a succession of related events over time, generally involving settings and characters (Norris, Guilbert, Smith, Hakimelahi, & Phillips, 2005). This usage includes a variety of genres such as stories (non-realistic, fantasy), realistic fiction, tales, science fiction, and so on. Only major text types will be considered in this paper. Of these, five were relatively uncontroversial and could be found in most previous studies of text types in basals: narrative, poem (including songs), play (including readers' theatre), biography or autobiography, and expository. Five other

Table 1 Number of Student Books and Selections by Grade and Publisher

	PUBLISHER							
	Gage		Ginn		Nelson		Total	
Grade	Books	Selections	Books	Selections	Books	Selections	Books	Selections
1	4	64	12	49	5	47	21	160
2	2	58	10	51	3	52	15	161
3	2	49	5	72	2	47	9	168
4	2	68	5	86	2	53	9	207
5	2	59	5	83	2	66	9	208
6	2	60	5	85	2	57	9	202
Total	14	358	42	426	16	322	72	1106

categories were included to accommodate texts that could not easily fit within such a limited scheme. These will be outlined after a brief discussion of some challenges with text classification.

A variety of conundrums emerged in the process of attempted categorization of selections. For simplicity's sake, these will be reduced to problems of (a) cross-classification, (b) multiple text selections, and (c) hybrid texts. Cross-classification arises because arguments can be made for consideration of a selection in more than one category. Smith (1991) identified this as a problem when "criteria for inclusion are not mutually exclusive" (p. 48). She did not, however, give specific examples or suggest guidelines for dealing with the difficulty. In our data, we experienced cross-classification problems both at the level of major text types and subtypes. For example, biography is generally considered a different subgenre from narrative although, depending on the nature of the information presented, it can sometimes be difficult to distinguish a biographical piece from a narrative nonfiction selection. In such cases, we relied on the context of the text and the dominant textual aspects to make our judgment. Coders sometimes experienced difficulties, for example, distinguishing various subgenre types of tales (e.g., fairytales, folktales, tall tales, pourquoi tales) or differences between myths and legends. Although there may be theoretical differences and prototypical cases, many of the selections encountered were not clear-cut. In this particular case, we grouped all tales, myths, and legends as a single subcategory under narrative.

A second conundrum involved multiple-text selections. In these cases, there were clearly identifiable text types within a single selection, but it was not always clear whether one type was primary. In cases where one text type was clearly dominant, as in the case of a poetry selection embedded in a much longer narrative, the selection was coded for the overarching genre (narrative, in this case). In cases in which a selection contained more than one major text type and it could not be determined which type was overarching or dominant, the selection was judged as multi-text. For example, an article on endangered species consisting of a poem (with an expository function) and a description of each of four endangered species is a clear case of what we call a multi-text. In practice, however, it may be difficult to distinguish multi-texts from cases where texts are embedded or are hybrid.

The existence of hybrid texts has been recognized in most previous studies of genre in basals, but there has been no consensus as to treatment. Flood and Lapp (1987), for example, defined hybrids as texts "which have the form of a story and the function of an expository piece" (p. 301). They tabulated these separately but included them as a form of exposition when analyzing subtypes of writing. Other researchers have followed their lead in terms of definition but not necessarily in terms of treatment. Murphy (1991) included hybrids in her expository text counts whereas Moss and Newton (2002) rated hybrid texts "informational" when factual aspects were judged to be predominant and "fictional" when narrative aspects predominated. Smith (1991) used Flood and Lapp's 1987 definition and included "historical fiction, biographical fiction, and fact/information narrative" in her hybrid category.

We took an approach that recognized previous work but expanded the definition. Because the essence of a hybrid was a kind of form-function disjuncture, it seemed reasonable to include forms other than narrative that had obvious functions not generally associated with the form. For example, in addition to narratives, we found poems, cartoons, plays, and riddles with clear expository functions. There did not seem to be a clear rationale for excluding these forms, which are not used primarily to convey factual information, while considering narratives with such a function to be hybrids. We therefore expanded the definition of hybrid to include other forms that had informational functions not generally associated with the form, although this approach was also not without difficulties. The prototypical personal letter, for example, is generally not written with the purpose of conveying information, although there is no reason why this form could not serve such a purpose (other than that it can result in a somewhat stilted personal letter). Thus, although fairly clear cases of hybrids could be found, the fact that many forms can serve various functions means that "hybrid" is often a relative notion.

In consideration of categories used in previous studies and in light of the conundrums identified, we included five additional major categories in our text coding scheme. A multi-text and hybrid category were included because they each represent different text types in the programs we examined. Three categories were added because their presence in our data suggested possibilities for study: pictorial texts, patterned texts, and other texts. Pictorial texts were defined as wordless pieces like photo essays and reprints of artwork that are not part of a larger text. In some of these cases, a caption, a line of print, or a short introductory section accompanied the images, but the intention of the selection was clearly to encourage the reader to examine the pictures/photographs. Patterned texts are repeated strings of text with some word/phrase substitutions. These repetitions of text patterns (non-rhyming or rhyming) generally show little meaning development as in this example from Nelson 1a: "Jump in the leaves. Jump in the snow. Jump in the puddles. Here we go" (pp. 4-7). In some cases, a repeated text pattern did contain rudimentary narrative elements or appear to have an expository purpose that made the coding decision more difficult as the cross-classification problem became more pronounced. To avoid proliferation of categories, simple early reading texts were included in the patterned text category. These were defined as texts that had an insufficient number of words to code for text type (e.g. Look! Look at …). Finally, like Murphy (1991), we utilized a catch-all *other* category to deal with a wide variety of low-frequency text forms such as interviews, diary excerpts, letters, reproduced advertisements, and resumes. The category of *other* was used also to code problematic cases that could not be handled by any of the other categories. With these five less orthodox categories and the traditional five noted earlier, our study thus utilized ten major text type categories: (a) narrative, (b) poem, (c) play, (d) auto/biography, (e) expository, (f) multi-text, (g) hybrid, (i) pictorial, (j) patterned, and (h) other.

Calculating Text Type Amounts

We utilized the dual method of calculating text type amounts described by Flood and Lapp (1987) and used in most subsequent studies: percent of selections and percent of pages devoted to each type of writing. A determination of page counts was complicated by the fact that most selections are accompanied by a variety of pedagogical materials that not only surround the selection (pre- and post- activities, for example) but frequently are integrated into the selections by means of textboxes, sidebars, and the like. Thus, such information often shares page space with actual selection material. In order to avoid inflating page counts for text types, we quantified the amount of space taken up by the pedagogical texts estimated to the nearest 1/4 page, subtracted from the selection page counts, and combined the pedagogical text counts for an estimate of the total amount of all such material. This material, designated *Other Instructional Elements* (OIE) in this paper, is thus a congeries consisting of introductory reading tips, author/illustrator information, responding activities, directions, student writings to accompany a selection, and a variety of other materials presumably intended to aid literacy development.

Procedure and Reliability

The text categorization scheme described above was developed using an iterative procedure. The final coding scheme was adopted only after all team members were in agreement and high levels of inter-rater reliability were demonstrated. All selections were then assigned to two trained coders in a stratified random manner that ensured that selections from each grade and publisher were equally divided between the coders.

After all selections had been coded, a random sample of 10% of selections from each grade and publisher was chosen. Selections in this sample were coded independently. Using a match-mismatch inter-rater reliability procedure, agreement on major text type category was determined to be 84% percent.

RESULTS

Percent of Selections Overall

Figure 1 shows the quantity of each text type as an average percentage of total selections across all grades and publishers. The data showed that there were more narratives than other text types, although poetry ran a close second. Together they accounted for 54% of all selections. Expository/informational texts were the third most frequent of all selections. The results for the remainder of selections can be viewed as falling into two groups. The percentages for three categories were roughly comparable: other, hybrid, and multi-text. Together, these accounted for the same percentage of selections as expository texts. The remaining four categories made up only 10% of all selections: auto/biographical, patterned, plays, and pictorial. Of these, only plays were found at each grade level, patterned texts were found almost exclusively in Grade 1, and pictorial texts were most frequent in Grades 1 and 2, where no auto/biographical texts were found. These data suggest a dominant literary emphasis in commercial anthologies, when *literary* is defined as narrative and poetic selections, as together, they accounted for 8% more than the eight remaining text types (46%).

Percent of Pages Overall

The data on percentage of pages devoted to each text type indicated a similar pattern to the data on percentage of selections with a few interesting differences (see Figure 2). Narratives occupied more pages than any other type. Poetry, however, dropped from second to fourth place because, although poetry accounted for 26% of all selections, texts of this type tend to be short and thus took up only 8% of all pages. Literary selections (i.e. narratives and poetry) still dominated at 44% of pages compared to 54% of selections.

The second most abundant text type reported was not one of the ten major text types but the other instructional elements (OIE) that were interspersed throughout the selections. Among text types, expository occupied the second highest number of pages, accounting for fewer than half the pages taken by narratives. Beyond these text types and instructional elements that took up 77% of all pages, two groupings of results again occurred. Other, multi-text, and hybrid types collectively accounted for the same percentage of pages (15%) as expository texts. The remaining four text types (patterned, play, auto/biographies, and pictorial) together accounted for the same percentage of pages as poetry (8%), but had the uneven distribution patterns by grade as noted above.

Figure 1 Percentage of Selections by Text Type across Grades and Programs

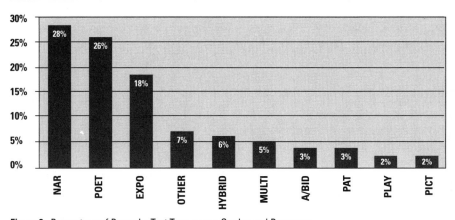

Figure 2 Percentage of Pages by Text Type across Grades and Programs

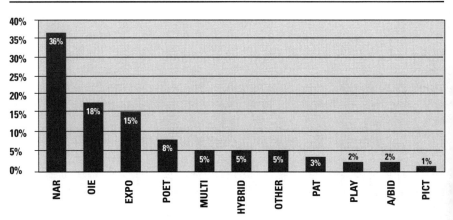

Narrative and Expository Text Amounts by Grade

We were particularly interested in the amount of narrative relative to *informational* text in commercial reading programs. Although uses of the term informational in the literacy field do not necessarily map exactly onto the meaning of expository text, we took this category to be the major discourse type that most accurately represented such informational text. Some studies (e.g., Flood & Lapp, 1987) noted a decrease in narrative and a corresponding increase in exposition with grade level. Figure 3 summarizes the quantity of narrative texts in the three programs in our study by grade. There was a similar pattern in the page and selection percentages with the higher percentages being found in Grades 2 and 3. The fact that Grade 1 percentages were lower than Grades 2 and 3 may be explained by the fact that patterned texts, which were found almost exclusively in Grade 1, made up 17% of the selections and pages in that grade. There was no clear evidence in our study, however, of a decreasing number of narratives with grade advancement, as percentages simply peaked at Grades 2 and 3, and leveled off at Grade 4. Overall, our data suggest that roughly a third of all pages and selections were devoted to narratives, with the lowest percentages at the highest grades. The fact that the page percentages were larger than the selection percentages indicates that narratives tended to be longer than other text types.

Expository/informational text amounts by grade are summarized in Figure 4. The means indicate, on average, fewer than 1/5th of selections and 1/6th of pages were devoted to expository texts. In contrast to the pattern shown for narratives, the selection percentages were higher than the page percentages, indicating that expository passages tended to be short. By grade, the patterns for page and selection percentages were very similar with the fewest selections and pages devoted to exposition at Grade 1. These percentages increased dramatically at Grades 2 and 3 and then decreased considerably by Grade 4, never to recover the percentages found at the second and third

Figure 3 Percentage of Narrative by Pages and by Selections by Grade across Programs

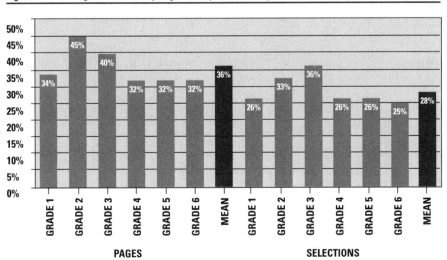

grade. Thus, these data do not show a gradual increase in exposition as did the data reported by Flood and Lapp in 1987.

Percentages of Multi-Text, Hybrid Text, Other Text Types, and OIE by Grade

Overall percentages indicated that three categories (multi-text, hybrid, and other) accounted for as much material as expository text (18% of selections, 15% of pages). Additionally, 18% of all pages consisted of pedagogical material (OIE). As indicated in Table 2, there were more multi-text types and other text types at the upper elementary grades (4th, 5th, and 6th) than at the early elementary grades (1st, 2nd, and 3rd). Hybrid texts, however, tended to decrease with grade. OIE material appeared least in Grade 1 (7% of pages). There was a substantial increase in Grade 2

Table 2 Selection and Page Percentages of Multi-Text, Hybrid Text, Other Text Types, and OIE by Grade

Grade	Multi-Text		Hybrid Text		Other Text Types		OIE
	% Sels	% Pgs	% Sels	% Pgs	% Sels	% Pgs	% Pgs
1	4	4	9	8	6	5	7
2	6	5	8	6	4	3	11
3	2	1	8	4	4	4	22
4	6	7	4	5	10	6	23
5	6	6	5	4	10	7	24
6	7	7	4	2	8	7	22

Figure 4 Percentage of Expository Text by Pages and by Selections by Grade across Programs

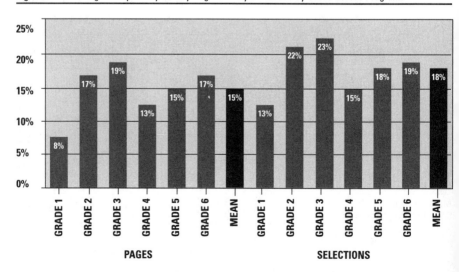

PAGES　　　　　　　　　　　　　　　　　SELECTIONS

(11%), after which the amount of OIE material more than doubled (22-24% of pages) for Grades 3 to 6.

Comparison to Previous Studies

In order to determine whether there have been noticeable changes in the literary emphasis of commercial reading programs during the last decade, we investigated the differences between our results and those of previous studies of text types. Exact comparisons were not possible due to differences in methodology and study foci. Moss and Newton (2002) for example, reported on the presence of fiction and informational literature, categories that we would expect largely to overlap with the narrative and expository categories we used in our study, although not entirely, given that their definition of *informational* included hybrids. Also, they appear to have counted only selections with trade book counterparts, whereas our analysis used all selections regardless of origin. These comparisons must therefore be interpreted with these differences in mind.

The summary of studies presented in Table 3 shows that our results report the lowest percentages, both in terms of pages and of selections, for narratives of all the studies compared here. As noted above, narratives were still the most prevalent text type at all grade levels, but the amount of narrative in our study was far below previously reported levels. Earlier studies reported that up to 2/3 of all text (by page counts) in reading programs was narrative, whereas our numbers suggest that roughly 1/3 was narrative.

DISCUSSION

We began this study with the question of whether the amount of narrative has decreased in commercial reading programs, and if so, what is replacing the narrative content? In comparison to previous studies, our results support the conclusion that narrative has diminished dramatically, with little or no increase in informational/expository text. How can we understand these results given that there has been a widespread call for more informational text?

Table 3 Comparison of Percentage Narratives and Expository Texts in Other Studies

Comparative Studies	Narratives		Expository Texts	
	% Pages	% Selections	% Pages	% Selections
Flood & Lapp (1987) (1983 Program Date)	66	41	11	18
Smith (1991) 1989-1991 Program Dates)	57	37	19	27
Murphy (1991) (1983-1988 Program Dates)	60	32	12	14
Moss & Newton (2002) (1995-1997 Program Dates)	66	45	20	18
Our Study (1996-2001 Program Dates)	36	28	15	18

Understanding Estimates of Narrative

Several plausible explanations can be invoked to explain the differences between our results and those of previous studies. First, the phenomenon of fewer narratives may, to some extent, result from methodological differences between studies. We utilized more categories than other studies because of the difficulties we experienced with simple categorization. As a result, some texts that were coded hybrids or patterned text, for example, may have been considered narratives in other studies. This methodological difference alone would not account for such large differences, however, because patterned texts were found only at Grade 1 and most studies claimed to have considered hybrids as expository texts. In any case, our hybrid category was broader than narratives with expository functions and, even if all selections coded hybrids in our study were added to narrative, the total narrative percentages would still not be as large as those reported in previous studies. Thus, methodology alone seems an inadequate explanation of the large differences in results.

A second difference between other studies and ours is program publication dates, with some published as long ago as 1983 and as recently as 1997, and ours in 2001. In the intervening time, the literacy field witnessed a groundswell in the direction of increasing children's exposure to informational texts in the elementary grades. Thus, a second explanation for our results is that the phenomenon of fewer narratives in commercial programs is real, a reflection of publishers' responses to criticisms of narrative-dominated programs and the informational-text move of the past decade. This explanation cannot account for differences between our results and those of Moss and Newton (2002), however, and leaves unanswered the lack of change that we found in the amount of informational text. Perhaps the most significant difference between us and Moss and Newton is that they counted only selections with trade book counterparts and we counted all selections.

As shown in Table 3, the selection percentages we found for expository text are exactly the same as two previous studies, and page percentages are within a 5% range of all previous studies noted here. Thus, there is some consensus with all studies reporting expository page amounts of 20% or less (range: 11% - 20%). We conclude from these results that informational/expository text amounts have not increased in response to the decrease in narrative texts that we reported.

Although we take the meaning of expository to overlap with what is meant by informational text, we believe that it is by no means clear exactly how these terms overlap in actual usage. In an attempt to elucidate the relationship between expository and informational text types, we perused the research and professional literature. Although we found a strong convergence in notions of informational, expository, and nonfiction texts, there was by no means consensus in how these terms were used. In many cases, the terms were used interchangeably, whereas in other cases, writers were careful to make distinctions. Duke and Bennett-Armistead (2003) and Lukens (2003), for example, pointed out that informational text is a type of nonfiction that is distinguishable from other forms of nonfiction such as biography. Narrative is often juxtaposed with expository to delineate two major text structures, while expository is equated with informational text (e.g.

Gambrell, 2002). For some, however, informational text is not necessarily expository, nor does the term expository exclude text with narrative characteristics. Moss, Leone, and Dipillo (1997), for example, noted that exposition is "found in information trade books" but such books "need not be exclusively expository in nature" because "more and more titles blur the lines between two or more genres or combine narrative and exposition in unique and creative ways" (p. 420). Thus, at least some hybrids and mixed-genre texts could well be considered informational text by some definitions.

Reference books were not particularly helpful in clarifying the relationship between the meanings of expository and informational text. An early dictionary of reading (Harris & Hodges, 1981), for example, defined both exposition and narration as "one of the four traditional forms of composition in speech and writing" (presumably, these are argumentation, description, exposition, and narration). They stated, the "primary purpose" of exposition, however, is "to set forth or explain," and "it may include *limited* (italics ours) amounts of argumentation, description, and narration to achieve this purpose"(p. 111). The same dictionary defined "information book" as "a nonfiction book of facts about a subject" (p. 155). Surprisingly, given the attention directed to informational text over the past decade, a more recent literacy encyclopedia (Guzzetti, 2002) does not include a separate entry for informational text. The term is, however, more or less equated with expository text in the entry on narrative and expository text (Gambrell, 2002, pp. 385-388). Expository texts "inform, explain, or persuade" (p. 385) and communicate "information about the natural or social world" (p. 386). Expository texts "make use of a number of text structures such as cause-effect, compare-contrast, time-order, simple listing, and problem-solution" (p. 386-387). Texts that "combine qualities of both narrative and expository texts" (biographies, autobiographies, and historical fiction are given as examples) are referred to as "hybrid texts ... 'soft' expository and infotainment text" (p. 385). Thus, by this definition, informational text would appear to exclude hybrids and other possibly mixed genre or "other" forms with a variety of functions.

An answer to the question of whether informational text has increased in commercial reading programs depends to a large extent on the definition(s) one employs and the text categorization schemes that one uses. Because the determination of text types is somewhat controversial, we cannot say definitively that quantities of informational text have not increased in commercial reading programs. However, although expository text counts do not show an appreciable increase, at least some of the texts that fell into our categories of hybrid, multi-text, and other texts may be considered informational by some standards. These three text categories made up 18% of all selections and 15% of all pages.

Our results suggest that text types in commercial reading programs are diversifying and that at least some of this diversification is related to the informational text movement. Several observations converge to bolster this hypothesis. First, earlier studies found narrative domination to a far greater extent than we did. Second, with the exception of brief mentions of hybrids, most often defined as texts that have the form of narrative and the function of exposition, previous studies reported little difficulty with fairly straightforward categorization schemes compared to the difficulty we experienced with a more elaborate scheme. Moss and Newton (2002) reported 85%

agreement on assignment of selections to categories, a figure not unlike ours (84%). Although our methodology and terminology differed (they focused on informational and fictional texts), we attempted to reflect the complexity of texts that are found in more recent anthologies and the difficulties of categorizing selections that can be seen as having multiple purposes and blurred text types. We may have found more blurring than was the case in the past.

Although expository percentages have generally not increased, our results also suggest that publishers have attempted to integrate selections with informational purposes into their programs through a wider variety of text types. In this study, for example, most hybrids had an informational purpose, although they may have taken a variety of forms (e.g. narrative, poem, cartoon, etc.). Interestingly, there tended to be more of these texts in the early elementary grades suggesting an underlying belief that information is more understandable, engaging, or otherwise effective in these forms than in clear expository forms at these grades. Conversely, multi-texts and other text forms tended to be more plentiful in the upper elementary grades, a finding that suggests increasing diversity in text forms, and presumably functions, at higher levels. At least some of the forms and functions in these groupings are informational in nature. We found, for example, interviews, letters, and personal commentaries that appeared to have informational purposes, although they would not be considered informational text by some definitions.

Our study raises a number of questions and issues for further investigation. Are texts in commercial reading programs generally more diverse with an increased infusion of selections with informational characteristics? Are there more multi-genre and hybrid text types than in the past? Can the characteristics of these text types be better delineated? Beyond these questions is a host of issues concerning the implications of these texts for the reading process and the teaching of reading. Advocacy for experience with a wide variety of text types at earlier ages is by now fairly commonplace, but what do we know about how students process and learn from texts that obscure or mix genres and text types? Reading acquisition and learning from texts cannot be viewed apart from instruction, raising questions about the most effective use of these texts. Will the contents of these commercial reading programs be more effective than their predecessors in advancing literacy? Clearly, if text offerings in these widely used reading programs are diversifying as this study suggests, there is plenty of room for further investigation and, possibly, for new concerns.

CONCLUSIONS AND IMPLICATIONS

Calls for increased experience with informational text in the elementary grades have intensified in the past several decades. Most previous studies have shown that basal reading series consisted primarily of narrative text selections with few informational text offerings. This examination of the text types present in the three most widely used Canadian commercial reading programs found that, although narrative was the most prevalent text type, the amount was considerably less than previously reported. This finding suggests that publishers have responded to the information text movement by decreasing narrative content. The question raised by the decrease, however, is whether informational text has increased. Our results may be considered to be both optimistic and pessimistic. The good news, at one level, is that narrative content has decreased. The bad news is that a well-known genre, narrative, has decreased and has been replaced by text types that blur the boundaries of ready text recognition for struggling emergent readers. The mixture of informational content evident in the programs we analyzed appears to have switched, imported, and transformed the conventions of text types. We see no educational issue in such deviations for advanced readers; we do see some potential problems for emerging readers, however, who are struggling to read and to identify the conventions of text types. The familiarity of text type affords young readers the power of predictability, an ease of decoding, and a grasp of form, function, and purpose. Diversity of text is important in the reading repertoires of young children. However, whether rare and infrequent exposure to such hybrid texts and types increases children's reading ability is a pertinent and pressing question. Our study also highlighted, albeit indirectly, the glaring absence of attention to two of the major types of discourse: descriptive and argumentative texts. The rationale for increased diversity of text types applies also to descriptive and argumentative texts through which children acquire expertise to experience school and life success in an even broader range of text types. Our current findings show a decrease in narrative and an increase in diverse text types and point to the need for further research on the effects of such changes for children being instructed with current commercial reading programs.

REFERENCES

Christie, F. (1987). Genres as choice. In I. Reid (Ed.), *The place of genre in learning: Current debates* (pp. 22-34). Victoria, AU: Deakin University (Centre for Studies in Literacy Education).

Collections. (1996-2000). Scarborough, ON: Prentice Hall Ginn Canada.

Cornerstones: Canadian Language Arts. (1998-2001). Toronto, ON: Gage.

Cullinan, B. E. (1987). Inviting readers to literature. In B. E. Cullinan (Ed.), *Children's literature in the reading program* (pp. 2-13). Newark, DE: International Reading Association.

Doiron, R. (1994). Using nonfiction in a read-aloud program: Letting the facts speak for themselves. *The Reading Teacher, 47,* 616-624.

Dole, J. A., & Osborn, J. (2003). Elementary language arts textbooks: A decade of change. In J. Flood, D. Lapp, J. R. Squire & J. M. Jensen (Eds.), *Handbook of research on teaching the English language arts* (2nd ed., pp. 631-639). Mahwah, NJ: Erlbaum.

Duke, N. K. (2000). 3.6 minutes per day: The scarcity of informational texts in first grade. *Reading Research Quarterly, 35,* 202-224.

Duke, N. K., & Bennett-Armistead, S. (2003). *Reading and writing informational text in the primary grades: Research-based practices.* New York: Scholastic.

Duthie, C. (1994). Nonfiction: A genre study for the primary classroom. *Language Arts, 71,* 588-595.

Flood, J., & Lapp, D. (1987). Forms of discourse in basal readers. *The Elementary School Journal, 87,* 299-306.

Flood, J., Lapp, D., & Flood, S. (1984). Types of writing found in the early levels of basal reading programs: Preprimers through second-grade readers. *Annals of Dyslexia, 34,* 241-255.

Gambrell, L. B. (2002). Narrative and expository text. In B.J. Guzzetti (Ed.), *Literacy in America: An encyclopedia of history, theory, and practice* (pp. 385-388). Santa Barbara, CA: ABC-CLIO.

Guthrie, J. T., Van Meter, O., McCann, A. D., Wigfield, A., Bennett, L., Poundstone, C., et al., (1996). Growth of literacy engagement: Changes in motivation and strategies during concept-oriented reading instruction. *Reading Research Quarterly, 31,* 306-333.

Guzzetti, B. J. (Ed.). (2002). *Literacy in America: An encyclopedia of history, theory, and practice.* Santa Barbara, CA: ABC-CLIO.

Harris, T. L., & Hodges, R. E. (Eds.). (1981). *A dictionary of reading and related terms.* Newark, DE: International Reading Association.

Hoffman, J. V., McCarthey, S. J., Abbott, J., Christian, C., Corman, L., Curry, C., et al. (1994). So what's new in the new basals? A focus on first grade. *Journal of Reading Behavior, 26,* 47-73.

Littlefair, A. B. (1991). *Reading all types of writing: The importance of genre and register for reading development.* Bristol, PA: Open University Press.

Lukens, R. J. (2003). *A critical handbook of children's literature* (7th ed.). Boston, MA: Pearson Education.

McCarthey, S. J., Hoffman, J. V., Abbott, J., Elliott, B., Stahle, D., Price, D., et al. (1995). Learning to read with the "new" literature-based basal reading programs: Some initial findings. In K. A. Hinchman, D. J. Leu, & C. K. Kinzer (Eds.), *Perspectives on literacy research and practice* (pp. 295-304). Chicago, Il: National Reading Conference.

Millard, E. (1997). *Differently literate.* London, UK: Falmer Press.

Morrow, L. M., & Gambrell, L. B. (2000). Literature-based reading instruction. In M. L. Kamil, P. B. Mosenthal, P. D. Pearson, & R. Barr (Eds.), *Handbook of reading research* (Vol. III, pp. 563-586). Mahwah, NJ: Erlbaum.

Moss, B., Leone, S., & Dipillo, M. (1997). Exploring the literature of fact: Linking reading and writing through information trade books. *Language Arts, 74,* 418-429.

Moss, B., & Newton, E. (2002). An examination of the informational text genre in basal readers. *Reading Psychology, 23,* 1-13.

Murphy, S. (1991). Authorship and discourse types in Canadian basal reading programs. *Reflections on Canadian Literacy, 9,* 133-138.

Nelson Language Arts. (1998-2001). Scarborough, ON: Nelson Thomson Learning.

Neuendorf, K. A. (2002). *The content analysis guidebook.* Thousand Oaks, CA: Sage Publications.

Norris, S. P., Guilbert, S. M., Smith, M. L., Hakimelahi, S., & Phillips, L. M. (2005). A theoretical framework for narrative explanation in science. *Science Education, 89,* 535-563.

Pappas, C. C. (1991). Fostering full access to literacy by including information books. *Language Arts, 68,* 449-462.

Reutzel, D. R., & Larsen, N. S. (1995). Look what they've done to real children's books in the new basal readers! *Language Arts, 72,* 495-507.

Schmidt, W. H., Caul, J., Byers, J. L., & Buchmann, M. (1984). Content of basal text selections: Implications for comprehension instruction. In G. G. Duffy, L. R. Roehler, & J. Mason (Eds.), *Comprehension instruction: Perspectives and suggestions* (pp. 144-162). New York: Longman.

Smith, B. D. (1991). *A descriptive analysis of the content in three basal readers.* Ann Arbor, MI: University Microfilms.

Smith, M. L., Phillips, L. M., Leithead, M., & Norris, S. P. (2004). Story and illustration reconstituted: Children's literature in Canadian reading programs. *Alberta Journal of Educational Research, 50,* 391-410.

Yopp, R. H., & Yopp, H. K. (2000). Sharing informational text with young children. *The Reading Teacher, 53,* 410-423.

Young Children Learn to Read Chapter Books

Nancy L. Roser

University of Texas at Austin

Miriam Martinez

University of Texas at San Antonio

Kathleen McDonnold
Charles Fuhrken

University of Texas at Austin

Chapter books or novels appear, on the surface at least, to present young readers with greater difficulties than do the picturebooks that initiate most children into reading. At a glance, chapter books appear longer, are less supported by pictures, and are more demanding in terms of vocabulary and memory load. Although language, content, and text difficulty vary widely in picturebooks, with some too mature and complex for young readers, picture storybooks most often offer a single story line, relatively few characters, supportive visuals, and plot resolution, all within 32 pages. By definition, a picture storybook is interpreted and elaborated by its illustrations that, in turn, help children make meaning from the text (Kiefer, 1995; Sipe, 2000). By contrast, chapter book texts can mean more complex plots, more (and more well-developed) characters, little support from illustration, and the likelihood of more details for the reader to process and remember. To succeed with chapter books, children seem (minimally) to need the kinds of skills and strategies they rely on to read picturebooks successfully, but they may need more or different strategies and stances as well. For example, readers of chapter books must sustain attention to multiple events over time while remaining uncertain of their relative importance.

Although there is good evidence that reading picturebooks *to* children builds a vocabulary/comprehension foundation for their own independent reading of those books (Dickinson & Smith, 1994; Elley, 1989; Sipe, 2000), it also seems important to explore how reading aloud can help children acquire strategies for reading longer narratives strategically and well. Although the results of the National Reading Panel Report (National Institute of Child Health and Human Development [NICHHD], 2000) underscored the need for multiple strategy instruction and flexibility in application of comprehension strategies, Pressley (2001) argued that

> with respect to the higher-order competence of comprehension, the Panel emphasized the teaching of individual strategies more than the teaching of the entire complicated processing that sophisticated readers employ when they read challenging texts. (pp. 8-9)

Winograd and Johnston (1987) also contended that researchers need to consider the complexities of teaching and learning when they called for more direct instruction or direct explanation of comprehension processes. One of those complexities is, of course, the text itself. Perhaps more than any other aspect of comprehension, the Panel report skirted consideration of the particular demands of text, and the ways in which different text forms challenge readers' meaning constructions differently. Even so, the National Panel Report emphasized that comprehension instruction should weave strategies together, occur in natural settings, and be available for all readers (NICCHD, 2000).

Toward understanding how readers' gears may need to shift as instructional terrains (texts) become more rugged or unfamiliar, we investigated the natural integration of demonstration, enlistment, and application of meaning-making strategies as children were introduced to chapter books, first, as their teacher read aloud to them, and second, as they selected and read chapter books for themselves.

Although the investigation of effective comprehension instruction has well-developed roots (Dole & Duffy, 1991; Fielding & Pearson, 1994; Pressley, 2000), we continue to need to learn more about the introduction of new forms of texts as well as the cusps and transitions between different kinds of texts and tasks within literacy programs, such as movement from narrative to information text (Duke, Bennett-Armistead, & Roberts, 2002; Smolkin & Donovan, 2001), from teacher-led to student-led discussions of text forms (Jewell & Pratt, 1999; Maloch, 2004; Short, Kauffman, Kaser, Kahn, & Crawford, 1999), from learning to read and write texts in one language to learning to read and write in two (Moll, Saez, & Dworin, 2001), as well as how children learn to negotiate meaning-making as they meet lengthier text such as their first chapter books. Toward deepening our understanding of the acquisition of reading comprehension strategies (Smolkin & Donovan, 2001) particular to reading chapter texts or novels, we have looked closely at this latter cusp, at the ways in which an effective teacher helps children make sense of longer, more complex narrative. Recently, young children have been offered some additional scaffolding into chapter books by the proliferation of "easy-to-read" chapter books in the trade market. To date, however, there has been very little agreement as to the distinguishing features of these easy-to-read chapter books (Graves & Liang, 2004), nor systematic inspection of their influence on children's movement into novels (Roser, Martinez, McDonnold, & Fuhrken, 2004).

We approached our investigation by investigating how one experienced teacher (Kathleen McDonnold) helped children move through their first in-school chapter book, gaining understanding of its format, its plot strands, its multiple characters, its vocabulary demands, and its failure to resolve after one storytime session. We wanted to observe the processes she used, as well as keep close watch on her children's responses through their talk and writing and eventual movement into transitional chapter books. So, for this initial phase of a longer study, we observed Kathleen's classroom of first graders across the reading of one chapter book lasting nearly eight weeks. We wanted to understand the guidance and teaching she provided to help her children reason their way actively through a challenging text and cope with its new format, features, and demands. We asked: In what ways does an experienced first grade teacher support her children's meaning-making through their first chapter book? By close inspection of the conversations, instruction, and writing that occurred before, during, and after the reading of a complex narrative, we hoped to build a better understanding of what it means to learn to read within a chapter book when supported by a natural, highly-integrated, and purposeful instructional setting.

METHOD

Participants

The children. The elementary school in which Kathleen worked is set within a middle-class neighborhood in a southwestern city. The school of approximately 600 children serves a predominantly white and Asian pre-kindergarten through grade five population. Many of the children have two-parent families, with both parents working, and live in single-family homes, apartments, and duplexes. Kathleen's first-grade classroom had 11 girls and 11 boys. Of the 22 children, 16 were white, 5 were recent Asian immigrants, and one was Latina. Six of the students were learning English as a second language. These children had first languages of Korean, Japanese, Bengali, and Portuguese. None of Kathleen's children received free lunch. The children's mid-year *Developmental Reading Assessment* (Beaver, 2001) scores ranged from Level 4 to Level 44, or from emergent reader to an approximate fourth grade reading level, with an average score at about one year above grade placement. By the end of the year, the range of DRA scores was from 14 to 44, with nearly 50% of the children reaching the ceiling score. Thus, although not all children entered first grade as strong readers, most made normal to strong growth across the year, as judged by DRA scores. Further, the children were already showing interest in and ability to tackle longer texts, but none had read a chapter book as part of the regular school curriculum. Although we recognized that children typically make the transition to chapter books during the second or third grade rather than the first, we wanted to capture the discussion of an entire class being introduced to their very *first* chapter book, so we chose second semester first graders. Although it is possible that a few of the children had had some form of a lengthy text read to them at home, the novel length fantasy *The Castle in the Attic* (Winthrop, 1985) was the children's first experience in school with this text form, length, and complexity of plot.

The teacher. We chose a veteran teacher with over 20 years of experience with first graders to gain what Sipe (2000) calls an "intensive" sample, one very likely to show wellsprings of understanding of helping young children make meaning. Even so, Kathleen admitted to having much more experience helping children access picturebooks than chapter books. Our university's teacher education program had placed many student teachers in Kathleen's classroom, and during the two semesters in which data were collected, she and two of the researchers co-taught field-based university courses in her school. At the time of the study, Kathleen was a doctoral student and an active member of the research team. She also served as a chronicler of her own responses to the storytime events, as an interpreter of her children's talk, and a source of data verification along the way.

The classroom. Kathleen's classroom library collection was not limited to one space, so books of current study were on the chalk ledge, other books were grouped in tubs by topic or genre, and still others occupied classroom bookshelves. In addition, within the cupboards that lined one wall of the classroom, white cardboard boxes held multiple copies of picturebooks labeled by their contents (e.g., the works of authors such as Denise Fleming and Leo Lionni; sets of books to support content study, such as "Bats" and "Presidents"; and books organized for "genre" study, such as Poetry and Folktales). These boxes served as learning materials throughout the year and also provided multiple copies of texts for storytime, such as, for example, the 22 paperback copies of *Lunch* (Fleming, 1998) filed inside the Denise Fleming cardboard box. Kathleen often used what she called "a read-aloud/read-along" model with many of the picturebooks in her class. Over the years, she had gathered sufficient class sets of picturebooks so that at least once or twice each week during storytime, every child held a copy of the book being read and talked over.

University-based researchers. In addition to Kathleen, the university researchers included two teacher educators and a doctoral student in language and literacy studies. At least one of the researchers was in the classroom each day audio- and videotaping, taking fieldnotes, and debriefing. Except for Kathleen, researchers served more as observers than participants in this classroom, although occasionally they answered questions, monitored journal writing, and contributed realia, such as a "tapestry" jacket, an enlarged map of the novel's setting, and a tiny lead knight, in anticipation or in answer to children's needs.

Procedure

Our full investigation was a semester-long observational study of how children are helped to achieve the transition to successful independent chapter book reading. We gathered and interpreted the teaching strategies that seemed to support children as they worked together to make meaning of a chapter book, the children's oral and written responses to a chapter book read aloud, as well as their first attempts at selecting, reading, and discussing easy-to-read chapter books. So, although the study had several phases including the collection of baseline storybook reading procedures, the introduction of the chapter book, the collection of children's written responses to the chapters, as well as their movement into self-selected chapter books, we report here only the second phase of the investigation, the children's introduction to and discussion of a lengthy chapter book. In this phase, we observed the strategies and combinations of strategies an experienced teacher emphasized that appeared related to helping children negotiate the complexity, length, and demands of a chapter book.

The introduction, reading, and discussion of the children's first in-school chapter book followed the read-aloud/read-along model with which they were familiar. For two weeks prior to beginning the chapter book, picturebooks and information texts about castles, knights, and dragons were shared in storytime. As the children were introduced to their first chapter book, they sat on the story rug, adhering to their typical procedures for storytime. Each was handed an individual copy of Elizabeth Winthrop's (1985) *The Castle in the Attic* to follow along if they chose as Kathleen read. The chapter book reading, or the discussion of the text or response journals, began at approximately 8:30 a.m. and lasted approximately 45 minutes. Kathleen introduced the chapter book in late January and completed it in mid-March, reading two to three chapters per week. Book conversation occurred before, during, and after each chapter. In addition, the children wrote in a special "castle" response journal after each chapter was completed. As the first graders became more immersed in the chapter book, the talk, reading, and writing stretched past its original time frame. Although not every part of the instructional sequence (reading, talking, writing, and sharing) happened daily, some activity related to the chapter book occurred each day. The typical time allotments were as follows: pre-reading discussion: 10 minutes, oral reading and discussion: 30 minutes, journal writing: 20 minutes, and journal sharing: 30 minutes.

Across this observational inquiry, most of the children, regardless of native language, were able to follow along in the chapter book as Kathleen read. To help ensure understanding, following the reading of each of the first three chapters, one of the researchers guided those children with developing English through a retelling of the chapter, clarifying the plotline by using a flannel storyboard with cut-out characters and elements of the setting (house, attic, castle).

Data Sources

For the approximately eight weeks of chapter book study, we audiotaped and videotaped the ways in which Kathleen introduced, read aloud, and invited discussion of each chapter of the children's first chapter book. As the camera and recorders ran, we took fieldnotes, highlighting aspects of the conversations that introduced, interrupted, or reflected on the chapter's meanings. We also kept notes from follow-up conversations with Kathleen. To examine the potential complexity of the teacher's verbal moves as she helped children reason actively, we transcribed each day's talk. The transcriptions, fieldnotes, and debriefings, as well as the teacher's own journal, were the major data sources for this phase of the larger study.

Data Analysis

Data were drawn from complete transcriptions of the read-aloud, the discussions, as well as from the children's oral sharing of their written responses. One researcher who knew the names and recognized the voices of each child transcribed the majority of tapes; others of the research team listened to the tapes while reading the transcripts to verify accuracy of the transcriptions. Transcripts were intended as verbatim accounts of chapter and journal discussions in terms of repeated words, false starts, pauses, overlapping talk, and audible sounds. Perhaps because the tapes were collected in the classroom of an experienced teacher whose students had been read to both at home and at school, there was little management or off-task talk; the children were, for the most part, focused and engaged with the story, as evidenced by the nature and direction of their talk.

Once transcribed, each researcher read and reread all of the transcriptions and then independently wrote descriptive summaries of the ways the teacher and children seemed to work to make meaning from this chapter book. We compared our descriptions by reading aloud to one another both from the summaries and from the transcripts to build an initial general description of Kathleen and her children at work comprehending a lengthy narrative. In this discussion, we included our broad impressions of procedures, demonstrations of community, uses of materials and methods, and sustained and open-ended inquiry.

We then identified as the unit of analysis a teacher *move* defined as an utterance that appeared intended to support children's meaning-making in the chapter book. For example, in one transcript, the question, "What do you think?" was identified as a move. The question opened an extended transaction related to the hero's unexpected duplicity and resulted in children's text-based conjectures or judgments: "It's a half lie," Allie (pseudonym) explained in response, "Part lie, part true." Yet, whether or not sustained talk resulted, we identified each speech act that seemed intent on garnering or creating meanings as a precipitating move.

We coded the moves using the constant comparative method of Glaser and Strauss (1967), modifying or creating categories when they failed to account for or confirm identified teacher action. We initially coded and developed descriptions for 35 teacher moves that seemed to offer instructional support to children's meaning-making. Through rereading, alignment, and connection, we were able to develop more comprehensive conceptual categories "… to form more precise and complete explanations" (Strauss & Corbin, 1998, p.124). Thus, we arrived at eight broad categories of teacher moves, what we saw as the "instructional acts" Kathleen employed to help children become better comprehenders (see Table 1).

Kathleen's experienced teacher language also seemed to stretch a net of supportive *strategies* children could use to make meaning. In our second round of coding, we aimed to identify the task or strategy the children were being offered (or were attempting), a strategy that children could potentially appropriate for their own meaning-making. We attended to how the precipitating move, situated within the topic unit (the related talk contributed by children and teacher), revealed the underlying instructional strategy being offered. By examining the surrounding talk, we drew inferences about the strategy being demonstrated or offered. Although a teacher's instructional goals for comprehension and children's incorporation of comprehension strategies can seem to blur, we attempted to peel apart instructional goal from instructional strategy. For example, a teacher's instructional goal (move) for comprehension instruction may be to *determine how well readers are understanding* a complex timeline, but within that goal frame, she may be helping readers to *monitor their reading* for fuzziness or discomfiture, and then equipping them with some ways of coping with or repairing the confusion they encounter while interpreting the timeline. As another example, a teacher intent on helping children "step into the story world," an instructional move, as a way of comprehending deeply, might give invitation or practice or direction to help students "make mental images," a strategy they could eventually employ on their own. To identify how the children were offered instructional support that could become strategic for them, we used axial coding as described by Strauss and Corbin (1990) to achieve nine broad conceptual categories that subsumed the 38 instructional supports we had initially identified (see Table 2).

To manage the complexity of the discourse, we relied on a database that permitted us to identify and sort the teacher's instructional *moves* from the *strategies* that could eventually be turned over to child readers for their own use. The database also permitted us to re-inspect the categorized moves or strategies within the context of the surrounding discourse.

In addition, because we were intent on capturing the import of the text itself in these exchanges, we coded the literary focus of the talk (Eeds & Wells, 1989; Martinez & Roser, 1994; Sipe, 2000). That is, we inspected the instructional move and strategy support to determine what literary aspect of the text was being attended to through the talk, whether character, setting, plot, etc. Two researchers recoded portions of the data with the final set of categories with over 90% agreement.

Table 1 Definitions of Teacher's Moves

TEACHER MOVE	DEFINING FEATURES	EXAMPLE
Emphasizing important content	Pointing out the salience of a text to the unfolding action.	"She felt homesick. That's important."
Encouraging a speculative/ critical stance	Musings, questions, and pauses that invite children to enter into the construction of meaning, to fill inevitable gaps in text, and to approach text as something to be solved, as well as lived in.	"Kind of a puzzle, isn't it? Let's think about it. Is Mrs. Phillips his grandmother?"
Determining understanding	Probes, questions, and invitations indicating the necessity for checking to see if readers are successfully remembering and interpreting text.	"Let's share everything we can think of that Shari needs to know about William."
Providing/ inviting explanation	Drawing expertise from children, or providing definitions, explanations, or concrete representations (realia) at points of perceived complexity, difficulty, or opaqueness of text.	"What do you think that might mean? 'He has sucked out her heart and replaced it with a stone.' ... Nadia, do you have an idea about that?"
Inviting into the story world	Using the platform of the text as a staging for the invitation into the drama. Children act, move, read, or speak from within the story, especially from the perspective of the character.	"I think I want to do that part again. Maybe you could do that with me? Just like you were Alastor saying that? (together) 'I control you...'"
Modeling active/responsive listening	Body position, facial expression, murmurs, and pauses indicate room for listeners to join into the working out of meanings. Also, the teacher's probes, restatements, and requests for clarification indicate deep attention to what children offer.	C: He did that so she can't love anybody. T: Hmmmm. So, now, because the love would come from her heart and now that it's like a stone, she couldn't love anymore. That's a different way to think about it.
Modeling active/ responsive reading	Making the thoughtful aspects of reading more visible, including efforts to untangle meanings, express satisfaction or engagement, demonstrate inferences, and indicate how the unfolding story affects (confirms or shifts) meaning-making.	T: (reading): "You have inside you the heart and soul of a knight." That gives me bumps. Does it kind of give you bumps? I want to hear that part again.
Threading across content	Attempts to untangle plot lines or draw character actions together (and forward), possibly helping track important elements. Includes efforts to re-enter the story (recall, re-collect, plot trace).	C: Maybe he's the other person in the riddle. T: The other person in the riddle. We have the lady... C: The squire. T: The squire? C: Yeah. T: (reading): "The lady doth ply her needle. And the lord his doth test. Then the squire will cross the drawbridge." So, we know who the lady is...and we know who the lord is....

Table 2 Strategies Young Readers Could Use for Comprehending

WHAT YOUNG COMPREHENDERS ARE INVITED TO DO/TAKE OVER	DEFINITION	EXAMPLE
Elaborate and support; give evidence	Attempts to support one's ideas, positions, or developing notions by relying on text.	T: How is he gonna warn [his dad]?... C: Yell at his dad.... C: ...in one of the chapters, it said to warn Sir Simon, William could knock on the wall.
Connect	Awareness that the action or events in the story can be viewed through one's own experience. Conversely, the effect of the text on shaping a new awareness or understanding.	T: Now, let me just ask a question for some of our gymnastic experts...Before you do your routine, William was going to be warming up and stretching out his muscles. Is that something that you would do?
Conjecture	Efforts to reason actively within the text to make hypotheses about the action or characters.	T: [Reading]: "William leaned down to listen." Now let me think about this: Why is he having to lean down so far to listen?
Write and draw responsively	Offering ideas, images, interpretations that are profoundly personal or idiosyncratic through writing and illustration.	T: Okay. You've made this knight small like the coin. And tell us about your illustrations...Made the knight tiny. Very tiny.
Recall/Summarize	Attempts to rely on prior text to interpret	T: So what else do we know about Mrs. Phillips?
Make mental images	A conscious or habituated response to text that involves picturing the action, images, words, or emotions or mood being evoked; an attempt to step into the perspective of a character.	T: [Reading]: "His right hand was raised with a clenched fist, as if he were challenging some unseen enemy." Do you have that picture in your mind? That fist like that with the knight? Okay?
Monitor for meaning	Attention to the developing sense of a text, reinforcing readers' right to build meaning, question sense, and repair their reading by backing up, seeking help, or looking up.	T: Before we start reading (inaudible), can you think of any question you have about Chapter 8 that you think we need to talk about before we continue to read?"
Clarify and bring meanings to critically important text	Identifying, clarifying critically important portions of texts, pointing toward critically important text. Could involve restating the text in simpler terms or supplying the meaning of a term.	T: [Reading]: "'Jason, what if you had a friend who really needed your help, but you couldn't help him unless you changed yourself?' said William." That's a hard question, isn't it? I'm going to ask that question again. That's a tough one. T: Do you know that word pacing?
Make judgments, that is, evaluate the morality, veracity, validity, or worth of what is read	Response to text that questions, evaluates, or weighs. In literary texts, the judgments may be of craft or character action; in information text, it may be of the credibility or accuracy; in all texts forms, it could be judgments of the likelihood.	T: Do you think she should tell him?

We also looked for the shifts in talk across time. For this analysis, we compared the talk from the beginning, middle, and end of the story. Ultimately, through a multi-dimensional comparison (goal by strategy by literary focus by time, early, mid, and late in the book), we inspected how one experienced teacher (a) *aims* comprehension *instruction* to (b) *support* young readers' use of meaning-making *strategies* toward (c) particular *aspects of text*, and (d) across *time* (the chapters of a lengthy text).

Finally, we looked toward the talk that focused specifically on challenges of the chapter book form—its length that made finding and refinding one's "place" not to be taken for granted, the notion of chapters as structure for the book, and such unexpected discoveries as the passage of time marked by a row of asterisks.

RESULTS

Moves

To understand better how teachers work with naïve readers to help them construct meaning with longer and more difficult texts, we identified eight categories of Kathleen's talk that appeared intentional toward helping readers make meaning in chapter books. The eight included: (a) emphasizing important content; (b) encouraging a speculative/critical stance; (c) determining understanding; (d) providing/inviting explanations; (e) inviting readers into the story world; (f) modeling active/responsive listening; (g) modeling active/responsive reading; and (h) threading across content (see Table 1 for definitions and examples). By inspecting for these moves across the chapters, we gained perspective on their relative emphasis as the plot developed (see Table 3).

For example, the most prevalent kind of teacher support across the chapter book we eventually categorized as threading, by which we meant a deliberate attempt to untangle plot lines or draw character actions together (and forward), possibly helping children track important elements. Across the chapters of The Castle in the Attic, the teacher directed 25% of her comprehension talk toward these threadings, which included helping children recollect, recall,

Table 3 Number and Percentage of Teacher Moves Across Chapters

TEACHER'S STRATEGIC MOVES	EARLY	MID	END	TOTAL	%-AGE
Threading across content	61	24	31	116	25
Encouraging speculative/critical stance	7	50	40	97	21
Modeling active/responsive reading	12	31	23	66	14
Modeling active/responsive listening	1	12	45	58	13
Providing/inviting explanation	15	8	47	40	9
Inviting into the story world	7	10	19	36	8
Emphasizing important content	10	5	10	25	5
Determining understanding	3	15	5	23	5
TOTAL	**116**	**155**	**190**	**461**	**100**

weigh, and re-enter their reading. At the beginning of the book, threading talk accounted for 55% of the teacher's moves. Kathleen, for example, helped the children hold onto a rhyming riddle, "The lady doth ply her needle. And the lord his sword doth test. Then the squire will cross the drawbridge…," with ambiguous clues that were unveiled across the text:

- *That riddle is just really difficult. There's something special about that riddle. And you thought about that in Chapter 7* [Transcript chapter 9, p. 2].

Later, speaking musingly, she again hinted at the need to gather clues:

- *… The other person in the riddle. We have the lady…* [Transcript chapter 9, p. 13]

Still later, she added:

- *…so we know who the lady is and who the lord is …*[Transcript chapter 9, p. 14].

Along the way, children took up the threading by working with the tasks of comprehension: recollecting, drawing on clues, and speculating (from Transcript chapter 9, pp. 13-14):

- *Hey, maybe he's* [the lead character, William] *the…uh…other person…maybe he's the other person in the riddle.*

- *Fifty-three!* [referring to the page long past on which the riddle first appeared].

- *And maybe he's the one to cross the drawbridge.*

- *And then Mrs. Phillips is the lady!*

- *That's what I said.*

Both at the middle and end of the chapter book, the teacher's emphasis appeared to be on encouraging the children to be speculative, engaged, and extremely active in their meaning-making, as when she said, "Why is that? Why didn't William really want to take the knight the wood that he asked for?" Modeling or encouraging a speculative/critical stance accounted for 21% of the teacher's moves across the text. However, by the end of the book, Kathleen seemed intent on making even more room for children's speculative talk. Thus, the instances of talk in which she "received" children's speculations and responses, *listening actively/responsively,* accounted for 13% of her total instructional moves, but increased to account for 24% of her total moves in chapter 15 alone. Overall, 14% of Kathleen's instructional intents seemed directed toward modeling active/responsive reading. In this "participant" role, she became a "co-responder" to the text (Maloch, 2004; Roser & Martinez, 1985; Short, Kauffman, Kaser, Kahn, & Crawford, 1999), sharing genuine puzzlements, responses, or connections:

- *Weird. It kind of gives me the shivers just to think about it.* [Transcript chapter 15, p. 18).

- *Can you WAIT to read chapter 16?* [Transcript chapter 15, p. 29].

- *I think I gotta keep reading. I'm confused, too.* [Transcript chapter 15, p. 26]

- *Kind of a puzzle, isn't it? Let's think about it. Is Mrs. Phillips his grandmother?* [Transcript chapter 3, p. 3].

Further, in a text devoid of pictures, *entering the story world* seemed both important and enjoyable as a way of understanding its intricacies, the characters' actions, feelings, and the significance of events. From inside the story world, children could create their own envisionments (Langer, 1994). Overall, *entering the story world* accounted for 8% of the talk:

- *Oh! Might be angry. I can tell you this. I would be angry if someone were going up in my attic and setting fires. How would your parents feel about someone setting fires in your attic?* [Transcript chapter 9, p. 5].

- *Are you thinking what the knight is thinking?* [Transcript chapter 9, p. 12].

- *In fact, let's practice that first. A terrified face. Pretend you're the knight. You're being lifted up. The whole castle is being lifted up. So scary* [Transcript chapter 9, p. 19].

Thus, Kathleen's instructional moves focused predominantly on threading or keeping track, making speculations about unresolved outcomes, thinking purposefully aloud, and helping children step inside the story. These prevalent instructional acts seemed intended to help children make meaning with longer texts.

Support for Strategies

The strategies Kathleen offered to children were most evident in the seamless discussion of literature, that is, a flow from story to the modeling/demonstration, casual asides, genuine probes, and invitations to share thinking and process. During discussion in which the focus was on the story world, the strategy support never took the form of a heuristic. Rather, supports were used and re-used to serve meaning-making. Repeating the demonstrations of successful readers in new contexts was more likely to occur than specific strategy instruction. In a follow-up video interview, Kathleen anticipated that more "coaching" and direct explanation would come later, at points of need in children's reading, including their reading of still other chapter books.

As transcript data seemed to support, making and inviting conjectures was important in Kathleen's classroom, occurring in 26% of the coded talk (see Table 4). Her stance toward this fantasy novel was one of helping readers make sense of an unfamiliar story world with its unexpected shifts in chronological time, relative sizes, and power. One way in which she did this was by encouraging *conjecture*, the conceptual category that included inviting and modeling inferences, inviting and modeling predictions, as well as wondering/puzzling:

- *All right, there's a problem here with Jason coming to see the castle, and you're saying... Karrie, you're saying he didn't want him to find out about the Silver Knight. Hmmmm.* [Transcript Chapter 9, p. 3].

- *I think he also might be feeling a little badly. Might be feeling a little badly about this mess that's been created.* [Transcript chapter 9, p. 21].

Table 4 Number and Percentage of Supporting Strategies Across Chapters

SUPPORTING STRATEGY	EARLY	MID	END	TOTAL	%-AGE
Conjecture	10	66	45	121	26
Identify important text/ meanings	18	10	52	80	17
Give evidence/elaborate	17	27	18	62	13
Recall	31	13	6	50	11
Make mental images	7	6	35	48	11
Write and draw	18	11	17	46	10
Connect	12	15	10	37	8
Monitor	2	6	4	12	3
Make judgments	1	1	3	5	1
TOTAL	**116**	**155**	**190**	**461**	**100**

- *What was that about? "No blood" on that dagger.* [Transcript chapter 15, p. 7]

Seemingly critical, too, to comprehending lengthy text is being able to recognize or intuit when an author is offering essential clues, details, meanings, or evidence. In a narrative text, important words/concepts are clarified. Kathleen shared concrete examples (a portcullis on a toy castle, a wok, a windflute) at appropriate points in the story, helped children to add their understandings so as to work out meanings, and alerted them to the most significant junctures, terms, metaphoric language, and plot intricacies in 17% of the coded data:

- *Allie and Nadia have both noticed...* [Transcript chapter 15, p. 13].

- *Hmmmm. So, now, because the love would come from her heart and now that it's like a stone, she couldn't love anymore...* [Transcript chapter 15, p. 16].

- *Usually when you're pacing, you're thinking about something. You're worried about something, and you're thinking about it deeply. ...* [Transcript chapter 9, p. 11].

- *This is the minstrels' gallery right up here. And this is where the musicians and the court jesters would be and then they...there would be dancing and big parties and things there, and that would be (inaudible) the Great Hall.* [Transcript chapter 3, p. 9].

The ability to give evidence for conjectures, or to clarify one's opinions with text and discussion is essential to Rosenblatt's "evoked poem" (Farrell & Squire, 1990, p. x). In 13% of the strategy talk, the first graders in Kathleen's discussion circle were invited to view evidence, to elaborate their own ideas, or to contribute to a justification. The attention to elaborated, evidentiary talk increased across the chapters:

- *Why would she be sad? ...* [Transcript chapter 9, p. 8].

- *Karrie, did you want to add to that? ...* [Transcript chapter 9, p. 8].

- *Todd, did you have another idea about that? ...* [Transcript chapter 9, p. 20].

It should be noted that during discussions in which children were contributing evidence, each instance of Kathleen's inviting a child into the discussion by speaking the child's name with a questioning inflection, as when she said, "Mara?" "Todd?" "Joon?", was coded as an instance of seeking evidence or elaboration.

Kathleen also appeared ready to show readers how to pull essential ideas together or reconstruct elements of plot. Summarizing or recalling, whether asked for or demonstrated, accounted for 11% of the strategy talk and occurred prominently during the chapter book's opening chapters:

- *So, part of her is happy that William has the castle, and part of her is sad because she's (inaudible). Good point. Thank you, Mara.* [Transcript chapter 3, p. 16].

- *And, what's the name of this chapter?...The name of the title...the title of the story is all that the author shares with us, and there's just numbers for chapters. We don't have a name. So, we think of what's happening in the chapter as we read.* [Transcript chapter 3, p. 24].

- *Before we start our next chapter, and before we share our journals, we need to kinda catch Celia up. Because she wasn't here for chapter 1 or 2. And Mara wasn't here for chapter 2. So, let's sorta review and remember what we know so...it will kind of make sense* [Transcript chapter 3, p. 1].

Seemingly important, too, was the children's ability to visualize the text to be comprehended. The strategy of mental image-making occurred in 11% of Kathleen's read-aloud talk and increased markedly by the book's end. We defined it broadly to include all efforts to help children see the story from the inside out:

- *While he's getting his illustration to show you...I want you to pretend right now that you're William, and you have scooped down and picked up Mrs. Phillips, and here she is in your hand, and you're putting her in that ...pocket. Can you imagine? That was somebody my size that now you would be able to pick up and put in your pocket.* [Transcript chapter 9, p. 1].

- *All right. I think I want to do that part again. Maybe you could do that with me? Just like you were Alastor saying that?* [Transcript chapter 15, p. 16].

Focus of Talk

In our third pass through the data, we used the traditional elements of narrative to determine on which aspects of text the comprehension talk focused. That is, we mapped each purposive teacher move and instructional support with the part of the text toward which the support seemed to be pointing to learn that the preponderance of talk pointed to character as this teacher helped children make their way through a complex text. When the specific story elements are grouped for inspection across the beginning, middle, and end of the chapter book, *character* again superseded *plot* as the center of talk (see Figure 1). It is possibly through character that children can identify, care about, and come to understand longer narratives:

Figure 1 Incidence of Talk Focused on Story Elements Across a Chapter Book

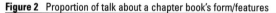

Figure 2 Proportion of talk about a chapter book's form/features

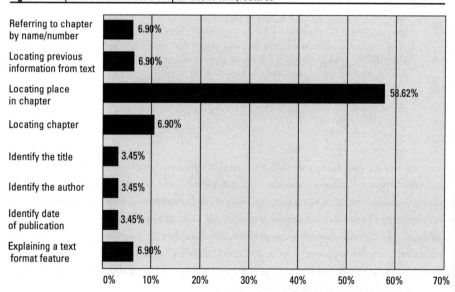

- *A terrified face. Why would this knight be so terrified? So scared.* [Transcript chapter 9, p. 21].

- *Why is William gonna start to cry? What's the sad part here? Why is he gonna cry?* [Transcript chapter 9, p. 21].

- *Okay, kinda think... about how it would feel.* [Transcript chapter 9, p. 19].

Negotiating Text Features

When readers meet a new form of text, they must learn to navigate its features. Questions and help for the features of a first chapter book ranged from the teacher and children referring to "chapters" to locating a page in previously read chapters to explaining a text feature format, such as a row of asterisks to mark the passage of time. In the analysis of three chapters, there were 29 separate incidents of support for the use of the chapter book form. Over half of that talk (59%) was related to being guided to the "place" in response to "Where are we?" (see Figure 2):

- *All right. I'm here in the middle of the page 20. Are you right there with me?* [Transcript chapter 3, p. 27].

- *Chapter 5. Another good chapter* [Transcript chapter 9, p. 3].

DISCUSSION

The purpose of this observational study was to describe and document how young children and their teacher approach meaning-making with their first in-school chapter book. We examined the acts of introducing and reading a novel-length text with first grade children for the first time. We collected and analyzed the story discussions that occurred in conjunction with the book as the teacher read it aloud (with children following in their own copies of the book as best they could) to identify the goals, instructional strategies, and focus of the talk the teacher used to help children reason actively as they read a challenging text. Many of the instructional strategies the teacher demonstrated or asked children to perform are ones that have been identified in previous studies, such as monitoring and summarizing. However, the teacher also provided support in ways that may have particular potential to help readers negotiate longer narratives, such as reaching back through story content to prepare for re-entering the text, helping children visualize and enact the story when illustrations are unavailable, lifting and identifying important plot details they may have overlooked, and calling attention to the form/format of chapter book layout.

In a recent survey of practice, Baumann, Hoffman, Duffy-Hester, and Ro (2000) determined that a significant number of elementary teachers (83%) offer children opportunities to read novels in addition to adopted basal texts. Existing research, however, has provided little insight as to what specifically children may require to move successfully into complex narratives. This experienced teacher appeared to support the reading of difficult text in myriad ways. These included modeling meaning-making; monitoring children's understanding; eliciting children's input; serving as an appreciative co-responder; acting the meanings of story words, phrases, and feelings; inviting child enactments; serving as expert strategist; negotiating divergent explanations; reacting, and withholding reactions, to children's responses; and serving as a focusing agent. We watched her gather purposeful recountings of previous chapters (using, for example, a child's previous absence as a reason to ask for a retelling of a previous read-aloud); wonder aloud in ways that encouraged students' own puzzling; introduce realia to make the reading "sense-able" (a recorder, a castle map); receive questions and leave them open for conjecture; use the power of the pause, "hmmmm," to make space for thinking; provide for research by asking such questions as "What *is* a tunic?"; appreciate expressive language aloud; reread for real reasons; look back for clarification; accept speculations but ask for support; read expressively; provide "just right" help at the appropriate time, as when she asked, "What about this word *apparition*? Do we need to talk about it?"; share personal responses and value the responses of others; link with the children's lives; help students focus on some aspect of the artistry or craft of the text; listen carefully; draw children's ideas together; and weave random noticings into literary conversations.

Surely, as we continue to examine children's meaning-making, the forms and purposes of their literacy will demand more well-understood and more finely tuned ideas of appropriate instructional strategies for specific text forms. As Winograd and Johnston (1987) posited, the largest portion of children's reading is fantasy, requiring not just the traditional recall/restate demands of school-like reading, but a suspension of disbelief, an application of "what-if," and an imaginative play that involves "decontextualization and recontextualization, processes that seem to be at the heart of comprehension" (p. 219). As teachers help children make transitions to new (to them) text forms, their instructional moves must acknowledge the strategies children will require.

REFERENCES

Baumann, J. F., Hoffman, J. V., Duffy-Hester, A. M., & Ro, J. M. (2000). The First R yesterday and today: U.S. elementary reading instruction practices reported by teachers and administrators. *Reading Research Quarterly, 35*, 338-377.

Beaver, J. (2001). *Developmental reading assessment.* Parsippany, N.J.: Pearson.

Dickinson, D. K., & Smith, M. W. (1994). Long-term effects of preschool teachers' book readings on low-income children's vocabulary and story comprehension. *Reading Research Quarterly, 29*, 104-122.

Dole, J. A., & Duffy, G. G. (1991). Moving from the old to the new: Research on reading comprehension instruction. *Review of Educational Research, 61*, 239-264.

Duke, N., Bennett-Armistead, V. S., & Roberts, E. (2002). Bridging the gap between learning to read and reading to learn. In D. Barone & L. M. Morrow (Eds.), *Literacy and young children: Research-based practices* (pp. 226-242). New York: Guilford.

Eeds, M., & Well, D. (1989) Grand conversations: An exploration of meaning construction in literature study groups. *Research in the Teaching of English, 23*, 4-29.

Elley, W. B. (1989). Vocabulary acquisition from listening to stories. *Reading Research Quarterly, 24*, 174-187.

Farrell, E., & Squire, J. (1990). *Transactions with literature: A fifty-year perspective.* Urbana, IL: National Council of Teachers of English.

Fielding, L. G., & Pearson, P. D. (1994). Reading comprehension: What works. *Educational Leadership, 51*(5), 62-68.

Fleming, D. (1998). *Lunch.* New York: Henry Holt.

Glaser, B. G., & Strauss, A. L. (1967). *The discovery of grounded theory: Strategies for qualitative research.* Chicago: Aldine.

Graves, B., & Liang, L. A. (2004). Transitional chapter books: An update. *Book Links, 13*, 12-16.

Jewell, T., & Pratt, D. (1999). Literature discussions in the primary grades: Children's thoughtful discourse about books and what teachers can do to make it happen. *The Reading Teacher, 52*, 842-850.

Kiefer, B. Z. (1995). *The potential of picturebooks: From visual literacy to aesthetic understanding.* Englewood Cliffs, NJ: Merrill.

Langer, J. A. (1994). A response-based approach to reading literature. *Language Arts, 71*, 203-211.

Maloch, B. (2004). One teacher's journey: Transitioning into literature discussion groups. *Language Arts, 81*, 312-322.

Martinez, M., & Roser, N. L. (1994). Children's responses to a chapter book across grade levels: Implications for sustained text. In C. K. Kinzer & D. J. Leu (Eds.), *Multidimensional aspects of literacy research, theory, and practice. Forty-third Yearbook of the National Reading Conference* (pp. 317-324). Chicago: National Reading Conference.

Moll, L., Saez, R., & Dworin, J. (2001). Exploring biliteracy: Two student case examples of writing as a social process. *Elementary School Journal, 10*, 435-449.

National Institute of Child Health and Human Development. (2000). *Report of the National Reading Panel. Teaching children to read: An evidence-based assessment of the scientific research literature on reading and its implications for reading instruction: Reports of the subgroups* (NIH Publication No. 00-4754). Washington, DC: U.S. Government Printing Office.

Pressley, M. (2000). What should comprehension instruction be the instruction of? In M. L. Kamil, P. B. Mosenthal, P. D. Pearson, & R. Barr (Eds.), *Handbook of reading research* (Vol. III, pp. 361-379). Mahwah, NJ: Erlbaum.

Pressley, M. (2001). *Effective beginning reading instruction.* Executive summary and paper commissioned by the National Reading Conference. Chicago, IL: National Reading Conference.

Roser, N., & Martinez, M. G. (1985). Roles adults play in preschoolers' responses to literature. *Language Arts, 62*, 485-490.

Roser, N., Martinez, M. G., McDonnold, K., & Fuhrken, C. (2004). Beginning chapter books: Their features and their support of children's reading. *Yearbook of the National Reading Conference, 53*, 308-320.

Short, K., Kauffman, G., Kaser, S., Kahn, L., & Crawford, K. (1999). Teacher watching: Examining teacher talk in literature circles. *Language Arts, 76*, 377-385.

Sipe, L. (2000). The construction of literary understanding by first and second graders in oral responses to picture storybook readalouds. *Reading Research Quarterly, 35*, 252-275.

Smolkin, L. B., & Donovan, C. A. (2001). The contexts of comprehension: The information book read aloud, comprehension acquisition, and comprehension instruction in a first grade classroom. *Elementary School Journal, 102*, 97-122.

Strauss, A., & Corbin, J. (1998). *Basics of qualitative research: Techniques and procedures for developing grounded theory* (2nd ed.). Thousand Oaks, CA: Sage.

Winograd, P., & Johnston, P. (1987). Some considerations for advancing the teaching of reading comprehension. *Educational Psychologist, 22*, 213-230.

Winthrop, E. (1985). *The castle in the attic.* New York: Yearling.

Analyzing the Production of Third Space in Classroom Literacy Events

Deborah Wells Rowe
Kevin M. Leander
Vanderbilt University

Despite the growing interest in third space theory, only a few studies in literacy education have empirically described the production of third space literacy environments in classrooms (e.g., Dyson, 1997; Gutierrez, Baquedano-Lopez, & Turner, 1997; Leander, 2002b; Sheehy, 2002). Gutierrez and her colleagues have led the way in this effort but have primarily focused on the discursive aspects of interaction. In this paper, we present a theoretical framework for analyzing material and embodied features of third space events and then use one example from a first grade classroom to illustrate how such analyses can provide insights into students' hybrid literacy performances.

THEORETICAL CONCEPTIONS OF THIRD SPACE

"Thirdness:" Hybridity, Contest, Transformation

The notion of third space has been in circulation in education (e.g., Gutierrez, Rymes, & Larson, 1995; Moje et al., 2004), cultural geography (Soja, 1996), and cultural studies (Bhabha, 1994) for some time. Because of the varying theoretical and empirical interests of researchers, third space has been conceptualized in a variety of ways (as have first and second space for that matter). Nevertheless, common across these disparate traditions is a view of third space as places for critical coming together (Soja, 1996). Hybridity is a defining characteristic of third space. A recent review of this work by Moje et al. (2004) has noted that third space may bring together texts, contexts, relationships, identities, and material spaces from a variety of Discourse (Gee, 1999) communities. Third space is the borderland (Wilson, 2000) or in-between space that is produced in the articulation of cultural differences (Bhabha, 1994). Such spaces oppose the notion of binaries such as out-of-school/in-school or spontaneous concepts/academic concepts (Bhabha, 1994; Moje et al., 2004; Soja, 1996). Third space draws selectively from binary categories, and through creative recombination of these perspectives, creates new modes of thinking that extend beyond them (Soja, 1996). For this reason, third space remains open and resistant to closure.

At the same time, third space is often associated with contest. Third space is created as people resist cultural authority and bring different experiences to bear on their interpretation of cultural events and symbols (Bhabha, 1994; Soja, 1996; Wilson, 2004). Soja, in particular, viewed third spaces as " 'counterspaces,' . . . of resistance to the dominant order" (p. 68) that come into being because of the subordinate or marginalized positions of participants. Not surprisingly, third space's challenges to recognized boundaries (e.g., between home and school knowledge, or between traditional roles of teacher and learner) may be met with increased concern by dominant groups who hold to traditional categories and modes of thinking (Sheehy, 2002), making them sites of tension and struggle.

A number of writers have highlighted the possibility that the tensions inherent in third space can be generative exactly because of creative hybridity and contest. Soja (1996) argued that the process of "critical thirding" (p. 5) at work in third space involves a kind of restructuring of existing knowledge. By drawing selectively from opposing categories, new alternatives are created. In producing third spaces, people draw from the resources of existing spaces and Discourses, but imaginatively rework them to create hybridized practices that transform the practices and ideologies from which they were formed (Dyson, 1999; Wilson, 2000). Such interactions create new sociocultural terrain by altering what counts as knowledge and as representations of knowledge. From this perspective, third space interactions have the potential to propel learning and promote cultural and educational change (Gutierrez et al., 1997). Difference is seen as a major resource for learning rather than as a deficit to be overcome (Gutierrez, 2000; Kress, 1997).

Conceptions of "Space"

The foregoing discussion of third space focused on cross-disciplinary views of "thirdness" that revolve around hybridity, social struggle, and learning through imaginative transformation of existing cultural resources. Yet to be addressed are the varying views of "space"—material, discursive, or imagined—that are implicit in the theoretical and empirical work reviewed.

Perhaps not surprisingly, third space research conducted by literacy educators has often focused on "discursive spaces" (Gutierrez, Baquedano-Lopez, & Alvarez, 2001; Leander, 2001; Sheehy, 2002.) That is, the term "space" is used to refer to patterns of talk and interaction rather than as a reference to material or embodied features of space. For example, in an influential line of third space research, Gutierrez and Stone (2000) focused on "social space," linking it to Bourdieu's (1991) notion of habitus. For them, third space was defined as a "discursive space in which alternative and competing discourses and positionings transform conflict and difference into rich zones of collaboration and learning" (Gutierrez & Stone, 2000, p. 157). While they mentioned material and embodied features of these social spaces such as gaze and gesture, for the most part, the focus of their analysis remained on varying patterns of talk and what counted as knowledge in different kinds of classroom interactions.

Recently, however, several literacy researchers (e.g., Leander, 2002a, 2004; Sheehy, 2004; Wilson, 2000, 2004) have begun to examine literacy interactions through the trialectics of Lefebvre (1991) and Soja (1996), including the three-way relations of first, second, and third spaces as well as the interactions among sociality, historicality, and spatiality. Lefebvre has eloquently made the case for the importance of a spatial analysis of human life. He argued that most critical inquiry into human experience has focused on the elements of time and social relations, while "the spatiality of history and social life was, for the most part, frozen into the background as an 'external' container, stage, or environment for social action" (Soja, 1996, p. 44). Challenging the ways in which space was either avoided, set apart, or moved to the background in social analysis, Lefebvre argued that the social and spatial aspects of human life are mutually constitutive, with social life routinely producing spatiality and with spatiality producing social life. Further, he argued that non-verbal (material and spatial) aspects of life are not fully captured by language, with its sequential, historical narratives.

In this article, we will argue that spatial analysis is particularly important for research on third space events in classrooms. When students create points of contact between dominant school Discourse and that of their peer groups and homes, they draw not only on the linguistic resources of these Discourses, but also on embodied and spatial ways of making meaning. The results are hybridized performances that often challenge teachers' expectations about school literacy. In order for educators to capitalize on the generative nature of third space events, they need ways of interpreting the socio-spatial frames indexed and of understanding how students combine them and shift between them.

THEORETICAL FRAMEWORK FOR MATERIAL/ SPATIAL ANALYSIS OF THIRD SPACE

The Social Production of Space

Social and critical geographers such as LeFebvre (1991) and Soja (1989; 1996) have argued that material space is not a given, but instead is socially produced through the operation of a variety of social practices that underlie and structure it. They have problematized simple notions of the material world as "real" and objectively knowable and have argued instead for a trialectical perspective on space as it is *perceived* by the senses, cognitively *conceived*, and *lived* by participants. Soja (1996), following LeFebvre, has referred to these types of space, respectively, as first space, second space, and third space. Table 1 provides an overview of the defining characteristics of each type of space. Briefly, *first space* includes the aspects of the material world that are directly sensible (or seem so) and are open to

Table 1 LeFebvre[1] and Soja's[2] Trialectical Perspective on Spatiality

SPATIAL PERSPECTIVE		
First Space	**Second Space**	**Third Space**
Perceived space	Conceived space	Lived space
Materialized spatial practice	Representations of Space	Spaces of Representation
"Real" space	Imagined space	"Real" & imagined
The material world that is directly sensible and open to measurement and description	Discursively devised representations of space and spatial representations of power	Forms that draw on material and represented space but extend beyond them
Examples: Built Environment Objects Embodiment Spatial Relations of objects and people in places Movement	Examples: Maps Conceptions of space in laws, rules, and norms regulating spatial access and arrangement	Examples: Imaginative use of objects and bodies to appropriate and change dominant representations of space; Recasting pop culture superheroes as characters in school writing (Dyson, 2003)

[1]Lefebvre, 1991
[2]Soja, 1996

measurement and description. *Second space* involves mental representations of space that are often expressed visually in the creation of maps and images or verbally in laws, rules, and norms about the distribution of and access to spaces. Soja noted that conceived (or second) space, what he called "the imagined geography" (p. 79), tends to become the "real" geography because representations of space often have a powerful role in ordering spatial practice. An example is the way that road maps channel traffic into a set of visually represented (but not totally inclusive) routes. *Third space* uses imagination to appropriate first space places, objects, and bodies along with second space representations of them in order to create a "counterspace" of resistance to the dominant order.

This trialectical perspective on spatiality has been a powerful heuristic for helping us form research questions for the spatial analyses of classroom literacy events. Our analysis of first space involves describing material features of classroom events. Second space analysis involves identification of dominant and marginalized rules, norms, and representations that shape spatial practice. Third space analysis involves identifying hybrid spaces where multiple Discourses are present and then identifying which cultural frames are being indexed. In addition, we examine the extent to which non-dominant practices are publicly introduced into dominant school events and how they are valued by various groups of participants.

Frames

Overall, the goal of our spatial analysis of classroom literacy events is first to understand how arrangements of places, bodies, and objects are produced by, and productive of, social conceptions and representations of space and, second, to explore how third space events use multiple cultural frames as resources for learning and social participation. (One of the ironies of first space analyses is that material space is necessarily described from some second space vantage point; that is, descriptions of physical and embodied features of classroom interaction must be constructed in terms of some conception of space.) We might consider the analysis of space in terms of "framings" as a close cousin to the analysis of recurrent patterns of social practice within a Discourse (Gee, 1990). The configuration signals how social life organizes a whole host of elements, including "people, artifacts, symbols, tools, technologies, actions, interactions, times, places, and ways of speaking, listening, writing, feeling, believing, thinking and valuing" (Gee, 2000, p. 191). In the configuration, "literacy bits" (Gee, 2000, p. 193) are produced in relation to everything else.

To consider more fully the spatial features of classroom configurations, we have found Goffman's (1974) approach to frame analysis helpful. He argued that people understand everyday interactions in relation to frames or schemata that consist of their social knowledge about the linguistic and material organization of socio-spatial events. These frames are "not merely a matter of the mind" (p. 247), however, because they correspond to the material organization of activity and because people use them to shape the way they present themselves to others. In particular, frames guide the production of the "personal front," the social roles people "put on or enact through the use of conventionalized sign equipment, gesture, posture, dress, use of material objects, and aspects of our surroundings" (Scollon & Scollon, 2003, p. 74).

Goffman's (1974) analyses also revealed that participants frequently shifted between multiple, co-present frames for interaction, creating laminated social spaces (e.g., Prior, 1998). He termed unexpected or unauthorized moves between frames variously as "breaking frame" or as shifts in the "footing" of the event (Goffman, 1974, 1981). Shifts in footing produce different social relations and recruit different forms of embodiment and arrangements of objects. Shifts in footing provide crucial moments for examining frames for interaction and the facets of the personal front by which they are performed (Goffman, 1974; Scollon & Scollon, 2003). Contrastive analysis of embodiment and spatial relations before and after frame breaks highlights the spatial norms and rules implicit in social interaction.

Indexicality

Scollon and Scollon's (2003) recent work on geosemiotics has provided additional grounding for studying spatial features of classroom literacy events. They noted that it matters where signs are located in the world stating, "Indexicality, action, and identity are all anchored in the physical spaces and real times of our material world" (p. 14). Social practices are indexical to the spaces where they are emplaced in the world and therefore should be analyzed "in place." Scollon and Scollon have highlighted two types of sign functioning, both of which involve indexicality. Some signs (e.g. printed text, actions, objects) "point to" the physical spaces where they are located. For example, school materials such as pointed "teacher" scissors and smaller, blunt-tipped "kid" scissors are understandable in relation to their emplacement in classrooms where the difference in the physical size of adults and children is marked as an important attribute and where adults are assumed capable of handling sharp objects and children are not. Signs can also symbolically index spaces not physically present. For example, adult scissors can index home or peer spaces where children are presumed competent to use them.

DATA ANALYSIS PROCEDURES

Data Source

We launched the Talking Spaces Project to study the embodied and spatial features of literacy learning in classrooms and to explore the variation and similarity in literacy practices for K-12 students of different ages. Data analyzed for the larger project were drawn from two year-long ethnographies of literacy learning in public school classrooms at the high school (Leander, 2002b) and elementary school levels (Rowe, Fitch, & Bass, 2003). For this paper, illustrations are drawn from micro-analyses of data collected by Rowe in a first grade writer's workshop and reported elsewhere with a different emphasis (Rowe, Fitch, & Bass, 2001, 2003).

Analysis of Frame Breaks

Analysis of frame breaks was guided by the research questions generated to tap first and second space perspectives on classroom interactions. Questions about first space included: How can the built environment, embodiment, spatial relations, and movement be described for this literacy event? How are bodies and objects rearranged over time? Second space questions included: What dominant and marginalized frames (i.e., ideas, rules, norms) for spatial practice are present? Are there shifts/breaks in expected frames for spatial practice? How do frames shape embodiment and physical spaces? To address these questions, narrative transcripts and videotapes were reviewed to identify *frame breaks* or shifts in footing. Goffman (1974) noted that when frame breaks occur, participants are aware that something new or different is happening. Following suggestions by Scollon and Scollon (2003), we looked for moments of realignment or management of the personal front, transitions between front and backstage, and out-of-character or discrepant roles. Cues for boundary movements included changes in the personal front as evidenced by changes in gaze, gesture, posture, ways of speaking, objects/clothing carried or set aside, interpersonal distance, and movements in space.

From still images recorded at these transitions, we created *filtered stills* by sketching the relative positions of key objects and people (see Figure 1, for example). We also created F-formation maps (Kendon, 1990, 1992; Leander, 2002b) showing spatial and orientational relationships between participants through overhead mapping of the relative location of people, the orientation of their bodies, and the direction of their gaze (see Figure 2). According to Kendon (1990), an F-formation arises as people create spatial and orientational relationships to each other that indicate who is included in the interaction. Kendon argued that the orientation of the lower body strongly determines the orientation of individuals and, therefore, F-formations can be largely traced along the lines of this lower-body orientation.

Figure 1 Launching *Edward Scissorsman*: Embodied and spatial relations for "giving a play."

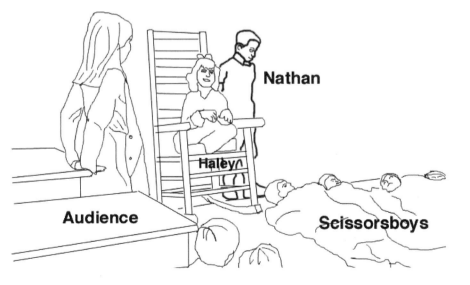

Indexicality Analysis

Indexicality analysis was guided by research questions generated to explore third space perspectives and focused on inferring the Discourses and socially produced spaces being indexed in each performance. Specifically we asked: Are multiple frames indexed? Are dominant frames contested? Are first and second space resources appropriated and rearticulated? To what extent are third space interactions made public? To what extent are third space knowledge and forms of representation valued? Inferences were based both upon our ethnographic understandings of the history of participants, objects, and space in these classrooms and our microanalyses of discursive and spatial practices, especially at frame breaks.

We chose to examine indexicality at frame breaks because they represented points of transition and sometimes points of tension. For these events, school frames (e.g., "giving a play," "writer's workshop") were identified as dominant because of the powerful institutional forces working to construct and maintain them. We then identified other frames being indexed and noted to whom they were made available. Gutierrez and her colleagues (Gutierrez, Larson, & Kreuter, 1995; Gutierrez et al., 1997; Gutierrez, Rymes, & Larson, 1995) have suggested that third space events in classrooms are most powerful when competing scripts or frames are made public for discussion and become resources for learning. To this end, we looked for hybrid practices that publicly incorporated

Figure 2 Overhead map of embodied positions, orientations, and movement during *Edward Scissorsman.*

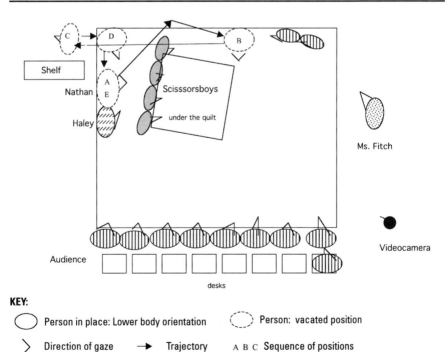

multiple social and cultural frames. Then, we examined the video and field note data for cues as to how the classroom teacher, students, and ourselves as researcher/participants reacted to third space practices. Finally, we considered in what ways third space knowledge and forms of representation were valued and/or remained sites of tension and contest.

FINDINGS: A SPATIAL ANALYSIS OF THE *EDWARD SCISSORSMAN* PLAY

To illustrate the potentials of material and spatial analyses of third space events, we present a brief discussion of a student drama performance recorded in a first grade classroom where Rowe conducted a year-long study of connections between drama and literacy learning (Rowe et al., 2003). Drama was introduced as an option in writer's workshop from the beginning of the year, and the ethnography tracked the ways children took up invitations to include drama in their reading and writing activities. Children often chose to write and informally perform plays for their classmates during the Author's Chair sharing time at the end of each writer's workshop period. By the January 10 performance of the *Edward Scissorsman* play, children had considerable shared history to define what "giving a play" or "being an audience" meant in this classroom.

Nathan: "The Original Tool and Scissors Man"

The strand of analysis presented here focuses on Nathan, the child who played the lead role of Edward Scissorsman in the play. Some background is necessary to understand why and how the role of Edward Scissorsman was created and how this role reflected important aspects of Nathan's history with his teacher and peers. From the beginning of the year, Nathan was the most resistant writer in the class. He had developed a number of avoidance strategies that allowed him to be peripherally engaged in writing activities during workshop time without having to put pen to paper. The most persistent and publicly discussed was his strategy of using scissors to cut paper shapes. When Ms. Fitch, his teacher, talked with him about the relation of his cutting to writing or reading, he claimed he planned to use the cutouts to illustrate a book or perhaps as a prop for a to-be-written playscript. Although Ms. Fitch pushed him toward print, he remained quite resistant to writing. To lighten the tone of their writing conferences, she celebrated his unquestioned skill with scissors and, with a touch of humor, called him the "Scissorsman." In January, she suggested that they co-author the *Edward Scissorsman* play in a purposeful attempt to connect his resistant Scissorsman persona to the drama and writing practices of the workshop.

Before turning to the performance itself, it is important to note that Nathan's affinity for scissors figured into his interactions with peers as well. Scissors were not only a symbol of academic resistance but also a symbol of power in the peer world. For several months, Nathan had been in the habit of borrowing Ms. Fitch's large "teacher scissors" from the workbasket behind her desk. Although this was technically allowed, there was a largely unenforced rule that children should use child-sized scissors unless a special task required the larger pointed version usually reserved for adults. Nathan stretched this rule by finding numerous tasks that required the use of adult scissors. In peer interactions recorded during the workshop, Nathan used the adult scissors as a means of establishing a power hierarchy in the peer group. Therefore, scissors, as material objects, had a history in both the workshop and peer interactions. In the following sections, we briefly describe spatial and verbal features of the *Edward Scissorsman* play and then discuss how spatial analyses helped us understand the work Nathan accomplished with this hybrid literacy performance.

The Edward Scissorsman Play

As the play opened, a row of children stood or sat on the floor facing the rug area serving as the stage (see Figure 1.) Haley, playing the mother role, sat in Ms. Fitch's rocking chair at stage left. Nathan stood at stage left (Figure 2, location "A") beside the four Scissorsboys (babies) who were lying on the floor under a quilt ready for the production to begin. Behind his back, he held two pairs of adult-sized scissors representing his character's scissor-hands. When Ms. Fitch asked Nathan to begin the performance, the classroom lights were turned off by another student. In a dramatic announcer's voice, Nathan introduced the play, "Presenting Edward Scissorsman!"

When the lights were turned on, Nathan stood center stage in the back (Figure 2, location B). He looked out into the audience and spoke loudly, "No, I'm not *that* guy!" He shifted his gaze to the off-stage region and began to move off stage left in a swaggering walk (Figure 2, location C). His voice trailed off unintelligibly, "I'm just the guy that . . ." (see Figure 3).

Snapping her fingers, Ms. Fitch called his name. She extended her arm, pointing to him, and motioned for him to put his hands behind his back. Nathan moved on stage at left back (Figure 2, location D), put his hands behind his back and momentarily faced the audience. He adopted a "silly" pose (see Figure 4). Smiling, he tilted his head to the side. With feet stationary, he swayed his hips side to side. Then he moved to stand beside and behind Haley seated in the rocking chair at stage left

Figure 3 Breaking Frame: Embodied and spatial cues for "fooling around."

(Figure 2, location E). He turned his body to face Ms. Fitch standing at stage right. Holding his body still and upright, he then dropped his gaze to the floor as Haley began to speak her first line of dialogue.

Space does not allow description of the entire performance, but near the end of the play, Nathan's embodiment of Edward Scissorsman became particularly dramatic. As Ms. Fitch read the final line of narration, Nathan turned stage right in a sweeping circle, stepping and moving his arms in a rhythmic dance displaying the opening and closing scissors. He ended in a pose with one leg raised to tip toe, arms pointing diagonally down toward his feet, and his head lowered to gaze down at the scissors. With appreciative audience applause and catcalls in the background, he shifted to his writer's workshop role as director of the play. He authoritatively pointed the scissors at each actor as he introduced the child's real name and role in the play. As he began to lose audience attention, he crouched down and rhythmically moved to stage left. Then, standing erect, he faced the audience with his chin up. He swung his body side to side, smiling mischievously. He had now regained the audience's attention. He pranced stage right several steps. Then with a quick swivel of his hip, he turned back to grin at Ms. Fitch as he announced, "*I* was Edward Smartypants!"

Frame Breaks and Hybridity

The opening segment of this play contained several frame breaks. Once both actors and audience were in place, Ms. Fitch invited Nathan to repeat his announcement of the title of the drama, a kind of formal bracketing of the shift from writer's workshop to the "giving a play" frame. Once the lights were turned back on, the actors were, by the conventions of the play performance frame, assumed to be in the story world. Nathan, however, created an immediate shift of footing by

Figure 4 Nathan's "silly" pose: Performing hybridity across "fooling around" and "giving a play" frames.

gazing directly at the audience and engaging them in conversation about his character: "No, I'm not *that* guy . . . " It was not his words but, instead, his facial expression, body posture, and gait as he moved off stage that provided the most important cues for interpreting his performance (see Figure 3). Nathan did not address the audience from an official workshop role as an actor or as the director of the play, another role he legitimately held. Neither did he address the audience from his starring role as Edward, Senior. Instead, Nathan's swaggering walk was a direct call to his classmates within a familiar peer frame for "fooling around." He intentionally upstaged the other actors. His actions and comments were an example of "flooding out" (Goffman, 1974), an occasion where an actor breaks from the drama frame in an unexpected or unauthorized way to address the audience. In doing so, he momentarily created a laminated space that foregrounded a new F-formation with the audience (Figure 1, location B), and that backgrounded the F-formation constructed by the actors ready for their first lines.

Ms. Fitch's verbal reprimand and gestured directives show she was aware of this shift in footing. Nathan's response to Ms. Fitch was mixed. Although he moved back on stage and put his hands behind his back as directed, the orientation of his trunk was open to his peers but not his teacher (see Figure 2, location D, and Figure 4). Rather than reconstructing the F-formation with Ms. Fitch and the other actors, he used facial expression, gaze, and body posture to construct the "fooling around" frame with his peers. Here, he once again violated the convention of backgrounding his interactions to that of the actor who was about to speak on stage. At the same time, the hybridity of his performance was evident in his body posture. With hands behind his back, he had begun to take up the role of Edward. Following this brief moment of flooding out, he moved back into the F-formation with the other actors and awaited his entrance to the scene (see Figure 2, location E).

Constructing a Hybrid Space

Long-term ethnographic description in this first grade classroom made it possible to uncover some of the ways that Nathan's choices of dramatic props and arrangement of his body indexed a number of co-present frames. For the *Edward Scissorsman* play, these included the school frame for "giving a play" in Ms. Fitch's writer's workshop, a peer frame for "fooling around," and, of course, the imagined story frame where Edward, Sr., and his children lived. The construction of these frames was accomplished using embodied, spatial, and material resources with histories in previous interactions. The scissors, for example, had a history in writer's workshop as literacy tools, as material evidence of differences in adult and child roles, and as the preferred tools of Nathan's resistance to writing. In peer interactions, large scissors were constructed as symbols of power. As props within this first grade play, they indexed popular culture images from the movie, *Edward Scissorhands* (Burton, DiNovi, & Thompson, 1990) and from martial arts shows. Nathan's use of scissors in the play allowed him to construct a hybrid space where he could simultaneously participate and resist.

Contested Spaces

Although Nathan had, indeed, adopted powerful literate roles as the co-author and director of the play and had allowed his role as a performer in a writer's workshop play to position him as a good student, he had not entirely "played it straight" during the performance. Nathan refused to be completely co-opted into the dominant frame for school plays. Instead, he used the dramatic performance as an opportunity to rearticulate elements of school and peer frames to create a hybrid event that was less serious than school and more literate than his usual play with peers. His "Edward Smartypants" comment was telling in that Nathan publicly acknowledged that he had been parodying his role as Edward for the enjoyment of his peers. With this statement, he was no longer simply fooling around for the enjoyment of his peers but also challenging Ms. Fitch's efforts to tame his Scissorsman persona and his performance of resistance by incorporating it into the dominant school frame.

Nathan constructed the social space of the play as both a site of contest and of participation in school literacy. Where, one moment, he directly addressed his peers with exaggerated movements and "silly" gestures, in the next he stood quietly on stage waiting for the entrance of his character in the story world. By turns, he was a "cool kid," an actor playing Edward Scissorsman, a director, and a playwright. This was a "both/and" performance, drawing on the cultural resources available in different cultural spaces and re-articulating them. These resources were as much spatial and embodied as they were discursive.

Reactions to Nathan's Third Space Performance

A final aspect of our analysis of third space events involved examining the extent to which third space interactions were valued (or not) as opportunities for learning. Adult reactions are particularly important in school contexts because teachers, researchers, and parents have considerable power over the structure of classroom events and what counts as literacy there. Conclusions related to this research question were drawn from analysis of the video data of the event, data recorded in previous and subsequent events, and interviews of key participants.

In this case, it was clear that Ms. Fitch thoughtfully and purposefully created an opportunity for Nathan to bring his resistant "scissorsman" persona into mainstream school literacy practices, hoping that his success in this event would motivate future writing. However, while she hoped Nathan would draw on his existing frames in order to participate in school literacy events, at the time, neither she nor Rowe (as participant/observer) fully anticipated or perhaps fully appreciated the type of hybrid spaces he created. Field notes record Ms. Fitch's excitement about Nathan's participation as a writer and actor but also her observation that he had tended to be "silly" during the play, a term she and Rowe had often used to describe behaviors designed to gain peer attention. Neither Ms. Fitch nor Rowe could fully understand why Nathan had continued to "fool around" in the play. In a pre-performance conversation, Ms. Fitch had explicitly told Nathan that she was trying to find ways to interest him in reading and writing and that they had based the play on his ideas for this reason. She had asked for his help and asked him not to act "silly." In retrospect, it appears that while Ms. Fitch and Rowe sanctioned and encouraged Nathan's use of resources from peer culture, they hoped he would reframe these resources within the dominant school frame. This expectation is seen in the writing of the script where Ms. Fitch was influential in recasting Nathan's Scissorsman character as cooperative rather than resistant. Nathan, however, gave the role of Edward, Sr., a more humorous and resistant reading, largely through embodied features of the performance.

At the time, neither Ms. Fitch nor Rowe could fully explain their discomfort with Nathan's hybrid performance, though they continued to value it because it had lured him into reading and writing. While they anticipated the need for curricular third spaces, they did not predict the kinds of hybrid and contested spaces that might be created. Spatial microanalyses of the sort conducted here, have, in retrospect, provided a means of explicitly examining the ways by which Nathan imaginatively created a hybrid space allowing both participation and resistance.

CONCLUSION

With the increasing multimodality of classroom literacy practices, an important problem in literacy research is how to interpret student performances and compositions. What is it that students are making and doing in what we deem to be literacy events? How do current means of understanding these events constrain or enable us as educators? How, in particular, do we interpret those events that produce something new, unanticipated? In this paper, we have argued that the analysis of third space provides an important means of critically and creatively interpreting such events. We have further argued that third space analysis necessarily involves interpretation of the relations of textual and discursive practices to material resources and practices (e.g., material texts and tools, embodied posture, gait, gesture, and position). In order to understand literacy events, we need to disrupt a text-centric and logo-centric perspective and move toward a broader semiotic and embodied analysis of meaning making. Through such analyses, we may better understand that literacy is intertwined with material, spatial, and embodied practices and cannot be understood apart from them.

Beyond arguing for the value of third space analysis, in this paper we have begun to sketch one methodological approach. If third space is a "critical coming together," then what means do we use to read creative recombinations? In rejecting binaries, how do we interpret the in-betweenness of social and cultural borderlands in literate activity? We have recovered two familiar constructs from communication studies and have reworked them for our own ends. We have made use of *frame* and *framing*, but loosened these relatively undeveloped constructs from a strong psychological sense (as in *schema*). Drawing on Goffman's (1974) insight that frames are akin to interactional *footings*, our analyses examine the ways multimodal resources are brought to bear as resources for framing. We read *frames* as configurations of semiotic and embodied relations that provide participants with cues that reveal when an event and its relations of power and meaning have changed. Like participants in the events, our analysis of frames as social spaces makes use of our implicit sense of when a new frame is being composed, either visually or auditorily. Of course, even among the research team, our implicit senses of when new frames appear are not always in agreement. Although this disagreement may be considered an analytical problem, it is also a resource. The various interpretations of framing and frame breaks demonstrate one of our central points: frames do not appear singularly but rather, like other expressions of social space, appear in multiples. Classroom spaces are complex configurations of co-present frames that provide multiple possibilities for making meaning.

In our analysis of third space, we have also attempted to describe how frames have social and cultural histories in specific places: "giving a play" in Ms. Fitch's class reconstituted a particular kind of space-time or frame. Similarly, we have examined indexical relations as a broad expression of the inter-textuality, or rather, inter-spatiality, produced between focal events and widely circulating meanings, discourses, and objects. Nathan's scissors are a key example in this regard. The scissors are indexical to bodies, other objects, and bits of talk in the configuration of the play performance and yet are also indexical to the social spaces of *Edward Scissorhands* (Burton, DiNovi, & Thompson, 1990) as a film, to writer's workshop as a school literacy event, to peer interactions with scissors, and to popular culture images of martial arts as symbols of power. For us, third space analysis is about interpreting the production of the dynamic relations among social spaces of all varieties and of all time spans, including those produced on the fly and those that are geographically and temporally attenuated.

The notion of multiple framings also raises some methodological issues to be considered in future research. In particular, researchers need to analyze how children, their peers, and teachers position themselves in relation to one another. Our analyses, here, have focused almost exclusively on Nathan, in part, because of limitations on the size of this report, but also because the focus of the single camera used to record the *Edward Scissorsman* play followed the student actors while presenting only partial views of the audience and Ms. Fitch. In future studies, we plan to use multiple cameras to record classroom interactions in order to capture more of this complexity. At the same time, we recognize that it is important to analyze carefully the conceptions of (second) space implicit in research decisions about camera positioning and focus.

Lastly, our analysis suggests insights relevant to literacy teaching and research. First, when Ms. Fitch imagined and worked to create a space for Nathan to succeed in the classroom, she constructed this space, on the one hand, as an alternative distinct from that of the classroom (i.e., a bracketed, "special" space for the resistant student.) On the other hand, she constructed it as a space very much like the usual classroom space for "giving a play." Nathan, however, was less interested in producing a performance in a familiar space than in working the borders between spaces—in hybridizing. We interpret his Edward Scissorsman performance as a call for us to consider critically how spaces for struggling, diverse, or resistant students are bracketed and dominated by school space. Even with innovative teaching that provides support for a broad range of literacy performances to "take place" or make space, the curricular drive toward new space may unintentionally reproduce old space (Sheehy, 2004).

Moreover, across a range of classrooms, and especially in multicultural classrooms, we need a better understanding of the linguistic and embodied literacy practices that are present and how these practices are regulated and valued. The analyses presented in this article show that even in classrooms with a comparatively low degree of cultural diversity, it can be difficult to understand adequately students' embodied practices without close analysis. It is likely that many embodied aspects of interaction involving students from diverse backgrounds are all the more undervalued or misunderstood. Culturally sensitive observation of embodied and spatial cues may help teachers reflect on the nature of hybrid environments and enable them to expect and value the different practices and forms of knowledge that necessarily result.

REFERENCES

Bhabha, H. K. (1994). *The location of culture.* New York: Routledge.

Bourdieu, P. (1991). *Language and symbolic power* (J. B. Thompson, G. Raymond, & M. Adamson, Trans.). Cambridge, MA: Harvard University Press.

Burton, T. (Producer/Director/Writer), DiNovi, D. (Producer), & Thompson, C. (Writer). (1990). *Edward Scissorhands* [motion picture], United States: 20th Century Fox.

Dyson, A. (1997). *Writing superheroes. Contemporary childhood, popular culture, and classroom literacy.* New York: Teacher College Press.

Dyson, A. (1999). Transforming transfer: Unruly children, contrary texts, and the persistence of the pedagogical order. *Review of Research in Education, 24,* 141-171.

Dyson, A. (2003). *The brothers and sisters learn to write: Popular literacies in childhood and school cultures.* New York: Teachers College Press.

Gee, J. P. (1990). *Social linguistics and literacies: Ideology in discourses.* New York: The Falmer Press.

Gee, J. P. (1999). *An introduction to discourse analysis: Theory and method.* London: Routledge.

Gee, J. P. (2000). The New Literacy Studies: From 'socially situated' to the work of the social. In D. Barton, M. Hamilton, & R. Ivanic (Eds.), *Situated literacies: Reading and writing in context* (pp. 180-196). New York: Routledge.

Goffman, E. (1974). *Frame analysis. An essay on the organization of experience.* Boston: Northeastern University Press.

Goffman, E. (1981). *Forms of talk.* Philadelphia: University of Pennsylvania Press.

Gutierrez, K. (2000). Teaching and learning in the 21st century. *English Education, 32,* 290-298.

Gutierrez, K., Baquedano-Lopez, P., & Alvarez, H. (2001). Literacy as hybridity. In M. de la Luz Reyes & J. H. Halcon (Eds.), *The best for our children. Critical perspectives on literacy for Latino students* (pp. 122-141). New York: Teachers College Press.

Gutierrez, K., Baquedano-Lopez, P., & Turner, M. G. (1997). Putting language back into language arts: When the radical middle meets the third space. *Language Arts, 74,* 368-378.

Gutierrez, K., Larson, J., & Kreuter, B. (1995). Cultural tensions in the scripted classroom: The value of the subjugated perspective. *Urban Education, 29,* 410-442.

Gutierrez, K., Rymes, B., & Larson, J. (1995). Script, counterscript, and underlife in the classroom: James Brown versus Brown v. Board of Education. *Harvard Educational Review, 65,* 445-471.

Gutierrez, K., & Stone, L. D. (2000). Synchronic and diachronic dimensions of social practice: An emerging methodology for cultural-historical perspectives on literacy learning. In C. D. Lee & P. Smagorinsky *(Eds.), Vygotskian perspectives on literacy research. Constructing meaning through collaborative inquiry* (pp. 150-164). Cambridge, England: Cambridge University Press.

Kendon, A. (1990). *Conducting interaction: Patterns of behavior in focused encounters.* Cambridge, England: Cambridge University Press.

Kendon, A. (1992). The negotiation of context in face to face interaction. In A. Duranti & C. Goodwin (Eds.), *Rethinking context: Language as an interactive phenomenon* (pp. 323-334). Cambridge, England: Cambridge University Press.

Kress, G. (1997). *Before writing: Rethinking the paths to literacy.* London: Routledge.

Leander, K. M. (2001). "This is our freedom bus going home right now": Producing and hybridizing space-time contexts in pedagogical discourse. *Journal of Literacy Research, 33,* 637-679.

Leander, K. M. (2002a). Polycontextual construction zones: Mapping the expansion of schooled space and identity. *Mind, Culture, and Activity, 9,* 211-237.

Leander, K. M. (2002b). Silencing in classroom interaction: Producing and relating social spaces. *Discourse Processes, 34,* 193-235.

Leander, K. M. (2004). Reading the spatial histories of positioning. In K. Leander & M. Sheehy (Eds.), *Spatializing literacy research and practice* (pp. 115-142). New York: Peter Lang.

Lefebvre, H. (1991). *The production of space* (D. Nicholson-Smith, Trans.). Oxford, England: Blackwell.

Moje, E. B., Ciechanowski, K. M., Kramer, K., Ellis, L., Carrillo, R., & Collazo, T. (2004). Working toward third space in content area literacy: An examination of everyday funds of knowledge and Discourse. *Reading Research Quarterly, 39,* 38-70.

Prior, P. (1998). *Writing/disciplinarity: A sociohistoric account of literate activity in the academy.* Mahwah, NJ: Lawrence Erlbaum.

Rowe, D. W., Fitch, J. D., & Bass, A. S. (2001). Power, identity, and instructional stance in the writers' workshop. *Language Arts, 78,* 426-434.

Rowe, D. W., Fitch, J. D., & Bass, A. S. (2003). Toy stories as opportunities for imagination and reflection in writers' workshop. *Language Arts, 80,* 363-374.

Scollon, R., & Scollon, S. W. (2003). *Discourses in place: Language in the material world.* London: Routledge.

Sheehy, M. (2002). Illuminating constructivism: Structure, discourse, and subjectivity in a middle school classroom. *Reading Research Quarterly, 37,* 278-308.

Sheehy, M. (2004). Between a thick and a thin place: Changing literacy practices. In K. Leander & M. Sheehy (Eds.), *Spatializing literacy research and practice* (pp. 91-114). New York: Peter Lang.

Soja, E. W. (1989). *Postmodern geographies: The reassertion of space in critical social theory.* London: Verso.

Soja, E. W. (1996). *Thirdspace: Journeys to Los Angeles and other real-and-imagined places.* Malden, MA: Blackwell Publishers.

Wilson, A. (2000). There is no escape from third-space theory: Borderland Discourse and the in-between literacies of prisons. In D. Barton, M. Hamilton, & R. Ivanic (Eds.), *Situated literacies: Reading and writing in context* (pp. 45-69). London: Routledge.

Wilson, A. (2004). Four days and a breakfast: Time, space and literacy/ies in the prison community. In K. Leander & M. Sheehy (Eds.), *Spatializing literacy research and practice* (pp. 67-90). New York: Peter Lang.

Development of a New Framework for the NAEP Reading Assessment

Terry Salinger
American Institutes for Research

Michael Kamil
Stanford University

Barbara Kapinus
National Education Association

Peter Afflerbach
University of Maryland

In this article, we describe the development of the Framework for the 2009 National Assessment of Educational Progress in Reading and its key design features; it also provides a contrast between the 1992 Framework and the new Framework. The authors bring different perspectives and experiences to the development process. Terry Salinger directed the project that is described and had directed the development of the 1990 NAEP Reading Assessment. Michael Kamil was the chair of the Planning Committee for the development of the 2009 NAEP Reading. Barbara Kapinus directed the development of the framework and specifications for the 1992 NAEP Reading, which the new one replaces. Peter Afflerbach has served on NAEP development and advisory committees for more than a decade; he was a member of the 2009 Planning Committee.

Since 1969, the National Assessment of Educational Progress (NAEP) has been the major ongoing national indicator of what American students know and can do in numerous subjects, including reading. In the "Nation's Reading Report Card," NAEP chronicles students' performance as they read texts and respond to multiple-choice and constructed-response questions. Since its initiation, NAEP Reading has been administered on a regular schedule to students in grades 4, 8, and 12.

NAEP data are intended to help educators, policymakers, and the public understand student reading performance and make informed decisions about educational choices and expenditures. Data are available for the nation as a whole, for states, and recently, for large urban school districts. Data can be disaggregated by state, region, type/size of school, gender, race/ethnicity, and socioeconomic level, but by law, scores are not available for schools or individual students. Responses to teacher, student, and administrator questionnaires have, over the years, allowed for secondary data analysis. Among the most interesting of these secondary analyses are those that attempt to relate reading achievement to issues of resource provisions in schools, instructional practices, and students' reading behaviors both in and out of school.

NAEP is sometimes referred to as the "gold standard" of achievement testing because the assessments rigorously measure what students learn, while steering clear of curricular trends or identifiable instructional programs. NAEP reading, even at grade 4, assesses comprehension of fairly long, intact passages similar to what students encounter in their school and out-of-school reading. For many years, NAEP has asked students to respond to multiple choice items and also to write both short- and extended-constructed responses to questions. NAEP has also included "intertextual" item sets that require students to read two passages on a similar topic or theme and answer questions that require them to make links across what they read. The achievement levels--basic, proficient, and advanced--with which NAEP is reported set high standards in all content areas. The generic achievement levels approved by the National Assessment Governing Board (NAGB) state that performance at the advanced level "signifies superior performance," at the proficient level "represents solid academic performance . . . students reaching this level have demonstrated competency over challenging subject matter," and at the basic level "denotes partial mastery of prerequisite knowledge and skills that are fundamental for proficient work" (AIR, 2004, p. 44).

DEVELOPING THE FRAMEWORK

In 2002, the National Assessment Governing Board (NAGB), which oversees NAEP, awarded a contract to the American Institutes for Research (AIR), a Washington research firm, to develop a framework and specifications to replace those used since 1992. NAEP frameworks provide the theoretical and empirical base for assessments and describe the contents of the stimulus material and items used at each grade. AIR was also charged with developing detailed specifications to guide the reading item development contractor, Educational Testing Service (ETS).

The Political Context

Work on the Framework took place within the complex political world of the *No Child Left Behind Act* (NCLB) and increased attention to the "science" of reading research (NICHD, 2000). Under the *No Child Left Behind Act of 2001* (NCLB, 2001), NAEP will assess reading in grades 4 and 8 every two years and will also measure reading in grade 12 every four years. NCLB stipulates that state participation in NAEP is a prerequisite for Title I funding; and districts selected for inclusion in the NAEP sample must also participate or forfeit Title I funds. Although NAEP data cannot by law be disaggregated to determine the progress of individual schools toward their Adequate Yearly Progress (AYP) goals, state results on NAEP are considered important indicators of upward or downward achievement "trends" and often provide a sobering contrast to inflated state reading test scores. The seriousness with which NAEP data are viewed is suggested by a change in the timeline for the framework development. When it became clear that changes in the NAEP design would necessitate "breaking the trend line," NAGB delayed the first administration of the "new" NAEP from 2007 to 2009 so that states would have three data points to report under NCLB--2003, 2005, and 2007.

This implementation change, which occurred midway in the development cycle, was perhaps the most dramatic reflection of the political world but was hardly the first. NAGB had initially requested proposals for the framework project in winter 2002, but the procurement was unexpectedly withdrawn the day before proposals were due. The RFP was reissued the following summer, and two contracts were awarded: one to AIR, and the other to the Thomas B. Fordham Foundation and the Education Leaders Council (ELC). The ELC is a group of chief state school officers who had broken away from the Council of Chief State School Officers (CCSSO) reputedly because of CCSSO's more liberal attitudes toward education.

According to the contract, AIR would develop the framework and specifications needed for the new assessment, but only after both AIR and ELC had developed and presented a literature review and "issues paper" laying out what each considered the major issues in reading to consider in designing the new assessment. NAGB had required issues papers for other subjects, but commissioning two papers that might be pitted against each other was unique. In preparing its issues paper, the Fordham/ELC group contracted with the firm RMC and was advised by a group that included researchers and policymakers with a decidedly conservative perspective on reading.

The two issues papers presented visions for the new assessment. Even while agreeing that the 1992 Framework had proven to be vague in many ways (National Research Council, 1999), the two papers had substantive differences. The Fordham/ELC (Educational Leaders Council, 2002) paper identified as a major issue NAEP's historical emphasis on assessing only comprehension. The paper recommended that NAEP assess decoding at grade 4 and fluency and vocabulary at all grades. Fluency would be assessed with a one-minute "oral read" to be administered to all students who sat for the assessment. Both rate and accuracy would be determined and used as a proxy for comprehension. No plan was presented for assessing vocabulary; however, a statement in the paper suggests that definitions might be assessed in isolation: "Since it is not clear from the research exactly which words should be learned at which grade levels, a matrix sampling procedure would allow for testing various sets of vocabulary words at each grade level, 4, 8, and 12, in order to identify the set that most strongly relates to comprehension skills at the respective grade level" (Education Leaders Council, 2002, p. 11-12). AIR's paper began by reaffirming the importance of measuring students' comprehension of diverse genres with lengthy, intact, authentic passages and with both multiple choice and constructed response items. Inclusion of both literary and informational text was stressed, and the paper recommended that the planning committees for the framework consider how students' reading is influenced by computer technology and media. Without overtly recommending that the assessment be given on-line, AIR suggested the consideration of "new text types, new item types, and indeed new modes of administering NAEP" (American Institute for Research, 2002, 13).

AIR also stressed the importance of developing instruments that would gather information about all students who are assessed, including the increasing numbers of English language learners, students with special needs, and students who score "below basic" on NAEP. The "below basic" students are the ones who garner most of the headlines when NAEP data are released because the press, and ultimately the public, regard these students are virtually illiterate. In reality, the students at the "below basic" level can read, albeit mostly at the literal level. AIR's issue, then, was that the new NAEP have enough "floor" in terms of accessible stimulus material and items that those students who were previously designated as "below basic" would have a chance to show what they know and can do on grade-appropriate material.

Most significantly perhaps, AIR recommended a move from the 1992 taxonomy of reading, which reflected a reader response theoretical base, to a taxonomy grounded in cognitive science. The need for clear specification of the cognitive demands of items was emphasized (e.g., reading to locate information, integrate ideas across texts, etc.). Items targeting specific behaviors produce substantively different reports than those from an assessment whose items focus on "reading for a literary experience" or "to perform a task," as was the case with the previous framework (National Research Council, 1999).

Moving Beyond the Issues Papers

The two issues papers were presented to NAGB in November 2002, and the differences were ultimately reconciled through tactful editing by NAGB staff. AIR then began the task of convening three committees to advise the development process--a Planning Committee, to be headed by Michael Kamil; a Steering Committee to provide general direction to and reviews of the Planning Committee's work; and a Technical Advisory Panel of testing experts. Determining membership involved attending to political and ideological perspectives, as well as achieving the desired geographic, gender, and racial balance of researchers, teacher educators, classroom teachers, policy makers, and representatives of the literacy-related business community. The resulting committees included individuals who had advised the Fordham/ELC effort, as well as a few people who had been involved with NAEP in many roles since before the 1992 framework was developed. There were also some newcomers--people who knew about NAEP and its uses but had never been involved in framework development. Planning and Steering Committees members are listed in Table 1.

The committees met numerous times. At the first meeting, the Steering Committee laid forth its charge to the Planning Committee, including among other directives: developing an acceptable definition of reading; using as reference points state reading/English language arts standards and the international reading assessments PISA and PIRLS; and considering the feasibility of assessing vocabulary and fluency. At a minimum, the committee was to consider repeating the special studies of fluency that had been conducted with grade 4 students in 1992 and 2003 (Pinnell, Pilkulski, Wixson, Campbell, Gough, & Beatty, 1995).

Committee meetings were often spirited, especially when the Steering Committee was in attendance. Members took quite literally the statement written into the NAEP enabling legislation that they had to reflect the best that is known about reading research and practice but did not have to reach consensus (National Assessment Governing Board, 2002). Tempers sometimes flared, and both personal opinions and research interests were frequently voiced. AIR staff played many roles ranging from the "devil's advocate" in discussions, to referee, to provider of research, and to "ghost writers" who turned notes and ideas into texts that were sent back to committee members for what seemed like endless rounds of review. Decisions were made, revoked, reconsidered, documented, and finally translated to texts that were reviewed by the Assessment Development Committee (ADC) of the National Assessment Governing Board.

DESIGN OF THE 2009 NAEP ASSESSMENT

Per the Steering Committee's directive, a clear definition of reading was an essential starting point. The Planning Committee considered many existing definitions, both those derived from research and those designed for test development. Because NAEP is primarily concerned with reading comprehension, the Committee began with the RAND Reading Study Group (RAND, 2002) definition of comprehension, which emphasizes the reader, the text, and the activity--or purpose--as important elements of reading: "The process of simultaneously extracting and constructing meaning through interaction and involvement with written language" (p. 11). Some committee members resisted the use of the word "extracting" in this sense, but the search for a seminal definition was only beginning.

Figure 1   Members of the Steering and Planning Committees

Steering Committee Members
Marilyn Adams, Soliloquy Learning Corporation
Phyllis Aldrich, Saratoga-Warren BOCES, Saratoga
  Springs, NY
Francie Alexander, Scholastic, Inc.
Patricia Alexander, University of Maryland
Lance Balla, Teacher, Snohomish High School, WA
Wanda Brooks, University of Maryland,
  Baltimore County
Leila Christenbury, Virginia Commonwealth University
Mary Beth Curtis, Lesley University
JoAnne Eresh, Achieve, Inc.
Alan Farstrup, International Reading Association
Mike Frye (Retired), North Carolina Department of
  Public Instruction
Margo Gottlieb, Assessment and Evaluation
Illinois Resource Center, Des Plaines, IL
Jane Hileman, 100 Book Challenge Company,
  King of Prussia, PA
Billie J. Orr, Education Leaders Council
Melvina Pritchett-Phillips, National Association of
  Secondary School Principals
Sandra Stotsky, Northeastern University
Cynthia Teter Bowlin, Dallas County Community
  College
Julie Walker, American Association of School
  Librarians, a Division of the American Library
  Association

Planning Committee Members
Michael Kamil, Stanford University, Chair
Peter Afflerbach, University of Maryland
Donna Alvermann, University of Georgia
Amy Benedicty, Peninsula High School, San Bruno, CA
Robert Calfee, University of California-Riverside
Mitchell Chester, Assistant Superintendent,
  Ohio Department of Education
Barbara Foorman,University of Texas-Houston
Irene Gaskins, Benchmark School, Media, PA
Carol Jago, Santa Monica High School, CA
Jolene Jenkins, Mahaffey Middle School,
  Fort Campbell, KY
Janet Jones, Berry Elementary School, Waldorf, MD
Marilyn Joyce, Brewer High School, Brewer, ME
Michael Kibby, SUNY Buffalo, Amherst, NY
Margaret McKeown, Learning Research and
  Development Center, University of Pittsburgh
Paula Moseley, Los Angeles Unified School District
Jean Osborn, Champaign, IL
Charles Peters, University of Michigan
Carol Santa, Montana Academy, Kalispell, MT
Karen Wixson, University of Michigan
Junko Yokota, National-Louis University

External Reviewers
Dennis J. Kear, Wichita State University, Chair
Ellin O. Keene, University of Pennsylvania
Katherine A. Mitchell, Alabama State Department
  of Education
Keith E. Stanovich, University of Toronto
Joanna P. Williams, Teachers College, Columbia
  University

The search then moved to definitions used in the two international literacy assessments. The Program for International Student Assessment or PISA (Campbell, Kelly, Mullis, Martin, & Sainsbury, 2001, p. 3), which assesses the mathematical, scientific, and reading literacy of fifteen-year-olds, relied on the following definition for item development and reporting: "Reading literacy is understanding, using, and reflecting on written texts, in order to achieve one's goals, to develop one's knowledge and potential, and to participate in society." This definition emphasizes reading as a social and goal-directed activity, a factor that is difficult to explore on an assessment such as NAEP. The second international assessment definition was that of the Progress in International Reading Literacy Study or PIRLS, which is given to nine-year-olds. Its definition is: "The ability to understand and use those written language forms required by society and/or valued by the individual. Young readers can construct meaning from a variety of texts. They read to learn, to participate in communities of readers, and for enjoyment" (Organization for Economic Co-operation and Development, 2000, p. 18). This definition also emphasizes the social and community aspects of reading and also was considered somewhat beyond the scope of what could be assessed authentically on a paper-and-pencil test.

After much discussion, the Planning Committee recommended the following definition of reading to the Steering Committee for their approval: "Reading is an active and complex process that involves: understanding written text, developing and interpreting meaning, and using meaning as appropriate to type of text, purpose, and situation" (AIR, 2004, p. 2). This definition acknowledges the critical elements of the other definitions while recognizing their limitations to guide assessment development. It views reading as involving the reader, texts, and purposes--three elements of the definition have direct implications for the construction of the 2009 NAEP assessment items.

Reviewers of drafts of the framework had stressed the need for clear language and transparent definitions of what might be considered "insider terminology" if the framework were to be useful to a wide range of users. To that end, elaborations and clarification were provided for many of the terms in the definition of reading. For example, *using meaning* was defined as follows: "Readers draw on the ideas and information they have acquired from text to meet a particular purpose or situational need. The 'use' of text may be as straightforward as knowing the time when a train will leave a particular station or may involve more complex behaviors such as analyzing how an author developed a character's motivation or evaluating the quality of evidence presented in an argument" (AIR, 2004, p. 3).

Additionally, the definition of *purpose* for reading generated considerable interesting debate. Planning Committee members argued that an expanded definition was needed; some thought it should cover all reading activities, while others argued that the purpose and situation for reading on a test--even NAEP--was merely to take the test. The expanded definition of *purpose* recognizes this reality: "Students' purpose for reading the passages presented on NAEP is determined by the assessment context; thus, the influence of purpose on readers' comprehension is somewhat limited" (AIR, 2004, p. 3).

Further, as committee members debated the distinction between literary and informational text, they revisited the purposes for reading in an effort to make a crisp distinction between the two genres. This led to a workable definition of *literary nonfiction* and the further expansion of purpose, which stated that "differences in reading *purpose* are, of course, permeable. For example, well-crafted informational text is often read for appreciation and enjoyment, in addition to obtaining the information that the text can provide" (AIR, 2004, p. 8).

Much of the discussion at committee meetings was genuinely exciting, heady, and intellectual, as members debated topics such as: the difference between a definition of reading for an assessment and for a broader context; the very identity of NAEP as an assessment of reading *qua* reading or of literature; the ways technology has come to influence reading; and possible methods for simulating web searches on a standardized assessment. The debate about technology was temporarily resolved by proposing that a special study be conducted to investigate the issue.

Many of the discussions concerned the nature of the taxonomy of reading behaviors that would drive item development. This was an important topic because movement away from the taxonomy used for item development starting in 1992 would change NAEP dramatically enough that the "trend line" of data would have to be "broken," even though "bridging studies" could link the older assessment results to new results. Movement away from the former taxonomy would also represent a change in theoretical base from reader response to cognitive science. Eventually, committee members proposed that NAEP assess reading according to a series of "cognitive targets" for item development (discussed below) that distinguish among behaviors specific for comprehending literary or informational texts and those that are common across text type.

REVIEWS AND APPROVAL OF THE FRAMEWORK

Reviews are always an integral part of the NAEP development process. The Steering Committee reviewed the Planning Committee's work at every stage. Emerging documents were vetted with NAEP state directors and state English language arts and assessment directors. NAGB's Assessment Development Committee reviewed numerous drafts and provided feedback, and AIR posted the draft framework on a dedicated website. NAGB also launched a new review process with the reading framework. The framework, in a near final draft, was sent to a panel of five external reviewers (see Table 1), whose recommendations were presented to NAGB and to AIR for action. On the whole, the reviewers affirmed the direction the framework had taken and suggested only minor changes--with the exception of elimination of the recommended special study on technology and reading. Panel members echoed the enthusiasm of other reviewers over plans to assess vocabulary and supported a developmental special study to investigate the validity of this new assessment component.

The final step in the process was approval by NAGB. The Framework had been reviewed numerous times by the Assessment Development Committee, and their recommendations had been thoughtful and constructive. When the ADC presented the Framework to the full NAGB membership, they gave it their full approval.

WHAT'S NEW IN THE 2009 NAEP FRAMEWORK?

The 2009 Framework includes several new features that have the potential to yield new kinds of information about students' reading.

Vocabulary Assessment

The assessment of vocabulary in a systematic way is a major new feature of the 2009 NAEP Framework. Previously, vocabulary was one of many possible "targets" for item writing, but few vocabulary items were actually included. A subgroup of the Planning Committee crafted a definition of *meaning vocabulary* as "the application of one's understanding of word meanings to passage comprehension" (AIR, 2004, p.12). They developed a rubric for selecting target words for item writing to help test developers identify the appropriate "tier two" words for inclusion on the assessment (Beck, McKeown, & Omanson, 1987; Beck, Perfetti, & McKeown, 1982) and drafted statements of basic, proficient, and advanced performance in using vocabulary as a tool to aid comprehension.

NAEP will assess vocabulary within the context of the passages students have read, and vocabulary items will function both as a measure of passage comprehension and as a test of readers' specific knowledge of the word's meaning as intended by the passage author. The Planning Committee recommended that two vocabulary items be developed for each stimulus. Even though there is concern that two items per NAEP "block" of items will be too few to generate a valid subscore for vocabulary, new and valuable information about students' use of their vocabulary knowledge will be gained from this new component of the assessment.

Distinctions Among Text Types

The 2009 NAEP Framework clearly differentiates items across three types of text: literary text, characterized by the use of story structures; literary nonfiction, including narrative essays, speeches, and autobiographies or biographies; and poetry, which will be included at all grades. Poems may be used at all grades and especially in conjunction with prose pieces on a similar theme or topic in "intertextual item sets" that include items asking about each distinct stimuli and requiring thinking across the two texts. The inclusion of literary nonfiction is an attempt to resolve confusion about uses of the terms "story" and "narrative," recognizing that not all narratives are stories. Poetry is included at all grades because it typically requires a different set of cognitive skills from other types of text.

Similarly, informational text is also differentiated as follows: exposition, which primarily presents information through various structural patterns; argumentation and persuasive text, which are distinguished by their intent to convince or to present an argument and by the features that authors select to accomplish their goals; and procedural text and documents. Procedural texts convey information in the form of discrete steps conveying directions for accomplishing a task. Documents include graphical representations, often as multimedia elements that require readers to draw on information presented as short continuous prose and also as columns, matrices, or other formats. Detailed exhibits in the framework and specifications provide examples of each kind of informational text to guide the selection of stimulus material for the assessment.

Decisions about text categorization and ultimately about text selection for the assessment encouraged discussion about unique text characteristics, the kinds of thinking each engenders, and the extent of use in schools across grades 4, 8, and 12. Many committee members advocated for increasing amounts of diverse informational text in the upper grades, while others wanted a strong emphasis on the primacy of literature. The final recommendations for the distribution of text types in the NAEP Framework increases from an even balance at grade 4 to a 60-40 split favoring information text at grade 12. These percentages represent estimates of what students at these grade levels encounter in their school and out-of-school reading. As these percentages were presented to state reading and assessment directors, there was almost unanimous approval for this recommendation.

Cognitive Targets

The Committee members were fully aware of the critiques of the way in which the 1992 Framework operationalized reading through an item development taxonomy based on reading purpose, genres, and aspects for reading (National Research Council, 1999). The AIR issues paper had taken a strong stand on the need to root the taxonomy more firmly in research on the nature of the reading process. The 2009 Framework lays out a new taxonomy based on the following "cognitive targets"--or behaviors and skills: Locate/Recall, Integrate/Interpret, and Critique/Evaluate. These so-called "cognitive targets" for item development illustrate the complex nature of the reading process. The framework distinguishes these behaviors in three ways: those common across text types, those specific to literary texts, and those elicited specifically by informational texts.

To measure these cognitive skills, students will respond to both multiple-choice and short- and long-constructed-response items, with varying distributions by grade level. Students in grade 4 will spend approximately half of the assessment time responding to multiple-choice items and half responding to constructed-response items. Students in grades 8 and 12 will spend a greater amount of time on constructed-response items.

Recommended Special Studies

Special studies are often conducted in conjunction with NAEP to investigate to specific aspects of reading that are not assessed on main NAEP. Fluency was, as noted earlier, the focus for special studies in 1992 and 2003. Having excluded the technology special study, the committees recommended three special studies, subject to approval and availability of resources. The first is a developmental study to be conducted in advance of actual item development for the 2009 assessment. This study will explore the effectiveness of item types to assess vocabulary in the way recommended by the framework. The study will test the limitations of the multiple choice item format to assess meaning vocabulary and investigate the extent to which passages at appropriate levels of difficulty can be found from which ten or so rich comprehension and two vocabulary items can be developed. The study will provide valuable information needed to make the vocabulary assessment a permanent part of NAEP Reading.

The second and third studies involve secondary analysis of NAEP data. One study will look at differentials in girls' and boys' reading scores by examining how differences in themes, gender of characters in stories (or individuals mentioned in informational text) and genre in general might influence the reading performance. The second study will examine the scores of students identified as second language learners by focusing especially on the time elapsed between when they exited bilingual or ESL instruction and the time at which they take NAEP.

What's Missing in the 2009 Framework?

There are limits to what can be assessed on the NAEP, given the burden of testing time for students, the resources available for a large-scale assessment, and the requirement for quick reporting of results. Despite a great deal of committee debate about the inclusion of an assessment of electronic multimedia text, the framework does not recommend assessing reading of this type of text, at least not in 2009. Technical problems of computer access were deemed too great to undertake such a task at this time, especially if the assessment were to be an authentic test of students' abilities to read this kind of test, rather than a manufactured situation with very controlled conditions.

Additionally, the 2009 NAEP will not assess fluency, either in a special study or as part of the full assessment. Special studies of students' oral reading had been conducted previously, and the results of those studies convinced the committees that there was minimal additional information to be gained by assessing fluency on the 2009 NAEP. The 1992 study, for example, concluded that "higher levels of fluency were also associated with increasingly higher overall reading proficiency" (Pinnell et al., 1995, p. 23).

COMPARING NAEP 1992 WITH NAEP 2009

Work on the 1992 Reading Framework took place amid concern about the overuse of large-scale assessment and the reduction of reading achievement to a set of discrete skills. The National Assessment Governing Board (NAGB) had recently been developed as a non-partisan body to provide oversight to the development contractor, Educational Testing Service. In broad strokes, NAGB consisted of nonpartisan appointees and a group of staff members who served as the full-time administrators for framework development, reporting, and contractual issues. In previous framework development efforts, the item development contractor had convened committees and drafted frameworks for the National Center for Education Statistics. Under NAGB, the framework development would be external to the item development contractor. CCSSO received the contract to develop the 1992 framework, convened committees, and subcontracted for some of the work with AIR.

For the first time in NAEP's history, state-by-state comparative information would be provided about reading performance of grade 4 students. Many educators believed this new function for NAEP was the beginning of a national curriculum and would lead to all sorts of misuses of the NAEP data. In this context, the framework development group set out to design an assessment that would be acceptable to a wide range of educators and still meet the demands of policymakers. Some of the most interesting aspects of the assessment grew out of the effort to address the many specific demands placed on the assessment because of its new use as a state-by-state comparison measure.

In the early 1990s many reading tests did, in fact, reduce reading to a set of discrete skills, often defined by Bloom's taxonomy. In an effort to counter these concerns, the taxonomy of reading behaviors developed for the 1992 assessment emphasized readers' responses to text, not their specific strategies for deriving information from text. This perspective won acceptance from many, but it also garnered numerous criticisms. One particular design feature reflects what can happen when this theoretical perspective is operationalized in a test. As shown in Table 2, the types of texts were classified according to purpose and genre, as a reflection of the reader, text, and context/purpose paradigm making its way from research into practice. Just as happened during the 2009 Planning Committee discussions, some members of the 1992 Framework development committee had pointed out that the real purpose of NAEP is to answer test questions; but majority opinion prevailed in 1992, and the resulting Framework included purpose--even on a test--as significant factor in reading performance. Items were classified according to "stances" or "aspects of reading." Decisions were strongly influenced by the work of Judith Langer (described fully in Langer, 1995). The theoretical premise was that reading consisted of a series of "movements" in and out of text as understanding was constructed and then standing back to examine both the text and the meaning that had been constructed (Langer, 1995).

The underlying theory of reading, for all its elegance, proved difficult to operationalize with items that could be reliably classified according to the taxonomy (Pearson & DeStefano, 1994). The labels of the "stances" in the first iteration of the 1992 framework illustrates the imprecision that concerned critics: 1) initial understanding [of the text]; 2) developing an interpretation; 3) personal reflection [on] and response to text]; and 4) demonstrating a critical stance [toward the text]. Table 2 presents the terms that eventually replaced the original names in an effort to convey more clearly what was being measured. Nonetheless, as the framework was operationized in item development, it was possible (although unlikely) that items could be written that asked a student to "provide a personal response" or "take a critical stance" about a description of scientific procedure or even a bus schedule. The use of "cognitive targets" to guide item development for 2009 NAEP is, then, a major difference between the previous and proposed frameworks--one that will increase the likelihood that items can be developed to measure reading precisely.

Several other components of the 1992 assessment represented new ways of thinking about large-scale reading assessment. For example, the 1992 Framework recommended an increase in the number of constructed-response items, with twelfth graders spending as much as fifty percent of their time writing about what they read. Use of short- and extended-constructed-response items, which require hand scoring and extend the time between test administration and score reporting, has become fairly common in state and commercial tests and will go forward in the 2009 assessment. The 1992 Framework also stressed the use of relatively long passages that had received little or no editing.

In response to a group within the reading community that wanted information not just on comprehension, but also on students' reading of distinct words, the 1992 Framework recommended an oral reading fluency study. Grade 4 students read a passage orally that they had read silently on NAEP; their reading was recorded and evaluated using a "fluency scale" that provided benchmark descriptors for oral reading at four levels ranging from word-by-word reading to reading in large, meaningful phrase groups. Fluency scores were compared with the students' overall NAEP scores (Pinnell, et al., 1995; see p. 15 for the fluency scale). The study also involved collecting "portfolios" of students' classroom work in reading and interviewing them about their work. These data produced interesting information about what goes on in classrooms and the kinds of choices students have in their reading. For example, students whose oral reading was scored as "fluent" were far more likely to report that they read books they had chosen themselves than were students whose reading was scored as nonfluent (Pinnell, et. al, 1995, p. 28).

The fluency special study from the 1992 assessment had real impact on the field and was repeated in 2002 (although results had not been made public at the time of the 2009 Framework development, they were summarized for the Planning Committee members). The study drew attention to fluency long before the introduction of NCLB, provided a tool to measure fluency, and suggested that "reading outside of school for enjoyment and reading self-selected books in school may be related to reading fluency" (Pinnell, et al., p. 59). As stated previously, the findings of the studies were convincing evidence that the fluency study did not need to be repeated.

The 2009 Framework honors many aspects of the previous Framework but also introduces some changes that have the potential to lead to better measurement and more precise reporting of assessment results. Further, just as the grounding in reader response reflects research and theory in the early 1990s, the new Framework bows to scientific research and the demands of *No Child Left Behind*. Key similarities and differences between the two frameworks are presented in Figure 2.

VALUE OF THE 2009 FRAMEWORK FOR THE FIELD

The 1992 NAEP Reading Framework was influential in its time and became the model for many state and commercial tests throughout the 1990s. Developers of the 2009 Framework hope that the new vision for NAEP will be equally influential. The Framework provides considerable detail, all the way from guidelines for selecting different kinds of texts to directions for selecting "tier two" words and writing distractors for vocabulary items. Such information has previously been included only in test specification documents that are not widely distributed. The distinctions made across text types can sharpen thinking about students' reading material, either for in-class reading or for assessment stimulus material. Further, the distinction of cognitive targets by text types can provide valuable information about the nature of comprehension processes and means for assessing them.

The 2009 Framework is grounded in research and features a hefty, current bibliography and detailed glossary. It formalizes procedures for vocabulary assessment in NAEP, continues NAEP's emphasis on comprehension, and lays out specific guidelines for developing assessment items that

Figure 2 Similarities and Differences between the 1992 and 2009 NAEP Reading Frameworks

1993 – 2007 NAEP READING CHARACTERISTICS		2009 NAEP READING CHARACTERISTICS	
CONTENT OF ASSESSMENT			
Stimulus material • Literary texts, including poetry at grades 8 and 12 • Informational texts • Document texts	Contexts for reading on assessment: • For literary experience • For information • To perform a task	Literary text • Fiction • Literary nonfiction • Poetry at all grade levels	Informational texts • Exposition • Argumentation and persuasive texts • Procedural texts and documents
COGNITIVE PROCESSES ASSESSED			
Stances/aspects of reading (terminology used in recent versions of the Framework): • Forming a general understanding • Developing interpretation • Making reader/text connections • Examining content and structure		Cognitive targets, distinguished by text type	
		Locate/recall · Integrate/interpret · Critique/evaluate	
VOCABULARY			
Vocabulary as a "target" of item development, with no information reported on students' use of vocabulary knowledge in comprehending what they read		Systematic approach to assessing "meaning vocabulary" with two items per passage	
SELECTION OF PASSAGES TO BE USED AS STIMULUS MATERIAL			
• Use of intact, authentic stimulus material • Expert judgment as sole criterion for passage selection		• Use of authentic stimulus material with some flexibility in excerpting so long as integrity of the material is maintained • Expert judgment as primary criterion, plus use of at least two research-based readability formulas	
PASSAGE LENGTH			
Grade 4: 250–800 Grade 8: 400–1,000 Grade 12: 500–1,500		Grade 4: 200–800 Grade 8: 400–1,000 Grade 12: 500–1,500	
ITEM TYPE			
Multiple-choice and constructed-response items included at all grades		Multiple-choice and constructed-response items included at all grades	

reflect the ways students read literary and informational text. Moreover, the Framework is as user-friendly as possible; indeed, many reviewers commented affirmatively on efforts to achieve a lucid, jargon-free presentation. Detailed exhibits of text and item characteristics promise to make the Framework accessible to educators and test developers seeking a model for a sophisticated and nonideological assessment of comprehension.

What's Next for the 2009 Framework

The first administration of the new NAEP will be in 2009. In the meantime, NAGB has been responding to the report of a special commission convened to consider student performance on grade 12 NAEP assessments (National Commission on NAEP 12th Grade Assessment and Reporting, 2004). The report, issued before the end of the Framework project, recommended a "new vision" for NAEP at grade 12, a test that could report on students' preparedness for college, work, and the military. It was reasoned that such a test would have wide value, even though individual scores would still not be available. The Planning Committee affirmed that the proposed assessment was rigorous and relevant enough to provide useful information about students' readiness and noted that the historic high omission rates on NAEP probably reflected students' lack of motivation on a test with no stakes administered in the second semester of grade 12. Still, the possibility existed that the design of grade 12 NAEP reading might have to be changed to accommodate the Commission's recommendations.

NAGB subsequently asked Achieve to convene a small group of experts to consider whether the framework should indeed be altered to measure students' preparedness (Achieve, 2005). They affirmed the rigor and usefulness of the Framework and the grade 12 assessment it would produce. Additionally, their first major recommendation echoed debates in the committee meetings: "Given that the reading demands high school graduates face are overwhelmingly informational in nature and that informational literacy is a vital 21st century skill, NAEP should increase the percent of informational text on the new NAEP from 60 percent formally used in the NAEP Reading Assessment to 70 percent" (p. 5). Thus, the 12th Grade Commission report could be seen not as a threat to the work of the Planning Committee, but instead as a support for the amounts of informational text proportionate to the informational texts students encounter in grades 8 and 12.

REFERENCES

Achieve. (2005). *Analysis of the 2009 Reading Framework in the context of the college and workplace preparedness benchmarks of the American Diploma Project: Report of the major recommendations of the Achieve panel.* Washington, DC: Author.

American Institutes for Research. (2002, November). *Issues Paper for the 2007 National Assessment of Educational Progress in Reading.* Prepared for the National Assessment Governing Board in Support of Contract # ED-02-R-0007. Washington, DC: Author.

American Institutes for Research (AIR). (2004, September). *Reading Framework for the 2009 National Assessment of Educational Progress.* Prepared for the National Assessment Governing Board in Support of Contract # ED-02-R-0007. Washington, DC: Author.

Beck, I.J., McKeown, M.G., & Omanson, R.C. (1987). The effects and use of diverse vocabulary instructional techniques. In M.G. McKeown & M. Curtis (Eds.), *The nature of vocabulary acquisition* (pp. 147–163). Hillsdale, NJ: Erlbaum.

Beck, I.L., Perfetti, C.A., & McKeown, M.G. (1982). Effects of long-term vocabulary instruction on lexical access and reading comprehension. *Journal of Educational Psychology, 74*(4), 506–521.

Campbell, J.R., Kelly, D.L., Mullis, I.V.S., Martin, M.O., & Sainsbury, M. (2001, March). *Framework and specifications for PIRLS Assessment 2001.* Chestnut Hill, MA: Boston College, Lynch School of Education, PIRLS International Study Center.

Educational Leaders Council. (2002, November). *Issues Paper Prepared for the 2007 National Assessment of Educational Progress in Reading.* Washington, DC: Author.

McKeown, M.G., Beck, I. L., Omanson, R.C., & Perfetti, C.A. (1983). The effects of long-term vocabulary instruction on reading comprehension: A replication. *Journal of Reading Behavior, 15*(1), 3–18.

Langer, J. A. (1995). *Envisioning literature: Literacy understanding and literacy instruction.* New York: Teachers College Press.

National Assessment Governing Board. (May 2002). *National Assessment Governing Board Policy on Framework Development.* Washington, DC: Author.

National Commission on NAEP 12th Grade Assessment and Reporting. (March 2004). *12th grade student achievement in America: A new vision for NAEP.* Washington DC: National Assessment Governing Board.

National Institute of Child Health and Human Development. (2000). *Report of the National Reading Panel.* Washington, DC: Author.

National Research Council. (1999). *Grading the Nation's Report Card: Evaluating NAEP and transforming the assessment of educational progress.* Washington, DC: Author.

No Child Left Behind Act (NCLB) of 2001, P.L. 107-110, signed by President George W. Bush, January 8, 2002.

Organisation for Economic Co-operation and Development. (2000). *Measuring student knowledge and skill: The PISA 2000 assessment of reading, mathematical and scientific literacy.* Paris: Author.

Pearson, P.D., & DeStefano, L. (1994). Content validation of the 1992 NAEP in reading: Classifying items according to the reading framework. (pp. 285-314). In R., Glaser, R. Linn, & G. Bohrnstedt (Eds.) *The trial state assessment: Prospects and realities: Background Studies.* Stanford, CA: National Academy of Education.

Pearson, P.D., & Camperell, K. (1994). Comprehension of text structures. In R.B. Ruddell, M.R. Ruddell, & H. Singer (Eds.), *Theoretical models and processes of reading* (4th ed., pp. 448–468). Newark, DE: International Reading Association.

Pinnell, G.S., Pikulski, J.J., Wixson, K.K., Campbell, J.R., Gough, P.B., & Beatty, A.S. (January 1995). *Listening to children read aloud: Data from NAEP's Integrated Reading Performance Record (IRPR) at Grade 4.* Washington, DC: National Center for Education Statistics.

RAND *Reading Study Group (2002). Reading for understanding: Toward an R&D program in reading comprehension.* Santa Monica, CA: RAND.

Young Children's Visual Meaning-Making During Readalouds of Picture Storybooks

Lawrence R. Sipe
Anne E. Brightman
University of Pennsylvania

INTRODUCTION AND THEORETICAL FRAME

This article reports on a study that explored the ways in which a class of first-grade children constructed meaning from the visual features of four picture storybooks that were read aloud to them. We know that, in a well-wrought picturebook, the illustrations and other visual features are important and necessary components of the story (Kiefer, 1995; Stewig, 1995); the pictures give us information that the words do not give us, and the words supply information that the pictures lack, filling in each other's gaps (Nodelman, 1988). Indeed, in many cases, understanding the words of the story is only a small part of the total experience of a picturebook as an aesthetic object (Marantz, 1977). All the components of a picturebook, including the dustjacket and endflaps, front and back covers, the endpages, the frontispiece, the title page, the dedication page, and the pages containing the publishing information (called the "peritext" [Genette, 1997a; Higonnet, 1990]), as well as the verbal text and the accompanying illustrations, are designed as an aesthetic whole; in other words, readers must interpret and integrate information across all these components in order to have the richest experience. In a similar way, a semiotic perspective on picturebooks (Golden & Gerber, 1990) suggests that the array of visual features in the book constitutes a system of visual signs, just as the arrangement of words constitutes a system of verbal signs, and that readers can explore the complex relationship between these sign systems by interpreting the visual signs in terms of the verbal signs, and the verbal signs in terms of the visual signs, in the process of transmediation (Sipe, 1998; Suhor, 1984). William Moebius (1986) lists a number of clusters of conventional signs in picturebooks, calling them "codes," such as the code of color to represent certain emotions or moods.

In many primary classrooms, children engage with literature mainly in the form of picturebooks; visual interpretation is thus a crucial component of their developing literary understanding and their development as astute and skilled readers. Moreover, since stories "lean" on other stories (Yolen, 1981) we would expect that children would draw on their prior experiences with visual interpretation in their construction of meaning for any given picturebook. This integration with prior knowledge is a form of intertextual linking (Harris, Trezise, & Winser, 2002). One powerful way of encouraging this intertextual linking is to expose children to "text sets" (Harste, Short, & Burke, 1988; Short, 1992), sets of books that share a similar topic, or books that are recognizable variants of the same story. For example, reading and discussing several versions of the story of *Rapunzel* has been shown to help young children build up knowledge across cases, as cognitive flexibility theory (Spiro, Coulson, Feltovich, & Anderson, 1994) suggests, thereby resulting in higher-level thinking and comprehension (Sipe, 2001).

Despite calls from senior literacy researchers to include examination of meaning-making from the illustrations (and other visual components) in discussions of children's responses to picturebooks (Flood & Lapp, 1995), there is a relatively small body of empirical research that specifically focuses on the affordances (Gibson, 1979) of the visual features of picturebooks for young children's literary interpretation. Kiefer's (1982) classroom research studied the responses of first and second graders to picturebook illustrations, adapting Halliday's (1975) categories of the functions of language, and described four types of response: informative, imaginative, heuristic, and personal. In informative response, children described the contents of the picture or compared and contrasted the picture to the real world. In heuristic response, children speculated and made inferences about the events depicted in the illustrations, how illustrations were made, and predicted outcomes or events. In imaginative response, children entered the story world or created figurative images to describe it. In personal response, children made connections between their own life experiences and the book, or evaluated the story. Golden and Gerber's (1990) research examined the responses of Native American second graders to Maurice Sendak's (1963) *Where the Wild Things Are*, considering the children's responses as "realized text" evoked by the "potential text" of the visual and verbal sign systems of the book. Drawing on the work of Flinders and Eisner (1994) on the stages of the development of visual art criticism, Madura (1997) explored four patterns used by young children in talking about picturebooks: description, interpretation, evaluation, and thematic issues.

Pantaleo's in-depth studies (2002, 2003, 2004a, 2004b) of first grade children's responses to postmodern picturebooks with multiple plots, multiple narrators, and metafictive devices (Lewis, 2001; Trites, 1994) provide evidence for the potential sophistication of young children in using text and illustrations to fill in each others' indeterminacies (Iser, 1978). The children in Pantaleo's studies constructed semiotic significance from visual details such as different font sizes; used illustrations to make connections among the multiple narratives; understood how the illustrations represented, complemented, extended, and sometimes contradicted the text; and used visual peritextual features of the books to predict the plot and to interpret the relationships among storybook characters.

METHOD

The research question for this study was: In a first grade classroom, what ways do children use visual features of picture storybooks to construct meaning during readalouds of four versions of the same traditional tale? The participants in the study were the members of a first-grade class of thirteen children (seven boys and six girls) in a pre-kindergarten through sixth grade elementary public school located in a middle-class suburban community in the Northeastern United States. Their self-contained classroom was a print-enriched environment, and they were actively engaged in meaningful literacy experiences throughout the school day. They began each morning with a community meeting that included interactive writing, language and word plays, and a readaloud. For the remainder of the morning the students participated in Language and Word Study, Reading Workshop, and Writing Workshop. Their afternoon included Math, Science, and Social Studies.

The students participated in two storybook readalouds each day. Ms. Blair, their classroom teacher, read to the children at the end of the morning community meeting and after lunch. During these readalouds, the students were encouraged to respond orally to the text and illustrations in an interactive manner (Barrentine, 1996; Morrow & Smith, 1990); that is, they responded during the reading of the story as well as before and afterwards. The children directed their comments to one another as well as to their teacher. Ms. Blair allowed the discussion to proceed as long as the children continued to contribute meaningful thoughts and ideas to the conversation. Ms. Brightman, the second author of this study, volunteered in Ms. Blair's first grade classroom two days each week from January through May. She explored a variety of literacy activities with the students, including reading aloud to them. Thus, by March, when the data for this study were collected, the children knew Ms. Brightman well and were comfortable in discussing stories with her, and had experienced a great many readalouds with Ms. Blair. Data consisted of complete transcripts of Ms. Brightman's reading, and discussion with the children, of a text set of four variants of *The Three Pigs* by Marshall (1989), Kellogg (1997), Scieszka (1989), and Wiesner (2001), read in this order. This sequence was chosen so that children would engage with texts that increasingly departed from the traditional form of this tale, ending with Wiesner's complex postmodern version (Pantaleo, 2002). This created an environment in which the students could utilize what they already knew about the tale to engage with the unique and atypical ideas, characters, plot, and format presented in the subsequent texts. These four versions were also chosen for their very different illustration styles, and it was hypothesized that these diverse styles would evoke a rich variety of responses. The four readings were done within a short time frame of two weeks, so as to maximize the connections children might make among the texts.

During each readaloud, Ms. Brightman sat in a rocking chair in the library corner of the classroom and the children gathered on the carpet at her feet so as to be close to the book. Before each readaloud, she reminded the children that they could speak freely and comment on anything they noticed in the illustrations or heard in the text, and that it was not necessary to raise their hands before they spoke. Her general pattern was to pause before and after reading the text on each page, as an invitation for students to comment. She also spent time encouraging interpretation, speculation and prediction based on the front and back covers, dust jackets, endpages, title pages, and other peritextual features of the books. By far the most common type of teacher turn was to simply read the words of the story, to call on children and otherwise manage the discussion, and to invite more comments ("What else?" "Any other ideas?"). Ms. Brightman repeated or restated children's comments, clarified or extended a child's idea, connected children's ideas with one another, and positively reinforced children's ideas. Her approach was neither laissez-faire nor rigidly controlling; she became more directive at crucial points, for example in emphasizing visual and textual connections among the four stories to assist children in refining and extending their story schemata. She was careful to extend children's comments relating to the visual features of the books, by probing and asking for clarification, and by asking children to comment on the visual meaning-making of their classmates ("That's interesting; does anyone have a comment about what Mandy said?").

In the text set we used, *The Three Little Pigs* by James Marshall (1989) is the most traditional retelling of this familiar tale. The text deviates little from the well-known versions of the story;

rather, the illustrations of the text add originality to the narration. The illustrations of the three pigs encourage the reader to describe the first pig (sleeping in a hammock) as lazy, the second pig (holding a balloon and listening to wind chimes) as whimsical or artsy, and the third pig (wearing a three-piece suit) as savvy and practical. In addition, the illustrations depict the wolf as mischievous and thug-like.

In *The Three Little Pigs* by Steven Kellogg (1997), the three pigs run their mom's waffle-making business and attempt to elude the big bad wolf. The wolf is depicted as a tough biker "dude." There is abundant humor in both the text and illustrations in this variant and children must explore this book visually to appreciate Kellogg's humorous twists.

The True Story of the Three Little Pigs by Jon Scieszka (1989) is told from the perspective of the wolf. According to Alexander Wolf, he only wanted to borrow a cup of sugar from his neighbors, and blowing down the pigs' houses was only the accidental result of a bad cold. This variant is intriguing for elementary children as it allows the reader to "understand what the author has done with the structure of a familiar tale and begin to see the events through the eyes of a new narrator" (Huck et al., 2004, p. 40). As with Kellogg's version, as the children carefully explore both the text and the illustrations, they continually uncover the richness of this book.

The Three Pigs by David Wiesner (2001) is a fascinating and somewhat chaotic postmodern version of this familiar tale. The pigs are literally blown out of their own story by the huffing and puffing of the wolf, and go an adventure together. Folding one of the pages of their story into a paper airplane, the three pigs travel to other stories and take several of the characters they encounter back to their own tale to defeat the wolf. Children must interact very actively with this text to "tell the story" and appreciate the intricacies of the illustrations.

Ms. Brightman audiotaped the four conversations and transcribed them, assigning pseudonyms to the children to ensure anonymity. The readalouds each lasted an average of 25 minutes and the children enthusiastically contributed to the conversations.

Using the children's conversational turns (Sinclair & Coulthard, 1975) as the unit of analysis, a first pass through the data was made by coding the conversational turns using a typology of literary understanding that had been shown to be generally applicable to young children's talk about picture storybooks (Sipe, 2000; 2001; 2003). Following this, the subset of conversational turns having to do with visual analysis and interpretation (hereafter called "visual talk") was extracted and analyzed by the creation of conceptual categories that emerged by the constant comparative method (Glaser & Strauss, 1967), using the three-stage qualitative analytic model of Strauss and Corbin (1990), which involves successively higher levels of generalization and the specification of ever-broader patterns of relationships. Out of a total of 918 conversational turns by the children during the four readings, 388 (42%) were identifiable as responses to the visual features of the storybooks. The first author and two graduate students read the transcripts together and assigned conceptual labels to each of the 388 conversational turns ("open coding," according to Strauss and Corbin). After combining similar conceptual labels to create a list of codes ("axial coding"), the three of us then independently coded the data again. Interrater realiability among the three of us was 91%. We then met again as a group to achieve consensus on the coding for all the conversational turns on which there had been disagreement. Finally, we compared proportions of the codes within each readaloud transcript as well as across all four transcripts in order to relate the codes to each other and to comprehensively describe the use the children made of visual information in interpreting the four stories (Strauss and Corbin's "selective coding").

FINDINGS

The content analysis of the data revealed eight ways in which the children used visual features of the storybooks to create meaning.

Setting/Background

The children described, labeled, or made inferences about details in the setting or background of the illustrations. A little over one third (35%) of their conversational turns having to do with visual features of the stories involved these close observations. Young children are quite adept at observing visual detail, and frequently focus on parts of an illustration rather than the whole (Huck, Kiefer, Hepler, & Hickman, 2004). In the discussion of the Kellogg version, for example, the children wanted to describe the background of the double page spread depicting the houses built by the three pigs, set on three different hills, as well as other details:

> Tina: It has a bridge and um, they have hills and mountains.
> Unidentified child: They have tunnels.
> Steven: That could be a bridge.
> Tina: And they have rivers.
> Steven: They have bridges, they have mountains, and they're making waffles and they have a waffle stand.
> Nathan: There's two turtles in there.
> Manuel: Three, four, five
> Melanie: One, two, three, four, five [counting the five turtles]

Character: Appearance

Children identified main characters present in the illustrations and described their appearance. About one fifth (19%) of the visual talk was in this category. For example, when Ms. Brightman showed the children the front and back covers of the Marshall version, the children commented:

> Dominique: There's pigs facing that way and there's pigs facing the other way.
> Nathan: They're wearing clothes.
> Melanie: One has a flower and one has a hat.
> Rob: That one is wearing funny clothes.
> Manuel: What? Which one?
> Rob: The middle pig

Character: Action/Movement

Children also described and interpreted the main characters' movements and actions. About 5% of the visual talk focused on these descriptions of action. For example, during the reading of the Scieszka version, the children delightedly observed that the cake the wolf makes for his "dear old granny" contains some unusual ingredients:

> Mary: He's cooking bunny ears!

In a later illustration, they also described the pig with his razor:

> Steven: He's shaving. But he forgot the shaving cream!

Character: Inner State

About 2% of the visual talk involved interpreting or inferring characters' feelings, thoughts, disposition, and personality. For example, the back cover of the Kellogg version shows a reformed wolf (the badness steamed out of him by being pressed in the waffle iron!), standing on a beach, wearing a t-shirt with the words "Thugs need hugs, too." His arms are outstretched toward several pigs, who look anxious and concerned. Melanie, Dominique, and Rob commented on this illustration, interpreting the wolf's change of heart:

> Melanie: He's like, "Hey, Piggy!" on the back right here. "I'm not bad at all."
> Dominique: 'Cuz he's nice.
> Rob: He's nice now.

Prediction/Confirmation of Plot

About 4% of the visual talk was concerned with using the illustrations to predict what might happen in the story or to confirm predictions. For example, in looking at the title page for the Wiesner version, which depicts the three pigs with the materials (straw, sticks, and bricks) they will use to build their houses, the children noticed that the sequence of actions—first, the house of straw, then the house of sticks, and finally the house of bricks—was prefigured in a subtle way by the illustration:

> Norman: They all, they all have the things that they make their house out of.
> Steve: The grey one is the third one.
> Manuel: Sticks and bricks and straw.
> Alex: I bet I know why the, that one, the straw is in the middle [pointing to the pig in the middle]
> Teacher: Why?
> Alex: Because that one comes first and then if you look right there it's a little bit closer because it goes second, and that one [pointing to the pig on the right] is far and it's third.
> Steve: The grey one is the smart one.

In this example, we see that Wiesner has placed the "straw pig" in the center, closest to the viewer; the "sticks pig" is placed to the left, a little further away from the viewer; and the "bricks pig" is on the right, furthest in the plane of the picture. Thus, as Alex notices, it's not a left-to-right sequence, but the foreground to background sequence that prefigures the order in which the pigs will build their houses in the story.

Integration

The children understood that all the components of the picturebook had to work together to produce a unified aesthetic whole. Thus, another type of visual talk (about 10% of the total visual talk) concerned their urge to relate the various components to each other so as to integrate their knowledge and literary interpretation. For example, during the reading of the first few pages of the Kellogg version, the children speculated about why the endpages are light blue in color:

> Alex: Um, can you show the cover for a minute? Because um this thing [points to the picture of the waffle truck], I bet they were making pizza in it and it's blue.
> Morgan: The color is blue because…'cuz they're at the beach [on the back cover].
> Steven: The water's blue.
> Dominique: Can you turn it back [to the front cover] again? That blue umbrella.
> Melanie: The sky is blue, and the hats are blue, and the shirt. [first page of story]

Here we see children struggling to connect the color of the endpages to some of the prominent objects on the front cover, and also making connections to the sky and the ocean in the illustration on the back cover. Also, as the story begins, they are still thinking about the endpages and how the color blue is carried over into the illustration of the mother pig. The children were proceding on the assumption that everything in the picturebook has meaning, even the color of the endpages, and that everything must make sense in terms of everything else. This type of speculation was also present in the discussion of the Marshall version, where the children interpreted the rust-red colored endpages as a representation of the curtains (of the same color) which they had just seen on the front cover.

Comparison

Children compared visual elements in several illustrations in the story or across stories. In this type of response (about 15% of the total visual talk), the children made intratextual connections among illustrations in one story or made intertextual connections across stories. In the discussion of the Kellogg version (the second book in the text set), there were 17 conversational turns that compared the visual information in the Kellogg version to the visual information in the previously read Marshall version. In the third discussion (Scieszka), there were 12 comparisons to the Kellogg and Marshall versions, and in the fourth discussion (Wiesner), there were 24 comparisons to the three previous versions. For example, in the Wiesner version, the discussion of the front cover included the following:

> Nathan: They're *real* pigs. … They're, they look like real three pigs. And in the other stories, the other pigs didn't really look a lot like real pigs.
> Morgan: They're pigs like animal pigs and the other ones are like people pigs.
> Teacher: These are animal or people pigs, oh, what do you mean by people pigs?
> Steve: Like they walk on their two feet…they talk.

Mandy: And they wear clothes.
Nathan: These are going to die.

This vignette shows the children's surprise that, in contrast to the illustrations for the three previous versions they had examined (Marshall, Kellogg, and Scieszka), David Wiesner chose to depict the pigs realistically. In fact, Wiesner has stated that he based his illustrations on three actual breeds of pigs, so the children are quite correct. The children have noticed this switch from "people pigs"—pigs that are not realistically portrayed and that can only exist in stories, because they act like people—to "animal pigs": images of pigs as animals in the real world. "People pigs" wear clothing, walk upright like humans, and talk. It's interesting that Nathan's prediction here, that the pigs in this story "are going to die," seems directly connected to the idea that these are "animal pigs." Realism in the illustrations, in other words, suggests to Nathan that the narrative will be realistic as well.

Story Boundaries

The fourth and last discussion (of the Wiesner version) contained a type of visual response found only during that readaloud. Because the book centrally concerns the pigs moving out of their own story, into several other stories, and back again to their own tale, children used the illustrations to interpret this difficult concept of moving across story boundaries or borders (Mackey, 2003a). This represents a playful "blurring" of the world of reality and the world of the story; it is a form of metafiction, a self-referential way that the text calls attention to itself as an artifice, rather than drawing readers completely into its "secondary world" (Benton, 1992) for a "lived-through" experience (Rosenblatt, 1978) of the story. This is a complicated idea even for adults, as Pantaleo (2002) has pointed out. Though peculiar to the readaloud of the Wiesner version, this special type of talk comprised a significant amount (10%) of the total visual talk across all the discussions.

The first instance of "story boundary" talk occurred early in the book at the words, "So the wolf huffed and he puffed, and he blew the house in…" The accompanying illustration shows straw flying everywhere, and the first pig breaking the lower right-hand frame of the illustration. The pig seems nearer to us, the viewers, and thus appears to be falling off the page. The pig's speech balloon reads, "Hey! He blew me right out of the story!" At this point, the children's comments suggest cognitive dissonance and puzzlement:

Steven: It looks like he's falling out of the story.
Melanie: It says "I'll blow your house in" like the other one.
Anthony: I don't think he's in the story.
Steven: Let's see.
Teacher: That's a good question. The pig just said, "He blew me right out of the story!"
Steven: 'Cuz it looks like he's falling.
Manuel: It looks like he's falling…out.
Dominique: 'Cuz, 'cuz, 'cuz, if he was in the, 'cuz, it kinda looks like…
Manuel: It doesn't make sense.

Eventually, all three pigs move out of their own story; they fold a paper airplane from a page of their story and sail into blank space—a "space between" stories. Then they enter another book, which seems to be a collection of nursery rhymes, on the page for the rhyme, "Hey, diddle, diddle." When they enter the story, their appearance changes from "animal pigs" to "people pigs": they walk on two feet, their features appear more cartoon-like, and their bodies have less realistic colors (or, as Dominique suggested, "marker colors"). At this point, Keith hypothesized, "I bet they're in another story," and Manuel speculated that "It might be another three little pigs story." The pigs, however, do not spend much time in this story; yelling, "Let's get out of here!" they race off the right-hand side of the page. As they leave the story, they become "animal pigs" once again. At this point, the pigs are in another blank "space between," and they have the choice of going into a number of different stories, as Alex and Dominique realized:

Alex: They fell out of the story and they're coming up to another story.
Dominique: Um, I, there's a bunch of story frames and they might bump into a bunch of them.

The children were beginning to articulate the logic of story boundary- crossing:

Alex: Can you turn the page back? [Teacher turns back page] It was showing their like story color and he's walking out of it and it's like the regular color and right there's story color.

Here, Alex notices that, when the pigs are in the "space between," they appear as they did in their own story; but when they are in another story, their appearance conforms to that story's illustration style. This was confirmed to the children when the pigs enter yet *another* story, illustrated in black and white. The pigs become black and white line drawings. When they leave, they take a dragon with them, and the dragon changes from a black and white drawing to appear in the same realistic style as the pigs. In the strangest of their adventures, the pigs seem to come to a veritable library of stories, where there are no fixed boundaries at all:

Manuel: This is weird because this story's [points to the picture] going into this story. And this is another one. The fish are like floating in nowhere.
Dominique: It's like a bunch of pictures.
Manuel: This story is going into every story. The fish are going crazy and going everywhere!
Teacher: You're right.
Manuel: In that picture and in that picture!
Dominique: It's like a bunch of picture frames all over the place.

Even though the above examples relate only a small part of the children's excited discussion, they do serve to indicate some of the complicated lines of hypotheses and reasoning as these first graders engaged in Wiesner's postmodern tale.

CONCLUSION AND IMPLICATIONS FOR TEACHING AND FUTURE RESEARCH

This study suggests the importance of visual interpretation in children's literary understanding of picturebooks, and highlights the power of text sets in developing these interpretive skills. Children used visual information to describe details of the setting and background of illustrations, to interpret story characters' appearance, actions, relationships, feelings, intentions, and motivations, and to predict and confirm the plot. They also worked to integrate the meanings gleaned from various components of the picturebook into more complex and holistic significance. They made comparisons between illustrations within the same book and also compared and contrasted visual features across the four stories. Finally, they took on the challenge of a complicated version of *The Three Pigs* (Wiesner) by grappling with the idea of story boundaries. Teachers and other practitioners may want to closely examine their own class discussions about picturebooks to determine how their students are using visual information in comparison to the eight uses made by the children in this study. For example, if students are utilizing visual information to describe story characters' appearance and actions, but not to interpret the characters' inner thoughts or feelings, teachers can ask, "What might this character be thinking or feeling right now?" Children should also be encouraged to forge connections across visual information in the illustration sequence, in order to perceive changes or commonalities in the plot or character development during the course of the story. As they discuss visual information, teachers may well discover additional uses children make of visual elements, as they expand their repertoire of visual meaning making.

The study was based on a text set of four versions of *The Three Pigs*, chosen carefully to represent a variety of illustration styles and a variety of texts that varied in details, tone, and plot. Thus, even though all the stories were recognizable as variants of *The Three Pigs*, the text set afforded an opportunity for children to make interesting comparisons and contrasts. We suggest choosing four or five versions to create an intertextually rich environment. Our choice was also based on our desire to include a variety of illustrational styles by recognized artists; all four of the artists represented had won Caldecott awards, and all four were quite distinct. The intertextually rich environment was thus *visually* rich, as well, with James Marshall's deceptively simple and gently humorous outline drawings; Stephen Kellogg's more detailed and exuberant pen-and-ink illustrations; Lane Smith's wry and sardonic images that matched the tongue-in-cheek quality of Jon Scieskza's text; and David Wiesner's dramatic use of white space to represent the "space between stories" and multiple illustration styles that changed as the pigs went from story to story. If teachers choose similar contrasting artistic styles for text sets, children may be more likely to be drawn into discussing visual similarities and differences, and engaging in high levels of visual interpretation. Because some of the books used in this study seemed to elicit different and unique types of visual talk, teachers' choice of books is crucial. Books that represent a broad range of high-quality illustration styles and books that represent postmodern departures from conventions of genre and form will be likely to elicit richer discussion and more sophisticated literary understanding (Mackey, 2003b).

The sequence in which the variants are presented is also quite important. In this study, we used the principle of proceeding from the known to the new and from the simple to the complex, and therefore began with a version (Marshall) whose story line was probably familiar to the children. The subsequent variants were successively further departures from this starting point. The Kellogg version added the mother pig as another significant character as well as the plot element of making waffles. The Scieszka version changed the entire point of view from which the story was told; and the Wiesner version added the surprising metafictive element of the pigs leaving their own story and coming back again. Thus, teachers can think about the ways in which the plot, setting, characters, and points of view vary among the books they have chosen, and arrange them in an order that will allow for broadening and deepening children's schemata for stories.

In this study, children relied heavily on the peritextual features of the books (for example, the dust jacket, front and back covers, endpages, title page, and dedication page) in their discussion, showing the strong potential of these features for meaning-making. Teachers can make full use of all these components of picturebooks, spending time in each readaloud discussing one or two of them. In this way, they could (over time) teach children to consider picturebooks as aesthetic objects, in which every part of the total design (for example, the color of the endpages) is the result of an artistic decision, thereby encouraging critical thinking through building hypotheses about the decisions made by authors, illustrators, and editors.

Some stories (for example, *Cinderella*) exist in literally hundreds of forms from a diverse spectrum of countries and cultures, illustrated in a multitude of different styles and media; it is possible that a much longer literary study, with a larger number of variants, could result in a significant deepening of children's interpretive abilities. Further research might examine children's responses to visual material in a more extensive text set of more books over a longer period of time in order to more closely examine the ways in which visual talk develops and builds on previous knowledge. Such research could (1) refine and extend our understanding of the eight types of visual talk identified in this study, and (2) identify additional ways in which children use visual information in literary meaning making. Finally, the present study did not consider what the adult who read the story did to scaffold the children's visual talk—the questions she asked, the ways in which she restated (and expanded on) the children's comments, or re-directed the conversation. Analysis of this or similar data sets from this perspective would greatly extend our understanding of pedagogical practice that enhances children's visual meaning making.

REFERENCES

Barrentine, S. J. (1996). Engaging with reading through interactive read-alouds. *Reading Teacher, 50,* 36-43.

Benton, M. (1992). *Secondary worlds: Literature teaching and the visual arts.* Buckingham, UK: Open University Press.

Flinders, D. J., & Eisner, E. W. (1994). Educational criticism as a form of qualitative inquiry. *Research in the Teaching of English, 28,* 341-357.

Flood, J., & Lapp. D. (1995). Broadening the lens: Toward an expanded conceptualization of literacy. *Yearbook of the National Reading Conference, 44,* 1-16.

Genette, G. (1997a). *Paratexts: Thresholds of interpretation* (J. Lewin, Trans.). New York: Cambridge University Press.

Gibson, J. J. (1979). *The ecological approach to visual perception.* Boston: Houghton Mifflin.

Glaser, B., & Strauss, A. (1967). *The discovery of grounded theory.* Chicago: Aldine.

Golden, J., & Gerber, A. (1990). A semiotic perspective of text: The picture story book event. *Journal of Reading Behavior, 22,* 203-219.

Halliday, M. A. K. (1975). *Learning how to mean: Explorations in the development of language.* London: Longman Group Ltd.

Harris, P., Trezise, J., & Winsor, W. N. (2002). "Is the story on my face?": Intertextual conflicts during teacher-class interactions around texts in early grade classrooms. *Research in the Teaching of English, 37,* 9-54.

Harste, J., Short, K., & Burke, C. (1988). *Creating classrooms for authors.* Portsmouth, NH: Heinemann.

Higonnet, M. (1990). The playground of the peritext. *Children's Literature Association Quarterly, 15,* 47-49.

Huck, C. S., Kiefer, B. Z., Hepler, S., & Hickman, J. (2004). *Children's literature in the elementary school.* Boston: McGraw Hill.

Iser, W. (1978). *The act of reading.* Baltimore, MD: Johns Hopkins University Press.

Kellogg, S. (1997). *The three little pigs.* New York: Morrow Junior Books.

Kiefer, B. (1982). *The response of primary children to picture books.* Unpublished doctoral dissertation, The Ohio State University, Columbus, OH.

Kiefer, B. Z. (1995). *The potential of picturebooks: From visual literacy to aesthetic understanding.* Englewood Cliffs, NJ: Prentice-Hall, Inc.

Lewis, D. (2001). *Reading contemporary picturebooks: Picturing text.* New York: Routledge/Falmer.

Mackey, M. (2003a). At play on the borders of the diegetic: Story boundaries and narrative interpretation. *Journal of Literacy Research, 35,* 591-632.

Mackey, M. (2003b). Researching new forms of literacy. *Reading Research Quarterly, 38,* 403-407.

Madura, S. (1997, December). *An artistic element: Four transitional readers and writers respond to the picture books of Patricia Polacco and Gerald McDermott.* Paper presented at the National Reading Conference, Scottsdale, AZ.

Marantz, K. (1977). The picturebook as art object: A call for balanced reviewing. *The Wilson Library Bulletin,* 148-151.

Marshall, J. (1989). *The three little pigs.* New York: Dial Books for Young Readers.

Moebius, W. (1986). Introduction to picturebook codes. *Word and Image, 2,* 141-158.

Morrow, L. M., & Smith, J. K. (1990). The effects of group size on interactive storybook reading. *Reading Research Quarterly, 25,* 214-231.

Nodelman, P. (1988). *Words about pictures: The narrative art of children's picture books.* Athens, GA: The University of Georgia Press.

Pantaleo, S. (2002). Grade 1 students meet David Wiesner's Three Pigs. *Journal of Children's Literature, 28,* 72-84.

Pantaleo, S. (2003). "Godzilla lives in New York": Grade 1 students and the peritextual features of picture books. *Journal of Children's Literature, 29,* 66-77.

Pantaleo, S. (2004a). The long, long way: Young children explore the fabula and syuzhet of *Shortcut. Children's Literature in Education, 35,* 1-20.

Pantaleo, S. (2004b). Young children interpret the metafictive in Anthony Browne's *Voices in the Park. Journal of Early Childhood Literacy, 4,* 211-233.

Rosenblatt, L. M. (1978). *The reader, the text, the poem: The transactional theory of the literary work.* Carbondale, IL: Southern Illinois University Press.

Scieszka, J. (1989). *The true story of the three little pigs.* New York: Penguin Books.

Sendak, M. (1963). *Where the wild things are.* New York: HarperCollins.

Short, K. G. (1992). Researching intertexuality within collaborative classroom learning environments. *Linguistics and Education, 4,* 313-333.

Sinclair, J. M. & Coulthard, M. (1975). *Towards an analysis of discourse: The English used by teachers and pupils.* London: Oxford University Press.

Sipe, L. R. (1998). How picture books work: A semiotically framed theory of text-picture relationships. *Children's Literature in Education, 29,* 97-108.

Sipe, L. R. (2000). The construction of literary understanding by first and second graders in oral response to picture storybook readalouds. *Reading Research Quarterly, 35,* 252-275.

Sipe, L. R. (2001). A palimpsest of stories: Young children's intertextual links during readalouds of fairytale variants. *Reading Research and Instruction, 40,* 333-352.

Sipe, L. R. (2003). It's a matter of style: One teacher's storybook reading in an urban classroom. *The New Advocate, 10,* 55-66.

Sipe, L. R., & Bauer, J. (2001). Urban Kindergarteners' literary understanding of picture storybooks. *The New

Advocate, 14, 329-342.

Spiro, R., Coulson, R. L., Feltovich, P. J., & Anderson, D. K. (1994). Cognitive flexibility theory: Advanced knowledge acquisition in ill-structured domains. In R. B. Ruddell, M. R. Ruddell, & H. Singer (Eds.), *Theoretical models and processes of reading* (4th Ed.) (pp. 602-615). Newark, DE: International Reading Association.

Stewig, J. (1995). *Looking at picture books.* Fort Atkinson, WI: Highsmith.

Strauss, A., & Corbin, J. (1990). *Basics of qualitative research: Grounded theory procedures and techniques.* Newbury Park, CA: Sage.

Suhor, C. (1984). Towards a semiotic-based curriculum. *Journal of Curriculum Studies, 16,* 247-257.

Trites, R. S. (1994). Manifold narratives: Metafiction and ideology in picture books. *Children's Literature in Education, 25,* 225-242.

Wiesner, D. (2001). *The three pigs.* New York: Clarion Books.

Yolen, J. (1981). *Touch magic: Fantasy, faerie and folklore in the literature of children.* New York: Philomel.

"We Feel Like We're Separating Us":
Sixth Grade Girls Respond to Multicultural Literature

Sally A. Smith

Hofstra University

Mari: I think that we're afraid, when we say Black, like...

Tara: You shouldn't be afraid.

Mari: No, it's not that we're racists. We feel weird saying it, cause we're...

Suzanna: We feel like we're *separating* us...

In this conversation, occurring in the final session of a semester long book club, the sixth grade book club members negotiate identities as White and African American girls. Mari and Suzanna are reluctant to name differences, while Tara, who is African American, reassures her White friends. Listening in to literature discussions such as these provides adults with the opportunity to see response and identity negotiation made visible. To examine the processes of gender and racial identity development in early adolescent girls, I turned to the rich opportunities provided by small group discussions of well-written young adult novels with diverse perspectives. A number of studies of book talk in classrooms (Beach, 1997; Cherland, 2000; Enciso, 1997; Fox & Short, 2003; Moller, 2001) shed light on these opportunities, but few studies have explored the book conversations of a racially and ethnically diverse group of students out of the confines of the classroom.

To understand and describe the complexity of my participants' identity development, I used poststructuralist frames that highlight the socially constructed nature of racial and gender development. These theories describe identity as a fluid and contradictory process (Weedon, 1987) that is best examined by means of qualitative data. My study looked at one group of sixth grade girls and their responses to young adult novels read in the after school book group. My analysis focuses on two texts read in book club, *I Hadn't Meant to Tell You This* and *Maizon at Blue Hill*. Both titles are by an African American author, Jacqueline Woodson.

RESEARCH FRAMEWORK

Reading as a Site for Engagement and Critical Reflection

Research on readers' engagement, dispositions, and discussions about texts highlights the role that the reading transaction has in reflection on self and world. The "personally-lived through" response to literature that Rosenblatt describes as aesthetic, engaged reading (1976, p. 388) is influenced by the literary conventions of fiction and the stance and expectation of the reader (Finders, 1997; Langer, 1990; Purves, 1972; Rosenblatt, 1976). This transaction provides a space for considering one's own and other lives and is influenced by the reader's contexts, including gender, race, class, and education. Talking about books in social settings such as classrooms and discussion groups further affects these influences. Because the interchanges that occur in book talk influence and expand response opportunities for members of the reading group, the readers may begin to renegotiate and situate their identities in reaction to a text. This process contributes to the "polyphony" of multiple discourses and experiences (Broughton, 2002; Eeds & Wells, 1989; Enciso, 1997; Schweickart & Flynn, 2004). Engaging in collaborative talk, readers use the text to make sense of the world, and their talk about texts makes this process visible (Bakhtin, 1981; Vygotsky, 1986).

Multicultural texts and meaning making. The text itself is a crucial element in the reading transaction. Studies of multicultural texts in literature discussion groups indicate that multicultural picture books, as well as realistic and historical fiction, have the potential to further stimulate personal responses and foreground critique. When African American children and adolescents read literature by and about African Americans, they are able to make personal connections and envision possible lives, possible selves, and other lives (Broughton, 2002; Lewis, 1997; McGinley & Kamberelis, 1996). Mainstream and multicultural literature contribute to the images of color and culture available to all children, along with music videos, teen magazines, and television. Engaged, adult-facilitated discussions about such texts can facilitate the process of negotiating these multivocal and contradictory images and meanings (Cherland, 2000; Moller, 2001).

For White readers, more used to seeing themselves and their families in books, literature written from alternate perspectives introduces opportunities for vicariously experiencing the world as an outsider and for positioning themselves in a world both unfamiliar and familiar. Talk may be used as an opportunity to explore and clarify these portrayals, and may provide a forum for examining different cultural positions and reading strategies (Smith, 2000).

Racial Identity Construction in Early Adolescence

To understand my early adolescent participants' complex histories and responses to literature, I used Weedon's conceptual framework for "seeing" the identity negations of this age group to consider the importance of what Weedon terms "subjectivity," that fluid self "which is precarious, contradictory, and in process, constantly being reconstituted in discourse each time [they] speak" (Weedon, 1987, p. 33). According to this model, we all occupy different positions in different contexts and at different times as gendered and racial beings. In a similar vein, Egan-Robertson employs the notion of "personhood" (1998). This concept also highlights the reality that a person's identity positions often contradict themselves, depending on the situation, as they are socially constructed against a backdrop of cultural, academic, community, and global perspectives. Yet, they all fit into an individual's fluid, context-related self, or personhood. The book club study, situated in an unofficial reading setting, became a place for the construction of discourse that temporarily positioned these early adolescents as they constructed their views of themselves in their world against the background of young adult novels. I am aware that studies using categories such as gender or race as aspects of analysis run the risk of treating that category as an embodied social construction. I acknowledge this risk, and attempted to honor the fleeting, ever-changing identities observed in my study.

Race and difference. Racial differences become a salient issue in early adolescence (Leadbeater & Way, 1996; Tatum, 1997) as choices and expectations, cultural values and experiences, and norms for literacy shape young people's lives. Racial and ethnic group memberships have significant psychological implications in U.S. society. African Americans, Latinos, Native Americans, and Asian Americans must resist negative stereotypes to develop a positive sense of self within the multiple contexts of their lives.

As in all other aspects of identity development, the process of forming and reforming a racial identity is complex and nonlinear. Its progression is deeply influenced by subjective aspects such as social circumstances and experiences. For Whites, the process of forming a racial identity involves developing a sense of self that is based on reality in personal, political, and institutional contexts, rather than on assumed superiority (Helms, 1990; Tatum, 1997). White individuals' discourse about race highlights a tendency to "paper over" racism and to focus on well-meaning colorblindness (McIntyre, 1997). Helms (1990) developed a six-part theory of identity development for Whites that proposes a move from being unaware of themselves as racial beings to an autonomous stage free from White denial.

Cross (1991) and Tatum (1997) identified early stages of racial development for African American and White children as the pre-encounter stage, when they absorb many of the beliefs and values of the dominant culture. At this stage, the personal and social significance of one's racial group membership has not yet been realized and racial identity is not being examined.

In middle to late elementary school, the transition for African American children to the encounter stage is generally precipitated by an event or series of events that force the young person to acknowledge the personal impact of racism (Cross, 1991; Tatum, 1997). The impact of society's messages about what it means to be African American is lessened for young people whose parents encourage them to identify with positive cultural images and messages. African American parents who are race-conscious (Tatum, 1997) actively seek to provide and encourage positive cultural images and messages about what it means to be African American.

Studies indicate that while White adolescents are beginning to think about ethnic identity there is a more active search by African American students, especially females (Phinney & Tarver 1988). Eventually, both African American and White young people are forced to recognize the personal impact of racism. Children entering middle school, where tracking is common and dating begins, often recognize institutional patterns as well as personal racism. Cross & Tatum's studies speak to the importance of further examination of African American and White girls at early adolescence in settings that may allow these girls to share their observations and experiences, and to testify to their beliefs.

Talking about race. Children and young adults do not enter into new settings with set gender (or racial) positions. Rather they "(take) up and experimented with discourses that were made available to them in an attempt to negotiate power relations within the classroom" (Gallas 1998 p. 5-6). New and unfamiliar contexts--such as a book club--call for new responses to the shifting meanings of categories of identity like race. These new spaces allow students to assume certain identities or take up certain positions made available by discourses about race, and to take responsibility for these positions (Ellsworth, 1997; Fine, 1997). This necessarily implies critiquing institutional practices set up through modern bureaucracies like schools, both private and public.

In her study of private schools, Duesterberg (1999) examines the ways in which the liberal discourses of such schools work to position youth. She stresses that "while White adolescents actively remake themselves in relation to prevailing meanings and practices institutionalized in a largely white, upper-middle class school setting, Black students in White schools must continually negotiate and reposition themselves in relation to institutionalized discourses of race oriented around white, middle class norms, values, and expectations" (1999, p.776). The expectations of teachers and peers force students to take positions toward the social codes and discourses in academic and social settings. These positions and expectations are further complicated by the circumstances of class. Twine's (1997) study of girls of color raised in affluent White suburban settings indicated that during early adolescence, they seemed superficially to inhabit the same world as their European-American peers.

METHOD

Study Context: An Urban Independent School.

The setting for book club was an independent, or private, middle school in a large Northeastern city. The majority of the student body came from a middle-class to affluent European American neighborhood, but also included those from outlying areas with more diversity of class and race. As a researcher from outside the school community, I offered an on-going book club as an after school option for sixth grade girls, and eight eleven and twelve-year old girls volunteered to attend the after school activity. We discussed four novels selected by the girls, and two novels read in language arts classes, at our weekly meetings from 3:15 to 4:30 in an empty middle school classroom.

In the present study I focus on conversations by six of the book club members over five sessions. Two other book club members were absent during four of the five sessions. Two of the six focal participants were African American, one was Latina, one had a European American father and Latina mother, and two were European American. The book club members perceived themselves as savvy urban girls and their conversations in book club and interviews supported this perception, as they talked about gay culture, AIDS, sexual abuse, racial attitudes, and school gender relations with authority, humor, and developing understanding. Like the suburban girls of color studied by Twine (1997), the middle to upper middle class backgrounds the girls shared tended to flatten some racial and cultural differences, particularly for the two Latina girls.

Participants

One sixth grader, Suzanna, read widely and was a close friend of several girls in the group. Her mother is Latina and her father European American; she described speaking Spanish at home. Another, Nereida, has parents who are bilingual Latinos and she described herself as aware of her identity as a Latina in a "gringo" society. She was an intensely engaged reader.

Luann, a third participant, is African American. She lived far from the school in an African American neighborhood, and in an interview described her transition from the world of home and school each day: "And when I'm here I talk one way, and then at home, I get into the other way... by the time I'm home, I'm talking like me, like my family and friends." Luann was an articulate member of the group who got along with each of the other members.

Mari, a European American girl, was a member with insightful comments, usually delivered in a quiet, voice. Despite her quiet demeanor, Mari seemed at ease in book club. Allison was new to the school. She is White, and at twelve, was one of the oldest members of the group. She spoke to me (in interviews) of having lost her father when she was younger, and her conversations contributed a serious tone to the book club discussions. The sixth participant, Tara, is African American. She held strong opinions and brought these--such as "I just can't really take stereotypes!" to our discussions. Though sometimes off-task in book club, when her attention was focused, she was a vibrant and thoughtful member.

From the mainstream. I am a White woman and a parent, but not of these girls. I am a teacher, but not in this setting. Book discussions and talking about discrimination were familiar territory for me after many years' work in classrooms and libraries talking about stereotyping. While this experience provided me with a level of comfort in facilitating discussions about race, my Whiteness often positioned me as "other," limiting responses of students of color to me and to the curriculum. As we speak and interact with others, we take up positions in relation to their expectations, as well as to the social codes and discourses that are familiar to us (Lewis, 1997). As a White adult, I took part in and performed my own meanings about race based on my particular historical and social contexts (Ellsworth, 1997), as did my former students and my book club participants.

Diverse perspectives. The novels were also key participants in the book club, contributing powerfully to the polyphony of ideas, images, and voices in book club discussions. *I Hadn't Meant To Tell You This* (Woodson, 1994) is an intimate first person narrative that invites the reader into the world of middle class Marie, an African American girl, and her new friend Lena. Lena, poor and White, confides that she is being sexually abused by her father. *Maizon at Blue Hill* (1992) depicts a girl from an inner city neighborhood who goes to a White boarding school in the countryside where she must confront her ambivalent feelings about "fitting in." Pivotal scenes in both texts involve conversations about race and prejudice. As we finished reading these two novels, the author visited the school and spoke to book club members.

Data Collection and Analysis

My data sources consisted of a constant comparison method (Ely, Anzul, Friedman, Garner, & Steinmetz, 1991; Strauss & Corbin, 1990) to track emerging themes, and a discourse analysis to identify categories of response and the construction of a discourse community (Barnes, 1993; Barnes & Todd, 1995; Lemke, 1995). Data analysis was ongoing as the study progressed, and triangulation of data occurred through sharing transcripts with my participants in sessions and interviews, participant feedback, and through my analytic memos and field notes.

I conducted individual interviews at four intervals to obtain perspectives on reading, book club, family contexts, and school contexts. The first interviews occurred during the first and second month of book club; the fourth group of interviews occurred in September of the following year. I used aspects of a Listener's Guide protocol (Brown & Gilligan, 1992) to analyze interview data. The guide format enables listener and speaker to produce a narrative account which takes into consideration the researcher's questions, the experiences of the person being interviewed, as well as the "social location" of both (Taylor, 1996). Because the focus of my meta-analysis was on the group members' interactions with texts, I employed this guide solely for the interview data.

To best examine the identity processes of early adolescent girls in a small group setting, I analyzed the larger discourse patterns and conversational topics that emerged from the data, and explored the interaction between patterns and conversational topics. Topic analysis tracked the girls' on-going meaning making in relation to race. Three categories of discourse emerged that contributed to my examination of the construction and enactment of these themes. These categories were exploratory talk, storytelling, and testifying.

Exploratory talk. For the analysis of this category of discourse, I was guided by Barnes' (1993) and Barnes and Todd's (1995) studies of the small group discourse of British school children. Barnes and Todd identify exploratory talk as a significant characteristic of small group conversations. They characterize exploratory talk as typically occurring as participants engage in examining topics both personal and academic. This framework helped me recognize the texture and focus of the exploratory talk and how it contributed to the topic themes. This mode of analysis also enabled me to track changes in discourse patterns, and to attend to the development of talk as the group formed its own culture. Discourse patterns that became visible through my analysis were the participants' use of exploratory talk to share the floor with each other to build on and enlarge each other's interpretations to make meaning based on the text and their lived experiences (Cazden, 1998), and to raise queries, both heuristic and practical, about race.

Book club meetings often began with the sixth grade girls "reexperiencing" their response to a character or passage and "sorting-out" meaning together (categories described by Douglas Barnes in *Cycles of Meaning*, 1993, and further clarified in a personal communication in 1997) as the sixth grade girls shared and compared their immediate understanding of a text, and confirmed their individual responses to it. There were frequent questions, summaries, and explanations, and the viewpoints of some group members were internalized by others in the group. Exploratory talk often moved to identifying and evaluating the verisimilitude of the text, which in turn could lead to personal reflections. For example, at one point in the eighth session, Luann, an African American book club member, asked for clarification about the conversation on racism between two characters in *I Hadn't Meant to Tell You This.* She and other book club members subsequently related it to their understanding of racism following her comment.

Storytelling rounds. Although exploratory talk and some instances of storytelling were evident in the first six book club sessions as members discussed other novels, storytelling and testifying became significant characteristics of the discourse at the juncture of the seventh and eighth sessions when Tara and Allison, new members, joined book club and the girls met the author Jacqueline

Woodson. Data revealed that the girls used storytelling and testifying as ways to clarify communicate, and bridge gaps of experience. Storytelling involved sharing—sometime "matching"—personal or heard experiences that reinforced a theme in the text, or served to verify or contrast with a previous story (Tannen, 1984). An example of storytelling that reinforced a theme and also established a context of racial identity occurred when one new participant, Tara described a "back of the bus" experience of her grandfather. This was followed by two other stories from Tara and from Luann, the other African American group member.

Testifying to one's beliefs. Testifying emerged as a minor discourse mode in which one member of the group, in the midst of a discussion, put her values and beliefs on the table as a way of defining who she was (Smitherman, 1977). Tara and Luann, both African American members of the group often shared wisdom or opinions in this way, in the heat of conversation. For example Luann described the interracial make-up of her mother's church and then stated, "I'm used to getting along with everybody here."

When experiences are similar, in terms of race, culture, and class, the necessity for using story-telling and testifying to explain and connect to experiences and texts may not exist. However story-telling for meaning-making concerns difference, and attempting to both illustrate and bridge that difference. Book club members explored their racial identities through the employment of the above-mentioned response and discourse strategies, talk they also used to interrogate and comment on societal norms.

RESULTS

Using excerpts from book discussions I suggest ways the textual content engaged readers in examining and comparing their own racial positions, which they explored through sharing stories and testifying to their beliefs.

In the seventh session of the book club, Tara, an African American sixth grader, and Allison who is White, joined the original group of six participants in book club. The addition of a second African American book club member who freely shared her family's stories and beliefs may have had an impact on the frequency with which discussions of race, including storytelling and testifying, became an important component of response throughout the remainder of the sessions. Allison, the new White member, was also comfortable talking about race and was an acute observer of her new school and city.

The girls had just begun to read the first of two provocative novels. The original group of six book club members selected *I Hadn't Meant to Tell You This* by African American author, Jacqueline Woodson because the author was about to visit the middle school. Book club members also read another of the author's novels, *Maizon at Blue Hill.*

Jacqueline Woodson spoke to the assembled middle school as we were completing these two novels and met alone with book club members for about twenty minutes. Meeting Woodson, a strong and outspoken African American woman, seemed to help to focus the girls on her explicit portrayals of race. As they reflected on their meeting with Woodson, Tara remarked, "She really relates to topics that I can *understand.* Because it's around me, like *racism,* or like, the bad people in this world, that are racist..." They were also interested in the idea that a Black author would include fully developed White characters in her novels. As Tara concluded, "She's not just writing about Blacks, she's writing for everybody."

Illustrating and Bridging Differences

The intersection of the author visit and the girls' engagement in three novels with African American characters who talk about race, highlighted this topic. In addition to these circumstances, the informal, intimate out-of-class setting of our meetings, which contrasted with typical classroom contexts, provided ample access to the "floor" for these girls (Cazden, 1998; Sadker & Sadker, 1994). They were able to take the time to tell stories, to respond at length, to interrupt and to build on one another's themes.

In the seventh session, members' summary of the novel's plot became a prompt for stories and storytelling in book club as members shared vignettes about family, neighbors, and the media. Tara began this talk by describing a "fair-complected" cousin who was harassed by her darker skinned peers at her all African American college several years ago due to her looks and demeanor. She continued with another family story from the pre-Civil Rights 1950's:

Tara: And another thing, it's really screwed up, but my grandfather, he's really light complected, and he was riding the bus, and the bus driver said, 'Mr. you can sit in the front, because White people aren't supposed to sit in the back." And he said, "That's okay, I'm *Black.*"

Nereida: You'd think he'd sit up front!

Facilitator: That must have been hard for him to say...

Tara: Yeah, it was. It was just weird—like that whole Rosa Parks thing.

Tara's story, delivered in a dramatic manner, illuminates the complexity of racial markers in the U.S., markers that she and her family discuss. She may have assumed that all group members would understand the racial positions of that time. Nereida's comment indicates that she did not fully understand the import of the story. This vignette was followed by a similar story by Luann about a present day cousin in North Carolina who is very light-skinned and, passing for White, became a police officer. She hastily completed her story: "and blah, blah, blah, and so they realized that he was African American, and so they burned something next to his house... they tried to burn his house down."

These stories seemed to take on several functions during this first session of eight members. Using the experiences of relatives, two African American book club members describe a territory familiar to them, a context that describes and extends their families and defines them. The stories are revealing for the White and Latina members of the group--my notes for the session describe their attentiveness as Tara and Luann were speaking. Luann had not shared this kind of story in previous meetings. The topic itself, new to the group, charged the atmosphere. There is much more in these conversations than response to a novel.

The two girls' family stories created a layered, complex historical understanding of racism in the United States. These stories complicate the understandings of their White classmates, whose family stories speak to very different lives. Tara's vignette makes vivid a people's lived experience. She defines herself here as a person whose family is proud to be African American. The other group members responded to these stories with questions about "acting White." Their questions continue the exploration of the complexity of race and the somewhat distanced stance of the White group members. It may be an attempt by these girls to reposition themselves to better explore these new issues:

> Allison: I guess it's when you hang out with White people and Black people together. And if you would hang out mostly with the opposite race, I suppose you would *act...* more like them.
>
> Nereida: Yeah, I know a girl, she's White and most of her friends are African American, so she did her hair the way *they* did and she wore her clothes the way *they* did, and it was weird.
>
> Mari: It's weird that doing your hair means "acting Black..."
>
> Nereida: I don't know why people call it 'acting Black.' Is it that more Black people act that way than White people or something? But then I guess, if somebody of the opposite race acts like the opposite race or whatever, would it be like, "Oh my God, they're not supposed to do that"...it's like not *politically correct* to do that, you know?

In the exploratory talk above, the White and Latina girls begin to comment on and interrogate societal norms from their own points of view. With support from Tara and Luann's stories and facilitator questions, they examine society's use of superficial markers to define individuals in limited and oppositional ways. The girls themselves inadvertently introduce vocabulary of separation: Allison speaks of the "opposite" race, and Nereida incorporates the term in her own query. Neither African American girl joins the conversation. We do not know how they feel, but their stories indicate that their families have shared the lore of racism with them, and that their knowledge is based on an encounter with both the historical and the personal impact of racism (Helms, 1990; Tatum, 1997). The White group members may be in a transition stage, questioning societal givens, as they listen to their peers' experiences and attempt to construct a nonracist personhood.

Exploring Identities

By the next session, the two new members had caught up with the reading of the Woodson novel. This session followed the Woodson visit. Tara began the session by commenting on the author's themes, and Luann immediately turned to the book.

> Luann: Wait, I have a question. In *I Hadn't*, I know that her father's like a racist. But that part didn't make sense to me.
>
> Suzanna: Well I think he's, he's been discriminated for so long; and now he has

something to hate back.

Mari: I think it's not okay to say that they're bad (racist), but they need to have something to blame things on, and so that's why they say that.

Luann: And, I think it was this book, yeah, um. This book said something about, he grew up, he didn't know about racism? And then when he grew up, it just came with the territory.

In this conversation about *I Hadn't Meant to Tell you This*, Luann poses a question to the other members of the group, who propose their interpretations, based on their reading and experiences. Luann, African American, completes the interchange by using Suzanna and Mari's clarification to confirm that the book contributes to and confirms her own knowledge about racism--it just comes with the territory.

Luann's willingness to speak openly about race as well as the volatile aspect of her positionality is revealed in response to the novel *Maizon at Blue Hill* (also by Woodson). Luann said:

> I think that in *Maizon at Blue Hill*, like, I don't consider myself as an 'Oreo,' or that kind of person...But Pauli's the girl that um, like that all the African American girls don't like, cause she acts like she's White. I feel a little bit bad, cause at times I actually feel like Pauli.

Luann may be using her reading of this novel to further develop and make sense of her own position as an African American person in a White setting. She verbalizes one aspect of the process of negotiating her own role. In this statement, she is questioning and confronting her peers with her concerns. In her abrupt statement of emerging feelings, she seems to want to elicit reactions from the group. This question, to her African American and White and Latina peers, illustrates the fluid and often-contradictory process, of racial identity construction. As she speaks, Luann "reconstitute(s)" (Weedon, 1997, p. 33) herself as an Oreo, as unsure of identity as an African American person in that moment and that setting, precipitated by her reading of the novel. This is in contrast to her confident statement to me in an interview about her ability to be bidialectical, successful, and comfortable in the school setting, and at home with friends and relatives in an African American community. She occupies different positions in different contexts and at different times as a racial being.

White and Latina girls also described aspects of themselves in relation to their understanding of their racial positions, speaking of visiting relatives in all-White communities and how strange it seemed after their diverse urban neighborhood. Luann completed their story rounds with her own story of neighborhoods:

> Nereida knows this; there aren't many African American people at my country house. It's so funny, when little kids see me, they like look and say, "Look, Mommy, her skin!" Yeah, it's *real.* [Laughter] I've never really been in situations like all African American or basically all White. I'm *used* to everybody here.

Luann concludes her story with her own take on the "diversity" her White and Latina classmates feel comfortable with. Her telling ostensibly places her in the position of comfort in a White setting, yet her example, couched as a funny story, suggests the painful experience the reaction to her skin color--and her very identity--must be.

These matching stories also serve as a vehicle that allows the girls to testify to their beliefs about race. But they are telling different stories. The White and Latina girls have the freedom to come to this awareness, to revel in and value an interracial context. Luann makes clear in her story that she does not. From a much earlier time in her life, she had to get "used to everybody here" even when her color isolated her.

In the final sessions of book club, members continued to explore their positions as African American, White, and Latina within the context of their society and their connection to one another. While they worked together to make meaning of racism, the following excerpt reveals that meanings could differ depending on the race and culture of the speaker.

The following conversation occurred in the final session of book club. As they discussed a range of issues from the race of dolls to the media, the girls moved closer to examining their own experiences and context. The girls commented at length on racist portrayals, using the terms Black and White as they spoke. Suddenly, Mari, who is White interrupted:

Mari: I think that we're afraid, when we say "Black," like...

Tara: You shouldn't be afraid.

Mari: No, it's not that we're racists. We feel weird saying it, cause we're...

Suzanna: We feel like we're *separating* us...

Mari: Well yeah, like we're either separating, or like we're racist, or, it's hard to describe like, anyone, if you say White or *we* say...

Allison: See!

Mari: I know!

Tara: I think speech just segregates...

Allison: It's not just you.

Tara: It's weird; you say *we're*...

Suzanna: But when you describe someone, you have to add their color, because you can't see a person without it.

In this conversation White and Latina girls Mari, Allison, and Suzanna, articulate their discomfort at the separation that words bring about. Tara, who is African American, seems to be telling them not to be afraid to acknowledge race. Susanna does not like feeling separate, yet she continues to speak in terms of "we" and "you," as Allison and Tara both point out. Susanna concludes by insisting that you cannot see people without color. The girls have moved from swapping stories and discussing interpretations of characters to looking closely at themselves. In the context of the vivid stories and honest questions posed by Tara and Luann, the White and Latina group members seem to be involved in a tentative examination of their own feelings about race, about shared contexts, and their fears of separation.

DISCUSSION

The White and Latina girls' conversations reveal identities that are contradictory. They are in the process of reconstituting personas against the discourse about race in an intimate interracial setting but remain deeply influenced by their cultural communities and global perspectives. The circumstances of living in a city where racial diversity was ever present, reading novels that highlighted race, meeting a memorable African American author, and sharing friendships with the "opposite race," gave these girls an opportunity to reconstruct their own identities. For the African American girls, sharing stories and values in a supportive setting could replace the negative critique of the larger society with positive recognition and affirmation. Luann was able to question her role in the school as she wondered if she was an "Oreo," to affirm her position as a member of a diverse society, and also to share obliquely her pain at reactions to her skin color. Yet, in an interview, Luann indicated that often such conversations in an interracial group are more beneficial to White participants than to herself. Because she is usually one of the only African Americans in her class and school, she said, "I think I know them better than they know me." The two African American book club girls retain their positions as knowledgeable others.

For all of the girls, being able to speak out on a topic that was silenced or ignored in school provided an opportunity to both articulate their own emerging views and hear from the "opposite" race in a safe and friendly place. The exploratory talk, storytelling and shared beliefs or testimonies seemed to equip them to peel away, up to a point, layers of attitudes and expectations about race.

Should conversations such as these be part of the school curriculum? The study foregrounds how texts can stimulate intense reflection and critical connections for young readers about unsanctioned topics such as race. These conversations may be most successful in a small group setting, a setting without curriculum goals. Yet implications for classroom literacy practices are significant. Teaching critical reading through think-aloud protocols, questioning, and comprehension strategies, common in today's classrooms, is limited to helping students acquire structured higher level cognitive skills. Goals do not include "critical" and compassionate reading necessary in a democratic, diverse society. The use of texts that challenge prevailing discourses about race, class, and gender can provoke thoughtful discussions about the history and authenticity of cultural representations.

Selection of texts for literature discussion can also be informed by the study. These African American, White, and Latina girls felt "savvy" and sophisticated as they read and discussed serious issues that they knew firsthand. The seriousness and contemporaneity of these issues served to focus their attention and created deeply personal responses that began to impact on their identities as racial beings. The study also highlights the role that discourse modes such as story telling and the opportunity to testify to one's values and beliefs, have on creating personal meaning and in supporting early adolescents' exploration of identity and understanding of their world. These modes, often considered essentialist and "female," should be honored as useful classroom discourse.

REFERENCES

Bakhtin, M. (1981). *The dialogic imagination: Four essays.* (M. Holquist, Ed.). Austin, TX: University of Texas Press.

Barnes, D. (1993). Supporting exploratory talk for learning. In K. M. Pierce & C. Gilles (Eds.), *Cycles of meaning: Exploring the potential of talk in learning communities* (pp. 17-34). Portsmouth, NH: Heinemann.

Barnes, D., & Todd, F. (1995). *Communication and learning in small groups revisited: Making meaning through talk.* Portsmouth, NH: Heinemann.

Beach, R. (1997). Students' resistance to engagement with multicultural literature. In T. Rogers & A. Soter (Eds.), *Reading across cultures: Teaching literature in a diverse society* (pp. 69-94). New York: Teachers College Press.

Broughton, M.A. (2002). The performance and construction of subjectivities of early adolescent girls in book club discussion groups. *Journal of Literacy Research, 34,* 1-38.

Brown, L. M., & Gilligan, C. (1992). *Meeting at the crossroads: Women's psychology and girls' development.* Cambridge, MA: Harvard University Press.

Cazden, C. (1998). *Classroom Discourse: The language of teaching and learning.* Portsmouth, NH: Heinemann.

Cherland, M. R. (2000). Young adolescents constructing identity: Reading gender. In C. Courtland & T. Gambell (Eds.), *Intersections: Young adolescents meet literature.* Vancouver, B.C.: Pacific Educational Press.

Cross, W.E. (1991). *Shades of Black: Diversity in African-American identity.* Philadelphia, PA: Temple University Press.

Duesterberg, L. (1999). Theorizing race in the context of learning to teach. *Teachers College Record, 100,* 751-775.

Egan-Robertson, A. (1998). We must ask our questions and tell our stories. In A. Egan-Robertson & D. Bloome (Eds.), *Students as researchers of culture and language in their own communities* (pp. 261-284). Cresskill, NJ: Hampton Press.

Eeds, M., & Wells, D. (1989). Grand conversations: An exploration of meaning construction in literature study groups. *Research in the Teaching of English, 23,* 4-29.

Ellsworth, E. (1997). Double binds of whiteness. In M. Fine, L. Powell, L. Weis, & L. Mun Wong (Eds.), *Off-White: Readings on race, power and society* (pp. 259-269). New York: Routledge.

Ely, M., Anzul, M., Friedman, T., Garner, D., & Steinmetz, A.M. (1991). *On writing qualitative research: Living by words.* New York: Falmer Press.

Enciso, P. (1997). Negotiating the meaning of difference: Talking back to multicultural literature. In T. Rogers & A. Soter (Eds.), *Reading across cultures: Teaching literature in a diverse society* (pp. 13-41). New York: Teachers College Press/NCTE.

Finders, M. (1997). *Just girls: Hidden literacies and life in junior high.* New York: Teachers College Press.

Fine, M. (1997). Witnessing whiteness. In M. Fine, L. Powell, L. Weis, & L. Mun Wong (Eds.), *Off-White: Readings on race, power and society* (pp.57-66). New York: Routledge.

Gallas, K. (1998). *Sometimes I can be anything.* New York: Teachers College Press.

Helms, J.E. (Ed). (1990). *African American and White racial identity: Theory, research, and practice.* Westport, CT: Greenwood.

Langer, J. (1990). The process of understanding: Reading for literary and informative purposes. *Research in the Teaching of English, 24,* 220-257.

Leadbeater, B.J., & Way, N. (Eds.). (1996). *Urban girls: Resisting stereotypes, creating identities.* New York: New York University Press.

Lemke, J.L. (1995). *Textual Politics, discourse, and social dynamics.* London: Taylor & Francis.

Lewis, C. (1997). The social drama of literature discussions in a fifth/sixth grade classroom. *Research in the Teaching of English, 31,* 163-204.

McGinley, W., & Kamberelis, G. (1996). Maniac Magee and Ragtime Tumpie: Children negotiating self and world through reading and writing. *Research in the Teaching of English. 30,* 75-113.

McIntyre, A. (1997). *Making meaning of whiteness: Exploring racial identity with white teachers.* Albany, NY:

State University of New York Press.

Moller, K. (2001). "They're not 'them' and we're not 'us'": Addressing racism, ethnocentrism, and fear in response to Joseph Bruchac's *The Heart of a Chief*. Presented at the National Reading Conference, San Antonio, TX, December 2001.

Phinney, S.J.S., & Tarver, S. (1988). Ethnic identity search and commitment in Black and White eighth graders. *Journal of Early Adolescence 8*, 265-77.

Purves, A. (1972). *How porcupines make love.* Lexington, MA: Xerox Publishing.

Rosenblatt, L. (1938/1976). *Literature as exploration.* New York: Modern Language Association.

Sadker, M., & Sadker, D. (1994). *Failing at fairness: How America's schools cheat girls.* New York: Charles Scribner's Sons.

Schweickart, P., & Flynn, E. (2004). *Reading sites: Social difference and reader response.* New York: Modern Language Association.

Smith, S. (2000). Talking about "real stuff": Explorations of agency and romance in an all-girls' book club. *Language Arts, 78*, 30-38.

Smitherman, G. (1977). *Talkin' and testifyin.'* Boston: Houghton Mifflin.

Strauss, A., & Corbin, J. (1990). *Basics of qualitative research: Grounded theory and procedures and techniques.* Newbury Park, CA: Sage.

Tannen, D. (1984). *Conversational styles: Analyzing talk among friends.* Norwood, NJ: Ablex.

Tatum, B. (1997). *"Why are all the Black kids sitting together in the cafeteria?" and other conversations about race.* New York: Basic Books.

Taylor, J. M. (1996). Cultural stories: Latina and Portuguese daughters and mothers. In B.J.R. Leadbeater & N. Way (Eds.), *Urban girls: Resisting stereotypes, creating identities.* (pp.117-131) New York: New York University Press.

Twine, F. W. (1997). Brown-skinned white girls: Class, culture and the construction of white identity in suburban communities. In R. Frankenberg (Ed.), *Displacing whiteness: Essays in social and cultural criticism* (pp. 214-243). Durham, NC: Duke University Press.

Vygotsky, L. (1986). *Thought and language.* (A. Kozulin, Ed and Trans.). Cambridge, MA: MIT Press. (Original work published 1934)

Weedon, C. (1987). F*eminist practice and poststructural theory.* New York: Basil Blackwell.

Woodson, J. (1994). *I hadn't meant to tell you this.* New York: Delacorte.

Woodson, J. (1992). *Maizon at Blue Hill.* New York: Dell-Yearling.

A Good Daughter and an Independent Woman: Mapping one Student's Responses to Literature through her Negotiations of Competing Cultural Models

Amanda Haertling Thein

University of Pittsburgh

The notion of individualized learning has in many ways served to create more effective pedagogical practices in our schools. Traditional "aesthetic" theories of reader-response (Rosenblatt, 1995) have embraced this focus on the individual by encouraging readers to relate their "personal" experiences directly to the text. The result, according to Pirie (1997), is that "In English classrooms, we no longer see students as receptacles of knowledge, but rather as young people responding out of uniquely personal depths" (p. 9). However, while acknowledging the positive aspects of what Pirie calls the "cult of the individual," he and others (Lewis, 2000) have questioned whether a view of response as uniquely individual is a responsible means of teaching and interpreting literature. Recent postmodern theories of identity challenge the notion of the individual, suggesting that identity be viewed not as fixed or static, but rather as fluid and constituted by a variety of social practices adopted in certain social and cultural contexts. Gee (1999) suggested that people adopt "socially-situated identities" through participation in social practices. Other theorists refer similarly to "figured worlds" (Holland, Lachicotte, Skinner, & Cain, 2001) and "activity systems" (Engestrom, 1987)—all of which suggest fluid social worlds that are layered and competing in the lived experiences of individuals.

In understanding identity as shifting and adopted through social practices of various social worlds, sociocultural theories of response to literature (Galda & Beach, 2000) are interested not only in the ways that students relate their personal *experiences* to the text, but also in the *interpretive processes* students use to construct and negotiate their identities and social worlds in their lived experiences. In other words, this view of response understands readers as constructing norms operating in text worlds by drawing on their experiences with inferring norms that operate in their lived worlds.

A sociocultural theory of response is particularly relevant in examining discourses (Fairclough, 2003) and cultural models (Gee, 1999) related to gender. In viewing gender as socially and culturally constructed as opposed to biological, Davies (2003) suggested that "gendered persons" are constructed through discourses that are socially and historically produced. As readers, we tend to take up these discourses and storylines as if they were our own individual storylines; we do this because "we produce ourselves and our identities within the discourses that are available to us" (p. 14).

In exploring discourses available to girls and women in texts and in lived worlds, it is important to note that such discourses do not operate discretely, but rather they interact with other local, context-bound discourses. While acknowledging that constructs such as race, class, and gender cannot be separated from one another, this study foregrounds social and cultural discourses of gender as they are manifested in one girl's responses to literature read inside and outside of the classroom in an urban, working-class community.

The purpose of this ethnographic case-study was to examine how one high school girl's responses to classroom literature could be understood through her negotiations of cultural models acquired and explored through participation in social, cultural, family, and text worlds.

THEORETICAL FRAME

Reading and response practices of women and girls are in many ways gendered. Girls experience particular discourses of femininity in lived worlds that may lead them to interpret texts through particular stances of femininity (Davies, 2003; Greer, 2004). Likewise, discourses presented to girls through textual positioning often reinforce discourses of femininity experienced in lived worlds (Christian-Smith, 1990).

Outside of class, girls often read popular fiction and magazines to construct and appropriate norms of femininity (Finders, 1997). Additionally, reading of popular fiction often mediates social relationships for girls (Cherland, 1994; Enciso, 1998). For example, while boys tend to select reading material based on genre and utility, girls tend to read what their friends are reading and use those texts as touchstones in their peer-groups (Simpson, 1996). Reading "confessional" literature about women who have experienced difficult life circumstances is often an activity that mediates relationships for women. In fact it has been argued that confessional magazines of the 1950s created spaces for new discourses related to previously taboo subjects, such as unplanned pregnancy (Greer, 2004). In other cases this "dialogic" (Bakhtin, 1981) reading creates spaces for girls to negotiate social practices (Finders, 1997), and to deconstruct gender binaries (Davies, 2003; Ensico, 1998). Finally, while "feminine" texts such as series romance novels can serve to socialize girls into traditional feminine roles, these practices can also serve as safe places for resisting expectations and experimenting with roles and relationships (Cherland, 1994; Christian-Smith, 1990).

Within the English classroom, girls' reading and response practices are equally complex. Female characters encountered in school-sanctioned literature are often rejected by girls, who view them as "poor, uneducated, unemployed, and dependent on men," (Hartman, 2001, p. 221). However, girls hold ambivalent stances toward strong female characters as well (Davies, 1989; DeBlase, 2003; Trousdale, 1995). Deborah Hicks' (2004) study of working-class girls found that, even when presented with stories of female protagonists living in situations similar to their own, they often resist such "middle-brow" novels because the discourses of the text and the teacher-generated discussions about the text are unfamiliar to girls from working-class backgrounds.

Breggren (2004) posited that in reading "like a woman" women tend to read in ways that are "personal, accepting, emotional, addictive," rather than the "critical, cognitive" approaches that are typically valued in academic settings (p. 167). These personal purposes often work against academic literacy practices. Rather than acknowledging the value of women's reading practices, academics and teachers often focus their efforts on modifying these practices. Hicks (2004) suggested, however, that we take girls' reading practices more seriously by acknowledging the social and cultural power of popular fiction in their lives. She proposed that because popular fiction is a familiar genre for many girls, it may be a useful place to begin in teaching them to critically examine both literature and their lives.

In theorizing the social and cultural aspects of girls' reading practices, I draw on Gee's (1999) theory of discourse practices with a particular emphasis on the concept of "cultural models." Gee explained that cultural models can be understood as "images or storylines or descriptions of simplified worlds in which prototypical events unfold. They are our 'first thoughts' or taken-for-granted assumptions about what is 'typical' or 'normal'" (p. 59). He also explained that cultural models are our tacit, often unconscious theories about what counts as relevant or irrelevant in certain contexts or situations (Gee, 2004, p. 45).

The concept of cultural models is particularly useful in understanding how people navigate competing discourses in social worlds of texts and lived experiences because they can be flexible, changeable, inconsistent, and even incomplete. Gee (1999) stated that, "The partiality and inconsistency of cultural models reflect the fact that we have all had a great many diverse and conflicting experiences; we all belong to different, sometimes conflicting groups; and we are all influenced by a wide array of groups, texts institutions, and media…" (p. 70). Additionally, Gee explains that cultural models often appear inconsistent or partial because the models we enact are often inconsistent with those we espouse and those by which we judge ourselves and others (p.68). As I will demonstrate in my interpretations, Lia was a person whose experiences in school and family settings were often conflicting. Therefore, identifying cultural models that Lia appropriated and/or constructed helps me unravel and make sense of some of the complexity, inconsistency, and partiality in her responses to literature.

This body of research on the practices and stances women and girls take toward literature suggests a need to examine more closely the intersection of the dynamic ways high school girls use reading and response practices both outside and inside of the English classroom to navigate their social worlds and to constitute their gender identities. Such research may shed further light on discourses and cultural models that girls use in positioning their stances toward literature read in the classroom. In addition, this research may yield implications for choice of classroom texts and pedagogical practices in teaching literature that may be more equitable to all students.

METHOD

Participants and Data Sources

Research for this study was conducted over the course of one school year in a diverse, urban high school in a working-class neighborhood of a large, Midwestern city. Qualitative, critical ethnographic research (Carspecken, 1996) was conducted within the community, the high school, and one eleventh grade, advanced placement English classroom. Students in this class primarily read texts written by white males, with the exception of a text by the female, African American writer, Toni Morrison. Participants in this study include female students enrolled in the course, nine of whom were Asian American, six of whom were White, and one of whom was Latina. My stance as a researcher in this study was primarily one of "observer" rather than "participant" (Graue

& Walsh 1998; Spradley 1980).

Procedure

Lia, the focal student in this paper, was selected because of her passion for reading, her strong opinions about literature read in class, and the conflict she often expressed between home and school worlds (Phelan, Davidson, & Yu, 1998). In constructing a case study about Lia, I drew on transcripts and field notes from small and large group classroom literature discussions; a transcript of a focus group discussion in which Lia and three of her female classmates discussed their thoughts on texts read both inside and outside of class; transcripts of two, hour-long interviews conducted with Lia (see Appendix A for interview questions); copies of Lia's journal responses to novels read in class; and copies of several of Lia's writing assignments. While I often observed Lia in larger school contexts, such as in the cafeteria or at pep assemblies, my primary knowledge of Lia comes from my observations of and interactions with Lia in focus group, interview, and classroom settings, rather than work, community, or family settings.

Data Analysis

In analyzing the data I collected on Lia, my goal was to identify values, beliefs, and norms that Lia used in negotiating and interpreting her lived worlds and the worlds of texts read both inside and outside of classroom. In doing so, I hoped to illuminate some of complex social and cultural ways that Lia read and interpreted school-sanctioned literature.

I began my analysis through a systematic, inductive process of thematic coding (Emerson, Fretz, & Shaw, 1995), using QSR NVIVO software. I used this form of analysis both to help me sort the data and to help me identify broad discourses that Lia drew from in interpreting and negotiating text and lived worlds (see Appendix B for coding categories). As a second, related inquiry tool, I used Gee's (1996, 1999, 2004) theory of cultural models to help me pinpoint the beliefs, norms, and values that Lia appropriated and constructed through the broad discourses identified in the thematic coding.

In identifying cultural models that Lia used in negotiating competing discourses and social worlds I read the coded data through the lens of several questions that Gee (1999, p. 78) suggested as inquiry questions for identifying cultural models (see Appendix C). These questions not only helped me identify Lia's uses of cultural models, but they also helped me to see spaces where these models conflict, where they may be inconsistent, and where Lia struggles to revise and reshape them.

FINDINGS

Lia was an academically successful Asian-American student at Thompson High School (all names are pseudonyms). A vibrant girl, Lia often wore trendy clothes, hip glasses, and her long, dark hair in curls and barrettes. She was talkative in her eleventh-grade Advanced Placement (AP) English class both in discussions with other students from her small group and in larger class discussions and was not afraid to speak her mind, yet was comfortable asking questions about things she didn't understand. Lia was often the first to volunteer to read aloud in class; when called upon, she projected her voice in an articulate, confident manner. In constructing her identity as a self-assured, independent person, Lia negotiated her identity across many competing discourses and cultural models. In this paper I focus on cultural models embedded in two broad discourse communities that Lia negotiated in her lived experiences – discourses of family and traditional Hmong culture and discourses of a de-industrialized working-class community. Within these two discourse communities, Lia constructed her identity in relation to competing cultural models about what it means to be a young woman in a changing world. In reading and responding to literature read in and outside of class, Lia found spaces to construct her own model for negotiating across competing discourses in her lived worlds.

Flexibility and Cultural Models

Lia's parents were Hmong immigrants who came to the U.S. from Thailand soon after Lia was born and settled in a changing, de-industrialized, working-class neighborhood in a large Midwestern city. Although Lia attended public schools, grew up speaking English, and participating in American popular culture, she also lived in a family with traditional beliefs about culture, family, and women's domestic roles. Lia's parents expected that she would spend the majority of her free time helping around the house, caring for siblings, or helping her parents with their janitorial work. While Lia sought to please her family and worked hard to be a good daughter, she also negotiated space for her involvement in other possible worlds.

When I asked Lia what she wanted for her future, she explained to me that she had been granted a competitive internship with a major corporation based in the state for the following summer. She said that she hoped this position would help her get a scholarship to college in San Diego where she hoped to study to be a child psychiatrist. Following college, Lia said that she planned to travel to Japan to teach English for a year. After she talked about her plans, I asked whether she had any interest in marriage. Lia told me that she was in fact engaged to a much older man who was "half Mexican and half White." She explained that her family disapproved of this situation and that they expected her to marry a man whom they had approved from a Hmong background. While traveling and studying, marrying an older man, and performing a traditional role as a Hmong woman are three possible futures that might conflict with one another, Lia actively took steps toward enacting cultural models consistent with each of these scenarios.

Lia's active experimentation with cultural models across discourse communities may be understood in part through her experiences in a changing working-class neighborhood. Studies of working-class girls living in postindustrial economic times propose that as working-class girls see economic instability and divorce in the lives of their families and friends, they come to the conclusion that men cannot be relied upon for financial stability (Griffin, 1987; Weis, 1990). These girls often expect to marry, yet they see marriage as inevitable and not necessarily a positive, romantic venture. Likewise, these girls understand that in an unpredictable world, they must find ways of being responsible for their own financial and emotional stability, and they must be flexible in their plans for the future. This is consistent with Greer's (2004) theory of "flexible moral realism" which suggests that working-class women often interpret lived and text worlds through a stance that is flexible in terms of understanding women's negotiations of roles and relationships. Through this stance, women are realistic about the difficulties of marriage and other relationships, and focus on the notion that despite mishaps, moral and ethical lapses, and other struggles, it's still possible to find resolution and maintain a moral, happy life (p.148).

In listening to Lia's ideas about her future goals and expectations, her stance can be theorized as one that was flexible and one through which she did the active and sophisticated work of negotiating several competing cultural models about her identity at one time. For instance, Lia often expressed a desire to live up to the model of a "good daughter" in a Hmong family by carrying out her household duties, putting family needs before individual wants, and potentially submitting to an arranged marriage. Other times she spoke of wanting the freedom to be an "independent woman," a model that included attending college away from home, being self reliant, and/or marrying a man of her own choosing. In her lived experiences Lia enacted practices associated with each of these models in constructing her identity as a young woman.

A Good Daughter and an Independent Woman?

One way that competing cultural models manifested in Lia's lived worlds was in her juggling of home duties and school work. In one-on-one interviews, Lia spoke at length about her struggle to negotiate her role both as a "good daughter" who fulfills domestic obligations expected by her family, and as a "good student" who looks for independence through education, and potentially through attending college (Hartman, 2001). The following exchange highlighted some of the ways these competing cultural models functioned in Lia's lived worlds:

L: When I'm at school, you can't do the things that you do at home 'cause it's two totally different places…at home you have chores and you come to school and you have homework. And then you have to try to do your best here at school then you try to do what your respective role is as a girl at home cause that's how it is in our culture and stuff.

A: So what do you think your role is at home as a girl?

L: Umm (brief pause), when I try to read books, my mom, she, she doesn't really like the fact that I, you know, do it cause she doesn't really understand that cause all I'm expected to do is work, work, work, cook, clean, watch the kids, and when I spend a lot of time in my bed just reading it's like, then it's I'm a bad daughter and I'm just kind of slacking off on my duties and stuff, so when I try to read, I just try to read when nobody's home.

A: Is there a lot of time when nobody's home?

L: Not a lot.

A: Do you read like at night, before you go to bed?

L: Um, (pause), the only time when I think that I read is when I'm assigned books because I know that those are what I have to do…And other than that, I just try to do what I can, like what I'm expected at home and stuff.

This excerpt suggests that Lia was caught between two worlds and two different cultural models related to her role as a young woman. Lia wanted to be both a good daughter and a good student. Being a good daughter for many girls includes being a good student. For Lia, being a good student was less associated with being a good daughter than it was with being an independent woman. Lia strived to do well in school by completing homework and reading both for school and for pleasure. However, reading, viewed through the cultural model of "good daughter" in her family, was seen as a leisure activity, one that her took away from expected duties and may have caused Lia to be seen as a bad daughter. Thus, trying to be a "good daughter" and at the same time hoping to become an "independent woman," Lia often performed competing and conflicting roles. Understanding how cultural models competed in Lia's lived worlds help us better understand her responses to texts read in and out of the classroom.

Responding to Texts Outside of Class

In theorizing ways that Lia's responses to characters and situations in text worlds reflected her negotiations of cultural models in her lived worlds, I look first at Lia's responses to a text of her own choosing, Nicholas Sparks' novel, *A Walk to Remember* (1999). Lia cited this novel as one of her favorites and explained that she saw this novel as one that brought her "positive energy" through a female character that is both good and strong.

In this novel, set in the 1950s, Jamie, the misfit daughter of the town minister, is befriended by Landon, the rich, handsome star of the football team. Landon falls in love with Jamie and soon comes to see her as the kind of person he wants to be--someone who gives to others, has faith in God, has strict moral convictions, and believes in the goodness of all people. Unfortunately, Jamie is dying of Leukemia. As a final gift to Jamie, Landon decides to fulfill her fondest wish--he marries her in her home church, just months before she dies.

In discussing this book in both interview and focus groups settings, Lia explained that she found this book "heartbreaking," and yet "inspiring." She explained:

> A really good book is when you can like relate to it...I liked *A Walk to Remember*. It captures your attention and your heart when you read the book and stuff because the book is like it's really sad, the girl, she's really sweet and good and you know, she dies and all that stuff and it's heartbreaking. I think it's a good book.

In describing what she liked about this book, Lia mentioned many times that Jamie's goodness and sweetness inspired her. Lia said that she admired Jamie because she remained positive and true to her convictions despite the fact that she is a misfit at school and despite the fact that she is terminally ill. In the following excerpt from an interview Lia described Jamie:

> She's the priest's daughter. She seems like this really thin, fragile person...and then she's this godly person who's like into church and stuff and then she's really poor and her mother died and the guy who she, she falls in love with, they've been to school ever since elementary, all the way to high school and he never really liked her, but then he got her to help him with the school play and somehow they connected and they fell in love.

Here Lia pointed out that while Jamie "seems fragile" and has been through difficult times in her family, she still has the strength of character to actively participate in her faith and simultaneously participate in a school play that leads her to fall in love with a popular student. Being good helps her be successful on all of these levels.

On one level, it's easy to see that *A Walk to Remember* is a text with an explicit moral stance related to being a good girl and a good daughter. Jamie is depicted as a girl who takes care of her father, helps the poor (despite the fact that she is poor herself), loves children, is faithful to God, never gets angry, and helps others to be better people. On this level we could see Lia as having been acted upon by cultural models that suggest simplified binary notions of girls as either all good or all bad (Davies, 2003; Walkerdine, 1990). In other words, we could see Lia as having engaged with this text because the character of Jamie fits a cultural model related to being a perfect, good girl and daughter.

On another level, we can see this text as a space where Lia negotiated competing cultural models related to being both a good girl and an independent woman. As Lia's above comments suggest, she was particularly interested in how Jamie appears weak, but is actually strong. She pointed out that while Jamie seeks to please others, she does so by being true to her own convictions and beliefs. For example, Jamie's father does not want her to date Landon, but Jamie intuits that Landon is a good person and eventually convinces her father to accept him and even love him. Conversely, Landon does not understand why Jamie is so caught up in her religious faith. Jamie insists that having faith and caring about others is where Landon will find true fulfillment in life; eventually Landon finds that this is true and comes to join Jamie in her faith. In these matters, Jamie had intuition, persistence, and agency. Jamie is successful in negotiating across the competing cultural models and social worlds in her life, something Lia struggled to do. This text may have served as a space where she could envision constructions of her identity that fit cultural models from both her home world and her school and social worlds.

Responding to School-Sanctioned Texts

In reading and responding to school-sanctioned literature, Lia encountered characters and situations that were often more ambiguous and complex than those found in *A Walk to Remember*. In examining how Lia constructed some of these texts through these same cultural models, we may understand more about why she resisted certain texts and why she engaged with others.

Toni Morrison's novel *Beloved* (1987) was the text that Lia responded to most strongly and most negatively in her AP English class. In thinking about Lia's responses to this text, I want to begin by pointing out that *Beloved* was, on several levels, a difficult novel for many students in Lia's class to understand. Morrison's sophisticated, and at times opaque narrative style was more complex than the students in this class were accustomed to reading. As a result, many students, including Lia, came to class confused not only about thematic issues in the text but also about plot points. Students in this class expressed resistance to *Beloved*, particularly for the first few chapters, because they often did not understand the circular narrative style, and as a result, had trouble understanding what had actually occurred and to whom in particular scenes. Additionally, students were often surprised or confused by unfamiliar situations in this text, particularly in terms of depictions of sexuality.

In discussing a scene in *Beloved* involving bestiality, Lia explained that she was shocked by what she read. However, Lia was perhaps more bothered by her initial lack of comprehension of this scene. Lia stated, "I'm reading stuff and we'd come into class and everybody's like 'Oh, the men were having sex with cows,' and like because, just, I just, I never thought that and I read it and I didn't see it there and then it was like shocking to me...." This quote suggests that while Lia was shocked by what she read in this scene, she was surprised not as much by the sexuality itself as she was by the fact that she had not *noticed* the sexuality in this scene. Lia was perhaps frustrated less by the sexual situations in the scene and more by discovering that others in the class understood this situation on a literal level, while she did not.

Even as the above quote from Lia suggests that she was sometimes frustrated by finding she had misread sections of *Beloved*, this may not be an adequate explanation for Lia's resistance to this text. In fact Lia was a very careful and thorough reader and although she found the text confusing, she worked through it carefully and said that she found it satisfying to finally make sense of the text. She explained:

> It was very confusing because sometimes, cause it's not like 'Beloved said,' or like 'so and so replied,' you know you just kind of like have to figure out like because of this person's personality and because of how they viewed this, you just have to figure out like this is them talking because it's something they would say and stuff... but then because of how the storyline was and all that like phenomenal stuff it was very interesting to see how Morrison put everything together to make it make sense.

Indeed, in my interviews with Lia, she expressed a certain amount of pride in finishing and in understanding this novel. However, despite her ultimate success with *Beloved* she still described the novel as the worst she had ever read. The basis for Lia's resistance to this novel may in fact be found in competing cultural models about being a good girl and an independent woman that Lia negotiated in her lived worlds.

In *Beloved*, Toni Morrison depicts female characters as multifaceted people. None of these female characters is depicted as either "good" or "bad" per se, but rather as markedly complex and even problematic. It is these problematic characters that Lia found most frustrating in reading this text; she explained that the characters made her very angry. In her journal, she stated the following about Beloved, the "ghost" daughter who has returned to her mother, Sethe, and her sister, Denver:

> It makes me very mad at Beloved that she would turn her back on Sethe and try to choke her. Not only that, but she has sex with Paul D., the man that Sethe wants in her life...She is a person who should never have been helped. Denver and Sethe did a good deed, but in return only got hurt...how could a girl like Beloved who is so sweet and brought happiness back into their life possibly want to kill Sethe and hurt Denver, the person who loves and admires her most?

In this journal entry, Lia expressed frustration with the text and its characters because it did not make sense to her that Sethe and Denver would do a "good deed" and be punished rather than rewarded. Lia also found it confusing that Beloved would seem sweet and good, yet would actually try to hurt Sethe and Denver. One reason Lia might have responded to these characters with confusion and frustration is that in struggling to be a good girl and a good daughter in her family and cultural worlds, Lia was hesitant to identify with female characters that make complex and ambiguous moral decisions. Characters, such as Jamie in *A Walk to Remember*, who are depicted as always being good, may be somewhat safer and easier for Lia to understand.

However, Lia's negative response to *Beloved* cannot be explained solely as resistance to characters that seem good but have flaws, but rather her response may also have been a resistance to characters who she perceived as lacking independence and moral consistency – qualities that she saw as valuable in becoming an independent woman. In an interview, Lia talked at length about the character of Sethe and explained that she liked Sethe but found her to be inconsistent and "weak." She stated:

> I thought that she was really strong but there was some things that she did that it was just, you know, were not appropriate…And because she feels that she has to give back what she's taken she's letting the girl take control of her, which weakens her as a character.

During the course of this interview Lia continued to explain that she admired Sethe because of her strength, but at the same time felt angry with her in part because she was at times inappropriate (she specifically mentioned Sethe killing her baby), but primarily because her strength and morality were inconsistent. Lia was particularly frustrated with Sethe's willingness to allow Beloved to control her and create havoc in her life.

Although Lia's responses to *Beloved* were constructed through a number of factors including the difficulty of the text itself, I want to suggest that Lia's negotiations of cultural models in her lived worlds were a critical factor in her interpretations of this text – particularly in terms of her resistance to the text. As Lia struggled to construct an identity in which she was both "good" and "independent," she may have resisted the female characters in *Beloved* because their complexity allows them to be neither of these things in full at any one time. Again, this is a contrast to Jamie in *A Walk to Remember* who is consistently both good and independent. Lia's responses to other female characters read in class provide further evidence that her negotiations of these same cultural models were at play in her willingness to engage in classroom literature.

For example, one novel from class with which Lia was deeply engaged was *The Scarlet Letter* (Hawthorne, 1850). Lia was particularly interested in discussing the character of Hester Prynne, a woman who is shunned by her town for committing adultery yet maintains self-reliance and dignity throughout the text. Lia expressed admiration for Hester, not only because she is consistent in her moral stance but also because she is an example of how women can retain independence from men, despite difficult circumstances. Lia stated:

> She [Hester] kind of like inspires you that, you know, that you have to stand up for yourself and you have to be independent sometimes. And guys are not always gonna be there, sometimes they mess things up, they can take things that you had in your life and um that sometimes, you know, you might not know who you are in the world, but you always gotta, you know, be strong, you have to stick up for yourself when you don't have anybody.

In responding to *The Scarlet Letter*, Lia expressed that she felt inspired by Hester because, despite the questionable morality of Hester's affair and out-of-wedlock pregnancy, she is depicted as a good person who is kind to other people and knows how to take care of herself. Even though Hester could be seen as taking a moral misstep in committing adultery, she is consistent in her strength of character and in her moral stance following her mistake (which takes place prior to the start of the novel). In this sense, Hester is a contrast to Sethe in *Beloved* who Lia viewed as inconsistent in her strength of character and morality, while somewhat similar to Jamie in her steadfast convictions.

While Lia was engaged with literature in which women are depicted as morally "good," she was *most* engaged with literature that depicted good women who were also consistently strong and independent. Such literature may be a space where Lia could find possibilities for reshaping cultural models to bridge across the discourse communities in her lived worlds.

DISCUSSION

A Walk to Remember is a novel that offers Lia a somewhat idealized picture of what it might look like to successfully navigate across the competing cultural models in her lived worlds and discourse communities. Despite its moral and thematic simplicity, this novel is one that Lia found deeply engaging, and as such provides a useful place to begin to understand her responses to literature read in classroom. Providing Lia with the opportunity to seriously and critically examine the texts she finds most engaging outside of class may offer teachers a means to help her become more critically aware of the socially and culturally constructed nature of cultural models in both text and lived worlds. Lia's interpretations and responses to school-sanctioned texts might have become more sophisticated, critical, and meaningful a result. Studying the cultural models about women and girls forwarded in *A Walk to Remember* for example, in juxtaposition with those in *Beloved* or *The Scarlet Letter*, might offer a student like Lia opportunities to continue trying on new, and reshaping old discourses and cultural models related to the roles women play in family and society. This kind of textual exploration may ultimately offer Lia further agency in constructing her own identity as a young woman.

This research suggests that by understanding the social worlds and discourse communities that girls inhabit in their lived worlds, we can begin to understand the stances by which girls interpret literature. Additionally, this research demonstrates that in examining the ways that girls map cultural models onto texts of their choosing, we can better understand how they map such models onto the literature they read in class and perhaps better understand the reasons why they often resist such literature. In providing girls with opportunities to critically examine cultural models in both their lived and text world experiences, we can help them become agents in amending, deconstructing, and reconstructing their identities and relationships in their lived worlds. The worlds of literature and the worlds of our English classrooms are important spaces where this work can be imagined.

REFERENCES

Bakhtin, M. M. (1981). *The dialogic imagination.* (M. Holquist, Ed.; C. Emerson & M. Holquist, Trans.). Austin: University of Texas Press.

Breggren, A. (2004). Reading like a woman. In P. Scheickart & E. Flynn (Eds.), *Reading sites: Social difference and reader response* (pp. 135-165). New York: Modern Language Association.

Carspecken, P. F. (1996). *Critical ethnography in educational research.* New York: Routledge.

Cherland, M. (1994). *Private practices: Girls reading fiction and constructing identity.* London: Taylor & Francis.

Christian-Smith, L. (1990). *Becoming a woman through romance.* New York: Routledge.

Davies, B. (2003). *Shards of glass: Children reading and writing beyond gendered identities.* Cresskill, NJ: Hampton Press.

Davies, B. (1989). *Frogs and snails and feminist tales: Preschool children and gender.* Sydney, Australia: Allen & Unwin.

DeBlase, G. (2003). Acknowledging agency while accommodating romance: Girls negotiating meaning in literacy transactions. *Journal of Adolescent & Adult Literacy. 46,* 624-635.

Engestrom, Y. (1987). *Learning by expanding: An activity theoretical approach to developmental research.* Helsinki: Orienta-Konsultit.

Ensico, P. (1998). "Good/bad girls read together: pre-adolescent girls' co-authorship of feminine subject positions during a shared reading event. *English Education. 30,* 44-63.

Emerson, R., Fretz, R., & Shaw, L. (1995). *Writing ethnographic fieldnotes.* Chicago: University of Chicago Press.

Fairclough, N. (2003). *Analysing discourse: Text analysis for social research.* New York: Routledge.

Finders, M. (1997). *Just girls: Hidden literacies and life in junior high.* New York: Teachers College Press.

Galda, L., & Beach, R. (2000). Response to literature as a cultural activity. *Theory into Practice, 30*(1), 64-73.

Gee, J. P. (1996). *Sociolinguistics and literacies: Ideology in discourses* (2nd. Ed.). New York: Falmer.

Gee, J. P. (1999). *An introduction to discourse analysis: Theory and method.* New York: Routledge.

Graue, M. E., & Walsh, D. (1998). *Studying children in context: Theories, methods, and ethnics.* Thousands Oaks, CA: Sage publications.

Greer, J. (2004). "Some of their stories are like my life, I guess": Working-class women readers and confessional magazine. In P. Scheickart & E. Flynn (Eds.), *Reading sites: Social difference and reader response* (pp. 135-165). New York: Modern Language Association.

Griffin C. (1989). *Typical girls? Young women from school to the job market.* London: Routledge.

Hartman, P. (2001). *Academically successful working-class girls constructing gender and literacy.* Unpublished doctoral dissertation, State University of New York, Buffalo.

Hawthorne, N. (1850). *The scarlet letter.* Boston: Ticknor, Reed, & Fields.

Hicks, D. (2004). Back to Oz? Rethinking the literary in a critical study of reading. *Research in the Teaching of English. 40,* 63-84.

Holland, D. & Eisenhart, M. (1990). *Educated in romance: Women, achievement, and college culture.* Chicago: University of Chicago Press.

Holland, D., Lachicotte, W., Skinner, D., & Cain, C. (2001). *Identity and agency in cultural worlds.* Cambridge, MA: Harvard University Press.

Lewis, C. (2000). Limits of identification: The personal, pleasurable, and the critical in reader response. *Journal of Literacy Research. 32,* 253-266.

Morrison, T. (1987). *Beloved.* New York: Knopf.

Phelan, P., Davidson, A. L., & Yu, H. C. (1998). *Adolescents' worlds: Negotiating family peers and school.* New York: Teachers College Press.

Pirie, B. (1997). *Reshaping high school English.* New York: Teachers College Press.

Rosenblatt, L. (1995). *Literature as exploration* (4th ed.). New York: Modern Language Association.

Simpson, A. (1996). Fiction and facts: An investigation of the reading practices of girls and boys. *English Journal, 28*(4), 268-279.

Sparks, N. (1999). *A walk to remember.* New York: Warner Books.

Spradley, J. P. (1980). *Participant observation.* New York, Harcourt Brace Jovanovich.

Trousdale, A. (1995). I'd rather be normal: A young girl's response to "feminist" fairy tales. *The New Advocate,* *8,* 167-182.

Walkerdine, V (1990). *Schoolgirl fictions.* London: Verso.

Weis, L. (1990). *Working class without work: High school students in a de-industrializing economy.* New York: Routledge.

APPENDIX A: INTERVIEW QUESTIONS FOR STUDENTS

Students will be told: "The responses you give to these questions will not be shared with Ms. Mathison, so whatever you say will not bias her perception or evaluation of you one way or the other."

In Reference to Novels Studied in Class:

1. What was your reaction to the novel?

2. In reading the novel, what were some things about how it was written that made it easy to comprehend or understand? What were some things about how it was written that made it difficult to comprehend or understand?

3. How would you describe the cultural world or worlds portrayed in the novel? What were some things about the cultural worlds that were familiar or easy to understand? What were some things about the cultural worlds that were puzzling or difficult to understand?

4. What are some of the rules or norms as to appropriate behavior operating in the world of the novel? What are some specific things in the novel that suggest these rules or norms? What are some beliefs or attitudes operating in this world? What are some specific things in the novel that suggest these beliefs or attitudes?

5. How do you perceive the world of this novel as similar to or different from the worlds of other novels in the course? In what ways are they similar or different?

6. Did characters, conflicts, situations or resolutions portrayed in the novel remind you of any experiences in your own world? How were these experiences similar to or different from those portrayed in the novel?

7. What do you perceive to be some key issues or problems portrayed in the novel? What are some of the reasons why you may consider these issues or problems important to you?

8. In studying the novel, what were some classroom activities that were helpful for you in understanding the novel and why? What activities, if any, did you find less than helpful?

In Reference to Participation in Class in General:

1. People play lots of different roles in different situations. What kind of a role do you see yourself playing in class? What about in discussion in particular?

2. In class discussion, in what ways do the responses of other students affect what you are willing to say?

3. In class discussion, in what ways do you think your responses might affect what other students are willing to say?

4. What are some things that make class discussion a safe place for everyone to share ideas? What are some things that make it less than safe?

5. If you could design this course, what kinds of topics would you cover? What kinds of texts would you choose?

6. In what ways, if any, do you think being female affects who you are at school? In this class? In class discussions?

7. In what ways, if any, do you think your friends affect who you are at school? In this class? In class discussions?

In Reference to Literacy Practices Outside of the Classroom:

1. Do you read books outside of the classroom? What kinds of books do you like? What do you think you get from these books?

2. What kinds of television programs do you enjoy? What do you like about these programs?

3. What are some of your favorite movies? What appeals to you about these movies?

4. Do you read any magazines or newspapers? If so, what do you get from these magazines and newspapers? Do you prefer to read them alone or with friends? Why?

5. Thinking as broadly as you can, what are other ways you use writing in your life? Do you write notes to your friends? Keep a diary? Copy down song lyrics? Talk about what you think you get out of each of these activities.

6. Again, thinking broadly, what are other things you might read in your life? Notes from friends? Email? Talk about what you think you get out of each of these activities.

APPENDIX B: THEMATIC CODING CATEGORIES

Adapted from Beach, Thein, & Parks (in press)

1. Participant

1.1   Lia

1.2   Molly

1.3   Betty

1.4   Davie

1.5   Vickie

1.6   Joan

2. Text

2.1   The Scarlet Letter

2. 2   The Things They Carried

2. 3   The Great Gatsby

2. 4   Hamlet

2. 5   The Catcher in the Rye

2. 6   The Crucible

2. 7   Beloved

3. Student discussion/positioning strategies

3.1   challenging/disagreeing with other students/group

3.2   affirming others' stances/shared thinking

3.3   making connections to other texts, personal experiences, previous discussion

3.4   formulating lengthy, original interpretation

3.5   voices teacher words or actions or displays instructional strategies

4. Voicing/adopting stances/lenses/discourses related to:

4. 1   gender

4. 2   class

4. 3   race

4. 4   sports/athletics

4. 5   school/education/socialization

4. 6   historical/cultural analysis in general

4. 7   social groups/activities

4. 8   family/religion/cultural

5. Contextualizing/constructing text worlds in terms of:

5. 1   norms, conventions, beliefs, values in the text

6. Categorizing/defines perceptions of self, others, and characters

6. 1   categorizes self or others or describes perceptions of self and other in terms of identity, role, ability, status, beliefs;

6. 2   categorizes or describes perceptions of characters in terms of identity, role, ability, status, beliefs

APPENDIX C: QUESTIONS FOR IDENTIFYING CULTURAL MODELS (FROM GEE 1999, P. 78)

- What cultural models are relevant here? What must I, as an analyst, assume people feel, value, and believe, consciously or not, in order to talk (write), act, and/or interact in this way?

- Are there differences here between the cultural models that are affecting espoused beliefs and those that are affecting actions and practices? What sorts of cultural models, if any, are being used here to make value judgments about oneself or others?

• How consistent are the relevant cultural models here? Are there competing or conflicting cultural models at play? Whose interests are the cultural models representing?

• What other cultural models are related to the ones most active here? Are there "master models" at work?

• What sorts of texts, media, experiences, interactions, and/or institutions could have given rise to these cultural models?

• How are the relevant cultural models here helping to reproduce, transform, or create social, cultural, institutional, and/or political relationships? What Discourses and Conversations are these cultural models helping to reproduce, transform, or create?

How Literacy History Is Told: Approaches and Lenses for Historical Access

J Patrick Tiedemann
Jim S. Furman
Julie Ellison Justice
Jason F. Lovvorn
Victoria J. Risko
Peabody College of Vanderbilt University

Nila Banton Smith's *American Reading Instruction* was first printed in 1934 by Silver Burdett publishers. Two revised editions and a special edition, published by the International Reading Association, came out in 1965, 1986, and 2002, respectively. The book began as historical research for Smith's doctoral dissertation while she was a student at Teachers' College, Columbia University. Her work documented trends and issues and traced theoretical and research contributions of prominent literacy educators from the early 1600s through 1965. *American Reading Instruction* was the only comprehensive history of reading text focused on American reading instruction for at least 50 years after it was first printed, and it remains an important foundational text for theorists and researchers of the 21st century (Stahl, 2002).

In her introductory section Smith discusses the importance of considering the history of reading instruction. She argues that the story of reading instruction be told, "not only as a matter of information and for the light it throws on the history of education, but also as an aid in giving a clearer perspective on current practices in this significant field" (p. xv). Our own approach to the study of Smith's work has a similar purpose. As participants (four graduate students and one professor, the course instructor) in a graduate seminar entitled *Issues and Trends in Literacy Instruction,* we read *American Reading Instruction* as a primary reference. Accepting the premise that examining and analyzing historical trends across time is one way to inform our approach to contemporary problems in our field, we studied the content (i.e., what was told) of Smith's text and the form or organization of this content (i.e., how the story was told). In order to supplement our reading of *American Reading Instruction,* we read several seminal papers written by authors referenced by Smith along with other similar works (e.g., Huey, 1908; Durkin, 1979; Rosenblatt, 1978). We also examined some of the actual artifacts (e.g., basal readers, materials from early phonics programs, and assessment tools) Smith described in her text. We expected that our inquiry into perspectives, trends, and issues that affected the roots of U.S. literacy instruction would provide explanatory power for policy and research paradigms that continue to affect contemporary practice and curriculum content.

The problems and questions raised during this process led to the line of inquiry that we report in this paper. Our approach followed two paths. First, we reread Smith's text from the perspective that it is not definitive, but is itself a literary artifact. We utilized White's (1978) concept of *emplotment* to analyze Smith's configuration of historical events into a recognizable plotline. We began to uncover the ways that Smith had applied literary structures for storytelling to bring coherence and explanatory meaning to a select series of events and material artifacts. We also analyzed the rhetorical devices she used to establish an authoritative voice and to position her work as a substantiated explication of the history of reading instruction.

Second, our initial search for supplementary readings changed to a search for information not represented in *American Reading Instruction.* Smith, like any author, constructs a meaningful story by ignoring and subordinating certain events while emphasizing others (White, 1978). We therefore sought to identify alternative perspectives on the course of literacy instruction in the United States (e.g. Hogan, 1917; Weber, 1993; Willis, 2002). It became clear to us that Smith's account privileged a particular version of history based on sources that were widely accessible or made public in some way (e.g., published commercial materials, published research). These accounts did not necessarily represent "timeless truth" (Gutierrez & Rogoff, 2003, p. 23).

In this paper we consider both the affordances and marginalizations of Smith's approach to the history of reading instruction. Specifically, we analyze her use of chronological periods of social emphasis as a means of emplotting or organizing her report, her detailed attention to a particular set of artifacts, and her rhetorical and discursive devices employed to substantiate her authority. Then, presenting an alternative approach to the telling of history, we focus on "Literacy at Calhoun Colored School 1892-1945" (Willis, 2002) and analyze the same features in order to compare the affordances of each historical lens.

NILA BANTON SMITH'S *AMERICAN READING INSTRUCTION*

From the outset it is important to note that we are examining *American Reading Instruction* as a lens through which we can gain one perspective on the history of our field. Our purpose is not to contextualize the piece and critique the degree to which Smith conforms to the norms of her period. Neither is our goal to critique her in hindsight according to current academic values and expectations. Rather, we seek to present an analysis of the book's value as a macro-history of reading instruction. Early in our examination of Smith's text, we recognized and appreciated, as did Smith, the difficult task she had undertaken in "organizing the unwieldy body of historical facts" (p. xvii). We also recognized the magnitude of the contributions of this work to a field of instruction that had no other comprehensive account of its history. While we may critique and question the focus of Smith's history and the structure of her narrative, we continue to affirm its importance and its status as an artifact of a certain time and purpose.

Historic Periods: Depicting the Social and Political Influences on Reading Instruction

Smith began her research by identifying "the fundamental influences...responsible for bringing about change" as a way of "pointing up trends and drawing fairly clear lines of demarcation" (p. xviii) between distinct periods of reading instruction. She sought to determine loose starting and ending points for periods of educational emphasis. This approach is evident in the titles and dates assigned to her eight chapters--for example, "Chapter Two: The Period of

Religious Emphasis in Reading Instruction" or "Chapter Five: The Period of Emphasis on Reading as a Cultural Asset." Each of these chapters locates reading instruction within broader cultural trends of American society and then discusses the materials and methods that developed in response to each trend. For example, in chapter five Smith states, "With the success of the American democracy assured, with threats of major wars no longer impending, and with a population comfortable in a prosperous economy, a new trend emerged that affected the nature of reading instruction" (p. 108). Specifically, according to Smith, reading instruction became concerned with the quality of literature being read and the ability to interpret that literature correctly. This view of reading emphasized a privileged view of what counts as culture, literature, and literary interpretation. However, this same period of supposed stability, comfort, and prosperity for the country came on the heels of Emancipation and Reconstruction, national events with profound ramifications. Yet these events go unmentioned by Smith.

The direction of Smith's plot becomes evident as three of the final four periods in Smith's history focus heavily on scientifically based reading research. Smith introduces "The Period of Emphasis on Scientific Investigation in Reading" (1910-1924) by saying, "The dramatic period beginning in 1910 ushered in the first truly great break-through in American reading instruction. . . A new development suddenly shaped up that had startling effects in changing reading methods and materials" (p. 148). In much of what follows, Smith's concern moves from the influence of cultural concerns on reading instruction toward the influence of scientifically-based reading research. Put another way, the plot of her history builds to this "break-through," and this climactic building of events is the means by which the author tells a meaningful story.

White (1978) explains that emplotment is accomplished as "certain events or sets of events in the series... are endowed with explanatory force" (p. 92). If the first event in a chronology is emphasized, White argues that this event has original power and produces a deterministic history. Smith structures individual chapters in this manner, frontloading a cultural condition and then detailing its effects. In similar fashion, her overall history of reading instruction emphasizes in scientific research, a movement she believes will determine the future of reading instruction. As she argues in the final section of her book,

> Perhaps the supreme achievement for which this century always will be distinguished is that it brought to us the gift of scientific investigation. With instruments of measurement and diagnosis, we no longer need to depend solely upon judgment in assessing the needs of those whom we instruct or the effectiveness of theories, methods, and materials that we use. We can now obtain objective data in regard to many aspects of reading. This is an accomplishment of great magnitude. (p. 392)

While the beginning of empirical investigations into reading instruction is indeed important, Smith's emplotment leads us to believe that the advent of scientific inquiry in the field paves the way for steady, and perhaps unhindered, progress.

Smith's method is useful for organizing broad sets of information and general trends, but her periodization reduces literacy history to a grand narrative of only large-scale paradigmatic changes. Keenly absent is a conception of change located in the daily negotiations and struggles over literacy and instruction. Also missing in Smith's account is a cultural historical analysis--the kind of analysis that could help us understand literacy practices as variable, complex, and changeable. Smith's emplotment leaves certain questions unanswered: How was literacy defined locally by changing economic needs? What were the literacy practices of ethnically and linguistically diverse individuals and groups, those individuals and groups that we believed were not represented in the dominant accounts of schooling described by Smith? What were the contradictions to the dominant view, and what were the contributions of dissenting voices? Would we expect, as Graff (1995) suggests, that the study of such contradictions would enable us to address more clearly contemporary (and longstanding) problems associated with our ineffectual instruction of ethnically and linguistically diverse youth? As Meacham (2001) inquires, could current policy discussions that rarely acknowledge cultural diversity be informed by taking a broader and more inclusive look at our history?

Constructing a History Through Material Artifacts

Smith's obsession with the artifacts of reading instruction is a striking element of her book, and in some ways, given the author's methodologies, this aspect comes as little surprise. In her original preface Smith speaks to her methods and notes, "Most of the books described in the first five periods were selected on the basis of their popularity as determined by ascertaining the number of copies sold or, when this information was lacking, the number of editions published" (p. xvi). Regarding the last four periods treated in her text, Smith points out, "The writer conscientiously culled from the great masses of materials in present use those that to her seemed representative in that they conveyed ideas that were found again and again in many different and contemporary sources" (p. xvii). The issue Smith treats here is one of *selection*, and her straightforward assessment of technique provides a reader with a sense of both affordance and limitation. Using publication figures, for example, is a way to get at *reception*--of how often and long texts were taken up by an American populace. Such methods square well, in fact, with the scientific bias of Smith's own era. Looking for the most popular and representative examples of instructional readers gives the author of this history a valuable way to impose some order over the complexities of a vast topic. Such representation affords the ability to identify patterns that, in turn, become organizational markers in Smith's text.

As a result, however, cultural emphases are often overshadowed by measurements of texts, descriptions of their physical features, and categorizations of their content. For example, in chapter five, she makes the case that "The concern for cultural development resulted in an emphasis on the use of reading as medium for awakening a permanent interest in literary material that would be a cultural asset to the individual in adult life" (p. 108). What we find, however, as this chapter progresses, is a very homogenized, almost flat, sense of culture within the period. Smith's approach instead gives reading practice and literacy an oddly materialistic and limited feel. In place of a rich description of American culture and its connections to reading tastes, the reader encounters Smith's typical attentiveness to the material presence of a book. For instance, regarding Ward's Readers, we find Smith's thick description of the books themselves, complete with their "neutral tan color," "heavy cloth at the joints," and "55 pages of fables, folktales, and fairy stories; 47 pages of poetry 42 pages of realistic stories" (pp. 127 and 130). But what of the culture in the late 1800s? Where is the connection to the social conditions that warrant a category like "reading as a cultural asset" Who were these readers? And how is culture defined here?

Smith's fascination with describing physical texts and quantifying their contents misse something, particularly in a chapter that is purportedly directed at an assessment of culture Moreover, the cultural emphases we do encounter are, as Smith herself reminds us in her methods the emphases of the popular--of the most-read texts. Where then do we find counter cultures o the texts that shore them up? In *American Reading Instruction*, they simply do not exist. Because Smith's gaze is so sharply focused upon the texts themselves, to the extent that material details echo throughout her book, she depicts a fairly narrow conception of literacy practice. As astute readers we should recognize that Smith is painting a swath through American reading instruction in broac brush strokes, particularly when it comes to social context. This text/context divide reverberate throughout *American Reading Instruction*, which gives particular attention to the former and glosses over the latter with a nod here and a nod there--mostly in the headings and introductor sections of chapters.

Authoritative Voice and the Substantiation of Literacy History

Smith's rhetorical and discursive devices work to establish an authentic and authoritativ portrayal of reading instruction history. Understanding Smith's use of language allows readers t take a critical stance toward her claim to authentic, definitive history. Moreover, such understanding repositions the work as one possible perspective from which to read the story of ou past and to re-contextualize our present.

As explained above, Smith works from the basic assumption that her task of interpretatio as an historian is to organize the large body of facts she accumulated in such a way as to revea historic trends and delineate between successive periods of development. In other words, Smith operates from a naturalized definition of histories as explanations of the causal (or deterministic relationships between events. If the reader also accepts this definition of "histories" as natural and obvious, then the authenticity of Smith's work depends on presenting a convincing characterizatio of the social and political conditions that determined approaches to reading instruction. If she ha accurately characterized the trends, then her history is authentic. In this manner, the book i ultimately authenticated according to its own definition of histories. Smith intends a authoritative account of reading instruction in America according to a causal model of history, and she adopts a rhetorical style that reflects this stance. We analyze the ways that Smith's rhetoric and discourse are structured to present a convincing picture of the causes of trends in readin instruction.

One distinct feature of Smith's text is her use of rhetoric that naturalizes particula understandings of events and makes them seem definite and obvious. Smith repeatedly establishe her arguments through a structural method of exemplification and assertion. That is, Smith make statements about the relationship between influences and trends, provides representative example from the artifacts of the period, and tells the reader the definitive and proper understanding. Her method of analysis is simply to let the examples speak for themselves as if their relationship to the historic trend is self-evident. For example, in chapter five, Smith asserts that while Herbartianism's proliferation in the U.S. did not precede the nation's newest emphasis, and thus cannot be shown to be directly causal, "it seems more than likely that the movement later was accentuated by Herbartian principles" (p. 110). After providing some brief information naming people and publications associated with the movement, Smith continues: "Now let's see how Herbartianism may have accentuated the already existing emphasis. . ." (p. 111). This is followed by a page-length quote from Herbart's writings. Then comes a rhetorical practice that exemplifies Smith's approach to analysis: "After reading only this one quotation, it *becomes quite evident* that there was a similarity between Herbart's principles and the new type of reading instruction" (p. 112, emphasis added). That there *is* a similarity is asserted, not demonstrated, and then the similarity between the ideas in the passage from Herbart and the trend she has identified is assumed to exemplify cause and effect.

This meaning does not arise from the artifacts themselves, as she implies, but is constructed by her own model of historic emplotment, structuring of text, and statement that it is so. In keeping with this analysis through the structure of a cause and effect emplotment, Smith naturalizes the course of events as inevitable, "with the issuance of new materials and the formulation of new methods, it was *natural* that entire treatises should appear" (p. 115, emphasis added). Having once established these causal relationships through such rhetoric, Smith refers to earlier assertions as established and given: "We noted in the preceding period that the birth of our nation was followed by an emotional outburst of patriotism" (p. 69).

Another key feature of the text is the prevalent use of the pronouns *we* and *us*. The effect is to draw the reader into sharing Smith's interpretations and to authorize her historical analysis. This pronoun usage rhetorically positions the telling of the story as what we both, reader and Smith, have *seen to be true*. This is not just Smith's interpretation or version of the story. The conclusions are clear and inevitable and incumbent upon any reader who is following the line of analysis, the logic of the emplotment. For example, throughout an entire page Smith employs the device in a way that positions the reader as already having come to specific conclusions regarding trends: "We noted in chapter three some indication of this trend," "We saw that," and "We find the intense patriotic type of materials" (p. 78). Due to the structure of the emplotment and Smith's use of authoritative rhetoric, the reader is told what she or he noted, saw, and found in the artifacts. In effect the reader is told the inevitable conclusions, conclusions that are inescapable.

ARLETTE INGRAM WILLIS'S "LITERACY AT CALHOUN COLORED SCHOOL 1892-1945"

Willis's (2002) historical account of literacy at the Calhoun Colored School (CCS) is an alternative narrative using techniques and theoretical frames that contrast with those of Smith. Willis's approach provides a lens for accessing situated and local contexts where literacy is an emergent set of socio-cultural practices. Her multi-focal study of literacy education is valuable, in part, because we know that the historic colonization and neglect of marginalized groups remains a vital issue in many parts of the U. S. today (Grant, 2001). To unpack Willis's approach, we provide an analysis of the same dimensions that we examined in Smith's text: methods of emplotment, sources and materials accessed, and the work accomplished by the use of particular rhetoric and discourses.

Willis argues that recent histories have provided uncritical accounts of dominant literacy experiences, minimizing issues of literacy, knowledge, privilege, and power that work to marginalize particular groups and maintain cultural hegemony. Other historical accounts, among which she seeks to situate her own work, have been able to document the ways in which literacy has been restricted to certain groups based on gender, class, race, religion, geography, or other social distinctions. Willis asserts that, in order to understand how access to literacy has been historically constructed, we must study history locally, in specific and rich contexts. Rather than focusing on the whole of America, her text provides a thorough telling and analysis of the history of one particular school and its offshoots.

Willis characterizes her literacy history as "a genealogy of the literacy programs and practices at Calhoun Colored School (CCS) in the rural African American community of Calhoun, Alabama, from 1892 to 1945" (p. 11). The use of Foucault's genealogical method allows Willis to tell a narrative of reading instruction in ways not valued as better, but certainly valued as different, privileging aspects of history that were not privileged in Smith's text. She organizes her narrative around the voices and actions of key participants, examining the beliefs and accomplishments of influential people over a span of years as a primary means of discovering "the discourse, political and social contexts, and power/knowledge relations that influenced literacy access at CCS" (p. 13). Thus she is interested in exploring not only literacy instruction at the school, but also the negotiations and manifestations of power that shape the course of literacy instruction. Willis depicts one particular situation in its dynamic complexity. One key principle behind this method is the idea of *convergence*--of showing how a wide array of historical forces coalesces around, and give shape to, a single space and time. Rabinow (as cited in Willis 2002) describes this method quite nicely, noting how a genealogical construction "presents a series of discrete elements that, while following their own periodicity and their own dynamics, assemble at the same conjuncture." Thus, multiple struggles for power fill her history as individuals and institutions in the narrative wrestle for control of literacy curricula and literacy access for the local children and community. It is through this genealogical approach, we argue, that Willis's piece exemplifies the sort of alternative lens required for a broader view of literacy education history.

Historical People: Depicting the Local Struggle over Access to Literacy

Willis's genealogical narrative revolves around a continuously shifting network of power and knowledge relations, the local struggle involving the Hampton-Tuskegee model, the needs and motivations of the African-American community, and national literacy trends. Willis's emplotment depicts the contexts, discourses, and practices involved in "the shift from the Hampton-Tuskegee model to one that resembled the best of northern schools" (p. 38). She uses a Foucaultian lens to conclude that "the nexus of power/knowledge relations within social institutions and their discursive practices controlled how people constructed African American intelligence and worthiness" (p. 38) and retained a pervasive, though not unchallenged, influence on literacy education at CCS. Her narrative, therefore, entails a representation of a larger societal racism, exploring systematic social and economic oppression that existed throughout the period under study.

Willis situates the school's foundational educational policies and practices within the broader societal discourse on African-American education. Referencing the educational philosophies of Booker T. Washington and Samuel C. Armstrong, the author highlights the ways in which the Hampton-Tuskegee model of literacy was used as a form of social control. "The influence of Armstrong and Washington," she asserts, "in what has come to be known as the Hampton-Tuskegee model of education, designed to support the southern economy and instill African American submission, is unfathomable" (p. 16). This model becomes the reference point for her analysis of educational philosophies and practices at CCS, and across the time span of the school's existence, Willis consistently tracks variations from the Hampton-Tuskegee model.

Strongly connected to these shifting philosophies and practices are the ideas and actions of individual persons. Whereas Smith emplots her narrative around national emphases and trends, Willis organizes her history around people such as Samuel Armstrong, Booker T. Washington, Charlotte Thorn, Mabel Dillingham, Susan S. Showers, Clara Hart, Mabel Edna Brown, Jessie E. Guernsey, Edward M. Allen, and R. Luella Jones. The names reflect influential leaders, teachers, and administrators who were central to either the founding of CCS or to its day-to-day operations. Willis admits that this organization around individuals does not fit a strictly Foucaultian, genealogical analysis. In fact, she diverges from Foucault's model and instead follows Best and Kellner (1991), who argue that Foucault "occludes the extent to which power is still controlled and administered by specific and identifiable agents in positions of economic and political power" (quoted in Willis, p. 37). For Willis, who is interested in uncovering the veiled dynamics surrounding African-American literacy at CCS, much of this power was wielded by administrators who made key choices about the school and its practices.

Constructing a History through Multiple Artifacts

Willis produces a literacy history predicated upon multiple perspectives, offering insight into the larger social forces that shaped CCS and providing an *in-close, contextual* look at the school. This macro/micro view is a product of two impulses: (1) Willis's theory of historical construction and analysis that privileges the contextual and the discursive; and (2) her usage of source materials appropriate to such theorizing. These two elements work in conjunction, informing and building upon one another as the history emerges. In Foucaultian fashion, Willis collects a wide range of discursive artifacts from which she constructs her history of power dynamics. Willis therefore is tracking much more than texts; she is trying to overlay a range of historical narratives and voices, juxtaposing them so that, ultimately, they construct a meaningful picture of CCS. As Willis herself puts it, "genealogies focus on the continuities and discontinuities of history that include 'overlapping, interaction, and echoes'" (p. 13).

Willis's theory and approach reflect one another, for her data itself was "collected in interwoven and overlapping steps" (p. 12). Unlike Smith, whose methods concerned literacy texts and their reception, Willis attempts to describe literacy at CCS from a broader range of perspectives, some expansive and at a distance, others smaller and focused tightly on CCS. This task called for data that varied in both type and scope. Thus Willis's data set involved "an extensive review of available primary and secondary sources on the history of African-American education and CCS" (p. 12). Among the many primary sources used by Willis were files from the General Education Board, the property deed for CCS, annual reports written for the CCS Board of Trustees, correspondences, photographs, journal articles, and newspaper accounts. Secondary sources included other historical accounts of CCS as well as numerous journal articles, testimonials, letters, editorials, and essays.

Using multiple artifacts allows Willis to present the kind of social and cultural context that Smith's book overlooks. For instance, she locates literacy instruction at CCS within larger issues of access and denial that affected all African-Americans in the latter part of the nineteenth century. She traces the discursive practices that kept African-Americans in subservient positions, showing how such practices were inevitably connected to restrictions placed on African-American literacy. As she weaves this larger narrative across individuals and institutions, Willis connects these social conditions and cultural practices to the founding and administering of CCS.

Voice, Rhetoric, and the Genealogical Analysis of Literacy History

Willis's piece is written in a contemporary academic voice. Her careful qualification of the analysis and her acknowledgement of personal and professional interests are in keeping with a larger discourse appropriate to Foucaultian historical analysis (Hoy, 1986). She uses language that establishes her as a biased researcher exploring a topic, that identifies her paper as interpretative history, and that positions the reader as a fellow researcher interested in the pursuit of equitable literacy education.

Throughout the opening pages of the article Willis is clear about her theoretical and personal biases as an author. She ties the methodology and theory to her own position as a researcher through a consistent use of the pronoun *I*. She describes her professional purpose as providing the academic community with an "alternative perspective of the early history of literacy in the U.S." (p.14). Further, she is clear about her personal motivations as an historian, explaining that her interests in CCS first arose upon hearing family recollections, and that she initially wished to confirm their fond memories.

The language used throughout the article establishes it as a descriptive analysis based on the theoretical positions and judgment of the author. Rather than use the definitive rhetoric of Smith, Willis qualifies her genealogical analysis of literacy history at CCS as "but one possible interpretation" (p. 37). Through repeated use of the terms "suggests" and "possible" her analysis is positioned as grounded and plausible, but open to dissent and alternative perspectives. She often admits when the reasons for events are "not known" (e.g., p. 24, 31) or "not clear" (e.g., p. 24). This careful choice of wording positions her work as subject to peer review and open to critique and alternative perspectives.

Finally, by using first-person, plural pronouns in her discussion, Willis enlists the reader as a member of her academic circle.   For instance she states that her paper adds to "our understanding" (p. 36) and is an alternative to deficit thinking in "our field" (p. 39). She also asks the reader, "What is our role as a community of researchers who declare to have the best interests of all children. . .at heart to promote change?" (p. 39). Thus Willis's text strategically positions the reader in the discussion, but unlike Smith, Willis never attempts to draw the reader to definitive conclusions. Instead, the reader is invited to occupy a position better described as *coworker* rather than *follower*.

CONCLUSION

No approach tells a complete history. In fact, no history is exhaustive. There will always be persons, events, and artifacts omitted or marginalized in any telling. Yet, no matter how historians emplot their narratives, historical construction is always an act of meaning making with particular affordances. Put another way, every design offers a potentially valuable perspective on the past. In the case of *American Reading Instruction*, Smith's approach provides a story that is *broad* and *national*, taking on the Herculean task of characterizing literacy across three-and-a-half centuries and an entire country. This approach also allows her to discern, in a *unified* and *orderly* manner, the common elements in a complex mixture of people and events. Out of what would otherwise be an unintelligible and overwhelming body of facts, the reader is able to discern literacy trends. Such trends appear *definitive* and *uniform* due to the author's rhetorical strategies. Smith's work thus remains as one relevant step in exploring how history has led to the current moment in literacy education.

Willis's approach to history is *situated* and *local*. She is not challenged to understand the literacy history of an entire nation, and is therefore able to focus on the ideological struggles of a small group of people in one particular context. Likewise, her history is *personal* and *multi-vocal*. She is able to provide a richer history that includes the literacy experiences of traditionally silenced groups complete with their histories, ideological positions, values, intentions and goals. Willis avoids the position of relating events with a detached or official voice; rather, she is able to tell her history through the voices of the actual participants. Additionally, a genealogical approach allows Willis to tell a history that is *dynamic* and *problematic*. Hers is not a history of a straight-line progression toward a goal; rather, her narrative indicates historical paths filled with difficulties, wrong turns, and reversals. Finally, this particular history is *agonistic*. Struggles for power fill her history, as individuals in the narrative wrestle for control of literacy curricula and access of the children and community.

Our concluding thoughts are well summarized by Best and Kellner as quoted by Willis (2002): "no single theory or method of interpretation by itself can grasp the plurality of discourses, institutions, and modes of power that constitute modern society" (p. 37). We formulated this study on just this concept. No single approach to the telling of the history of literacy instruction can provide the type of rich understandings needed if we are to chart where we have been in order to contextualize the places in which we currently find ourselves. We believe that history can best serve the present and future when a multiplicity of voices that have come before us are drawn forth to tell their stories. A broad range of those diverse stories will never be accessed through a single paradigm, approach, or theoretical lens. Instead, we have come to believe that the complex history of our field can only be accessed by those willing to bridge paradigms. Examining only two works established a complex and sometimes contradictory picture, but thus is the nature of the history of literacy education.

REFERENCES

Durkin, D. (1979). *Teaching them to read.* Boston, Ma: Allen and Bacon, Inc.

Graff, H. J. (1995). *The labyrinth of literacy: Reflections on literacy past and present.* Pittsburgh: University of Pittsburgh Press.

Grant, C. (2001). Teachers and linking literacies of yesterday and today with literacies of tomorrow: The need for education that is multicultural and social reconstructionist. In J. Hoffman, D. Schallert, C. Fairbanks, J. Worthy, & B. Maloch (Eds.), *50th Yearbook of the National Reading Conference* (pp.63-81). Chicago: NRC.

Gutierrez, K. D., & Rogoff, B. (2003). Cultural ways of learning: Individual traits or repertoires of practice. *Educational Researcher, 32*(5), 19-25.

Hogan, W. E. (1917). *Changing conceptions of the aim of Negro education, as seen in the history of colored schools in Nashville, Tennessee.* Unpublished Masters thesis, George Peabody College for Teachers.

Hoy, D. C. (Ed.) (1986). *Foucault: A critical reader.* Oxford. Basil Blackwell.

Huey, E. B. (1908). *The psychology and pedagogy of reading.* NY: Macmillan. (Revised 1912, 1915).

Meacham, S. J. (2001). Literacy at the crossroads: Movement, connection, and communication within the research literature on literacy and cultural diversity. In W.G. Secada (Ed.), *Review of Research in Education, 25,* (pp. 181–208). Washington, DC: American Education Research Association.

Rosenblatt, L. (1978). *The reader, the text, the poem: The transactional theory of the literary work.* Carbondale, IL: Southern Illinois Press.

Smith, N. B. (2002). *American reading instruction.* Newark, DE: International Reading Association.

Stahl, N.A. (2002). Epilogue. In N.B. Smith, *America Reading Instruction* (special edition, pp. 413-418). Newark, DE: International Reading Association.

Weber, R. (1993). Even in the midst of work: Reading among turn-of-the century farmers' wives. *Reading Research Quarterly, 28,* 293-302.

White, H. (1978). *Tropics of discourse: Essays in cultural criticism.* Baltimore: Johns Hopkins University Press.

Willis, A. I. (2002). Literacy at Calhoun Colored School 1892-1945. *Reading Research Quarterly, 37*(1), 8-44.

Crossing Over to Canaan: Engaging Distinguished Women and/or Minority Literacy Scholars in Critical Tenure Conversations

Jennifer D. Turner
University of Maryland at College Park

Doris Walker-Dalhouse
Minnesota State University Moorhead

Gwendolyn Thompson McMillon
Oakland University

Crossing over to Canaan is a biblical metaphor that signifies the courage, resilience, and fortitude necessary for entering into the "Promised Land," a land flowing with milk and honey. According to the Old Testament story, the Israelites were promised the land of Canaan, but they were afraid of its many mighty inhabitants. As a result of their fear, they did not take the land, and spent many desperate years wandering in the desert.

In many ways, the professional experiences of junior women and/or minority faculty parallel the Israelites' journey into Canaan. Although women and minority scholars often attain tenure-track positions in literacy and other disciplinary fields, a significant number do not cross into the "Promised Land." Thus, members of the Ethnicity, Race, and Multilingualism Committee of the National Reading Conference (NRC) thought it imperative to initiate a dialogue about tenure with prominent women and/or minority literacy scholars. At the NRC 2004 Annual Meeting, we convened a symposium on race, gender, and tenure that featured five distinguished literacy scholars: Donna Alvermann, Kathryn Au, Patricia Edwards, Jane Hansen, and Robert Rueda. In this paper, we present the scholars' compelling tenure stories. We share their critical observations about tenure as a means for stimulating conversation and action that supports emerging literacy scholars from underrepresented groups "crossing over to Canaan" at major research universities within the United States.

ENTERING THE "PROMISED LAND" OF TENURE

Tenure is defined by the American Association of University Women (2004) as "the promise of lifetime employment awarded to professors who demonstrate excellence in scholarship, teaching, and service" (p.2). The concept of tenure is predicated upon egalitarianism, yet gender, racial, and cultural disparities in tenure rates suggest that equal opportunity has not easily translated to junior women and/or minority faculty (Aguirre, 2000; Perna, 2001). In 1998-1999, the National Center for Educational Statistics (NCES) reported that 64% of full-time faculty had tenure, and of those tenured faculty, 71% of men enjoyed tenure compared to only 52% of their female colleagues. Women comprise 18% of full professors and 30% of associate professors but constitute over 40% of assistant professors and more than 50% of instructional lecturers (Aguirre, 2000).

Ropers-Huilman (2003) contends that the gender gap in academia may be the result of the professional and personal dilemmas that women faculty encounter when their biological clocks conflict with their tenure clocks. It is estimated that one-third of women faculty have children, and many have experienced serious obstacles in their attempts to manage career demands and family responsibilities, negotiate the tenure review process, and develop supportive networks (Alfred, 2001; Gregory, 2001). Recent studies (e.g., Aguirre, 2000) also show that women faculty, especially those with children, report low levels of job satisfaction because institutional policies and practices that are intended to be "gender-neutral" often silence critical conversations about balancing work and family lives.

Entering the "Promised Land" appears to be even more difficult for scholars of color; only 14% of full-time faculty members are scholars of color, and less than half receive tenure (Hutchenson, 2004). The American Association of University Women (2004) recently reported that the majority of tenured faculty are White (87.7%), with significantly smaller proportions of Asian-Americans (5.8%), African-Americans (3.9%), and Hispanics (2.1%). It is important to note that significantly fewer females in all minority groups were represented at each rank. Mabokela and Green (2001) speculate that women scholars of color have difficulty fully participating in the academy because they experience significant pressure to choose between their personal affiliations (e.g., family, community) and their professional lives in academe.

Research on gender and racial group differences in tenure and promotion rates suggests that these inequities may be exacerbated by the "haphazard" nature of the tenure process (Tierney & Bensimon, 1996). In a study of junior faculty's perceptions of the tenure process in several major research universities, Verrier (1992) found that most were unclear about the process, were preoccupied with knowing where they stood in the process, and desired specific criteria or clearly defined road maps to gauge their progress. Perna (2001) contends that the absence of clearly defined performance and procedural requirements for tenure may be especially detrimental to junior women and/or minority faculty, because they are less likely than White men to be integrated into their departments and institutions, and have less access to professional information and networks.

Importantly, Alfred's (2001) study of tenured African-American female faculty revealed that knowledge about the tenure process (e.g., institutional expectations and promotion criteria) greatly contributed to their success in the academy. Bearing this in mind, we organized an NRC symposium to make the rules, expectations, and procedures of the tenure process more explicit, particularly for junior women and/or minority scholars. To accomplish this goal, we asked that our distinguished panelists respond to five key questions: (a) What general tenure advice do you have for junior women and/or minority scholars? (b) How do you balance research, teaching, and service? (c) What should junior women and/or minority faculty do if they are told that they have been engaged in activities which "don't count" towards tenure (e.g., spending significant time advising students of color or doing community work)? (d) What course of action should junior women and/or minority faculty take if they believe that their tenure review was unfair?, and (e) What can tenured literacy scholars do to support junior women and/or minority colleagues?

During the symposium, the distinguished scholars had 10-12 minutes to share their own personal tenure stories, as well as insights based upon their extensive work on tenure committees.

Inspired by these stories of determination and hope, we wanted this paper to reflect the multilayered complexity of the scholars' tenure experiences using their own voices. To this end, we asked the distinguished scholars for the notes that they prepared for their presentations. Shorter texts (e.g., Alvermann, Rueda) are presented in their entirety, while longer stories have been edited due to space constraints. As a formal member check, we returned all of the edited texts to the scholars to ensure that these representations were accurate. In the section that follows, we briefly share scholars' tenure stories.

THE TRAILBLAZERS: VOICES OF DISTINGUISHED LITERACY SCHOLARS WHO HAVE CROSSED INTO CANAAN

Donna Alvermann

Donna Alvermann is Distinguished Research Professor of Language and Literacy Education and a Fellow in the Institute for Behavioral Research at the University of Georgia. She has been president of the NRC, was elected to the Reading Hall of Fame in 1999, and was a recipient of NRC's Oscar S. Causey Award for Outstanding Contributions to Reading Research and the College Reading Association's Laureate Award.

"When I went up for tenure at the University of Georgia in the mid '80s, the rule of thumb was that 'successful candidates' had to have 25 refereed/published articles (which averaged out to five publications for every year in rank) inasmuch as five years was the average number of years spent in rank at the assistant professor level at that time."

"The magical (perhaps even mythical) number of 25 publications in five years is no longer bandied about; however, it continues to be the unspoken norm that while quality counts (as evidenced by the number of citations to one's works – not counting self-citations—that are recorded in the Social Sciences Citation Index), quantity is still a factor."

"Teaching evaluations, of course, have to be good, and service is expected, regardless of whether one has budgeted time for service; still, the bottom line is scholarship, and peer-refereed articles in highly prestigious journals 'count more' than chapters or books."

Kathryn Au

Kathy Au is a Professor at the University of Hawaii. She served as President of NRC in 1996 and has served as a board member of the International Reading Association.

"My own experience in gaining tenure is not a typical one, because I was already an established scholar when I took my first position at a university. However, I want to make one point about my own tenure experience: Minority scholars must become comfortable with bragging and selfishness in order to obtain tenure. Let me explain."

"I had prepared my papers with care, so I was surprised by the feedback given to me by my liaison from the department personnel committee. 'Kathy,' she said, 'you have done so many great things, but that doesn't come across in your papers. You're understating your accomplishments.' I was stunned by this feedback, but then realized what had happened. I was raised to value accomplishment but to look down on those who felt the need to brag about their accomplishments. I came to understand that in the university, which is run according to mainstream values, bragging is a necessary part of gaining tenure."

"Until you receive tenure, your number one priority must be research and publication. As a female, minority scholar, and as a mentor to quite a number of female, minority scholars, I know how difficult it is to make the decision to focus on research and writing when others are so clearly in need of your help. Focusing on your own research and writing seems like the worst kind of selfishness. The way to think about this situation is to understand that you are going to be in a better position to help others and to influence change if you become a tenured professor. Therefore, until you obtain tenure, you must engage in this kind of selfishness."

"Remember that service in the context of receiving tenure is defined at most institutions as service to the university, not to minority communities. Service to the university is lower on my list of priorities than service to Hawaiian communities and public schools, so I'm selective about the committees on which I serve. Each year, I serve on one university-wide committee, one committee at the college level, and one department committee. Given a choice, I think it's a good idea to serve on the most influential or prestigious committees. For example, I would choose the university research committee over the academic grievance committee."

"Obtaining tenure is a game with definite rules. Remember that in the context of obtaining tenure, you must play by the rules of the university as a mainstream institution. In this context, bragging and selfishness are necessary for winning the game."

Patricia Edwards

Pat Edwards is Professor of Language and Literacy at Michigan State University. She served on the Board of Directors of the International Reading Association and was recently elected vice-president of NRC.

"After completing my doctorate I felt that I needed a slower pace than the one I had encountered at the University of Wisconsin-Madison. Even though I felt that I had been well-prepared to conduct research and had gained some strategies for functioning at a major research institution, I still did not feel confident in my ability to achieve tenure. My decision not to pursue employment at a research institution received a strong reaction from my UW-Madison professors. One chilling comment was 'Pat, if you make the move to a small teachers' college, I strongly doubt that you will realize your dream of working at a major research institution.' Despite all of the warnings I received, I decided to spend two years teaching at a historically Black college and five years at a predominately midsize White teachers' college. At my second institution, I began to seriously think about what I needed to do in order to seek employment as well as tenure at a major research institution. For example, I assumed leadership roles in my local and state reading association, developed strong professional relationships with researchers by attending the National Reading Conference, and received a W. K. Kellogg Fellowship, which provided the opportunity for me to gain several mentors (i.e., Barbara Rogoff, Eugene Garcia, Dorothy Strickland, Shirley Brice

Heath). I feel that these mentors gave me what I call 'tenure training.' They helped me to feel confident by providing invaluable experiences for me, such as the opportunity to serve on national boards, publishing experiences, and introductions to key reading educators around the country."

"I cannot overemphasize the importance of mentors. I cannot emphasize enough that your mentors do not have to be ethnic researchers. I firmly believe that ethnic researchers choosing to pursue ethnic scholarship must not be concerned about the small number of ethnic academicians who are available to serve as mentors. Instead ethnic researchers should come to understand and believe that there are several nonethnic peers and faculty available and willing to serve as mentors if they choose to pursue an ethnic-related interest for their research. My ethnic mentors (Drs. Garcia & Strickland) and my nonethnic mentors (Drs. Brice Heath, Evans and Rogoff) all helped me to focus my research agenda."

"Seven years after completing graduate school, when my dream of working at a major research institution became a reality, I felt confident. When I met my department chairperson at Louisiana State University, and he began to share with me what was expected, I was not nervous, because I had heard this information from my mentors. I had a research plan and I followed it. I felt that my teaching was good, because I had had seven years of focusing on my teaching and service. So I was well on my way towards tenure and promotion. More importantly, I felt confident that I could be successful in achieving my goal."

Jane Hansen

Jane Hansen is professor at the University of Virginia. She earned her Ph.D. from the University of Minnesota in 1979 and began her academic career at the University of New Hampshire that same year. An active member of NRC since graduate school, Jane served as President of NRC in 1995.

"I was the first woman to become full professor in education at UNH. In the fall of my first year, my department chair advised me: 'Jane, we don't have a point system for tenure but, if we did, let's say it would be a 9-point system. Then 4 = teaching, 4 = scholarship, 1 = service.' I devoted myself to teaching and scholarship. I wrote a proposal for local funds, and collected data in the spring of my first year. For service, I was already active in NRC. I didn't step forward to serve on UNH committees. I knew my chair would assign me to a few tasks, and he did. He ensured I was in good shape, service-wise."

"A kind, full professor in the education department, not in my program, took me aside one day during my first semester at UNH to advise me. His words reinforced those of my department chair. This is what the professor said: 'Jane, your teaching will be fine. People who have trouble with tenure have those difficulties because of scholarship. If you publish two articles a year, you won't have to worry about tenure.'

"I decided to have three publications per year, and that worked. I never worried about tenure at all. I didn't get caught up in any of the tenure frenzy. I arrived at UNH with a research project, a follow-up to my dissertation that I was ready to implement. P. David Pearson, my advisor for my dissertation, had advised me to conduct a follow-up, and that is what I carried out in the spring of my first year."

"Also, at the time I came to UNH, several new professors arrived in the education department. We met for lunch once a week in a private room of the faculty center. The friendships we formed remained important throughout my career at UNH, and I value them to this day."

"During my first year, I looked around at what was going on at UNH that interested me. I visited research sites of other professors, met with the researchers, and learned about their projects. Mainly, I became interested in the work of Don Graves and worked with him on reading-writing research for years. Also, he and I engaged in a close working relationship with colleagues in the English Department who devoted their careers to the study of writing. My niche became the cross-over between reading-writing and English-Education."

"What made it all possible? In my case, men of power (such as Don Graves, Don Murray and Tom Newkirk) brought me in, mentored me, ensured that I succeeded, and insisted that I move forward. I entered academia ready to go, collected data my first year, published, disciplined myself, and worked within a network of supporters. I am committed. Yes, I am passionate about the importance of reading-writing to teachers and students."

Robert Rueda

Robert Rueda is a professor in Educational Psychology at the University of Southern California. He has been a senior researcher for the Center of the Improvement of Early Reading Achievement (CIERA).

"My own entry into academia was pure accident, as I was the first in my family to go for an advanced degree, and I did not have any models to draw from. I continued going to school because I was better at that than at fixing cars or doing other things that everyone else in my old neighborhood could do well. So, even though I did not have much of an idea of what a Ph.D. was, purely by accident I met Dr. Jack Share, a faculty member from UCLA who said, 'Have you ever thought of applying for a Ph.D.?'...and I did. Hopefully your career choice has been more deliberate and informed than mine. In any case, upon finishing my degree, since I still could not fix cars well, academia seemed like a logical choice."

"I can't emphasize enough two factors that have been key in my academic career. The first is good mentors. Bud Mehan and Michael Cole were two very strong influences on my early work, and later Ron Gallimore—all were struggling in different ways to integrate ideas about culture and sociocultural processes into teaching and learning. Another mentor I have learned a great deal from is Gene Garcia, one of the best administrators I know, but also a good scholar. The second factor, in addition to mentors, is the social networks I created or joined. During graduate school, I had a small network of peers that were a tremendous source of support. Some of them, like Luis Moll, have gone on to stellar careers. After graduate school, these networks, both formal and informal, have continued to be an important part of my academic career."

FOLLOWING IN THEIR FOOTSTEPS:
CRITICAL LESSONS LEARNED FROM THE TRAILBLAZERS

After the distinguished scholars' presentations, a lively exchange ensued. Audience members asked questions and raised important issues, and several junior faculty of color passionately requested a set of clearly defined strategies to help them through the tenure process. Thus, we synthesized the scholars' stories and developed a "road map" to show them how to begin their journey towards Canaan. Our road map consists of five critical lessons that were developed using an adaptation of Patton's (1990) qualitative content analytic process. In the first phase, informal analysis, we extensively discussed our notes on the symposium to identify key categories across the scholars' stories and in their dialogue with audience members (e.g., mentoring, time management). In the second phase, category formation, we used these categories, as well as others from the research literature (e.g., institutional culture), to collectively code the scholars' written stories. Throughout this process, we discussed how various categories could be combined to reflect significant themes across scholars' stories (e.g., "being a strategic scholar" included relevant topics like publishing, research, and national reputation). In the third phase, category confirmation, we confirmed these overarching themes by asking the distinguished scholars to review them. Our analyses yielded five critical lessons: (a) know the politics of your institution, (b) find mentors, (c) prepare early for tenure, (d) be a strategic scholar, and (e) work towards balance.

Lesson 1: Know the politics of your institution

Understand the culture of tenure. All five distinguished panelists encouraged women and/or minority junior faculty to learn about the culture of tenure at their particular institutions. Here, we use the term "culture of tenure" to refer to the norms, expectations, and behaviors that are associated with a favorable outcome as defined by a particular university, school, and department. Research (e.g., Aguirre, 2000) shows that cultures of tenure vary according to institutional type (e.g., major research university/teaching university), institutional prestige (e.g., public/private), and employment opportunity (i.e., availability of tenure-track versus non-tenure track positions). Often, there are also unwritten rules (or what Rueda called the "hidden curriculum") within institutions that are crucial for success within the tenure process. Thus, women and/or minority junior faculty should talk to successful candidates and review their materials, as well as consult with their department chairs, in order to make the culture of tenure more "visible."

Know the historical trends. Another critical aspect of understanding the culture of tenure is knowing the historical trends around tenure in your department, school, and university. Hansen, for example, talked with women who had not been successful in becoming full professors when she decided to submit her promotion papers at the University of New Hampshire. They all encouraged her to "go for it," and she became the first female full professor in education at UNH.

Be a good colleague. Once junior women and/or minority faculty understand the culture of tenure at their university, they can use this knowledge to become what Alfred (2001) calls "visible in the academic community" (p. 68). One way to become more visible is to *be a good colleague.* At many universities, tenure is not only about scholarship and productivity; tenured faculty members have to *want* junior faculty to be their colleagues. Thus, Edwards encouraged junior women and/or minority faculty to become "good departmental citizens." In order to garner the support of their peers during the tenure process, junior faculty must demonstrate that they are able to work well with others. Equally important, being a good departmental citizen means not "chicken fighting" with colleagues. Rueda encouraged junior faculty to "pick your battles well... Don't let minor things upset you, and don't waste your time on every little (or even moderate) injustice."

Lesson 2: Find mentors who will guide you through the tenure process

All five of the distinguished scholars in our symposium spoke passionately about the importance of mentorship within the academy. For women and/or minority assistant professors, it is important to remember that mentors come in all packages. Au put it succinctly: "It is an advantage for a minority scholar to be mentored by a minority scholar, but it is not a necessity." This does not mean that universities should forsake commitments to increasing the number of women scholars and scholars of color within literacy departments; the presence of these scholars would clearly provide significant support and inspiration to new faculty members. However, given the low numbers of women and/or minority scholars within the academy, our distinguished panelists urged junior faculty to be open to receiving mentorship from a wide variety of colleagues in the literacy field.

Be "mentorable." Openness is a fundamental aspect of a personality trait that Edwards called "being mentorable." She explained that sometimes junior faculty who are women or from culturally diverse backgrounds can unintentionally isolate themselves; they want to be accepted amongst the literacy faculty, but rather than being assertive, they wait for the "red carpet" to be rolled out for them. Edwards suggested that junior faculty of color take the initiative and introduce themselves to the literacy faculty in their departments, and those they meet at national conferences like NRC.

Use multiple mentors. Research studies have shown that junior women and/or minority faculty need multiple mentors to help them navigate the tenure process (Mabokela & Green, 2001). This finding strongly resonates with the scholars' stories. Edwards, for example, observed that it is helpful for junior faculty to have a mentor in the area of teaching, because they often need someone to provide substantive feedback and guidance about their course syllabi, teaching style, and course assignments. Similarly, Au suggested that having a variety of mentors will allow women and/or minority junior faculty to attain the moral and technical support necessary for achieving tenure. Hansen reminded junior faculty that they can be successfully mentored and supported by other junior faculty, noting that the friendships she formed with junior colleagues as a new assistant professor at UNH have remained important throughout her career.

Lesson 3: Prepare early for the tenure process

Understand the rules of tenure at your institution. Au described tenure as a "game with definite rules," and we felt this metaphor was very useful because knowing that women and/or minority scholars can learn these rules helped to demystify the process. A critical aspect of knowing the rules of tenure is developing an understanding of what is valued by your institution; at major research universities, it is often the case that scholarship (i.e., publications in refereed journals) takes precedence over teaching and service. However, as the panelists observed, universities vary in their weighting of scholarship, teaching, and service. Traditionally, the tenure "formula" has been 40% research, 40% teaching, and 20% service, yet Rueda mentioned that some universities may have "unofficial" proportions that are much more skewed towards scholarship (e.g., 90% scholarship, 10% teaching and service). Taking the initiative to obtain these tenure requirements is extremely important for junior women and/or minority faculty, because higher education research suggests that they have less access to critical professional information (Perna, 2001; Tierney & Bensimon, 1996).

Document everything in your dossier. All five distinguished scholars noted the critical role of the dossier. Rueda asserted that junior faculty should begin preparing their dossiers *before* the day they are hired at a major research university, and that they should see the dossier as a "work in progress" rather than a document that is begun right before it is due. Alvermann emphasized two important points in preparing your dossier: (a) Demonstrate your productivity in a way that clearly delineates how your department or college would be hard pressed to do without your services. For example, in your summary statement of your accomplishments (or in whatever document it is that your university requires), discuss how your scholarship and teaching support your college/university's mission; and (b) Group publications and grants rather than simply listing them so that their impact is clear in terms of the institution's mission statement. Women and/or minority scholars may particularly feel uncomfortable with highlighting their accomplishments in these ways, but as Au suggested, bragging is a critical part of achieving tenure.

Select good external reviewers. While selecting external reviewers might not seem like a top priority, it is an aspect of the tenure process that should not be overlooked. Alvermann explained that external letters of support are extremely important to members of university-wide committees because typically these members will not know a candidate's area of expertise well enough to be able to judge it appropriately. Thus, a letter from a senior person in the field who is familiar with your work can go a long way toward convincing the committee to vote positively on your tenure decision. Alvermann suggested that junior faculty should select external reviewers who are knowledgeable but "distant" rather than selecting scholars who know them well (e.g., dissertation advisors/committee members, co-authors/co-editors). She also noted that it is a good practice for junior faculty to summarize the accomplishments of each of their external reviewers in order to let the university-wide committee make its own judgment as to whether to trust a reviewer's opinions about them. These summaries are extremely important because some universities evaluate external reviewers based upon their institution's national ranking; Rueda recalled one case where an external evaluation was discounted by the Tenure and Promotions Committee, because the external reviewer was at a low-ranking university, even though he/she was a top person in the field.

Lesson 4: Be a strategic scholar

Publications. Au emphasized the importance of setting specific goals to publish in quality journals, because tenure decisions are based on quantity and quality. Journal quality is often judged by the rejection rate (e.g., *Reading Research Quarterly*'s rejection rate is greater than 90%), and also by the circulation size. During the tenure process, many universities construct a table of the rejection and circulation rates for each journal. With regard to journal quality, Rueda also noted that junior faculty should be "be aware of the climate on your campus" because many tenure committees discount publications in "ethnic" journals or outlets, or discount scholarship related to ethnic issues.

Research. All five distinguished scholars discussed the importance of having a research program that is focused, programmatic, and funded. Based upon her own experiences as an assistant professor, Alvermann cautioned junior faculty not to become "opportunistic authors" who have a high number of publications that are not thematic or related because this does not signify serious scholarship to tenure committees. Hansen shared an important piece of advice for establishing a strong research program from Donald Graves: "Work on one research project at a time."

National reputation. Panelists outlined several strategies for establishing a national reputation: (a) Be active in professional organizations, such as the National Reading Conference (NRC), the International Reading Association (IRA) and the American Educational Research Association (AERA); (b) Get to know the work of people in national centers, such as the Center for the Improvement of Early Reading Achievement (CIERA) and the Center for Research on Education, Diversity, and Excellence (CREDE), because these are existing networks of people with interests in the same area that can provide national connections for you and your students; and (c) Get to know the work of the top scholars in your area of interest, and get to know them personally.

Lesson 5: Work towards balance

Time management. All five distinguished panelists strongly suggested that junior faculty become effective time managers, because there are so many professional activities that require significant time and energy. Aguirre (2000) observed that high demands are often placed on junior women and/or minority faculty for committee work and other service requirements.

Rueda noted that these competing demands include: (a) demands to represent the Department, School, and University on everything and anything related to diversity; (b) demands from the community to be involved in activities, events, and projects that do not "count" for tenure; and (c) teaching and/or service assignments that no one else wants to do but may be hard to turn down for political reasons. To counterbalance some of these demands, Edwards noted that teaching should be linked to research if at all possible. Similarly, Au suggested that junior faculty protect their time by serving on the most prestigious college-wide and university-wide committees as they possibly can, and turning down other service opportunities.

Balancing professional and personal lives. Achieving balance in professional and personal lives was not a theme elaborated upon by all five panelists, suggesting that individual scholars must consider the place of tenure within their own personal preferences and priorities. Edwards argued that while it takes significant time, energy, and attention to earn tenure, academicians should strive to create "parallel lives" for balance between personal and professional responsibilities. For women scholars of color, this means learning to operate in two worlds: one world reflecting their culture, family, and community, the other representing the "Ivory Tower" of academe (Mabokela & Green, 2001). According to Alfred (2001), junior women and/or minority faculty must continuously assess "balance" according to their personal and professional goals, and determine how to achieve it within their own lives.

A CALL TO ACTION

This paper presents the experiences and insights of five distinguished women and/or minority literacy scholars who have "crossed over" to Canaan and achieved tenure at major research institutions in the United States. By sharing these scholars' "wisdom stories," we hope to demystify the tenure process. As African-American literacy scholars, we view the "culture of tenure" as a form of the "culture of power" (Delpit, 1995), and as such, we believe it should be made visible to junior women and/or minority scholars. Providing access to the rules of the "tenure game" is critical, because junior women and/or minority faculty who have knowledge about the tenure process are empowered to develop and follow a plan of action for achieving tenure at their university (Alfred, 2001; Ropers-Huilman, 2003).

Although we offer a road map describing critical tenure instructions as a means of supporting junior women and/or minority faculty as they "cross into Canaan," we also recognize that there may be "mighty inhabitants," or discriminatory forces such as sexism and racism, serving as gatekeepers at some major research universities. Knowledge about tenure is a necessary, but not sufficient, condition for attaining tenure, and there may be instances where junior women and/or minority scholars are highly productive, yet still receive an unfavorable tenure decision. During the symposium, Alvermann strongly suggested that in these cases assistant professors consider initiating an appeal; all institutions have an appeal process designed to ascertain the fairness of tenure proceedings. This is an extremely difficult decision to make, but Alvermann encouraged junior faculty not to "be discouraged or afraid to use the appeal process should the need arise."

Given the reality of gender and racial inequity within higher education, we recognize that junior women and/or minority faculty cannot shoulder all the responsibility for achieving tenure at major research institutions. NRC and other professional organizations must develop multiple opportunities and experiences that help junior women and/or minority scholars navigate the tenure process. Conference sessions around writing for literacy publications at NRC, as well as the new series on methodology that was initiated at the 2004 Annual Meeting by Marla Marlette and Nell Duke, are wonderful professional development opportunities, but we must do more. Making the tenure process a topic of discussion at Vital Issues, for example, might not only extend the dialogue about the tenure process into the broader NRC audience, but it may also provide a "safe space" for emerging women and minority scholars to meet informally and make connections with distinguished literacy scholars. Appointing junior women and/or minority scholars to key leadership positions and committees would provide opportunities for them to get to know leading scholars on a personal basis, and give them credit for service to a national organization that could be included in their dossier. Organizations must also provide multiple opportunities for junior women and/or minority scholars to present their research ideas, and to receive constructive feedback from leading scholars in the field—all of which help emerging women and/or scholars of color to enhance funding and publishing possibilities.

Equally important, NRC can initiate and support research on various factors that contribute to junior scholars' successful navigation of the tenure process. Faculty mentorships may be one promising area of inquiry because, as Alvermann and Hruby (2000) point out, the study of mentoring within literacy teacher education is virtually nonexistent. We need to know much more about how mentorships are formed between junior faculty and established scholars, how they enhance (or inhibit) junior faculty's navigation of the tenure process, and how they change over the course of the professorial lifespan. Additionally, in an effort to increase the number of tenured literacy researchers from diverse backgrounds, Au and Raphael (2000) advance a research agenda that includes studying professional settings that support or fail to support women and scholars of color.

Lastly, NRC members serving as deans, department chairs, and faculty mentors can use this paper to initiate conversations about tenure with women and/or minority assistant professors from the moment they are hired. Many literacy faculty members *hire* women and/or minority junior faculty because they are strongly committed to diversity in higher education, but they might not know how to *retain* these scholars. Making the tenure process more visible is one way to enhance retention efforts. Institutions also need to change their perspective from "fixing" junior women and/or minority faculty through orientation programs and other interventions to adjusting departmental policies and practices in ways that honor gender and cultural differences. To this end, we recommend that literacy faculty members read and discuss books like *Sisters in the Academy: Emergent Black Women Scholars in Higher Education* (Mabokela & Green, 2001) and *"Strangers" of the Academy: Asian Female Scholars in Higher Education* (Li & Beckett, in press) that further illuminate the professional struggles and triumphs of female faculty of color at various institutions. Discussions around these texts may enhance literacy faculty members' awareness of how contextual (e.g., university setting), professional (e.g., job responsibilities), and personal (e.g., gender, race, culture) factors shape the tenure experiences of junior women faculty and scholars of color.

For many junior women and/or minority literacy scholars, "crossing over to Canaan" at institutions of higher education may be a difficult and uncertain journey, across mountainous terrain, or through valleys of flooded plains. We close with the hope that all literacy scholars will join us in making the path toward tenure more equitable for junior women and/or minority faculty.

REFERENCES

Aguirre, A. (2000). *Women and minority faculty in the academic workplace: recruitment, retention, and academic culture.* San Francisco: Jossey-Bass.

Alfred, M. (2001). Success in the Ivory tower: Lessons from black tenured female faculty at a major research university. In R.O. Mabokela and A. Green (Eds.), *Sisters in the Academy: Emergent black women scholars in higher education* (pp. 56-79). Virginia: Stylus Publishing, Co.

Alvermann, D.E. & Hruby, G.G. (2000). Mentoring and reporting research: A concern for aesthetics. In J.E. Readence & D. Barone (Eds.), *Envisioning the future of literacy: Themed Issue of Reading Research Quarterly* (pp.33-48). Newark, DE: International Reading Association.

American Association of University Women. (2004). *Tenure denied: Cases of sex discrimination in academia.* Washington, D.C.: American Association of University Women Educational Foundation and the American Association of University Women Legal Advocacy Fund.

Au, K.H. & Raphael, T.E. (2000). Equity and literacy in the next millennium. In J.E. Readence & D. Barone (Eds.), *Envisioning the future of literacy: Themed Issue of Reading Research Quarterly* (pp. 143-159). Newark, DE: International Reading Association.

Delpit, L. (1995). *Other people's words: Cultural conflict in the classroom.* The New Press: New York.

Gregory, S. (2001). Black faculty women in the academy: History, status and future. *The Journal of Negro Education, 70,* 124-138.

Hutchenson, P.A. (2004). Faculty tenure: Myth and reality 1974 to 1992. *The NEA Higher Educational Journal, 1,* 7-16. Retrieved December 28, 2004, from http://www2.nea.org/he.

Li, G. and Beckett, G. (Eds.) (in press). *"Strangers" of the academy: Asian female scholars in higher education.* Sterling, VA: Stylus Publishing, LLC.

Mabokela, R. O. and Green, A. L. (Eds.) (2001). *Sisters of the academy: Emergent Black women scholars in higher education.* Sterling, VA: Stylus Publishing, LLC.

National Center for Education Statistics. (2003). *Integrated Postsecondary Education Data System (IPEDS): Fall Staff surveys, 1993-94, 1997-98, and 1999-2000, and Winter 2001-02 survey.* Retrieved December 28, 2004 from http://nces.ed.gov/ipeds/.

Patton, M.Q. (1990). *Qualitative evaluation and research methods* (2nd Ed.). Newbury Park, CA: Sage.

Perna, L.W. (2001). Sex and race differences in faculty tenure and promotion. *Research in Higher Education, 42*(5), 541-567.

Ropers-Huilman, B. (Ed.). (2003). *Gendered futures in higher education: Critical perspectives for change.* Albany, NY: Albany State University of New York Press.

Tierney, W.G. & Bensimon, E.M. (1996). *Promotion and tenure: Community and socialization in academe.* Albany: State University of New York Press.

Verrier, D.A. (1992). *On becoming tenured: Acquiring academic tenure at a research university.* East Lansing, MI: Association for the Study of Higher Education. (ERIC Document Reproduction Service No. ED352908)

AUTHORS' NOTE

The authors wish to thank Donna Alvermann, Kathy Au, Pat Edwards, Jane Hansen, and Robert Rueda for participating in the symposium sponsored by the Ethnicity, Race, and Multilingualism Committee of the National Reading Conference. We also thank these distinguished scholars for sharing their compelling tenure stories, keen insights, and perceptive observations about the tenure process as a part of this paper.

Two Experienced Content Teachers' Use of Multiple Texts in Economics and English

Nancy T. Walker
University of La Verne

Thomas W. Bean
Benita Dillard
University of Nevada, Las Vegas

The learning and practice of teaching are situated processes shaped by numerous sociocultural and historical factors, including teachers using texts in their classrooms (Beach, 2000; Lewis, 2001; Walker & Bean, 2004). Texts, as defined by Wade and Moje (2000) are "organized networks that people generate or use to make meaning either for themselves or for others" (p. 610). Expanded definitions of text are consistent with recent efforts to reconceptualize secondary and content area reading within an adolescent literacy framework that acknowledges multiple literacies (Behrman, 2003: Readence, Bean & Baldwin, 2004). This research suggests that the nature of content area teaching is shifting from an older reliance on single texts toward a more constructivist, inquiry-based curriculum that requires the consideration of multiple texts (e.g. Behrman, 2003; New London Group, 1996; Shanahan, 2004; Stahl & Shanahan, 2004).

Indeed, the decision to use multiple texts in a classroom is very likely to result in a different, expanded form of classroom discourse that spans intertextual and critical connections that are quite different from the discourse derived from consideration of a single content text (Bean, 2002; Behrman, 2003; Hynd, 2002). We know from recent research that constructivist and inquiry-based units in science and social studies can be created around multiple texts including primary documents, as well as oral and digital forms of texts (Behrman, 2003; Shanahan, 2004; Stahl & Shanahan, 2004). However, we know far less about the sociocultural dimensions that influence content teachers' efforts to use multiple texts in their classrooms, particularly in a "No Child Left Behind" climate that narrows curricular activity. Inquiring into the decision-making process of teachers illuminates craft knowledge or the "accumulated wisdom derived from teachers' and practice-oriented researchers' understandings of the meanings ascribed to the many dilemmas inherent in teaching" (Grimmet & MacKinnon, 1992, p. 428). Thus, we conducted a multiple case study of 2 content area teachers, one in middle school and one in high school, to examine how multiple texts were used in their classrooms. This study is part of an ongoing series of studies we are conducting aimed at describing and interpreting teachers' beliefs and practices surrounding the use of multiple texts in various content area classrooms (Walker & Bean, 2004; Walker & Bean, 2003). Their stories are important sources of data for other teachers and researchers undertaking modifications to their curriculum that expand students' analysis, synthesis, and critique of the increasingly wide range of text forms they are likely to encounter in and out of school.

THEORETICAL FRAMEWORK

Content Area Literacy and Multiple Texts

In general, reviews of research in content area literacy point to the historical dominance of single text use in many middle and secondary content classrooms (Alvermann & Moore, 1991; Bean, 2001; Hynd, 1999). In contrast, more recent research shows that in some cases content area literacy teachers use a wide variety of texts (Behrman, 2003; Dillon, O'Brien, & Volkmann, 2001; Stahl & Shanahan, 2004; Wade & Moje, 2000). This inquiry challenged the narrow notion that content area teachers rely on traditional forms of texts as the primary source of information in the classroom. Also, the historical notion of content teachers relying on single texts (textbooks) may be shifting, partially driven by sociocultural dimensions and influenced by technology innovations (O'Brien, 2003).

Wade and Moje (2000) noted that a variety of texts are used and produced in the classroom by teachers and students and by students outside the classroom setting. Yet, in-depth studies of content teachers' use of multiple texts (i.e. outside materials such as newspapers, magazines, and technology) are rare (Bean, 2002; Behrman, 2003; Palmer & Stewart, 1997; Walker & Bean, 2004). In a commissioned paper released by the Carnegie Corporation of New York titled *Principled Practices for a Literate America: A Framework for Literacy and Learning in the Upper Grades*, the researchers noted that content area instruction should focus on utilizing multiple texts in varying contexts and grades (Alvermann, Boyd, Brozo, Hinchman, Moore, & Sturtevant, 2002). These texts can include "film, CD-ROM, Internet, music, television, magazines newspapers and adolescents own cultural understandings" (Phelps, 1998, p. 2). It is critical that we explore these new avenues of text usage in classrooms because students are faced with complex challenges that include a "globalized economy, the emergence of new, hybrid forms of identities, and new technologies that are transforming traditional print" (Luke, 1998, p. 306). Furthermore, the use of multiple texts "teaches adolescents that all texts, including their textbooks, routinely promote or silence particular views (Alvermann, 2002, p. 198).

Many traditional classrooms that support the textbook/worksheet format limit literacy interactions. O'Brien (1998) noted that "by the time students reach adolescence, their experiences with reading materials and practices in school have taught them to dislike literacy activities" (p. 29). Many of these activities may be due to state-mandated standards that often create a mismatch between student interests and content requirements (Ivey & Broaddus, 2001). Therefore school literacy runs the risk of being an arena for answering questions for content area texts (Bean, Bean, & Bean, 1999) that places adolescents in passive roles. These are heavily ingrained practices that are difficult to alter and affect the way in which students approach multiple texts. For example, Palmer and Stewart (1997) found that middle school students read multiple texts in social studies in exactly the same fashion they read more traditional textbooks. That is, they engaged in a search-for-the-answer style of reading rather than reading deeply and critically in nonfiction trade books. Thus, the process of using multiple texts is more complex than simply adopting materials.

In addition, teacher beliefs about literacy play a substantial role in how they use texts in various content areas. Research shows how secondary teachers' beliefs develop over time and impact literacy practices in the classroom (Alvermann & Moore, 1991). Agee (2000) found that beliefs emerged from background experiences and university coursework. Similarly, Sturtevant (1996) found that elementary and secondary teacher memories play a role in constructing beliefs about instruction. Bridging the disconnect that exists between teachers, texts, and students is a concern of educators.

When teachers use multiple texts strategically they are helping students make intertextual links by reading, critiquing, and synthesizing concepts across various sources (Rogers & Tierney, 2002). From this standpoint, intertextuality can be understood as "texts created in response to other texts and are part of a larger network of meaning" (Rogers & Tierney, p. 258). Bloome and Egan-Robertson (1993) viewed the social construction of intertextuality as a way to reveal the literacy learning and instructional experiences of both teachers and students. In our study, we highlight the intertextual possibilities that occur with multiple text usage.

In this study, we examined two experienced teachers' use of multiple texts along with their philosophical views of teaching with multiple texts. Our approach relied on classroom observations and interviews consistent with multiple case study analysis.

METHOD

Participants

Our earlier work focused on new teachers' use of multiple texts in the classroom. Early in their career, these teachers exhibited activities and materials that demonstrated a variety of multiple text usage (Walker & Bean, 2004). The present study examined two experienced teachers' use of multiple texts and inquiry into the notion of how experience in the classroom impacts text choice. Due to limited resources and extensive time needed to examine the use of multiple texts in classrooms at different sites, we limited our study to two experienced teachers so that we could explore their instruction and use of texts in-depth and over time. Our purposeful sampling (Patton, 1990) of these two teachers centered on the print rich content areas of Economics and English. Both teachers were introduced to us by the new teachers in our earlier study (Walker & Bean, 2004) when we expressed interest in continuing our work with experienced teachers who had taught across multiple content areas. In addition, they were willing to participate in our study, allowing us to observe them in their classrooms, and reflect on their teaching in interviews. In order to situate ourselves in the context of this research, we briefly describe our biographies as co-researchers on this project before describing the data sources and analysis.

Researchers

The first author is a Caucasian female associate professor employed at a west coast university. She taught middle school for eight years, and her current research interests include content area reading instruction and reading policy. The second author is a European American senior professor at a public southwestern university with specializations in content area literacy and classroom-based research in teacher education. The third author is an African American female graduate student who is currently working on a Ph.D. in Curriculum and Instruction with an emphasis in literacy.

Data Sources and Analysis

Given our interest in understanding how and why content teachers use multiple texts we constructed a descriptive qualitative multiple case study to describe the use of multiple texts in the classroom setting. Studying the use of multiple texts by teachers during their classroom instruction allowed us to capture this phenomenon as it occurred in context (Marshall and Rossman, 1995).

We drew on four data sources that included five observations, fieldnotes, classroom artifacts, and five semi-structured interviews collected over a three month period. Classroom observations focused on the use of multiple texts during instruction. Fieldnotes were made capturing the interaction of students and informal conversations with the teachers and researchers. Classroom artifacts included samples of additional texts, comprehension, and vocabulary aids (Patton, 1990) and photographs of bulletin boards, simulation materials, and student products. Semistructured interviews focused on educational history, teaching beliefs, and purposes for using multiple texts. During this time, we shared, questioned, and triangulated data with the teachers.

Pattern analysis (Yin, 1994) was used to analyze and interpret our data sets. Pattern analysis involved reading and rereading the transcribed fieldnotes and interview transcripts that were organized in data binders along with artifacts and photographs. This process was followed by several meetings of the three researchers to discuss the transcripts, which were cross-referenced with the artifacts and photographs for types of text, student simulations, and student products. Tentative categories emerged reflecting classroom activities, assessment, intertextual connections, and text modification. These categories were coded and followed by additional readings of the data which led to metathemes (Merriam, 1998) including classrooms as space for curricular creativity, state standards, metacognitive coaching, and interdisciplinary teaching. These metathemes resulted in the metaphor of teacher as field guide to "provide a different way of perceiving the reality" (Munby, 1986, p. 199) of these teachers and their classroom instruction.

Trustworthiness of the data was achieved by triangulating information from the data collection methods (specifically classroom observations, fieldnotes, artifacts, and semistructured interviews) and through the perspective of different participants (the researchers and teacher participants). In addition, we further triangulated the data with member checks (Merriam, 1998) conducted using key quotes from our transcripts and artifacts. These quotes captured the beliefs and practices of both teachers and included their respective rationales for multiple text use, along with references to pedagogical practices (e.g. simulations). Member checks revealed underlying issues and allowed the researchers to check for understanding. These checks provided opportunities for teachers to reflect on the teaching, learning, and curriculum and for the researchers to learn from the process. We wrote descriptive case studies of each teacher's use of multiple texts to answer our research question: How do experienced secondary content area teachers use and view multiple texts in their classrooms?

Two Cases

The findings from this study are presented with a brief description of each school, teacher, and class. We begin by highlighting metathemes and the metaphor we created to encompass the philosophical nature of the two teachers' beliefs about the role of multiple texts in students' content learning. Metaphors raise the level of interpretative abstraction to crystallize the data and provide a way to "comprehend a teacher's construction of professional knowledge" (Munby, 1986, p. 206). We then offer an in-depth look at the two content area teachers' use of multiple texts. Teacher names are pseudonyms and both schools are located on the west coast.

Kenneth

Kenneth teaches high school economics for seniors. He has been teaching for over 21 years in many subjects including mathematics, computers, drawing, ceramics, civil and criminal law, government, geography, and United States history. Like many of his colleagues, Kenneth is European American. His students' ethnicities include Caucasian (53%), Hispanic (23%), African American (10%), Asian (11%), and American Indian, Pacific Islander, and Filipino. Senior economics is required for graduation in this state.

Teacher As Field Guide. Kenneth's teaching can be encapsulated in the metaphor, teacher as Field Guide. Our creation of this metaphor to characterize Kenneth's use of multiple texts was based on a recognition that Kenneth thought about the teaching of economics as a kind of enculturation in what it means to think like an economist. Kenneth chose to engage students in discipline-based inquiry into economic dilemmas surrounding issues of supply and demand, scarcity, and opportunity cost. He consciously chose not to merely lecture or deliver information. Rather, he created scenarios that afforded students opportunities to make tough decisions about resources and then consider the economic principles that might support their thinking. He tried not simply to give them easy answers to difficult issues.

Since he viewed the core economics text, *Economics in Our Times* (Arnold, 1999) as limited, Kenneth saw curriculum design as a space for pedagogical creativity. The text was, in his view, unable to extend students' understanding of economics to real life, day-to-day decisions. As a result, Kenneth developed an array of economics simulations that tapped into multiple texts including the *Los Angeles Times* and *Reader's Digest*. He viewed these sources as more readable and accessible for his students than the core text. For example, in order to make students more aware of complex economic principles such as opportunity cost and scarcity, Kenneth created a case-based simulation about heart transplants with a related news article entitled: "Who gets a heart?" Students rank ordered various patients in terms of compelling reasons for each person to receive a heart transplant, thus making critical choices and decisions for a scarce critical resource. In one of his interview reflections on teaching, Kenneth commented, "I try to give them multiple ways of acquiring the concepts. I try to get them involved in simulations, group work, and talking to each other because I am not the fountain of all wisdom."

As a Field Guide, Kenneth saw his teaching as creative space to orchestrate opportunities for students to use multiple texts in the pursuit of concept learning in economics. Like many other teachers in our studies (Walker & Bean, 2003, 2004), Kenneth saw the end result of this hands-on, activity based teaching as an increase in students' understanding of economics and successful state test scores. He commented, "If I look at my Golden State results I bet that I have the highest pass rate of any teacher in this school." He attributed his success to both students' grasp of economics concepts and the metacognitive coaching he offered them. In essence, his view of teaching as Field Guide led him to help students with study strategies and connections between concepts in economics and the state graduation test. He infused study strategies including graphic organizers, herringbone, and note taking with his lectures. "I make them take all these notes and condense them down into 3 X 5 note cards. They have to analyze what they have, evaluate it, synthesize it, and put it in the note card. It's a sneaky way to get them to look again at their notes and try and make some sense out of it."

Kenneth argued that the most interesting economic conundrums were not in the text. He viewed its major function as a reference point for rereading and as a valuable resource for second language students. But simulations were always at the center of his teaching, "I want them to think of what we did in simulation; what you wrote in your journal….If they can read it, hear it and once they do it, it seems to stick with them. When I ask questions on the test I will ask them to think back to something or a simulation to respond to the questions."

Ultimately, Kenneth viewed economics as a dialogic process involving critical choices by individuals, communities, and governments. In his words, "I want the kids to be aware in the beginning that economics is not the study of money." During the course of our interviews Kenneth noted the following five limitations of a single text approach to his field: (a) the text fails to meet content standards; (b) the text is not that interesting; (c) the text is merely one tool; (d) the text information is too static and frequently wrong; and (e) the text requires guidance from the teacher to get students to read against the grain when the text is in error.

Although we have organized these comments in lists, they emerged in the course of interview conversations and member checks with Kenneth over time and in a less tidy fashion than these lists suggest. Kenneth, as an experienced teacher and Field Guide in economics, also noted the following eight advantages to using multiple texts: (a) high interest readings from day-to-day life are more engaging; (b) primary sources are crucial to read and not well-represented in contemporary textbooks in economics; (c) multiple texts from the newspaper and magazines are more readable than the adopted text; (d) multiple texts connect to real life economic dilemmas and choices (e.g. rent control), and the adopted text rarely addresses these issues; (e) multiple texts that students produce (e.g. via simulations of productivity where they act as publishers of books) engage students in concept learning and are likely to be recalled on state assessments; (f) multiple texts can be integrated with teaching students functional metacognitive reading strategies like herringbone (←←←←) and note taking systems for mapping key concepts; (g) multiple texts offer an opportunity to integrate learning across disparate content areas such as economics and literature; and (h) multiple text use is actually supported by the content standards, not inhibited by them as many might argue.

Clearly, Kenneth's teaching relies on his 21 years of experience across multiple fields, and it represents a rich source of intertextual material he taps for creative simulations that capture students' interest. Nevertheless, reading remains at the center of learning in his classroom. In order to participate in the simulations, students must read the multiple texts, and they must survive the state assessment. "Many of them are looking for that Golden State Diploma. It is a validation, too. I can find out statistically how I'm doing as a teacher by finding out my pass record for the kids getting through the GSE." As an experienced teacher, Kenneth manages the tensions between multiple text use, pedagogical creativity, and external high stakes assessment. With his teacher as Field Guide approach, he offers a strong model of hope for other teachers trying to cope with increasing high stakes testing while teaching complex content domains in the most principled way possible. Indeed, Kenneth had a beginning teacher colleague elect to spend prep periods shadowing his use of various metacognitive coaching strategies. Kenneth's style in this mentoring role was also consistent with the Field Guide metaphor. "My way may work for me. It may not work for somebody else…I don't say you should do this with kids."

Phyllis

Phyllis teaches middle school regular English for eighth grade. She has been teaching for 31 years with appointments in United States History, Gifted and Talented English, and regular English courses that include a mixture of struggling readers and grade-level readers. Like many of her colleagues, Phyllis is European American. Her students' ethnicities include Caucasian (26.4%), Latino (36.4%), Asian (17.4%), African American (12.8%), Filipino (6.6%), and American Indian (1%). Regular eighth-grade English is a literature based course that is designed to help students respond to questions on standardized tests and develop an understanding and appreciation for the power of literature.

Teacher as Interdisciplinary Field Guild. Our metaphor for Phyllis's teaching is teacher as Interdisciplinary Field Guide. Much like Kenneth, Phyllis sought ways to engage her middle school English students in literature beyond the boundaries of a traditional anthology. She tapped into her history teaching background to help students create intertextual connections between English and history through projects involving writing, research, and reading of multiple texts.

She saw limitations in the core English textbook and used it with her students infrequently as noted in our observations. In one of her interview reflections, she noted similar reservations about the history text, "So often the history textbook doesn't excite the kids. They were just memorizing the material to the test with no real life questions, and that drove me crazy. I want kids to make real life connections. Education is not just studying. Education is going beyond. That is my goal. To wake them up."

Phyllis created an array of activities that engaged students in reading multiple texts and voicing their views about current events and issues. For example, she used articles from *Time*, *Newsweek*, and the *Los Angeles Times* where students considered writers taking different positions on unmanned space flights. She also used a jigsaw format, assigning different groups to read and report on various articles about unmanned space flights. Phyllis commented: "I would like the students to get different perspectives so they can see the different perspectives clearly." In another simulation in history, students became publishers of a newspaper in a frontier town. The class broke into small groups and explored the Internet, encyclopedias, and books to check on the authenticity of the material they included in their newspaper. In one of her interview reflections on teaching, Phyllis commented, "We need to take the interest to be informed citizens."

Phyllis used various novels to illuminate historical events. For example, Mildred Taylor's *Roll of Thunder Hear My Cry* offers students a powerful look at the Civil War and sharecropping. In addition, Phyllis's interest in social justice issues surrounding exclusionary policies led to the development of a unit on immigrants. "They are going to read about Chinese Americans and working on the transcontinental railroad. They will read about exclusionary acts that were in place."

Phyllis was dedicated to student engagement in English and social studies; she used the district standards as a starting point and her rich pedagogical content knowledge as the center of creative lesson development. For example, one of the standards required Phyllis to teach the students to recognize and understand the difference between several types of poetry: ballads, sonnets, and so forth. Phyllis taught the terms and showed examples of the different types of poetry. Since the students were working on publishing a newspaper for a frontier town, Phyllis allowed the students to decide on the components of the newsletter. Utilizing her Interdisciplinary Field Guide approach, the students had the option to write one of the types of poems that included information on the Civil War or to find a poem about the Civil War.

As an Interdisciplinary Field Guide, Phyllis saw her teaching as a creative space to orchestrate opportunities for students to make intertextual connections. She stated, "The kids were talking about the movie *Holes* and they said it was a flashback to frontier times." Moreover, Phyllis saw her teaching as an opportunity to help students make connections with multiple texts and the standards. In one of her interview reflections on teaching, Phyllis stated, "I wanted to give these kids the opportunity to show that they really know dialogue, soliloquy that goes along with a dramatic presentation, so that if there are questions like that on the standardized test, they could respond." Her view of teaching as Interdisciplinary Field Guide led her to use many eclectic strategies to help struggling readers develop an appreciation for literature. "I try to pair up kids who are at grade level with struggling kids. I make sure they have time to read to each other. I try to do things that would make it fun for them in the class… reading out loud, acting it out, readers' theater, and popcorn reading."

Phyllis argued that both the English textbook and traditional social studies textbook did not include a variety of good readings and writings. She viewed the major function of the English textbook as a good resource to retrieve literature on the Civil War and the social studies textbook as a good resource to retrieve factual information. However, teaching students to love reading and writing were always at the center of her teaching: "I want kids to discover how wonderful it is to sit down with a good book to read a piece of nonfiction and learn about something that you had little knowledge about. You just open up your mind and open up your world."

Phyllis connected nonfiction books with historical fiction novels in order to expose students to different kinds of reading. In her words, "I am trying to call their attention to good writing so they can choose their own." Phyllis noted the following three limitations of single text use in English and social studies: (a) the core text does not address the standards; (b) the core text does not provide multiple perspectives on the Civil War; and (c) the core text is not high interest.

These lists were compiled over time from the interviews and member checks. She noted the following five advantages of a multiple text approach: (a) nonfiction and historical fiction novels are activity based; (b) nonfiction and historical fiction novels make students want to read more; (c) these novels engage higher readers but are easy enough for struggling readers; (d) multiple texts offer the possibility for intertextual connections; and (e) note taking and other strategies serve real reading purposes with multiple texts.

Phyllis described her overall goal as a teacher in a way that placed reading at the center of the curriculum in middle school. As an Interdisciplinary Field Guide, Phyllis sought to help students see "ordinary people who had accomplished extraordinary things." Clearly, Phyllis's teaching relies on her 31 years of experience across multiple fields and interactions with students who read on different levels. As an experienced teacher, Phyllis managed the tensions between multiple text use, adhering to the standards, and pedagogical creativity. With her Interdisciplinary Field Guide approach, Phyllis also offered a strong model of hope for other teachers trying to adhere to standards while at the same time teaching students how to develop an understanding and appreciation for the power of literature.

DISCUSSION

What have we learned about experienced teachers' choices of texts? Our data analysis revealed connections between teachers' beliefs and text choice. Both Kenneth's and Phyllis's beliefs about instruction developed over their years in the classroom (Alvermann & Moore, 1991) and are tied to their own educational experiences and teacher development (Agee, 2000; Sturtevant, 1996). Both teachers reflected on their use of multiple texts using discourse that falls within what Grimmet and MacKinnon (1992) characterized as "craft knowledge." Grimmet and MacKinnon (1992) argued for the importance of experience in the development of craft knowledge. This knowledge, for both experienced teachers, is deeply contextualized and specific to the local sites of their classrooms. Indeed, in both their beliefs and their discourse related to teaching, they embodied a connection to lived experience as the main route to accomplished practice (Hiebert, Gallimore, & Stigler, 2002).

We would argue that their deep, often interdisciplinary, experience might best be characterized under the broader label of "intertextual craft knowledge." That is, both Kenneth's and Phyllis's discourse and praxis with multiple texts in their classrooms borrowed heavily from their experiences teaching other disciplines including social studies and science, as well as outside authoritative educational reports encouraging intertextual connections and critical analysis of secondary sources (National Research Council [NRC], 1996. p. 33).

Kenneth and Phyllis strived to increase students' learning beyond what a single text might offer. Their stories illuminate the "Teacher as Field Guide" metaphor because existing single text adoptions are often flawed. Instead, they selected primary sources that were likely to engage students' interests and curiosity, as well as offer rich conceptual information. Therefore, they used curriculum design as a creative space where they could make decisions to go beyond the limits of the adopted text in the best interest of their students. Both teachers managed to resist or disrupt strong institutional forces while using texts to produce an environment that valued students' interests outside the classroom. In the case of Kenneth, outside texts in simulations and group work connected to students' popular culture, which made the classroom content more memorable than the standard text would allow. In her classroom, Phyllis chose texts that excited students and allowed them to make intertextual connections. In essence, they were engaging in what some researchers have termed "principled practices" (Alvermann, Boyd, Brozo, Hinchman, Moore, & Sturtevant, 2002).

This study was limited by the fact that we studied only two experienced teachers, yet we acknowledge that other teachers (both new and experienced) utilize multiple texts in their classrooms. We also acknowledge that just because a teacher uses multiple texts there is no guarantee that student learning will be enhanced. For example, Palmer and Stewart (1997) explored nonfiction trade book use in two middle school classrooms. They found that when multiple texts are used in traditional ways, where students simply search for answers to low level questions, students read the same way they would for any textbook reading assignment. Teacher development, scaffolding, and guidance are needed to move students toward intertextual connections and critical reading with multiple texts. The two teachers in our study were well versed in setting up learning scenarios and simulations where students constructed their own insights and intertextual connections. Both teachers had many years of classroom experience across various content areas and this depth of experience and craft knowledge undoubtedly contributed to the relative ease they displayed in using multiple texts. Nevertheless, any curricular innovation is often more complex and demanding than it looks on the surface, and we would argue that this holds for content teachers who move away from a reliance on a single textbook toward the use of multiple texts.

This study contributes to existing knowledge of multiple text use by showing how two teachers created learning conditions where students could make intertextual connections. By including multiple texts, simulations, and metacognitive learning strategies (e.g. herringbone), students grappled with elements of provisional truth in English, economics and history. Both Kenneth and Phyllis provided opportunities for students to think like economists or historians through the introduction of problem-based learning scenarios with no easy answers. Our hope is that other teachers may be encouraged to attempt the use of multiple texts, recognizing that these two experienced teachers were able to tap a wide array of cross-disciplinary resources in economics, English, history and other fields of knowledge. Work by Behrman (2003), Hynd (1999, 2004), and others have offered useful guidelines for undertaking multiple text use in science and social studies. These studies suggest that regardless of the difficulties that face teachers attempting to move away from a reliance on single texts, this transformation is worth pursuing. Moreover, as students encounter an increasing array of digital texts, they need strategies for critically reading and evaluating this barrage of information. This finding begs the researchable question, how can multiple texts become an integral part of more content area classrooms and what might the outcome be in terms of student learning?

REFERENCES

Agee, J. (2000). What is effective literature instruction? A study of experienced high school English teachers in differing grade-and ability-level classes. *Journal of Literacy Research, 32*, 303-348.

Alvermann, D. (2002). Effective literacy instruction for adolescents. *Journal of Literacy Research, 34*, 189-208.

Alvermann, D., Boyd, F., Brozo, W., Hinchman, K., Moore, D., & Sturtevant, E., (2002). *Principled practices for a literate America: A framework for literacy and learning in the upper grades.* New York: Carnegie Corporation.

Alvermann, D. E., & Moore, D. W. (1991). Secondary school reading. In R. Barr, M. L. Kamil, P. Mosenthal, & P. D. Pearson (Eds.), *Handbook of reading research* (Vol. 2, pp. 951-983). New York: Longman.

Arnold, R. (1999). *Economics in our times.* Cincinnati: West Educational Publishing.

Beach, R. (2000). Critical issues: Reading and responding to literature at the level of activity. *Journal of Literacy Research, 32*, 237-251.

Bean, T. W. (2002). Text comprehension: The role of activity theory in navigating students' prior knowledge in content teaching. In C. Roller (Ed.), *Reading research 2001* (pp. 133-147). Newark, DE: International Reading Association.

Bean, T. W. (2001). Reading in the content areas: Social constructivist dimensions. In M. L. Kamil, P. B. Mosenthal, P. D. Pearson, & R. Barr (Eds.), *Handbook of reading research* (Vol 3, pp. 629-644). Mahwah, NJ: Lawrence Erlbaum.

Bean, T. W., Bean, S. K., & Bean, K. F. (1999). Intergenerational conversations and two adolescents' multiple literacies: Implications for redefining content area literacy. *Journal of Adolescent & Adult Literacy, 42*, 438-448.

Behrman, E. H. (2003). Reconciling content literacy with adolescent literacy: Expanding literacy opportunities in a community-focused biology class. *Reading Research and Instruction, 43*, 1-30.

Bloome, D., & Egan-Robertson, A. (1993). The social construction of intertextuality in classroom reading and writing lessons. *Reading Research Quarterly, 28*, 305-333.

Dillon, D. R., O'Brien, D. G., & Volkmann, M. (2001). Reading, writing, and talking to get work done in biology. In E. B. Moje and D. G. O'Brien (Eds.), *Constructions of literacy* (pp. 51-75). Mahwah, New Jersey: Lawrence Erlbaum.

Grimmet, P. P., & MacKinnon, A. M. (1992). Craft knowledge and the education of teachers. *Review of Research in Education, 18*, 385-456.

Hiebert, J., Gallimore, R., & Stigler, J. W. (2002). A knowledge base for the teaching profession: What would it look like and how can we get one? *Educational Researcher, 31*, 3-15.

Hynd-Shanahan, S., Holschuh, J.P., & Hubbard, B. (2004). Thinking like a historian: College students' reading of multiple historical documents. *Journal of Literacy Research, 36*, 141-176.

Hynd, C. R. (2002). Using multiple texts to teach content. Paper presented at the North Central Regional Laboratory Annual Literacy Research Network Conference. Naperville, Illinois.

Hynd, C.R. (1999). Teaching students to think critically using multiple texts in history. *Journal of Adolescent & Adult Literacy, 42*, 428-436.

Ivey, G., & Broaddus, K. (2001). "Just plain reading": A survey of what makes students want to read in middle school classrooms. *Journal of Adolescent & Adult Literacy, 36*, 350-377.

Lewis, C. (2001). *Literacy practices as social acts: Power, status, and cultural norms in the classroom.* Mahwah, NJ: Lawrence Erlbaum.

Luke, A. (1998). Getting over method: Literacy teaching as work in new times. *Language arts, 75*, 305-313.

Marshall, C., & Rossman, G.B. (1995). *Designing qualitative research.* Thousand Oaks, CA: SAGE.

Merriam, S.B. (1998). *Qualitative research and case study applications in education.* San Francisco: Jossey-Bass.

Munby, H. (1986). Metaphor in the thinking of teachers: An exploratory study. *Journal of Curriculum Studies, 18*, 197-209.

National Research Council. (1996). *National science education standards.* Washington, DC: National Academy Press.

New London Group (1996). A pedagogy of multiliteracies: Designing social futures. *Harvard Educational Review, 66*, 60-92.

O'Brien, D.G. (1998). Multiple literacies in a high-school program for at-risk adolescents. In D. E. Alvermann, K. A. Hinchman, D. W. Moore, S. F. Phelps, & D. R. Waff (Eds.), *Reconceptualizing the literacies in adolescents' lives* (pp. 27-50). Mahwah, NJ: Erlbaum.

O'Brien, D. G. (2003, March). Juxtaposing traditional and intermedial literacies to redefine the competence of struggling adolescents. *Reading Online.* Online journal of the International Reading Association. Retrieved December 10, 2004, from http://readingonline.org/newliteracies/obrien1/

Palmer, R. G., & Stewart, R. A. (1997). Nonfiction trade books in content area instruction: Realities and potential. *Journal of Adolescent & Adult Literacy, 40*, 630-641.

Patton, M. Q. (1990). *Qualitative evaluation and research methods.* Newbury Park: SAGE.

Phelps, S.F. (1998). Adolescents and Their Multiple Literacies. In D. E. Alvermann, K. A. Hinchman, D. W. Moore, S. F. Phelps, & D. R. Waff (Eds.), *Reconceptualizing the literacies in adolescents' lives* (p. 2). Mahwah, NJ: Erlbaum.

Readence, J. E., Bean, T. W., & Baldwin, R. S. (2004). *Content area literacy: An integrated approach* (8th ed.). Dubuque, Iowa: Kendall Hunt.

Rogers, T., & Tierney, R. J. (2002). Intertextuality. In B. Guzzetti (Ed.), *Literacy in America: An encyclopedia of history, theory, and practice* (p. 258). Santa Barbara, CA: ABC CLIO.

Shanahan, C. (2004). Teaching science through literacy. In T. L. Jetton, & J. A. Dole (Eds.), *Adolescent literacy research and practice* (pp. 75-93). New York: The Guilford Press.

Stahl, S. A., & Shanahan, C. (2004). Learning to think like a historian: Disciplinary knowledge through a critical analysis of multiple documents. In T. L. Jetton, & J. A. Dole (Eds.), *Adolescent literacy research and practice* (pp. 94-115). New York: The Guilford Press.

Sturtevant, E. G. (1996). Lifetime influences on the literacy-related instructional beliefs of experienced high school history teachers: Two comparative case studies. *Journal of Literacy Research, 28*, 227-257.

Wade, S. E., & Moje, E. B. (2000). The role of text in classroom learning. In M. L.Kamil, P. B. Mosenthal, P. D. Pearson, & R. Barr (Eds.), *Handbook of reading research* (Vol. 3, pp. 609-628). Mahwah, NJ: Lawrence Erlbaum.

Walker, N., & Bean, T. W. (2004). Using multiple texts in content area classrooms. *Journal of Content Area Reading, 3*(1), 23-35.

Walker, N., & Bean, T. (2003, April). Multiple uses of texts in content area teachers' classrooms. Paper presented at the American Educational Research Association Conference, Chicago, Il.

Yin, R. (1994). *Case study research: Design and methods.* Thousand Oaks: SAGE.

Prediction of First Grade Reading Achievement:
A Comparison of Kindergarten Predictors

Heather P. Warley
Timothy J. Landrum
Marcia A. Invernizzi
University of Virginia

Research over the past two decades indicates that children who start behind their peers in development of reading skills in the early primary grades have a difficult time "catching up" (Juel, 1988; Stanovich, 1986). Discrepancies among the reading achievement of children have been well-documented beginning in the first grade year, with recent data showing that a significant proportion of American school-children fail to achieve adequately by the later elementary grades (National Assessment of Educational Progress [NAEP], 2003). Children who are poor, who are learning English as a second language, and who are ethnic and racial minorities are particularly vulnerable for underachievement in reading skills (NAEP, 2003).

Some experts contend that early differences among students grow larger over time, a phenomenon Stanovich describes as the Matthew Effect (Stanovich, 1986). Students who are classified as reading disabled tend to maintain that classification anywhere from two to six years later (Juel, 1988; Satz, Fletcher, Clark, & Morris, 1981; see Scarborough, 1998 for a summary). The wealth of research on this topic has led to an emphasis on early identification and intervention for students who are at-risk for later reading problems, a proactive paradigm shift emphasizing the need to "catch children *before* they fall" (Torgesen, 1998). Indeed, a variety of current national and state educational policies reflect this paradigm shift to reduce early disparities in reading development in preschool and early elementary students (e.g., *Early Reading First, No Child Left Behind Act of 2001*).

Of relevance to current initiatives regarding the prevention of reading difficulties is early identification of those students who are most at risk for experiencing reading problems. Much research has focused on phonological awareness as a potential predictor of reading achievement. For example, children's facility with rhyme and their beginning sound awareness have been shown to be significant predictors of reading outcomes (Bradley & Bryant, 1983, 1985; Swank & Catts, 1994). Nursery rhyme knowledge, a proxy for phonological awareness, was found to be a powerful predictor of reading achievement "even after differences in social background, IQ, and the children's phonological skills at the start of the project" were taken into account (Bryant, Bradley, Maclean, & Crossland, 1989, p. 407). Furthermore, training in phonological awareness has been associated with improved performance in reading and spelling (Bradley & Bryant, 1985).

Two important meta-analyses represent recent attempts to parse out the most powerful predictors of reading achievement from kindergarten, and these analyses suggest that phonological awareness measures may have a limited life span in predicting reading achievement (Hammill, 2004; Scarborough, 1998). That is, while phonological awareness measures are powerful predictors when sampling children prior to kindergarten, print-related measures contribute more consistently to these predictions as students get closer to first grade. Prior to entering kindergarten, both phonological awareness and print-related measures provide unique contributions to predicting children's elementary-grade reading achievement, as shown by the meta-analysis of the National Early Literacy Panel (NELP) (National Center for Family Literacy, 2003), which examined specific emergent literacy skills and their predictive power for school-age reading achievement.

Measures used to assess young children's print-related knowledge typically include environmental print reading, name writing, concepts about print, and alphabet knowledge (e.g., Justice & Ezell, 2001), and the mean correlation between these four measures and later decoding ability as averaged across studies is .52, .50, .46, and .45, respectively (NELP, 2003). By contrast, the mean correlation between measures of phonological awareness and later decoding is .44, and .38 for measures of oral language and later decoding. When using kindergarten samples, Hammill (2004) and Scarborough (1998) suggest that the strongest predictors of later reading achievement may be print-related measures. Scarborough (1998) found that oral language measures, including phonological awareness, were less predictive than print-related measures such as letter identification, letter-sound knowledge, and print concepts. In a meta-analysis of early predictors of later reading, Hammill (2004) found print knowledge or "graphological" skills to be the best predictors of reading. In short, a child's cumulative knowledge about print forms and functions is one of the most reliable and robust indicators of the ease with which she or he will progress as a reader.

Morris, Bloodgood, and Perney's (2003) recent modeling of kindergarten predictors of first-grade achievement supports the findings of these meta-analyses. Morris, Bloodgood, and Perney (2003) examined the predictive power of specific tasks at the beginning, middle, and end of the kindergarten year, namely alphabet recognition, beginning consonant awareness, concept of word in text, spelling with beginning and ending consonants, phoneme segmentation, and word recognition. Only alphabet recognition and concept of word predicted first-grade reading achievement at all three points in the kindergarten year. In addition, spelling was a significant predictor in both the middle and end of the year, whereas word recognition and beginning consonant awareness were significant predictors at the end of the year only. It is interesting to note that "two seldom-used print-related variables (concept of word in text and spelling) were better predictors than two widely used phonological variables (beginning consonant awareness and phoneme segmentation)" (Morris, Bloodgood, & Perney, p. 102).

Furthermore, these studies suggest that no single task can sufficiently predict reading performance. Scarborough's (1998) meta-analysis indicated that a combination of measures provides greater predictive power than a single measure. Similarly, Morris, Bloodgood and Perney (2003) found that a combination of measures is necessary at different points in the kindergarten year to accurately predict first-grade reading performance. These findings echo results from the Cooperative Research Program in First Grade Reading Instruction (i.e., the "First Grade Studies") (Bond & Dykstra, 1967). Because no one instructional program or method produced better results than another, it was suggested that a combination of approaches may be superior to any single approach (Bond & Dykstra, 1967). Moreover, the results of the First Grade Studies suggest that multiple measures may be preferable to a single measure when assessing a complex phenomenon such as reading (Pearson, 1997).

The focus of these studies during the kindergarten year is well warranted. With the knowledge that first grade students who start behind generally stay behind, any early efforts to enhance the skills of struggling readers to more closely match the levels of their peers would seem to be advantageous. The kindergarten year can be described as a highly transitional time in the student's life; a time when patterns of interaction between students, teachers, and parents are apt to change (Rimm-Kaufman & Pianta, 2000). Indeed, "minor adjustments in the trajectory of development in this period may have disproportionate effects on the direction of the child's school career" (Rimm-Kaufman & Pianta, p. 494). By the second year of schooling, many of these patterns become fixed.

The present study is an effort to replicate and expand upon the findings of Morris, Bloodgood, and Perney (2003) using a statewide sample to examine the generalizability of findings to a longitudinal statewide data set of more than 50,000 students of varying demographic characteristics. In this study we address two major questions: (a) What kindergarten literacy skills best predict first-grade reading achievement, and (b) Does the predictive power of these skills vary depending on the point during the kindergarten year at which they are assessed? We hypothesize that a combination of literacy skills will provide the most predictive power, and that the specific combination of these skills will vary across the kindergarten year.

METHOD

Participants

The sample consisted of 54,084 students (51% males, 49% females) who participated in a statewide literacy screening conducted during the years 2002, 2003, and 2004. The mean student age was 5 years, 6 months in the fall of kindergarten; 6 years, 2 months in the spring of kindergarten; and 7 years 2 months in the spring of first grade.

Participants were students attending public schools in the Commonwealth of Virginia who completed screening at three points in time: fall of kindergarten 2002, spring of kindergarten 2003, and spring of first grade 2004. The original sample consisted of 74,833 students. Students were excluded from the data set if they did not have scores from all three assessment points. Potential reasons for students not having all three sets of scores included retention or moving out of the state. Additionally, some students were not screened if specific provisions in the student's IEP, or the student's level of English proficiency made literacy assessment with this particular screening tool inappropriate. Thirty percent of this cohort was receiving some sort of service, such as special education, Title I, speech-language, or tutoring in the fall of first grade.

The ethnicity of the sample mirrored that of Virginia's statewide school enrollment. In the sample, 64% of the students were non-Hispanic Caucasian, 27% were African-American, 5% were Hispanic Caucasian, and 2% were Asian/Pacific Islander (students with ethnic identies other than these four groups comprised an additional 2% of the sample). Data on socio-economic level were not available at the individual student level, so school-level free and reduced lunch counts were used as a proxy. The median percentage of students receiving free and reduced lunch was 35%, and ranged from 0% to 97%.

Measures

In the state of Virginia, students are administered the *Phonological Awareness Literacy Screening (PALS)* (Invernizzi, Meier, & Juel, 2004; Invernizzi, Swank, Juel, & Meier, 2004) in kindergarten through third grades. Each instrument is administered by students' teachers (or other professionals, such as aides) during a specified screening window. Subsequent to screening all students in a classroom, the teacher enters scores into an online centralized database, and receives score reports for his or her class as a whole, as well as students individually. *PALS-K* is administered in the fall and spring of the kindergarten year. *PALS 1-3* is administered in the spring of the first and second grade years, with fall administration optional. The development and implementation of the literacy screening is supported by Virginia's Early Intervention Reading Initiative (EIRI), the purposes of which are to identify students who are at-risk for reading difficulties and to provide diagnostic information that teachers may use to target instruction toward the areas where students need extra help.

Both instruments have good evidence of inter-rater reliability (r = .93 - .99), test-retest reliability (r = .78 - .97), and internal consistency (r = .79 - .96). A variety of data analyses support the content, construct, and criterion-related validity of both instruments (see Invernizzi, Justice, Landrum, & Booker, 2004; Invernizzi, Meier, & Juel, 2004; Invernizzi, Swank, et al., 2004). Of particular relevance to this study is the issue of inter-rater reliability. Because classroom teachers are responsible for administering the *PALS* instruments, it is reasonable to question the extent to which screening is standardized in its administration, scoring, and score reporting across students, classrooms, and schools. Training videotapes and detailed directions for administration and scoring are provided to administrators to enhance standardization. The inter-rater reliability coefficients reported above support that both *PALS* instruments can be reliably administered and scored (see Invernizzi, Meier, & Juel, 2004; Invernizzi, Swank, et al., 2004).

Additional quality control of the data is maintained via the mechanism by which teachers report assessment data. Teachers enter their data via a secure, password-protected website. To ensure that only valid scores are entered, the online score entry procedure is programmed to indicate to the user when a score falling outside the possible range of points is entered, and such scores are not accepted by the website. Additional checks of the reliability of data entry are conducted each year, with a random sample of teachers' paper score sheets checked against the scores they entered online. These internet reliability checks have consistently yielded error rates of less than 1%.

From the kindergarten screening, the two phonological awareness measures are Rhyme Awareness and Beginning Sound Awareness. Kindergarten print-related measures include Alphabet Recognition, Letter Sounds, Spelling, and Concept of Word in text. Each task is administered in the fall and spring of the kindergarten year. Two tasks administered in the spring of the first grade year, and relevant to this study, are Word Recognition in Isolation and Oral Reading in Context. A brief description of tasks follows.

Rhyme awareness. Out of a set of three pictures, students are asked to find and circle the picture that rhymes with the target picture. Students are administered this task in small groups of five or fewer students. Ten points are possible.

Beginning sound awareness. Out of a set of three pictures, students are asked to find and circle the picture that has the same beginning sound as the target picture. Students are administered this task in small groups of five or fewer students. Ten points are possible. Teachers are instructed to administer the Rhyme Awareness and Beginning Sound Awareness tasks on different days due to the similar format of the tasks.

Alphabet recognition. The student is asked to name all twenty-six lower-case letters of the alphabet, arranged in random order. Twenty-six points are possible.

Letter sounds. The student is asked to say the sound for twenty-three letters of the alphabet, plus three digraphs (Sh, Ch, Th). The letter sounds for X and Q are not assessed, and M is used as the practice item. The letters are presented in upper-case form and arranged in random order. Twenty-six points are possible.

Spelling. Students are asked to spell five consonant-vowel-consonant (CVC) words, such as "mat." Students are awarded credit for beginning and ending consonants, and medial vowels. Phonetically acceptable representations receive credit (i.e., "v" for "f"); a bonus point is awarded for accurate conventional spelling. Twenty points are possible.

Concept of word. After memorizing a familiar rhyme such as "Humpty Dumpty" using picture prompts, the student is asked to repeat the rhyme while pointing to each word in the text (presented in booklet format). The student receives one point if he or she points to each word in the line correctly. Next, the administrator points to a word in the rhyme and the student is asked to identify the word. Two words per line are assessed and one point per word identified is awarded. Lastly, the student is presented with a list of ten words in isolation from the nursery rhyme. The student is asked to read the words for a total of ten possible points. The three subtest scores are combined for a Concept of Word total score.

Word recognition in isolation. In the spring of first grade, students are administered grade-level word lists. Each list contains twenty words that are representative of that level. Each first grade student in the spring begins with the first grade word list. Students scoring less than fifteen on the list are administered the primer word list. Students scoring fifteen or greater on the first grade list are administered the second grade word list. Administration of lists continues in this manner until the administrator finds the highest list on which the student scores fifteen or higher (in this study, the lists ranged from preprimer to fourth grade level). Twenty points per list are possible.

Oral reading in context. In the spring of first grade, students are administered one or more oral reading passages based on their scores from the Word Recognition in Isolation task. Each student reads the oral reading passage that corresponds to the highest word list on which he or she scored fifteen or higher, while the administrator takes a running record and scores the passage for percent accuracy. Administrators are encouraged to administer higher or lower level passages until the highest instructional level passage (90-97% accuracy) is determined. In this study, passages ranged from readiness to fourth grade level. Administrators are also encouraged to time the student's oral reading to determine a reading rate, assign a qualitative level of fluency (i.e., expression and phrasing), and administer the multiple choice comprehension questions accompanying the primer and higher passages.

An algorithm was programmed into the score entry and reporting website in order to determine an oral reading level for each student in the spring of first grade. An oral reading level was established for each student by considering both word recognition in isolation from grade-level lists as well as word recognition accuracy in context from grade-level expository passages. Although comprehension is assessed in *PALS 1-3* via multiple choice questions, comprehension scores were not used in the determination of oral reading level (for further discussion see Sweet & Snow, 2003).

RESULTS

Because the kindergarten variables used in this study are highly intercorrelated, it is difficult to completely tease out the unique contribution of any one variable to the prediction of reading success. The nature of intercorrelated predictor variables means that the relative contribution of any one variable may be masked by other predictors that share variance with that variable. This notion suggests simply that all the variables assessed here are related, to some extent, to the general construct of early literacy.

In order to gain insight into the relationship of these kindergarten predictors to the dependent measure of oral reading level in first grade, we subjected the data to two separate analyses. First, we computed a multiple regression equation using stepwise entry of variables. This analysis was intended to provide the best overall statistical prediction of oral reading level based on the kindergarten predictor variables. While we predicted that the order of importance of the predictor variables would change across the kindergarten year, we did not have a hypothesis about the relative order of contribution, making stepwise regression an appropriate statistical technique. Stepwise regression first locates the most powerful predictor of the outcome variable based on simple correlation, and then adds other variables if they contribute additional predictive power to the regression equation, after taking into account the variance accounted for by variables already in the equation. In this way, stepwise regression addresses the problem of intercorrelation among predictor variables by only allowing variables to enter the equation if they add predictive power not already accounted for by variables in the equation.

While stepwise regression analysis establishes the most parsimonious prediction model, it is limited in two ways with regard to the questions we posed. First, stepwise regression does not necessarily leave all variables in the equation if their inclusion does not enhance predictive power. Second, the results of stepwise regression do not speak fully to the relative contributions of variables that are intercorrelated. If one of two highly intercorrelated variables enters the equation first, for example, the second variable to enter may appear to add relatively little predictive power, when in fact it may have nearly as strong a relationship to the outcome measure as the first variable.

To address these concerns, we also used discriminant analysis (DA) to assess the extent to which a discriminant function equation, based on the kindergarten predictors, would accurately classify students as on or above grade level oral reading versus below grade level oral reading in first grade. Examination of the discriminant function(s) allows an assessment of the relative contribution of individual kindergarten predictors to the discrimination between groups.

As seen in Table 1, all kindergarten predictor variables were significantly intercorrelated ($p<$ .01). In the fall, the highest intercorrelated variables were Letter Sounds and Spelling ($r = .78$), Alphabet Recognition and Letter Sounds ($r = .73$), Concept of Word and Spelling ($r = .68$), Concept of Word and Letter Sounds ($r = .67$), and Alphabet Recognition and Spelling ($r = .62$). The highest intercorrelations in the spring can be seen between Letter Sounds and Spelling ($r = .71$), Concept of Word and Spelling ($r = .67$), Concept of Word and Letter Sounds ($r = .67$), and Letter Sounds and Spelling ($r = .63$).

Table 2 shows the Pearson correlation coefficient of each kindergarten variable with the outcome measure, oral reading level. All correlations were significant ($p< .01$), and in the moderate range (from .35 to .51 in fall and from .28 to .61 in spring). In the fall of kindergarten, Concept of Word had the highest correlation to spring first grade oral reading level ($r = .51$), but five of the six predictors had similar correlations, between .45 and .51. Rhyme Awareness yielded the lowest correlation to spring first grade oral reading level ($r = .35$). In the spring of kindergarten, Concept of Word again had the strongest correlation with spring first grade oral reading level ($r = .61$), followed by Letter Sounds ($r = .53$) and Spelling ($r = .52$). In contrast, Alphabet Recognition,

Table 1 Inter-correlations among Kindergarten Predictor Variables Expressed as Pearson Correlation Coefficient

PREDICTOR VARIABLES	1	2	3	4	5	6
		Fall kindergarten				
1. Rhyme Awareness	---	.58*	.39*	.39*	.40*	.40*
2. Beginning Sound Awareness		---	52*	.59*	.56*	.53*
3. Alphabet Recognition			---	.73*	.62*	.57*
4. Letter Sounds				---	.78*	.67*
5. Spelling					---	.68*
6. Concept of Word						---
		Spring kindergarten				
1. Rhyme Awareness	---	.44*	.27*	.35*	.39*	.36*
2. Beginning Sound Awareness		---	.39*	.49*	.52*	.48*
3. Alphabet Recognition			---	.63*	.49*	.47*
4. Letter Sounds				---	.71*	.67*
5. Spelling					---	.67*
6. Concept of Word						---

$*p <.01$

Beginning Sound Awareness, and Rhyme Awareness yielded relatively weak correlations with spring first grade oral reading level (see Table 2).

Overall Prediction of Oral Reading Level

As seen in Table 3, all six fall kindergarten variables were statistically significant (at ∞ = .049 for entry and ∞ = .050 for removal) and thus entered into the regression model. Stepwise regression resulted in a regression equation that accounted for more than one-third of the variance in spring first grade oral reading level (R^2 = .35) based on the fall kindergarten predictor variables.

Examination of the stepwise regression equation provides some indication of the importance of predictors, both through standardized Beta weights and R^2 change values (see Table 3). In the fall, Concept of Word emerged as the strongest predictor of oral reading level, by itself accounting for 26% of the variance in oral reading level. The stepwise procedure then added Alphabet Recognition to the equation, which increased the amount of variance explained by approximately 7%, followed by Beginning Sound Awareness, which added another 2%. The three additional predictor variables (Rhyme Awareness, Spelling, and Letter Sounds) also entered the regression equation because they added statistically significant explanatory power, but the amounts of variance accounted for were less than 0.2% for each of these remaining variables.

Four variables were statistically significant (at ∞ = .049 for entry and ∞ = .050 for removal) in the spring of kindergarten: Concept of Word, Letter Sounds, Spelling, and Rhyme Awareness. The four variables in the regression model for spring kindergarten account for 40% of the variance

Table 2 Pearson Correlation Coefficients for Kindergarten Predictor Variables with Spring First Grade Oral Reading Level

	Fall kindergarten	
Concept of Word	.51*	
Alphabet Recognition	.50*	
Letter Sounds	.49*	
Spelling	.48*	
Beginning Sound Awareness	.45*	
Rhyme Awareness	.35*	

	Spring kindergarten	
Concept of Word	.61*	
Letter Sounds	.53*	
Spelling	.52*	
Alphabet Recognition	.36*	
Beginning Sound Awareness	.34*	
Rhyme Awareness	.28*	

*p <.01

in spring first grade oral reading level (R^2 = .40).

Among the spring of kindergarten predictors, Concept of Word again was identified as the best predictor of spring first grade oral reading level, individually accounting for 37% of the variance. Letter Sounds entered the equation next, adding an additional 3% to the variance explained. Spelling and Rhyme Awareness were entered into the equation, again because the tasks added statistically significant explanatory power, but the amounts of additional variance explained were slight (0.7% and 0.1%, respectively). Beginning Sound Awareness and Alphabet Recognition did not enter the equation because they did not add statistically significant power to the prediction.

Contribution of Variables to the Prediction of On-Grade Level Oral Reading

The data were also examined in terms of students who were reading on or above grade level as compared to students reading below grade level in spring of first grade. "On or above grade level" was defined as an oral reading level of first grade or higher. "Below grade level" was defined as an oral reading level below first grade (e.g., primer, preprimer, or readiness level). Discriminant analysis (DA) was used to determine whether a discriminant function based on students' kindergarten scores would accurately classify the students into the two groups: (a) on or above grade level oral reading and (b) below grade level oral reading. The resulting discriminant function was significant (Wilk's lambda = .82, p< .001) indicating that the function accurately classified students into these groups better than chance. Based on the combination of fall kindergarten

Table 3 Prediction Models of First Grade Oral Reading Level Based on Stepwise Regression

	Fall kindergarten							
Model	COW	ABC	Beg. Sound	Rhyme	Spelling	LS	R^2 change	Beta
1	+						.256**	.224**
2	+	+					.068**	.230**
3	+	+	+				.021**	.129**
4	+	+	+	+			.002**	.061**
5	+	+	+	+	+		.002**	.067**
6	+	+	+	+	+	+	<.001**	.017*

	Spring kindergarten					
Model	COW	LS	Spelling	Rhyme	R^2 change	Beta
1	+				.370**	.412**
2	+	+			.025**	.152**
3	+	+	+		.007**	.122**
4	+	+	+	+	.001**	.033**

$*p$ =.01. ** p <.0001

Note: Beg. Sound = Beginning Sound Awareness   ABC = Alphabet Recognition
LS = Letter Sounds   COW = Concept of Word

variables, 73% of the students were classified into the correct category.

We examined the individual correlations between predictor variables and the discriminant function to assess the importance of each variable to this discrimination between below grade level versus on or above grade level groups. Table 4 displays these correlations. In the fall, Alphabet Recognition had the highest correlation with the discriminant function ($r = .88$). As can be seen in Table 4, all other variables, especially Beginning Sound Awareness, Letter Sounds, and Concept of Word also had relatively high correlations with the discriminant function.

Discriminant analysis using the spring of kindergarten predictors also produced a statistically significant discriminant function (Wilk's lambda = .74, $p<.001$), which accurately classified 80% of the students into the correct category. For the spring variables, Concept of Word yielded the highest correlation with the discriminant function ($r = .94$), followed by Letter Sounds ($r = .78$) and Spelling ($r = .76$). Alphabet Recognition and the two phonological awareness measures, Rhyme Awareness, and Beginning Sound Awareness had the lowest relative correlations to the discriminant function (see Table 4).

DISCUSSION

In this study we examined the extent to which fall and spring kindergarten variables predicted end of first grade oral reading level. We discuss our findings in terms of the importance of the overall prediction of reading level, as well as the importance of individual variables. We also discuss the importance of our findings in relation to previous research on predicting reading

Table 4 Correlation of Predictor Variables to Discriminant Function

Fall kindergarten predictor variables	Correlation between predictor variables and discriminant function
Alphabet Recognition	.88
Beginning Sound Awareness	.75
Letter Sounds	.73
Concept of Word	.72
Spelling	.68
Rhyme Awareness	.59

Spring kindergarten predictor variables	Correlation between predictor variables and discriminant function
Concept of Word	.94
Letter Sounds	.78
Spelling	.76
Alphabet Recognition	.54
Beginning Sound Awareness	.53
Rhyme Awareness	.41

outcomes. Finally, we consider limitations of the present study, including the statistical issues involved in predicting any outcome with a set of highly intercorrelated variables.

Overall Prediction of Oral Reading Level

With respect to an overall prediction of reading level, 35% of the variance in spring first grade oral reading level was accounted for by the combination of fall kindergarten variables. With only Concept of Word and Alphabet Recognition as predictors, 33% of the variance was accounted for. Thus, the combination of all other variables only accounted for an additional 2% of the variance. In the spring of kindergarten, 40% of the variance in spring first grade oral reading level was accounted for by the combination of all kindergarten variables. Concept of Word and Letter Sounds alone, however, accounted for nearly all of this explained variance, with Spelling and Rhyme Awareness contributing less than 1% combined.

The proportion of variance accounted for in this study is similar to that found by Morris, Bloodgood, and Perney (2003). In their study, 30% of the variance in spring first grade passage reading and 31% of the variance in spring first grade comprehension were accounted for by the combination of the fall predictors. This is nearly identical to the results of the present study. In the spring of kindergarten, Morris, Bloodgood, and Perney (2003) found that 59% of the variance in passage reading and 53% of the variance in comprehension were accounted for by the combination of spring kindergarten predictors. These values are somewhat higher than those obtained in the present study. It is unclear why the Morris, Bloodgood, and Perney (2003) model accounted for substantially more variance than the model from the current study in the spring of kindergarten. One potential source of the difference may be that although the same skills were assessed in both studies, the tasks differed slightly in form. Two notable differences were that the Morris, Bloodgood, and Perney (2003) study included a measure of word recognition and did not include a direct measure of letter sound knowledge.

The results from the present study support the First Grade Studies' (Bond & Dykstra, 1967) and Scarborough's (1998) findings that a combination of measures provides a stronger prediction than a single measure. However, when the variables are highly intercorrelated as they are in the present study, the combination of a small number of predictors may account for a large portion of variance, while additional variables that might be statistically significant add little additional explanatory power.

Importance of Individual Predictor Variables

Taken together, our results point to some indications of the relative importance of the predictors we examined, and further highlight that the predictive power of these variables may be different from fall to spring in the kindergarten year. Results from the fall kindergarten stepwise regression analyses indicate that Concept of Word has the highest zero-order correlation with spring first grade oral reading level. However, Alphabet Recognition was entered second into the fall kindergarten regression equation, and has the highest correlation with the discriminant function ($r = .88$). Beginning Sound Awareness also adds a substantial amount of predictive power to the regression equation in the fall of kindergarten, and has a high correlation with the discriminant function (r = .75).

In the spring of kindergarten, Concept of Word is the strongest predictor of spring first grade oral reading level. This is evident not only in that Concept of Word entered the stepwise regression equation first, and accounted for 37% of the variance in reading level, but also in the high correlation (r = .94) of this variable with the spring discriminant function. Letter Sounds and Spelling also add some predictive power to the regression equation in the spring of kindergarten and yield high correlations with the discriminant function (r = .78 and r = .76, respectively).

It is also noteworthy that in the spring of kindergarten the two phonological awareness tasks, Beginning Sound Awareness and Rhyme Awareness, had the lowest correlations with spring oral reading level (r = .34 and r = .28, respectively) and with the spring discriminant function (r = .53 and r = .41, respectively). Further, Beginning Sound Awareness in the spring of kindergarten did not add statistically significant power to the prediction equation. While Rhyme Awareness did add statistically significant power to the equation, its contribution was small (R^2 change = .001). These findings suggest that, in the spring of kindergarten, print skills show a stronger relationship to first grade oral reading achievement than phonological awareness skills. It should be noted that the phonological awareness skills in the present study were generally less advanced phonological awareness skills. Different results may be obtained if more advanced phonological awareness skills such as blending and segmenting were used.

Relation to Previous Research

Morris, Bloodgood, and Perney (2003) found that only alphabet recognition and concept of word predicted first grade reading achievement in the beginning, middle, and end of kindergarten. Our results support the Morris, Bloodgood, and Perney (2003) findings of the predictive power of Concept of Word in both the fall and spring of kindergarten. Alphabet Recognition was also found as a powerful predictor in the fall of kindergarten. However, Letter Sounds (which was highly correlated with Alphabet Recognition) emerged as a powerful predictor in spring of kindergarten. Morris, Bloodgood, and Perney (2003) also reported spelling and beginning consonant awareness as significant predictors in the spring of kindergarten. While Spelling emerged as a significant predictor in the present study, its contribution was minimal. The spring predictive power of both Spelling and Beginning Sound Awareness was likely diminished in the presence of the highly-correlated Letter Sounds task, a task that Morris, Bloodgood, and Perney (2003) did not include.

With respect to concept of word, the similarity in findings of the present study and the Morris, Bloodgood, and Perney (2003) study are striking. Recall that the Concept of Word task taps a student's ability to track words in print and to identify words both within and out of context. This skill is directly related to a student's ability to use beginning sound knowledge to read words and remember them as sight words (Morris, Bloodgood, Lomax, & Perney, 2003). These findings may suggest that the closer the spring kindergarten task is to actual reading, the better it will predict future reading performance. Historically, concept of word has been overlooked as a predictor of reading achievement. The results of the present study and the Morris, Bloodgood, and Perney (2003) study suggest that this task warrants a prominent position in future research efforts.

Limitations

The difficulty of predicting outcomes with highly intercorrelated variables means that no one statistical procedure can fully answer the prediction questions we posed. For example, while stepwise regression provides the best mathematical prediction from a set of predictors, a limitation is that a variable with potential predictive power may be essentially eliminated if a highly correlated variable enters the regression equation. Consider Letter Sounds and Alphabet Recognition in the fall of kindergarten. The tasks have nearly identical correlations to oral reading level (Letter Sounds: $r = .49$, Alphabet Recognition: $r = .50$). However, because Alphabet Recognition and Letters Sounds are highly intercorrelated ($r = .78$), when Alphabet Recognition is included in the regression equation, Letter Sounds is reduced in importance to the extent that it contributes very little to the equation (R^2 change $< .001$). More advanced statistical procedures that address the influence of intercorrelated variables on one another, such as structural equation modeling, may be powerful in advancing our understanding of this research question.

Other limitations pertain to the sample size and our determination of oral reading level. The sample size in this study is exceptionally large. Because of this, some relationships between the predictor and outcome variables are statistically significant, yet provide little meaningful information. Additionally, reading rates were not considered in establishing the oral reading level used as the outcome measure. Reading rate is a crucial component of oral reading fluency, but since there is a lack of consensus on expected oral reading rates for different instructional levels (Gummere, 2003; Howell, 2005), we did not include them in determining the oral reading level. It is possible that the study would have yielded different predictors if we had done so.

CONCLUSION

To conclude, we offer an important caveat related to the intended use of an assessment. At first glance, the results of this study could be interpreted to mean that the inclusion of all kindergarten variables we examined may not be necessary if simple prediction of a student's first grade oral reading level is the goal. However, there is great instructional merit in administering many, if not all, of the tasks described herein to a kindergarten student. Although the most parsimonious model in the spring of kindergarten indicates that only four variables should be included in the model, it is important for kindergarten teachers to understand their students' development in all aspects of emergent reading behaviors in order to plan appropriate instruction. The intercorrelations among these tasks argue for a symbiotic view of literacy development in which one skill or behavior depends critically on another.

The results of this study reaffirm that a combination of measures provides greater power than any single measure in predicting reading outcomes. That being said, the Concept of Word task consistently yielded a high degree of power in this study, especially in the spring of kindergarten. Given the fact that concept of word is a complex amalgam of phonological and print skills, this is not a surprising result. A concept of word in text entails synchronizing units of speech with printed units on the page. To achieve a concept of word, children must be able to isolate the beginning phoneme of spoken words and simultaneously match it to a recognized letter at the beginning of a printed word boundary. Thus, to attain a concept of word, children must have a certain degree of phonological awareness, automatic alphabet and letter sound recognition, and other concepts of print. Achieving a concept of word entails the coalescence of all of these interrelated subskills.

Research in the past twenty years has emphasized the importance of phonological awareness in predicting reading outcomes. This line of research has contributed invaluable insight into the nature of early reading difficulties and awakened the educational community to the importance of teaching phonological awareness skills as early as preschool and kindergarten. The results of this study suggest that it is equally important to consider the development of print-related skills over time and the coalescence of these two important domains across the kindergarten year.

REFERENCES

Bond, G., & Dykstra, R. (1967). The cooperative research program in first-grade reading instruction. *Reading Research Quarterly, 2*(4), 5-142.

Bradley, L., & Bryant, P. (1983). Categorizing sounds and learning to read: A causal connection. *Nature, 30*, 419-421.

Bradley, L., & Bryant, P. (1985). *Rhyme and reason in reading and spelling.* Ann Arbor, MI: University of Michigan Press.

Bryant, P.E., Bradley, L., MacLean, M., & Crossland, J. (1989). Nursery rhymes, phonological skills and reading. *Child Language, 301*, 419-421.

Gummere, S. (2003). Measuring oral reading fluency: How accurate are we?. *Reading in Virginia, 27*, 47-54.

Hammill, D.D. (2004). What we know about correlates of reading. *Exceptional Reading, 70*(4), 453-469.

Howell, J.H. (2005). *Oral reading rates: An examination by grade level, instructional level, and age.* Unpublished doctoral dissertation, University of Virginia, Charlottesville.

Invernizzi, M., Justice, L., Landrum, T., & Booker, K. (2004). Early literacy screening in kindergarten: Widespread implementation in Virginia. *Journal of Literacy Research, 36* (4), 479-500.

Invernizzi, M., Meier, J. D., & Juel, C. (2004). *Phonological awareness literacy screening: Grades 1-3.* Charlottesville, VA: University Printing Services.

Invernizzi, M., Swank, L., Juel, C., & Meier, J. D. (2004). *PALS: Phonological awareness literacy screening: Kindergarten.* Charlottesville, VA: University Printing Services.

Juel, C. (1988). Learning to read and write: A longitudinal study of fifty-four children from first through fourth grades. *Journal of Educational Psychology, 80*(4), 437-447.

Justice, L.M., & Ezell, H.K. (2001). Word and print awareness in 4-year-old children. *Child Language Teaching and Therapy, 17*, 207-225.

LaBerge, D., & Samuels, S.J. (1974). Toward a theory of automatic information processing in reading. *Cognitive Psychology, 6*, 293-323.

Morris, D., Bloodgood, J., Lomax, R. & Perney, J. (2003). Developmental steps in learning to read: A longitudinal study in kindergarten and first grade. *Reading Research Quarterly, 38*, 302-328.

Morris, D., Bloodgood, J., & Perney, J. (2003). Kindergarten predictors of first- and second- grade reading achievement. *The Elementary School Journal, 104*(2), 93-109.

National Assessment of Educational Progress (NAEP). U.S. Department of Education, Institute of Education Sciences, National Center for Education Statistics, 2003.

National Center for Family Literacy (2003). *Synthesis of Scientific Research on Development of Early Literacy in Young Children.* National Early Literacy Panel (NELP).

Pearson, D. (1997). The first grade studies: A personal reflection. *Reading Research Quarterly, 32*(4), 428-432.

Rimm-Kaufman, S.E., & Pianta, R.C. (2000). An ecological perspective on the transition to kindergarten: A theoretical framework to guide empirical research. *Journal of Applied Developmental Psychology, 21*(5), 491-511.

Satz, P., Fletcher, J., Clark, W., & Morris, R. (1981). Lag, deficit, rate, and delay constructs in specific learning disabilities: A reexamination. In A. Ansara, N. Geschwind, A. Galaburda, M. Albert, & N. Gartrell. (Eds.), *Sex differences in dyslexia* (pp 129-150). Towson, MD: The Orton Dyslexia Society.

Scarborough, H.S. (1998).   Early identification of children at risk for reading disabilities: Phonological awareness and some other promising predictors. In B.K. Shapiro, P.J. Accardo, & A.J. Capute (Eds.), *Specific reading disability: A view of the spectrum* (pp. 75-119). Timonium, MD: York Press.

Stanovich, K. (1986). Matthew effects in reading: Some consequences of individual differences in the acquisition of literacy. *Reading Research Quarterly, 21*, 360-406.

Swank, L.K., & Catts, H.W. (1994). Phonological awareness and written word decoding. *Language, Speech, and Hearing Services in Schools, 25*, 9-14.

Sweet, A.P., & Snow, C.E. (Eds.) (2003). *Rethinking reading comprehension.* New York: Guilford.

Torgesen, J. (1998). Catch them before they fall. *American Educator, 22* (1&2), 32-39.

Viewing Professional Development Through the Lens of Technology Integration: How do Beginning Teachers Navigate the Use of Technology and New Literacies?

Susan Watts-Taffe
Independent Literacy Researcher

Carolyn B. Gwinn
Independent Literacy Researcher

We have much to learn about the ways in which teachers integrate technology into their instruction (Zhao & Frank, 2003) and even more to learn about what constitutes meaningful integration and how teachers come to personal understandings of what this means (Watts-Taffe, Gwinn, Johnson, & Horn, 2003). According to the CEO Forum (1999) and the U.S. Department of Education (1999), much of the investment in technology in the schools has been in hardware and software, rather than teacher professional development. In a survey conducted by the National Center for Education Statistics (2000), most teachers reported feeling less than well prepared to effectively integrate computers and the Internet into their instruction. Studies of inservice and preservice teachers suggest wide variation in instructional practices and beliefs about the role of technology in literacy instruction across the continuum (Fisher, Lapp, & Flood, 2000; Karchmer, 2001; McGrail, 2004; Richards, 2001).

Current notions of teacher professional development assert that classroom practice improves when teacher education is ongoing, scaffolded, context-specific, and marked by teacher ownership and investment (Ball & Cohen, 1999; Borko, Davinroy, Bliem, & Cumbo, 2000). The ever-changing nature of technology demands new approaches to teacher professional development (Leu & Kinzer, 2000). Citing Senge (1990), Fawcett and Snyder (1998) suggest that professional development must focus on "capacity building, where capacity is defined as the ability to continuously learn" (p. 122). Further, it is particularly important to take into account teachers' multiple realities, given the wide variation in classroom resources and teacher expertise in the area of technology (Labbo & Reinking, 1999).

This study was designed to explore the ways in which beginning teachers navigate the use of technology and new literacies, as they simultaneously construct their understandings of effective literacy instruction. The Encarta World English Dictionary (1999) lists as the first definition of *navigate*, "to find a way through a place, or direct the course of something." We use this word to represent the journey into new territory, from traditional technologies (e.g., books, paper, pencil) to new technologies (e.g., the Internet, software for reading, writing, and communicating) and from traditional literacies to new literacies. One of the hallmarks of the new information and communication technologies (ICTs) is the unprecedented rate at which they are continuously changing. Thus, it is difficult to precisely capture a definition of *new literacies*. As an initial conception, Leu, Kinzer, Coiro, and Cammack (2004) suggest that new literacies "include the skills, strategies, and dispositions necessary to successfully use and adapt to the rapidly changing information and communication technologies and contexts that continuously emerge in our world and influence all areas of our personal and professional lives" (p. 1572). These new literacies go beyond the traditional literacies associated with books, paper, and pencil to include the reading, writing, viewing, and communication skills required by the Internet and other ICTs (Karchmer, Mallette, Kara-Soteriou, & Leu, 2005).

Our line of inquiry, begun in the Fall of 2000, grew out of our desire to learn about ways in which we could improve the preparation of preservice teachers in our literacy methods courses for classrooms of the 21st century. In the phase of the study reported here, we investigated the professional development of first-year and third-year teachers as they planned for and implemented literacy-technology integration in their classrooms. This paper addresses two of the central questions guiding our investigation: (a) How do participating teachers navigate the use of technology in their literacy instruction? and (b) What is the influence of participation in this research project on teacher professional development?

PARTICIPATING TEACHERS

Joan and Jack were selected from among six teachers, representing grades 2-8 in five midwestern school districts, who took part in this study. All participants were former preservice teacher education students of the authors and had learned about and applied methods of technology integration as part of their literacy methods courses. Four were in their first year of teaching. The remaining teachers, in their third year of teaching, had been involved in this study since the start of their careers. A case study approach (Stake, 2003) was used to understand the experiences of two teachers, one in her first year of teaching and one in his third.

Joan and Jack (self-selected pseudonyms) were selected for in-depth study for two reasons. First, these were teachers for whom we had the widest breadth and the greatest depth of data. As described in the next section, our techniques for data generation included teacher submission of information. Both the quantity and quality (i.e., precision and detail of description) of Joan's and Jack's submissions were such that in-depth analyses were facilitated. Second, their teaching settings were demographically similar and both had a high level of technology support available in their schools, providing each of them with a wide array of possibilities relative to other participating teachers.

As a first-year teacher, Joan taught third-grade in a school with a high level of technology support. Of her 25 students, 1 qualified for free or reduced price lunch, 8 received Title I services, and 4 were English Language Learners. Building demographic information listed seventeen of Joan's students as Caucasian, 2 as African American, and 3 as East Indian. Three students were classified as "Other."

Jack was in his third year of teaching second-grade. His school also was equipped with rich resources for technology integration. In his classroom of 22 students, 7 qualified for free or reduced price lunch, 11 received Title I services, and 2 were English Language Learners. According to building demographics, 19 of his students were Caucasian, 1 was African American, 1 was Russian, and 1 was Hmong. Both Joan and Jack are Caucasian.

METHODS OF DATA GENERATION AND ANALYSIS

Our methods of data generation were designed both to provide information about, and contribute to, the ongoing professional development of teachers as they moved from our preservice literacy methods courses into their first years of teaching. The data reported here were generated from September 2003 through May 2004.

Processes of Data Generation

Fieldnotes and transcripts of focus group meetings. Over the course of the year, three 90-minute meetings provided a forum for planning, sharing work, and describing perspectives on project involvement. During two meetings, each teacher was asked to describe a literacy-technology integration experience that she or he felt was particularly meaningful and to further discuss why it was meaningful.

Written responses. As part of each of the group meetings, teachers responded to questions related to hopes, plans, and resources for technology integration (Fall), the evaluation of student work related to technology integration (Winter), and the evolution of hopes and plans, as well as reflections on challenges encountered and teacher self-growth over the course of the year (Spring).

Electronic instructional planning grids. This grid allowed teachers to share with us their plans and their work on a monthly basis. Each month, teachers filled in the following: (a) *student objectives* related to lessons involving technology; (b) *preparation:* ways of gathering knowledge or materials to inform instruction; (c) *specific applications* used for preparation and instruction; (d) *evidence of student learning:* observations or documentation related to the degree to which instructional objectives were met; and (e) *future instructional plans* based on lesson outcomes.

Instructional observation and follow-up debriefing. Each teacher was observed teaching a lesson involving technology. Fieldnotes were taken, using an observation protocol that focused the observer's attention on the knowledge and skills being taught, the learning environment, and the technology integration. Aspects of the learning environment that were considered include student self-sufficiency and control, equity of access, teacher management of equipment and materials, student grouping patterns, teacher modeling, and meeting the needs of diverse learners. Afterward, teachers shared their own observations of the lesson in a follow-up interview.

Anecdotal logs. Each teacher kept an anecdotal log to record any ideas, observations, plans, questions, or notes related to her/his literacy-technology integration efforts. All teachers wrote free hand and used the log to suit their individual purposes. Some used the log primarily to brainstorm ideas and list potential plans, while others used the log to record notes about instruction or observations about student performance and student response related to instruction.

Process of Data Analysis

Following the guidelines of constructivist grounded theory (Charmaz, 2003; Strauss, 1987), data analysis was continuous and cumulative. We used field texts and analytical tools in the form of observer comments, personal memos, and methodological notes; analytic narratives; e-mail dialogue and conversation; and analytic grids (Richardson, 2000; Stake, 2003; Wolcott, 1994). Our approach was marked by two phases of analysis. The first phase consisted of our initial coding of written responses, meeting transcripts, and electronic instructional planning grids, and occurred as these documents were collected throughout the school year. At this time, what we learned from teacher comments during each of the focus group meetings helped inform the questions we asked during successive meetings. As needed, we used e-mail to get clarification on information provided by teachers in their instructional planning grids.

We began the second phase of analysis by reading through all of the data, narrowing our focus to the two teachers for whom we had the most data, and proceeding to make notes, write narratives, and construct analytic grids. Our analytic grids were central to the use of constant-comparative methods that allowed us to compare data in the following ways: (a) both within and between teachers, (b) across time, and (c) against our developing coding scheme (Charmaz, 2003). We created individual grids for the focus group meeting transcripts in which we described and coded teacher talk related to meaningful technology integration, student learning objectives, the evaluation of student work, and professional development over the course of the year. We used the same approach for the written responses, using the focal questions on these responses as the organizing framework for the grid. For the Instructional Planning Grids, we recorded observations, questions, and interpretations in narrative form, using the grid categories of student objectives, preparation, and evidence of learning to organize our notes.

FINDINGS

How Did Joan and Jack Navigate the use of Technology in Their Literacy Instruction?

We will address this complex question in two ways. First, we will present a concrete example from each teacher's classroom, satisfying two criteria. Each example of instruction is (a) identified by the teacher as particularly meaningful, and (b) one that we believe typifies that teacher's literacy-technology integration efforts over the course of the year.

We will then present themes that we identified to characterize the ways in which Joan and Jack navigated the use of technology in their literacy instruction. While Joan's and Jack's approaches to literacy-technology integration were unique, and the two teachers differed in grade level taught and years of teaching experience, our analysis revealed strong commonalities which are illustrated in the six themes.

Reading, Researching, and Writing with the Internet in Joan's Third Grade Classroom

In November, as part of a five-week unit of study focusing on the history and people of the Northwest Coastal region, Joan's students spent several days accessing information on the Internet. Specifically, Joan's objectives state that, "students will find information about their Native American tribes and their styles of homes. They will be asked to analyze why the styles varied from those in the NW Coastal region. Ex: materials available, climate, etc." (Instructional Planning Grid, November). Joan entered into these lessons with the intent of laying a foundation for using the Internet, and an integral part of this series of lessons was a focus on "how to look at a website filled with a lot of information" (Meeting Transcript Grid, p. 2). Joan's students needed to read and comprehend the information presented on websites, make notes, compare and contrast, and present their findings in a report that included text and pictures. Among the reasons Joan articulated for viewing this as a meaningful series of lessons was the high level of student excitement and engagement.

Reading and Writing Across Texts in Jack's Second Grade Classroom

In January, Jack's students participated in a series of lessons involving shared readings of two traditional fairy tales, *Cinderella* and *Yeh Shen*, followed by the creation of their own fairy tales. They read *Yeh Shen* in big book format, then read *Cinderella*, as it appears in *Claris Works for Kids*, projected on a large screen. Students were asked to compare and contrast the two stories, then write and illustrate their own fairy tales, using the *Amazing Writing Machine* (Microlytics/Broderbund) software. As stated in Jack's objectives, "Students will write and illustrate their own fairy tale, gaining further practice in properly writing a title, complete sentences, and a story with a setting, characters, a problem, and a resolution while learning important technology skills" (Jack's Instructional Planning Grid, January). The primary reason Jack saw this as a meaningful lesson was that he saw academic progress in his lower achieving students.

Shared Themes in Joan's and Jack's Instruction

In this section, we will address the following ways in which we characterize Joan's and Jack's work: (a) integration of conventional and new literacies, (b) promotion of critical thinking, (c) multifaceted preparation for instruction, (d) attention to social interaction and grouping, (e) active decision-making, and (f) differentiation of instruction.

Integration of conventional and new literacies. Joan and Jack used technology to meet a wide range of student objectives including those related to traditional or conventional literacy learning (e.g., "improving phonics skills") and those related to technological literacy (e.g., "students will become familiar with finding the program on the server") (Jack's Instructional Planning Grid, September). Both teachers moved students cohesively between and among electronic and paper texts, as well as the reading and writing of a variety of genres in each medium.

An example of the way in which a conventional literacy skill is juxtaposed with a new literacy skill is found in Jack's classroom. After reading aloud the story *Cloudy with a Chance of Meatballs* (Barrett, 1978), Jack informed students that they would be using *ClarisWorks for Kids* to create pictographs of Breakfast Precipitation. He then modeled this process for his students, using a think-aloud procedure. As he showed them how to make a capital letter on the keyboard, he said, "If the light is on, you'll have all capital letters. . . .Why capitalize the 'M' on Monday?" In this example, taken from his observed lesson, Jack fostered understanding of both the keyboarding mechanics of creating a capital letter as well as the concept of capitalization.

Promotion of critical thinking. Although technology was used to support students in the acquisition and review of what might be called "basic skills," such as sounding out words and answering literal-level comprehension questions, as well as writing conventions such as capitalization, the vast majority of literacy-technology integration occurring in Joan's and Jack's classrooms promoted higher level comprehension and critical thinking. Students were engaged in reading and thinking across texts, synthesizing information from multiple sources, and using technology to create and convey information using text and graphics. In addition, both Joan and Jack discussed the fact that one or more students who struggled in other areas of the classroom literacy program found success when literacy and technology were integrated.

For example, Joan's students learned to access and read websites to retrieve specific information, make decisions about which types of information matched their purposes for reading, compare and contrast across texts (both electronic and paper) and convey information to others. Several of these processes are evident in the example "Reading, Researching, and Writing with the Internet in Joan's Third Grade Classroom," presented earlier.

Multifaceted preparation for instruction. Preparation was a significant part of Joan's and Jack's work to utilize technology and address new literacies in their classrooms. Joan and Jack engaged in preparation that was multifaceted, involving layers of activity beyond that associated with traditional lesson planning. In addition to exploring websites and software, as well as learning about hardware capabilities, they prepared materials to guide their students through various aspects of new literacies. For example, Joan created graphic organizers for her students to use as they conducted online information searches. Both spent time making sure that the appropriate software was installed on each student computer and/or that websites had been bookmarked and could be accessed easily.

Another dimension of preparation involved collaboration with building and district-level support staff. For Joan, collaboration with the building technology support person was critical and occurred regularly. Not only did she collaborate on matters of hardware and software, but also on matters of curriculum and pedagogy, as in the creation of her graphic organizers. Jack also collaborated with his technology support person when needed, and he was assisted in his preparation by district-level inservice workshops.

Attention to social interaction and grouping. A commitment to foster social interaction and establish effective grouping patterns was demonstrated by Joan and Jack. This was clear in their instruction and was even made explicit in several of Jack's student objectives, in which he indicated how students would collaborate. Observation and teacher comments attest to the sense of community maintained by Joan and Jack and reveal that students were motivated by the opportunity to collectively engage in literacy-technology experiences. Even when working individually, children regularly helped one another. In Jack's classroom, for example, one child circulated to help others during the *Cloudy With a Chance of Meatballs* lesson. Similarly, "Children depend on each other while waiting to work with Joan" (Observation Fieldnotes, 2/18/04, p. 2). It was clear from Joan's and Jack's instructional plans, and reflections on their instruction, that grouping patterns and social interaction were an integral part of their literacy-technology integration efforts.

Active decision-making. Joan and Jack were engaged in decision-making during all phases of instruction: before, during, and after. In addition, both teachers addressed the inherent risk of system crashes and online connection failures, with decision-making that was "right there," and "in the moment." In the preparation, implementation, and reflection phases of instruction, their work seemed to rest on the fundamental question: Is this enhancing my instruction? Both Joan and Jack underscored the idea that they do not "do technology, just to do it. You think about what you want to teach and then how does technology make it better?" (Joan, Spring Meeting Transcript, p. 11)

Jack illustrated the purposeful, progressive nature of his *planning* as he described the ways in which a unit on monarch butterflies, culminating in student-designed KidPix slideshows, was intended to prepare students for more sophisticated work with technology including graphing information and locating information online. Joan demonstrated active decision-making *during* a series of lessons by suggesting the use of a different website with easier text for students having difficulty locating information. This decision-making continued *after* the lesson, as Joan reflected upon the ability of two students, representing different levels of achievement, to successfully gather online information for the assignment. She realized the need to accommodate "all levels of learners" by providing websites of varying levels of difficulty and complexity for research purposes. In this example, we see that teacher decision-making was both proactive and responsive.

Differentiated instruction. Throughout the course of the year, we gained an understanding of how Joan and Jack worked to meet the varying instructional needs of their students. Both teachers viewed technology as useful in assisting students who struggle with literacy tasks presented in traditional formats. When asked what makes a literacy-technology integration lesson meaningful, both Joan and Jack routinely referenced struggling readers and writers. Through technology, Joan and Jack saw ways of reaching students who may have seemed inaccessible otherwise. As a third year teacher, Jack began the year with a proactive stance toward meeting the needs of lower achieving students. For Joan, this stance developed over time, in tandem with the revelations afforded her by student engagement in and performance on literacy-technology activities.

During the Winter meeting, Jack described the experience of his "most challenging student, as far as ability level," with the creation of his own fairy tale as part of the *Cinderella/Yeh Shen* lesson series described earlier in this paper:

> It's like pulling teeth to get him to journal or something like that. But when we went in the computer [lab] and did this, he was on fire. He was on fire to make the pictures. He has a para[professional] that works with him, but he was able to spell the words, several of them, to the para [and] told her what to write. . . He was the first one done and wanted to show everybody, and then was making another one. So that was really exciting because like I said it's been so hard to get him to write." (p. 9)

Both Joan and Jack suggested that technology allows for "a more level playing field" (Jack, Winter Meeting Transcript, p. 16) for their students, shifting the dynamics between high and low achievers and allowing them, as teachers, to see greater possibilities for their lower achieving students.

In the Spring, Joan made this observation about a special education student in her classroom:

When this kid can do more of his word processing on the computer, he's going to soar, because he's got the ideas up here [tapping her temple], but physically can't write them on paper. He doesn't have the patience or the small motor skills to do it, even in third grade. . . Some of these kids will fly on the computer where they can't in the regular classroom and I see that in [the] small amounts that I've done with the technology. That's very important." (p. 15)

As Joan realized the need to differentiate her instruction, her objectives began to reflect this awareness.

What Is the Influence of Participation in This Research Project on Teacher Professional Development?

Our goal for this project was to engage teachers in activities that would not only cast light on their work for our purposes, but would also illuminate and encourage their work in ways that they would find beneficial. Joan and Jack were eager to share their work during the three focus group meetings, actively engaging in conversation about what they were each doing, related to the infusion of technology into literacy, and how they were doing it. During the Spring meeting, they shared their thoughts regarding the role of this project in their professional development. We identified four themes in their talk about project participation, all from the Spring meeting transcripts: motivation and accountability, application and reflection, confidence, and collaboration. As evidenced in their language, these themes often overlap and there are some themes that represent a combination of constructs.

Motivation and accountability. Joan and Jack felt that participation with other teachers and monthly communication with us motivated them to address technology and new literacies more than they otherwise might have. Jack described the influence of his project involvement as "huge. . .just giving me the confidence to do it, the motivation to do it, and knowing that accountability is there because I know I'm going to be talking about what I've been doing and sharing that. . . ." (p. 8). Joan agreed with another participant who said that project involvement sparked teaching ideas, adding, "It made me think about it [ways to integrate technology] because I really don't think I would have this first year . . .there are so many other things that you're doing that you just get overwhelmed" (p. 11).

The notion of accountability was also an influential factor. Jack said that it was "healthy to be accountable . . . That was helpful to kind of see. They're going to be looking at these [Instructional Planning Grids] each month" (p. 8). Joan suggested that involvement in the project "made me do it. I think it would have probably been a back burner thing because I'm not really comfortable with it and it's not something that I think of right away" (p. 11).

Application and reflection. Joan and Jack highlighted application and reflection as important ways in which their project involvement had impacted them. They believed that their work in the project helped them to apply what they had learned as preservice teachers, as well as what they were learning in staff development workshops, and that these applications provided fertile ground for reflection. Jack, for example, developed several units in which students used *KidPix* software to compose stories or communicate information. He began with an adaptation of a lesson presented in our methods courses, then used ideas generated by project participation to develop increasingly sophisticated experiences for his students. These lessons were among those he found to be the most meaningful, and he spent time discussing them in all three focus group meetings. In Joan's words:

> We've been learning all the theory and it's nice to see the actual practical experience of it. . . . It was so nice to talk about it, apply it, and then come back and say, 'This is what I did.' I think if you just meet once and just talk about it, it's great but [to] really apply it, come back, and reflect on it, it's so much more meaningful..." (p. 12)

According to Jack, involvement in this project challenged him to be "more reflective" than any other professional development activity he had engaged in (p. 8).

Collaboration. When asked to compare their participation in this project to other professional development experiences they'd had during the year, Joan and Jack viewed this project as unique. Jack valued the collaboration, saying ". . .what I liked probably most about it was learning from other teachers and having that chance to share . . .it's just good to collaborate with other teachers" (p. 8). Joan described the meaningfulness of meeting with her former classmates, now classroom teachers, to exchange ideas: "I see things that we've done and I've tried different things that we've done through the program and I see you guys trying too. It works. I just think it's been great to touch base and really see each other doing it that whole first year" (pp. 12-13). It is clear that Joan and Jack valued this project in large part because of the way in which individuals in the group supported one another in their individual efforts and because of the mutual exchange of information.

Confidence. As stated earlier, Jack described the influence of his project involvement as "huge. . .just giving me the confidence to do it. . ." (p. 8). In response to the question, "What have you learned about yourself as a teacher with the increased emphasis on technology integration?" Joan said, "I can do it" (p. 14). Given the intrinsic relationship between confidence and teacher self-efficacy, Jack's and Joan's reference to confidence as an outgrowth of the project is intriguing.

DISCUSSION

Leu, Kinzer, Coiro, and Cammack (2004) suggest that the teacher's role changes, becoming more important in new literacies classrooms. We studied two teachers who had been exposed to conceptual and practical ideas related to technology integration in their teacher preparation program and who were teaching in environments that provided a high level of support for technology integration. Our focus on teachers who are relatively early in their careers complements other research, which has focused on more experienced or "expert" teachers (see for example, Karchmer, 2001; Wepner and Tao, 2002). Our findings suggest directions for the design of teacher professional development experiences as well as preservice teacher education.

Implications for What Teachers Need to Learn

We identified six conceptual categories to describe the ways in which Joan and Jack navigated technology in their literacy instruction. These categories are not mutually exclusive and we see many links between and among them. We found that these early career teachers do much of what the literature indicates will be required of all teachers, as technology becomes a more integral part of the school day. Jack's and Joan's integration of conventional and new literacies represents what Labbo (2005) refers to as comfort with being on the cutting edge, a key characteristic of teachers who effectively integrate technology with literacy. Joan's and Jack's promotion of students' critical thinking, as well as their attention to social interaction and grouping, reflect two other important characteristics of effective new literacies classrooms (Coiro, 2003; Karchmer, 2001, Wepner & Tao, 2002). In fact, Leu, Kinzer, Coiro, and Cammack (2004) list critical thinking and learning that is socially constructed as two of the central principles of their new literacies perspective.

In addition to learning what Joan and Jack did in their classrooms, we learned how principles of effective instruction were manifested within the context of literacy-technology integration. Just as researchers are in the initial stages of conceptualizing the parameters of the new literacies themselves, we, as a field, are in the infant stages of identifying the skills, strategies, and dispositions necessary to teach in new literacies classrooms. Our findings highlight characteristics of instruction that were important in Joan's and Jack's literacy-technology integration efforts. More importantly, they begin to answer critical questions such as: What does preparation for instruction entail when technology is integrated into the literacy program? What sorts of decisions are required of teachers as they integrate technology and address new literacies? What are the possibilities for differentiated instruction through literacy-technology integration? Our findings suggest that it is important for teachers to learn both about the specific ways in which they might effectively integrate technology into their literacy teaching, as well as the instructional strategies and dispositions required for optimal student learning.

Implications for How Teachers Need to Learn

This project affirms the importance of inservice teacher development that is ongoing and teacher-based. While there are many robust examples of such work, our experiences, and that of our teacher colleagues, suggest the preeminence of large-group, single session workshops in which the limited time available is spent by teachers listening without having the opportunity to share their personal professional concerns and questions, hear from their colleagues, or apply and reflect upon what they've learned in the session. This approach does not allow for capacity-building, which is central to effective professional development related to technology integration (Coiro, 2005). In our model, teachers regularly talked and listened within a community of peers (focus group meetings). Throughout the year, they used writing as a way to plan, document, and communicate what they were doing in the classroom (instructional planning grids, anecdotal logs). These written records helped them to talk about their work in focus group meetings. Together, the written records and regular meetings served as a catalyst for applying ideas and reflecting upon instruction. Teachers valued this long-term process, specific to their own classrooms, that allowed for collaborative learning. Structured writing, talking, application, and reflection hold promise for models of professional development aimed at supporting literacy-technology integration.

Directions for Future Research

This study was limited to two teachers, sharing similar teacher preparation experiences, technology resources, .and classroom demographics. We look forward to a broader investigation involving members of our study cohort who taught in very different contexts. For example, two participants teach in urban, alternative schools with scarce technology resources. For both of these teachers, the power of technology to motivate, engage, and jumpstart learning appears to have been magnified as was the leadership role required of them to obtain up-to-date, relevant hardware and software for their students. A look at our entire study cohort also suggests differences between first- and third-year teachers in both the possibilities and the challenges of literacy-technology integration. A more in-depth analysis may enable us to better understand the continuum of teacher development related to literacy-technology integration, as well as the longitudinal impact of participation in our professional development project.

REFERENCES

Ball, D. L., & Cohen, D. K. (1999). Developing practice, developing practitioners: Toward a practice-based theory of professional education. In L. Darling-Hammond & G. Sykes (Eds.), *Teaching as the learning profession: Handbook of policy and practice* (pp. 3-32). San Francisco: Jossey-Bass.

Barrett, J. (1978). *Cloudy with a chance of meatballs.* New York: Scholastic.

Borko, H., Davinroy, K. H., Bliem, C. L., & Cumbo, K. B. (2000). Exploring and supporting teacher change: Two third-grade teachers' experiences in a mathematics and literacy staff development project. *The Elementary School Journal, 100,* 273-306.

CEO Forum. (1999). Professional development: A link to better learning. Retrieved November 11, 2002 from http://www.ceoforum.org/reports.cfm?RID=2

Charmaz, K. (2003). Grounded theory: Objectivist and constructivist methods. In N. K. Denzin & Y. S. Lincoln (Eds.), *Strategies of qualitative inquiry* (2nd ed.) (pp. 249-291). Thousand Oaks, CA: Sage.

Coiro, J. L. (2003). Reading comprehension on the Internet: Expanding our understanding of reading comprehension to encompass new literacies. *The Reading Teacher, 56,* 458-464.

Coiro, J. L. (2005). Every teacher a Miss Rumphius: Empowering teachers with effective professional development. In R. A. Karchmer, M. H. Mallette, J. Kara-Soteriou, & D. J. Leu, Jr.(Eds). *Innovative approaches to literacy education: Using the Internet to support new literacies* (pp. 199-219). Newark, DE: International Reading Association.

Encarta World English Dictionary (1999). Microsoft Corporation.

Fawcett, G., & Snyder, S. (1998). Transforming schools through systemic change: New work, new knowledge, new technology. In D. Reinking, M. C. McKenna, L. D. Labbo, & R. D. Kieffer (Eds.), *Handbook of literacy and technology: Transformation in a post-typographic world* (pp. 115-127). Mahwah, NJ: Erlbaum.

Fisher, D., Lapp, D., & Flood, J. (2000). How is technology really used for literacy instruction in elementary and middle-school classrooms? *National Reading Conference Yearbook, 49,* 464-476.

Karchmer, R. A. (2001). The journey ahead: Thirteen teachers report how the Internet influences literacy and literacy instruction in their K-12 classrooms. *Reading Research Quarterly, 36,* 442-466.

Labbo, L. D. (2005). Fundamental qualities of effective literacy instruction: An exploration of worthwhile classroom practices. In R. A. Karchmer, M. H. Mallette, J. Kara-Soteriou, & D. J. Leu, Jr. (Eds). *Innovative approaches to literacy education: Using the Internet to support new literacies* (pp. 165-179). Newark, DE: International Reading Association.

Labbo, L. D., & Reinking, D. (1999). Negotiating the multiple realities of technology in literacy research and instruction. *Reading Research Quarterly, 34,* 478-492.

Leu, D., & Kinzer, C. (2000). The convergence of literacy instruction with networked technologies for information and communication. *Reading Research Quarterly, 35*, 108-127.

Leu, D., Kinzer, C., Coiro, J. & Cammack, D. (2004). Toward a theory of new literacies emerging from the Internet and other ICT. In R. R. Ruddell & N. J. Unrauh (Eds.), *Theoretical models and processes of reading* (5th ed.) (pp. 1570-1613). Newark, DE: International Reading Association.

Leu, D., Mallette, M. H., Karchmer, R. A., & Kara-Soteriou, J. (2005). Contextualizing the new literacies of information and communication technologies in theory, research, and practice. In R. A. Karchmer, M. H. Mallette, J. Kara-Soteriou, & D. J. Leu, Jr.(Eds). *Innovative approaches to literacy education: Using the Internet to support new literacies* (pp. 1-10). Newark, DE: International Reading Association.

McGrail, E. (December, 2004). *Lids up, lids down: Three teachers grapple with laptop technology in the high school English Language Arts classroom.* Paper presented at the meeting of the National Reading Conference, San Antonio, TX.

National Center for Education Statistics (2000). *Teachers' tools for the 21st century: A report on teachers' use of technology.* Washington, DC: U.S. Department of Education.

Richards, J. (2001). "I did not plan ahead": Preservice teachers' concerns integrating print-based lessons with computer technology. *National Reading Conference Yearbook, 50*, 507-518.

Richardson, L. (2000). Writing: A method of inquiry. In N. K. Denzin & Y. S. Lincoln (Eds.), *Handbook of qualitative research* (2nd ed.) (pp. 923-948). Thousand Oaks, CA: Sage.

Senge, P. M. (1990). *The fifth discipline.* New York: Doubleday.

Stake, R. E. (2003). Case studies. In N. K. Denzin & Y. S. Lincoln (Eds.), *Strategies of qualitative inquiry* (2nd ed.) (pp. 134-164). Thousand Oaks, CA: Sage.

Strauss, A. S. (1987). *Qualitative analysis for social scientists.* Cambridge, UK: Cambridge University Press.

U. S. Department of Education (1999). Getting America's students ready for the 21st century: Meeting the technology literacy challenge. Retrieved July 8, 2002, from the World Wide Web: http://www.ed.gov/Technology/Plan/NatTechPlan/

Watts-Taffe, S., Gwinn, C. B., Johnson, J. R., & Horn, M. L. (2003). Preparing preservice teachers to integrate technology into the elementary literacy program. *The Reading Teacher, 57*, 130-138.

Wepner, S. B., & Tao, L. (2002). From master teacher to master novice: Shifting responsibilities in technology-infused classrooms. *The Reading Teacher, 55*, 642-651.

Wolcott, H. F. (1994). *Transforming qualitative data: Description, analysis, and interpretation.* Thousand Oaks, CA: Sage.

Zhao, Y., & Frank, K. A. (2003). Factors affecting technology use in schools: An ecological perspective. *American Educational Research Journal, 40*, 807-840.

AUTHOR NOTES

We thank Karen Jorgensen for her research assistance on this project, as well as William Teale, Ruby Sanny, and the anonymous reviewers for their valuable comments on earlier versions of this manuscript.

54ᵗʰ Annual Meeting of the
National Reading Conference

December 1-4, 2004 • San Antonio, Texas

The 54th annual National Reading Conference was held in San Antonio, Texas from December 1-4, 2004 with a total conference attendance of approximately 1,350 in the newly renovated Crowne Plaza Riverwalk. A record number of proposals were submitted this year (502), with 381 papers, symposia, and round tables accepted. Our area chairs accomplished the first submission and review process that took place completely online. The new online submission and review system, developed by Roy Smith at TEI, worked well.

The San Antonio conference reminded us of the changing nature of our organization: we experienced more international speakers and attendees than ever before; we benefited from greater participation and involvement by graduate students; colleagues presented more rigorous research papers; and we gained new insights from an exceptional methodology series organized by Marla Mallette and Nell Duke. San Antonio was also a reminder of the traditionally supportive community that defines our organization. Everyone helped out, assisting us in various venues—from the Newcomer's Luncheon, hosted by our outgoing Field Council Chair, Joyce Many; to the graduate pizza luncheon with over 250 participants, hosted by our outgoing Chair of the Student Research Award Committee, Josephine Peyton Young; to the Annual Town Meeting, so wonderfully hosted by our colleagues Kelly Chandler-Olcott and Michael McKenna.

The conference began by celebrating the lives of five NRC colleagues who had passed away during the previous year: Ron Carver, Ted Grace, Peter Mosenthal, Steve Stahl, and Dick Venezky. Each of these exceptional colleagues devoted their time and intellect to our organization. They will be missed.

This year, the conference was organized around daily "Conversational Questions of the Day." Wednesday was devoted to "What defines literacy's past and present?" Lea McGee delivered the Presidential Address." The Role of Wisdom in Evidence-based Reading Programs." Gunther Kress also shared his important insights about multi-modal texts in his Distinguished International Scholar Address "Cultural Technologies of Representation and Communication: Reading and Writing in the Era of the New Screens." In the evening, we began an important initiative to reconstitute Vital Issues. P. David Pearson, Deborah R. Dillon, Taffy Raphael, Richard Allington, and Douglas Hartman initiated the conversation, helping us to understand both the past and present in literacy research, before we retired to the lobby for additional conversation.

On Thursday, the question was: "How do we achieve excellence in literacy research?" Michele Knobel and Colin Lankshear delivered a plenary address, "From Pencilvania to Pixelandia: Mapping the terrain of new literacies research." Robert Calfee, University of California, Riverside, delivered the Oscar Causey Address, "Exploring the Mind and Heart of the Reading Teacher." Ilana Snyder, Monash University, Australia delivered a second Distinguished International Scholar Address, "Doing Technoliteracy in Schools: Perspectives from Down Under." In addition, we held our annual Town Meeting, celebrating the true NRC spirit of common commitment and conversation. This Town Meeting prompted important conversation about our name. Nell Duke, along with others, raised a central issue – our name is beginning to seem somewhat distant from the true nature of our research community today. They noted that we are international in our membership, not national; we report research on a range of literacy issues, not simply reading issues; and we are much more of a permanent organization, not simply a one-week conference. Names, though, carry so many important meanings and such important history with them. In the evening, Donna Alvermann, David Reinking, Betty Sturdevant, Diane Schallert, Jo Worthy, Colin Harrison, and Kathleen Hinchman concluded our day with a Vital Issues session. We explored achieving excellence in literacy research.

Friday, the conversational question of the day was: "What will define the future of literacy research?" Peggy McCardle, from NICHD, and Elizabeth Albro, from the Institute for Educational Science, shared federal funding opportunities in reading and literacy with our membership. NRC Colleagues who are helping to frame the National Assessment of Educational Progress presented the session "The National Assessment of Educational Progress Reading Framework for 2009 and Beyond." In addition, the National Early Literacy Panel presented its research review findings and Michele Foster, from Claremont Graduate School, gave the plenary address: "What contemporary policy reveals about educational research and the struggle for education 50 years after Brown." In the evening, our final Vital Issues session was held, led by Michele Knobel, Colin Lankshear, Michele Foster, and Ilana Snyder who explored the future of literacy research.

On Saturday, Annemarie Sullivan Palincsar and Bridget Dalton delivered the NRC Annual Research Address, "Speaking literacy and learning to technology: Speaking technology to literacy and learning." Saturday was also devoted to our Research into Practice Conference for Texas educators. Gay Su Pinnell delivered the keynote address for this conference, "Research as a Foundation for Teaching" and we presented sessions on exceptional classroom practices, derived from research. These were led by Elizabeth Moje, Sharon Vaughn, Sylvia Linan-Thompson, Patricia Mathes, Sharolyn Pollard-Durodola, Elsa Cardenas Hagan, Shelley Xu, Nell K. Duke, Julie Coiro, Elizabeth Schmar-Dobler, Keonya Booker, Marcia Invernizzi, Montanna McCormick, Linda Kucan, and Larry Sipe.

Our distinguished award winners this year included: Peter B. Mosenthal for the Albert J. Kingston Award, Courtney B. Cazden for the Distinguished Scholar for Lifetime Achievement Award, Rebecca Rogers for the Early Achievement Award, Michael L. Kamil, Peter B. Mosenthal, P. David Pearson, and Rebecca Barr for the Edward Fry Book Award, Steven Stahl and Victoria Purcell-Gates for the Oscar Causey Award, and Rebecca Deffes Silverman for the Student Outstanding Research Award.

For more than 50 years, NRC has attracted scholars to a warm location during the first week in December, where we engage in spirited debate, dialogue, and conversation about the research we conduct. We work hard to mentor new members and graduate students into our research community and we provide local literacy educators with a special, one-day conference linking our research with promising instructional practices. Finally, we always manage to have a bit of fun, enjoying the pleasures of seeing friends and colleagues and meeting new ones. Thanks to our Area Chairs, we managed to accomplish this and much, much more. I want to thank them for their exceptional work in helping to put this program together: Margaret Finders, Jamie Meyers, Douglas Fisher, Marla Mallette, Sarah McCarthey, Elizabeth Baker, Rachel Brown, Julia Kara-Soteriou, Fenice Boyd, Zhihui Fang, Dana Grisham, Denise Johnson, Douglas Kaufman, Jeanne Swafford, Mark Dressman, Gay Ivey, Josephine Young, Renee Casbergue, Kelly Chandler-Olcot, Milly Gort, Karla Moller, Majorie Orellana, Wendy Glenn, Laura Smolkin, Bridget Dalton, Rachel Karchmer, Julie Coiro, Margaret Hagood, Catherine Kurkjian, Dana Cammack, and Carol Donovan. Thank you, from all of us!

Donald J. Leu
2004 Program Chair
University of Connecticut

In Memoriam
A toast to Dick, to Ron, to Ted, to Steve, to Peter

To the memories of colleagues
Who blessed our lives with their presence,
Who made us wiser,
Who supported and deepened our commitment to our work,
With their work, their words,
Their lives, and their legacies.

May we remember them
May we remember what they did, what they wrote, what they said,
As we face the challenges, the uncertainties, and the possibilities
Of fostering
A love of literacy among the teachers
Who work with the parents, and students,
Who depend upon schools, and the scholarship that supports our schools
To learn how to read, write, and think.

Thank you, friends, for all you did for us. We shall not forget you.

Written by P. David Pearson (2004)

Ron Carver
University of Missouri, Kansas City

Columbus (Ted) Grace
Syracuse University

Peter B. Mosenthal
Syracuse University

Steven Stahl
University of Illinois, Urbana-Champaign

Richard Venezky
University of Delaware

National Reading Conference Program
54th Annual Meeting

CONVERSATIONAL ISSUE OF THE DAY: *What Defines Literacy's Past and Present?*

Roundtables
Performance and Perspectives: Two Assessments of Federal Prisoners in Literacy Programs, **William R. Muth,** U.S. Federal Bureau of Prisons; *Do teacher's personal reading habits affect their classroom instructional practices?;* **Sharon S. McKool,** Rider University, **Susan D. Sundin,** Baty Elementary, Del Valle Independent School District; *Examining Effective Literacy Practices for ELL's in a Multi-age Urban Classroom,* **Sharon Ulanoff,** California State University, Los Angeles, **Ambika Gopalakrishnen,** California State University, Los Angeles, **Diane Brantley,** California State University, San Bernardino, **Susan Courtney,** LA Unified School District, **Richard Rogers,** LA Unified School District; *Exploring Students' Developing Understandings of Culture,* **Melanie D. Koss,** University of Illinois at Chicago; *Overcoming The Negative Writing Attitudes of Future Writing Teachers In University Methods Courses,* **Chris Street,** California State University, Fullerton; *Immigrant Mexicano Adolescents: Literacy, Discourses, and Hybrid Identities,* **María del Rosario Barillas,** University of Southern California, **Laurie MacGillivray,** University of Southern California; *Third Graders' Aesthetic Response to Multicultural Literature,* **Lauren J. Behar,** Ball State University, **Linda E. Martin,** Ball State University

Roundtables
"I Had Trouble Today": Concerns and Accomplishments of Preservice Teachers in a Laptop Computer Cohort, **Janet C. Richards,** University of South Florida, **Barry Morris,** University of South Florida, **Kim Schwartz,** University of South Florida; *Finding a Book for Eric: A First Grader "Struggles" to Read,* **Amma K. Akrofi,** Texas Tech University; *Literacy Portfolios for High School Seniors In A Non-Academic Track Class: Validation for Everyone;* **Carole Janisch,** Texas Tech University, **Xiaoming Liu,** Texas Tech University; *Shifting and Merging Realities: Examining the Interplay of Teacher and Student Perceptions of Reading Instruction in the Middle Grades,* **Deanna M. Stoube,** St. Ambrose University; *Teachers' Attitudes and Perceptions: The Effects of the I-READ Grant,* **Sherry Kragler,** University of Maryland; *What's the Meaning of All This? Preservice Teachers' Interpretations of Teaching Comprehension,* **Joan Leikam Theurer,** California State University, Long Beach, **Karen A. Onofrey,** Arizona State University West; *Transforming identities and redefining literate understandings with pre-service and in-service teachers,* **Sharon M. Peck,** SUNY Geneseo, **Koomi Kim,** SUNY Geneseo, **Joby Copenhaver,** SUNY Geneseo

Understanding the Role of Metacognition in Literacy Learning
Chair: Susan E. Israel, University of Dayton, **Discussant: Michael Pressley,** Michigan State University; *Metacognitive Literacy Instruction,* **Priscilla L. Griffith,** University of Oklahoma, **Jiening Ruan,** University of Oklahoma; *Metacognition's Contributions to Vocabulary and Comprehension Achievement,* **Cathy Collins Block,** Texas Christian University; *Metacognitive Instructional Strategies,* **Peter Afflerbach,** University of Maryland, **Kevin Meuwissen,** University of Maryland

Technology and the Education of Literacy Teachers: Opportunities and Challenges
Chair & Discussant: Junko Yokota, National-Louis University; *Overview of CTELL (Case Technologies for Enhacing Literacy Learning) and the Symposium,* **Linda D. Labbo,** University of Georgia, **Mary Love,** University of Georgia; *Realities, Complexities, Possibilities: Exploring the Use of the CTELL Cases in Pre-service Literacy Methods Courses,* **Ruby Sanny,** University of Illinois at Chicago, **William H. Teale,** University of Illinois at Chicago; *Panel Discussion: Opportunities and Challenges of Using Web-Based Video Cases in Pre-Service Literacy Courses: Voices of the Instructors,* **Joanne Ratliff,** University of Georgia, **Becky Alexander,** Middle Tennessee State University, **Francine C. Falk-Ross,** Northern Illinois University, **Catherine Kurkjian,** Central Connecticut State University, **Victoria G. Ridgeway,** Clemson University; *Panel Discussion: Opportunities and Challenges Related to Researching the Use of Web-Based Video Cases in Pre-Service Literacy Courses: Voices of the Principal Investigators,* **Linda D. Labbo,** University of Georgia, **Charles**

K. Kinzer, Teachers College, Columbia University, Donald J. Leu, University of Connecticut, William H. Teale, University of Illinois at Chicago

The Illinois Snapshots of Early Literacy: A Family of Standardized Instructionally Focused Early Literacy Assessments
Chair: Camille Blachowicz, National-Louis University, Discussant: Darrell Morris, Appalachian State University; *State policy issues and the initial plan for the ISEL,* Michael Dunn, National-Louis University; *The ISEL: Design, validation and change,* Roberta Buhle, Naperville, Il District 203, Therese Pigott, Loyola University; *"What About Second Grade? The ISEL-2,"* Diane Sullivan, National-Louis University, Therese Pigott, Loyola University; *"Are we done yet?" Responding to state needs and the issue of "completion,"* Camille Blachowicz, National-Louis University

Early Steps to Literacy: The Impact of Professional Development on Preschool Teachers and the Children in Their Classrooms
Chair: Ruth Ann Ball, University of Oklahoma, Discussant: Belinda Biscoe, University of Oklahoma; Susan Kimmel, University of Oklahoma; Loraine Dunn, University of Oklahoma; Sara Ann Beach, University of Oklahoma; *Who are teachers of preschool children of poverty?, What are effects of different literacy professional development interventions on the teachers?, How do the interventions affect the learning of the preschool children?*

Life in the Third Space: Constructing Identities through Story, Culture and Language
Chair & Discussant: Kathy G. Short, University of Arizona, *Exploring the Third Space Created by Children during a Literature Discussion: Young Children's Use of Story as a Meaning Making Device,* Julia Lopez-Robertson, University of Arizona; *Third Space: Families Finding a Voice at Home and at School,* Jeanne Fain, Arizona State University; *Creating a Comfortable Space in the Midst of Critical Conversations: How Students Resist Discussing Issues of Race and Culture,* Janine Schall, University of Arizona

Young Children Read and Write: Critical Lessons in Early Literacy Research
Chair: Prisca Martens, Towson University; *Why Research on Early Literacy,* Yetta Goodman, University of Arizona; *Making Meaning Visible: Sarah Learns to Write,* Prisca Martens, Towson University; *Literacy Capital in Kindergarten: Writing for Profit,* Rick Meyer, University of New Mexico; *The Ideological Force of Cultural Models and Social Practices in Literacy Learning,* Susan Adamson, Indiana University

Learning on the Line: When is Computer-Mediated Instruction a True Educational Experience?
Chairs: Diane L. Schallert, University of Texas, Suzanne E. Wade, University of Utah, Discussant: Janice F. Almasi, University of Kentucky; *What do Prospective Teachers Learn from Participating in Online Discussions?,* Presenters: Suzanne E. Wade, University of Utah, Janice Fauske, University of South Florida; *Aligning preservice teachers and elementary school students in an online book club: A focus on what is learned,* Presenter: Jennifer C. Wilson, University of Texas at Austin; *Online learning or learning on the line: Do students learn anything of value in a CMD?,* Presenters: Diane L. Schallert, University of Texas at Austin, JoyLynn H. Reed, The University of Phoenix Online, Minseong Kim, University of Texas at Austin, Alicia Beth, University of Texas at Austin, Yu-Jung Chen, University of Texas at Austin, Ming-Lung Yang, University of Texas at Austin

We Have Stories to Tell: Spirits, History and Humor in African American Children's Literature
Chair & Discussant: Violet J. Harris, University of Illinois at Urbana-Champaign; *"That's a spirit, not a ghost!" Unexpected responses to an "authentic" cultural depiction embedded within The House of Dies Drear,* Wanda Brooks, University of Maryland at Baltimore County; *"Pictures say so much more than words can": Adolescents respond to The Middle Passage: White Ships/Black Cargo,* Julia Connor, University of Illinois at Urbana-Champaign; *"I May Be Crackin', But Um Fackin'": The Utilization of Humor in The Watsons Go To Birmingham-1963,* Jonda C. McNair, Clemson University

Applying the ABC's Model in Teacher Education Classes Related to Literacy
Chair: **Caitlin McMunn Dooley,** University of Texas at Austin, **Discussant: Patricia Schmidt,** LeMoyne University; *Intercultural learning in online and face-to-face environments: Challenges to application and literacy research,* Claudia Finkbeiner, University of Kassel, Germany; *Relating Culture to Methods for Literacy Instruction,* **Lori Czop Assaf,** Texas State University; *The ELL Pen Pals Program,* **Maria Asplund,** Minnesota State University

Inquiries into Literacy Practices and Research
Chair: Julie L Pennington, University of Nevada, Reno, **Participants:. Julie L Pennington,** University of Nevada, Reno, **Marg Mast,** Goshen College, **Kathryn Prater,** University of Texas, Austin, **Sylvia Thompson,** University of Texas, Austin; *Inquiring Minds: Analysis of Four Pre-Service Teachers' Inquiry Stance; Teacher Inquiry as Research; The Veil of Professionalism: The Hyperpoliteness of White Talk in Research Inquiry*

Sustainable Teacher Research Networks: Researching the Conditions to Support Self-Organizing Professional Development Systems
Chair: **Margaret Hill,** University of Houston, Clear Lake, **Discussant: John Stansell,** University of North Texas; **Participants: Joan Curtis,** Dallas ISD, **Antoinette Duffey,** University of North Texas, **Paula Griffith,** Dickinson ISD, **Mary Harris,** University of North Texas, **Margaret Hill,** University of Houston, Clear Lake, **Jennifer Jackson,** University of North Texas, **Janelle Mathis,** University of North Texas, **Leslie Patterson,** University of North Texas, **Terisa Pearce,** University of North Texas, **Ruth Silva,** University of North Texas, **Liz Stephens,** Texas State University, San Marcos, **Nancy Votteler,** Clear Creek ISD, **Joan Parker Webster,** University of Alaska, Fairbanks, **Carol Wickstrom,** University of North Texas; *Teacher Voices; Researcher Voices: A Reader's Theater; Researching the Conditions to Support Sustainable Teacher Research Networks; Centering Resonance Analysis: A Method for Identifying and Interpreting Networks of Meaning in Text; Data Analysis Groups –Interpreting Networks of Meaning*

Alternatives to the Traditional Reading Clinic
Chair: **Dixie Massey,** North Carolina A & T State University **Discussant: Sam Miller,** University of North Carolina at Greensboro; *"I Know You" - Preservice Teachers Tutoring in an After-School Program,* **Dixie Massey,** North Carolina A & T State University; *Teachers as Tutors: An After-School Tutoring Program for Graduate Students,* **Theresa Deeney,** University of Rhode Island

A Higher Education Partnership to Better Prepare K-12 Literacy Preservice Teachers
Chair: **Deborah R. Dillon,** University of Minnesota, **Discussant: David G. O'Brien,** University of Minnesota, **Participants: Peggy DeLapp,** University of Minnesota, **Deborah R. Dillon,** University of Minnesota, **Mark Vagle,** University of Minnesota, **Lee Galda,** University of Minnesota, **Martha Bigelow,** University of Minnesota, **Joan Hughes,** University of Minnesota, **Richard Beach,** University of Minnesota, **Mary Jacobson,** Augsburg College, **Vicki Olson,** Augsburg College, **Bonnie Fisher,** College of St. Catherine, **Judith-Davidson Jenkins,** St. Cloud State University; *Developing K-12 Literacy Curriculum: Consensus Building on Key Content, Assignments, and Practica Experiences; Using Technologies to Transform vs. Amplify Reflective Activities in K-12 Preservice Literacy; Documenting Changes in University Faculty Members' Teaching Practices and Preservice Teachers' Learning as a Result of a Partnership to Renew Teacher Preparation*

Roundtables
Domain Specificity and Domain Generality of Inservice Teachers' Epistemological Beliefs: Their Role in Instructional Practices in Reading, **Gaoyin Qian,** City University of New York, **Liqing Tao,** City University of New York; *The Effects of Thinking Aloud in Expository Texts on Retelling and Comprehension,* **Lauren Leslie,** Marquette University, **JoAnne Caldwell,** Cardinal Stritch University, **Laura Hochmuth,** Marquette University, **Suzanne Warell,** Marquette University; *Preservice Teachers' Emerging Perspectives on Assessment and Remediation of Struggling Readers,* **Sunita Mayor,** West Chester University; *Story Time*

Literacy: Early Literacy Experiences at a Public Library, **Amy A. Howell,** University of Colorado at Boulder, **Steven R. Guberman,** University of Colorado at Boulder; *Teacher Candidates' Perspectives about Culturally Responsive Teaching,* **Wilma D. Kuhlman,** University of NE at Omaha, **Sarah K. Edwards,** University of NE at Omaha; *Using Transactional Inquiry to Capitalize on Key Events from Accidental Apprenticeships and Purposeful Practice,* **Catherine K. Zeek,** Texas Woman's University, **Carole Walker,** Texas A&M-Commerce

Roundtables

Comprehension in Secondary Content Areas – A Book Study, **Julia Reynolds,** Michigan State University/Aquinas College; *E-Merging Literacy:Assisting Parents to Scaffold the Emerging Literacy Skills of their Preschool Aged Children Through the use of Electronic Storybooks,* **Peggy Coyne,** Center for Applied Special Technologies; *Orality, Literacy, and the Internet: Reading and Learning in a Hypertext Environment,* **Edward H. Behrman,** National University, **Chris Street,** California State University, Fullerton; *Political Influences on Literacy Learning as Reported by Western Ukrainians,* **LaVerne Raine,** Texas A & M University - Commerce, **Alison A. Jones,** Texas A & M University - Commerce, **Wayne M. Linek,** Texas A & M University - Commerce; *Predicting Reading Comprehension Through Macro and Micro Analyses of Oral Story Retellings,* **Valerie J. Robnolt,** Virginia Commonwealth University; *Code switching and communities of practice for a multilingual adult,* **Dora F. Edu-Buandoh,** The University of Iowa

"Blogging the Way: Exploring New Literacies and New Media in Weblog"

Chair: Dana W. Cammack, Teachers College, Columbia University, **Discussant: Charles K. Kinzer,** Teachers College, Columbia University; *What in the world is a weblog? A feature analysis of weblogs and static websites,* **Sarah Lohnes,** Teachers College, Columbia University; *To blog is to be: And that is the question. An analysis of positioning and identity work in New York weblogs,* **Dana W. Cammack,** Teachers College, Columbia University; *The Sunnydale Sock Puppet Theatre Presents: Internet Literacies Take On Television Literacies,* **Gillian Andrews,** Teachers College, Columbia University

Teaching Children to Become Fluent Readers – Year 3

Chair: Melanie R. Kuhn, Rutgers, the State University of New Jersey, **Discussant: P. David Pearson,** University of California at Berkeley; *The ins and outs of fluency instruction: An observational study,* **Melanie R. Kuhn,** Rutgers, the State University of New Jersey, **Deborah Woo,** Rutgers, the State University of New Jersey, **Claire H. Smith,** University of Georgia, **Sunday Cummins,** University of Illinois, Urbana-Champaign, **Allison Friedman,** Rutgers, the State University of New Jersey; *Scaling-up: A pilot study Implications for practice,* **Lesley M. Morrow,** Rutgers, the State University of New Jersey, **Paula Schwanenflugel,** University of Georgia, **Franklin Turner,** Rutgers, the State University of New Jersey, **Rebecca Gara,** Rutgers, the State University of New Jersey; *Changes in Practice,* **Kay Stahl,** University of Illinois, Urbana-Champaign, **Bonnie Armbruster,** University of Illinois, Urbana-Champaign, **Julia Connor,** University of Illinois, Urbana-Champaign, **Steven A. Stahl,** University of Illinois, Urbana-Champaign (in memoriam); *A Tutoring Program for Children Receiving Fluency Oriented Instruction,* **Robin Morris,** Georgia State University, **Eileen Cohen,** Georgia State University, **Carolyn Groff,** Rutgers, the State University of New Jersey; *Word callers and teachers' perception of fluency and comprehension,* **Beth Meisinger,** University of Georgia, **Justin Miller,** University of Georgia

Digital Sources of Information and Students' Engagement With Academic Content

Chair: David Reinking, Clemson University, **Discussant: Donald J. Leu,** University of Connecticut; *College Students' Use of and Attributions to Online and Offline Sources of Information,* **David Reinking,** Clemson University, **Brenda Bennett,** Clemson University; *The Effects of Online Note Taking Among High-and Low-Achieving Students,* **Brent Igo,** Clemson University; *A Case Study of Literacy When Elementary School Students Collaborate to Create Web Pages in Science,* **Rewa Williams,** Clemson University

Young Children Read and Write: Critical Lessons in Early Literacy Research

Chair: Prisca Martens, Towson University, *An Analysis of the Text Characteristics of Four Trade Books, An*

Analysis of the Text Characteristics, Miscue Patterns, and Retellings Related to Four Trade Books, The Influence of Text Characteristics on Children's Readings of Authentic Literature, **Poonam Arya,** Towson University, **Lijun Jin,** Towson University, **Debora Lang,** Towson University, **Prisca Martens,** Towson University, **Pat Wilson,** University of South Florida

"This Isn't What We Normally Do," Or Is It?: Teaching Cases in Elementary Writing Instruction
Chair: Jenifer Jasinski Schneider, University of South Florida, Discussant: Marilyn Chapman University of British Columbia; *Myrmidon Fringe,* Steve Hart, University of South Florida, Vanessa Minick, University of South Florida; *Following the Child?,* Kim Shea, University of South Florida, Mary Huffstetter, University of South Florida, Marilyn Chapman, University of British Columbia; *Plop, Plop, Fizz,* Kim Schwartz, University of South Florida, Maura Santiago, University of South Florida, Susan Torpey, University of South Florida; *Sparked Imagination or Controlled Burning,* Mary Virginia Knowles, University of South Florida, Melinda Adams, University of South Florida

Legacy and Potential in K – 12 Literacy Development Research: Visceral, Personal, and Sociocultural Perspectives
Chair: George G. Hruby, Utah State University, Discussant: Jerry Harste, Indiana University, Bloomington; *Sociocultural Perspectives: Contributions Toward a Theory of Literacy Development,* Patricia L. Anders, The University of Arizona; *Implications of Developmental Models of Self for Emergent and Early Literacy,* Judith Lysaker, Butler University; *Transactional Dynamics in the Development of Language and Social Identity,* George G. Hruby, Utah State University

Shifting Roles and Identities of Literacy Specialists: Looking Inside Multiple Contexts Within a Large Federally Funded Project
Chair: Frank Serafini, University of Nevada Las Vegas, Discussant: Cathy Roller, Director of Research and Policy, International Reading Association; *The Emerging Role of the Literacy Specialist,* Frank Serafini, University of Nevada Las Vegas; *Developing and facilitating writing: Context and community matter,* Marilyn McKinney, University of Nevada Las Vegas, Cyndi Giorgis, University of Nevada Las Vegas; *Looking closely at one school: Literacy Specialists helping teachers teach writing through the writing traits,* Joann Ortiz, Martinez Elementary School, North Las Vegas

Navigating Technology and Professional Development
Chair: Susan Watts-Taffe, University of Minnesota, Discussants: William H. Teale, University of Illinois at Chicago, Ruby Sanny, University of Illinois at Chicago; *Viewing Professional Development through the Lens of Technology Integration: How do Beginning Teachers Navigate the Use of Technology and New Literacies?,* Susan Watts-Taffe, University of Minnesota, Carolyn B. Gwinn, University of Minnesota; *'Just Talk Among Yourselves': Professional Development Through Listserv Participation,* Rachel Brown, Syracuse University, Wendy Bunker, Syracuse University; *Lids up, lids down: Three teachers grapple with laptop technology in the high school English Language Arts classroom,* Ewa McGrail, Georgia State University, Atlanta

Using Digital Tools to Foster Teacher Professional Development and Reflection
Chair: David G. O'Brien, University of Minnesota, *Professional E-portfolios: Digital Tools and the New Media Literacies that Transform Teacher Reflection,* David G. O'Brien, University of Minnesota; *Teacher Development in Online Communities of Practice: Using Tappedin.org to Foster Reflection in a Graduate Media Studies Course,* Richard Beach, University of Minnesota; *Inservice Teachers' Social Interaction and Learning Through Mediated Chat Room Exchanges,* Tom Reinartz, University of Minnesota

Adolescents' Motivation to Read
Chair: Victoria G. Ridgeway, Clemson University, SC, Discussant: Linda Gambrell, Clemson University, SC; *Introduction and Welcome: Results of Motivation to Read Profile survey data analysis,* Chair: Victoria G. Ridgeway, Clemson University, SC; *Concurrent Sessions: What Adolescents Shared in the Conversational Interview,* Group A: Early Adolescents, ages 11-13, Elizabeth Sturtevant, George Mason

University, VA, **Merry Boggs,** Tarleton State University, TX, **Krishna Seunarinesingh,** University of the West Indies, St. Augustine, Trinidad & Tobago; *Group B: Middle Adolescents, ages 12-15,* **Victoria G. Ridgeway,** Clemson University, SC, **Pamela Dunston,** Clemson University, SC, **Nancy T. Walker,** University of LaVerne, CA, **Sharon M. Pitcher,** Towson University, MD; *Group C: Late Adolescents, ages 16-18,* **Carol Delaney,** Southern Illinois University, IL, **Lettie K. Albright,** Texas Woman's University, TX, **Kathy N. Headley,** Clemson University, SC; *Whole group share – designated reporters from each group*

Research Methodology Series: Experimental and Correlational Methodologies
Chairs: **Jill Castek,** University of Connecticut, **Ruby Sanny,** University of Illinois at Chicago, **Shenglan Zhang,** Michigan State University; *Experimental Methodologies in Literacy Research,* **Jonna Kulikowich,** Penn State University; *Correlational Methodologies in Literacy Research,* **Anne Cunningham,** University of California, Berkeley; *Using Structural Equation Modeling in Literacy Research,* **Richard Lomax,** University of Alabama

Critical Aspects of Reading: A Two Part Symposium
Part 1: Critical reading: Strategy, text and instruction; Chair: Peter Afflerbach, University of Maryland, **Discussant Part 1: P. David Pearson,** University of California, Berkeley; *How are 4th grade readers critical readers of history?,* **Peter Afflerbach,** University of Maryland,**Bruce VanSledright,** University of Maryland; *High school students reading civic texts designed to inform, argue, or explain: How does text design affect critical reading?,* **Marilyn Chambliss,** University of Maryland; *Informational text in the elementary school classroom: Crossing borders between critical reading and information literacy,* **Mariam Jean Dreher,** University of Maryland, **Sharon B. Kletzien,** West Chester University, **Heather Ruetschlin,** University of Maryland

Reading First: Research Issues in Policy and Implementation
Chair: **Haley Woodside-Jiron,** University of Vermont, **Discussant: Lea M. McGee,** University of Alabama; *Reading First: Complex Schools, Complex Policy Implementation,* **Haley Woodside-Jiron,** University of Vermont; *Reading First: Hidden Messages, Omissions, and Contradictions,* **Karen S. Evans,** Marquette University, **Nancy T. Walker,** University of La Verne; *Role of the Local Campus Coach in Reading First Schools During Year One Implementation,* **Doug Hamman,** Texas Tech University, **Arturo Olivarez,** Jr., Texas Tech University, **Julee Becker,** Lubbock Independent School District

Research on Initial Literacy Learners
Chair: **Mary Lou Morton,** University of South Florida, **Discussant: Michael Coyne,** University of Connecticut; *Non-Ability Grouping for Reading: Successes in an Urban First Grade Classroom,* **Mary Lou Morton,** University of South Florida; *I can't be promoted if I don't read at grade level: One principal's response to her state gateway promotion mandates,* **Sam Miller,** University of North Carolina at Greensboro; *"Read that one again:" The relationship between miscues, tutor responses, and immediate outcomes in adult literacy one-to-one tutoring contexts,* **Alisa Belzer,** Rutgers University

Research on Reading Fluency and Comprehension
Chair: **James Flood,** San Diego State University, *The Effects of the Neurological Impress Method on Third to Sixth Graders' Fluency and Comprehension,* **James Flood,** San Diego State University, **Diane Lapp,** San Diego State University, **Douglas Fisher,** San Diego State University, **Sharon Flood,** San Diego State University, **DiAnn Albert,** San Diego State University; *Developing Reading Fluency in the Middle School,* Peter Dewitz, Capital School District, **Kathleen L. Sullivan,** Omaha Public Schools, **Amy Tunning,** Omaha Public School; *The influence of text characteristics on the reading behaviors of first graders: Results of a longitudinal study,* **Heidi Mesmer,** Oklahoma State University

Reading Clinic/Literacy Lab to Classroom: Assessment of Learning and Evaluation of Professional Development
Chair: **Barbara Laster,** Towson University, **Discussant: Penny Freppon,** University of Cincinnati; *Literacy Lab via Distance Education: Linking Teacher Self-Evaluation, Reflection, and Instructional Goal*

Setting, **Jeanne Cobb,** University of Eastern New Mexico; *Making the Case for Multiple Assessments: Transfer from the Literacy Lab to the School Contexts,* **Cheryl Dozier,** University at Albany, **Ilene Rutten,** University at Albany; *Vocabulary Assessments in Reading Clinic and Beyond,* **Stephanie McAndrews,** Southern Illinois University Edwardsville, **Barbara Laster,** Towson University; *Application of Clinic-based Assessment Practices to Classrooms and Schools,* **Theresa Deeney,** University of Rhode Island; *Fourth Grade Teachers in a High Stakes Testing Environment,* **Lori Berman Wolf,** Adelphi University; *Analyzing Assessments in Classroom and Clinics,* **Barbara J. Walker,** Oklahoma State University; *Are Reading Clinics Preparing a Leadership Corp?,* **Margaret Hill,** University of Houston-Clear Lake, **Charlene Carter,** University of Houston-Clear Lake, **Lillian McEnery,** University of Houston-Clear Lake

Can They Teach Writing?: Preservice Teachers Learn to Teach and Assess Writing

Chair: Roger Bruning, University of Nebraska-Lincoln; *An Online Tool for Helping Literacy Teachers Learn to Rate Student Writing,* **Roger Bruning,** University of Nebraska-Lincoln, **Michael Dempsey,** University of Nebraska-Lincoln, **Lisa Pytlik Zillig,** University of Nebraska-Lincoln, **Mary Bodvarsson,** University of Nebraska-Lincoln; *Connecting Theory and Practice through Creative Writing: Multigenre Writing in the English Methods Class,* **Leslie S. Rush,** University of Wyoming; *Effective Methods for Teaching Preservice Teachers Writing,* **Susan A. Colby,** Appalachian State University, **Joy Stapleton,** East Carolina University

On Learning to Teach and Assess Reading

Chair: Dixie D. Massey, North Carolina A & T State University, **Discussant: Cathy Collins Block,** Texas Christian University; *Scaffolding Comprehension Instruction for Preservice Teachers: Tutoring in an After School,* **Dixie D. Massey,** North Carolina A & T State University; *The Effectiveness of Comprehension Strategy Instruction Training in Pre-service Teacher Education: A Research-in-Progress Report,* **Mary Kropiewnicki,** Wilkes University; *Improving Preservice Teachers' Ability to Determine Significant Miscues When Using an Informal Reading Inventory,* **Susan K. L'Allier,** Northern Illinois University, **Jerry L. Johns,** Northern Illinois University

Mentoring the Development of Literacy Researchers-Teacher Educators

Chair: Mona Matthews, Georgia State University, **Discussant: Joyce Many,** Georgia State University; *Mentoring within the Doctoral Program,* **Donna Taylor,** Georgia State University, **Mark Cobb,** Georgia State University, **Gwen Stanley,** Georgia State University; *Mentoring in the First Years of the Academy,* **Faith Wallace,** Kennesaw State University, **Ewa McGrail,** Georgia State University; *Mentoring in the Lives of Culturally Diverse Scholars,* **Gertrude Tinker Sachs,** Georgia State University, **Yan Wang,** Georgia State University; *After Tenure and Promotion - Re-examining our Needs,* **Dana Fox,** Georgia State University, **Joyce Many,** Georgia State University, **Mona Matthews,** Georgia State University

Teacher Talk to Support Professional Development

Chair: Judy M. Stephenson, Georgia State University, **Discussant: MaryEllen Vogt,** California State University, Long Beach; *Dialogue Dance: Teacher Talk in a Book Club used for Professional Development,* **Judy M. Stephenson,** Georgia State University; *Two Teachers Talking, Transcribing, and Thinking about Discussion and Comprehension,* **Linda Lucan,** Appalachian State; *Critical Conversations in a Teacher Study Group,* **Jean Ketter,** Grinnell College, **Cynthia Lewis,** University of Iowa

Studying Teachers' Beliefs and Decisions about Literacy Materials and Instruction

Chair: Cindi Davis Harris, San Diego State University, **Discussant: James Hoffman,** University of Texas; *Examining Teacher's Beliefs and Pedagogical Knowledge About Teaching Students To Write A Research Paper,* **Cindi Davis Harris,** San Diego State University; *Commercial literacy packages: School response to selection, use and evaluation in classroom contexts,* **Judy M Parr,** The University of Auckland, **Kathryn J Glasswell,** The University of Illinois at Chicago, **Margaret Aikman,** Auckland College of Education

Examining Critical Literacies within Teacher Education: Tensions, Possibilities, and Directions
Chair: Rosary V. Lalik, Virginia Tech; *Theoretical Framework,* Rosary V. Lalik, Virginia Tech; *Questioning Texts of Our Lives; Stepping into Critical Literacies through Exploration of Cultural Identity; Problematics of Problem-Based Teaching: Position, Epistemology, and Context;* Participants: Rosary V. Lalik, Virginia Tech, Ann Potts, Virginia Tech, Sandra J. Moore, Radford University, Kathleen Hinchman, Syracuse University, Josephine Young, Arizona State University

Roundtables
Assessing and Supporting Kindergarten Oral Language Development, Janet R. Young, Brigham Young University, Val Roberts, San Juan School District, Kendra Hall, Brigham Young University; *Connecting Teacher Beliefs and Practices in the Literacy Clinic and the Classroom,* Cassie Zippay, Western Kentucky University, Brittany Butler, Western Kentucky University; *Disrupting the Commonplace: Critical Literacy in First Grade;* Christine H. Leland, Indiana University, Kimberly Huber, North Salem Elementary School; *Giving Voice the Literacy Practices of Urban Third Graders,* Kim Boothroyd, University of New Hampshire; *If the kindergarten intervention was successful, why are they failing in first grade?,* Marla H. Mallette, Southern Illinois University Carbondale

Roundtables
Learning From Text: Instructional Significance for Under-represented First Grade Students in a University-Based Tutorial Program, Diane Brantley, California State University, San Bernardino, M. Alayne Sullivan, California State University, San Bernardino, Mary Jo Skillings, California State University, San Bernardino, Steve Comadena, California State University, San Bernardino; *Observations and Conversations: Constructing a theory of early readers and nonfiction texts,* Norrie Eure, Texas Woman's University; *Providing Third Space for Verifying Voice: Teachers as Writers and Inquirers,* Janelle Mathis, University of North Texas, Carol Wickstrom, University of North Texas, Leslie Patterson, University of North Texas; *To integrate or not to integrate: content area reading and secondary methods courses,* Nancy L. Michelson, Salisbury University, Monique C. Lynch, Salisbury University, Joel T. Jenne, Salisbury University, Starlin D. Weaver, Salisbury University, Arlene F. White, Salisbury University; *Understanding the Experiences and Needs of Mainstream Teachers of ESL Students,* Yan Wang, Georgia State University, Joyce Many, Georgia State University, Larry Krumenaker, Crosskeys High School; *High Achieving Readers in a Low Performing School,* Keli Garas, University at Buffalo; *Increasing skill and will in science writing,* Kathleen M. Wilson, University of Nebraska, Lincoln, Guy Trainin, University of Nebraska, Lincoln, Mimi Wickless, Folsom Children's Zoo and Botanical Gardens, David Brooks, University of Nebraska, Lincoln; *Instructional Actions of Exemplary Grades 2 and 5 Teachers Who Mediate Strategic Reading Behavior in Guided Reading,* Janine L. Batzle, University of Southern California, Robert Rueda, University of Southern California

Critical Aspects of Critical Reading Double Session
Part 2 Critical reading: Issues of race, ethnicity, sexuality and gender; Chair: Peter Afflerbach, University of Maryland, Discussant: Elizabeth Birr Moje, University of Michigan; *Reading girlhoods: Feminist poststructural literary theory as critical literacy practice,* Elizabeth Marshall, University of Maryland; *Critical text and teacher professional development,* Alfred Tatum, University of Maryland; *Becoming critical readers of the word and the world: Portraits of two European American elementary teachers in multicultural classrooms,* Jennifer Dandridge Turner, University of Maryland

The International Reading Association's Teacher Education Task Force: Supporting Teacher Preparation for Reading Instruction - Co-sponsored Session with IRA
Chair: Cathy Roller, International Reading Association, Participants and Teacher Education Task Force Members: Victoria Risko, Vanderbilt University, Patricia L. Anders, University of Arizona, Charline J. Barnes, Adelphi University, Rita M. L. Bean, University of Pittsburgh, Cathy Collins Block, Texas Christian University, Carrice Cummins, Louisana Tech Univesity, James Flood, San Diego State University, Lesley Mandel Morrow, Rutgers University, Timothy V. Rasinki, Kent State University,

MaryEllen Vogt, California State University, Long Beach, **Cathy Roller (ex officio),** International Reading Association

Current Perspectives on Literacy Development and Instructional Practices in International Contexts
Chair & Discussant: Colin Harrison, University of Nottingham; *Literacy Practices and Teacher Perspectives on Literacy Learning in Malawi,* **Mary Alice Barksdale,** Virginia Tech, **Denis Khasu,** Domasi College, Malawi; *Reading Instruction in China: A Case Study,* Jiening Ruan, University of Oklahoma, **Lijun Jin,** Towson University; *Literacy Learning in the Chinese Primary Grades,* **Nancy Pine,** Mount St. Mary's College; *Working with Burmese Indigenous Preservice Teachers on the Northern Burmese/ Thai Border,* **Janet C. Richards,** University of South Florida; *Reader Response in South African Classrooms,* **Misty Sailors,** University of Texas at San Antonio

Family and School as Contexts for Literacy Sponsorship
Chair: Carolyn Colvin, The University of Iowa; *Creating the "Ideal Reader,"* **Mark Reimer,** The University of Iowa; *"We would read and pretend to be intellectuals": Literacy Practices as Enactments of Identity,* **Michelle Holschuh Simmons,** The University of Iowa; *When school is not your sponsor: Responding to Limiting Literacy Contexts,* **Heidi Tafolla,** The University of Iowa; *Seeing Themselves as Literate: One Family's Intersecting Literacy Sponsors,* **Sheila Benson,** The University of Iowa

Teaching Comprehension Strategies in the Primary Grades: One Teacher's Journey
Chair & Discussant: MaryEllen Vogt, California State University, Long Beach; **Participants: Leslie Fisher,** Roxbury School District, Roxbury, NJ, **Glenn DeVoogd,** California State University, Fresco, **Maureen McLaughlin,** East Stroudsbury State University of PA; *Review of Current Research on Reading Comprehension; Teaching Reading Comprehension Strategies in the Primary Grades: One Teacher's Experiences; Examination of Teacher and Student Artifacts; Small Group Demonstrations of Teaching Reading Comprehension Strategies*

Research on Using Technology-based Approaches to Develop Effective Literacy Teachers
Chair: Mary Sheard, University of Nottingham, **Discussant: Erica Boling,** Rutgers University
The Affordances of Multimedia Storytelling and Social Science Writing: Undergraduates and Youth Creating Reciprocal Relationships, **Paige D. Ware,** Southern Methodist University, **Jessica C Zacher,** University of California, Berkeley; *A New Approach to Video-Case-Based Professional Development in Reading Comprehension Instruction Using Reciprocal Teaching: Developing Complex Understanding and Adaptive Flexibility with EASE Learning Environments,* **Annemarie Sullivan Palincsar,** University of Michigan, **Rand J. Spiro,** Michigan State University, **Shirley J. Magnusson,** University of Michigan, **Brian Collins,** Michigan State University, **Susanna Hapgood,** University of Michigan, **Aparna Ramchandran,** Michigan State University, **Nick Sheltrown,** Michigan State University; *Extending Learning Through Electronic Discourse,* **JoAnne Vazzano,** Oakland University

Becoming a Teacher: Negotiating New Identies
Chair: Cynthia A. Lassonde, State University of New York at Oneonta; *When I'M a Teacher…: Creating Teacher Identities Through Inquiry Groups,* **Cynthia A. Lassonde,** State University of New York at Oneonta, **Amy Muratore,** State University of New York at Oneonta, **Chelsey Smith,** State University of New York at Oneonta, **Glenda Vatovec,** State University of New York at Oneonta; *Teacher Identity on the Boundaries,* **Jean Ketter,** Grinnell College, **Kara L. Lycke,** Grinnell College, **Erin Stutelberg,** Grinnell College; *Preservice Teachers and New Literacies: Interning Pedagogical Possibilities in Teacher Education,* **Jory Brass,** Michigan State University

Methods and Issues in Current Genre Research
Chair: Charles A. Elster, Purdue University; *Four Principles for Measuring the Ability to Read and Write Particular Genres of Text,* **Victoria Purcell-Gates,** University of British Columbia, **Nell K. Duke,** Michigan State University; *Using Thematic Analysis to Assess Children's Knowledge of School-Based Genres,* **Zhihui Fang,** University of South Florida; *High School Students' Use of Genres to Mediate Dialogic Tensions in Lived & Text*

Worlds, **Richard Beach,** University of Minnesota; *Assessing the Development of Genre Knowledge in Preschool & Elementary Children,* **Charles A. Elster,** Purdue University

Reading Visual Text: What Literacy Researchers Can Learn from Reality TV
Chair: **Joanne Ratliff,** University of Georgia, **Discussant: George G. Hruby,** Utah State University; *Five Professors of Reading Teacher Education "Read" Joe Millionaire I and II,* **Donna Alvermann,** University of Georgia; *Results, Conclusions and Implications from Viewing Joe Millionaire I,* **Stephen Phelps,** Buffalo State College, **Josephine Young,** Arizona State University; *Cross Cultural Perspectives and Implications from "Reading" Joe Millionaire II,* **Linda D. Labbo,** University of Georgia, **Joanne Ratliff,** University of Georgia, **Kristiina Montero,** University of Georgia, **Hellen Inyega,** University of Georgia, **Hristina Keranova,** University of Georgia

Learning to Tutor: Preservice Teachers, Cooperating Teachers and Teacher Educators
Chair: **Dixie D. Massey,** North Carolina A & T State University, **Discussant: Deborah R. Dillon,** University of Minnesota; *When Teacher Educators Tutor: Influences on Preservice Teachers and Beyond,* **Dixie D. Massey,** North Carolina A & T State University, **Anthony Graham,** North Carolina A & T State University; *Partners in Practice: Reflective Partnerships in Literacy Education,* **Amy Seely Flint,** Georgia State University, **Katie Van Sluys,** DePaul University; *Moving Beyond the Literal Level: Facilitating Preservice Teachers' Ability to Reflect Critically on Their Tutoring of Struggling Readers,* **Kathy Ganske,** Rowan University

Frameworks for Facilitating Teacher Change
Chair: **Diane C. Nielsen,** University of Kansas, **Discussant: Dana Grisham,** San Diego State University; *Bringing the Knowledge of the Intervention Teacher To The Classroom Teacher: Effect on Student Achievement In An Urban District,* **Diane C. Nielsen,** University of Kansas, **Laurie Leiker Winter,** University of Kansas; *CIMS (Confidence, Independence, Metacognition, Stamina): A Literacy Framework for Effective Literacy Instruction,* **Karen F. Thomas,** Western Michigan University, **Lauren Freedman,** Western Michigan University, **Holly Johnson,** Texas Tech University; *A Comparison of Two Professional Development Models for Facilitating Teacher and Student Change,* **Latisha Hayes,** University of Virginia, **Valerie J. Robnolt,** Virginia Commonwealth University, **Jennifer Jones,** Radford University

Bridging Instruction in Literacy and Technology: Applications for New Literacies in Instructional Settings
Chair: **Denise Johnson,** William and Mary College, **Discussant: Bridget Dalton,** Center for Applied Special Technologies; *Exploring Teachers' Perceptions of Their Role in Preparing Students to Read Informational Text on the Internet,* **Beth Schmar-Dobler,** Emporia State University; *Information search strategies on the Internet,* **Laurie A. Henry,** University of Connecticut; *E-mail communication: Composing and comprehending as new literacy constructions,* **Jill Castek,** University of Connecticut; *Developing an assessment instrument for measuring reading comprehension on the Internet,* **Julie Coiro,** University of Connecticut; *Defining the digital divide and its impact on new literacies instruction,* **Clarisse Lima,** University of Connecticut

Special Methodology Series: Ethnography and Case Study Methodologies
Chairs: **Crystal Caffey,** Southern Illinois University Carbondale, **Dana W. Cammack,** Teachers College, **Jon Callow,** University of Western Sydney; *Qualitative Inquiry: Philosophical Foundations and Disciplinary Histories,* **George Kamberelis,** University at Albany, State University of New York, **Greg Dimitriadis,** University at Buffalo, State University of New York; *Ethnography and Case Study in Literacy Research,* **Diane Barone,** University of Nevada, Reno; *Using Digital Data in Literacy Research,* **Savilla Banister,** Bowling Green State University

Presidential Address
Chair: **Victoria Purcell-Gates,** University of British Columbia; *In Memoriam,* **Donald J. Leu,** University

of Connecticut; *Student Research Award Presentation*, **Josephine Peyton Young**, Arizona State University; *Introduction of the Speaker*, **Lee Gunderson**, University of British Columbia; *Presidential Address: The Role of Wisdom in Evidence-based Reading Programs*, **Lea M. McGee**, University of Alabama

Opening Night/Presidents' Reception
Master of Ceremonies: Lee Gunderson, University of British Columbia

Vital Issues: Panel and Audience Conversation Around the Issue of the Day: What Defines Literacy's Past and Present?
Chair: Donald J. Leu, University of Connecticut; **Discussion Panel: P. David Pearson**, University of California, Berkeley, **Deborah R. Dillon**, University of Minnesota. **Taffy Raphael**, University of Illinois, Chicago, **Richard Allington**, University of Florida, **Douglas Hartman**, University of Connecticut; *1. How has literacy been defined from various perspectives in the past? What reminders and connections do we see in today's research presentations?; 2. How well have we succeeded in answering central questions over the years? Is there forward movement or do we just shift location on the pendulum? Which questions have been marginalized?; 3. Are the definitions of literacy changing today? If so, how?; 4. How might we better respond to the questions that are most important for today ... and tomorrow?*

THURSDAY • DECEMBER 2, 2004
CONVERSATIONAL ISSUE OF THE DAY: *How Do We Achieve Excellence in Literacy Research?*

Roundtables
A tale of ten cities: The NAEP Trial Urban District Assessment, student exclusion rates and the (mis-) representation of 4th grade reading achievement; **Peter Afflerbach**, University of Maryland; *Comprehension strategy use during peer-led discussions of text: Ninth graders tackle The Lottery,* **Kathleen F. Clark**, Oakland University, **Jennifer I. Berne**, University of Illinois, Chicago; *Adult ESL Oral Reading Fluency and Silent Reading Comprehension,* **Kristin Lems**, National-Louis University; *Preschool literacy screening: Longitudinal predictors of early literacy achievement beyond alphabet knowledge and initial phoneme awareness,* **Minwha Yang**, University of Virginia, **Montana McCormick**, University of Virginia, **Karly Gellar**, University of Virginia, **Keonya Booker**, University of Virginia; *Prevalent Content Vocabulary Strategies and What Secondary Preservice Teachers Think About Them,* **Wanda B. Hedrick**, University of North Florida, **Janis M. Harmon**, University of Texas at San Antonio, **Karen D. Wood**, University of North Carolina at Charlotte; *School-College Collaboration in the Wireless Teacher-Education Classroom: Long-Term Effects for Student-Teacher Interns,* **Marion H. Fey**, SUNY Geneseo

Roundtables
"I'm Prepared for Anything Now": Student Teachers' and Cooperting Teachers' Perceptions of Developing Knowledge about Teaching Reading, **Mellinee Lesley**, Texas Tech University, **Doug Hamman**, Texas Tech University, **Arturo Olivarez**, Texas Tech University; *A Bilingual Child's Journey to Independent Biliteracy,* **Karen A. Jorgensen**, University of Minnesota; *One Size Does Not Fit All: Orthographic Development in Adolescents Who Struggle with School-based Literacies,* **Gwynne Ellen Ash**, Texas State University, San Marcos, **Deborah Knight**, University of Delaware; *"So it's not literacy...it's reading and writing": Diverging definitions of "literacy" among members of a teacher inquiry group,* **Amy Lassiter Ardell**, University of Southern California, **Margaret Curwen**, University of Southern California

International Symposium on the Assessment and Evaluation of Literacy Achievement
Chair: Gerry Duffy, University of North Carolina at Greensboro; *Investigating the role of awareness and multi-perspectives in content and language integrated literacy education across Europe; A national intervention programme to raise reading standards in under-achieving children in England; The e-China Project and the Teaching of Reading in English as a Foreign Language;* **Participants: Claudia Finkbeiner**, University of Kassel, Germany, **Roger Beard**, Leeds, UK, **Ian McGrath**, School of Education, University of

Nottingham, **Barbara Sinclair,** School of Education, University of Nottingham, **Colin Harrison,** School of Education, University of Nottingham

Special Invited Session
Chair: Michael McKenna, Georgia Southern University; *Multiple Visions of Multimedia Literacy: The Dynamics of an Emerging Field,* **Renee Hobbs,** Temple University

From the Margins to the Mainstream: Literacy Practices In and Out of School
Chair & Discussant: Kelly Chandler-Olcott, Syracuse University; *Making it to the Mainstream: Current and Former Students reflect on Adolescence, Schooling, and Real-World Literacy,* **Susan Hynds,** Syracuse University; *Culturally Conscious Hip-Hop and Spoken-Word Poetry: Attempting to Make Culturally Relevant Pedagogy Real for Urban Youth,* **Columbus (Ted) Grace,** Syracuse University,* Dr. Grace's work will be presented by **Fenice B. Boyd,** University of Buffalo; *"Reading 'Cause I Want To":Negotiating Adult Literacy Practices in Adolescence through Community Book Clubs,* **Deborah Appleman,** Carleton College, Northfield, MN

Findings From Across Five Urban Sites: New Insights Into the Reading Process
Chair: Barbara Laster, Towson University, **Discussant: Bess Altwerger,** Towson University; *The intersection of words and comprehension: What the miscues and retellings of second graders in four different reading programs tell us;* **Poonam Arya,** University of South Florida, **Prisca Martens,** University of South Florida, **G. Pat Wilson,** University of South Florida; *What is the significance of fluency? How does fluency correlate with miscues (including meaning construction), retellings, instructional model, specific texts, and oral language fluency?,* **Nancy Shelton,** Towson University, **Nancy Jordan,** Towson University, **Bess Altwerger,** Towson University; *Snapshots of the long-term effects of early literacy instruction: Ethnographic observations of 5th graders who were part of the 2nd grade study,* **Steve Mogge,** Towson University, **Shelly Huggins,** Towson University, **Deb Lang,** Towson University; *Conceptions and misconceptions of good reading: Metacognitive interviews at 2nd Grade and 5th Grade,* **Nancy Wiltz,** Towson University, **Barbara Laster,** Towson University

Research on Families and Literacy
Chair: Renée Rubin, University of Texas at Brownsville, **Discussant: Marla H. Mallette,** Southern Illinois University; *Lessons Learned: Involving Latino Families in their Children's School Literacy Development,* **Renée Rubin,** University of Texas at Brownsville, **Michelle Abrego,** University of Texas at Brownsville, **John Sutterby,** University of Texas at Brownsville; *Empowering Parents through Engagement in their Young Children's Literacy Development: Understanding what works in Family Literacy Programs, K-3,* **Deborah J. Romero,** University Nevada Las Vegas & Universidad Autónoma de Querétaro, México; *A Study of Latino parents' Hopes for Their Children's Educational Future: Messages of Perseverance, Self-Confidence and the Importance of Character,* **David B. Yaden, Jr.,** University of Southern California, **Enjolie Lafaurie,** University of Southern California

Young Children's Development of Literary Understanding in Varying Text Forms
Chair: Lawrence Sipe, University of Pennsylvania, **Discussant: Yetta Goodman,** University of Arizona; *Children's Responses to Hybrid Texts,* **Charles A. Elster,** Purdue University; *Young Children's Visual Meaning-Making During Readalouds of Picture Storybooks,* **Lawrence Sipe,** University of Pennsylvania, **Anne E. Brightman,** University of Pennsylvania; *Helping Young Children Learn to Read Chapter Books,* **Nancy Roser,** University of Texas at Austin, **Miriam Martinez,** University of Texas at San Antonio, **Kathleen McDonnold,** University of Texas at Austin, **Charles Fuhrken,** University of Texas at Austin, **Norma Carr,** University of Texas at Austin

Crossing Over to Canaan: Engaging Distinguished Women and/or Minority Scholars in Critical Conversations about Tenure
Chair: Jennifer Danridge Turner, University of Maryland at College Park, **Moderator: Doris Walker-Dalhouse,** Minnesota State University at Moorhead; **Panel: Donna Alvermann,** University of Georgia,

Kathryn Au, University of Hawaii, **Patricia A. Edwards,** Michigan State University, **Jane Hansen,** University of Virginia, **Robert Rueda,** University of Southern California

Writing Instruction and Performance in Multicultural and Multilingual Settings
Chair: **Beverly E. Cox,** Purdue University, Discussant: **Zhihui Fang,** University of Florida; *Genre and Register Knowledge Used by Culturally Diverse Kindergarteners,* **Beverly E. Cox,** Purdue University, **Jackie Covault,** Purdue University & Purdue North Central, **Melissa Shepson,** Purdue University; *Genre Usage in Bilingual and Multicultural Upper Elementary School Students,* **Jeni Arndt,** Purdue University; *Influence of Bilingual Instruction on Bilingual First Graders' Genre and Register Knowledge,* **Jiening Ruan,** Oklahoma University; *Collaborative Discussion's Effects on Culturally Diverse Community College Students' Writing,* **Sharon Snyders,** Purdue University & Ivy Tech Community College

The Storied Lives of Boys: Masculinities, Literacies and Schooling
Chair: **Michael D. Kehler,** University of Western Ontario, Discussant: **Michele Knobel,** Montclair State University; *The Literate Selves: Reading or misreading the textuality of high school boys,* **Michael D. Kehler,** University Of Western Ontario; *Reading Men Differently: Alternative portrayals of masculinity in contemporary young adult fiction,* **Tom Bean,** University of Nevada-Las Vegas, **Helen Harper,** University of Western Ontario; *Exploring The Socio-cultural Borderland: Journeying, navigating and embodying a male queer identity,* **Marc Davidson,** The University of New Mexico.

Teaching Against the Grain: Enacting Constructivist Beliefs Within Institutional Constraints
Chair: **Stacey Leftwich,** Rowan University, Discussant: **Cindi Hasit,** Rowan University; *Catching the Forgotten Ones: Framing a Course Around a Provocative Proposition,* **Marjorie E. Madden,** Rowan University; *Sharing the Reins: Transforming Students' Intellectual Passivity into Collaboratively Mediated Learning,* **Elaine S. Marker,** Rowan University, **Susan Browne,** Rowan University; *They Want Me to Transmit but I Want Them to Construct: Students Sharing Power in a Children's Literature Course,* **Stacey Leftwich,** Rowan University

Self-Organizing Networks of Meaning: How Do Competing Stakeholders Build Consensus about the Preparation of "Highly Qualified" Teachers?
Chair: **Leslie Patterson,** University of North Texas, Discussant: **Glenda Eoyang,** Human Systems Dynamics Institute; *Shaping Consensus Through Networks of Meaning: Applying Centering Resonance Analysis to Political Discourse,* **Leslie Patterson,** University of North Texas, **Kevin Dooley,** Arizona State University, **Royce Holladay,** Human Systems Dynamics Institute; *Analyzing Networks of Meaning in Official Discourse: What Is a "Highly Qualified Teacher?,"* **Leslie Patterson,** University of North Texas, **Shelia Baldwin,** Monmouth University, **Darcy Bradley,** R. C. Owens, Publishers, Inc., **Kevin Dooley,** Arizona State University, **Royce Holladay,** Human systems Dynamics Institute, **Ruth Silva,** University of North Texas, **Joan Parker Webster,** University of Alaska – Fairbanks; *Interpreting Networks of Meaning from a Critical Perspective: Practical Implications of the Official Definitions of "Highly Qualified" Teachers,* **Joan Parker Webster,** University of Alaska – Fairbanks, **Ruth Silva,** University of North Texas

Special Invited Session
Essential Perspectives on Literacy in a Diverse World
Chair: **Mileidis Gort,** University of Connecticut; *Transitions to Biliteracy: Skill, Strategies and Self,* **Kathy Escamilla,** University of Colorado, Boulder; *New tools for writing: Assistive technology for students with writing difficulties,* **Skip MacArthur,** University of Deleware

Special Methodology Series: Using Mixed Methodologies in Literacy Research
Chairs: **Laurie A. Henry,** University of Connecticut, **Mary Sheard,** University of Nottingham, **Jeremie Seror,** University of British Columbia; *What's Mixed in Mixed Methods?,* **Elizabeth Birr Moje,** University of Michigan, **Cathy Roller,** International Reading Association; *Formative Experiments as Mixed Methodology Research in Literacy,* **David Reinking,** Clemson University, **Barbara Bradely,** University of Georgia

Plenary Session
Chair: **Julie Coiro,** University of Connecticut; *Announcements,* **Donald J. Leu,** University of Connecticut; *Early Career Award Presentation,* **Wendy Kasten,** Kent State University, **Janet W. Bloodgood,** Appalachian State University; *Introduction of the Speakers,* **Julie Coiro,** University of Connecticut; *Plenary Address: From Pencilvania to Pixelandia: Mapping the terrain of new literacies research,* **Michele Knobel,** Montclair State University, **Colin Lankshear,** University of Ballarat and Central Queensland University

Research on Early Literacy Development
Chair: **Janice S. Eitelgeorge,** University of South Florida; *Multiple Continua of Writing Development in a First Grade Classroom,* **Janice S. Eitelgeorge,** University of South Florida; *The Coordination of Reading and Writing Abilities in First-grade, Emergent Bilingual Children: Patterns of Literacy Growth in Phonological Awareness, Orthographic Knowledge, Concept of Word, and Metalinguistic Awareness,* **Linda Gubler Junge,** Rossier School of Education, University of Southern California, **David B. Yaden, Jr.,** Rossier School of Education, University of Southern California; *Preliteracy Knowledge in Chinese and U.S. Preschoolers,* **Nancy Pine,** Mount St. Mary's College, Los Angeles

Distinguished International Scholar Address
Chair and Introduction of the Speaker: **Linda D. Labbo,** University of Georgia; *Pattern Recognition: Learning From the Technoliteracy Research,* **Ilana Synder,** Monash University, Australia

Studies on the Linguistic and Cognitive Aspects of Secondary Literacy
Chair: **William G. Brozo,** University of Tennessee, **Discussant: Tom Bean,** University of Nevada-Las Vegas; *Attribution Theory Reconsidered: Corroborating Struggling Readers' Explanations for Academic Failure,* **William G. Brozo,** University of Tennessee; *Tagging as a Situated Local Literacy Practice,* **Laurie MacGillivray,** University of Southern California, **Margaret Curwen,** University of Southern California

Historical Issues in Literacy Research
Chair: **Kimberly H. Creamer,** University of North Carolina-Chapel Hill, **Discussant: Norm A. Stahl,** Northern Illinois University; *Integration, Adaptation, and Change: An Ethno-history of Reading Instructional Methods at a Rural Primary School,* **Kimberly H. Creamer,** University of North Carolina-Chapel Hill; *Oral Histories of Low-income Neighborhoods,* **Eliane Rubinstein-Avila,** University of Arizona; *Defending Children's Right to Read in Cold War America: The "Business as Usual" Anti-Censorship Work of McCarthy Era Educators and Librarians,* **Christine A. Jenkins,** University of Illinois at Urbana-Champaign

Research on Literary Response and Discussion
Chair: **James Damico,** Michigan State University; *Engaging with Socially Complex Texts: Testimonial Reader Response with young readers,* **James Damico,** Michigan State University; *Literature Discussion: Taking-a-stand for Middle School Learners,* **Paula Costello,** The University at Albany/CELA, **Peter Johnston,** The University at Albany/CELA; *"We Feel Like We're Separating Us": Black, White and Latina Girls Respond to Multicultural Literature,* **Sally Smith,** Hofstra University

Researchers Examining Texts
Chair: **Linda M. Phillips,** University of Alberta; *Types of Texts in Commercial Elementary Reading Programs,* **Linda M. Phillips,** University of Alberta, **Martha L. Smith,** University of Alberta, **Stephen P. Norris,** University of Alberta, **Marion R. Leithead,** University of Alberta; *Prototypical written narrative genres: Comparative analysis of descriptive and evaluative functions in personal recount and fictional story picture books,* **Kathleen Cali,** University of North Carolina at Chapel Hill; *"Are we really addressing diversity in classrooms when we leave out so many voices?" Representations of families in literature and in our classrooms,* **Karla J. Möller,** University of Illinois at Urbana-Champaign

Research on Instructional Discussions
Chair: **Samantha Caughlan,** California State University, Fresno, **Discussant: Deborah Appleman,**

Carleton College; *The Dialogic Dance of Discussion,* **Samantha Caughlan,** University of Wisconsin-Madison; *Talking Ourselves to Understanding: Literature-Based Discussions as "Instructional Conversations,"* **Kristy L. Dunlap,** George Mason University; *When reading it wrong is getting it right: Shared evaluation pedagogy among struggling fifth grade readers,* **Maren Aukerman,** University of California, Berkeley

Issues in Literacy Learning and Instruction for English Learners
Chair: Hsiang-ju Ho, SUNY Fredonia, **Discussant:** Shelley Xu, California State University, Long Beach; *Best Approach to Literacy Instruction for English Language Learners: Mainstream Teachers' and Asian Parents' Perspectives,* **Guofang Li,** SUNY at Buffalo; *The Effect of Comprehension Strategies Instruction on Ghanaian English Language Learners' Comprehension Processes and Text Understanding,* **Kafui Etsey,** University of Iowa; *Latina/o adolescents' language and literacy practices as windows into identity (re)constructions,* **Alejandra Rodríguez-Galindo,** University of Texas at Austin

From Preschool to High School: Students Responding to Texts
Chair: Patricia E Enciso, The Ohio State University, **Discussant:** Susan Hynds, Syracuse University; *The Practice of Sociopolitical Theory: An introduction to Critically Engaged Reading Pedagogy,* **Patricia E Enciso,** The Ohio State University; *Discourses of Femininity? A Socio-cultural Analysis of Girls' Reading and Response Practices in Classroom, Focus-Group, and Interview Settings,* **Amanda Haertling Thein,** The University of Minnesota; *Poetry Read-Alouds and Preschool Children's Meaning-Making Responses,* **Diane Jackson Schnoor,** The University of Virginia

Beyond the Standard Form: Research on Multiple Text Types in Schooling
Chair: Wendy Glenn, University of Connecticut, **Discusssant:** Lawrence Sipe, University of Pennsylvania; *From Response to Interpretation to Appreciation: Listening to Novice and Expert Readers Make Sense of Poetry,* **Sarah W. Beck,** New York University; *Into a New Light: A Qualitative Investigation into the Genre of Biography within the Postmodern Educational Context,* **Karen A. Krasny,** Texas A&M University; *Enhancing Comprehension by "Reading" Multiple Texts: A Study of Social Inequality and School Desegregation,* **Fenice B. Boyd,** SUNY at Buffalo, **Chinwe Ikpeze,** SUNY at Buffalo

Perspectives on Critical Literacy and Social Change
Chair: Elizabeth Dutro, Cleveland State University, **Discussant:** Patricia Schmidt, Le Moyne College; *"We Didn't Fit the Category": Critical Literacy and the Interrogation of Racial Categories in an Urban Elementary Classroom,* **Elizabeth Dutro,** Cleveland State University, **Elham Kazemi,** University of Washington, **Ruth Balf,** Seattle Public Schools; *Examining Racism with Fresh Eyes: Sixth Graders and Pre-Service Teachers Scaffold Together to Become Agents of Change,* **Monica Taylor,** Montclair State University, **Gennifer Otinsky,** Grover Cleveland Middle School, **Eric Weiner,** Montclair State University; *Leaving Adults Behind: Developing Literacies of Social Justice in a Neoliberal Age,* **Eric J. Weiner,** Montclair State University

Dispelling Myths about Teacher Education in Literacy Myths: Learning from our Stories
Chair: Susan Davis Lenski, Portland State University, **Discussant:** Nancy Farnan, San Diego State University; **Participants:** Claudia Finkbeiner, University of Kassel, Germany, **Karen Smith,** University of Manitoba, **Linda Wold,** Purdue Calumet, **Dana Grisham,** San Diego State University, **Debra Wellman,** Rollins College, **Susan Davis Lenski,** Illinois State University, **Leslie Patterson,** University of North Texas, **Mary Strong,** Widener University, **Janet Young,** Brigham Young University, **Bette S. Bergeron,** Arizona State University, **Carole Rhodes,** Adelphi University

Special Invited Session
Struggling Adolescent Readers Across Instructional, Inservice, and Administrative Contexts: Researchers and Practitioners in Dialogue
Chair: Mark Dressman, University of Illinois, **Discussant:** Richard L. Allington, University of Florida; *Short Paper: Instructional Practice Short Paper,* **Donna Alvermann,** University of Georgia; *Dialogic Response,*

Josephine Young, Arizona State University, **Amy Komitzky,** Chandler High School, Chandler, AZ, Unified School District; *Inservice Teacher Education Short Paper,* **Colleen Fairbanks,** The University of Texas at Austin; *Dialogic Response,* **Gay Ivey,** James Madison University, **Sheri Sevenbergen,** Herbert Hoover High School, San Diego, CA; *Administration and Policy Short Paper,* **Elizabeth Birr Moje,** University of Michigan; *Dialogic Response,* **Mark Dressman,** University of Illinois at Urbana-Champaign, **Carolyn Schubach,** Murray, UT, School District

Roundtables
An Analysis of Strategy Instruction in Current Basal and Intervention Programs in Terms of the Research on Word Identification Strategies, **Thomas Gunning,** Central Connecticut State University; *From Easyrider to Easy Writer: An Examination of Non-Traditional Writers and Their Road to Literacy,* **Cheryl M. North-Coleman,** University of Delaware; *Literacy Teachers Making a Difference in Urban Schools,* **Althier M. Lazar,** Saint Joseph's University; *Service Learning in Preservice Teacher Education: Promoting a Culturally Responsive Stance Toward Reading Instruction,* **Beth Maloch,** The University of Texas at Austin, **James Hoffman,** The University of Texas at Austin, **Melissa Madison,** The University of Texas at Austin, **Laura A. May,** The University of Texas at Austin, **Carrie S. Bert,** The University of Texas at Austin

Roundtables
Establishing the Construct Validity of a Universally Accessible Word Recognition Assessment, **Karen Erickson,** University of North Carolina at Chapel Hill, **Stephanie Spadorcia,** Lesley University, **David Koppenhaver,** Appalachian State University, **James Cunningham,** University of North Carolina at Chapel Hill; *Our Journey Backward: Retrospective Analysis of the Development of Authentic Assessment for Teacher Candidate Reading Instruction,* **Brian Walker Johnson,** Principia College, **Katherine Beyer,** Principia College, **Libby Scheiern,** Principia College; *Spanish speakers learning to read in English: Results and implications from an early literacy assessment,* **Lori Helman,** The University of Nevada, Reno; *Teacher Educators: Acting in the Policy Realm,* **Devon Brenner,** Mississippi State University, **Terry Jayroe,** Mississippi State University, *The Teacher-Student Writing Conference: Exploring Ideas and Revising Text,* **Antony T. Smith,** University of Washington

Foregrounding the Complexity of Literacy Teaching
Chair: **Elizabeth G. Sturtevant,** George Mason University, **Discussant: Jane Hansen,** University of Virginia; *Literacy Coaches/Reading Specialists in Middle and High Schools: History and Current Policy Issues,* **Elizabeth G. Sturtevant,** George Mason University; *No Quick Fix: A Study of Change and Policy Implementation in a High-Poverty School on Probation,* **Kristin M. Gehsmann,** University of Vermont, **Haly Woodside-Jiron,** University of Vermont; *Standardized Assessment Practices in Reading and Writing with New Technologies: A Canadian Portrait,* **Marlene Asselin,** University of British Columbia, **Margaret Early,** University of British Columbia, **Margot J. Filipenko,** University of British Columbia

Special Invited Session
Reading at Risk: A Survey of Literary Reading in America from the National Endowment for the Arts
Chair: **Mark Bauerlein,** National Endowment for the Arts, **Discussants: Cathy Roller,** International Reading Association, **Mark Dressman,** University of Illinois, Urbana-Champaign, **Sandra Stotsky,** Northeastern University, **Bruce Gans,** Wright College

Comprehension Strategy Instruction or Cognitive Engagement?
Chair: **Georgia Garcia,** University of Illinois at Urbana-Champaign, **Participants: Georgia E. Garcia,** University of Illinois, Urbana-Champaign, **Jason Stegemoller,** University of Illinois, Urbana-Champaign, **Laura Engel,** University of Illinois, Urbana-Champaign, **Teresa Mendez Bray,** University of Illinois, Urbana-Champaign, **P. David Pearson,** University of California, Berkeley, **Vicki Benson,** University of California, Berkeley, **Barbara M. Taylor,** University of Minnesota, **Monica Marx,** University of Minnesota, **Ceil Critchley,** University of Minnesota, **Eurydice B. Bauer,** University of Illinois, Urbana-

Champaign, **Yvonne Lefcourt,** University of Illinois, Urbana-Champaign, **Kay Stahl,** University of Illinois, Urbana-Champaign, **Sunday Cummins,** University of Illinois, Urbana-Champaign, **Julia Johnson Connor,** University of Illinois, Urbana-Champaign

Research on Computer-Mediated Communication
Chair: **Alicia D. Beth,** University of Texas at Austin, **Discussant: Bridget Dalton,** Center for Applied Special Technologies; *"Somewhere Between Repartee and Discourse": Graduate Students' Experiences of Reading and Writing in a Computer-Mediated Discussion,* **Alicia D. Beth,** University of Texas at Austin; *Computer-mediated (mis)communication and second language learning: Examining sustained interaction in written conversations,* **Paige D. Ware,** Southern Methodist University; *Teaching-Learning Relationships: How Caring is Enacted in Computer-Mediated Communication,* **Minseong Kim,** University of Texas, Yoon-Hee Na, Chonnam National University

Research on Letter Sounds and Vocabulary Instruction in Kindergarten classrooms
Chair: **Rebecca Deffes,** Harvard Graduate School of Education, **Discussant: Susan Neuman,** University of Michigan; *Comparing Three Methods of Kindergarten Vocabulary Instruction,* **Rebecca Deffes,** Harvard Graduate School of Education; *Teaching Vocabulary to Kindergarten Students during Shared Storybook Readings,* **Michael Coyne,** University of Connecticut; *Articulation Attributes of Letter Sounds: Considering Manner, Place, and Voicing for Kindergarten Instruction,* **Terri L. Purcell,** Cleveland State University

Popular Culture, Culturally Relevant Pedagogy, and Third Space Theory: Honoring Funds of Knowledge
Chair: **Perry Marker,** Sonoma State University, **Discussant: Patricia A. Edwards,** Michigan State University; *Teachers Explore Culturally Responsive Teaching: Integration of Popular Culture Text in an Urban Setting,* **Shelley Hong Xu,** California State University at Long Beach; *Supporting Culturally Relevant Pedaogy: "It made the difference!,"* **Patricia Schmidt,** Le Moyne College; *Exploring Third Space: Alternatives to Business as Usual for Adolescent Learners,* **Brenda Shearer,** University of Wisconsin Oshkosh, **Martha Ruddell,** Sonoma State University

Reconsidering Efferent Reading and the Online Transaction
Chair: **John E. McEneaney,** Oakland University, **Discussant: Dana W. Cammack,** Columbia University; *Reconceptualizing the efferent transaction; A transactional systems approach to online literacy; Stance, navigation, recall, and comprehension in expository hypertext;* **Participants: Kristine Allen,** Oakland University, **Lizabeth A. Guzniczak,** Oakland University, **Ledong Li,** Oakland University, **John E. McEneaney,** Oakland University

Echoes and Reverberations: Social Narrative Writing and Identity Work in a Third Grade Classroom
Chair & Discussant: **Jerry Harste,** Indiana University; *The Tensions Between Transgression and Compliance: The Identity Work Taken On by One Third Grade Girl in Social Narrative Writing,* **Mitzi Lewison,** Indiana University, *Teaching My Brother About the Good Times and The Bad Times: Putting Social Narrative Writing To Work,* **Lee Heffernan,** Indiana University/Childs Elementary, *Trying On Gee's "Tools of Inquiry" for Analyzing Student Writing*

Understanding New Literacies
Chair: **Kimberly Lawless,** University of Illinois at Chicago; *Investigating how less-skilled readers use reading strategies while reading on the Internet,* **Julie Coiro,** University of Connecticut, **Elizabeth Dober,** Emporia State University; *Investigating Adolescents' Awareness of Critical Technological Literacy,* **Kelly Chandler-Olcott,** Syracuse University, **Donna Mahar,** Syracuse University; *The Development of Children's/Adolescents Critical Multiliteracies: Toward a Working Metatheoretical Framework,* **James R. Gavelek,** University of Illinois at Chicago, **Kimberly Lawless,** University of Illinois at Chicago

Research on Reading and Language in Preschool
Chair: Barbara A. Bradley, University of Kansas; *A Formative Experiment to Enhance Verbal Interactions in a Preschool Classroom,* **Barbara A. Bradley,** University of Kansas; *Preschoolers' Acquisition of Vocabulary from Participation in Repeated Read-Aloud Events and Retellings Involving Informational Picture Books about Light and Color,* **Cynthia B. Leung,** University of South Florida, St. Petersburg; *The Development of Knowledge about Environmental Print, the Alphabet and Word Reading: A First Look at a Longitudinal Study,* **Sherri L. Horner,** Bowling Green State University

Research on Teachers Learning About Culture and Literacy
Chair: Caitlin McMunn Dooley, University of Texas at Austin, **Discussant: Kathryn Au,** University of Hawaii; *Teachers' Transforming Understandings about Culture and Literacy: An Exploration of Teacher Learning,* **Caitlin McMunn Dooley,** University of Texas at Austin; *Developing Understandings of Cultural and Linguistic Diversity through Family Stories,* **Julie Kidd,** George Mason University, **Sylvia Y. Sanchez,** George Mason University, **Eva K. Thorp,** George Mason University, *Supporting Culturally and linguistically Diverse Learners in a Mainstream 5th Grade Classroom,* **Sandra M. Webb,** University of North Carolina-Greensboro

Issues, Opportunities, and Initiatives in Literacy Education
Chair: George G. Hruby, Utah State University, **Discussant: Mark W. Conley,** Michigan State University; *Reading Wars, Paradigms, and Pepperian Hypotheses: A Formal Content Analysis of Literacy Research Motifs,* **George G. Hruby,** Utah State University, **Peggie Clelland,** Utah State University; *An Analysis of the Employment Opportunities for Reading, Language Arts, and Literacy Faculty in Higher Education During the 2003-2004 Academic Year,* **Douglas Hartman,** University of Connecticut; *Literacy Initiatives at the Top 50 Education Schools,* **Catherine M. Bohn,** University of Minnesota, **Steven R. Yussen,** University of Minnesota, **Anthony D. Pellegrini,** University of Minnesota

Research Methodology Series: Discourse Analysis
Chairs: Annie Moses, Michigan State University, **Katina Zammit,** University of Western Sydney; *Discourse Analysis in Literacy Research,* **Susan Florio-Ruane,** Michigan State University; *Critical Discourse Analysis in Literacy Research,* **Ernest Morrell,** Michigan State University, **Leslie Burns,** Michigan State University

Oscar Causey Award Presentation and Address
Chair: Lea M. McGee, University of Alabama; *Announcement of the Distinguished Scholar Award,* **William Teale,** University of Illinois, Chicago; *Oscar Causey Award Presentation for 2004,* **Mark W. Conley,** Michigan State University; *Introduction of the Speaker,* **Connie Juel,** Stanford University; *2004 Oscar Causey Address: Exploring the Mind and Heart of the Reading Teacher,* **Robert Calfee,** University of California Riverside

Town Meeting
Facilitators: Kelly Chandler-Olcott, Syracuse University, **Michael McKenna,** Georgia Southern University

Vital Issues: Panel and Audience Conversation Around the Issue of the Day: How Do We Achieve Excellence in Literacy Research?
Chair: Laurie A. Henry, University of Connecticut, **Discussion Panel: Donna Alvermann,** University of Georgia, **David Reinking,** Clemson University, **Elizabeth Sturdevant,** George Mason University, **Diane L. Schallert,** University of Texas, Austin, **Jo Worthy,** University of Texas, **Colin Harrison,** University of Nottingham, **Kathleen Hinchman,** Syracuse University; *What qualities should characterize exemplary research in our field?; What must we do as an organization and as individuals to improve the quality of literacy research? Why?; To what extent does technology change our understanding of reading? Writing? Literacy?; How must the nature of our research change in order to more directly impact public policy? Why?; Which sessions from today represent exemplary models of literacy research for our field? Why?*

FRIDAY • DECEMBER 3, 2004
CONVERSATIONAL ISSUE OF THE DAY: *What Will Define the Future of Literacy Research?*

Roundtables
The Effects of Bilingual and Multilingual Environments on the Metalinguistic Awareness of Young Children: Implications for Practitioners, **Tina Tsai,** University of Southern California, **David B. Yaden,** University of Southern California; *Does the Road to Professionalism Leak Back to Self?,* **Margaret A. Gallego,** San Diego State University, **Sandra Hollingsworth,** San Jose State University; *Doing the hard work of reflection: Using narrative and non-narrative texts to explore literacy, race, class, and culture with preservice and inservice teachers,* **Mary McVee,** University at Buffalo/SUNY, **Maria Baldassarre,** University at Buffalo/SUNY; *Investigating Teacher and Adminstrator Change in a Professional Development School,* **Roxanne Henkin,** The University of Texas at San Antonio, **Lorri Davis,** National-Louis University, Chicago, Illinois; *Teach, Read, & Succeed: Pre-service Teacher Education Making a Difference in Early Field Experiences for Assessment & Instruction,* **Verlinda Angell,** Southern Utah University; *The influence of a university-school partnership project on preservice elementary teachers' efficacy for inquiry and student-centered decision-making in literacy instruction,* **Denise Johnson,** The College of William & Mary

Roundtables
"That's how you know:" Exploring Young Children's Roles in Meaning Construction, **Anne E. Gregory,** Boise State University;.*Children's Contemporary Realistic Fiction Portraying Struggling Readers: An Analysis of the Issues Confronted by the Characters,* **Jennifer L. Altieri,** The Citadel; *Creating Contexts for Education and Literacy at the Crossroads: A Case Study of Anglos, Latinos, and Literacy in Rural America,* **Jennifer Schmidt,** the University of Iowa, **Carolyn Colvin,** the University of Iowa; *Literacy by Design: A Universally Designed Reading Environment for Students with Cognitive Disabilities,* **Peggy Coyne,** Center for Applied Special Technologies; *Early Adolescent Emerging Readers: A Story of Strengths,* **Robin C. Thompson,** University of South Florida; *Revisiting the Philosophical Orientation to Literacy Learning (POLL) Questionnaire: The Impact of Data Collection on Instrumentation,* **Kimberly L. Klakamp,** Texas A&M University - Commerce, **LaVerne Raine,** Texas A&M University - Commerce, **Wayne M. Linek,** Texas A&M University - Commerce, **Mary Beth Sampson,** Texas A&M University - Commerce, **Patricia E. Linder,** Texas A&M University - Commerce, **Crystal Torti,** Texas A&M University - Commerce, **Ceretha Levingston,** Texas A&M University - Commerce

No Teacher Left Behind? Investigating Professional Development of the Reading First Initiative as an Innovation for Change
Chair & Disscuant: Kenneth Schatmeyer, Wright State University, **Participants:**
Cynthia Bertelsen, Bowling Green State University, **JoAnn Dugan,** Ohio University, **Sharon Walpole,** University of Delaware; *Literacy Specialists: A Catalyst for Change; Mirrors of Change: Transforming Literacy Education through Authentic Dialogue, Reflection and Action; Changing the Culture of the School to Improve Literacy Teaching and Learning; Shared Responsibility: Principals, Literacy Coaches, and Federal Reform Dollars*

Figuring Out Literacy Engagement for Adolescent Latino Students Just Beginning to Read and Write English
Chair: Gay Ivey, James Madison University, **Discussants: Peter Afflerbach,** University of Maryland, **Richard Allington,** University of Florida, **Kathleen Hinchman,** Syracuse University, **Robert Rueda,** University of Southern California, **Participants: Gay Ivey,** James Madison University, **Karen Broaddus,** James Madison University, **Tu Phillips,** Eastern Mennonite University; *A Formative Experiment of Older Language Minority Students Beginning to Read and Write English: Case #1: Connecting with Rosa and Sandra: Finding a Point of Entry, Case #2: Answering Questions with Alejandro: Uncovering the Need to Know, Case #3: Laughing with Tony: Revealing the Complexity of Individual Literacy*

Three Years of Growth: Tracing Individual, Group, and Teacher Development while Participating in Peer Discussions of Text
Chair & Discussant: John F. O'Flahavan, University of Maryland; *One Cohort's Social, Cognitive, and*

Affective Development Across Grades 1-3, **Janice F. Almasi,** University of Kentucky, **Hyunhee Cho,** University at Buffalo, SUNY, **Keli Garas,** University at Buffalo, SUNY, **Wen Ma,** LeMoyne College, **Lynn Shanahan,** Daemen College, **Amy Augustino,** University at Buffalo, SUNY; *Teacher Change in Peer Discussion Classrooms,* **Barbara Martin Palmer,** Mt. St. Mary's College; *Achieving Social Status Among Peers: The Case of Aliya,* **Keli Garas,** University at Buffalo, SUNY, **Janice F. Almasi,** University of Kentucky

Critical Perspectives on Literacy Instruction in Classroom Contexts
Chair: Deborah Wells Rowe, Vanderbilt University, **Discussant: Beth Maloch,** University of Texas at Austin; *Analyzing the Production of Third Space in Classroom Literacy Events,* **Deborah Wells Rowe,** Vanderbilt University; *Tracking by Any Other Name: Teachers' Descriptions of "Regular" and "Honors" Language Arts Classes,* **Jo Worthy,** The University of Texas at Austin, **Jessica Mejia,** The University of Texas at Austin, **Norma Carr,** The University of Texas at Austin, North East Independent School District, **Heather Bland-Ho,** The University of Texas at Austin; *Black and Latina Children's Critical Literacies in Early Childhood and Elementary School Contexts,* **Nadjwa E.L. Norton,** City College, CUNY

Benchmark School: Teaching Struggling Readers to Read Is Just the Beginning of Recovery
Chair: Irene Gaskins, Benchmark School, **Participants: Michael Pressley,** Michigan State University, **Irene Gaskins,** Benchmark School, **Katie Solic,** University of Florida, **Stephanie Collins,** Michigan State University, **Richard C. Anderson,** University of Illinois, **Linnea Ehri,** CUNY Graduate Center, **Linda Six,** Benchmark School, **Sally Laird,** Benchmark School

Emergent Literacy in Early Reading First Sites
Chair: Elizabeth Sulzby, University of Michigan/CIERA, **Discussants: Dorothy Strickland,** Rutgers University, **Mary Ann Colbert,** Region One, New York City Public Schools; *Implementation of Emergent Reading and Writing in an Early Reading First Site in New York City,* **Elizabeth Sulzby,** University of Michigan/CIERA; *Bookreading and Classroom Literacy Environments: Changes During Early Implementation,* **Deanna Birdyshaw,** University of Michigan/CIERA, **Elizabeth Sulzby,** University of Michigan/CIERA; *"Come Read With Me": Meaningful Early Literacy Assessment,.* **Andrea DeBruin-Parecki,** High/Scope Literacy Research Institute, **Marjata Daniel-Echols,** High/Scope Educational Research Foundation; *Meaningful Writing: Invented Spelling and its Antecedents,* **Donald J. Richgels,** Northern Illinois University

Social and Cultural Identity Issues of ENL Students in New Literacy Acquisition
Chair: Guofang Li, SUNY at Buffalo, **Discussant: Charles A. Elster,** Purdue University; *Social Identity Construction in ENL Learners,* **Xiaoning Chen,** Purdue University; *Academic Discourse and Cultural Identity of Female Asian High School Students,* **Reiko Habuto Ileleji,** Purdue University; *Picture Books and ENL Students: Theory and Practice,* **Olha Tsarykovska,** Purdue University

Integrating Technology in Teacher Education: A Socio-Cultural Perspective
Chair & Discussant: Dana Grisham, San Diego State University, **Participants: Rebecca S. Anderson,** The University of Memphis, **Gary B. Moorman,** Appalachian State University, **Jane B. Puckett,** The University of Memphis, **Laura S. Roehler,** Michigan State University

"They Learned a Lot...and So Did I!" Preservice Teachers Encounter Multicultural Picture Books.
Chair & Discussant: Ann Powell-Brown, Central Missouri State University; *Overview of the studies, data collection and analysis,* **Kathryn Chapman Carr,** Central Missouri State University; *Three trends in pre-service teachers' thinking,* **T. Gail Pritchard,** University of Alabama; *Visual literacy as an instructional tool* **Dawna Lisa Buchanan,** Central Missouri State University

Research on Literacy and Identity
Chair: Iris Dixon Taylor, Teachers College, Columbia University, **Discussant: Sara Ann Beach,** University of Oklahoma; *Contextualizing the Interplay of Critical Literacies and Identities of African American*

Youth, **Iris Dixon Taylor,** Teachers College, Columbia University; *"That's the Way It Is for Us Too": Reading to Construct Identities,* **Jessica Zacher,** University of California, Berkeley, **Julia Menard-Warwick,** University of California, Davis; *Boys' Literacy Spaces Under Construction,* **Sandra M. Webb,** University of North Carolina-Greensboro

Effective Literacy Practices Across Languages and Cultures
Chair: **Youb Kim,** Michigan State University, **Discussant: Aydin Durgunoglu,** University of Minnesota, Duluth (unable to attend); *Mandarin Students' Development as Writers in English and Chinese,* **Sarah J. McCarthey,** University of Illinois at Urbana-Champaign, **Yi-Huey Guo,** University of Illinois at Urbana-Champaign; *Examining the role of syntactic proficiency in second-language reading comprehension: Studies of Spanish and German learners,* **Elizabeth B Bernhardt,** Stanford University, *Language and literacy practices in Mexico,* **Robert T. Jimenez,** University of Illinois at Urbana-Champaign, **Patrick H. Smith,** University of the Americas, Puebla

Do Try This at Home: Training Parents in Phoneme Awareness Activities
Chair: **Keonya C. Booker,** University of Virginia, **Discussant: Patricia A. Edwards,** Michigan State University; *"Kiss Your Brain": A Closer Look at Successful Literacy Gains in Impoverished Elementary Schools,* **Keonya C. Booker,** University of Virginia, **Marcia A. Invernizzi,** University of Virginia, **Montana McCormick,** University of Virginia; *Do try this at home: Training parents in phoneme awareness and reading aloud,* **Shannon Coman Henderson,** Auburn University, **Bruce A. Murray,** Auburn University, **Connie Buskist,** Auburn University, **Edna Greene Brabham,** Auburn University; *The Effect of an After-School Intervention Programme on Children Experiencing Reading Difficulties,* **Susan J. Dymock,** University of Waikato, New Zealand

Research Methodology Series: Looking forward into our Future — Upcoming Methodologies and Issues with New Definitions of Literacy
Chairs: **Julie Coiro,** University of Connecticut, **Katherine Hilden,** Michigan State University, **Mary Love,** University of Georgia; *Considering paradigms and possiblilites for research in electronic environments,* **Charles K. Kinzer,** Teachers College, Columbia University; *Examining Electronic Data Collection: Benefits, Concerns, and Future Possibilities,* **Rachel Karchmer,** University of Delaware; *Bringing together screen and talk data in digital research: a multimethod approach to investigating how students engage as users and creators of curricular knowledge,* **Claire Wyatt-Smith,** Griffith University

Roundtables
A Multidimensional Model of Past, Current, and Future Adolescent Literacy Research, **Roger A. Stewart,** Boise State University, **David G. O'Brien,** University of Minnesota; *Examining Communication Interactions of a Korean L2 Child, the Parents, and Teachers,* **Jennifer Battle,** Texas State University-San Marcos, **Won Gyoung Kim-Choi,** Texas State University-San Marcos; *Snapshots of Literacy: Using Photographs to Capture and Define Adolescent Literacy Events,* **Deanna M. Stoube,** St. Ambrose University; *Storyteller as Cultural Tool: The Use of Storytelling in Early Literacy Environments,* **L. Marie Lavallee,** University of Louisville; *The use of Multicultural Children's Literature in six Primary-Grade Classrooms,* **Bena R. Hefflin,** University of Pittsburgh

Roundtables
Exploring the Emotions of "Struggling" Readers: Influences of School Contexts, Curriculum, and Relationships, **Cheri F. Triplett,** Virginia Tech (cancelled); *Family Involvement in Literacy Education: An Analysis of Preservice Teachers' Knowledge, Perspectives, and Plans,* **Laurie Elish-Piper,** Northern Illinois University; *Individualized Instruction in an Urban Middle School: Improving Reading for Students who Experience Significant Delays,* **Nancy Frey,** San Diego State University, **Douglas Fisher,** San Diego State University, **Diane Lapp,** San Diego State University, **James Flood,** San Diego State University; *The Power of the Pencil: A preschooler explores genre and social positioning through writing,* **Heather E. Bland-Ho,** The University of Texas at Austin; *Friendships As Catalysts To Literacy Learning,* **Huei-Hsuan Lin,** Syracuse University, **Jolene T. Malavasic,** Syracuse University and Baldwinsville School District

Using Technology to (Re)Conceptualize Literacy Teacher Education: Considerations of Design, Pedagogy and Research
Chair: Colin Harrison, University of Nottingham, England, UK, **Discussant: Elizabeth Baker,** University of Missouri; *'P, not–P and perhaps Q': How the Interactive Classroom Explorer (ICE) Interface can Support Teacher Professional Development,* **Colin Harrison,** University of Nottingham, England, UK, **Daniel Pead,** University of Nottingham, England, UK, **Mary Sheard,** University of Nottingham, England, UK; *Considerations of Pedagogy and Research using Reading Classroom Explorer (RCE),* **Erica Boling,** Rutgers University, **Suzanne Knezek,** Michigan State University, **Sharman Siebenthal,** University of Michigan, Flint, **Aman Yadav,** Michigan State University; *Considerations of Design, Pedagogy and Research using Case-based Technologies to Enhance Literacy Learning (CTELL),* **Charles K. Kinzer,** Teachers College, Columbia University, **Dana W. Cammack,** Teachers College, Columbia University, **Donald J. Leu,** University of Connecticut, **William Teale,** University of Illinois, Chicago, **Linda D. Labbo,** University of Georgia

The National Assessment of Educational Progress Reading Framework for 2009 and Beyond
Chair: Terry Salinger, American Institutes for Research; *The Process of Creating the New NAEP Framework,* **Terry Salinger,** American Institutes for Research; *The NAEP Framework for 2009 and Beyond,* **Michael L. Kamil,** Stanford University; *Comparison of the 1992 and 2009 NAEP Reading Frameworks,* **Barbara Kapinus,** National Education Association; *Panel Discussion and Question and Answer Session,* **Peter Afflerbach,** University of Maryland, **Charles W. Peters,** University of Michigan, **Karen Wixson,** University of Michigan

Policies and Research on Retention, Assessment, and Early Literacy Instruction
Chair: Anne McGill-Franzen, University of Florida, **Discussant: Sheila W. Valencia,** University of Washington, Seattle; *Questioning the Confluence of Two Policy Mandates: Core Reading Programs & 3rd Grade Retention,* **Anne McGill-Franzen,** University of Florida, **Courtney C. Zmach,** University of Florida, **Katie Solic,** University of Florida, **Jacqueline Love Zeig,** University of Florida; *Readiness, Policy Guidelines, and Reading Gains: Factors Affecting Teachers' Decisions to Retain or Promote Elementary Students (4-91),* **Alysia D. Roehrig,** Florida State University; *Stability of Early Literacy Skills: A Comparison of Kindergarten and First Grade (4-511),* **Heather Patridge,** University of Virginia, **Laura Justice,** University of Virginia, **Jennifer Howell,** University of Virginia, **Karly Geller,** University of Virginia

Central Issues in New Literacies
Chair: Katina Zammit, University of Western Sydney, **Discussant: Michael McKenna,** Georgia Southern University; *Engaging students from disadvantaged backgrounds in learning: Using multiliteracies, technology and popular culture in an Australian elementary classroom,* **Katina Zammit,** University of Western Sydney; *Pen Pals Without Borders: A Cultural Exchange of Teaching and Learning,* **Gwendolyn Thompson McMillon,** Oakland University Rochester, Michigan; *Impact of Technology and Media on Literacy Learning of Adolescent Boys and Girls,* **Kathy Sanford,** University of Victoria

Professional Development in Literacy Instruction: Reports from Two Partnerships Designed to Support Teacher Learning and Student Achievement
Chair: Kathleen M. Collins, University of San Diego; *Six in the City: Examining the Usefulness of Six Traits Writing for Improving Writing about Reading in Urban Schools,* **James L. Collins,** State University of New York, Buffalo; *Contexts of Promise: Teachers and Artists Collaborating to Support Student Success Through Integrated Arts Instruction,* **Kathleen M. Collins,** University of San Diego; *Component Research Reports: Tricks or Traits: The Research Basis for Six Traits Writing in the Context of Writing About Reading,* **James Collins,** The State University of New York at Buffalo; *The Influence of Professional Development: How Teachers Take Up Six Trait Writing in Content Area Classrooms,* **Kim Leavitt,** The State University of New York at Buffalo; *The Influence of Writing Instruction: Case Studies of Writers Before and After Six Traits Writing Instruction,* **Pauline Skowron,** The State University of New York at Buffalo; *The Influence of Six Traits Writing with Special Needs Children: A comparison of Peer and Independent Methods to Promote Meaningful*

Revision, **Corinne Kindzierski,** State University of New York, Buffalo; *Every Picture Tells a Story: Drawing on Visual Thinking Strategies to Support Students' Development of Text-Based, Academic Literacies,* **Melissa Showman,** Finney Elementary School, **Danielle Michaelis,** Community/Teachers/Artists, **Kelly Rampino,** University of San Diego; *Building a Battery: Sculpting, Modeling and Movement as Scaffolds for Students' Understanding of Matter and Energy in Third Grade Science,* **Kathy Busser,** Rogers Elementary School, **Elizabeth Bennett,** University of San Diego, **Renee Weisenberger,** Community/Teachers/Artists; *The Play's the Thing: Second Grade Students' Use of Drama to Construct*

Contemporary Issues in Reading Research
Chair: **Annemarie Sullivan Palincsar,** University of Michigan; *Investigating verbal protocols for what they reveal about upper elementary students' text processing across narrative and informational texts,* **Annemarie Sullivan Palincsar,** University of Michigan, **Bridget Dalton,** Center for Applied Special Technologies, **Shirley J. Magnusson,** University of Michigan, **Nancy Defrance,** University of Michigan, **Adrienne Gelpi-Lomangino,** University of Michigan, **Susanna Hapgood,** University of Michigan; *Effects of K-1st, 2nd-3rd, and 4th-5th grade looping on reading comprehension,* **Gretchen C. Guitard,** Southwest Missouri State University, **Cynthia J. MacGregor,** Southwest Missouri State University; *Playing Within and Beyond Text: Examining the Book-Related Pretend Play of At-Risk Preschoolers,* **Jodi G. Welsch,** Frostburg State University

Studies in Comprehension and Composing
Chair: **Janice F. Almasi,** University of Kentucky, Discussant: **Nell K. Duke,** Michigan State University; *The Impact of Peer Discussion on Social, Cognitive, and Affective Growth in Literacy,* **Janice F. Almasi,** University of Kentucky, **Hyunhee Cho,** University at Buffalo, SUNY, **Keli Garas,** University at Buffalo, SUNY, **Lynn Shanahan,** Daemen College, **Wen Ma,** University at Buffalo, SUNY, **Amy Augustino,** University at Buffalo, SUNY; *Developing Independence in Writing: The Journeys of Six Young Writers,* **Karen L. Fischer,** University of New Mexico, **John F. O'Flahavan,** University of Maryland; *Exploring texts: The uses of informational texts in a second grade classroom,* **Beth Maloch,** University of Texas at Austin

Assessing Elementary ESL and Native English Speaking Students' Oral Reading Fluency and Orthography
Chair: **Woodrow Trathen,** Appalachian State University, Discussant: **Jerry Zutell,** The Ohio State University; *Utility of Oral Reading Fluency and Spelling Measures: Contrastive Cases,* **Darrell Morris,** Appalachian State University, **Woodrow Trathen,** Appalachian State University; *The Relationship Between Presentation Durations of a Word Recognition Inventory (WRI) and Other Measures of Reading,* **Elizabeth Frye,** Appalachian State University; *ESL Students' Acquisition of English Orthography and Its Relationship to Reading Performance,* **Laurie Palmer,** Hickory City Schools, **Woodrow Trathen,** Appalachian State University

Research on Preservice Teacher Education
Chair: **Julia Kara-Soteriou,** University of Bridgeport, Discussant: **Rachel Karchmer,** University of Delaware; *A Longitudinal Study of the Self-Assessment of Preservice Literacy Teaching,* **Linda S. Wold,** Purdue University Calumet; *The Integration of the Miss Rumphius Award Winning Web Sites in a Language Arts Course: A Study With Pre-Service Teachers,* **Julia Kara-Soteriou,** University of Bridgeport; *Validating Literacy Engagements that Support Teacher Resiliency: Preservice Teachers Create Multicultural Text Sets,* **Janelle Mathis,** University of North Texas, **Diana Bernshausen,** University of North Texas

The Complexity of the Instruction-Achievement Relationship in Early Reading
Chair: **Ellen McIntyre,** University of Louisville, Discussant: **Laurie MacGillivray,** University of Southern California; *The Complexity of the Instruction-Achievement Relationship in Early Reading,* **Ellen McIntyre,** University of Louisville; *How Much Should Emerge Readers Read?,* **Ellen McIntyre,** University of Louisville, **Sherry Powers,** Western Kentucky University; *Fighting Boredom: High and Low Literacy Engagement in Classrooms,* **Rebecca Powell,** Georgetown College; *How Direct is Direct Instruction Anyway? The Enactment of SRA in Different Settings,* **Elizabeth Rightmyer,** University of Louisville

Adolescents' Perceptions of Literacy
Chair: **Lisa Patel Stevens,** University of Queensland, **Discussant: Gay Ivey,** James Madison University; *What's So 'Adolescent' about Adolescent Literacy?,* **Lisa Patel Stevens,** University of Queensland; *Classroom Case Studies in Multiliteracy Research: Working from an Asset Model of Young Adolescent Literacy,* **Jill Kedersha McClay,** University of Alberta; *High School High Achievers Who Say They Hate to Read: A Close Up Look at Their Reading Journeys,* **Adnan Salhi,** Saginaw Valley State University

Theoretical and Methodological Perspectives on Literacy Research
Chair: **Mark Dressman,** University of Illinois at Urbana-Champaign, **Discussant: George G. Hruby,** Utah State University; *Framing School Literacy Research as Rhetorical Practice,* **Mark Dressman,** University of Illinois at Urbana-Champaign; *Discussing Shiloh: A Conversation Beyond the Book Using Critical Discourse Analysis to Investigate Student Discussions,* **Lane W. Clarke,** University of Cincinnati; *Co-Researcher Methodologies with Black and Latina Early Childhood and Elementary Age Children,* **Nadjwa E.L. Norton,** City College, CUNY

Research Methodology Series: What Makes for Excellence in Literacy Research Methodology?
Chairs: Deborah Golos, University of Georgia, **Kristen Perry,** Michigan State University; *Perspectives from the Editors of Reading Research Quarterly,* **Donna Alvermann,** University of Georgia, **David Reinking,** Clemson University; *Perspectives from the Journal of Literacy Research,* **Nancy Padak,** Kent State University; *Understanding Methodology in Grant Writing,* **Richard Anderson,** University of Illinois

Roundtables
Examining the role of the literacy practicum in transforming literacy representations: A symbolic interaction perspective, **Linda Bausch,** Southampton College, Long Island University, **Julio Gonzalez,** Southampton College, Long Island University, **Susan Voorhees,** Dowling College, Oakdale, N.Y.; *In search of the elementary multicultural literary canon: A cross-site exploration,* **Deborah L. Thompson,** The College of New Jersey, **Susan S. Lehr,** Skidmore College; *Positioning Theory as a Critical Lens to Guide Analysis and Discussion of Young-Adult Literature,* **Kendra Sisserson,** University of San Diego; *Pre-Service Teachers' Perspectives and Responses in a Children's Literature Course: Moving Beyond "I Loved this Book,"* **Susan King Fullerton,** Clemson University; *The Promise of Cooperative Inquiry to Locate Texts and Literacy in Content-Area Classrooms,* **Roni Jo Draper,** Brigham Young University, **Daniel Siebert,** Brigham Young University; *Writing prompts: Do they help students improve writing skills?,* **Karin Huttsell,** NWAC Schools, **Kathryn Bauserman,** Indiana State University

Roundtables
Beyond Intensive Tutoring: Facilitating Effective Partnership with Parents in Clinical Remediation, **Chinwe Ikpeze,** University at Buffalo, State University of New York; *Instruction of Reading Comprehension: Understanding How Teachers Come to Teach Cognitive Engagement,* **Eurydice Bouchereau Bauer,** University of Illinois at Urbana-Champaign, **Joan Primeaux,** University of Illinois at Urbana-Champaign; *Interactive Assessment: Portfolios as Tools for Inquiry into Literacy Learning,* **Thomas P. Crumpler,** Ilinois State University; *Non-Fiction Study Group: A Portfolio of Primary Literacy Curriculum Development,* **Beverly J. Bruneau,** Kent State University; *Teachers' Beliefs About Reading Instruction: Contrasting Preservice Teachers' Conceptions with Experienced Teachers' Conventions,* **Jerrell C. Cassady,** Ball State University, **Lawrence L. Smith,** Ball State University; *Vocabulary-Comprehension Relationships: A Retrospective Research Review* **James F. Baumann,** University of Georgia

Approaches to the History of Literacy: Cases in What is Learned, Silenced, and Privileged
Chair: **Victoria Risko,** Peabody College of Vanderbilt University, **Discussant: Janice F. Almasi,** University of Kentucky; *How History is Told: Approaches and Lenses for Historical Access,* **Jim Furman,** Peabody College of Vanderbilt University, **Julie Justice,** Peabody College of Vanderbilt University, **Jason Lovvorn,** Peabody College of Vanderbilt University, **Patrick Tiedemann,** Peabody College of Vanderbilt University, **Victoria Risko,** Peabody College of Vanderbilt University; *Collecting Oral History Evidence in*

Literacy Contexts: Is it the Talk or is it the Text?, **Norman Stahl,** Northern Illinois University, **James R. King,** University of South Florida; *An Organizational History of Literacy: What is Learned, Silenced, and Privileged in Complementary Institutional Narratives,* **Douglas Hartman,** University of Connecticut, **Lou Ann Sears,** University of Pittsburgh

The Potential of Technology in Principal Dimensions of Literacy Instruction
Chair: Michael McKenna, Georgia Southern University; *Information Communication Technology and Adolescent Literacy,* **Donna E. Alvermann,** University of Georgia; *Technology and the Literacy Achievement Gap,* **Kathryn H. Au,** University of Hawai'i; *Comprehension and Technology,* **Nell K. Duke,** Michigan State University, **Beth Schmar-Dobler,** Emporia State University, **Shenglan Zhang,** Michigan State University; *Can Technology Support Emergent Reading and Writing?: Directions for the Future,* **Lea M. McGee,** University of Alabama, **Donald. J. Richgels,** Northern Illinois University; *Integrating Reading Assessment and Technology,* **Barbara J. Walker,** Oklahoma State University, **Sandra K. Goetze,** Oklahoma State University; *Vocabulary Development and Technology: Teaching and Transformation,* **Camille L.Z. Blachowicz,** National-Louis University, **Peter Fisher,** National-Louis University; *Real and Imagined Roles for Technology in Acquiring Second-Language Literacy,* **Elizabeth Bernhardt,** Stanford University; *Technology and the Engaged Literacy Learner,* **Linda Gambrell,** Clemson University; *The Role of Technology in Family Literacy,* **Patricia A. Edwards,** Michigan State University; *Spelling and Technology: It's More than Just Encoding,* **Shane Templeton,** University of Nevada, Reno; *The Potential of Technology in Fluency, Phonics and Phonemic Awareness Instruction,* **Melanie R. Kuhn,** Rutgers University, **Steven A. Stahl,** University of Illinois (in memorium); **Panelists: Julie Coiro,** University of Connecticut, **Richard E. Ferdig,** University of Florida, **Colin Harrison,** University of Nottingham, UK, **Renee Hobbs,** Temple University, **Rachel Karchmer,** University of Delaware, **Ronald Kieffer,** Ohio State University at Lima, **Linda D. Labbo,** University of Georgia, **David Reinking,** Clemson University, **Rand Spiro,** Michigan State University, **Sharon Walpole,** University of Delaware

Research on Reading Fluency Assessment
Chair: Sheila W. Valencia, University of Washington, Seattle, **Discussant: Peter Afflerbach,** University of Maryland; *The Rush for Oral Reading Fluency: Issues of Assessment and Implications for Classroom Instruction,* **Sheila W. Valencia,** University of Washington, Seattle, **Antony Smith,** University of Washington, Seattle, **Heather Newman,** University of Washington, Seattle, **Anne Reece,** University of Washington, Seattle, **Kelley Archer,** Univeristy of Washington, Seattle, **Karen K. Wixson,** University of Michigan; *A Psychometric Study of Two Methods of Measuring Reading Rates,* **Jennifer Howell,** University of Virginia, **Timothy J. Landrum,** University of Virginia, **Marcia A. Invernizzi,** University of Virginia

Contemporary Perspectives on Reading Models and Strategies
Chair: Kevin Flanigan, West Chester University, **Discussant: Lauren A. Liang,** University of Utah; *A Concept of Word in Text: A Pivotal Event in Early Reading Acquisition,* **Kevin Flanigan,** West Chester University; *Reading Strategies Revealed in Chinese Children's Oral Reading,* **Xiaoying Wu,** University of Illinois at Urbana-Champaign, **Richard C. Anderson,** University of Illinois at Urbana-Champaign; *The Development of Reading-Specific Representational Flexibility and its Contribution to Reading Comprehension in Beginning Readers,* **Kelly B. Cartwright,** Christopher Newport University, **Kristina Dandy,** Christopher Newport University, **Marisa Isaac,** Christopher Newport University, **Timothy R. Marshall,** Christopher Newport University

Studying Central Issues in Writing
Chair: Douglas Kaufman, University of Connecticut, **Discussant: Jane Hansen,** University of Virginia; *Growth in Written Reflections in Journal Writing over Traditional and E-mail List Serves,* **Diane S. Kaplan,** Texas A&M University; *Learning about Language: Written Conversations in Multilingual Classrooms,* **Katie Van Sluys,** DePaul University, **Tasha Tropp Laman,** Indiana University; *Pre-service Teachers Perceptions of Learning Through Personal Writing in the Language Arts Methods Classroom,* **Douglas Kaufman,** University of Connecticut

Negotiating and Co-constructing Research with "Struggling" Middle School Readers and Writers
Chair & Discussant: **Rebecca Rogers,** Washington University; *Listening to the Voices of Middle School Readers and Writers,* **Christine Woodcock,** Massachusetts College of Liberal Arts/CELA, **Elizabeth Yanoff,** The University at Albany/CELA, **James Collins,** The University at Albany/CELA, **Cheryl Dozier,** The University at Albany/CELA; *Methodological Issues: Examining the Research Process,* **Paula Costello,** The University at Albany/CELA, **Peter Johnston,** The University at Albany/CELA; *Negotiating Literacy Across Communities: Case Studies from Two Longitudinal Studies,* **Virginia Goatley,** The University at Albany/CELA, **Erin McCloskey,** Kingston City School District; *"That was Then, This is Now": Time, Place, and Shifting Experiences of Literacy in Rural Learning and Teaching,* **Marta Albert,** The University at Albany/CELA, **Mark Jury,** The University at Albany/CELA

Roundtables
Research on Teacher Change
Chair: **Dana Grisham,** San Diego State University, Discussant: **Deborah Appleman,** Carleton College; *The Role of University Professional Development in Perceptions of Self-Efficacy of Experienced Literacy Teachers,* **Dana Grisham,** San Diego State University, **Evangelina Bustamante-Jones,** San Diego State University; *Caught in the Middle: Teachers' Collaboration for Students with Language/Literacy Difficulties in Grades 6-7,* **Francine C. Falk-Ross,** Northern Illinois University; *Teacher Interruption Behaviors with Minority Students and Students from Low Socioeconomic Backgrounds,* **Tania Mertzman,** University of Wisconsin, Milwaukee

A Moment in Time: The Influence of History, Gender, and Power on Literate Identity
Chair: **Sara Ann Beach,** University of Oklahoma, Participants: **Sara Ann Beach,** University of Oklahoma, **Angela Ward,** University of Saskatchewan, **Sapargul Mirseitova,** Kazakstan Reading Association

Transforming Literacy Instruction
Chair: **Laura B. Smolkin,** University of Virginia, Discussant: **Trika Smith-Burke,** New York University; *Scientific Reasoning during Science Trade Book Read Alouds,* **Laura B. Smolkin,** University of Virginia, **Carol A. Donovan,** University of Alabama; *Under Pressure: Controlling Factors Faced by Classroom Literacy Teachers as They Work through a Professional Development Program,* **Faith H. Wallace,** Kennesaw State University, *Bumps in the Road: Challenges in Learning to Teach Literacy,* **Stephen White,** George Mason University, **Debby Deal,** Loyola College in Maryland

Preparing to Teach in an Information Age
Chair: **Mary Sheard,** University of Nottingham, England, UK , Discussant: **Linda D. Labbo,** University of Georgia; *Envisionments in Pre-service: Examining the Impact of Web-based Technology on Curriculum and Pedagogy,* **Ruby Sanny,** University of Illinois at Chicago; *Learning to teach literacy in a digital age: A narrative analysis of literacy stories,* **Amy Suzanne Johnson,** University of Wisconsin-Madison; *First Graders' Reading and Writing Preferences in Information-literacy Rich Classrooms,* **Marilyn L. Chapman,** University of British Columbia, **Jon Shapiro,** University of British Columbia, **Margot J. Filipenko,** University of British Columbia, **Marianne McTavish,** University of British Columbia

Central Research Issues in Professional Development
Chair: **Katherine Hilden,** Michigan State University, Discussant: **Erica Boling,** Rutgers University; *Stories of Obstacles and Success: Teachers' Experiences in Professional Development of Reading Comprehension Instruction,* **Katherine Hilden,** Michigan State University, **Michael Pressley,** Michigan State University; *Exploring Comprehension Instruction: The Effects of a Clinical Practicum on Teacher Practices,* **Pamela Ross,** San Diego State University, **Cynthia McDaniel,** San Diego State University; *"Becoming': a Literacy Coach: The First Year in Reading First Schools,* **Rita M. Bean,** University of Pittsburgh, **Kathy Carroll,** University of Pittsburgh, **Allison Swan,** West Virginia University, **Naomi Zigmond,** University of Pittsburgh

Special Invited Session
Recent Research on New Literacies
Chair: Denise Johnson, The College of William & Mary; *The promise of electronic storybooks for young children at- risk: Outcomes of two emergent literacy experiments,* **Adriana Bus,** Leiden University, Netherlands, **Maria DeJong,** Leiden University, Netherlands; *Children's Reading of Commercials: A Post-Developmental Perspective,* **Joe Tobin,** Arizona State University

Roundtables – Area 10
Investigating Teacher Change through Online Professional Development, **Charlotte J. Boling,** The University of West Florida; *Pictures and Text: Portrayal of African American Children in Picture Books,* **Wendy M. Smith,** Loyola College in Maryland, **Margaret Musgrove,** Loyola College in Maryland; *Preschool Children's Emergent Understanding of Global Structures and Linguistic Registers of Information Book Genre,* **Ida Maduram,** North Park University; *Rereading with Audio Models and Verbal Discussion Prompts: Extending Comprehension Instruction into the Homes of Diverse Learners,* **Irene H. Blum,** Literacy Partners International, **Patricia S. Koskinen,** Literacy Partners International; *Significant Stories: The Figured Worlds of White Teachers,* **Audrey Appelsies,** University of Minnesota; *The Role of a Teacher Observation Tool in Guiding the Professional Development of Preschool Teachers in Early Literacy,* **Shelly McNerney,** University of Kansas, **Diane C. Nielsen,** University of Kansas; *Handheld Computers and Electronic Portfolios: Enhancing Literacy Assessment and Instruction,* **Elaine Roberts,** State University of West Georgia, **Cathleen Doheny,** State University of West Georgia

Roundtables – Area 2
"Do you want me to explain that?": A Seventh Grade Remedial Reader's Experiences in Mathematics, **Leigh A. Hall,** Michigan State University; *"Getting Along in the World": Exploring Preservice Teachers' Responses to Children's Literature through a Framework of Critical Literacy,* **Cynthia McDaniel,** San Diego State University; *Beginning Teachers' Interpretations of Balanced Literacy Theory and Practice,* **Lois A. Groth,** George Mason University; *The Initial Development of a Reading Self-Perception Scale for Use in Secondary Grades,* **William A. Henk,** Southern Illinois University (unable to attend), **Steven A. Melnick,** Penn State Capital College; *The Standardized Assessment of Phonological Awareness: Validity, Reliability, & Usability,* **Jerrell C. Cassady,** Ball State University, **Lawrence L. Smith,** Ball State University, **Linda Huber,** Ball State University; *Decoding & Metacognition: One 5-year old's Journey,* **Roya Q. Leiphart,** The University of North Carolina at Greensboro & Winston-Salem/Forsyth County Schools

Exploring New Issues in Literacy Research
Chair: Lauren A. Liang, University of Utah; *Scaffolding Middle School Students' Comprehension of and Response to Narrative Text,* **Lauren A. Liang,** University of Utah; *A Tale of Two Teachers: Facilitated Reflection to Support Professional Change,* **Eileen Kaiser,** Wisconsin Department of Public Instruction

Research on New Literacies in Classroom Contexts
Chair: Dana Grisham, San Diego State University, **Discussant: Richard E. Ferdua,** University of Florida; *Creating a Middle School Learning Community with Technology,* **Dana Grisham,** San Diego State University **T. Devere Wolsey,** Lake Elsinore USD; *Integrating Literacy and Technology: How Classroom Teachers are Using their own Web Pages,* **Elizabeth (Betsy) A Baker,** University of Missouri-Columbia, **Soon-Wha Kim,** University of Missouri-Columbia; *Investigating digital literacies: resolving dilemmas of researching multimodal technologically-mediated literacy practices,* **Geraldine Castleton,** University College, Worcester, UK, **Claire Wyatt-Smith,** Griffith University, Australia

Research on Identity and Response in Adolescent Literacy Contexts
Chair: Loukia K. Sarroub, University of Nebraska - Lincoln; *I Was Bitten by a Scorpion: Reading and Masculinity In and Out of School in a Refugee's Life,* **Loukia K. Sarroub,** University of Nebraska - Lincoln, **Todd Pernicek,** Teach for America, **Tracy Sweeny,** Rancocas Valley Regional High School, Mount Holly, NJ; *Reading Race: Constructing Self and Other In and Through Narrative Discourse,* **Laura Schneider,**

VanDerPloeg, University of Michigan, **Elizabeth Birr Moje,** University of Michigan; *Reading and Writing Texts with Radical Change Characteristics,* **Sylvia Pantaleo,** University of Victoria, **Heather Sandquist,** University of Victoria

Research on Reading and Writing Practices Among Adolescents and Adults
Chair: **Thomas W. Bean,** University of Nevada, Las Vegas; *Sociocultural Dimensions of Multiple Texts in Two Experienced Content Teachers' Classrooms,* **Nancy T. Walker,** University of La Verne, **Thomas W. Bean,** University of Nevada, Las Vegas; *Reading in a High School: Mapping the Terrain of Students' Reading Across Content Areas,* **Bruce Taylor,** University of North Carolina at Charlotte; *The Writing Lives of Women Scholars in Education,* **Elizabeth Noll,** University of New Mexico, **Dana Fox,** Georgia State University

Research on Spelling Instruction and Development
Chair: **Mark Sadoski,** Texas A&M University; *Orthographic and Semantic Predictors of Spelling Performance,* **Mark Sadoski,** Texas A&M University, **Victor L. Willson,** Texas A&M University, **Angelia Holcomb,** Texas A&M University, **Regina Boulware-Gooden,** Nehaus Educational Center; *Which Way is Best?: One District's Pursuit of Effective Spelling Instruction,* **Donita Massengill,** University of Kansas, **Sharon Green,** University of Kansas; *Spelling Development in Korean Orthography: Grades 1 through 6,* **Minwha Yang,** University of Virginia

Special Invited Session
Federal Research Grant Funding Opportunities
Chair: **David Reinking,** Clemson University; *Building the Evidentiary Base in Literacy:, and Gaining Grant Support to Make it Possible,* **Peggy McCardle,** Child Development & Behavior Branch, National Institute of Child Health and Human Development; *Funding Opportunities for Reading Research and Evaluation at IES,* **Elizabeth R. Albro,** National Center for Education Research, Institute of Education Sciences, U.S. Department of Education

New perspectives on Research in Literacy Learning
Chair: **Sharon Vaughn,** The University of Texas; *Enhancing the Literacy and Oracy Development of English Langauage Learners,* **Sylvia F. Linan-Thompson,** The University of Texas, **Sharon Vaughn,** The University of Texas; *Building Early Literacy Skills: An Integrated, Theme-Based Approach,* **Kendra Hall,** Brigham Young University, **Brenda Sabey,** Brigham Young University, **Barbara Culatta,** Brigham Young University; *Developing an Arts Integrated Reading Comprehension Program for Less Proficient Third and Fourth Grade Readers,* **Kari-Lynn Winters,** University of British Columbia

Critical Perspectives on Reading and the Teaching of Literature
Chair: **Jen Turner,** University of Maryland, **Discussant: Violet J. Harris,** University of Illinois at Urbana-Champaign; *"If there was still slavery…": Reading Sojourner Truth in a Diverse 5th-Grade Classroom,* **Jessica C. Zacher,** The University of California, Berkeley, Graduate School of Education, *"Mocking" the Other: Pre-Service Teachers Negotiating Subjectivity, Identity and Representation in High School Reading Practices;* **Ingrid Johnston,** University of Alberta, **Jyoti Mangat,** University of Alberta; *Fictional Boys Defying Patriarchal Expectation: A Feminist Critical Analysis of the YA Novels of Karen Hesse,* **Wendy Glenn,** University of Connecticut

Technology Infusion: Helping Preservice Teachers Integrate Technology into Literacy Learning in Meaningful Ways
Chair: **Amy Andersen,** West Texas A&M University, **Dicussant: Eddie Henderson,** West Texas A&M University; *Improving the Technology Skills of Preservice Teachers; Read All About It: Infusing Technology into a Children's Literature Course; Integration of Technology into a Language Arts Methods Course; Cause and Effect: Preservice Teacher Technology Integration and How it Impacts Inservice Technology Integration;* **Participants: Kathy Burleson,** Datatrac Information Services, **Suzanne Monroe,** West Texas A&M University, **Buddy Fox,** West Texas A&M University, **Amy Andersen,** West Texas A&M University

Research on Multiliteracies and Multimodality
Chair: **Melissa McMullan**, University of Connecticut, Discussant: **Katina Zammit**, University of Western Sydney; *Critical Multimedia Literacy: student Subjectivities and Agency in Multiple Modalities,* **Eli Tucker-Raymond**, University of Illinois at Chicago; *Literacies in the Art museum: Examining the Theories, Spaces, Conditions, and Possibilities for Multimodal Literacy Learning and Subject Formation,* **Jonathan Eakle**, University of Georgia; *Educating Ourselves: Teacher Educators and Graduate Students Explore the Multiliteracies of Local Adolescents,* **Heather Sheridan-Thomas**, Binghamton University, **Jennifer Moon Ro**, Binghamton University, **Karen Bromley**, Binghamton University

Multiple Perspectives on Literacy Research
Chair: **Renita R. Schmidt**, University of Iowa, Discussant: **George G. Hruby**, Utah State University; *Broken Trust: Teachers' Talk about Literacy Teaching in Times of Mandates,* **Renita R. Schmidt**, University of Iowa; *Critical Interactions: Teenage Mothers' Interrogations of Texts and Lives,* **Kara L. Lycke**, Grinnell College; *When "Home" is a Homeless Shelter: Mothers' Literacy Practices in a Public Space,* **Laurie MacGillivray**, University of Southern California, **Amy Ardell**, University of Southern California

Studies of Literacy Practices across Contexts
Chair: **Patricia A. Young**, Howard University, Discussant: **William H. Teale**, University of Illinois at Chicago; *Boys and Girls in the Reading Club: Conversations about Gender and Reading in an Urban Elementary School,* **Lyndsay Moffatt**, Toronto District School Board and University of British Columbia; *Power and Agency in the Importation and Exportation of Literacy Practices Across School, Community, Language, and Cultural Borders,* **Kristen Perry**, Michigan State University, **Victoria Purcell-Gates**, University of British Columbia; *Bridge: A Cross-Culture Reading Program (1977): Rediscovering A Technology Of Literacy Made By And For African Americans,* **Patricia A. Young**, Howard University

Plenary Address
Chair: Sarah J. McCarthey, University of Illinois; *Announcements,* **Donald J. Leu**, University of Connecticut; *Edward B. Fry Book Award Presentation: About the Edward B. Fry Book Award,* **Edward B. Fry**; *Presentation of the Award,* **Janice Strop**, Cardinal Stritch University; *Introduction of the Speaker,* **Sarah J. McCarthey**, University of Illinois; *Leaving too many students behind: What contemporary policy reveals about educational research and the struggle for education 50 years after Brown,* **Michele Foster**, Claremont Graduate School

NRC Yearbook and Journal of Literacy Research Reception

Annual Business Meeting

Vital Issues: Panel and Audience Conversation Around the Issue of the Day: What Will Define the Future of Literacy Research?
Chair: **Jill Castek**, University of Connecticut, Discussion Panel: *Plenary Speakers and Distinguished International Scholars,* **Colin Lankshear**, University of Ballarat and Central Queensland University, **Michele Knobel**, Montclair State University, **Michele Foster**, Claremont Graduate School, **Ilana Snyder**, Monash University, Australia; *1. What will be the most important issue for our field ten years from now?; 2. Given the nature of the changes taking place, what questions have we failed to ask in our research?; 3. What implications do changes hold for our own research and for our organization?; 4. What should we do as an organization and as individuals to improve the quality of our research in the future?; 5. How must our organization change in order for our research to more directly influence public policy? What are the risks in moving in this direction?; 6. Which sessions have challenged you to think differently about literacy instruction and research?*

SATURDAY • DECEMBER 4, 2004

Improving Literacy Achievement by Investing in Teachers Versus Programs: Research on Three Promising Initiatives
Chair: **Samantha Bowers Welte,** University of Illinois at Chicago, **Discussants: Karen Wixson,** University of Michigan, **P. David Pearson,** University of California, Berkeley; *Experiences with the Standards Based-Change Process: What It Takes for Schools to Make a Difference in Students' Literacy Achievement,* **Kathryn H. Au,** University of Hawaii; *Focus on Professional Learning Communities: Implementation and Evaluation of a Standards-Based Change Process in an Urban Setting,* **Taffy Raphael,** University of Illinois at Chicago, **Susan Goldman,** University of Illinois at Chicago, **Samantha Bowers Welte,** University of Illinois at Chicago, **Hongmei Dong,** University of Illinois at Chicago, **Ji Yon Kim,** University of Illinois at Chicago, **Andrea Brown,** University of Illinois at Chicago, **Catherine M. Weber,** University of Illinois at Chicago, **Nance Wilson,** University of Illinois at Chicago; *Focus on Professional Learning Communities: Implementation and Evaluation of a Standards-Based Change Process in an Urban Setting,* **Barbara M. Taylor,** University of Minnesota

The National Early Literacy Panel: Findings from a Synthesis of Scientific Research on Early Literacy Development
Chair: Timothy Shananan, University of Illinois at Chicago, **Discussant: Laura Westberg,** National Center for Family Literacy; *Methodology for the Synthesis of Scientific Research on Early Literacy Development; The Early Literacy Skills that Predict Later Reading Achievement; Identifying Effective Programs and Interventions that Impact Early Literacy; Implicatons for Educational Research, Policy and Practice;* **Participants: Victoria Molfese,** University of Louisville, **Christopher J. Lonigan,** Florida State University, **Anne Cunningham,** University of California at Berkeley, **Dorothy Strickland,** Rutgers University

Becoming Critically Literate Across the Lifespan
Chair: **Rebecca Rogers,** Washington University in St. Louis, **Discussant: Peter Johnston,** University at Albany; *Roundtable Discussions: Critical Literacy in a White, Working Class Classroom,* **Rebecca Rogers,** Washington University in St. Louis, **Melissa Mosley,** Washington University in St. Louis; *What Difference Does Critical Literacy Make for Adolescents?; "As if you heard it from your momma": Reconstructing Histories of Participation with Literacy Education in an Adult Education Class,* **Rebecca Rogers,** Washington University in St. Louis, **Carolyn Fuller,** Adult Education and Literacy, St. Louis Public Schools; *Talking of Change: A Study of a Teacher Education Critical Study Group,* **Margaret Finders,** Washington University in St. Louis; *Discussant's Discussion of the Papers,* **Peter Johnston,** University at Albany; *Open Dialogue with Session Participants and Presenters*

Stances of Situated Literacy: Moving from Situation to Situation
Chair: **Sherry L. Macaul,** University of Wisconsin, Eau Claire, **Discussant: Jamie Myers,** Pennsylvania State University; *From Fringe to Center of a Situated Literacy Event: Where are the Critical Moments of Learning?,* **Karen E. Smith,** University of Manitoba; *Stances During Mediated Digital Video Self-Evaluation,* **Ronald Kieffer,** The Ohio State University, Lima; *New Literacies & Media Literacy Assignments and Assessments in Teacher Education,* **Sherry L. Macaul,** University of Wisconsin, Eau Claire; *Changing Views about Critical Thinking Over Time and in Intentional Spaces in Pre-service Technology Pedagogy Courses,* **David M. Lund,** Southern Utah University

Evidence-Based Research: Internalization and Transfer of Comprehension Processes
Chair: **Margaret Taylor Stewart,** Louisiana State University, **Discussant: Michael Pressley,** Michigan State University; *Internalization and Transfer of Comprehension Processes: Integrated Strategies Using the GO!Chart - Impact on Instruction, Learning, and Motivation,* **Carrice Cummins,** Louisiana Tech University; *Internalization and Transfer of Comprehension Processes: Integrated Strategies Using Bookmarks and Post-It Notes – Impact on Instruction, Learning, and Motivation,* **Cathy Collins Block,** Texas

Christian University; *Internalization and Transfer of Comprehension Processes: Impact of Informational Text and Comprehension Strategies Instruction on Vocabulary Learning,* **Margaret Taylor Stewart,** Louisiana State University

Applying a Transactional Framework to Research in Online Reading
Web-level Transactions: Inquiry-oriented search as an expression of stance, **Maya Eagleton,** Center for Applied Special Technologies; *Site Level Transactions: User navigation as an expression of the evocation,* **John E. McEneaney,** Oakland University; *Page Level Transactions 1: Eye movements as an expression of selective attention,* **Bob Dolan,** Center for Applied Special Technologies; *Page Level Transactions 2: Supporting and warranting the evocation,* **Bridget Dalton,** Center for Applied Special Technologies

Exploring the Interface of Technology and Tutoring for Literacy Learning
Chair: Michelle Commeyras, University of Georgia; *Overview,* **Michelle Commeyras,** University of Georgia; *Technology Poster Presentations,* **Jane Middleton,** University of Georgia, **Tanya Dwight,** University of Georgia, **Nancy Edwards,** University of Georgia, **Tammy Ryan,** University of Georgia, **Mary Love,** University of Georgia, **Kathleen Waugh,** University of Georgia, **Gary Fogarty,** University of Georgia, **Mary Roe,** Washington State University, **Gerald Maring,** Washington State University, **John Doty,** Washington State University, **Michelle Fickle,** Washington State University; *Grand Conversation,* **Linda D. Labbo** (Discussion Leader), University of Georgia

Teens, Preservice and Inservice Teachers Interact with Everyday Texts in Various Settings
Chair: Josephine Peyton Young, Arizona State University, **Discussant: Donna Alvermann,** University of Georgia; *Adolescents' Punk Rock Fandom: Construction, Deconstruction, and Production of Lyrical Texts,* **Barbara Guzzetti,** Arizona State University, **Sheila Fram-Kulik,** Arizona State University, **Yunjung Yang,** Arizona State University; *Preservice Teachers Seek a Connection between Popular Culture Texts and Children's Literature Texts,* **Shelley Hong Xu,** California State University, Long Beach; *In-Service Teachers and Graduate Students Make Inquiries into the New Literacies,* **Jennifer Moon Ro,** Binghamton University-SUNY

Constructing Responses to Postmodern Children's Picturebooks
Chair: Frank Serafini, University of Nevada, Las Vegas, **Discussant: Theresa Rogers,** University of British Columbia; *What is "Postmodern" about Postmodern Children's Picturebooks?,* **Lawrence Sipe,** University of Pennsylvania; *Entertaining Ambiguity – Readers Respond to Postmodern Picturebooks,* **Frank Serafini,** University of Nevada, Las Vegas; *The Role of Postmodern Picturebooks in the Elementary Reading Curriculum,* **Suzette Youngs,** University of Nevada, Reno

Through the Picture Frame: Children's Drawings and Their Responses to International Literature
Chair & Discussant:: T. Gail Pritchard, University of Alabama; *Review of the study, data collection and analysis,* **Kathryn Chapman Carr,** Central Missouri State University; *Exploring the visual: Reviewing selected samples of children's drawings,* **Dawna Lisa Buchanan;** *Implications and suggestions for teachers,* **Ann Powell Brown,** Central Missouri State University

Holding the Beast at Bay (and Maybe Even Taming It): Grammar and the Preservice Teacher
Chair: Janet W. Bloodgood, Appalachian State University, **Discussant: Charles Duke,** Appalachian State University; *The Beast: Grammar through Preservice Teachers' Eyes,* **Linda C. Pacifici,** Appalachian State University; *Some Background: A History of Grammar Instruction,* **Lynne Bercaw,** Appalachian State University; *The Magic Wand: Grammar through Skills-DOL and Grammar with a Grin,* **Ellen Pesko,** Appalachian State University; *The Crystal: Grammar through Literature,* **Linda Kucan,** Appalachian State University; *The Sword: Grammar through Writing,* **Susan A. Colby,** Appalachian State University; *The Juggler: Inductive Grammar through Sentence Reconstruction,* **Janet W. Bloodgood,** Appalachian State University

We're in This Thing Together: Collaborating to Implement Statewide Change in Literacy Instruction
Chair: Janice Almasi, University of Kentucky, **Discussant: Ellen McIntyre,** University of Louisville; *Introduction to the Kentucky Reading Project,* **Susan Cantrell,** Collaborative Center for Literacy Development, University of Kentucky; *Statewide Trends in Instruction and Achievement,* **Kaye Lowe,** University of Kentucky, **Shani Yero,** National Center for Family Literacy; *Case Studies from Kentucky,* **Mary Shake,** University of Kentucky, **Michele Bowling,** Fayette County Schools, **Stephanie Haggard,** Fayette County Schools, **Goria Quinn Wright,** Fayette County Schools, **Beverly Walker,** Fayette County Schools, **Shirley Long,** Eastern Kentucky University, **Margaret Davis,** Eastern Kentucky University, **Faye Newsome,** Eastern Kentucky University, **Michelle Lemmon,** Model Lab School, **Sherry Powers,** Western Kentucky University

Research Methodolgy Series: Questions and Conversation with the Series Participants
Chairs: Donald J. Leu, University of Connecticut, **Marla H. Mallette,** Southern Illinois University, **Nell K. Duke,** Michigan State University, **Panel: Jonna Kulikowich,** Penn State University, **Anne Cunningham,** University of California, Berkeley, **Richard Lomax,** University of Alabama, **George Kamberelis,** State University of New York, Albany, **Greg Dimitriadis,** State University of New York, Buffalo, **Diane Barone,** University of Nevada, Reno, **Savilla Banister,** Bowling Green State University, **Elizabeth Birr Moje,** University of Michigan, **Cathy Roller,** International Reading Association, **David Reinking,** Clemson University, **Barbara Bradely,** University of Georgia, **Susan Florio-Ruane,** Michigan State University, **Ernest Morrell,** Michigan State University, **Leslie Burns,** Michigan State University, **Charles K. Kinzer,** Teacher College, Columbia University, **Rachel Karchmer,** University of Delaware, **Claire Wyatt-Smith,** Griffith University, **Donna Alvermann,** University of Georgia, **Nancy Padak,** Kent State University, **Richard Anderson,** University of Illinois

NRC Annual Research Address
Chair: Kathleen Hinchman, Syracuse University; *Albert J. Kingston Award,* **Laura Smolkin,** University of Virgina; *Introduction of the Award Winner,* **Martha Ruddell,** Sonoma State University; *Introduction of the Speakers,* **Charles K. Kinzer,** Teachers College, Columbia University; *2004 NRC Research Address: Speaking literacy and learning to technology; Speaking technology to literacy and learning,* **Annemarie Sullivan Palincsar,** University of Michigan, **Bridget Dalton,** Center for Applied Special Technology

Afternoon Research Keynote Address
Chair: Leigh A. Hall, Michigan State University; *Research as a Foundation for Teaching,* **Gay Su Pinnell,** Ohio State University

Research-Based Practices in Literacy Instruction

Building Comprehension of Informational Text
Chair and Introduction: Annie Moses, Michigan State University; **Nell K. Duke,** Michigan State University

Another Look at Content Area Literacy: How to Connect the Literacy Lives of Adolescents to the Literacy Goals of Content Area Classrooms
Chair and Introduction: Mary Kay Johnson, Michigan State University; **Elizabeth Birr Moje,** University of Michigan

Providing Reading Interventions to Primary Grade EL Learners at Risk for Reading Difficulties
Chair and Introduction: Linda Golson, University of Alabama; **Sharon Vaughn,** University of Texas, **Sylvia F. Linan-Thompson,** University of Texas, **Patricia Mathes,** Southern Methodist University, **Sharolyn Pollard-Durodola,** Texas A&M University, **Elsa Cardenas Hagan,** University of Houston

Two Urban Teachers' Experiences with an Integration of Students' Popular Culture Texts into Literacy Curriculum
Chair and Introduction: **Jory Brass,** Michigan State University; **Shelley Xu,** California State University at Long Beach

Instructional Strategies for Addressing the Challenges of Reading for Information on the Internet
Chair and Introduction: Alison K. Billman, Michigan State University; **Julie Coiro,** University of Connecticut; Beth Schmar-Dobler, Emporia State University

The Stories Behind the Scores: High Literacy Gains in High Poverty Schools
Chair and Introduction: Katherine Hilden, Michigan State University; **Keonya Booker,** Randolph-Macon Woman's College, **Marcia A. Invernizzi,** University of Virginia, **Montanna McCormick,** University of Virginia

Some Suggestions for Meaningful Talk About Texts
Chair and Introduction: Julia Reynolds, Michigan State University; **Linda Kucan,** Appalachian State University

The Power of Text Sets: Encouraging First-Graders' Responses to Four Versions of *The Three Little Pigs*
Chair and Introduction: David Gallagher, Michigan State University; **Larry Sipe,** University of Pennsylvania, **Anne Brighton,** University of Pennsylvania